APPREHENDING THE INACCESSIBLE

Northwestern University
Studies in Phenomenology
and
Existential Philosophy

Founding Editor †James M. Edie

General Editor Anthony J. Steinbock

Associate Editor John McCumber

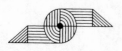

APPREHENDING THE INACCESSIBLE

Freudian Psychoanalysis and Existential Phenomenology

Richard Askay and
Jensen Farquhar

Northwestern University Press
Evanston, Illinois

Northwestern University Press
Evanston, Illinois 60208-4170

Copyright © 2006 by Northwestern University Press.
Published 2006. All rights reserved.

Printed in the United States of America

10   9   8   7   6   5   4   3   2   1

ISBN 0-8101-1900-5 (cloth)
ISBN 0-8101-2228-6 (paper)

Library of Congress Cataloging-in-Publication Data

Askay, Richard.
　　Apprehending the inaccessible : Freudian psychoanalysis and existential
phenomenology / Richard Askay and Jensen Farquhar.
　　　　p. cm. — (Northwestern University studies in phenomenology and
existential philosophy)
　　Includes bibliographical references and index.
　　ISBN 0-8101-1900-5 (alk. paper) — ISBN 0-8101-2228-6 (pbk. : alk. paper)
　　1. Psychoanalysis. 2. Existential phenomenology. 3. Psychoanalysis and
philosophy. I. Farquhar, Jensen. II. Title. III. Northwestern University studies
in phenomenology & existential philosophy.
　　BF173.F85A825 2005
　　150.19'52—dc22

　　　　　　　　　　　　　　　　　　　　　　　　　　　　　　　　　　2005007765

♾ The paper used in this publication meets the minimum requirements of the
American National Standard for Information Sciences—Permanence of Paper
for Printed Library Materials, ANSI Z39.48-1992.

This book is dedicated with deep respect and love to
Dr. Elizabeth Swenson for her invaluable insights, suggestions,
support, and assistance on this text as well as in life. She is a
remarkable woman who has shown us both the profound role
the emotions play in the human condition.

Contents

Preface

This book explores several major ways of approaching the theme of apprehending the inaccessible—the hidden dimensions of human experience—within the Western tradition. While doing this, we will take as our focal point the historical and philosophical engagement of Freudian psychoanalysis with Husserlian phenomenology and the various primary forms of existential phenomenology.[1]

We have selected Freudian metapsychological theory and therapeutic practice as our primary catalyst for exploring this theme for several reasons. First, it is a remarkable fact that no one has clearly, carefully, systematically, and succinctly delineated the most fundamental philosophical presuppositions underlying the philosophical-historical influences on Freudian psychoanalysis. Uncovering Freud's philosophical presuppositions and influences allows us to understand Freud more clearly, and assess critiques of his psychoanalysis.[2] Second, it is important to note that although society (even today) ostensibly acknowledges Freud's great contributions toward understanding human nature, few are aware of the extent to which Freudian psychoanalysis was an accumulation, cultivation, and synthesis of many great ideas throughout history.[3] Even those scholars who have studied Freud's work have, for the most part, confined their research into the historical influences on psychoanalysis within the scientific sphere.[4] These have most often included Ernest Brücke's hard laboratory science, Josef Breuer's preference for physiological theory, the physicalistic principles of the Helmholtz school, Darwinian evolutionary theory, and so on (to which Freud himself often referred). Yet it is also the case that Freud had clearly been affected (consciously and unconsciously) by the philosophical worldviews/traditions which underlie and are transcendentally prior to the various scientific positions.[5] As his major translator, James Strachey once observed, on a conscious level

> Freud was a striking example of a man equally at home in both of what have been called the "two cultures." He was not only an expert neuro-anatomist and physiologist; he was also widely read in the Greek and

Latin classics as well as in the literatures of his own language and in those of England, France, Italy, and Spain.[6]

This is corroborated by the fact that the books surviving from Freud's libraries are equally divided between the humanities and the sciences.[7] To extend Strachey's point, it is important to note that there are a good number of *philosophical* works in his highly selective library (books to which Freud had obviously become very attached). They include, among others, works by Plato, Montaigne, Bacon, Locke, Hume, Kant, Goethe, Feuerbach, Schopenhauer, Nietzsche, and Theodor Lipps. It surely is no coincidence that of those relatively select few whom Freud took to be *the* exemplars of genuine greatness were Plato, Bacon, Goethe, Kant, Voltaire, Darwin, Schopenhauer, and Nietzsche.[8]

Third, it is undeniable that Freud made powerful contributions toward our understanding of some of the hidden dimensions of human experience which arguably have still not been sufficiently understood or appreciated within the philosophical community or by popular culture. For example, as the influential philosopher, Richard Rorty, recently declared: "I think we have not even begun to assimilate Freud. Freud has been dead for fifty years but we intellectuals are barely beginning to come to terms with Freud."[9] Similarly, the intellectual historian Peter Gay remarked: "Yet while modern culture has largely absorbed Freud's ideas, and given them enormous influence, they are, strangely enough, really not very well known or fully appreciated."[10]

It must also be said that although some of Freud's discoveries and ideas have been assimilated into our culture at large, much has been forgotten or—even worse—distorted. The Freud who has entered public consciousness has become such a caricature that the actual Freud has virtually disappeared. What are arguably some of Freud's most important contributions—the unconscious, the Oedipus complex, sexual symbolism, the notion of a phylogenetic history, and so on—are no longer taken seriously by most. Having been reduced to punch lines in an array of bad jokes, these ideas are no longer taken as possible modes of apprehending the inaccessible. This is due, in part, to the uproar his theories and discoveries incited during his own lifetime. Many of the important scholars and thinkers of his time simply joined the crowd of outraged bystanders in dismissing his ideas as ludicrous. Yet one must ponder (as did Freud himself) how ideas so "obviously false" could incite such opposition. Why not simply and silently shake one's head and move on?

According to Freud's own theory, such hostile reactions are strong indicators of psychological resistance and an underlying concealment of an unconfrontable truth about ourselves. This was part of the basis for

Freud's frustration in his remark to his friend, Wilhelm Fliess, that "truth is not accessible, mankind does not deserve it."[11] In this respect, then, Freud may have posed a threat to our transparent visions of beauty and complacency as well as our philosophical systems which served, among other things, to raise humans to a level above basic animalistic instincts. Certainly, Freud's ideas threatened many philosophical and cultural perspectives.

Finally, to illustrate the import of Freud's contributions toward apprehending the inaccessible, we believe it is important to show how his approach engaged what many take to be one of his primary philosophical sets of competitors: Husserl's phenomenology and the giants of existential phenomenology—Martin Heidegger, Jean-Paul Sartre, and Maurice Merleau-Ponty. While doing so, one of our major concerns will be to disclose the mutual failures of understanding and missed opportunities for genuine engagement between Freud and Husserl, and the existential phenomenologists. By clearing up such misunderstandings, we believe that we can show what mutually significant contributions each tradition is in a position to offer the other. The result, we believe, will be a more holistic and cogent account of how to apprehend the inaccessible in human experience.

The Methodology Employed in the Approach to Apprehending the Inaccessible

In the first part of this book—to set the stage for the engagement between Freud and Husserl, and the existential phenomenologists—we adopt a method which has been employed by both existential phenomenologists and psychoanalysts to gain access to the hidden dimensions of the human psyche (both globally and individually). It is best described as a regressive, "archaeological"[12] approach: a penetration and plunging into a depth of existence. The approach is itself a phenomenological-philosophical application of psychoanalysis.

In the development of psychoanalysis it may be argued that Freud himself applied a regressive, "archaeological" methodology both in the therapeutic environment and in his research. In therapy, Freud began with the manifest material—that which was given on a surface level—of his patients. Yet early on, Freud realized that the manifest material was more akin to a set of clues (or symptoms) which gave him the tools for uncovering the more fundamental, unconscious latent material beneath.

Similarly, in his research, Freud frequently began with an idea from science only to revisit the wisdom of ancient and primitive people. Here he sought to reclaim those insights that had become concealed by a repressive process of social evolution. He would then return to science with the ancient wisdom in hand, and work to synthesize both toward a deeper understanding of the subject matter. Not unlike Freud (and, as we will see, some phenomenologists) then, this book approaches Freudian psychoanalysis philosophically in order to uncover both its manifest and latent content.

A closer look at Freud and his philosophical heritage serves many purposes, including these:

1. It facilitates a more profound understanding of Freud's theory by identifying the most powerful, formative philosophical influences on his synthesizing mind; for example, by distinguishing Freud as the conscious and unconscious outcome of Empedocles, Plato, Bacon, the Philosophes, Kant, Romanticism, Nietzsche, and, above all, Schopenhauer.
2. Directly applying Freud's own psychoanalytic method of returning to the "origin" helps to illustrate—and restore a sense of balance to, and renewed awareness of—important contributions made by Freudian psychoanalysis.
3. A deeper understanding of what Freud was attempting to convey (both unconsciously and consciously) puts us in a better position to evaluate to what extent Freud succeeded in enabling us to apprehend the inaccessible.
4. Providing the philosophical-historical context of Freudian psychoanalysis affords us the opportunity to evaluate more clearly the strength of existential phenomenological critiques, and to identify more easily the specific crucial themes which underlie that entire dialogue: the body, causality and freedom, meaning, unconscious phenomena, and so on.

Hence, throughout our discussion on Freud and the existential phenomenologists, we will be simultaneously conducting a genetic phenomenological and psychoanalytic investigation of the historical development of Freud's theory and practice.

Methodological Overview

We begin with an investigation (a "philosophography") into Freud as a synthesizing force in the history of ideas—ideas which have been percolating in their incubative state for millennia. In so doing, we consider Freud's ideas as immersed within the flow of Western philosophical traditions. To better grasp how Freud saw himself within this confluence, we will consider Freud's attitude toward philosophy in general, as well as his understanding of and familiarity with philosophy as a discipline. Next, we present a "surface" account of Freud's metapsychological theory and therapeutic approach, in order to generally establish the main points of Freud's grounding of psychoanalysis.

Following the regressive archaeological approach, we will then move from a surface presentation of Freud's psychoanalysis to examine his self-proclaimed scientific roots in the Enlightenment. Here we will see that even those scientific worldviews had at their foundation important historical ideas which may be traced back along Western lines to ancient Greek philosophy. Moving to a deeper level, we will consider the philosophical influences of Empedocles and Plato specifically, as they impacted Freud and Enlightenment figures as well. The romanticist philosophers reclaimed from the Greeks some fundamental holistic notions of nature which, in turn, influenced Freud on a deep level: his very choice to become a scientist was predicated on an essay reputedly authored by Goethe, which he heard as a young college student. Moving from the romanticists to Schopenhauer and Nietzsche, we make our ascent to the philosophical predecessors who pervaded the intellectual ambiance of Freud's formative years. Our historical-psychoanalytic-phenomenological investigation will then conclude with a discussion of some important contemporary thinkers who impacted both Freud and Husserl—the father of phenomenology—who exerted the greatest impact on existential phenomenology. This, then, leads us into the second primary section of our book: a discussion of the major existential phenomenologists' critique of Freudian psychoanalysis.

Since Freudian psychoanalysis and existential phenomenology were roughly contemporaneous, much of Freud's philosophical background drew from the same tradition out of which phenomenology and existential phenomenology emerged. Yet—as is most often the case—each tradition incorporated that which most closely approximated its own unique views of "human reality." Hence it will be seen that, in regards to apprehending the inaccessible, certain themes and areas of disagreement emerged between these two traditions: especially involving issues of freedom, bodily being, and the possibility/impossibility of an unconscious. Hopefully—in engaging in the dialogue between these two highly influential traditions—some synthesis and/or unification can be gleaned which may serve to further the progress each has made toward a human understanding of the inaccessible.

Logistical Constraints

Given the complicated nature of our approach it is necessary for this text to operate under certain logistical constraints:

1. We will reference a minimum of secondary source material. While we are certainly aware of the existence and value of such material, to include this would be to blur the lines of exploration with undue complexity and thereby transcend the scope of what is already an ambitious undertaking.

2. We have restricted ourselves to a consideration of the "classic" phenomenologists: Husserl and existential phenomenologists—Heidegger, Sartre, and Merleau-Ponty—all of whom engaged Freud in substantial ways.

3. Within the scope of this book, we are unable to take up the relatively recent spectrum of developments in psychoanalysis: ego psychology (Hartmann), object relations theory (Mahler, Fairbairn), two-factor theory (Modell's integration of object relations and Freudian instinct theory), interpersonal psychoanalysis (Sullivan), analytical psychology (Jung), Adlerian theory, Kohut's psychology of narcissism, Klein's reformulation of psychoanalytic theory, and so on.

4. In our historical account of Freud's philosophical influences—though we acknowledge the important impact they exerted on Freud—we do not spend much time on the positivists (except in broad brushstrokes) since this information has already been extensively and widely treated.

Acknowledgments

We are grateful to the University of Portland for funding a sabbatical during which we were able to assemble the formative elements of this text and a research trip to Europe where, among other opportunities, we worked at the Husserl Archive in Louvain, Belgium, and met with Dr. Medard Boss at his home in Zurich. Our discussions with Dr. Boss—on Heidegger and Freud, and the relationship between the two—proved invaluable to Richard Askay and Franz Mayr in translating the *Zollikon Seminars,* and in the development of this book. We feel especially privileged to have had access to Dr. Mayr's limitless knowledge of philosophy over the last two decades, and have deeply appreciated his humor and his friendship. In addition, we want to thank Ms. Rayne Funk for her ancillary services, and the editors at Northwestern University Press for all their work on this project.

Dr. Askay would also like to acknowledge the strong formative and seminal influences of Dr. Calvin O. Schrag and Dr. William L. McBride upon the emergence of this volume. Dr. Askay and Ms. Farquhar would both like to thank Dr. Larry Bowlden for his immense impact on their lives, philosophically and personally.

We are grateful to Dr. Wayne Swenson, whose background in physics compels him to insist that there is no unconscious, and to Dr. Elizabeth Swenson, who supports us in our passionate plea that there is. A special thanks to Nick and Carol Farquhar whose love and dedication have shown us the benefits of apprehending the inaccessible in our own lives.

Finally, we would like to express our appreciation and love to our sons Søren, Tyler, and Emerson for their enduring patience and understanding during the several years it has taken us to bring about the birth of this book. Hopefully they will find a way to forgive us for the numerous (and at times, apparently nonsensical) discussions that interrupted and impeded family interactions.

Abbreviations

Freud employed a number of abbreviations in discussing his topographical model of the mind. The following should suffice to orient readers who are unfamiliar with his usage:

Cs. = consciousness
Ucs. = unconscious
Pcs. = preconscious
Pcpt-Cs. = perceptual-conscious

APPREHENDING THE INACCESSIBLE

Introduction: The Theme of Apprehending the Inaccessible in Western Philosophy

In meditation as in action we must make a distinction between what is accessible and what is inaccessible; failing this, little can be accomplished either in life or in knowledge.
—Goethe

Man is very well defended against himself, against being reconnoitered and besieged by himself, he is usually able to perceive of himself only his outer walls. The actual fortress is inaccessible, even invisible to him, unless his friends and enemies play the traitor and conduct him in by a secret path.
—Nietzsche

Man carries the ultimate fundamental secrets within himself, and this fact is accessible to him in the most immediate way. Here only, therefore, can he hope to find the key to the riddle of the world, and obtain a clue to the inner nature of all things.
—Schopenhauer

[The id] is the dark, inaccessible part of our personality.
—Freud

What manifests itself as the inaccessible is the mystery.
—Heidegger

The "Inaccessible" in the History of Philosophy

Throughout the history of Western civilization, philosophers have relentlessly pursued what may be called "inaccessible domains." Many have suggested that such realms are rarely if ever open to direct (or even indirect) experience, and yet have also claimed that they form the very basis for all beings or Being. Such domains are taken by many to be of paramount importance. Furthermore, depending upon the orientation, these domains have been understood and approached in a variety of ways. It is not at all surprising, then, that one of the major functions of such disciplines as philosophy and psychoanalysis has been to disclose and elucidate, to whatever extent possible, inaccessible domains.

The pursuit of an underlying "something" or dimension has taken many forms throughout the history of Western philosophy.[1] Among the Presocratic philosophers there was a quest to ascertain that "substance" or being which underlies everything. Familiar examples come to mind: Anaximander spoke of *apeiron,* the "primordial stuff" (the limitless, eternal surrounding); Heraclitus pursued the eternal logos (the underlying principle governing all things);[2] Parmenides sought Being, the One; Plato spoke of a unifying principle (namely, the "Good") which makes possible and underlies all levels of knowledge and reality; Locke referred to "that, I know not what," which he believed must hold all of our sensations together. More recently, Kant's "Copernican revolution" played a crucially pivotal role in the metaphysical bifurcation of the universe into: that which we are able to experience (to access)—the phenomenal world; and that which *is* and yet we cannot experience (is inaccessible)—the noumenal world.

For the purposes of this text—that is, in light of the subsequent development of Freudian psychoanalysis—it was Kant's ideas that served as the fulcrum for future developments concerning the question of what is accessible and what is not. For the Kant of the first *Critique,* the noumenal world was considered to be utterly inaccessible to human beings. All we could hope for was to refine our understanding of the phenomenal world (to access our understanding of it in the appropriate manner via transcendental philosophy). Kant went even further, of course. He spoke of "discovering a [hidden] purpose in nature behind this senseless course of human events," and of humans "unconsciously promoting an end."[3] Transcending his earlier position, Kant continued in his third *Critique* to develop a view of the universe as including an emerging, sprawling *underneath* which ultimately comprised the ultimate foundational essence of who we are. Following this prodigious seed, the romanticists spoke of nature as spirit; Hegel discussed the cunning of reason which fulfills its own hidden purposes during the dynamic process of the Absolute Consciousness coming to know itself (although Hegel, of course, rejected Kant's noumenal world as inaccessible and thereby irrelevant); and Marx emphasized the functioning of "ideology" where the economic infrastructure controls our actions and governs our ideas without our even being aware of this.

Finally, both Schopenhauer and Nietzsche contended that there was a "hidden" to be uncovered (apprehended). For example, Schopenhauer sought to uncover the "cosmic will," and "unconscious desires." Schopenhauer wrote, "it can be explained that in all we know, a certain something remains hidden from us as being quite unfathomable."[4] Nietzsche sought to "uncover" the "will to power," "unconscious desires," the "id," and so on.[5] Nietzsche wrote, "[the human being] is a dark and veiled thing,"[6] and "everything is at the same time concealed, ulterior, subterranean."[7] Such ideas, of course, presaged Sigmund Freud's conceptions of the "unconscious" and the "id." In turn, Freud exerted an immense influence, positively and reactively, on the major strands of contemporary continental philosophy—critical theory, structuralism, postmodernism and poststructuralism, among others—especially existential phenomenology. Existential phenomenology has since evolved various strains which proceeded to develop their own accounts of the nature of inaccessible realms: for example, Heidegger's notions of the clearing and concealment; the later Sartre's account of le vécu (lived-experience); and Merleau-Ponty's focus on the pre-reflective nature of lived-body experience.

Obviously, throughout history many humans have shared a belief in something transcending or unfathomably immanent in the empirical world, something which may not be immediately accessible (or accessible at all). Many have emphasized that we must learn to apprehend in a new way so that we can reach the inaccessible on some level. Even those who have tended to reject the idea of an inaccessible domain have often found it necessary to—at the very least, by way of reaction—say something about such a notion, misguided though it may be. In response, some who have insisted upon the "reality" of the inaccessible have noted that even a denial in some sense legitimizes and confirms the inaccessible.

Freud and the Inaccessible

Freud has been a particularly pivotal figure in our culture on the issue of the inaccessible. As a highly influential figure in the history of Western thought, Freud brought one way of apprehending an inaccessible domain into the lives of individuals through the development of his extraordinary theory of human nature and the application of his therapeutic techniques. His conceptions of the id and the unconscious forced people to reconsider the idea, in a fresh and resilient way, that there were hidden worlds within the very essence of each human being. In a sense, then, Freud gave poets and artists the added weight of what he took to be science, when speaking of the most mysterious of all—our selves. Obviously, the influence of Freud's ideas have extended to and exerted an impact upon almost every realm of our everyday lives.

Freud and Existential Phenomenology

Freud, Husserl, and the primary figures in the tradition of existential phenomenology (Heidegger, Sartre, Merleau-Ponty) existed roughly within the same social-historical time period. They all shared a similar philosophical environment, and had friendships and associates which bridged the gap between philosophical differences. Both traditions were concerned with similar questions and, most important, shared a common philosophical heritage. Yet most advocates of existential phenomenology did not embrace Freudian psychoanalysis. In fact, according to Medard Boss, Heidegger's reading of Freud's metapsychological works rendered him physically "ill." Sartre displayed, at the very least, a profound ambivalence toward Freudian psychoanalysis. Although Merleau-Ponty seemed much more open to Freud's ideas, he too believed Freud to be a co-conspirator of mechanistic thinking, attempting to relegate human existence into the realm of "thing" ontology.

It may be argued that the existential phenomenologists in general approached Freud as a symbol of the scientistic materialism they so vehemently opposed; and—in accordance with Freud's own Oedipus complex—treated him as a scientistic authority figure whose primary purpose was to deprive them of their freedom and responsibility: their "patricide" assumed the form of critique. In so doing, the existential phenomenologists may have failed to honor their own demands that any theoretical framework be critiqued within the full flow of the historical context from which it arose. Freud's metapsychology was all too facilely dismissed as simply a snapshot, frozen in time, of scientistic thinking gone awry without sufficient consideration of the deep philosophical roots from which it emerged.

Of course, Freud himself was not exempt from blame for the existentialists' (mis)interpretation of his metapsychology: he did, at least prima facie, blatantly deny human freedom, reducing "free will" to a "psychical compulsion";[8] he also claimed that science had preferential rights and access to truth and knowledge, and that no matter how limited science's vision may be, philosophy was blind in comparison.[9] Hence, as is often the case, both positions contributed to and thereby exacerbated their mutual misunderstandings, despite their obviously similar pursuits. What remains is for us to attempt to reconcile the two, in hopes of discovering a more holistic approach to apprehending the inaccessible by considering what each tradition has to offer the other toward this end.

Preliminary Considerations of the Inaccessible

Before we proceed to consider the "inaccessible" with regard to Freudian psychoanalysis, its historical influences, and the various existential phenomenological reactions, it is important to stop and carefully consider the following question: What is meant by the term "inaccessible"? Literally, the term signifies something not capable of being approached, or reached. It derives from the Late Latin *inaccessibilis;* the Latin *accedere* (*accessus*), "to come near, approach"; and at its roots, *ad-* "toward" + *cedere* (*cessi*) "to go." Yet, crucial ambiguities are concealed in the deceptive simplicity of this definition. It is unclear, and susceptible to a variety of interpretations and/or levels of interpretation, some of which may be interrelated, taken discretely or taken together simultaneously.

There are three interrelated senses of the "inaccessible" which will play a major role throughout the course of this book. First, there is the "transcendent" sense of the inaccessible as that which can *never* become accessible to human beings: that which can never form a part of knowable human experience in any way whatsoever—for example, Kant's noumenal world. One might say that this sense of the inaccessible transcends the very limits of philosophy itself! Second, the inaccessible may manifest aspects or dimensions of itself to us in the past, present, and/or future, without allowing us to apprehend it *as it is in-itself.* On this "immanent" level, that which is real and that which appears (phenomenal) are indissolubly, ontologically inseparable. Our dealing with the inaccessible on this level, then, is necessarily limited. Finally, there is the "eliminable" sense in which something may have been or continues to be inaccessible because (1) we have yet to find suitable ways to approach it, and/or to discover it; (2) it has been blocked in some way—for example, we have a distorted way of looking at the world which serves to cover up the accessible, or something or someone else blocks it from us; (3) it has been forgotten for whatever reason, and yet could be recovered. Here, in this final sense, the inaccessible is available to us to some extent if we can find a way to "unlock the mysteries"—to find an approach that works, remove any occlusions to our approach, and/or recall what has been forgotten.

Each of the traditions we will consider in this text has in one way or another dealt with the above, interrelated senses of inaccessibility. In addition, it will be shown that there are important commonalities among Freud and Husserl, and the existential phenomenologists involving these notions of the inaccessible.

In view of how we defined the "inaccessible" above, one implicit application is to those aspects of each thinker's work that remain inaccessible to their own understanding. For example: the philosophical presuppositions embedded in Freudian metapsychology; or the underlying reasons (according to Merleau-Ponty) for Heidegger's not adequately addressing bodily existence in his philosophy. An inaccessible domain could also refer to entities, aspects, or dimensions of human nature (as in Freud). In contrast: an inaccessible domain could involve ontological considerations (as in Heidegger); the pre-reflective level of bodily existence in Merleau-Ponty; the pre-reflective manifestation of the pursuit of the fundamental project of becoming the in-itself-for-itself in Sartre, and so on. All of these different manifestations of the "inaccessible" resemble so many threads which weave together the various levels of meaning involved. Furthermore, they disclose the creativity of expression, and the "need" to at least say something about that which is elusive to human understanding.

Next, when we speak of "apprehending the inaccessible" an ostensible paradox immediately appears: if a realm is indeed inaccessible, how can it be apprehended at all? How can one "take to oneself (before)"—apprehend—a domain which one is unable "to move toward"? If a realm is apprehensible is it not then, necessarily *not* inaccessible? Or, the reverse: if one cannot "take to oneself from a domain," how is it possible to move toward it at all? One way to answer this question is to point out that it is possible to be aware of that which *involves* the inaccessible, and yet not know the inaccessible itself. It is also possible to be aware of the inaccessible or experience the inaccessible in some way, without knowing that one is doing so. Or, it is possible that the inaccessible might manifest aspects of itself without showing itself in its *totality*. What does any of this mean? Given that this is one of the underlying themes of Freudian psychoanalysis and phenomenology/existential phenomenology, some preliminary examples may be helpful.

In Freudian psychoanalysis, one of the primary goals of therapy is to make conscious the repressed material formed during early childhood and uncover and eliminate resistance, thereby enabling the analysand to achieve greater self-knowledge, and consequently increased self-control over his/her impulses.[10] Yet Freud persisted in conceiving of the id as existing "in forms unknown to us" in "an unimaginable substratum."[11] Another familiar example is that one could be anxious about an event, and yet not know of the repressed meaning that is responsible for the anxiety. In Sartre's existential psychoanalysis, one could be aware of a preference for *x*, without knowing that this actually involved an "original choice" in the face of our underlying, fundamental project of trying to become the in-itself-for-itself. Or, a person could act in bad faith and yet believe that she/he is always authentic. In each of these examples there is a sense of having access to something that, at the same time, remains a mystery to us; something ordinarily hidden manifests itself, or makes its presence felt. Furthermore, in each of these cases, the tools provided by the intellect seem inadequate at best. There is a need to transcend or "let go" of thinking in order to deepen our understanding, and yet the very act of describing this "phenomenon" necessarily involves the intellect. Hence, we see another major aspect of the paradoxical nature of the inaccessible.

In this book, then, we shall explore approaches to the question of how best to approach the inaccessible, taking Freudian psychoanalysis as our focal point and then placing it in dialogue with Husserlian phenomenology and the existential phenomenologists. By doing so, we will clarify two major configurations that have made substantial progress in apprehending the inaccessible. And we will show how placing them in dialogue enables each to be strengthened by the other, and to make possible even greater advances in apprehending the inaccessible.

Part 1

A Regressive Archaeological Exploration of the Dialectical Synthesis of Freud's Philosophical Heritage

1

The Atavistic Spirit or "the Monster of Energy": Origins of Freud's Synthesizing Mind

That individual philosophical concepts are not anything capricious or autonomously evolving, but grow up in connection and relationship with each other; that, however suddenly and arbitrarily they seem to appear in the history of thought, they nevertheless belong just as much to a system as all the members of the fauna of a continent—is betrayed in the end also by the fact that the most diverse philosophers keep filling in a definite fundamental scheme of possible philosophies. Under an invisible spell, they always revolve once more in the same orbit; however independent of each other they may feel themselves with their critical or systematic wills, something within them leads them, something impels them in a definite order, one after the other— to wit, the innate systematic structure and relationship of their concepts. Their thinking is, in fact, far less a discovery than a recognition, a remembering, a return and a homecoming to a remote, primordial, and inclusive household of the soul, out of which those concepts grew originally; philosophizing is to this extent a kind of atavism of the highest order.
    —Nietzsche

By then, there is usually also someone who becomes the recipient of great gratitude, not only for the good he himself has done but above all for the treasure of what is best and highest that has gradually been accumulated by his predecessors.
    —Nietzsche

I have been driven to realize that here once more we have one of those not infrequent cases in which an ancient and jealously held popular belief seems to be nearer the truth than the judgement of the prevalent science of to-day.
    —Freud

As Nietzsche so eloquently noted, the generation and evolution of ideas and even entire systems of thought rarely occur in a historical vacuum. More typically they incubate within the multifarious forces of abundant dynamic, historical environments, when at last they burst forth in a sudden flash of intricately synthesized insight.[1] Nietzsche created an even more powerful imagery in this respect:

> There are men who are the heirs and masters of this slowly-acquired manifold treasure of virtue and efficiency—because, through fortunate and reasonable marriages, and also through fortunate accidents, the acquired and stored-up energies of many generations have not been squandered and dispersed but linked together by a firm ring and by will. In the end there appears a man, a monster of energy, who demands a monster of a task.[2]

Freud may be said to have been a prototypical example of the "monster of energy" Nietzsche presaged. Furthermore, Freud fit Nietzsche's descriptions in another way as well:

> A higher culture must give to man a double-brain, as it were two brain-ventricles, one for the perceptions of science, the other for those of non-science: lying beside one another, not confused together, separable, capable of being shut off; this is a demand of health.[3]

Recall Strachey's earlier observation that Freud was "a man of two cultures" in precisely the above way.

To appreciate the nature and extent of Freud's synthesizing mind it is important to mention in a preliminary way some of the general characteristics of his specific historical context (the synchronic) and those historical influences exerted upon it (the diachronic), as well as the way in which he engaged them.

The historical context in which Freud worked was characterized by an especially tumultuous intellectual climate, and various fundamentally opposing and powerful conceptual viewpoints were operative. In the wake of the Philosophes and Comte, science was defined by Helmholtz in positivistic, physicalistic, and deterministic language. Darwin and Spencer (who were promoting the psychology of instincts) were especially prominent in this movement. While jointly opposing this worldview, nonscientistic philosophy was itself split into a spectrum of competing worldviews. As the pinnacle of German idealism, Hegelian philosophy was dominant during the nineteenth century: absolute consciousness was in the process of coming to know itself in the dialectical movement of the phenomenology of spirit. Contra Hegel, Schopenhauer and Nietzsche focused on the will, and will to power, as the underlying impetus for all that happened (yet each conceived this will in very different ways). As the heir to Kant's chair at Königsberg, Johann Herbart sought to develop a "mathematized" psychology that adequately took into account the "unconscious" in psychical life. Finally, in his fervent opposition to German idealism, Franz Brentano sought to bridge the gap between philosophy and science in protophenomenological terms. These philosophical currents permeated the intellectual atmosphere of Vienna during the time of Freud's formative development. Freud was influenced, consciously and unconsciously, by all of these orientations, as well as their philosophical ancestors.

On a more personal level, Freud's intellectual development was molded in part by his classical training. Freud's educational experiences gave him extensive, direct access to the wisdom of previous generations. It provided him with an immense pool of resources, that contained many historical and philosophical ideas. These ideas were consciously and unconsciously manifested in Freud's theory of human nature—hence, to truly understand what Freud had in mind when he generated his theory of human nature, it is helpful to consider the various philosophical ideas contributing to Freud's intellectual development and his formulation of psychoanalysis.[4]

Philosophy and Psychoanalysis

One of the claims made by Freud was that psychoanalysis had a great deal to offer philosophers by looking at the psychoanalytical underpinnings/ origins of their ideas (what he describes as a "psychography"). It is equally true, however, that philosophers have a great deal to offer psychoanalysis by considering the philosophical underpinnings/origins of its ideas (a "philosophography"). Ironically enough, by doing so, we may be in a better position to appreciate the *psychoanalytic* underpinnings of the development of any theory—and the theory of psychoanalysis itself.

When we inquire into the relationship between Freud and various historical figures, we will be addressing two interwoven questions. To what extent did philosopher X anticipate, or prediscover, Freud's ideas? And then, to what extent did philosopher X influence Freud? The latter question breaks down into a question of conscious versus unconscious influence: and the unconscious influences are crucially important, given Freud's own theory on the development of a thinker's ideas.

Unconscious Influences on Freud

First (and possibly foremost) Freud himself made the following essential point regarding the apprehension of the inaccessible within himself, as well as others: for the most part we are *unaware* of the origins of who we are, what we think, and why we think in the way we do.[5] Indeed, this was why Freud partially defined psychoanalysis as "a procedure for the investigation of mental processes which are almost inaccessible in any other way."[6] His metapsychology was designed to elucidate the very foundations of who we are, and the origin of meaning for human nature in general; while his therapeutic practice was meant to do this (resolve psychological problems) for the individual within his/her own idiosyncratic context. For our purposes, this applied to the very development of Freud's ideas (or those of anyone), for they were *always more* than he consciously understood them to be. As we shall see, *he* himself was largely unaware—that is, unconscious—of the origin and meaning of those ideas which made him who he was, and led him to think as he did.[7]

Freud clearly acknowledged this in his ambivalence concerning the claim of originality of his major ideas. As we shall see, Freud often denied having read various philosophers, for fear of their contaminating his own fresh discoveries, and asseverated that (at least some of) his ideas were truly original.[8] In 1927, he assumed the air of a solitary explorer blazing entirely new and original trails in human knowledge without the benefit of assistance from past explorers. For example, while contrasting the nature of his own investigations with those of Einstein's, Freud lamented:

> The lucky fellow has had a much easier time than I have. He has had the support of a long series of predecessors from Newton onward, while I have had to hack every step of my way through a tangled jungle alone.[9]

Yet it is also the case that at times Freud seemed to conveniently sacrifice his desire for originality of thought in order to seek the supportive "confirmation" afforded by great thinkers for some of his primary and more controversial insights. When psychoanalytic ideas incited disbelief and outrage from his audiences, Freud was more apt to concede the very real "possibility of cryptomnesia."[10] Freud realized that humans are often not fully conscious of the origin of their ideas (in this case, from other thinkers). His thoughts on this are both revealing and instructive:

> When some new idea comes up in science, which is hailed at first as a discovery and is also as a rule disputed as such, objective research soon afterward reveals that after all it was in fact no novelty. Usually the dis-

covery has already been made repeatedly and has afterward been forgotten, often at very long intervals of time. Or at least it has had forerunners, had been obscurely surmised or incompletely enunciated . . .

But the subjective side of originality also deserves consideration. A scientific worker may sometimes ask himself what was the source of the ideas peculiar to himself which he has applied to his material. As regards some of them he will discover without much reflection the hints from which they were derived, the statements made by other people which he has picked out and modified and whose implications he has elaborated . . .

Careful psychological investigation . . . reveals hidden and long-forgotten sources which gave the stimulus to the apparently original ideas, and it replaces the ostensible new creation by a revival of something forgotten applied to fresh material. There is nothing to regret in this; we had no right to expect that what was "original" could be untraceable and undetermined.[11]

This was a remarkably stark and intellectually honest statement by Freud. It conceded the very real possibility of unconscious influences upon his own work. Freud himself offered an example of this in 1914, when he acknowledged that some of his most important ideas (for example, the sexual etiology in neuroses) had a genesis which he initially thought to be "new and original," but later saw "by no means originated with [him]" but were "imparted to [him] by three people who commanded [his] deepest respect."[12] As was often the case, Freud's personal discovery gave him "valuable insight into the processes of human creative activity and the nature of human knowledge." One can be exposed to ideas which lie dormant until one day they emerge in the form of an "original" discovery.[13]

If one applies Freud's own insights of unconscious elements in the acquisition of human knowledge, it may be said that psychoanalysis was Freud's own original discovery that emerged as a culmination of numerous historical and philosophical insights. To some extent Freud was aware of this. Yet his attitude toward philosophy in general was ambivalent: he both embraced the *spirit* of philosophical thought and attacked the then-current general philosophical demeanor, which he at times perceived as an impediment toward the acquisition of "scientific" truth and therapeutic success.

Freud's Ambivalence toward Philosophy

It is an interesting fact that early in Freud's adult life, his self-ascribed "original goal" was to pursue philosophy and the insight it afforded.[14]

While under the influence of Brentano, at one point Freud had decided to take his Ph.D. in philosophy and zoology;[15] and from his student days until his early forties, philosophy clearly held an enormous attraction for him.[16] Indeed, Freud took himself to be pursuing philosophical goals throughout his career—in psychology.[17] Given this, one might even argue that through the development of his metapsychology (which was at times highly speculative) Freud was seeking to ground psychoanalysis on a philosophical level. Near the end of his career, Freud reflected that he was able to return to his "original purpose" which was "to understand something of the riddles of the world in which we live and perhaps even to contribute something to their solution."[18]

Yet it is commonly asserted that Freud exhibited nothing but *antipathy* toward philosophy. And many of his comments, throughout his lifetime of writings, do suggest a strong negative opinion of "philosophy."[19]

> We have nothing to expect from philosophy except that it will once again haughtily point out to us the intellectual inferiority of the object of our study.[20]

> Let us humbly accept the contempt with which [philosophers] look down on us from the vantage-ground of their superior needs.[21]

> We know well enough how little light science has so far been able to throw on the problems that surround us. But however much ado the philosophers may make cannot alter the situation . . . such a benighted traveller may sing aloud in the dark to deny his own fears but for all that, he will not see an inch further beyond his nose.[22]

> I not only have no capability for philosophy but also no respect for it . . . in secret, I cannot say this aloud, I believe that metaphysics will one day be seen as a nuisance, as a misuse of thought . . . and it will be judged thus.[23]

> As if the most useless things in the world were not arranged in the following order: shirt collars, philosophers, and monarchs.[24]

Freud's ambivalence toward philosophy was perhaps no better exemplified by the comments he made during discussions before the Vienna Psychoanalytic Society. In a 1908 discussion on Nietzsche's *Genealogy of Morals,* Freud made no bones about "his own peculiar relationship to philosophy; its abstract nature [was] so unpleasant to him, that he has renounced the study of philosophy."[25] Again, in a discussion in 1909 entitled

"Theory of Knowledge and Psychoanalysis," Freud ostensibly held the same line: "Personally, [I have] particular difficulty grasping such abstract ideas, ideas that should have been presented in a much more elementary manner."[26] However, Freud immediately pondered the following point:

> It would be interesting to find out whether a philosophic study [of a question] would yield more than a mere translation into a language difficult to understand, or whether one could perhaps expect a further simplification and the achievement of clear results . . . The philosophic mastery of our experiences is actually going to yield new results.[27]

To be sure, Freud was unsure whether or not "the time [was] ripe for it." It is clear, however, that Freud held out hope that it was not only possible but a valuable endeavor as well.

Given Freud's ambivalence toward philosophy, certain compelling questions emerge. For instance: To what extent was Freud familiar with philosophy, and how did his familiarity (or lack of familiarity) manifest itself in his theory of human nature? After all, it may be argued that the very fact that Freud developed a theory of human nature could not help but place him squarely within the domain of philosophy.

Freud's Familiarity and Involvement with Philosophy

It is natural to wonder how much philosophy Freud had actually read. Ernest Jones posed this very question to Freud himself. His response: "Very little. As a young man I felt a strong attraction toward speculation and ruthlessly checked it."[28] Furthermore, while speaking of the field of philosophy, Freud periodically claimed that he was simply not "well read."[29]

At times, as we noted earlier, Freud even emphasized the importance of *avoiding* reading philosophical works. He said that he was afraid of being hampered by the "anticipatory ideas" of the philosophers,[30] that they might "stir up too many thoughts and stint [him] of the satisfaction of discovery,"[31] and that they might contaminate his own clinical observations.[32] The crucial idea was that he had trained himself to "convert the facts that revealed themselves" to him in as "undisguised, unprejudiced, and unprepared" a form as possible. This was in accordance with the rigorous demands of "science" as Freud interpreted them.

Despite Freud's disclaimer, there is substantial evidence that Freud was nonetheless familiar with many philosophical works fairly early on in his career. Freud apparently read a great deal of philosophy during his university years (1873–82).[33] He felt confident enough to compose "a general introduction to philosophy"—which he called a "Philosophical

A.B.C."—for his fiancée, Martha Bernays, in 1882.[34] For at least five years, Freud actively participated in the "Reading Society of the German Students of Vienna" in which the philosophies of Schopenhauer and Nietzsche, among others, were discussed. Dozens of philosophical books remained in his final library in the Freud museum, some of which reveal his marginal notations to major philosophical treatises: Bacon's *Novum Organum,* Kant's *Critique of Pure Reason,* and Schopenhauer's *Fourfold Root of Sufficient Reason,* are but a few good examples of this which dated from this early period of his life. In a letter of 1873, Freud indicated that he was reading Feuerbach;[35] in 1879, Freud translated a volume of John Stuart Mill's political philosophy; and in a letter of 1898 to Fliess, Freud openly acknowledged: "I have set myself the task of making a bridge between my germinating metapsychology and what is in the books, and I have therefore plunged into the study of Lipps whom I suspect of being the best mind among present day philosophical writers."[36] Indeed, as we shall see later, Freud credited Theodor Lipps and Gustav Theodor Fechner—both renowned *philosophers* in their own right—for having anticipated some of his most important ideas, and with giving him the courage to pursue the path he had chosen in challenging the medical canon.

Furthermore, Freud voluntarily enrolled in several specialized philosophy seminars offered by a renowned philosopher of the time, Franz Brentano (one of which, for example, was on Aristotelian Logic). It is also the case that references to great philosophers are interspersed throughout Freud's writings: Aristotle, Augustine, Brentano, Descartes, Diderot, Empedocles, Epicurus, Galileo, Goethe, Kant, Leibniz, Marx, Nietzsche, Pascal, Plato, Schelling, Schiller, Schleiermacher, Schopenhauer, Spinoza, Voltaire, and so on. Freud denied having read Nietzsche, even in his later years;[37] yet it is significant to note that not only do some of the philosophical presuppositions of Freud's metapsychology closely parallel certain primary facets of Nietzsche's (and Schopenhauer's) philosophy, but that Freud was clearly aware of this (see chapters 6, 7, 8). It is irrefragable, then, that Freud had a substantial background in philosophy, despite his disclaimers.

Still, Freud was not a philosopher (in the conventional sense), nor did he purport to be. Given his self-attributed "constitutional incapacity" for philosophy[38] and lack of philosophical talent,[39] he simply did not believe that he was at all qualified or competent to critically evaluate philosophical systems.[40] In a letter to James Putnam, Freud was clear: "As you know, I comprehend very little of philosophy and with epistemology (with, not before), my interest ceases to function."[41] Furthermore, Freud did not engage in philosophical activities typical of the philosophers of his time.

In his writings Freud did not critically examine his own most fundamental philosophical presuppositions (as well as those of others), construct his own worldview, carefully define and examine his terms and concepts, inquire into the most basic philosophical questions, and so on. (Indeed, as we shall see, this is part of what complicates the debate between the existential phenomenologists and Freud later on!) In fact, some of the "mistakes" in reasoning or lack of careful articulation in his metapsychology may in fact be manifestations of his "lack of philosophical talent."

Freud's Self-Described Scientific Philosophy

Clearly Freud was no philosopher, though he did generate a powerful psychological theory of human nature. He did know enough about philosophy to formulate his philosophical position and, at times, acknowledge his philosophical roots. First, he was not (at least at times) reticent to advocate the rationalism/empiricism of the eighteenth-century Enlightenment (along with its seventeenth-century precursors and nineteenth-century heirs). Second, Freud openly acknowledged his immense debt on this score to his mentor Ernst Brücke, a nineteenth-century positivistic and materialistic scientist: in the tradition of Galileo and Newton, Brücke insisted on reducing natural phenomena to phenomena of motion. Freud consciously took himself to be a positivist, materialist, and rationalist, all of which provided the foundation for his scientific empiricism.[42]

Freud had a strong allegiance to science: "[psychoanalysis] is part of science and can adhere to the scientific Weltanschauung."[43] This science was firmly developed within a philosophical tradition which Freud admired and affirmed. Hence, it can be said that Freud consciously accepted philosophy insofar as it expressed the scientific worldview.

However, Freud had neither sympathy for nor attraction to what he considered "unsound philosophy." It is apparent that, following Brentano, what Freud rejected most was *metaphysics*. Interestingly, Freud noted the similarities between paranoids and philosophers on this score: "the delusions of paranoiacs have an unpalatable external similarity and internal kinship to the systems of our philosophers."[44] For, according to Freud, both the paranoid personality and *unsound* philosophy endeavored to construct complete, coherent, and comprehensive systems in which everything had its proper place. Freud wrote a general statement aimed at the metaphysician, claiming that philosophers made up

an intellectual construction which solves all the problems of our existence uniformly on the basis of one overriding hypothesis, which accord-

ingly, leaves no question unanswered and in which everything that interests us finds its fixed place.[45]

The problem with these *systems*[46] for Freud, was that they inevitably turned
out to be nothing more than dogmatic and artificial constructions.[47] Not
only did he believe that such constructions failed to contribute to genuine
knowledge, they inevitably "collapse with every fresh advance in our
knowledge."[48] Nevertheless, one might ask of Freud if he was not also par-
ticipating in the construction of a new Weltanschauung by *extending* the
resources of science to mental life and the unconscious, and by "filling in
the gaps in the phenomena of our consciousness." After all, Freud wrote
that psychoanalysis "ended by claiming to have set our whole view of mental life upon a new basis and therefore to be of importance for every field
of knowledge that is founded on psychology."[49] Indeed, according to
Freud this was precisely the contribution of psychoanalysis to science!

However, Freud felt justified in postulating an unconscious to account for human phenomena (parapraxes, neurotic symptoms, dreams,
and so on) which would otherwise go unexplained and inadequately considered. He believed that the unconscious was, in fact, implied through
empirical observation; most philosophers during Freud's time, on the
other hand, simply defined mental life as consciousness. The problem with
that, according to Freud, was that there was a major logical fallacy in such
a definitional approach: that is, it begged the question by asserting "conscious" to be a term identical with "psychical."[50] Because it assumed, a priori, consciousness to be identical with mental life (rather than proving it),
much philosophy outright rejected the notion of an unconscious.

Those philosophers and philosophical systems which had some
notion and acceptance of an unconscious mental life did so, generally
speaking, from an unscientific framework which rendered their concepts
"speculative" and "useless," according to Freud.[51] Hence, where the unconscious was concerned, Freud did not believe that philosophy contributed anything.[52]

> Either their unconscious has been something mystical, something intan-
> gible and undemonstrable, whose relation to the mind has remained
> obscure, or they have identified the mental with the conscious and have
> proceeded to infer from this definition that what is unconscious cannot
> be mental or a subject for psychology.[53]

The result was that unsound philosophy essentially rendered the "unconscious" a priori nonexistent, or altogether inaccessible.

In contrast to philosophy, psychoanalysis worked with imprecise concepts—such as the unconscious—with the intention of substantiating those concepts with empirical observation. Hence, general psychoanalytic concepts *out of necessity* were "always incomplete and always ready to modify its theories . . . [and] lack[ed] clarity and its postulates [were] provisional."[54] This was one of the beauties and contributions of science, according to Freud. If one were to side with the philosophers and claim completeness or comprehensiveness then this would, in Freud's mind, preclude the emergence of new discoveries and the advancement of knowledge. Yet, philosophers attacked psychoanalysis precisely for its lack of clarity and precision in its most general concepts.[55] Freud's ambivalence toward philosophers (and philosophy in general) was partly predicated on these differences of opinion and understanding.

But the conflict between Freud and philosophy went even deeper. On a more personal level, Freud's attitude toward philosophy reflected his own investment in the position psychoanalysis held: philosophy was another threat to that precarious position. Both medicine and philosophy, at the time, seemed closed-minded to psychoanalysis:

> So it comes about that psycho-analysis derives nothing but disadvantages from its middle position between medicine and philosophy. Doctors regard it as a speculative system and refuse to believe that, like every other natural science, it is based on a patient and tireless elaboration of the facts from the world of perception; philosophers, measuring it by the standard of their own artificially constructed systems, find that it starts from impossible premises and reproach it because its most general concepts (which are only now in process of evolution) lack clarity and precision.[56]

In short, Freud felt trapped between the demands of medicine and philosophy, in the development of psychoanalysis. Hence, the dilemma of psychoanalysis as Freud perceived it, was that he was caught between science (which criticized his concepts for being philosophically speculative) and philosophy (which criticized his concepts for lack of clarity and linguistic precision). Exacerbating this situation were the facts (as he interpreted them) that (1) he sought scientific respectability while trying to apply its methodology to domains not susceptible to direct observation, and (2) philosophers obfuscated the situation by either mystifying the unconscious or begging the question concerning its existence. Freud's challenge was to satisfy the demands of each discipline without sacrificing the integrity of his theory and concepts.

Freud as Scientist and Philosopher

It may be said that Freud's ultimate proclamation for uncovering the mysteries of human nature and mental illness was a scientific-philosophical "know thyself." Science could contribute through its emphasis on detailed and "objective" observation of the human species, and philosophy could provide the grounding for explaining and making sense of such observation. A complimentary combination of the two disciplines led Freud to one unavoidable conclusion: the human being is a complex organism with advanced mental functions that operate primarily on an unconscious level. And Freud's discoveries did not emerge out of nowhere.

It will be argued that Freud's psychoanalytic theory was a major culmination of one of the most prominent brushstrokes of history (where ideas have germinated, incubated, and evolved over the course of millennia). A more in-depth look into Freud's philosophical intellectual past reveals a confluence of ideas into Freud's theory from a variety of historical contexts: from antiquity, Empedocles and Plato; from the Renaissance, Bacon; from the Enlightenment, Diderot and Kant; from Romanticism, Goethe, Schiller, and Schelling; and from the philosophies of Schopenhauer and Nietzsche. It is interesting to note how each successive wave of philosophers has been powerfully influenced by its predecessors, in a flow which has both identity and difference. Some ideas remain roughly the same, others evolve; and yet the two form one primary brushstroke on the tightly woven fabric of the history of ideas.

In addition, we shall argue that Freud was also a great synthesizing mind in the Hegelian sense (though he was not attracted at all to Hegelian philosophy). Hegel, of course, was famous for his claim that

> [the fluid nature and] the diversity of philosophical systems as the progressive unfolding of truth . . . makes them moments of an organic unity in which they not only do not conflict, but in which each is as necessary as the other; and this mutual necessity alone constitutes the life of the whole.[57]

And again, "The True is the whole. But the whole is nothing other than the essence consummating itself through its development."[58] In fact, Hegelian philosophy was mentioned only once—in passing—in the *Standard Edition,* though Freud's remark revealed that he thought he had some understanding of Hegel's philosophy.[59] Yet Hegel's philosophy is remarkably pertinent to Freud and the development of psychoanalysis for a number of reasons. First, Hegel once remarked that the struggles between historical epochs also manifest in great individuals themselves. One clear example of this, as we shall see, is Freud as philosophe and positivist in the development of his metapsychological theory; and as romanticist and humanist—someone who cares deeply about the suffering in human existence, and seeks to do something about it—insofar as Freud was a concerned therapist. In reciprocal, dialectical fashion, there are times when Freud moved from the developing processes of individual consciousness to those of the consciousness of humanity. For example, Freud claimed that the "entire development of humanity" could be conceived as "an enlargement of the consciousness of mankind (analogous to the coming into consciousness of instincts and forces hitherto operating unconsciously) . . . repression that progresses through the centuries . . . more and more of our instincts become subject to repression."[60] When seen as part of an overall context of the dialectical movement toward the liberation of Absolute consciousness, such remarks take on, of course, a distinctively Hegelian flavor. Second, there were Freud's attempt to apprehend the inaccessible by pushing the methodological limits of science itself: science was understood by Freud to be an evolving being. Finally, there was the Hegelian idea that through "the cunning of reason" the purposes of history get manifested in the history of ideas in ostensibly contradictory ways. This is shown in the development of psychoanalysis via the emergence of certain apparent dialectical tendencies:[61]

1. Freud said a great deal in opposition to the field of philosophy and yet not only specified philosophy as his own original goal, but saw himself pursuing philosophical questions by doing psychology.

2. Freud said he was opposed to the completeness sought by the philosophers, yet his goal was to fill in the gaps of mental life, and to provide a metapsychological foundation which encompassed all of human experience.

3. Freud was opposed to the construction of Weltanschauungen as "fabrications" which can be left to the philosophers; yet he uncritically adopted scientific Weltanschauungen that were also constructed, to a great degree, by philosophers (Bacon, the Philosophes, and others).

4. Freud took himself to be a scientist—with observation as his foundation—and yet he extended the methods of science to unobservable realms (the unconscious, the instincts, the id, and so on), thereby seeking to push the edge of its methodological self-understanding.[62]

5. Freud said that he was anti-system, yet he constructed his metapsychology as the unifying, systematic foundation for psychoanalysis (and, arguably, according to Freud, anything else).

6. Freud said he was opposed to speculation but engaged in such when he speculated, for example, that there were two sets of instincts underlying all human activity.[63]

7. Freud used rationality to explore the irrational impulses of mankind and in turn witnessed their very impact on that rationality itself which had conducted the inquiry. "What is alone of value in mental life is rather the feelings."[64]

These issues are interwoven throughout the text, and form the dynamic, dialectical tendencies within Freud's mind. Throughout the text, it is important to consider the question to what extent Freud was able to resolve these apparent dialectical tendencies. It is also valuable to bear in mind certain other fundamental questions: To what extent did the historical forces operating on Freud necessitate these tendencies? How genuine (versus apparent) are they? And, how are they to be resolved?

2

Freud as "Meta-physician": Freudian Metapsychological Theory and Psychotherapeutic Practice

> My original purpose . . . was to understand something of the riddles of the world in which we live and perhaps even to contribute something to their solution.
> —Freud

> My worthy friend, gray is all theory, and green is alone Life's golden tree.
> —Goethe, quoted by Freud

Despite Freud's early aspirations toward philosophy, Freud sought his advanced training within the domain of science. Trained as a doctor, Freud encountered numerous maladies which appeared to be physiological in origin. Upon closer inspection Freud, among others, came to realize that—although some illnesses were very real in their physiological manifestation—the original "causes" were oftentimes not physiological at all. For instance, Freud witnessed humans who suffered from blindness whose eyes were functioning normally, and paralysis in patients whose legs were perfectly fit. Contrary to the attitude of his time, Freud did not believe that these patients were "faking" their illnesses, but rather pondered the possibility that physical suffering could have psychological origins. This was substantiated by the application of hypnosis; Freud found that long-standing illnesses could be magically eliminated within moments, simply by implanting a strong suggestion in a patient who was not wholly conscious. Yet, Freud also discovered that these suggestions only worked to eliminate particular symptoms. Most frequently, patients who had undergone hypnosis developed other symptoms shortly after being "cured."

Through his continual process of developing and refining his therapeutic technique in search of a cure for neurosis, Freud also sought to explain human mental functioning and its interrelated impact on physiological health. Thus, Freud sought to bridge the gap between mind and body, seeing both as organically based. With science as his tool (and his training) he attempted to apply its methodology to human nature in order to explain the interplay of organic and natural forces that he believed composed the essence of human beings and their potential for health.

Freud had confidence in scientific knowledge, and believed that he was a loyal follower of the scientific Weltanschauungen. While some would argue that his discoveries took him far beyond the confines of science, Freud held that he appropriately applied the scientific methodology of observation, the formation of hypotheses, and the process of scientific validation; if a patient showed significant improvement (his/her symptoms disappeared) through the administration of his therapeutic technique, his hypotheses were correct and thus his metapsychological theory held true. Freud hoped that the scientific community would be convinced by his discoveries and expand to include his account of human nature. Unfortunately, the scientific community refused to follow, and Freud was relegated to a kind of limbo, somewhere between science and philosophy— rejected by both disciplines for failing to conform to the demands of each.

Freud's Metapsychological Theory

According to Freud, psychoanalysis consisted of a number of diverse yet interrelated elements. He conceived it as consisting of a research procedure, a therapeutic method, and a collection of psychological information.[1] Yet, all of these were understood to exist in a unity; hence, psychoanalysis was conceived by Freud to be a unified science. This science, Freud believed, required an ultimate grounding in a comprehensive theory on human nature; thus he developed what he referred to as his "metapsychological theory."[2] Freud considered his metapsychology to be of the utmost importance, claiming that nothing could be achieved without consulting the "Witch Metapsychology": "without metapsychological speculation and theorizing . . . we shall not get another step forward."[3] He took his metapsychology to be a scientific attempt to rectify the abstruse fantasy-constructions of metaphysics by "transforming metaphysics into metapsychology."[4] Freud's metapsychological theory was designed "to clarify and carry deeper the theoretical assumptions on which a psychoanalytic system could be founded."[5] For him then, the doctrine of psycho-analysis was understood as a superstructure which would eventually have as its foundation an organic infrastructure described in his metapsychological theory.[6] In other words, through his theory, Freud asserted and, he believed, demonstrated that human meanings and/or ideas are ultimately grounded in biological processes.

Freud referred to his theory as "*meta*psychology" for obvious reasons. Although Freud believed that psychoanalysis, as a science, was constructed through and remained committed to empirical observation,[7] he was not satisfied with limiting psychoanalysis to purely empirical observation. It was Freud's observations, in fact, which compelled him to transcend what was actually perceived or experienced so that he could make sense of psychical processes more adequately. In other words, Freud's experience necessitated an exploration of the inaccessible as part of his psychoanalysis. For example, in justifying his metapsychological concept of the unconscious, he wrote: "A gain in meaning is a perfectly justifiable ground for going beyond the limits of direct experience."[8] Freud's theory, then, is "meta-" because psychoanalysis required a nonempirical—albeit scientific—foundation.

Freud explicitly defined his metapsychology as: "A method of approach according to which every mental process is considered in relation to three coordinates, which I described as dynamic, topographic, and economic."[9] Briefly, the *dynamic* standpoint is one which derives all psychical processes from the conflicting interplay of forces which are originally in the nature of instincts, and hence have an organic origin. They are represented mentally as images or ideas with an affective charge (cathexis). *Topographically*, the mental apparatus is a composite instrument composed of an "id," an "ego," and a "superego."[10] The processes in the id are completely unconscious, while consciousness is the function of the ego's most exterior layer, which is concerned with the perception of the external world. The *economic* viewpoint assumes that the mental representations of the instincts have an affective charge of definite quantities of energy, and that it is the purpose of the mental apparatus to prevent any occlusion of these energies, thus keeping the excitations at a minimal level. The mental processes, then, are incipiently directed by the "pleasure principle," but in the course of development they submit to modification upon confrontation with an external world, thus complying with the "reality principle" (the delay of instinctual gratification).

The genesis of the three dimensions of psychical apparatus is clearly interwoven in Freud's theory. The psychical apparatus has the id as the "true psychical reality": it represents the inner world of subjective experience and has no knowledge of, or contact with, "external" objective reality.

It is the reservoir of psychical energy, furnishing all fuel for the various psychical systems, and derives its energy from the somatic processes. The id, operating by the pleasure principle, seeks to reduce tension in the organism to a comfortably low level. It seeks to accomplish this either via reflex actions or the primary process (that is, by forming an image of the desired object that will reduce the tension, as in "wish-fulfillment"). Since the simple image formation of the desired object is unable to reduce tension by itself, a secondary process arises in the organism—the system of the ego. Being able to differentiate between the images of the subjective reality of the id and the entities of the objective external reality, the ego is able to match the image of the desired object with a "real" one of the external world, and thereby reduce tension. Hence, operating via the secondary process, the ego obeys the "reality principle." As "executive" of the personality, the ego's primary function is to act as a mediator between the instinctual desires of the organism and its surrounding environmental conditions. The ego determines which instincts will be satisfied, and how, where, and when. Subsequently a superego develops, which seeks to inhibit gratification of the id's instinctual impulses, to persuade the ego to substitute moralistic goals for them, and to strive for perfection.

There is a fourth standpoint which implicitly permeated Freud's metapsychology, since it was ubiquitous and intrinsic to the underlying assumptions of his psychoanalytic constructions: that is, the *genetic* viewpoint.[11] From the very first, Freud's theories of infantile sexuality, the specific stages of libidinal development, the etiology of neurosis, and so on, focused on the genetic causes in human development. In tracing one psychical structure back to another which was its antecedent and out of which it developed, Freud believed that it was possible to discover the genetic causes of neurotic (and other) symptoms.[12] Hence, Freud conceived of the psychical life as a continuous thread of activity. Furthermore, the genetic viewpoint incorporated two fundamental factors in Freud's theory: the predisposing influential experiences of early childhood and hereditary disposition (i.e., phylogenetic influences).[13] It is easy to see that this viewpoint connected with the other coordinates of Freud's metapsychology:

> We have been able to make our simple genetic formula more complete, without dropping it. Transference neuroses correspond to a conflict between the ego and the id; narcissistic neuroses, to a conflict between the ego and the super-ego; and psychoses to one between the ego and the external world.[14]

This, then, was the fundamental thrust of Freud's metapsychological theory. It would account for those universal and necessary conditions for the possibility of the emergence of meaning in our experience.

Freud's Therapeutic Approach

The application of Freud's metapsychological theory provided the philosophical-scientific foundation upon which his therapeutic approach was grounded. It offered an organic, biological, explanation of human nature that conceived of health and illness in terms of his dynamic, topographic, economic and genetic coordinates. For Freud, health and illness were considered a matter of degree and dependent upon one's ability to balance energies and establish an equilibrium among the various systems in relation to internal and external demands. More specifically, mental illness was conceived by Freud as an economical reaction to conflict and trauma—a person experiences a "flight into illness" because it is considered the most efficient way to protect oneself from a perceived threat.

> Falling ill involves a saving of psychical effort; it emerges as being economically the most convenient solution where there is a mental conflict (we speak of a "flight into illness"), even though in most cases the ineffectiveness of such an escape becomes manifest at a later stage.[15]

Thus, even when the original threat is removed, the memory-trace of the threat remains. Awareness of the threat, however, must be repressed insofar as it continues to be considered a threat. Hence, there arises a tension between a person's failure to remember (consciously) and an impossibility to forget (unconsciously); and the more this tension swells (the more often, for example, unconscious reactions are triggered) the more one must devote energy to the repression of the material. Consequently, the more energy devoted to repression, the less energy one has to go about one's every day activities. Psychotherapy, then, was developed as a means of freeing up the confined energies by bringing about an awareness of repressed material so as to reestablish an equilibrium in the body's mental systems.

The Task of Freudian Psychotherapy

Freud was quite explicit in his conception of the task of therapy:

> We have formulated our task as physicians thus: to bring to the patient's knowledge the unconscious, repressed impulses existing in him, and, for that purpose, to uncover the resistances that oppose this extension of his knowledge about himself.[16]

> From our point of view . . . the transformation of this unconscious material in the mind of the patient into conscious material must have the

result of correcting his deviation from normality and of lifting the compulsion to which his mind has been subjected. For conscious will-power governs only conscious mental processes, and every mental compulsion is rooted in the unconscious . . . It is only by the application of our highest mental functions, which are bound up with consciousness, that we can control all our impulses.[17]

We try to restore the ego, to free it from its restrictions, and to give it back the command over the id which it has lost owing to its early repressions.[18]

[Analysis will] thanks to having strengthened the patient's ego, succeed in replacing by a correct solution the inadequate decision made in his early life.[19]

The goal of Freud's therapy, then, was clear: by making conscious the repressed material formed primarily during early childhood and uncovering and eliminating the resistances, Freud enabled the analysand to achieve greater self-knowledge, and consequently an increase in self-control over his impulses.

To accomplish this overall goal, Freud employed numerous psychoanalytic techniques he developed and refined throughout his career. Early on, Freud conceived of psychoanalysis as a powerful form of suggestion. He felt strongly that physicians ought to become more adept at utilizing psychoanalytic techniques because by virtue of their medical position they were performing such techniques regardless of their awareness. Patients came to them seeking cures for their ailments, and the very nature of the healing relationship presumed a psychical interaction; patients would inevitably be affected, for better or worse, by the suggestions of their physicians.

All physicians, therefore, yourselves included, are continually practicing psychotherapy, even when you have no intention of doing so and are not aware of it . . . Is it not then a justifiable endeavor on the part of a physician to seek to obtain command of this factor [the psychical disposition of the patient], to use it with a purpose, and to direct and strengthen it? This and nothing else is what scientific psychotherapy proposes.[20]

The power of suggestion became blatantly clear to Freud, especially in the employment of his earlier methods of hypnosis. Freud came to realize that, simply by making strong suggestions to the patient in a hypnotic state, longstanding symptoms could be apparently eliminated. The success of this method, however, depended upon too many factors, including the patient's ability to be hypnotized and the strength of the physician's suggestion. All too often symptoms would return in some form. Freud wrote: "In every severe case I saw the suggestions which had been applied crumble away again; after which the disease or some substitute for it was back once more."[21]

Freud abandoned hypnosis early in his career (around 1896). He found that by relying on the therapist's suggestions, rather than encouraging the expression of unconscious material, other factors necessary in understanding the patient's illness became concealed. Freud used the analogy of painting versus sculpture. In the former, the artist applies a substance— "particles of colour"—whereas, in the latter case, the artist "takes away from the block of stone all that hides the surface of the statue contained in it."[22] Freud's conception of psychoanalysis, then, moved from the level of suggestion to the level of "analysis": a *regressive, archaeological approach.*

> The technique of suggestion aims at proceeding *per via di porre;* it is not concerned with the origin, strength and meaning of the morbid symptoms, but instead, it superimposes something—a suggestion—in the expectation that it will be strong enough to restrain the pathogenic idea from coming to expression. Analytic therapy, on the other hand, does not seek to add or to introduce anything new, but to take away something, to bring out something . . .[23]

Freud abandoned the use of hypnosis for other reasons as well. He came to realize, for instance, the importance of therapists' objectivity and neutrality. Instead of imposing a suggestion on the patient, Freud's therapeutic approach moved more and more toward the utilization of techniques which would allow the patient more freedom of expression whereby the unconscious could more fully show itself.

Freud came to rely heavily upon two therapeutic devices to accomplish a "cure": therapeutic interpretation (free association and dream analysis), and the "working through" of information. First, it was the "fundamental rule" which had "the greatest importance for cure":

> [The analysand] is to tell us not only what he can say intentionally and willingly, what will give him relief like a confession, but everything else as well that his self-observation yields him, everything that comes into his head, even if it is disagreeable for him to say it, even if it seems to him unimportant or actually nonsensical.[24]

Freud's method of free association required that the therapist encourage the patient to abandon all conscious control of ideas, and to give in to free and spontaneous associations. The goal was to uncover—via the psycho-analytic act of interpretation—the repressed unconscious content (the result of chosen childhood repressions, that had come to dominate the individual's psychical life). Later, by replacing the automatic restrictions of repression by conscious judgment, the therapist aimed to enable the patient to control (not eliminate) instinctual life. It is clear from its centrality why Freud thought that the "fundamental rule" was of "the greatest importance for cure."[25]

Dream interpretation

In the employment of the technique of free association, Freud noticed that rather than presenting their symptoms, patients often related their dreams to him. This frequent occurrence led Freud to study the significance of dreams both as a therapeutic technique and as a valuable tool for unlocking some of the mysteries of human existence. Once again, however, Freud stepped beyond the restricted boundaries of the science of his day and suffered the consequences. The scientific community failed to take Freud's work seriously: his most important work on dreams, *The Interpretation of Dreams,* only sold 351 copies over a six-year period, and those who took notice of the book had nothing positive to add. According to Freud,

> the few notices of it that have appeared in scientific periodicals show so much *lack* of understanding and so much *mis*understanding that my only reply to the critics would be to suggest their reading the book again—or perhaps, indeed, merely to suggest their reading it.[26]

In spite of the reception of his theory, Freud refused to give up on the importance of dreams. He asserted boldly:

> I have been driven to realize that here once more we have one of those not infrequent cases in which an ancient and jealously held popular belief seems to be nearer the truth than the judgment of the prevalent science of to-day. I must affirm that dreams really have a meaning and that a scientific procedure for interpreting them is possible.[27]

Freud believed that dreams afforded us access to what otherwise would remain hidden. However, the conveyance of the dream by itself did not necessarily reveal the true meaning of the dream: he believed dreams had both a manifest and latent content. The manifest content was what his patients presented to him in their retelling of their dreams during therapy. The significance of the manifest content was not readily apparent.

Freud found that, by applying his method of free association to the manifest content of the dream, oftentimes the underlying latent material would surface, and the actual meaning of the dream would be revealed in the context of the patient's life and illness. This latent material, Freud believed, was grounded in unconscious wishes that became more accessible during sleep, due to the relaxation of the censor.

During sleep, the censor's primary responsibilities were turned inward—focusing on the maintenance of sleep. The most likely material to be considered threatening to the sleeping state was the unconscious material which became all the more powerful during sleep; hence, in order to fulfill its function of promoting sleep, the censor created dream images which would satisfy the demands of unconscious desires (thus, dreams are "wish-fulfillments") while not allowing the "unacceptable" nature of the material to be revealed directly to the conscious mind (such shocking material would most likely awaken the dreamer and defeat the purpose of the dream).[28] Freud believed that the manifest dream, those images which the dreamer could recall, must have undergone various distortions prior to being admitted into consciousness. What had been concealed through this process of distortion were the unconscious, latent thoughts.

Freud's technique of free association applied to dreams was intended to uncover the latent thoughts responsible for the manifest dream. There seemed, however, to remain some dream material that repeatedly did not inspire any associations in Freud's patients. The fact that many patients had the same difficulty with the same dream-elements led Freud to speculate that a "fresh general principle is at work where we had begun by thinking we were only faced by an exceptional failure of technique."[29] Freud accumulated many similar cases of relatively few elements, and found that these same elements or *symbols* could be interpreted consistently in each case, that is, they presented the same difficulty in eliciting associations and had the same underlying meanings regardless of the patient's unique case.[30] This remarkable phenomenon led Freud to conclude that "we are faced by the fact that the dreamer has a symbolic mode of expression at his disposal which he does not know in waking life and does not recognize."[31] This discovery led Freud to speculate that something of the ancient continues to exist in us all: that the human unconscious not only retains all the childhood memories of the individual, but also of the human race.

> The prehistory into which the dream-work leads us back is of two
> kinds—on the one hand, into the individual's prehistory, his childhood,
> and on the other, in so far as each individual somehow recapitulates in

an abbreviated form the entire development of the human race, into phylogenetic prehistory too.[32]

Despite this exciting find, Freud never gave up his insistence that psychoanalytic dream interpretation should include the dreamer's associations and life context.

> Psycho-analysis follows the technique of getting the people under examination so far as possible themselves to produce the solution of their riddles. Thus, too, it is the dreamer himself who should tell us what his dream means.[33]

In fact, Freud repeatedly cautioned against the temptation to reduce psychoanalytic dream interpretation to a decoding of dream symbols.

> I should like to utter an express warning against over-estimating the importance of symbols in dream-interpretation, against restricting the work of translating dreams merely to translating symbols and against abandoning the technique of making use of the dreamer's associations. The two techniques of dream-interpretation must be complementary to each other; but both in practice and in theory the first place continues to be held by the procedure which I began by describing and which attributes a decisive significance to the comments made by the dreamer, while the translation of symbols, as I have explained it, is also at our disposal as an auxiliary method.[34]

Interpretation of dream symbols was to be considered a "supplement" only.

> Interpretation based on a knowledge of symbols is not a technique which can replace or compete with the associative one. It forms a supplement to the latter and yields results which are only of use when introduced into it.[35]

Implications of dreams

The study of dreams had implications other than their obvious therapeutic use. Through his investigations into dreaming, Freud believed that he had uncovered truths regarding human mental processes in general. Dreams were *"the royal road to a knowledge of the unconscious activities of the mind"*[36] precisely because they provided scientific evidence for unconscious mental activity in sleeping and waking states. Thus, all the elements discovered through his research into dream analysis were active in the waking state as well, only in a less obvious way. Hence, just as in dreaming, the waking mind had numerous demands placed upon it; and, just as in dreaming, the censor was responsible for interpreting information and when "necessary," distorting the "unacceptable" in order to reduce tension and establish an equilibrium of energies. What was deemed unacceptable in waking life also underwent a process of repression. Freud believed that this held true in both the neurotic and "healthy" person. In a sense, then, Freud's theory of the unconscious resulted in the view that all individuals unconsciously contribute toward the creation of their own reality by virtue of individual interpretations, distortions, and the selectivity of material. The unconscious represented individual—as well as phylogenetic—energies and material, from which the conscious mind received only a worked-over glimpse.

Working-Through and Transference

The employment of dream interpretation along with the utilization of free association during therapy afforded Freud special access to the analysand's unconscious and repressed childhood material. Once this material became available, Freud gained knowledge about the analysand by reconstructing the past from the present fragments and ascertaining the early childhood "decisions" concerning repressions. This enabled him to uncover the source of the analysand's resistance. Once the therapist had come to understand the causes for resistance, the problem remained of how and when to expose these findings to the analysand. Freud believed that, by giving the patient the "conscious anticipatory idea" (the idea of what he may expect to find) and the similarity of this with "the repressed unconscious idea in himself,"[37] the gap between unconscious and conscious material became bridged, and the patient could then overcome the inherent resistances. Freud learned, however, that simply giving the knowledge he had gained about the analysand was insufficient for cure (overcoming the resistance) to occur. He realized that the necessary condition was for that knowledge to be founded upon an inner change in the patient, a change which can only come about by a mental operation directed to that end.[38]

Freud recognized that the patient must "work through" (especially on an emotional level) the known resistance in order to overcome it. This "is a part of the work which effects the greatest changes in the patient and which distinguishes analytic treatment from any kind of treatment by suggestion."[39] Furthermore, the timing of the disclosure of knowledge to the analysand was considered crucial: these revelations should not occur until a well-developed rapport was established in the patient with the physician in transference.

> It remains the first aim of the treatment to attach [the patient] to it and
> to the person of the doctor . . . [the patient] will of himself form such an
> attachment and link the doctor up with one of the imagos of the people
> by whom he was accustomed to be treated with affection.[40]

Freud believed that it was necessary to establish a permissive atmosphere
within the therapeutic encounter in order for the patient to feel comfortable in expressing and exploring repressed emotional factors.[41] Subsequently, for Freud, it was natural for these emotions which manifested a
repetition of neurotic patterns gradually to become targeted directly at
the therapist: this occurrence Freud called "transference neurosis." The
working-through of transference was accompanied by a recollection of
forgotten infantile experiences—real or fantasized. By recovering and understanding the repressed experiences and conflictual occurrences that
had been left unresolved, and by living them through, the individual was
able to gain mastery of these early conflicts and grow as a human being.

According to Freud, transference was one of the strongest attempts
by the analysand's psyche to resist the therapeutic process. By projecting
onto the therapist the attributes of an important figure from the analysand's past, confronting unconscious material became more difficult, for
the analysand was directly faced with past difficulties in the current situation. (It is much harder to confront a real person than an image from the
past.) Hence, transference was also an indication of the success of treatment. Freud recognized that it was a kind of barrier the unconscious built
before the patient in an attempt to preclude further progress—and no
such barrier would be necessary unless there were something to hide.
How the therapist dealt with transference, then, was one of the most important issues in psychoanalysis.

Finally, it should be underscored that Freud conceived the role of
the therapist as crucial in the therapeutic encounter. The therapist was to
remain as objective and neutral as possible, so as not to contaminate the
process. Such a position was not an easy one: by virtue of their humanness,
therapists were subject to the same kind of phenomena as those they
treated; and a therapist could also become (unconsciously) influenced by
the patient. Hence, Freud believed that it was imperative for the therapist
to seriously consider "counter-transference," and to recognize and overcome this in himself or herself.

> We have noticed that no psycho-analyst goes further than his own com-
> plexes and internal resistances permit; and we consequently require that
> he shall begin his activity with a self-analysis and continually carry it
> deeper while he is making his observations on his patients.[42]

Freud felt this so strongly, in fact, that he asserted that anyone unable to undergo the kind of self-analysis of which he had in mind should "at once give up any idea of being able to treat patients by analysis."[43]

Clearly, then, Freud's therapeutic approach provided doctors with some of the necessary techniques to effect a cure in those patients whose sufferings were not helped by current medical procedures. He believed that the application of therapeutic techniques was successful precisely because the human mind was not separate from its bodily functioning—both were grounded in organic forces and processes. His metapsychological theory was an attempt to explain those processes *in scientific terms,* thereby accounting for mental illness and offering a potential cure for suffering.

3

The Ego as Master in Its Own House: Freud and the Enlightenment

The time will therefore come when the sun will shine only on free men who know no other master but their reason.
    —Condorcet

Our best hope for the future of the intellect—the scientific spirit, reason—may in the process of time establish a dictatorship in the mental life of man.
    —Freud

As a physician in search of a cure for neurosis, Freud took himself to be first and foremost a scientist. Freud believed and openly stated that science gave us greater access to knowledge of reality. For this reason, he ostensibly felt no need (nor even the ability) for psychoanalysis to attempt to create a worldview of its own. He wrote: "It does not need one; it is a part of science and can adhere to the scientific *Weltanschauung*."[1] Yet one might ask, from whence did this scientific worldview originate? Certainly Freud had some deeper knowledge of these historical sources, as indicated by his classical training and personal library. A closer look into the "scientific" influences on Freud reveals a wealth of underlying philosophical ideas which formed the ground of scientific thinking in Freud's time.

It was Enlightenment philosophy—as represented by Descartes, Bacon, Diderot, Voltaire, and Kant—that provided the philosophical infrastructure for Freud's scientism,[2] and which was later to be reinforced by Brentano's attempt to bridge the gap between philosophy and science (see chapter 9). In this chapter, we will focus on the primary philosophical influences that underlie, and led to the generation of, Freud's scientistic worldview. The following chapter will consider some specific Enlightenment figures, for whom Freud had the utmost respect and admiration.

Freud and Bacon

It has not been generally recognized just how influential (consciously or unconsciously) Sir Francis Bacon's philosophy was—as one of the major intellectual predecessors of the Philosophes—in Sigmund Freud's intellectual development. Although he did not often refer to Bacon in his writings, Freud ranked him as the intellectual rival of Da Vinci and Copernicus, in terms of importance for the development of intellectual history.[3] This was high praise indeed! One of Freud's mentors, Pierre Janet, often quoted Bacon; while another, Theodor Meynert, considered himself a "Baconian." In addition, and most significantly, there were clear reasons why Freud thought it important enough to retain Bacon's *Novum Organum* in his highly selective final library in London. It is not at all surprising to find that Freud shared (and identified with) many views put forth by Bacon; what is surprising is just how closely the content and tone of Freud's expressions approached those of Bacon.[4]

The highly significant similarities[5] between Bacon and Freud include that both (1) viewed the forces of nature as something to be understood and controlled, (2) viewed and articulated the nature and role of philosophy in similar (though not identical) ways, (3) sought a solid foundation for knowledge in genuine scientific philosophy, and (4) had a related notion of a hidden something to be discovered and explored. These similarities are explored below.

Bacon was, of course, famous for his claim that "Knowledge is power."[6] "Human knowledge and human power come to the same thing, for where the cause is not known the effect cannot be produced. We can only command Nature by obeying her."[7] Bacon defended science, then, as the ultimate dominion of humanity over nature. Similarly, Freud's view called for the scientific spirit to "establish a dictatorship in the mental life of man" so that humans could gain progressive control over themselves (their natural instincts) and, thereby, Nature as well.[8] Freud wrote: "Human civilization rests upon two pillars, of which one is the control of natural forces, and the other the restriction of our instincts."[9]

Most significantly, Freud and Bacon viewed the nature and role of philosophy in similar ways. Both distinguished between what they regarded as true and false philosophy. Though the root cause of error of false philosophy was more encompassing in Bacon than in Freud, they voiced similar objections in the same tenor: according to both, false philosophy occluded truth for much the same reasons.[10] For Bacon, metaphysicians were prey to *Idols of the Theater.* Like Freud, Bacon was completely opposed to the systems generated by metaphysicians—those constructed by Aristotle and Scholastic philosophers such as Anselm, Aquinas, and so on. Such systems involved the blind acceptance of authority and tradition, and hence, were dogmatic.[11] In addition, "all previous systems of philosophy" seemed to contrive "theatrical worlds" instead of dealing with the real one and, hence, were misleading and fanciful.[12] The result of such systems, according to Bacon, was that they blinded us to the truth.[13]

Bacon and Freud warned that we should be suspicious of sharply defined concepts that seek to grasp the universe. Here, Bacon argued that we have a tendency to fall prey to the *Idols of the Market-Place*.[14] Developing precise definitions, Bacon asserted, achieved nothing; words simply get defined by other words which share the same defects.[15] Hence: "words plainly do violence to the understanding and throw everything into confusion, and lead men into innumerable empty controversies and fictions."[16] The result was that they "render philosophy and science sophistical and inactive."[17] Freud must have been buoyed by Bacon's remark in the face of those philosophers and psychologists who simply equated mental life with consciousness:

> This evil lurks far more insidiously in philosophies and sciences, in
> which an opinion once adopted infects and brings under control all the
> rest, though the latter may be much firmer and better.[18]

Freud and Bacon shared an intense antipathy toward speculative philosophy in general. Bacon distrusted any appeal to supposedly self-evident truths which were intuited at the outset of inquiry; the use of deductive logic to ascend to hasty and insufficiently examined generalities served only to compound the error. Bacon conceived traditional metaphysical philosophers as spiders who spun webs of fantastic ingenuity and formal perfection.[19] The problem was that they had nothing to do with reality, and thereby rendered such philosophies irrelevant.

Both were firmly opposed to the practice of abstraction exhibited by philosophers, because it lacked practical value. Bacon observed: "The human understanding is of its own nature given to abstractions";[20] one problem which results is the tendency to mistake these abstractions for real things.[21] Furthermore, withdrawal to a world of abstract objects supposedly accessible to reason leads merely to illusion and the enunciation of empty generalities. Bacon eloquently expressed what he thought should be done with such theories: "But I say that those foolish and aping imitations of worlds which men's fancies have created in their philosophies must be utterly put to flight."[22] Such theories were considered fruitless and hence lacked value. Bacon, along with Freud, insisted that knowledge be useful: the primary goal was to exert power over nature in the service of humankind.[23] On a related point, one of Bacon's most important innovations was the close linking of theoretical and practical disciplines. In natural philosophy, each speculative discipline was to have its operative counterpart. Practitioners had made progress in a purely empirical way, while the philosophers—especially those in the universities— had disdained experience and spun metaphysical cobwebs. The only hope of progress lay in uniting the two approaches. In parallel fashion, Freud sought to make his metapsychology the grounding for everything (including observation), and reciprocally used observation to establish the truth of his most fundamental metapsychological concepts.

Bacon and Freud opposed the preconceived fancies generated by philosophers that tended to leave them less critically reflective about their own frameworks than they should have been. Through the *Idols of the Cave*, Bacon said that we falsify the light of nature because we become attached to particular contemplations.

> But men of this kind who apply themselves to philosophy and to contemplations of things in general, distort and corrupt them as a result of their preconceived fancies . . . who utterly enslaved his natural philosophy to his logic, rendering it more or less useless and contentious.[24]

Our preconceptions influence what we see, and, perhaps more important, what we do not see.[25] Freud wholeheartedly agreed:

> Unfortunately, however, people are seldom impartial where ultimate things, the great problems of science and life, are concerned. Each of us is governed in such cases by deep-rooted internal prejudices, into whose hands our speculation unwittingly plays.[26]

The result was that such approaches failed to subject themselves to genuine critical self-examinations. Bacon's remedy was that we "should be suspicious of whatever allures and captivates [our] understanding, and should be all the more cautious over theories of this kind, so that the understanding can be kept impartial and pure."[27] In the same spirit, Freud insisted that such theories should at best merely be regarded as "provisional."[28] Freud insisted that the most general ideas of psychoanalysis were "open to revision" and that since "its theoretical superstructure [was] incomplete" it remained "subject to constant alteration."[29]

Freud and Bacon both consciously sought a solid foundation for knowledge in genuine scientific philosophy.[30] Moreover, both firmly held that genuine scientific philosophy alone generated true knowledge, and shared a view of the proper scientific method to acquire that truth. Freud must have been especially impressed with Bacon's attempt to try to delineate the proper methods of science so that it could produce immense benefits for humanity. Bacon argued that, since the goal of science was to establish laws, it must consider an exhaustive enumeration of phenomena along with the ways in which they vary. Bacon drew up lists of facts with a given quality in common, of facts which lacked the quality, and of those which possessed the quality in varying degrees. He believed that such a collection of numerous facts would eventually lead to a useful generalization about the quality. People ought to collect data, conduct experiments, and thereby learn the secrets of nature by planned and organized observation of its regularities: this was what Bacon described as "the Great Instauration." Compare this to Freud:

> The true beginning of scientific activity consists rather in describing phenomena and then in proceeding to group, classify, and correlate them . . . repeated references to the material of observation from which they appear to have been imposed . . . It is only after more thorough investigation of the field of observation that we are able to formulate its basic scientific concepts with increased precision and progressively so to modify them that they become serviceable.[31]

This, for Bacon, was also the true way of acquiring scientific knowledge. Beginning with particulars, one was able to gradually ascend to knowledge of general qualities;[32] according to Bacon, this approach enabled us to "rise up gradually to those things that are more general in Nature."[33] While doing so, Bacon insisted that it must stick close to observation while recognizing that the latter is not always trustworthy; and reciprocally, he chastised the rationalists for failing to check their analysis with the use of observation.[34] Hence, Bacon insisted on the unification of the senses and reason:

> I have established for ever a true and lawful marriage between the empirical and the rational faculty, the unkind and ill-starred divorce and separation of which has thrown into confusion all the affairs of the human family.[35]

Freud as well, of course, insisted that we remain vigilant about recognizing the importance, yet obvious limitations, of reason, while supplementing it with the crucial data afforded by empirical observation.[36] Bacon and Freud, then, agreed that the "coherence" of a worldview did not involve rationality alone.

One of the most intriguing similarities between Bacon and Freud was that both sought to extend the reach of science to that which was beyond the directly observable. Both thought that it crucial to eschew an uncritical reliance upon sensory observation, because people tend to forget that their sense perceptions are at least partially dependent on their own minds, and that, thus, all sensory knowledge is relative.[37] Bacon and

Freud agreed that this tendency was responsible for the neglect of investigations into the nature of those things which were not directly observable; hence, both had some notion of a hidden something to be discovered and explored.[38] Bacon was acutely aware of the inadequacy of the senses to sufficiently discern the hidden operations of nature, though he believed that hidden processes could be inferred through observable consequences. In short, Bacon asserted that things ought not to be ignored simply because they cannot be directly perceived.[39]

It is interesting to note that there are a couple of passages in Bacon's writings in which he seemed even to anticipate some aspects of the Freudian notion of the unconscious; emotions, for example, often "pervade and infect" our understanding in imperceptible ways.[40]

> But by far the greatest impediment and aberration of the human understanding arises from the dullness and inadequacy and deceptions of the senses, in that those things which strike the sense outweigh things which, although they may be more important, do not strike it directly. Hence, contemplation usually ceases with seeing, so much so that little or no attention is paid to things invisible. Therefore every action of the spirits enclosed in material bodies lies hidden and escapes us.[41]

Freud could not have helped but applaud such insights! Freud was equally clear in emphasizing the occasional necessity to go beyond direct observation to account for how things really are (see his justification of the notion of the unconscious).

Furthermore, Bacon had divided natural philosophy into metaphysics and physics. Metaphysics, he argued, gives "us nothing": a comment with which, as we have seen, Freud would have been very sympathetic. Physics, on the other hand, was concerned with the investigation of processes that were not directly observable but needed to be discovered. The process of natural change depended on factors not immediately observed by the senses. It is interesting to note that when Freud spoke of the unobservable (for example, the unconscious) he used physics as an example of a science in the same predicament as psychoanalysis.

Freud and the French Enlightenment

Having been influenced by Bacon, it stands to reason that Freud would have been interested in the works of the two most influential French philosophes of the eighteenth century, Voltaire and Diderot.[42] Indeed, Freud had been especially impressed by Voltaire, so much so that he listed

Voltaire as one of a half-dozen or so men he considered "great."[43] The motivation behind Freud's appreciation of both Voltaire and Diderot seems reasonably clear: Bacon's reflections on science and philosophy, of course, had exerted an immense influence upon the two philosophes. Both advocated along Baconian lines that we, on the one hand, remain content with the limited and fallible knowledge we gather about nature via the careful application of empiricistic methodology; and, on the other, remain suspicious of the construction of abstract, metaphysical systems as nothing more than speculative (thus, feeble) attempts to generate all encompassing systematic accounts of the entire universe which lack foundation.[44] Voltaire described this approach as "sound philosophy" and hence accorded Bacon the status of "father" of "experimental philosophy."[45] Diderot extolled the Baconian formulation of the experimental method in his essay, "Thoughts on the Interpretation of Nature" (1754). In addition, he made the Baconian model of classification the basis of his organization of the *Encyclopédie*.[46]

Both (the mature) Voltaire and Diderot—as well as Rousseau—were scientific materialists, and thereby determinists who claimed that the laws of necessity which govern all of nature also govern human beings. Like any other animal, humans are determined by "instincts" and "ideas" which they have, yet over which they exert no (ultimate) control. Hence, human freedom is illusory.

Voltaire and Diderot also shared similar reservations about the potential for human progress. Both—again, with Rousseau—believed that various uncontrollable natural and human factors severely limited the historical potential for the development of human happiness. Voltaire stated this point in stark terms: "All history . . . is little else than a long succession of useless cruelties . . . history in general is a collection of crimes, follies, and misfortunes . . . a barren desert."[47] For his part, Diderot came to the conclusion that the achievements and benefits of civilization and morality came at the expense of man's natural happiness. More specifically, he held, in alignment with Rousseau, that there was an internal strife between man's natural instincts and the restrictions of morality. Regarding the instincts, Diderot was clear: "The propagation of beings is the greatest object of nature . . . reason, the slave of instinct, limits itself to serving the latter."[48] Morality, to the contrary, involved a renunciation of the instincts.[49] Hence, Diderot maintained, human beings were caught between their own human nature and a social morality which distorts it. No matter which prevailed, then, humans were doomed to unhappiness.

It is interesting to note as well that Freud referred to a passage in Diderot's "famous dialogue," *Le neveu de Rameau*, three times within the context of his discussions on the Oedipus complex. Diderot's famous passage was translated (by Strachey): "If the little savage were left to himself, preserving all his feebleness and adding to the small sense of a child in the cradle the violent passions of a man of thirty, he would strangle his father and lie with his mother."[50] Freud understood Diderot to be supplying historical evidence of the Oedipus complex, its "essential characteristics, its universality, its content and its fate."[51] It is clear that Freud believed Diderot to be among those great witnesses who had some recognition of the truth of the human condition, whether conscious or unconscious. Furthermore, Diderot's forceful and unpleasant realization of human fate (and unhappiness) was likewise reflected in Freud's own conclusions in *Civilization and Its Discontents.* The extent to which such reflections by the philosophes anticipated Freud's conclusions is remarkable to say the least.

Freud and Kant

The German Enlightenment exerted its impact on Freud predominantly via Kant's philosophy in extensive and often unrecognized ways. Freud was clearly quite familiar with Kant's philosophy: he was a participant in discussions involving Kant's philosophy during meetings of the Vienna Psychoanalytic Society.[52] References to various works by Kant—including the *Critique of Pure Reason* (which was retained and has marginal notes in Freud's library in London) and the *Critique of Judgement,* as well as other more esoteric Kantian works (some of which are very obscure)—appear throughout Freud's writings.[53] There were also specific Kantian ideas Freud acknowledged as having affected him. For example, one primary idea of Kant's epistemological theory that influenced Freud quite consciously was stated in his *Papers on Metapsychology:*

> In psycho-analysis there is no choice for us but to assert that mental processes are in themselves unconscious, and to liken the perception of them by means of consciousness to the perception of the external world by means of the sense-organs . . . The psycho-analytic assumption of unconscious mental activity appears to us . . . as an extension of the corrections undertaken by Kant of our views on external perception. Just as Kant warned us not to overlook the fact that our perceptions are subjectively conditioned and must not be regarded as identical with what is perceived though unknowable, so psycho-analysis warns us not to equate perceptions by means of consciousness with the unconscious mental processes which are their object. Like the physical, the psychical is not necessarily in reality what it appears to be.[54]

Indeed, Freud had already developed this idea *ob ovo* fifteen years earlier in his *Interpretation of Dreams:*

> The unconscious is the true psychical reality; *in its innermost nature it is as much unknown to us as the reality of the external world, and it is as incompletely presented by the data of consciousness as is the external world by the communications of our sense organs.*[55]

It is important to note that Freud was acknowledging two interrelated points here. First, that Kant had shown us that we do not know the external world directly through our senses. Second, and even more important, consciousness does not know the unconscious processes of the mind directly. On this point, Freud could not have failed to miss Kant's observations:

> We can be indirectly conscious of having an idea, although we are not conscious of it. Such ideas are obscure . . . Sense perceptions and sensations of which we are not aware but whose existence we can infer, that is, obscure ideas in both man and animals constitute an immeasurable field . . . It is as if just a few places on the vast map of the mind were illuminated . . .[56]

Freud also remarked on another specific aspect of Kantian epistemological theory:

> As a result of certain psycho-analytic discoveries, we are today in a position to embark on a discussion of the Kantian theorem that time and space are "necessary forms of thought." We have learnt that unconscious mental processes are in themselves "timeless." This means in the first place that they are not ordered temporally, that time does not change them in any way and that the idea of time cannot be applied to them. These are negative characteristics which can only be clearly understood if a comparison is made with conscious mental processes. On the other hand, our abstract idea of time seems to be wholly derived from the method of working of the system Pcpt-Cs. and to correspond to a perception on its own part of that method of working. This mode of functioning may perhaps constitute another way of providing a shield against stimuli.[57]

In accordance with Kant, who stated that "Time is nothing but the form of inner sense, that is, of the intuition of our inner state,"[58] Freud asserted that time was a vague awareness of our own mental functioning, that is, "the working of the system Pcpt-Cs." and "a perception on its own part of that method of working." Yet for Freud, the human mind also included an inner "noumenal world"—namely, the unconscious "id," from which consciousness springs—which is itself timeless and has no order in time.

> There is nothing in the id which corresponds to time; there is no recognition of the passage of time, and—a thing that is most remarkable and awaits consideration in philosophical thought—no alteration in its mental processes is produced by the passage of time.[59]

All of the above similarities between the Freudian and Kantian models of the mind are quite remarkable: in both, consciousness is severed from its source, in such a way that the source is inapprehensible. The result is that both Kant and Freud distinguished between reality as it actually is versus how it appears to us. Hence, the contents of Freudian consciousness correspond to Kantian phenomena; in the structural model of each, the ego is responsible for actively unifying and organizing one's experience.

It is important to note, however, that Freud also took himself to be transcending Kantian theory:

> There is an area whose frontiers belong both to the outer world and to the ego: our perceptual superficies. So it might be that the idea of time is connected with the work of the systemW-Bw [perceptual cs]. Kant would then be in the right if we replaced his old-fashioned "a priori" by our modern introspection of the psychical apparatus. It should be the same with space, causality, etc.[60]

In other words, Kant's "a priori"—his universal and necessary condition for knowledge—was to be considered within the context of human mental functioning. Space and time were conceived by Freud as projections of the functioning of our mental apparatus; they represented a vague awareness of how our minds work.[61] It is here where we encounter Freud's self-ascription of being a dualist:

> If [I] had to choose among the views of the philosophers, [I] would characterize [myself] as a dualist. No monism succeeds in doing away with the distinction between ideas and the objects they represent.[62]

> The explorer of nature, on the other hand, may, through practice, have sharpened his powers of observation to such an extent that he can apply them to the outside world. But the segment of the outside world which

he can understand still remains relatively small. The rest, he "thinks," will be as I am; that is, he becomes anthropomorphic in relation to the rest; the remainder, therefore, he replaces with the dim perception of his own psychic processes.[63]

Freud raised some points in relation to Kant's lesser-known works as well. For example, in the *Interpretation of Dreams,* Freud wrote: "Kant writes somewhere [1764]; 'The madman is a waking dreamer.' "[64] The quote to which Freud referred was actually written in a section of Kant's book *The Classifications of Mental Disorders* entitled, "The relations between dreams and mental diseases." It is likely that Freud had at one time or another encountered this obscure work by Kant. Freud also made reference to a passage in Kant's *Anthropologie* (1798), noting that Kant "declares that dreams seem to exist in order to show us our hidden natures and to reveal to us, not what we are, but what we might have been, if we had been brought up differently."[65]

Freud also sought to describe the psychological-historical origins of Kant's categorical imperative. In the preface to *Totem and Taboo,* Freud *reinterpreted* Kant's categorical imperative as that "which operates in a compulsive fashion and rejects any conscious motives."[66] Freud believed that:

> it may begin to dawn on us that the taboos of the savage Polynesians are after all not so remote from us as we were inclined to think at first, that the moral and conventional prohibitions by which we ourselves are governed may have some essential relationship with these primitive taboos and that an explanation of taboo might throw a light upon the obscure origin of our own "categorical imperative."[67]

Extending this thesis even further, Freud claimed that the Oedipus complex might be plausibly understood as at the root of Kant's categorical imperative:

> I may remind you of Kant's famous pronouncement in which he names, in a single breath, the starry heavens and the moral law within us. However strange this juxtaposition may sound—for what have the heavenly bodies to do with the question of whether one human creature loves another or kills him?—It nevertheless touches on a great psychological truth. The same father (or parental agency) which gave the child life and guarded him against its perils, taught him as well what he might do and what he must leave undone, instructed him that he must adapt himself to certain restrictions on his instinctual wishes, and made him understand what regard he was expected to have for his parents . . .[68]

The super-ego—the conscience at work in the ego—may then become harsh, cruel and inexorable against the ego which is in its charge. Kant's Categorical Imperative is thus the direct heir of the Oedipus complex.[69]

Here, of course, Freud was not only influenced by Kant, but sought to explain the very origins of one of his most important philosophical ideas as ultimately having its basis in the formation of the superego (one part of which is the conscience) via the Oedipus complex.[70]

Given Freud's obviously extensive familiarity with Kant's writings, it is remarkable that he unwittingly overlooked or failed to reference one of Kant's ideas that is quite supportive of his own teleological ideas regarding the unconscious and the collective mind. In his *Idea for a Universal History with a Cosmopolitan Purpose* (1784), Kant claimed that "individual men . . . are guided in their advance along a course intended by nature. They are unconsciously promoting an end . . ."[71] Furthermore, Kant (influenced, of course, by Rousseau) asserted that an antagonism existed between individual human desires and the constraints of society.[72]

In line with the Philosophes, Kant's optimism for potential human evolution only went so far:

> Dogmas and formulas, those mechanical instruments for rational use (or rather misuse) of his natural endowments, are the ball and chain of his permanent immaturity . . . Thus only a few, by cultivating their own minds, have succeeded in freeing themselves from immaturity and in continuing boldly on their way.[73]

Kant and Freud seemed to share a lack of optimism for the possibility of genuine progress.

Finally, given his familiarity with Kant's *Classifications of Mental Disorders* it is interesting to note that Freud failed to mention one of Kant's important observations: that "the therapeutic goal can be reached only through the use of the sufferer's own mental resources."[74] This is important, given Freud's idea of a therapeutic alliance between the analyst and some part of the analysand's ego.

Enlightenment Roots of Freud's Scientific Worldview

Arguably a preponderance of Freud's scientific worldview, then, was clearly manifested in the influence of and/or identification with certain specific philosophical themes of the Enlightenment. For example, Freud shared in the contempt the Enlightenment philosophers had for the construction of metaphysical systems and believed that metaphysics served more to retard than facilitate the advancement of knowledge. Similarly, both maintained that it was the application of scientific methodology that afforded human beings the opportunity to understand the world (including understanding those beings who themselves sought understanding).

It is important to point out that science itself was founded upon the ideas and theories of Enlightenment figures and predecessors. Yet science, during Freud's time, opposed his notion of unconscious mental processes. As we have seen, Freud's investigations into unconscious realms were actually quite consistent with the fathers of scientific methodology. Bacon especially warned against putting too much trust in what we can know purely through our senses, since our perceptions could only take us so far and could, in fact, mislead us. Kant was very vigorous in assessing the vital role mental functioning played in the development of our theories, dogmas, formulas, and so on. Freud's unconscious was a valid scientific step, given its grounding in philosophical-scientific tradition; and thus, even that which the scientists rejected in Freud (the unconscious) for its lack of scientific evidence, was well within the scientific tradition.

An historical glimpse at the Enlightenment figures, then, gives us further insight into "Freud the scientist." His metapsychological theory offered a clearly scientific account of human nature: Freud approached human beings as organic entities, composed of that which made up the same physical material being as everything else in nature. He wrote, "the intellect and the mind are objects for scientific research in exactly the same way as any non-human things."[75] Human existence was part and parcel of a fundamentally organized universe, in which everything was subject to rational understanding and thereby able to be controlled.

Given his scientific view of human nature, Freud firmly believed in the appropriate application of science to human mental functioning, and considered psychoanalysis to be an extension of science. He wrote that psychoanalysis's "contribution to science lies precisely in having extended research to the mental field."[76] Here, Freud believed that the sovereignty of reason would enable men to think and act appropriately. He also believed that continued careful observations enable human beings to identify the rational laws of the universe and correct their understanding of them: "[Psychoanalysis] asserts that there are no sources of knowledge of the universe other than the intellectual working-over of carefully scrutinized observations . . . no knowledge derived from revelation, intuition or divination."[77]

Hence, Freud shared a confidence in the universal, natural capacity of humans to use their reason and observation (exemplified in the works of Bacon, Locke and Newton through a commitment to natural science) to gain truth about the universe (which in itself was assumed to be rationally organized); and a universal human nature, especially its psychological, social, and political dimensions.

Such confidence in reason and observation was similarly manifested as a kind of optimism about the possibility of human progress.[78] Since human beings could make proper use of their rationality, and since the universe was comprehensible through the resources of reason, it was possible to achieve genuine progress. In *The Future of an Illusion* Freud wrote, "In the long run, nothing can withstand reason and experience."[79] To be sure, Freud alluded to the limitations of the capacity of the intellect; he also held the unshakeable conviction that ultimately reason could save us from ourselves.

4

Unity and Separation: Freud and Greek Philosophy

> For the wisdom of men grows according to what is before them.
> —Empedocles

> And no one can foresee in what guise the nucleus of truth contained in the theory of Empedocles will present itself to later understanding.
> —Freud

As we have seen, significant sources of Freud's scientific heritage come from the Enlightenment. However, if we dig deeper into what Freud himself understood to be his philosophical heritage, there is no doubt that he was influenced by early Greek philosophy. Indeed, when asked to name his favorite list of ten books, Freud included a book entitled *The Greek Thinkers*.[1] What was it that Freud felt was so significant about this book? The Greeks had clearly struck a primordial chord on a variety of levels.

It may be said that, for all of humanity's capacity to reason and understand the world, humans are never so far removed from Plato's cave. Freud, as a psychoanalytic archaeologist and synthesizing mind, believed that if we turned to make a descent back into our primitive past, we would find that the basic elements of our humanity and history remained virtually untouched. The early writings of Greek philosophy provided psychoanalytic archaeologists with the opportunity to reclaim those invaluable remnants. Freud speculated that such early insights were less concealed by the sociohistorical tendency to repress the truths of primitive man. The Oedipus complex was a prime example of this: Freud found in Sophocles the recognition of humankind's "fate" prior to social repression. It was Freud's realization that this phenomena extended back as far as ancient Greece,[2] in fact, that inspired the label "Oedipus complex" to describe what he believed was a universal pattern repeated in various forms throughout human history.[3] Thus, it is not surprising that Freud both

read and applied ancient Greek philosophy to his psychoanalytic conceptualization of human nature. In particular, Empedocles and Plato offered
insights Freud reclaimed and utilized to exemplify aspects of his theory.
As we shall see, such discoveries, most likely, also exerted an unconscious
influence in Freud's intellectual development.

Empedocles and Freud

Empedocles was the earliest Western philosopher to whom Freud referred. Freud considered him "one of the grandest and most remarkable
figures in the history of Greek civilization."[4] Freud undoubtedly identified
with some of Empedocles' intellectual methodological approaches: this
was first and foremost manifested by the fact that both sought a unified
account of human existence, the world, and nature, from several sources.
Empedocles synthesized the thoughts of his predecessors (Anaximander,
Xenophanes, Parmenides, Pythagoras, and others),[5] his experiences as a
physician,[6] and his observations on nature. Similarly, Freud unconsciously
and consciously synthesized the thoughts of his predecessors, his experiences as a psychoanalyst, and his observations of the universe.[7] Just as important, both sought to synthesize highly diverse areas of investigation.
Freud specifically admired this in Empedocles: "His mind seems to have
united the sharpest contrasts. He was exact and sober in his physical and
physiological researches, yet he did not shrink from the obscurities of mysticism."[8] Freud, of course, refused to shrink from the obscurities of that
which was unobservable in psychical life and showed how they related to
that which was directly observable.[9]

Both thinkers were highly speculative as to the underlying, most
fundamental forces operative in the universe. Freud himself characterized Empedocles' reflections as "cosmic speculations of astonishingly
imaginative boldness,"[10] while referring to his own reflections as *speculative*
throughout his final metapsychological work *(Beyond the Pleasure Principle)*.[11] However, it should be noted that Freud himself alluded to the speculations of Empedocles as "a cosmic phantasy" while stating that his were
"content to claim biological validity"[12] as a difference between their two
theories. Yet two points mitigated this difference. First of all, Freud accurately acknowledged "the fact that Empedocles ascribes to the universe
the same animate nature as to individual organisms robs this difference
of much of its importance."[13] In other words, given that Empedocles cos-
mologically projected the fundamental characteristics of individual organisms onto the universe as a whole, the conclusions at which he arrived

concerning the universe would necessarily apply to individual organisms. It could be argued, then, that Empedocles' insights were reasonably congruent with Freud's biological assessment of human beings: this was reciprocally reinforced by the fact that Freud extended the operation of the instincts to cover both the organic and inorganic regions of things. "The analogy of our two basic instincts extends from the sphere of living things to the pair of opposing forces—attraction and repulsion—which rule in the inorganic world."[14] This is a highly suggestive comment we will take up later (see chapter 5). Second, while it is true that Freud insisted throughout *Beyond the Pleasure Principle* that his speculative assumptions must ultimately be grounded in empirical observation, he also acknowledged that Empedocles was "exact and sober in his physical and physiological researches."[15] Furthermore, Freud was aware of the impact unconscious influences could have on speculation.

> Unfortunately, however, people are seldom impartial where ultimate things, the great problems of science and life, are concerned. Each of us is governed in such cases by deep-rooted internal prejudices, into whose hands our speculation unwittingly plays.[16]

Freud himself consciously employed the use of fantasies in application to psychoanalysis, for example, when he described

> a "taming" of the instinct. That is to say, the instinct is brought completely into the harmony of the ego, becomes accessible to all the influences of the other trends in the ego and no longer seeks to go its independent way to satisfaction. If we are asked by what methods and means this result is achieved, it is not easy to find an answer. We can only say: "We must call the Witch to our help after all!"[17]—the Witch Metapsychology. Without metapsychological speculation and theorizing—I had almost said "phantasying"—we shall not get another step forward.[18]

Freud would often himself examine the fantasies of his patients in order to better understand the nature of their worldview and liberate them from their own repressions—the exploration of fantasies often had immense therapeutic and theoretical value. For example, as Strachey noted: "Freud became aware of the part played by phantasy in mental events, and this opened the door to the discovery of infantile sexuality and of the Oedipal Complex."[19]

Hence, Freud's comparison of Empedocles' "cosmic phantasy" to his own speculations as having "biological validity," might best be seen as a diminution of what at first appeared to be a stark contrast. Given this, it is useful to compare the content of both theories in order to ascertain what specific influences Empedocles had on Freud's development of psychoanalysis.

Specific Similarities between Freud and Empedocles

Although Empedocles and Freud had, at times, very different ways of understanding the universe and human existence, Freud recognized in Empedocles some truths he consciously conceded and applied to his psychoanalytic theory. Other similarities—of which Freud was not necessarily conscious—are apparent as well.

Empedocles and Freud confronted and answered in the same way the fundamental question as to how to reconcile certain ostensibly opposing features of the universe: the problem for both was how to reconcile the dualistic features of (for example) permanence versus change, and unification versus separation. In order to account for the processes of the continual motion and change of things in the universe, Empedocles postulated the existence of two principles: the first principle, Strife (forces of repulsion), separated the elements; while the second principle, Love (forces of attraction), brought them together.[20] As such, Empedocles conceived these principles to be primordial and eternal;[21] along with the elements, they comprised all material reality.[22] Natural change consisted of the combination, separation, and recombination of permanent entities.[23] The processes of the universe, then, consisted of an interminable oscillation of periods between unity and separation in which one of the principles was dominant.[24]

Freud's reaction to Empedocles' theory was clear: "The two principles of Empedocles—Love and Strife—are, both in name and function, the same as our two primal instincts, Eros and destructiveness."[25] Freud had made this point even earlier (1923): "[The death instinct's] opposition to the libidinal instincts finds an expression in the familiar polarity of love and hate."[26] According to Freud, Eros aimed to bring unity into being, whereas Thanatos could only lead to disunity and destruction for the organic—namely, death.[27] Of particular interest to Freud must have been Empedocles' claim that "all things unite in one through Love."[28] As such, Love represented the power of organic unity and continuous creative combination.[29]

We should also note that Freud made one highly telling remark in his analysis of Empedocles' theory. He approvingly quoted a secondary source description of Empedocles' conceiving of the powers of love and strife as "natural forces operating like instincts, and by no means intelligences with a conscious purpose."[30] The instincts were believed to operate, then, on a level lacking a conscious purpose; obviously, such a comment must have been quite suggestive for Freud.

A second major commonality in terms of content involved the notion that the major principles and/or forces of life were considered to be cyclic in nature. For Empedocles, there were four periods to each cycle: initially the sphere contained all the elements mixed together in Love; eventually Strife entered, and gained on Love; Love then departed, leaving Strife to dominate; and, in the final period, Love reemerged and Strife departed.[31] This description of the dynamic interplay of forces was similar to Freud's:

> It is as though the life of the organism moved with a vacillating rhythm. One group of instincts rushes forward so as to reach the final aim of life as swiftly as possible; but when a particular stage in the advance has been reached, the other group jerks back to a certain point to make a fresh start and so prolong the journey.[32]

Obviously, however, the cycles were of a different sequence for Empedocles and Freud. In contrast to Empedocles, Freud contended that the two basic instincts acted concurrently, were mutually opposed in action, and each was alloyed with a certain quota from the other.[33] However, it is interesting that both accounts reflected a similar theme of unity to separation to unity.[34]

Our penultimate point regarding the cyclical nature of major principles or forces of life is not one of conscious commonality between Empedocles and Freud. The religious teachings of Empedocles were generally mystical given the influence of Orphism and Pythagoreanism. It was specifically under the influence of the Pythagoreans[35] that Empedocles subscribed to the doctrine of the transmigration of souls: souls are condemned to the cycle of birth and rebirth.[36] The exile and return of the individual soul (the "wheel of birth") was reflected in the cosmic movement from harmony to division to harmony. Empedocles preached release from the "wheel of birth" by purity and abstinence.[37] Freud, of course, rejected such mystical accounts of human existence, although he did not reject the idea that such accounts could be investigated as metaphorical insights (such insights lacked the scientific tools which could be used to reveal the underlying biological truths). Hence, although Empedocles spoke of a "transmigration of souls," Freud may have seen an opportunity to convert the underlying insights into scientific theory. It may be argued, for example, that Empedocles' "wheel of rebirth" was symbolic of an individual's "compulsion to repeat," something in which one is doomed to engage until the unconscious material is brought into consciousness. Similarly, Freud's own release from the wheel of repetition was accomplished through an awareness of unconscious desires and an ability to control and renounce those unacceptable impulses of the id through reason. In both cases, the aim was to achieve enlightenment.

Third, as Freud himself noted, Empedocles "included in his theoretical body of knowledge such modern ideas as the gradual evolution of living creatures, the survival of the fittest and a recognition of the part played by chance in that evolution."[38] One might argue that Empedocles had anticipated some aspects of Darwinian evolutionary theory, the latter of which of course exerted an immense influence on Freud.[39]

The philosophical speculations by Empedocles, then, had obviously exerted an influence on the development of Freud's thinking, yet this influence was dwarfed in comparison to the immense impact of Plato's philosophy and psychology.

Plato and Freud

Freud's familiarity with various basic ideas found in the writings of Plato's philosophy is concretely manifested by a number of circumstances. Certainly his classical education must have placed him in contact with some of Plato's dialogues relatively early on.[40] A specific example of this was that while Freud was a student at the Universität Wien taking classes from Franz Brentano, he read Brentano's book, *Psychology from the Empirical Standpoint;* in it, Brentano specifically discussed Plato's pioneering efforts in the fundamental classification of mental phenomenon. Brentano also stated that Plato had recognized internal conflict in man: "a conflict of opposites, first between the demands of reason, and physical desires, but also between physical desires themselves."[41]

It is also clear that Freud had a firm grasp on much of Plato's philosophy. Having been recommended by Brentano, Freud served as the translator to John Stuart Mill's *Grote's Plato.*[42] Freud was clearly familiar with Plato's *Republic,* and retained the *Symposium* in his library in London.[43] Indeed, in a discussion of the psychoanalytic society, Freud specifically alluded to the myth of Aristophanes as employed by Plato, in the *Symposium.*[44] Freud occasionally noted some of the similarities between Plato's ideas and his own throughout his psychoanalytic writings, reverentially alluding to Plato as "the divine Plato."

The relative infrequency of his references to Plato in the *Standard*

Edition is somewhat puzzling, then, and suggests that the major part of Plato's influence on Freud may have been largely unconscious or, as Freud put it, a result of "cryptomnesia." Freud once remarked in a highly significant passage, while contemplating some remarks made to him by Breuer and Charcot:

> At the time I heard them I did not understand what these authorities meant; indeed they had told me more than they knew themselves or were prepared to defend. What I heard from them lay dormant and inactive in me, until the chance of my cathartic experiments brought it out as an apparent original discovery.[45]

What was so remarkable about this passage? Immediately thereafter, Freud conceded that *this happened explicitly in the case of Plato*. What was it that specifically attracted Freud to Plato on, perhaps, an unconscious level? Certainly Plato was yet a synthesizing mind on an even grander scale than Empedocles: not only had he synthesized some of the highly influential positions of his Presocratic predecessors, he did so on a number of interwoven philosophical levels—metaphysics, epistemology, ethics, aesthetics, and so on.[46]

Freud surely must have had an awareness on some level that Plato had developed a psychological theory of human nature intrinsic to his philosophy, and that aspects of it closely (at times) resembled those of his own theory.[47] For example, Freud likely understood that Plato had anticipated some aspects of his theory of the unconscious: within the frameworks of both Freud and Plato, human beings were understood as having desires and ideas which were in some way inaccessible to them, and the challenge was to find a way to gain access. Indeed, as we shall see, Plato even alluded to a censor (not unlike Freud's) preventing such apprehension.

Plato's Acknowledged Influence on Freud

There were three fundamental ways in which Freud *consciously* recognized Plato's historical precedence and its subsequent impact on his thinking. They include Plato's theories of reminiscence, and of Eros, and comments on the importance of dreams and their role in disclosing to us the underlying meaning of our desires.

Theory of reminiscence

Freud directly acknowledged that he had been strongly impressed by Plato's theory of reminiscence and that it had provoked a great deal of thought in him.[48] Indeed, Freud indicated that he was so taken with some of Plato's ideas that he wove them into his most speculative work, *Beyond the Pleasure Principle*. There, Freud alluded to a famous myth told by Aristophanes in Plato's *Symposium* (189e), which Freud considered so valuable precisely because "it traces the origin of an instinct to *a need to restore an earlier state of things*."[49] The myth told of Zeus who cut into two separate parts, beings who were either man, woman, or both. Each being as a unity, originally had two sets of every bodily part; once cut, each of the two parts sought to grow into the other to regain its lost unity. This yearning, or desire, was Eros or love.[50] Freud asked:

> Shall we follow the hint given us by the poet-philosopher, and venture upon the hypothesis that living substance at the time of its coming to life was torn apart into small particles, which have ever since endeavored to reunite through the sexual instincts?[51]

This speculation takes on an interesting aspect if we compare it with a later comment by Freud: "we long ago discovered that what, in the conscious, is found split into a pair of opposites often occurs in the unconscious as a unity."[52] Given that Freud conceived of the unconscious as retaining our genetic prehistory, it should not surprise us that such a metaphor of an original unity and subsequent split would have enticed Freud to speculate that the Greeks may have had access to biological truths expressed metaphorically through their myths. Nonetheless, Freud's scientific mind quickly "checked" this speculation.[53]

Plato was also famous for holding his doctrine of reminiscence: that we know more than we think we know, and that we do not know what we think we know (see the *Meno*). One task of the philosopher, then, was to enable a person to regain lost knowledge—that is, to recollect a previously inaccessible memory—while eliminating inaccurate knowledge through dialogue.[54] The philosopher did this, Plato claimed, without instructing the person or trying to convince him/her about anything.[55] For Freud, what must have been striking (though on an incubative level of understanding) was how the above are all fundamentally characteristic of the psychotherapeutic process as Freud eventually came to conceive of it. Furthermore, even though Freud took himself to be discussing an intrinsically Lamarckian position (based on our phylogenetic history), there is at least one remarkably similar passage to Plato's ideas on this score:

> Thus in the id, which is capable of being inherited, are harboured residues of the existences of countless egos; and, when the ego forms its

super-ego out of the id, it may perhaps only be reviving shapes of former egos and be bringing them to resurrection.[56]

Hence, it is possible for us to retrieve "memories" from previous generations in an individual's present existence for Freud as well. However, we must not make too much out of this similarity of structure since the specific contexts involved differ so significantly.

Theory of Eros

Initially, Freud held more of a biological conception of the libido which emphasized the quantitative, energetic and initial stages as aspects of the instincts.[57] Freud equated "libido" with "the vicissitudes of sexual activity." Yet, Freud himself held (albeit, arguably erroneously) that Plato's concept of Eros and his own theory of libido were identical: "In its origin, function, and relation to sexual love, the 'Eros' of the philosopher Plato coincides exactly with the love-force, the libido of psychoanalysis."[58] Here, it is not altogether clear what Freud took the content of this identity to be; Freud claimed that this equivalence had been demonstrated by Oscar Pfister in an article of 1921.[59] In it, Pfister claimed: "According to [Plato], Eros, Love, is above all the instinct of sex or propagation." On the other hand, Freud wrote in 1925:

> What psycho-analysis called sexuality was by no means identical with the impulsion towards a union of the two sexes or towards producing a pleasurable sensation in the genitals; it had far more resemblance to the all-inclusive and all-preserving Eros in Plato's *Symposium*.[60]

In an earlier footnote, Freud offered an explanation for these apparent discrepancies in his comparison of Libido and Eros:

> [Our] terminology has undergone some development . . . We came to know what the "sexual instincts" were from their relation to the sexes and to the reproductive function. We retained this name after we had been obliged by the findings of psycho-analysis to connect them less closely with reproduction. With the hypothesis of narcissistic libido and the extension of the concept of libido to the individual cells, the sexual instinct was transformed for us into Eros, which seeks to force together and hold together the portions of living substance.[61]

According to Freud, both he and Plato sought to delimit the boundaries of an expanded sexuality[62] while preserving an essential unity afforded by Eros.[63] Freud was clear:

According to our hypothesis human instincts are of only two kinds: those
which seek to preserve and unite—which we call "erotic," exactly in the
sense in which Plato uses the word "Eros" in his *Symposium* . . .[64]

Eros, then, was "all-inclusive" and "all-preserving," seeking unity in all that
is, for Freud as well.[65] And this unity manifested itself in a myriad of ways
for Plato and Freud—that is, the goals and objects of erotic desire were
considered displaceable.[66]

Freud ostensibly interpreted Plato (at least at times) as presupposing an all-encompassing notion of Eros, which served as the common
source (the underlying unity of psychic energy) for the desires of the parts
of the self. With this view Freud explicated and identified his conception
of the libido as well.[67] Hence, each considered Eros as that source which
provided for the possibility of the development of any ideas, including
philosophy itself.[68]

The role of dreams

Freud also consciously shared some of Plato's ideas concerning the source
and role of dreams in our lives.[69] Plato and Freud distinguished between
dreams and reality in similar ways: Plato described dreams as "shadows
which the appetitive, deluded soul mistakes for reality"; Freud conceived
dreams as resulting from a primary process (as "wish-fulfilling" images,
meant to satisfy the active and unconscious id during sleep), while (external) reality was identified by the ego through the secondary process.[70]
Next, both understood that dreams involved the repression of desires and
yet served, at times, as the means of satisfaction for those desires. While
discussing wishes which were considered censored in dreams, Freud pondered:

> What does psychoanalysis do in this connection but confirm the old say-
> ing of Plato that the good are those who content themselves with dream-
> ing of what others, the wicked, actually do?[71]

Freud was thinking no doubt of such comments in the *Republic:* "the most
evil type of man. He is, I presume, the man who, in his waking hours, has
the qualities we found in his dream state."[72]

Furthermore, Freud clearly agreed with Plato that we all have desires that we consider to be shameful and are revealed only in dreams, and
this is possible because the rational part of us is slumbering, enabling our
lawless desires to gain greater expression.[73] Here we see Plato's anticipation of Freud's notion of a censor operative in mental life. In addition,
Plato may have, in a significant sense, anticipated Freud's formulation of

the Oedipus complex,[74] for at times, Plato directly spoke of some dreams as the manifestation of parricidal and incestuous desires.[75] Recall too, that Freud considered dreams as a means for unlocking the mysteries of both our individual histories and the phylogenetic history of the human unconscious. Plato (along with Sophocles) had the roots of the Oedipus complex prior to the social evolutionary process of repression. Thus, Plato's realization that parricidal and incestuous desires exist in us assisted Freud in his archaeological discoveries, by uncovering this past recognition of a human "fate"—a fate which Freud believed "constitute[d] the *nuclear complex* of every neurosis."[76]

Even more striking, Plato spoke of the distortion that occurred in dreams as a result of reflections in appetite of rational thoughts, and hence of a need for an interpretation of the content of dreams conducted by reason.[77] As we have noted (in chapter 2), Freud distinguished between the manifest and latent content of dreams, and applied free association to dreams as a means for interpretation.[78]

Plato's Unacknowledged Influence on Freud

The comments Freud made about his similarities to some of Plato's ideas were remarkable, given their historical influence, but perhaps *what he did not say* is even more striking! There were highly significant similarities, which went unacknowledged by Freud between Plato and his theories of human nature—particularly in terms of how they both conceived of Self. There were also striking parallels between Plato's methodological approach (namely, dialectic) and Freudian therapeutic practice.

A tripartite theory of the self

Surprisingly, given his own adoption of a tripartite theory of the self,[79] Freud was utterly silent about Plato's tripartite theory of the soul, even though aspects of it were powerfully developed in the *Phaedrus,* the *Republic,* and the *Timaeus.*[80] It is certainly plausible, in fact, that the influence of some key aspect of Plato's philosophy occurred on a subliminal level.[81]

It is not difficult to see the remarkable convergence between Plato's and Freud's tripartite theories of the self; consider Plato's famous description in the *Phaedrus:*

> Let [the soul] be likened to the union of powers in a team of winged steeds and their winged charioteer. Now all the gods' steeds and all their charioteers are good, and of good stock, but with other beings it is not wholly so. With us men, in the first place, it is a pair of steeds that the charioteer controls; moreover one of them is noble and good, and of

good stock, while the other has the opposite character, and his stock is opposite. Hence the task of our charioteer is difficult and troublesome.[82]

Compare this to Freud's description:

> Thus in its relation to the id [the ego] is like a man on horseback, who has to hold in check the superior strength of the horse . . . the ego is in the habit of transforming the id's will into action as if it were its own.[83]

And again,

> The ego's relation to the id might be compared with that of a rider to his horse. The horse supplies the locomotive energy, while the rider has the privilege of deciding on the goal and of guiding the powerful animal's movement. But only too often there arises between the ego and the id the not precisely ideal situation of the rider being obliged to guide the horse along the path by which it itself wants to go.[84]

In both, the rational parts of self seek to control as best as possible the other parts of the self which are often pulling in divergent directions. The goal for both, then, was clearly one of *self-mastery*.[85]

Similarities in schemata of self

Interestingly, both Freud and Plato developed theories of the self that involved multiple parts. Both shared a generalized notion of Eros as the common source for the desires of each part, and as such, Eros served as the underlying unity of psychic energy for the self.[86] Yet, each saw conflicts occurring in what must have been different parts of the self: clearly, Plato and Freud understood the self as having parts that were in conflict. This, then, is a general schema of the self that Freud and Plato shared:

1. *The self has parts.*[87] For Plato, spirit was differentiated from both desire and the calculating part of the self.[88] For Freud, "The ego represents what may be called reason and common sense, in contrast to the id, which contains the passions."[89] In addition, Freud, of course, characterized the split in the self in a variety of other interrelated ways: the conscious/unconscious, reason/instinct, and the primary/secondary processes.[90]

2. *There are higher and lower parts to the self.* Both thinkers agreed that the rational, more "mental" part of the self was higher; while the irrational, more "bodily" part of the self was considered lower.

3. *Conflicts occur among the parts of the self.*[91] There are times when the parts are in opposition to one another. Here, Plato approvingly quoted Heraclitus: "The one in conflict with itself is held together, like the harmony of the bow and of the lyre."[92] For example, according to both Plato and Freud, desire and calculating reason are opposed.[93]

4. *Higher parts of the self try to temper and train lower parts.*[94] Plato, of course, in the *Republic* argued that in order to get persons to want to see the truth and apprehend higher reality it was necessary for them to want to use the higher portion of the mind: "the soul of a man within him has a better part and a worse part, and the expression self-mastery means the control of the worse by the naturally better part."[95] And for Plato it was, of course, reason that was best suited to look after the whole person; it was reason that had the strongest ability to decide which of the desires to satisfy and when.[96] This was also why Freud regarded the ego as the executor of the personality.

5. *Parts of the self can and do form alliances with other parts.*[97] For Plato, the spirited part was the natural ally of reason.[98] For Freud, the ego and the superego could, for example, form an alliance against the id.[99]

6. *Any part of the self has the potential/capacity to become the dominant part.*[100]

7. *Different parts can and do dominate or rule the self at different times.*[101] This is made possible by the fact that energies are added to or taken away from different parts of the self at different times. The following remarkable quotation from Plato illustrates this point:

> When a person's desires incline strongly in one direction, we know that they will be weaker in other directions, like a stream of water directed off into one channel. So when someone's desires have set to flow towards learning and the like, they will be concerned with the pleasures of the soul itself by itself and will abandon the pleasures of the body, if he is truly a lover of wisdom.[102]

Freud's word for this was "displacement." Indeed, Freud asserted, "Without assuming the existence of a displaceable energy of this kind we can make no headway."[103] And while elucidating his concept of sublimation, Freud employed precisely the same analogy as Plato:

> Libidinal impulses . . . are related to one another like a network of communicating canals filled with fluid, these impulses display a great "capac-

ity for displacement," i.e., "sublimation." Here society will recognize the rechanneling as something "higher."[104]

For Plato and Freud, the most significant contributions to society developed because of this process. Both agreed, then, that the origins of philosophy (as one of the noblest activities of the human mind, according to Plato) stemmed from Eros.[105] Given that the primary purpose of Eros was to unite, sound philosophy served as the highest aim (Plato) and one of the highest intellectual pursuits (Freud).

8. *When the parts are out of balance, a person has an unhealthy self; reciprocally, when they are in harmony as a whole self, a person is deemed healthy.* For Freud, neurosis was an outcome of mental disharmony; for Plato, the "unjust" was characteristic of disharmony in the self. Both viewed mental maladjustment as unresolved conflict among the parts of the self.[106] Given the potential for conflict among the parts of the self, both examined malfunctioning personalities in order to ascertain those necessary conditions which would enable one to develop a healthy self whose parts were "harmoniously working together."[107] A corollary to this may be seen as an anticipation by Plato of what was, according to Freud, one of the most typical defense mechanisms humans employed—*reaction formation*. Plato wrote, "in truth, any excess is wont to bring about a corresponding reaction to the opposite in the seasons . . . and most especially in political societies."[108] In addition Plato (as well as Empedocles) shared with Freud the dialectical tension of polar opposites within the self—*attraction/repulsion*. Plato wrote, "Is it not that there is something in the soul that bids them drink and a something that forbids, a different something that masters that which bids"[109] and, "a desire to see them and a repugnance and aversion . . ."[110]

9. *The healthy person is one whose parts each fulfills their respective proper functions/tasks.*[111] In doing so, harmony is established by itself, within itself.

A comparison of parts of self

Given the above similarities of the schemata of the self, it is useful to consider a direct comparison and contrast between the respective parts of the self according to each thinker: namely, Plato's "appetites," "spirit," and "reason" and Freud's "id," "superego," and "ego."

The similarities between Freud's conception of the id and Plato's description of the appetites are especially remarkable (though the former was clearly more complicated).[112] Plato described the appetites as "the mass of the soul in each of us,"[113] its "chief and strongest element,"[114] and as much larger than reason;[115] while Freud described the id as "incomparably greater" and more imposing than the ego.[116] Plato described the appetitive part of the self as "fierce nestlings of desire" which "run wild";[117] he wrote, "in fact there exists in every one of us, even in some reputed most respectable, a terrible, fierce, and lawless brood of desires."[118] These desires, which lacked reason and were not able to satisfy themselves, were revealed in sleep according to Plato.[119] Furthermore, both Plato and Freud contended that desires conflict among themselves.[120] Freud wrote: "We explain the psychical splitting dynamically, from the conflict of opposing mental forces, and recognize it as the outcome of an active struggling on the part of two psychical groupings against each other."[121]

Further similarities exist between Plato's concept of the appetites and Freud's concept of the id. Both were considered (1) intimately connected to bodily influences;[122] (2) the source of diverse desires[123] (of hunger, love, and so on);[124] (3) to be seeking to gain pleasure, and avoid pain;[125] (4) capable of distorting perception in compliance with the desires; and (5) unruly and in need of being forcibly restrained.[126] Neither the appetites nor the id were believed to be aware of good versus evil in a moral sense,[127] nor capable of applying the principle of contradiction.[128]

A primary difference between Freud and Plato was that for Plato, a person was typically aware of the contents of his/her appetite; whereas for Freud, unlike the appetite, the id was considered to be intrinsically unconscious. Freud wrote, "we are 'lived' by unknown and uncontrollable forces."[129]

Nonetheless, the similarities between the appetites and the id are quite striking, especially when one compares each thinker's analysis of the impact of the appetites/id during sleep. Each spoke of the manifestation of desires during sleep as involving specific similar aims (for example, making love to one's mother),[130] as well as general ones (dreams as a means to satisfy desires); as unconstrained (for example, killing at will); and as distortions—and thereby repressions—of desires which required interpretation, by means of reason, of the underlying real meaning of dreams.[131]

The similarities between Plato's spirited element and Freud's conception of the superego are not nearly as powerful; yet there are some, which we should not fail to mention. For example, both saw their respective elements as nonrational, yet serving as the ally of reason and opposing appetites/instinctual impulses, and offering it a way to achieve good behavior;[132] as the origin of values (the just, honorable, and so on), as having been bred into children by their parents[133]—in Freudian terms, this was called "introjection"—and, when morality was not followed, as en-joining retributive forces; and as the source of anger and shame within the self.[134]

However, major differences can be discerned as well. Plato granted aggression an honorable status as one of the primary elements of the spirit, while Freud saw it as nothing more than a manifestation of the in-stincts. Like Kant and unlike Plato, Freud broke reason into two parts: one dealing with perception and intelligibility (the ego), and the other with moral judgments (the superego). Neither ego nor superego had knowl-edge of the Forms, and hence reason was of a lower nature for Freud in either function.

Finally, there are similarities in the functions of Plato's rational, cal-culating element and Freud's "ego." Both considered these respective parts as intrinsically involving reason;[135] as the most qualified and inclined to govern the well-being of the whole self, as well as mediate among each of its subsystems;[136] as having (as one of its responsibilities) the duty of decision among desires;[137] as falling asleep at night;[138] and as having as one of its chief functions that of strengthening reason's control over one's appetites/desires.[139]

This last point offers a particularly striking parallel between Plato and Freud, given how each explicitly made the point. Plato wrote, "[Man] is his own master when the part which is better [reason and temperament] by nature has the worse [appetite] under its control."[140] Compare this to Freud: "it is the task of psychoanalysis to strengthen the ego's hold on the id."[141] However, Freud did not at times share Plato's optimism:

> It is thus that psycho-analysis has sought to educate the ego. But these two discoveries—that the life of our sexual instincts cannot be wholly tamed, and that mental processes are in themselves unconscious and only reach the ego and come under its control through incomplete and untrustworthy perceptions—these two discoveries amount to a state-ment that *the ego is not master in its own house.*[142]

It is also true that Plato's belief that Reason is the highest function of the soul parallels Freud's hope that "the intellect will form a dictator-ship in the mind." The chief difference between the two being that, while each spoke of reason as placing oneself in contact with the "real," each meant something different by the real. For Plato it was knowledge of the Good, and the Forms; for Freud, ego was devoted to the reality prin-ciple—the necessity of recognizing the constraints of everyday reality on the demands of the id.[143]

Methodological Similarities between Plato and Freud

There are also truly remarkable similarities in the methodological approaches employed by each of these thinkers: Plato's "dialectic" and Freud's therapeutic process. Indeed, there is the following noteworthy (yet frequently neglected) passage in Plato:

> All . . . she now disdains, welcoming a slave's estate and any couch where she may be suffered to lie down close beside her darling, for besides her reverence for the possessor of beauty she has found in him the only physician for her grievous suffering.[144]

The similarities between Plato's dialectic approach and Freud's therapeutic approach are numerous, and include the following:

1. *Each was clearly seeking a way for individuals to be enabled to apprehend the inaccessible.* (The essence of what each conceived to be the nature of the inaccessible was, of course, quite different as we have seen.) Both shared a similar idea that memories were inaccessible.[145]

2. *The logistics of each involved a process occurring typically between two persons: for Freud the analyst/analysand, and for Plato the philosopher/student.* Each participated in a kind of dialogue to know the truth—to restore lost knowledge. Within these processes, each endeavored to reduce the difference in their respective understanding of the "subject" involved; and for each, this separation between persons was analogical to the separate parts of the psyche. For Plato, the philosopher stood in the same relation to other persons as the rational element stood to the appetitive. For Freud, the analyst stood in the same relation to the analysand as the ego stood to the id. Freud made this point directly: "This struggle between the doctor and the patient, between intellect and instinctual life . . ."[146] Furthermore, both claimed that no knowledge should be imposed during the dialectical/therapeutic process; neither the philosopher nor the analysand should see their task as trying to persuade the other person of something.[147]

3. *Both Plato and Freud acknowledged that recognition of the truth was often uncomfortable.*[148] Both held the idea that not only do we (at least at times) not know what we think we know, but we know more than we think we know. Both Plato and Freud understood that there were powerful resistances to knowing the truth—for example, continuing to hold beliefs with which one has become all too familiar and comfortable—and that these resist-

ances typically involved the fact that various parts of the self were working at cross purposes.

4. *Plato and Freud both acknowledge the need to restore knowledge.* The task of the analyst/philosopher was seen as providing those conditions conducive for the memory to be recalled. In Plato, ignorance was believed to arise from focusing attention upon the everyday, changing objects of perception and appetites; for Freud it occurred, for example, in hysteria, because one did not want to know.[149]

5. *Both Plato and Freud examined selves that were not working well in order to find a way to enable them to do so.* Intrinsic to the processes of dialectic/therapy was the idea that a person is, in the words of Plato, released from their bonds—one sense of the Greek word *analyein* is "to be released from one's chains"—and thus healed.[150] Freud clearly agreed: "Analysis does not set out to make pathological reactions impossible, but to give the patient's ego freedom to decide one way or the other."[151] For both, a "healthy" individual was one who was liberated and enabled to fulfill his/her own nature.

In summary, Freud was clearly familiar with a good deal of Plato's philosophy and liberally borrowed from him on both conscious and unconscious levels. The convergence of their theoretical constructs and methodological approaches—not to mention the very language they employed—testifies to this. Hence, Freud's application of his regressive archaeological method of retrieving the wisdom from past generations, found a wealth of information in the writings of Empedocles and Plato, which he was able to synthesize toward the development and documentation of his psychoanalytic discoveries.

Furthermore, Plato indirectly influenced Freud—as we shall see in the following chapters—in directly impacting the philosophies of the romanticists and, subsequently, Schopenhauer. These philosophical systems contributed their own insights toward Freudian psychoanalysis.

5

Freud's Romanticistic Overtures: Goethe, Schiller, Schelling

> Look within yourselves and you will find everything, and rejoice that out there . . . is nature which says an unconditional yes, assenting to all that you have found within yourselves. To see this, we must investigate experience as it is concretely lived on all levels, including the dark, hidden recesses of the mind.
> —Goethe

> We are now able to understand how it is the animal sensations have the power to drive the soul . . .
> —Schiller

> "Unheimlich" is the name for everything that ought to have remained . . . secret and hidden but has come to light.
> —Schelling

> The uncanny [*unheimlich*] is something which is secretly familiar, which has undergone repression and then returned from it.
> —Freud

At a pivotal point in his young life, Freud was faced with the decision of what career he should follow. Having shown much promise throughout his early education, his father had developed confidence in him and insisted that he should follow his own inclinations. Surprisingly, Freud had little interest in becoming a doctor. In his autobiographical study, Freud wrote: "Neither at that time, nor indeed in my later life, did I feel any particular predilection for the career of a doctor."[1] Rather, what moved him at the time—and throughout his life—was a curiosity "directed more towards human concerns than towards natural objects," and he was leaning in the direction of law and politics. Had it not been for the romanticist notion of Nature and a very powerful essay on the subject read aloud during a lecture young Freud attended, he could likely have chosen an entirely different direction in life.

Inspired by what he believed to be the words of Goethe, Freud listened attentively to the following passage, which helped determine his career path:

> Nature! We are surrounded and embraced by her—powerless to leave her and *powerless to enter her more deeply* . . . We live within her and are strangers to her. *She speaks perpetually with us and does not betray her secret.* We work on her constantly, and yet have no power over her. All her effort seems bent toward individuality, and she cares nothing for individuals. She builds always, destroys always, and her workshop is beyond our reach . . . *and yet all create a single whole* . . . She keeps to herself her own all-embracing thoughts which none may discover from her . . . *She wraps man in shadow and forever spurs him to find the light* [italics added].[2]

Ironically (and as a kind of metaphorical foreshadowing?) these words were attributed to Goethe (by Freud), when the essay was actually written by G. C. Tobler. According to a footnote in the *Standard Edition*[3] it appears that Goethe came across the essay and "by a paramnesia, included it among his own works."[4] Regardless of authorship, Goethe obviously endorsed its meaning; and Freud, having a great respect for Goethe, was deeply affected.

It is an interesting point—given that Freud is often characterized exclusively within the scientific tradition—that what brought him to science was such an emphatic, romantic, and personal exaltation of Nature. Perhaps "Goethe's" personification of Nature removed some of the barriers between "human concerns" and "natural objects" for Freud. Possibly Freud glimpsed an opening in science that could potentially satisfy his (philosophical) curiosity while at the same time give him access to the secrets of Nature as it related to human understanding and discovery.

Freud's Attitude toward Romanticism

Freud's general attitude toward the figures of German Romanticism—Goethe,[5] Schiller, and Schelling—was one of admiration.[6] Freud included them on his relatively brief list of great thinkers. He described Goethe as "the great universal personality,"[7] and Schiller as "one of the noblest personalities of the German nation."[8] Schelling was, of course, widely recognized at the time as the principal philosopher of German Romanticism.[9]

Despite his obvious respect for these men, however, Freud did not agree with everything they had to say. All of them were participants in a movement referred to as *Naturphilosophie*. Freud exhibited a clear ambivalence—one which once again manifested the dialectical nature of his philosophical temperament—toward this movement. On the one hand, he maintained works on the foundations of *Naturphilosophie* in his final library in London.[10] When it suited his purposes Freud referred to these writings to show how others had anticipated, reinforced, and elucidated his own ideas (and hence that he was not so crazy after all). At times, Freud even exhibited camaraderie with *Naturphilosophie*. For instance, in a paper entitled "Resistances to Psychoanalysis" Freud spoke about how his idea of the mind working on the physiological level of disturbances was rejected by the sciences and medical profession in the same way the scientific world had rejected the "philosophy of Nature" that dominated Germany in the first part of the nineteenth century.[11]

On the other hand, like most scientists of his time Freud tended to group *Naturphilosophie* with mysticism[12] and poetics, which were considered deficient in uncovering and expounding upon knowledge since they lacked the resources of the natural sciences.[13] For example, Freud did not explicitly share the romanticist general belief that all reality is ultimately the manifestation of a creative absolute spirit in nature that grounds everything, manifesting itself as an urge of self-expression and thereby self-realization (see chapter 4, on Empedocles). In this regard, Freud apparently maintained the scientific worldview which at least part of him would never give up.[14] Nor did he share the deep doubts by the romanticists about science, reason, and the intellect; and hence he also rejected their claim that the whole universe could be apprehended in its concrete immediacy or nature via sensuous intuition. Nonetheless, a closer look at the romanticists reveals many significant overlapping similarities and shared ideas.

Goethe's Influence in Freud's Life

That Freud was influenced by Goethe is undeniable. Freud had read Goethe extensively, referred to Goethe frequently throughout the *Standard Edition*, and his final library in London included the 126-volume set of his collected works. Freud was also the recipient of the "Goethe Prize" in 1930, which was awarded to "a personality of established achievement whose creative work is worthy of an honour dedicated to Goethe's memory."[15] This brought "great pleasure" to Freud, who wrote: "There is something about [the Goethe Prize] that especially fires the imagination and one of its stipulations dispels the feeling of humiliation which in other cases is a concomitant of such distinctions."[16] In his acceptance address, Freud described Goethe with admiration as "both artist and scientific investigator . . . In Goethe's life both personalities found room side by side: at different times each allowed the other to predominate."[17] This, of course, was commensurate with those sides of Freud's philosophical proclivities we discussed in the preface of this book.

Freud also articulated what he took to be "Goethe's connections to psychoanalysis." Freud stated that Goethe would have been at least amicable toward psychoanalysis since he also had similar insights, which psychoanalysis was later able to confirm (despite often unpleasant reactions from society).[18] For instance, Goethe recognized the unsurpassable power of emotional bonds among humans and realized (or rather, did not "deny") that these occur incipiently in the context of familial relations (for example, the Oedipus complex). Goethe also had an awareness that the maze of passions ultimately underlie the content of dreams—something of great significance to Freudian psychoanalysis. Freud believed that Goethe even anticipated and made use of certain methods of psychoanalytic technique: Goethe had concretely illustrated how the condition of genuine compassion could facilitate the possibility of a liberating cathartic experience; and he showed how directly talking about anxiety-producing ideas ("through a passionate outburst of feeling") could effect a "cure."[19] Finally, according to Freud, Goethe had succeeded in identifying the unity of Eros and its varied expressions on a par with Plato; indeed, Goethe had made clear that Plato served as the model for approaching the most difficult of philosophical questions.[20]

It is interesting to note that one similarity Freud failed to mention in his address for the Goethe Prize, was that Goethe had also anticipated his notion of the death instinct as beyond the pleasure principle.

> The moment of death, which is thus most appropriately called *dissolution,* is that in which the chief or ruling monad dismisses all those subordinate monads which have hitherto been vassals in her service. I therefore regard the quitting life, as well as the entering it, as a spontaneous act of this chief monad, whose very constitution is utterly unknown to us.[21]

Goethe had thus also anticipated Freud's idea that "the aim of all life is death."[22]

Not only did Freud have an immense respect for Goethe, he apparently identified with him as a kind of "father figure."[23] As mentioned earlier, Freud's decision to become a physician was due in part to an essay on Nature attributed to Goethe; Freud's own father had left the decision up to him as to what his future direction would be, and it was "Goethe" who provided that direction. Freud also admitted that he (and analysts in general) was guilty of applying psychoanalysis to his "hero," Goethe, in part out of a similar (psychological) ambivalence one has toward "fathers and teachers."[24]

Goethe's own insights disclose another interesting personal connection between he and Freud: Goethe apparently believed that he "had no sense for philosophy in the real meaning of the word." Goethe wrote: "when I philosophized about things in my own way I did so with unconscious naïveté."[25] Compare this with Freud's insecurity regarding his own philosophical acumen (see chapter 1). Goethe also openly conceded that he had no taste for logic and epistemology; recall that according to Freud philosophy "goes astray in its method by over-estimating the epistemological value of our logical operations,"[26] and Freud's comment that "with epistemology I lose all interest."[27] Nevertheless Goethe, like Freud, could not help himself—at least at times—when it came to addressing philosophical concerns. Both proceeded to see the necessity for and/or succumb to the temptation of engaging in metaphysical inquiry. Goethe wrote, "There are some problems in the natural sciences which cannot be adequately discussed without involving the help of metaphysics."[28] He proceeded to do this, for example, throughout his *Scientific Studies,* while Freud did so repeatedly in *Beyond the Pleasure Principle.*[29]

Freud and Goethe (as well as the romanticists in general) recognized the importance of historical tradition in the development of ideas, and both maintained a reverence for historically rooted ideas. For example, in his *Maxims and Reflections,* Goethe suggested,

> If we are to rescue ourselves from the boundless multiplicity, atomization and complexity of the modern natural sciences and get back to the realm of simplicity, we must always consider the question: how would Plato have reacted to nature, fundamentally one unity as it still is, how would he have viewed what may now appear to us as its greater complexity?[30]

As we have seen, Freud did just this throughout his writings: with Empedocles, Plato, Enlightenment thinkers, and the romanticists.

As we shall see more thoroughly in what follows, Freud also shared Goethe's new vision of science in its quest for archetypal phenomena[31] and primal polarities;[32] he also opposed the exclusive use of quantitative method in the theory and practice of science. For example, in the context of his discussion on hysteria, Freud emphasized the need for "the most sympathetic spirit of inquiry and not an attitude of superiority and contempt" (which science might adopt). Here Freud approvingly quoted Goethe: "Not Art and Science serve alone; Patience must in the work be shown."[33] Such a reminder suggests that Freud might have supported Goethe in his advocacy of a distinctively non-Newtonian conception of science.

Philosophical Similarities between Freud and German Romanticism

While they do not appear as often, Schiller and Schelling were employed by Freud when he felt the need for additional philosophical/poetic grounding. This is not at all surprising given the direct influence exerted by Goethe on Schiller (the two were close friends) and Schelling. Freud had recourse to Schiller's works throughout his writings: to illustrate definitions, examples, or experiences;[34] to show a basis in literature of some of Freud's ideas;[35] to show how Schiller's ideas were in line with some misguided ways of perceiving the world, and so on. Freud referred to Schelling less often; however, as we shall see, he shared some of his most powerful ideas as well.

A more in-depth consideration of some of the primary tenets of the romanticists provides us with the opportunity to ascertain the extent to which Freud was influenced by the romanticist movement. These similarities include issues regarding (1) reason and its place in human understanding, (2) the hidden self, (3) an organically unified, teleological conception of the universe, (4) the proper procedure for uncovering Nature's secrets, (5) Nature as a unified whole, (6) the Universe as governed by polarities, and (7) primordial phenomena.

Against the powerful currents of the Enlightenment in general, the romanticists emphasized the limited resources of reason in understanding the universe and insisted on elevating the importance of the passions in this regard. Goethe spoke of reason as a "pander" which exploited the weaknesses of the noblest and most vulgar of the instincts.[36] For Goethe, emotional experiences (the felt quality of the world) were deemed highly significant in enabling us to understand. Spontaneous emotional paroxysms would more effectively enable the self to reveal itself to itself. Along similar lines, Schiller suggested:

> Against an excess of the animal sensations the severest mental exertion
> in the end possesses no influence, as they continue to grow stronger, rea-
> son closes her ears, and the fettered soul moves but to subserve the pur-
> poses of the bodily organisation.[37]

Also, Schiller rejected Kant's sharp bifurcation of reason and desires (passions) as intolerable. In doing so, one might say he sought a synthesis between Goethe and Kant. For Schelling, since nature seeks to manifest
itself in the fullest possible way, we must come to realize that genuine
knowledge of it can be acquired not through rational means, but through
emotional-intuitive absorption within the process as it is lived.

In accord with the romanticists, Freud did not share the lack of
interest or even outright antipathy of most Enlightenment thinkers[38]
concerning the nonrational aspects of nature.[39] However, he also did not
entirely agree with the romanticists' assertion of the primacy of feeling, imagination, and sentiment in opposition to reason; instead, Freud
sought to use the resources of reason to investigate the nonrational nature of man. Freud recognized, like the romanticists, the importance of
not being constrained by reason or the intellect to discover what was real,
and giving the passions their due. Neither, of course, advocated forsaking
reason or the intellect altogether to become irrationalists, however Freud
(at least from a therapeutic stance) and the romanticists sought to avoid
being unduly constrained by it.[40]

The romanticists insisted that the most genuine path toward understanding the whole universe is through an examination of the rich and diverse experiences of the hidden, inner self.[41] It was Goethe who made this
point in a particularly striking way:

> Look within yourselves and you will find everything, and rejoice that out
> there . . . is nature which says an unconditional yes, assenting to all that
> you have found within yourselves. To see this, we must investigate experi-
> ence as it is concretely lived on all levels, including the dark, hidden
> recesses of the mind.[42]

As opposed to reason, ultimate reality was the individual will, which strives
for self-fulfillment. Hence, Goethe had an awareness that the sciences of
the time were insufficient for understanding the complexities of human
existence.

The romanticists were interested in the manifestation of the human
will in dreams, unconscious processes, mental illnesses, and so on. It was
in the romanticist movement (as influenced by Rousseau) that we find the
idea that in the unconscious mind lies the contact of the individual with

the universal powers of nature. The springs of human nature lie in the unconscious, for it links the individual with the universal—or at least the organic. It is felt to be the source of power, the active principle which leads us to feel, to imagine, to think, to act. Indeed, Goethe, Schiller, and Schelling were the first to popularize the term "unconscious" *(Unbewusstsein)* with meanings that approached Freud's in connection with the above point.[43]

It was Goethe who especially shifted our attention even further than his romantic predecessors from an emphasis on the cognitive toward the instinctive, latent elements of the mind:

> It is characteristic of man, an innate quality closely textured into the fabric of his being, that what is closest to him does not suffice for cognition.[44]

> Man cannot persist long in a conscious state, he must throw himself back into the unconscious, for his root lives there.[45]

> People are to be seen as organs of their century who, as a rule, act unconsciously.[46]

> Mood is something unconscious and is based on sensuality.[47]

> Every action, and so every talent, needs some inborn element which acts of itself, and unconsciously carries with it the necessary aptitudes . . . Here begin the manifold relations between the conscious and the unconscious.[48]

According to Goethe, the conscious and the unconscious were considered inseparable, indissolubly interwoven aspects of the mind, just as the mind was inseparable from nature. The cooperation of the two were believed to be the necessary condition for the great achievements in any discipline—Goethe went so far as to say that the mind's imaginative capacity operated "involuntarily, even against my will." He claimed to have written *The Sorrows of Young Werther* "practically unconsciously." Freud himself used Goethe's productive activity (along with Helmholtz's) as an example of the unconscious. Freud wrote: "what is essential and new in [his] creations came to [him] without premeditation and as an almost ready-made whole."[49]

Schiller, as well, referred to the hidden recesses of the mind when aroused by our passions:

> Although by the dim light of everyday emotions the secret working of
> the forces of desire remain hidden away from light, it becomes all the
> more conspicuous and stupendous when passion is strongly
> aroused . . .[50]

In addition, Schiller held that men act morally from the unconscious instinct and that poetry originates in the unconscious.[51] Freud also alluded
to the use of the word *heimlich* by Schiller as meaning "that which is obscure, inaccessible to knowledge."[52] We shall take up this point more thoroughly in subsequent sections.

However, among the romanticists, it was Schelling who incorporated an elaborate conception of the unconscious in his works.[53] We know
that Freud was specifically aware of Schelling's thoughts on the unconscious, given his reading of Eduard von Hartmann's *Philosophy of the Unconscious* (1869) where Schelling's ideas on the unconscious were discussed.[54] Schelling clearly conceived of dynamic unconscious forces
underlying self-consciousness:

> [Man's] noblest activity is that which is not aware of itself . . .[55]

> In all, even the commonest and most everyday [human] production,
> there cooperates with the conscious an unconscious activity . . . That
> which exists in me without consciousness is involuntary; that which exists
> with consciousness is in me through my willing.[56]

> identity of the conscious and the unconscious in the self . . . nature
> begins as unconscious and ends as conscious.[57]

Indeed, Schelling held that there was a hidden lawlessness of the unconscious, which guided the entire species.[58]

Like Freud, Schelling sought to explain how consciousness emerged
in nature. His explanation resembled Freud's insofar as he conceived of
the whole process in terms of the initial "I" splitting itself so that it comes
to know the world of nature. Two important parallels should be noted
here. First, Schelling, like the Freud of *Beyond the Pleasure Principle*, argued
that matter may be "brought to life" when the equilibrium of the expansive and constrictive forces were disturbed and a conflict of forces arose.[59]
Indeed, Schelling suggested, just as Plato had, "only in equilibrium of
forces is there *health.*"[60]

Second, Schelling believed that the incipient states which enabled
the material world of nature to come into being were unconscious. Hence,

Schelling and Freud shared the idea that thought is driven by forces which are not directly accessible to it so that it remains hidden, unconscious, and its operations remain forever enigmatic.[61]

In his *Philosophical Inquiries into the Nature of Human Freedom,*[62] Schelling—anticipating Schopenhauer (as Freud well knew from his reading of Hartmann)—claimed that all reality consists of an indeterminate, unconscious striving will.[63] He believed that this will created reason, ideas, and so on; hence, unconscious nature was regarded as potential mind, which becomes conscious through the ego. The world process consists of the interplay (sometimes conflicting and sometimes not) between this will and conscious reason (which always remains a secondary phenomenon).

> Man is born . . . to exert all his powers upon a world which has influence upon him, lets him feel its forces, and upon which he can react. Between him and the world, therefore, no rift must be established; contact and reciprocal action must be possible between the two, for only so does man become man.[64]

Reality, then, develops from a primordial striving will (or energies, forces) to rational self-knowledge and determination.

Moreover, the romanticists heavily influenced Freud in the generation of his theory of instincts. At the inception of this theory—which was so vital to psychoanalysis—Freud said he was perplexed as to how to proceed:

> Of all the slowly developed parts of analytic theory, the theory of the instincts is the one that has felt its way the most painfully forward. And yet that theory was so indispensable to the whole structure that something had to be put in its place.[65]

Freud credited Schiller's specific suggestion as the starting point for how to proceed in developing his theory of instincts: "Hunger and love: that, after all, is the true philosophy, as our Schiller has said."[66] For Freud, *hunger* stood for the "ego instincts" which strive after objects, and *love* stood for the "sexual instincts" which strive for preservation of the species. The two confront one another.[67] Far from the quantitative instinct theory that was becoming fashionable, Freud's speculations about life and death more clearly resembled, as we have seen, Empedocles, Plato, and the romanticists.

There is a point in an essay by Freud on the Uncanny *(Unheimlich)* where Freud made a very interesting reference to Schelling.[68]

In general we are reminded that the word "heimlich" is not unambiguous, but belongs to two sets of ideas, which, without being contradictory, are yet very different: on the one hand it means what is familiar and agreeable, and on the other, what is concealed and kept out of sight . . . what is the connection between the two? . . . Schelling says something which throws quite a new light on the concept of the Unheimlich, for which we were certainly not prepared. According to him, everything is unheimlich that ought to have remained secret and hidden but has come to light.[69]

What Schelling had in mind, Freud believed, was further explicated by the latter's concept of repression:

[If] psychoanalytic theory is correct in maintaining that every affect belonging to an emotional impulse, whatever its kind, is transformed, if it is repressed, into anxiety, then among instances of frightening things there must be one class in which the frightening element can be shown to be something repressed which recurs . . . if this is indeed the secret nature of the uncanny, we can understand why linguistic usage has extended das Heimliche ["homely"] into its opposite, das Unheimliche (p.226); for this uncanny is in reality nothing new or alien, but something which is familiar and old-established in the mind and which has become alienated from it only through the process of repression.[70]

For Freud, then, the "uncanny" *(unheimlich)* is something which is secretly familiar, which has undergone repression and then returned from it.

Freud agreed with the romanticists' thesis that humans are *not* separate from nature because of the human capacity to reason (as some Enlightenment thinkers had argued); rather, human reason was simply an outcome of biological processes. Hence, both the romanticists and Freud advocated a biological conception of the universe in which the organismic parts were seen as inseparable and interdependent parts of the whole.

Furthermore, the description of nature as wild and unruly resonated with Freud's description of the id within man quite nicely. As we have seen, the Kant of the *Critique of Judgement*—with whom Freud was familiar—provided the philosophical seed of this point. There, Kant presented a teleological picture of nature as an organic unity, an interrelated system, of a purposive, sprawling, growing, evolving, dynamic, and living universe in which man is fundamentally embedded. Schiller and Goethe shared the "growth metaphor" which had been drawn originally from Aristotelian cosmology, modernized by Kant, and more currently with the burgeoning developments in biology. It was Schiller who had made

Goethe aware of the importance of Kant in this respect and, subsequently, probably impacted Freud as well.[71] The result was that both Freud and the romanticists shared in an organically unified teleological conception of the universe; they viewed human life as nature, as intrinsically purposive and goal-directed.

Goethe viewed nature as a living unity in which mind and matter were indissolubly connected. He wrote, "It isn't possible to separate nature and idea without destroying . . . life";[72] and, "The things we call the parts in every living being are so inseparable from the whole that they may be understood only in and with the whole."[73]

Similarly, Schiller held that "[t]he wisest purpose is served by the power which the animal sensations possess over the perceptive faculty of the soul." "Physical phenomena express the emotions of the mind."[74] "And vice versa, mental pain undermines the welfare over the entire organism."[75] While showing this, his intent was to "re-establish the unity of human nature."[76]

For Schelling, the processes of nature and spirit (for example, thinking consciousness) were linked in a series of developments by unfolding powers together forming one great organism in which nature was dynamic visible spirit and spirit invisible nature.[77] Schelling's point was that one underlying organizing principle must pervade nature and consciousness, and that this principle operated without conscious awareness in determining the processes of nature. Of course, on this score, Freud was more comfortable remaining on the human level without speculating about "spirit" nor what must be the case in all of nature.[78] Yet the idea of an underlying principle or principles as governing the unconscious processes of mental life (as in Freud's "pleasure principle," and his later addition of Thanatos) certainly could have stemmed from this application of Schelling.

Goethe and Schelling shared the idea that Nature discloses her secrets only to an approach which resisted quantitative and mechanistic analysis:

> [The] leading scholars in the natural sciences declare . . . an interest in details. This, however is not thinkable without a method which reveals an interest in the whole.[79]

> Mechanism alone is far from being what constitutes Nature. For as soon as we enter the realm of *organic nature,* all mechanical linkage of cause and effect ceases for us. Every organic product exists *for itself;* its being is dependent on no other being . . . The organic, however, produces *itself,* arises *out of itself* . . .[80]

Similarly, Freud's entire approach to the study of human nature was based on analytical reasoning with its emphasis on detailed observation *within a recognition of the whole organic structure*. Freud clearly shared Goethe's contention that one must begin one's inquiry by simply describing phenomena:[81] "The true beginning of scientific activity consists rather in describing phenomena."[82] He also agreed with Goethe's contentions that "the observer never sees the pure phenomenon with his own eyes."[83] Freud acknowledged, for example,

> even at the stage of description it is not possible to avoid applying certain abstract ideas to the material in hand, ideas derived from somewhere or other but certainly not from the new observations alone. Such ideas—which will later become the basic concepts of the science—are still more indispensable as the material is further worked over. They must at first necessarily possess some degree of indefiniteness; there can be no question of any clear delimitation of their content. So long as they remain in this condition, we come to an understanding about their meaning by making repeated references to the material of observation from which they appear to have been derived, but upon which, in fact, they have been imposed.[84]

Compare Freud's recognition to Goethe's:

> The highest would be to realize that all so called facts are already theory-laden.[85]

> No phenomenon is explicable in and by itself; only many of them surveyed together, methodically arranged, can in the end amount to something which might be valid for a theory.[86]

In order to comprehend Nature, then, humans must recognize that they too are natural beings and contribute their own understanding of the "facts."

Freud's recognition of the above extended to his therapeutic practice in two fundamental ways: Freud conceived of the therapist's role to be that of a quiet compassionate observer, and he emphasized awareness of, for example, counter-transference in the therapeutic relationship. The role of observer allowed patients' unconscious material to emerge uninhibited through free association.[87] By becoming a "blank slate" for the patient she/he could project important images onto the therapist via the necessary process of transference. Freud recognized that therapists too were human and carried with them their own unresolved histories.

Hence, therapists would also form various attachments (namely, counter-transference) with their patients. For this reason, Freud frequently emphasized the need for therapists to continually undergo self-analysis in order to preserve the integrity of the therapeutic process. For a therapist's observations and interpretations were always bound up with his/her self-understanding (see chapter 2).

Both the romanticists and Freud believed that Nature (and humans, as natural beings) formed a unified whole. Not only did this view affect Freud's therapeutic technique, it helped form his very conception of health and illness along with the goals of therapy.

In his letters *On the Aesthetic Education of Man*,[88] Schiller focused on the development of the whole person: a being which he conceived as at one with itself, nature, and society; in which all dimensions (cognitive, ethical, aesthetic, and so on) of the person functioned harmoniously within the whole.[89] Goethe shared this view, and recognized that "freedom" was fundamentally a kind of resolution of self-imposed captivity, stemming from disturbances in one's equilibrium.[90] He wrote, "From the forces that all creatures bind, who overcomes himself his freedom finds."[91]

Schelling also believed that humans were originally whole, and that wholeness was essentially an "equilibrium of forces and of consciousness."[92] For Schelling, also, human "freedom" was bound up with the harmony and disruption of forces. "But he can upset this equilibrium through freedom, in order to reestablish it through freedom. But only in equilibrium of forces is there health."[93]

In line with this view, Freud saw the dynamic goal of therapy as a freeing up of energies with the intention of returning the biological mental energies to a balanced state whereby the ego was once again unified.

> The neurotic patient presents us with a torn mind, divided by resistances. As we analyse it and remove the resistances, it grows together; the great unity which we call his ego fits into itself all the instinctual impulses which before had been split off and held apart from it.[94]

And so, for the romanticists and Freud, health involved issues of freeing energies in order to reestablish equilibrium and, hence, regain the natural unity.

The romanticists believed the universe—for Freud, mental life—in its unified wholeness, was governed by certain underlying polarities (conflicting and complementary forces). Once again, it was Kant who served as a primary impetus for this idea: for example, Kant had claimed attraction and repulsion to be the only universal and necessary forces of matter.[95] Influenced by the Greeks,[96] Kant, Schelling, and Goethe conceived of nature as essentially a system of opposing forces: life/death, love/hate, light/dark, and so on.[97] Indeed, Goethe extensively used the idea of the polarity of attraction and repulsion as basic cosmic forces.[98]

Here, of course, Schelling had been especially influential on Goethe. First, in *On the World Soul* Schelling declared, "it is the first principle of a philosophical doctrine of nature to go in search of polarity and dualism throughout all nature."[99] As with Heraclitus and Empedocles (see chapter 4, on Freud and Greek philosophy), this emphasis on polarity was associated by Schelling with a conception of nature as a balance of opposed forces or tendencies that when disrupted led to strife and activity. Second, he had strongly influenced Goethe with his ideas of polarity and intensification as that which is rudimentary to the natural order, and that without opposites there could be no life:

> The two great driving forces in all nature: the concepts of polarity and intensification, the former a property of matter insofar as we think of it as material, the latter insofar as we think of it as spiritual. Polarity is a state of constant attraction and repulsion, while intensification is a state of ever-striving ascent. Since, however, matter can never exist and act without spirit, nor spirit without matter, matter is also capable of undergoing intensification, and spirit cannot be denied its attraction and repulsion. Similarly, the capacity to think is given only to someone who has made sufficient divisions to bring about a union, and who united sufficiently to seek further divisions.[100]

In addition, in his *Ages of the World*, Schelling described the intelligible world, including ourselves, as the result of an ongoing conflict between expansive and contractive forces.[101] Schelling had also emphasized that the reason and distinctions drawn in conscious life were merely emanations of an underlying unconscious turmoil, though one which formed a unity. This was an idea which—later, of course—was to exert immense influence on Schopenhauer, Nietzsche, and Freud.

As we have seen, Freud sought the unity of mental life as grounded in the underlying somatic processes in the development of his metapsychological theory. Also, in alignment with Schelling, Freud clearly saw the world as comprised of opposing polarities (id/superego, Eros/Thanatos, individual interests/societal constraints). The particular importance of polarities to Freud's metapsychological framework was clear:

> Our mental life as a whole is governed by three polarities, the antithesis Subject (ego)–Object (external world), Pleasure–Unpleasure, and Active–Passive . . . the essential feature in the vicissitudes undergone by

instincts lies in the subjection of the instinctual impulses to the influences of the three great polarities that dominate mental life.[102]

Freud concurred with Schelling's point concerning the distinctions of
conscious life versus the unity of the unconscious as well. Recall that
Freud wrote: "since we long ago discovered that what, in the conscious, is
found split into a pair of opposites, often occurs in the unconscious as a
unity."[103] For Freud, the unconscious id was the original, unified, and true
reality of the self out of which consciousness (and distinctions) emerged.
The ego, having been born out of the id, was also unified. Hence, for both
Freud and the romanticists, unity was the grounding of polarities.

Goethe and Freud also shared the conception of the major polarity
between the individual and society as well as some concerns resulting from
it: both saw a tragic opposition in individuals as freely striving for wholeness while suffering from the constraints imposed by societal norms
and/or moral conventions.[104]

Freud shared with the romanticists the claim that there are primordial phenomena which are intrinsic to the metamorphosis in man. Goethe
called such primal phenomena *Urphänomena:* archetypal forms of shapes
that revealed nature's secret principles via intellectual intuitions.[105]

Concurrently, Freud's id was a primary example of these primordial
phenomena in human beings. For (as we have discussed) the id not only
retained each individual's childhood memories, but retained memory
traces that recalled all of human history and hence contributed to the determination of the evolution of the species.[106] For instance, Freud's belief
that there was an original incidence of an actual killing of the "father" in
the early human primal horde provided the seed for what is now known
as the "Oedipus complex."[107] Precisely because nothing is ever lost, humans evolved as they have. Again, for Freud it was the human inability
to forget (on an unconscious level) along with a strong desire to not remember which formed the very foundation of individual, societal, and
cultural relationships.

Freud also shared the romanticists' observation that people react to
such primal phenomena with timidity or fear. Goethe wrote:

> When basic primitive phenomena appear unveiled to our perception,
> we feel a kind of timidity, even fear. Sense-bound people take refuge in
> astonishment; but along comes reason that busy pander hurrying to
> mediate in its own way between the noblest and the most vulgar
> instincts.[108]

Compare this with Freud's discussions of Eros (libido, sexuality) and the
Oedipus complex; for example, on the latter topic:

It cannot be said that the world has shown much gratitude to psychoanalytic research for its revelation of the Oedipus complex. On the contrary, the discovery has provoked the most violent opposition among
adults; and those who had neglected to take part in the repudiation of
this proscribed and tabooed emotional relationship made up for their
fault later by depriving the complex of its value through twisted re-
interpretations [reference is to Jung and Adler]. It is my unaltered conviction that there is nothing in this to be disavowed or glossed over. We
must reconcile ourselves to the fact which was recognized by the Greek
legend itself as an inevitable fate.[109]

In light of such profound similarities between Freud and the romanticists, one must ponder the extent to which Freud was simply—or
merely—a scientific thinker of his time. As we have seen in the previous
chapters, although Freud's scientific mind was philosophically grounded
in the enlightenment figures, his synthesizing mind also sought to reclaim
some concealed treasures from the early Greek philosophers and to ground
their ancient "fantasies" in a biological conception of humans. The impact
of Greek philosophy on the romanticists, as well as the romanticists' own
formulations of human existence—all of which, in turn, converged in the
philosophies of Schopenhauer and Nietzsche—impacted Freud's psychoanalysis. As we shall see in the following chapters, Freud was perhaps most
fundamentally impacted by Schopenhauer's philosophy.

A Case Study of Freud's Philosophical Repression: Schopenhauer and Nietzsche

> The large extent to which psycho-analysis coincides with the philosophy of Schopenhauer . . . is not to be traced to my acquaintance with his teaching. I read Schopenhauer very late in my life. Nietzsche, another philosopher whose guesses and intuitions often agree in the most astonishing way with the laborious findings of psycho-analysis, was for a long time avoided by me on that very account.
>
> —Freud

To be sure, Freud had his problems with the philosophers of his own time. The reason was clear: philosophers either conceived of the unconscious as "something mystical," or rejected the unconscious outright based on their prejudiced view which equated mental functioning with consciousness (see chapter 1). However, Freud himself acknowledged that Schopenhauer was one of the "few exceptions" among philosophers on this score; in fact, he bestowed on Schopenhauer the accolade of being *the* foremost philosophical forerunner of psychoanalysis.[1] Freud wrote, "There are famous philosophers who may be cited as forerunners [of psychoanalysis]— *above all* the great thinker Schopenhauer" [italics added].[2]

In Freud's view, Nietzsche was no intellectual slouch either. He wrote, "the degree of introspection achieved by Nietzsche had never been achieved by anyone, nor is it likely ever to be reached again"; and also, "In my youth, Nietzsche signified a nobility I could not attain."[3] Clearly, Freud had the greatest admiration and respect for both Schopenhauer and Nietzsche. He included *both* on his relatively brief list of six thinkers whom he considered to be "great," and works by each remained in his final library, in London.[4]

It is also clear that Freud identified (in the psychoanalytic sense of the term) with Schopenhauer and Nietzsche on a number of levels. First—and foremost—Freud must have identified with Schopenhauer's and Nietzsche's intellectual integrity and willingness to stand up and challenge the systematic philosophies of their time which had equated mental life with consciousness.[5] Schopenhauer and Nietzsche were among the very few to take on (and suffer the fallout from) *the* major philosophical juggernaut of his day—Hegel. It was only later that they received the recognition they deserved for their contributions toward understanding the place of human existence in the universe. For Freud this was directly analogous to his taking on the philosophical and scientific prejudices of his time (for example, the equation of consciousness with mental life by the philosophers).

Furthermore, Schopenhauer, Nietzsche, and Freud (see previous chapters) explicitly acknowledged that they owed highly significant debts of their intellectual heritage to Plato and Kant.[6] Indeed, references to the most formative philosophical influences on Freud's intellectual development—Plato, Descartes, Goethe, and Kant—received by far the most references throughout Schopenhauer's *The World as Will and Representation* and (in some cases) Nietzsche's work. Empedocles,[7] Bacon, Schelling, and Schiller permeated Schopenhauer's,[8] Nietzsche's, and Freud's works alike. It was as a result of these influential historical-philosophical figures that Schopenhauer and Freud sought to form coherent, unified interpretations of human existence, to identify the underlying reality (noumenal world), and uncover the relationship between the Kantian noumenal world and phenomena. Nietzsche radically departed from this endeavor by rejecting this distinction.[9]

Despite Freud's obvious admiration for—and identification with—Schopenhauer and Nietzsche, his "involvement" with these men (Schopenhauer in particular) was marked by an attitude of ambivalence. Freud liberally quoted and made use of Schopenhauer's metaphysical ideas while at the same time denying the extent to which they truly impacted his development of psychoanalysis. The following chapters will explore this ambivalence, as well as the overwhelming overlap between Freudian psychoanalysis and Schopenhauer's—and, to a lesser extent, Nietzsche's—philosophy.

Freud's Familiarity with Schopenhauer and Nietzsche

It is clear that Freud not only was, but could not have avoided being, aware of the ideas of Schopenhauer and Nietzsche. First we know that, early on in his intellectual development, Freud had been an active participant in a student society at the University of Vienna which met to discuss the major ideas and writings of the dominant intellectual figures of the day, which included, most notably, those of Schopenhauer and the early Nietzsche (namely, *The World as Will and Representation, The Birth of Tragedy* and *Unfashionable Observations*).[10] Also while at the University, one of Freud's most respected and influential teachers, Franz Brentano, had published his magnum opus, *Psychology from the Empirical Standpoint,* in which he discussed some of Schopenhauer's ideas. Brentano also commented on Eduard von Hartmann's *Philosophy of the Unconscious,* which explicitly involved Schopenhauer's philosophy on the topic of the unconscious.[11] More significantly, Freud himself quoted from von Hartmann's book in his *Interpretation of Dreams* (1900). Schopenhauer was depicted in von Hartmann as the natural historical outcome of a synthesis of the romanticists and Kant.[12] In addition, Freud was clearly acquainted with von Hartmann (as "the well-known philosopher") and acknowledged the relationship between von Hartmann and Schopenhauer via an example in his *Psychopathology of Everyday Life.*[13]

Freud surrounded himself with close friends who showed not only a keen interest in Schopenhauer's ideas, but also had the opportunity to form relationships with Nietzsche. For example, Freud maintained a close relationship with Lou Andreas-Salomé[14] and wrote about her and her friendship with Nietzsche (which abruptly ended when she refused Nietzsche's marriage proposal).[15] Another friend of Freud's, Josef Paneth, studied philosophy under Brentano with Freud at the University of Vienna. Paneth maintained an active interest in Schopenhauer's and Nietzsche's ideas and met Nietzsche in 1884. Paneth corresponded with Freud on his discussions with Nietzsche: unfortunately for our purposes, Freud apparently destroyed their correspondence.[16]

It is also well known that Schopenhauer and Nietzsche were among the most frequently discussed philosophers throughout the intellectual community in Europe in the latter part of the nineteenth century (from the 1880s on). This was clearly manifest in the intellectual circles with which Freud associated. One prominent set of these included, of course, the discussions of the meetings of the Vienna Psychoanalytic Society held between 1907 and 1922 (almost all of which were attended by Freud). During those meetings, the philosophies of Schopenhauer and Nietzsche served as among the most commonly held philosophical backdrops of their discussions.[17] Indeed, some entire sessions of the Society were devoted to Schopenhauer's or Nietzsche's philosophies and their relationship to psychoanalysis. For example, in 1912 Dr. Eduard Hitschmann presented a paper entitled "On Schopenhauer," examining the psychological genesis of Schopenhauer's basic ideas, and thereby exploring the feasibility of a psychoanalytic application to them.[18] Just as important, Hitschmann observed that Schopenhauer's ideas served as a precursor of such psychoanalytic conceptions as the significance of the instincts and sexuality for life, repression, and the unconscious.[19] Similarly, in 1909, Otto Rank had brought some passages from Schopenhauer's *World as Will and Representation*[20] to Freud's attention, on the former's anticipation of repression.[21] Subsequently, Hitschmann made a presentation along similar lines, entitled "Nietzsche's Ascetic Ideal," from section three of the *Genealogy of Morals*.[22] In this meeting, Adler argued that it was Nietzsche's way of thinking which was "closest" to psychoanalytic ideas:

> In Nietzsche's work, one finds almost on every page observations reminiscent of those we make in therapy, when the patient has come rather a long way and is capable of analyzing the undercurrents in his mind. Thus it was given to him to discover in all the manifold expressions of culture just that primal drive which has undergone a transformation of civilization.[23]

In 1908, Nietzsche's *Ecce Homo* was directly discussed by members of the society, including Freud himself; [24] and in 1911, A. von Winterstein read directly from a passage from Nietzsche's *Daybreak*[25] on the role of instincts in dreams.[26]

Clearly, Freud was not oblivious to the widespread discussions of the ideas of Schopenhauer and Nietzsche and the obvious influence they exerted.[27] What remains peculiar is that Freud himself denied any genuine acquaintance with the works of these two great thinkers. Freud claimed to have only read Schopenhauer very late in life.[28] In parallel fashion, Freud wrote that he "rejected the study of Nietzsche although—no, *because*—it was plain that I would find insights in [Nietzsche] very similar to psychoanalytic ones."[29] In 1908, Freud stridently maintained before the Vienna Psychoanalytic Society "that Nietzsche's ideas have had no influence whatsoever on my own work."[30] In addition, he offered a variety of reasons for his reticence of reading Schopenhauer and Nietzsche: indolence, being overwhelmed by Nietzsche's wealth of ideas, protecting the autonomy of his ideas,[31] being "smothered by an excess of interest,"[32] antipathy for their abstractness, fear of intellectual embarrassment, and so on.

All in all, Freud himself was never very specific as to which of their works he read or when he read them. In the light of this, the ineluctable question arises as to what Freud had actually read and when. Nietzsche's case is, to some extent, straightforward. As noted above, in 1908 Freud read sections of Nietzsche's *On the Genealogy of Morals* and *Ecce Homo,* and discussed them during meetings of the Vienna Psychoanalytic Society. While ostensible references are made to Nietzschean terms and phrases (will to power, transvaluation of values, superman, and so on) very occasionally in Freud's writings, there is no immediate, concrete evidence that Freud read other works by Nietzsche. The case of Schopenhauer, on the other hand, is unclear to say the least—especially given Freud's characterization of his own familiarity with Schopenhauer as someone he read only late in life. The problem is that Freud himself made references to—and quotes from—some of Schopenhauer's works as early as 1899 and subsequently throughout his writings.[33] This inconsistency in Freud's recollections and actions is worthy of further consideration.

Freud's References to Schopenhauer

Freud's earliest references to Schopenhauer occurred in *The Interpretation of Dreams* (1899).[34] In his first—and by far most extensive—reference, Freud gave a moderately detailed account of Schopenhauer's metaphysical theory as offering an account of the origin of dreams.[35] Later, he briefly referenced Schopenhauer's claim that anyone who appears in a dream conforms to their own character,[36] and his comparative analysis of the relationship between dreams and madness.[37] His next reference occurred in *Totem and Taboo,* in 1913, where he wrote: "Schopenhauer has said that the problem of death stands at the outset of every philosophy."[38] Next, Freud observed that Schopenhauer's concept of repression—this once having been shown to him by Rank (1909), from Schopenhauer's *World as Will and Representation*—"coincides with my concept of repression so completely."[39] Only a few years later, in 1917, Freud offered this highest tribute to Schopenhauer:

> Probably very few people can have realized the momentous significance for science and for life of the recognition of unconscious mental processes. It was not psycho-analysis, however, let us hasten to add, which first took this step. There are famous philosophers who may be cited as forerunners—*above all the great thinker Schopenhauer,* whose unconscious "Will" is equivalent to the mental instincts of psychoanalysis. It was this same thinker, moreover, who in words of unforgettable impressiveness admonished mankind of the importance, still so greatly under-estimated by it, of its sexual craving [italics added].[40]

Freud went on to acknowledge in 1920 and 1925 that "Schopenhauer showed mankind the extent to which he was determined by his sexual impulse."[41] In addition, Freud wrote,

> The large extent to which psycho-analysis coincides with the philosophy
> of Schopenhauer—not only did he assert the dominance of the emo-
> tions and the supreme importance of sexuality but he was even aware of
> the mechanism of repression.[42]

It was in *Beyond the Pleasure Principle* (1920), while discussing his dualistic
view of life as governed by the life instincts and the death instincts, that
Freud actually quoted from Schopenhauer's *Parerga und Paralipomena:*

> We have unwittingly steered our course into the harbours of Schopen-
> hauer's philosophy. For him death is the "true result and to that extent
> the purpose of life," while the sexual instinct is the embodiment of the
> will to live.[43]

However, Freud emphasized that Schopenhauer had only succeeded in
showing this merely "on an abstract basis"; it was left to psychoanalysis to
demonstrate this "in matters that touch every individual personally and
force him to take up some attitude towards these problems,"[44] and "confirm by sober and painstaking detailed research."[45] Hence, according to
Freud, any resemblances to Schopenhauer's philosophy were to be chalked
up to Schopenhauer guessing or intuiting,[46] on an abstract, metaphysically
speculative level, what psychoanalysis was later to establish on the concrete level of everyday life[47] using the proper method of careful, clinical
observation.[48]

However, Freud *vociferously denied* that any of the commonalities
psychoanalysis shared with Schopenhauer's philosophy were due to a familiarity with his writings. In his *Autobiography* Freud (somewhat self-
consciously) wrote:

> Even when I have moved away from observation, I have carefully avoided
> any contact with philosophy proper. This avoidance has been greatly
> facilitated by constitutional incapacity . . . The large extent to which
> psycho-analysis coincides with the philosophy of Schopenhauer—not
> only did he assert the dominance of the emotions and the supreme
> importance of sexuality but he was even aware of the mechanism of
> repression—is not to be traced to my acquaintance with his teaching. I
> read Schopenhauer very late in my life . . . I was less concerned with the
> question of priority than with keeping my mind unembarrassed.[49]

Hence, according to Freud, he delayed his reading of Schopenhauer to
avoid the intellectual embarrassment of possibly not understanding or
being unable to understand[50] Schopenhauer's philosophy and thereby
falling prey to his "constitutional incapacity" for philosophy.

Unfortunately, Freud's explanation runs counter to many cogent historical (and even psychoanalytical) considerations. First, it flies in the face of Freud's own insight that we are most typically unaware of the origin of our own ideas—his idea that we can never be certain that whatever ideas we have been exposed to, in whatever forms, have not had an impact on our thinking. Second, if it were true that Freud avoided Schopenhauer's writings or teachings for fear of intellectual embarrassment—to prevent his ideas from being side-tracked or contaminated by the philosopher's ideas, and to preserve the satisfaction from fresh discovery, as he himself said—such psychological concerns would presumably extend to other philosophical writings. Yet Freud never denied having read Plato, Kant, Bacon, and so on. Indeed, as far as the intimidation factor goes, Schopenhauer had a reputation for being among the *clearest* writers—and hence among *the most accessible* (a fact that was widely known)—in the history of German philosophy. The writings of Schopenhauer were not considered nearly as challenging as the works of Plato, Kant, and others—some of which Freud was clearly familiar with—even to professional philosophers. Indeed, as Schopenhauer demurred in his essay "Some Observations on my own Philosophy":

> There is scarcely a philosophical system so simple and composed of so few elements as mine; and so it can be taken in and comprehended at a glance. This is due ultimately to the complete unity and agreement of its fundamental ideas.[51]

This quote is from a volume of essays *(Parerga und Paralipomena)* with which we know Freud to have been very familiar early on in his intellectual development; so it is difficult to believe that Freud would have found Schopenhauer intimidating. Finally, Freud openly acknowledged having carefully read, and been influenced by, the philosophical ideas of Theodore Lipps and G. T. Fechner, two prominent philosophers of his day: indeed, Freud credited both with not only having closely anticipated his ideas, but spurring him on in his own development of them.[52] The obvious question is, why Freud's professed reasons for not reading Schopenhauer and Nietzsche did not apply to them as well?

What is especially interesting about this is the context in which Freud spoke about Fechner in his *Autobiography*:

> I have carefully avoided any contact with philosophy proper. This avoidance has been greatly facilitated by constitutional incapacity. I was always open to the ideas of G. T. Fechner and have followed that thinker upon many important points.[53]

Thereafter, Freud *immediately* denied having read Schopenhauer and Nietzsche. As early as 1898, Freud read Theodor Lipps without reticence, and experienced some unanticipated astonishment:

> I have set myself the task of making a bridge between my germinating metapsychology and what is *in the books,* and I have therefore plunged into the study of Lipps, whom I suspect of being *the best mind among present day philosophical writers.* So far he lends himself very well to *comprehension and translation into my terms* . . . In Lipps I have rediscovered my own principles quite clearly stated—perhaps rather more so than suited me. "The seeker often finds more than he seeks" . . . in details the correspondence is close too; perhaps the divergence of which I shall be able to base my own contribution will come later [italics added].[54]

In retrospect it is clear what must have been appealing to Freud about Fechner and Lipps: both saw the importance of the scientific study of the hidden processes of the mind. First, both had insisted on the scientific nature of psychology. Fechner composed numerous works in philosophy, which stayed within the boundaries of natural science; his treatises on psychophysics formed the foundations of the establishment of experimental psychology as a science. Lipps even more explicitly formulated the idea that "Psychology is philosophy made scientific."[55] Second, against the currents of their time which equated consciousness with mental life, Freud praised Fechner's and Lipps's recognition of the crucial importance of the hidden underlying currents in mental life. Fechner had referred to the mind as an iceberg, whose tip above the surface was directly available to observation and yet was moved by hidden currents.[56] Freud credited Lipps for being aware that, "The problem of the unconscious in psychology is . . . *the* problem of psychology."[57] Freud wrote: "A German philosopher, Theodore Lipps, asserted with the greatest explicitness that . . . the unconscious is the truly psychical."[58]

In light of the above, the further question arises: given that Freud was willing to read the philosophers Lipps and Fechner on these matters (all of whose works were composed at least sixteen years after Schopenhauer's last writings), why did he not do so with Schopenhauer, especially since the latter had just reached the peak of his prominent place within the intellectual community during the 1870s and thereafter? Why did he not seek "to make a bridge between his germinating metapsychology and what is in the books" of *Schopenhauer*—the most discussed philosophical writings of the time? Schopenhauer arguably trumped all of the above ideas of Fechner and Lipps, and—as we shall see—was even closer than they to Freud's position, globally and in detail.

Prima facie, it would seem reasonable to argue that Freud's early reading of Lipps and Fechner rather than Schopenhauer was attributable to Schopenhauer's well-known criticism of science, and the adherence to scientism by both Lipps and Fechner. But this speculation runs aground given that Freud's beloved Goethe had done precisely the same—and this had not prevented Freud from reading *him*!

To continue the historical sequence, in his fourth preface (1920) to the *Three Essays on Sexuality*—in an effort to mitigate some of the attacks he had been taking for decades for his assertion of the ubiquitous importance of sexuality in human existence—Freud observed with a tone of reassurance and satisfaction that it was Schopenhauer,[59] and not he, who first brought "the whole world of readers" face to face with this idea:

> It must also be remembered, however, that some of what this book contains—its insistence on the importance of sexuality in all human achievements and the attempt that it makes at enlarging the concept of sexuality—has from the first provided the strongest motives for the resistance against psycho-analysis . . . *We might be astonished at this, if we ourselves could forget the way in which emotional factors make people confused and forgetful.* For it is some time since Arthur Schopenhauer, the philosopher, showed mankind the extent to which their activities are determined by sexual impulses . . . It should surely have been impossible for a whole world of readers to banish such a startling piece of information so completely from their minds [italics added].[60]

For our purposes, what is most interesting is not so much the content of Freud's point, but the *way* in which he presented it. Arguably, Freud unwittingly offered evidence for his own "resistance" (in the psychoanalytic sense) to the idea that Schopenhauer had exerted an influence upon his intellectual development: presumably, Freud himself was among that "whole world of readers" to which he alluded in the above passage. And indeed, this point is reinforced by the observation that Freud sprinkled references to Schopenhauer's philosophy throughout his writings, treating them as *common intellectual knowledge*. In 1909, for example, Freud alluded to the everyday sense of "knowing Schopenhauer" due to this familiarity.[61]

It is important to note that Freud strongly insisted on the claim for "priority" or "originality" in his discovery of repression (as opposed to any familiarity with Schopenhauer). Why? The need to be original on "the cornerstone of psychoanalytic theory" surely could have plausibly provided sufficient impetus for "confusion and forgetfulness" (according to Freud's own theory). Hence, Freud's resistance to the point that Schopenhauer exerted any influence on his theory of repression. But why did Freud insist on priority here—in relation to Schopenhauer—while downplaying its importance earlier? All of this is fascinating, historically and psychoanalytically, given Freud's own relatively late observations on the claims to originality:

> Careful psychological investigation . . . reveals hidden and long-forgotten sources which gave the stimulus to the apparently original ideas, and it replaces the ostensible new creation by a revival of something forgotten applied to fresh material. There is nothing to regret in this; we had no right to expect that what was "original" could be untraceable and undetermined.[62]

We cannot help but pause here to note, once again, a highly relevant passage on this topic from an undated letter Freud had written to Fliess: "Whoever undertakes to write a biography binds himself to lying, to concealment, to flummery . . . Truth is not accessible; mankind does not deserve it." An irresistible observation to be made here is that Freud concealed from himself his knowledge of Schopenhauer's ideas—that is, the extent to which he was familiar with Schopenhauer's work—*in his autobiography*. We might simply chalk this up to Freud's "forgetting" having read Schopenhauer or being exposed to his ideas early on, but this would not do *even in Freudian terms*. He wrote: "it is our belief that no one forgets anything without some secret reason or hidden motive,"[63] and that forgetting is "determined by unconscious purpose(s)."[64] What could have motivated Freud's "forgetting" in this case? Freud himself offered a solution: "the purpose of avoiding arousing unpleasure by remembering is conspicuous,"[65] and "in every case the forgetting turned out to be based on a motive of unpleasure."[66] The claim of "originality" to the cornerstone of psychoanalysis (the theory of repression) obviously gave Freud a great deal of pleasure; else he would not have invested so much energy into it (indeed, this is the very point of the development of anticathexes in the first place, according to Freudian theory). Remembering his having read Schopenhauer or learned of his philosophy otherwise early on in his intellectual life would have been too much of a loss to withstand; and so, Freud denied what was verifiably true while remaining consciously oblivious to this fact (the classical marks of a defense mechanism). In this, Freud (inadvertently) offered a graphic, concrete illustration of his own theory of repression. The conclusion is unavoidable: *Freud repressed the true origin of his own theory of repression.*[67]

In applying psychoanalytic principles to Freud we are reminded of his own accolade:

> Psychoanalysis can supply some information which cannot be arrived at by other means, and can thus demonstrate new connecting threads in the "weaver's masterpiece" . . . it seems to me thanks are due to psychoanalysis if, when it is applied to a great man, it contributes to the understanding of his great achievement.[68]

> [Psychoanalysis] teaches us to recognize the affective units—the complexes dependent upon the instincts—whose presence is to be presumed in each individual, and it introduces us to the study of the transformations and end-products arising from these instinctual forces. It reveals the relations of a person's constitutional disposition and the events of his life to the achievements open to him owing to his peculiar gifts . . . psychoanalysis can indicate subjective and individual motives behind philosophical theories which have ostensibly sprung from impartial logical work.[69]

In the above, we have taken Freud's own methodology and applied it to him, finding that he was himself, albeit unwittingly, a concrete manifestation of his own methodological approach. Freud had sought, precisely for this reason, to prevent others from knowing too much about him.

This psychological analysis of Freud is further substantiated by Freud's later attitude toward Schopenhauer. In his *New Introductory Lectures on Psychoanalysis* (1933), Freud had apparently had enough of people equating his concepts with Schopenhauer's philosophy:

> You may perhaps shrug your shoulders and say: "That isn't natural science, it's Schopenhauer's philosophy!" But, Ladies and Gentlemen, why should not a bold thinker have guessed something that is afterwards confirmed by sober and painstaking detailed research? Moreover, there is nothing that has not been said already, and similar things had been said by many people before Schopenhauer. Furthermore, what we are saying is not even genuine Schopenhauer.[70]

Here, one is able to discern a certain sense of ambivalence expressed by Freud that is arguably a manifestation of "protesting too much." First, Schopenhauer was presented as having guessed it correctly; then Freud noted that others had already done so, hence his insight was not even an original one; and—oops—this was not "genuine Schopenhauer" at all, anyway. For a psychoanalyst, such mental gymnastics in so short a passage often indicates that unconscious motivations and/or defense mechanisms are clearly manifesting themselves in a not-so-subtle form. There is, *at the very least*, reasonable room for suspicion.

A particularly interesting example—quoted above—of Freud's relationship to Schopenhauer's thought occurred in 1920, in *Beyond the Pleasure Principle:*

> We have *unwittingly* steered our course into the harbour of Schopenhauer's philosophy. For him death is the "true result and to that extent the purpose of life," while the sexual instinct is the embodiment of the will to live.[71]

And then, in 1933:

> [But] why should not a bold thinker [Schopenhauer] have guessed something that is afterwards confirmed by sober and painstaking detailed research?[72]

It was as if, in Freud's mind, Schopenhauer had merely antecedently and inadvertently stumbled across ideas which Freud, then, had independently discovered; yet the historical context outlined above reveals that something more was involved. Freud had clearly indicated that he had *not* been able to bring himself to accept the existence of a death instinct, especially one that was on the same level as the libidinal instincts, as early as 1909.[73] Freud did not so much as mention this topic again in his published writings for over a decade—until he told Lou Salomé, in the summer of 1919 (in the wake of World War I), that he had come across an unusual idea involving the instincts while reading, among others, Schopenhauer. The outcome: Freud's analysis of the eternal struggle between Eros and Thanatos appeared shortly thereafter, in *Beyond the Pleasure Principle* (1920) and *The Ego and the Id* (1923). Given the above considerations alone, it is difficult to see how the confluence of Schopenhauer's and Freud's views on this topic "unwittingly" occurred; Freud had obviously been inspired by *someone.*

Nevertheless, to continue the sequence, it was not until 1930 (in chapter VI of *Civilization and Its Discontents*) that he first gave special attention to the destructive instincts. He offered later summaries of these again in 1933 (in the *New Introductory Lectures*) and 1938 (in chapter II of his *Outline of Psychoanalysis*). It became obvious that Freud had come to believe strongly in this new and strange idea, and that it played a central role in psychoanalytic theory.

Another fascinating aspect of this sequence is that Freud correctly formulated Schopenhauer's ideas when he thought that they were in agreement with his own and tended to misunderstand Schopenhauer when he thought they differed from one another. For example, Freud's description of Schopenhauer's ideas in *Beyond the Pleasure Principle* were correct; yet consider Freud's characterization in the face of the assertion that his theory of instincts was merely Schopenhauer's philosophy. Indeed, Freud was so self-consciously defensive about the suggestion that he went on in the very next paragraph to insist that "the starting-point of these reflections on the theory of the instincts . . . was . . . the impression derived from the work [case studies] of analysis."[74] Freud continued to assert that his theory fundamentally differed from Schopenhauer on the role of death instincts in human existence:

> What we are saying is not even genuine Schopenhauer. We are not asserting that death is the only aim of life; we are not overlooking the fact that there is life as well as death. We recognize two basic instincts and give each of them its own aim.[75]

Freud must have known full well—given his descriptions in *Beyond the Pleasure Principle*—that Schopenhauer had not "overlook[ed] the fact that there is life." And consider the following, emphasized by Schopenhauer:

> *The will-to-live* . . . is the only true description of the world's innermost nature. Everything presses and pushes towards *existence*, if possible towards *organic existence*, i.e., *life*, and then to the highest possible degree thereof.[76]

> Nature has only *one* purpose, namely that of *maintaining all the species* . . . she works toward this through the pressing intensity of the sexual impulse.[77]

> The will-to-live is . . . first and unconditioned, the premiss of all premisses, and for that reason that from which philosophy has to *start* . . . since the world appears in consequence of the will to live.[78]

Anyone, however remotely familiar with Schopenhauer's philosophy, could not miss his claim regarding the importance and primordiality of the life instincts as manifested in the will-to-live. It seems that Freud reverted to his "constitutional incapacity" for philosophy[79] and need for originality when it suited his needs, desires, and/or purposes.

In summary, we must consider Freud's claims to have read Schopenhauer only "late in life," and that Nietzsche exerted no influence on his thinking, with some suspicion. Given the above, the inexorable conclusion must be that Freud, despite his disclaimers, was (at the very least) quite familiar with these philosophers' ideas via a number of channels and on several related and mutually reinforcing levels.[80]

"Schopenhauer contra Nietzsche"

While numerous writers have recognized that Schopenhauer anticipated a number of the ideas basic to Freudian metapsychological theory, the extent to which Schopenhauer exerted a powerful influence on the global unity of Freudian theory has not, in our estimation, been sufficiently appreciated on the philosophical or psychoanalytic levels. This is, of course, less true of the exploration of the relationship between Nietzsche and Freud. We believe that it is important to take seriously Freud's insight that it was Schopenhauer (as opposed to Nietzsche, for example) who was "above all" the philosophical forerunner of psychoanalysis; hence, our primary emphasis in the following chapters is on demonstrating Schopenhauer's relationship to Freudian theory in a reasonably thorough way.[81] (Nietzsche's contributions are acknowledged as important, yet generally taken to be supplementary in nature.) While doing so we note, however, that there are a few topics on which Nietzsche had a great deal more than Schopenhauer to offer Freud.

In considering Schopenhauer's and Nietzsche's various contributions to Freudian psychoanalysis, a specific configuration surfaces in relation to the topic of this book. We cannot purport to be comprehensive in a few chapters, yet consideration of the general (and at times specific) similarities among these three thinkers offers valuable insights toward a more unified interpretation of psychoanalysis, as well as affording the opportunity to address later criticisms of psychoanalysis made by the existential phenomenologists: for it was in Schopenhauer's philosophy, in particular, that Freudian psychoanalysis had its most stable philosophical roots. (It is interesting to note that Schopenhauer and Nietzsche similarly influenced existential phenomenology, with at times very different results.) The topics covered in the following chapter will be those most pertinent to our purposes, including issues of the "in-itself" and the "will"; we will then be in a position to consider the views of Schopenhauer, Nietzsche, and Freud on unconscious phenomena, and issues relating to freedom and determinism, in the subsequent chapter.

7

The Masters of Suspicion: Schopenhauer and Freud on the Inaccessible Nature of Humanity

> [The will] is the point that remains for ever inaccessible to all human knowledge precisely as it is.
> —Schopenhauer

> [The id] is the dark, inaccessible part of our personality.
> —Freud

As a foremost "master of suspicion," Schopenhauer was one of the primary participants in the "unmasking" trend of the nineteenth century. He strove to uncover the very nature of even hidden dimensions of human experience; indeed, Schopenhauer emphasized that this goal explicitly formed the central endeavor of his entire unified philosophy:

> [It] can be explained that in all we know, a certain something remains hidden from us as being quite unfathomable, and we must confess that we are unable to understand even the commonest and simplest phenomena . . . it must be that things exhibit themselves in a manner quite different from their own inner nature, and that therefore they appear as through a mask. This mask enables us always merely to assume, never to know, what is hidden beneath it; and this something then gleams through as an inscrutable mystery.[1]

In Schopenhauer's endeavor to access the inaccessible nature of reality, he couched the problem explicitly in Kantian terms: "On the Possibility of Knowing the Thing-in-itself."[2] Schopenhauer found that intellect, reason and science all failed to access the thing-in-itself because they failed to recognize that the ultimate nature of reality is not representational:

> [That] about which we are enquiring must be by its whole nature com-
> pletely and fundamentally different from the representation; and so the
> forms and laws of the representation must be wholly foreign to it. We
> cannot, then, reach it from the representation under the guidance of
> those laws . . . the forms of the principle of sufficient reason.[3]

According to Schopenhauer, the mind constructs its world via representation and then forgets that this world is its own construction, thereby
misidentifying the latter as able to apprehend reality as it actually is. By
starting with representation we shall never get beyond the representation—that is, the phenomenal world. "We shall therefore remain at the
outside of things; we shall never be able to penetrate into their inner nature, and investigate what they are in themselves."[4]

Given that reason and science (which operates within the epistemological constraints of logic and empirical observation) fail to enable us to
apprehend the inaccessible, what else is there? The obvious candidate for
Schopenhauer was metaphysics, and he was staunch in his advocacy of
metaphysics as the way to apprehend the inaccessible:

> Our philosophy proceeds from the phenomenal appearance to that
> which appears, to that which is hidden behind the phenomenon; thus
> metaphysics.[5]

> By metaphysics I understand all so-called knowledge that goes beyond
> the possibility of experience, and so beyond nature or the given phe-
> nomenal appearance of things, in order to give information about that
> by which this experience or nature is conditioned . . . but that which is
> hidden behind nature, and renders nature possible.[6]

It was the responsibility of metaphysics to inquire into that hidden, "inexplicable something" which forms the "ultimate basis" upon which everything else is grounded.[7] Furthermore, when metaphysics was conjoined
with genius remarkable progress could be made in apprehending the inaccessible:

> The purely objective apprehension of the world, the apprehension of
> genius, is conditioned by a silencing of the will so profound that so long
> as it lasts, even the individuality disappears from consciousness, and the
> man remains *pure subject of knowing.*[8]

Yet Schopenhauer was equally clear—and this is a highly significant point
from Freud's perspective—that metaphysics "cannot be spun out of mere

abstract concepts, but must be based on observation and experience, both inner and outer."[9] Empirical observation must serve as the foundation of metaphysics.[10] Hence, science was not to be thrown out the window; rather, the conclusions of genuine philosophy and science must be consistent, thereby reinforcing one another. Indeed, Schopenhauer emphasized that this was what made his neglected work, *The Will in Nature,* of particularly crucial significance:

> For, starting from the purely empirical, from observations of impartial investigators of nature who pursue the line of their special science, I reach here directly the real core of my metaphysics; I indicate its points of contact with the natural sciences.[11]

> Physics itself, and therefore natural science generally, pursues its own paths in all its branches; it must ultimately reach a point where its explanations come to an end. This point is just the metaphysical, perceived by science merely as its boundary beyond which it cannot go. Science stops here, and now hands over its subject to metaphysics . . . Therefore, this something, inaccessible and unknown to physics, at which its investigations end and which is afterwards taken for granted by its explanations . . .[12]

Given this, Schopenhauer attempted to demonstrate that the findings of science were indeed consistent with his metaphysical theory in *The Will in Nature.* For example, in his chapter entitled "Physiology and Pathology" Schopenhauer adduced evidence from physiology to show that the unconscious will was agent in both voluntary and involuntary bodily functions.

However, Schopenhauer also incessantly underscored the point that we as investigators must not restrict ourselves to observation.[13] Recognizing this, metaphysics was in the unique position of being able to take that decisive step which would solve the riddle of the world by "combining at the right place outer experience with inner, and making the latter the key to the former."[14] To do so, it must decipher the cryptograph that is experience. The correctness of its solution would be confirmed by its congruity with the continuity, correspondences, consistency, and connections that manifested themselves ubiquitously throughout experience: "It must spread a uniform light over all the phenomena of the world."[15] Schopenhauer wrote, "Accordingly, philosophy is nothing but the correct and universal understanding of experience itself, the *true* interpretation of its meaning and content."[16] Metaphysics, at least for Schopenhauer, could give us truth concerning the nature of human experience.

It is crucial to note that in his analysis, Schopenhauer was quite careful to insist that one must never speak of the thing-in-itself (namely, the will) as if it is somehow separable from and transcendent to the phenomena through which it manifests: to do so would be to speak about that of which one can never have any experience. Metaphysics, then, could only address that of which we have experience:

> [In] this sense metaphysics goes beyond the phenomenon, i.e., nature, to what is concealed in or behind it, yet always regarding it only as that which appears in the phenomenon, not independently of phenomenon. Metaphysics thus remains immanent . . . it never speaks of the thing-in-itself otherwise than in its relation to the phenomenon.[17]

Part of the human condition, then, is that in a fundamental sense the noumenal world and the phenomenal world are never to be understood as separate from its experience. It is only to *the extent of this boundary* that we are able to apprehend the inaccessible. At this juncture, it is clear that Schopenhauer suggested that we could approach the inaccessible in the "immanent sense" discussed in the introduction to this book. However, what transcends this boundary is and will always be inaccessible for Schopenhauer:

> Whatever torch we kindle, and whatever space it may illuminate, our horizon will always remain encircled by the depth of night. For the ultimate solution of the riddle of the world would necessarily have to speak merely of things-in-themselves, no longer of phenomena . . . Therefore the actual, positive solution to the riddle of the world must be something that the human intellect is wholly incapable of grasping and conceiving.[18]

> The essence of things before or beyond the world, and consequently beyond the will, is not open to any investigation, because knowledge in general is itself only phenomenon, and therefore it takes place only in the world, just as the world comes to pass only in it. The inner being-in-itself of things is not something that knows, is not an intellect, but something without knowledge . . . This is why a perfect understanding of the existence, inner nature, and origin of the world, extending to the ultimate ground and meeting every requirement, is impossible. So much as regards the limits of my philosophy and of all philosophy.[19]

For Schopenhauer metaphysics, then, can only meaningfully speak of and approach the "inaccessible" in the *immanent* and *eliminable* senses of the term.

Schopenhauer's Will and Freud's Id

Schopenhauer believed that we do have some access to the thing-in-itself (through a proper application of metaphysics and "science"), however, the question remained: What was the "hidden" element which remained concealed beneath the mask of the phenomenal world? For Schopenhauer it was, of course, will. Schopenhauer's epiphany:

> [The will] alone gives [humankind] the key to his own phenomenon, reveals to him the significance and shows him the inner mechanism of his being, his actions, his movements.[20]

> [W]e ourselves are the thing-in-itself. Consequently, a way from within stands open to us to that real inner nature of things to which we cannot penetrate from without. It is, so to speak, a subterranean passage, a secret alliance, which, as if by treachery, places us all at once in the fortress that could not be taken by attack from without. Precisely as such, the thing-in-itself can come into consciousness only quite directly, namely by it itself being conscious of itself.[21]

> The will is first and original; knowledge is merely added to it as an instrument belonging to the phenomenon of the will. Therefore every man is what he is through his will, and his character is original, for willing is the basis of his inner being.[22]

> The transition from the noumenal world to the phenomenal world occurs directly through the "emergence of an act of will" from the obscure depths of our inner being into the knowing consciousness.[23]

Hence, for Schopenhauer, the inner nature of human beings is will, the thing-in-itself, the noumenal world of Kant. Obviously, Freud was not unaware of the importance of Schopenhauer's notion of will to psychoanalysis; nor was he oblivious to the pivotal role played by Schopenhauer. Consider again, Freud's remarks on Schopenhauer:

> There are famous philosophers who may be cited as forerunners [to psychoanalysis]—*above all* the great thinker Schopenhauer, whose unconscious "Will" is equivalent to the mental instincts of psychoanalysis [italics added].[24]

To be sure, Freud was over sixty years of age when he penned this line; however, it is equally clear that the notion of will played a crucial (albeit slightly different) role in psychoanalysis from its inception. In his first theoretical work, *Project for a Scientific Psychology* (1895), a much younger Freud wrote: "it is thus that in the interior of the system there arises the impulsion which sustains all psychic activity. We know this power as the *will*—the derivative of the *instincts*."[25]

What is remarkable is just how closely Schopenhauer's descriptions of the will corresponded to Freud's descriptions of the id. In their respective systems each considered the will/id to be (1) the true core of our inner being; (2) the most fundamental aspect of our existence while remaining hidden and ultimately unknowable; (3) the underlying being which makes consciousness possible, yet itself is lacking in consciousness; (4) the precondition of everything that happens in accordance with cause and effect; (5) merely concerned with willing and not willing, while striving to bring about the satisfaction of instinctual needs; (6) pre-personal; (7) primitive; (8) lacking in any kind of organization; (9) lacking contact with the "external" world, while at the same time, a precondition for the phenomenal world; (10) organically based and survival-directed; (11) operating according to principles of tension and pleasure; (12) manifested in the body; and (13) a force with which to be reconciled in order to function in society. Each of these assertions merits scrutiny.

1. *Will/id is the true core of our inner being.*[26] This assertion of course was a natural outcome from Schopenhauer's and Freud's mutual, self-acknowledged roots in Platonic and Kant's later philosophy (as we have seen previously). It is important to note, however, that while it is true that for Schopenhauer the will was conceived as the original root of our being—the source from which we come—strictly speaking, for Freud it was the instincts, Eros and Thanatos, which served as the source of our being.[27] For Freud it was through the id that the instincts operated; hence the will was the "derivative" of the instincts.

2. *Will/id is the most fundamental aspect of our existence, yet lies hidden—is obscure and opaque.*[28] For Schopenhauer and Freud, the will/id was hidden and difficult to access. Yet both also asserted that we have some immediate awareness of it[29] and are afforded clues which can further access it.[30] For example, Freud discussed dreams, jokes, parapraxes, and so on. Hence, for both Schopenhauer and Freud, it was through self-consciousness that we are afforded the opportunity of such access.[31] Yet both also acknowledged that our access was limited,[32] that some aspects are and would forever be closed to us[33] and "absolutely inscrutable."[34] We can never know will/id completely.[35] Schopenhauer stressed that if we persist in asking what the will ultimately and absolutely is, we are asking a

question which can never be answered. The will as it is, independently of us, is "unknowable and incomprehensible." As such, "it is the point that remains for ever inaccessible to all human knowledge precisely as it is."[36]

3. *Will/id is the underlying being that makes consciousness possible; hence forms the basis for the development of the intellect/ego, which arises out of it.*[37] Will/id itself, however, lacks consciousness.[38]

4. *Will/id is a precondition for everything that happens.* It is crucial to note that there is a different notion of "cause and effect" employed in Schopenhauer's and Freud's conception of will/id: as *a precondition,* the will/id does not determine what happens. This has significant implications for the issue of freedom and determinism to be discussed in the following chapter.

5. *Will/id is capable of only willing and not willing in its endeavor to bring about the satisfaction of instinctual needs.* Schopenhauer described the instincts as "decided impulses of the will,"[39] and conceived them to be "the innermost impulse and urge of our true nature,"[40] "the inner operating and guiding principle."[41] In concert with Schopenhauer, Freud described instincts as "the mainspring of the psychical mechanism."[42] Hence, each viewed their respective entity (will or id) as the primary impetus, source, and/or container of the instincts.[43] Each held that the instincts were internal sources of excitation and forces originating from within the body,[44] and yet argued that to act, the instincts had to engage external circumstances.[45] Each thinker saw the (unconsciously motivated)[46] aim of instincts as "what is useful to the will"[47]—that is, what will satisfy the needs of the will/id.[48] Freud wrote, "The aim of an instinct is in every instance satisfaction, which can only be obtained by removing the state of stimulation at the source of the instinct."[49] As a result, each viewed the instincts as dominating the intellect/ego.[50] Each also held there to be essentially two classes of instincts—life[51] and death.[52] As Freud himself noted: "For [Schopenhauer] death is the 'true result and to that extent the purpose of life,' while the sexual instinct is the embodiment of the will to live."[53] This mirrored Freud's own account of life (or sexual) instincts and death (or ego)[54] instincts.[55] Finally, both agreed that the two classes of instincts inevitably conflict with one another.[56]

6. *Will/id is pre-personal yet manifesting itself, in each of us, as individual will.* It is clear that Schopenhauer conceived of the will as one unified being: it must be, he reasoned, because (for example) number and the drawing of distinctions/differences are operations of the intellect, and hence not characteristic of the thing-in-itself. If we "conceptually subtract" spatial,

temporal, and causal relations, Schopenhauer was convinced that the will must necessarily be one. And yet, insofar as individuals are manifestations of will, there are individual wills that have as their source the "Cosmic Will." Similarly for Freud, Eros and Thanatos (and their derivatives) have a pre-personal characteristic and yet manifest themselves only in individual ids.[57] In addition, there is the following remarkable claim by Freud in *Totem and Taboo:*

> I have taken as the basis of my whole position the existence of *a collective mind,* in which mental processes occur just as they do in the mind of the individual. In particular, I have supposed that the sense of guilt for an action has persisted for many generations which can have had no knowledge of that action [italics added].[58]

Here Freud is referring, of course, to the "phylogenetic acquisition"[59] of the Oedipal complex, and so on. He wrote in *Moses and Monotheism:* "The content of the unconscious, indeed, is in any case a collective, universal property of mankind."[60] Along similar lines, he wrote in *An Outline of Psychoanalysis:*

> [The id] contains everything that is inherited that is present at birth, that is laid down in the constitution—above all, therefore, the instincts, which originate from the somatic organization and which find a first psychical expression here [in the id] in forms unknown to us.[61]

The pre-personal nature of will/id is a natural outcome of the fact that Schopenhauer and Freud shared (with the German idealists Kant, Schelling, and Hegel) the cosmic view of the universal as manifesting itself through us. Like Schelling, Schopenhauer and Freud shared a concern for the "biological studies" that were emerging in the nineteenth century as well. Both fused these orientations in the construction of their systems.

7. *Will/id is "primitive."* Schopenhauer pointed out that as a comparatively primitive part of human beings, will lacked the sophistication to react to imaginary ideas in a different way from genuine beliefs.[62] Freud made a similar point when it came to religious beliefs and neurotic symptoms. Schopenhauer wrote that this primitive quality within us all "rages like a prisoner against the walls and bars of its dungeon."[63] Similarly, Freud employed the analogy of "a cauldron full of seething excitations."[64]

8. *Will/id is lacking any kind of organizing function.* The laws of thought (the laws of contradiction, identity, and so on) did not apply to the will's/id's

strivings; similarly, will/id was conceived as lying outside the forms of temporality and spatiality.[65] Hence, the will/id was considered by both Schopenhauer and Freud to be unchanging, identical with itself, and ubiquitously what it is in itself.[66]

9. *Will/id has no contact with the "external" world in which its objects lie.* In this sense, will/id is the thing-in-itself, from which the phenomenal world is an expression or manifestation. In other words, insofar as will/id is noumenon, it manifests itself in our world as energy—blind forces which strive. These forces act as the precondition for the phenomenal world. One of the implications of this view is that the phenomenal world, which is manifested through the will/id, has illusory characteristics.

10. *Will/id is organically based and survival-directed.* Recall that the id has no way to satisfy its own instinctual desires: no contact with the "external" world, no intellect, no consciousness, and so on. All of these necessary tools (reason, intellect, consciousness, and so on) developed out of a need to survive, a means to satisfy the instinctual demands of the id. Given this view of human beings, both Schopenhauer and Freud recognized the limitations of the intellect. Seeing the will/id as fundamental and primordial to reason and even consciousness, both considered the intellect to be superficial and an outcome of organically based instincts: consciousness (which does not belong to the id, but develops out of the id via the ego) only develops out of a need to increase one's likelihood of survival. Furthermore, given that the primary focus of the will/id is survival, it naturally follows that sexuality plays a primary role at the core of the human psyche. In fact, Freud believed that the *sexual instincts were the source of the fundamental energy and agency of unconscious psychical reality.* His belief was that sexuality is so basic to our nature because it begins from the inception of our existence, does not willingly accept blockages to its tension-reduction, and is easily molded to almost anything in life—that is, it assumes many forms and has a wide variety of potential objects. Given this, Freud found it necessary to "enlarge the concept of sexuality."[67]

Like Freud, Schopenhauer considered sexuality to be primordial to human existence:

> In *this* [sexual] *act* the inner nature of the world most distinctly expresses itself . . . Therefore that act, as the most distinct expression of the will, *is the kernel, the compendium, the quintessence of the world.* Hence we obtain through it a light as to the true nature and tendency of the world; it is the solution to the riddle [italics added].[68]

The sexual impulse in general . . . is in itself . . . the will-to-live.[69]

The sexual impulse is the focus of the will . . .[70]

Hence the sexual impulse "springs from the depths of our inner nature."[71] Indeed, a quarter of a century earlier, Schopenhauer had boldly proclaimed: "The sexual impulse is . . . [man's] final end and highest goal."[72]

> The satisfaction [of the sexual impulse] . . . is the summit and crown of his happiness, the ultimate goal of his natural endeavours, with whose attainment everything seems to him to be attained, and with the missing of which everything seems to have been missed.[73]

> Because the inner being of nature, the will-to-live, expresses itself most strongly in the sexual impulse, the ancient poets and philosophers— Hesiod and Parmenides—said very significantly that Eros is the first, that which creates, the principle from which all things emerge.[74]

> Eros [is] the excessive power of the procreative impulse . . .[75]

Recall Freud's observation earlier that his notion of libido coincided exactly with the notion of Eros;[76] as such, the sexual impulse was considered to be the central yet "invisible point of all action and conduct."[77]

The sexual impulse/instinct is the strongest impetus in life[78] and has "*primacy* over all other natural desires"; "we see it take its seat at every moment as the real and hereditary lord of the world."[79] All other functions were, for Schopenhauer and Freud, secondary:

> The sexual impulse is the kernel of the will-to-live, and consequently the concentration of all willing . . . Indeed, it may be said that man is concrete sexual impulse . . . this impulse alone perpetuates and holds together the whole of his phenomenal appearance . . . The sexual impulse is therefore the most complete manifestation of the will-to-live . . . The sexual impulse is the most vehement of cravings, the desire of desires, the concentration of all our willing.[80]

> It is clear why sexual desire bears a character very different from that of any other; it is not only the strongest of desires, but is even specifically of a more powerful kind than all the others are. It is everywhere tacitly assumed as necessary and inevitable, and is not, like other desires, a matter of taste and caprice. For it is the desire that constitutes even the very

nature of man. In conflict with it, no motive is so strong as to be certain of victory. It is so very much the chief thing, that no other pleasures make up for the deprivation of its satisfaction.[81]

Not only must man serve the sexual impulse against his will "he cannot aspire to anything more."[82] This is yet another reason why Freud ultimately agreed that "the ego is not master in its own house": "Anyone who promises to mankind liberation from the hardships of sex will be hailed as a hero, let him talk whatever nonsense he chooses."[83] Freud later softened somewhat on this point, but his sentiments were essentially the same:

> The task of subduing so powerful an instinct as the sexual impulse, otherwise than by giving it satisfaction, is one which may employ the whole strength of a man. Subjugation through sublimation, by guiding the sexual forces into higher civilizational paths, may succeed with a minority, and even with these only for a time . . . Experience shows that the majority of people constituting your society are constitutionally unequal to the task.[84]

Given the primacy, pervasiveness, and strength of the sexual impulse, both thinkers continually underscored that *sexual energy is ultimately the basis of all human activity.*

Interestingly, Schopenhauer and Freud mentioned the same kinds of examples. For both, sexuality (along with the death instinct) was the underlying basis of war;[85] it was the root of "all secret signs and suggestions"[86] which Freud saw as the basis of parapraxes (mistakes that really signify something else) and jokes.[87] For Freud, "Jokes make possible the satisfaction of an instinct (whether lustful or hostile) in the face of an obstacle that stands in the way."[88] Schopenhauer was also aware of the sexual element in jokes. He wrote: "[they are] the inexhaustible source of wit . . . the ever ready material for a joke, only because the profoundest seriousness lies at its root";[89] and sexuality provided the basis of "the constantly recurring *reverie* of the chaste even against their will."[90] Compare Freud's suggestion that hysterical symptoms are a realization of sexual fantasies[91] and that sexual fantasies have their basis in instincts.[92] Freud went further, of course, than Schopenhauer, contending that sexuality is "the essential factor in the causation of neuroses . . . and psychoneuroses."[93]

Schopenhauer and Freud emphasized that the most fundamental goal of sexuality was the propagation of the species (though they both also referred to its manifestations on the level of the individual).[94] Schopenhauer wrote:

> In all sexual love, instinct holds the reins . . . since for nature the interest of the species takes precedence over all others . . .[95]

> Pleasure in the other sex . . . [is] merely disguised instinct . . . the purpose that unconsciously guides us is clearly the possibility of procreation in general.[96]

> The vehemence of the sexual impulse is . . . [that] everything . . . has to be staked on the maintenance of the species.[97]

Freud wrote:

> Biology teaches that sexuality is not to be put on a par with other functions of the individual; for its purposes go beyond the individual and have as their content the production of new individuals—that is, the preservation of the species . . . the individual is a temporary and transient appendage to the quasi-immortal germ-plasm, which is entrusted to him by the process of generation.[98]

And the role that the sexual *body* plays in all of this is, of course plain for Schopenhauer: "the genitals are objectified sexual impulse."[99]

> Far more than any other external member of the body, the genitals are subject merely to the will . . . the genitals are the real focus of the will.[100]

> The genitals are the life-preserving principle assuring to time endless life.[101]

Freud as well, of course, saw the genitals as the manifestation of sexual instinct[102] and viewed the genital organization of the libido as having "primacy" vis-à-vis the id's desires.[103]

Finally, and most important, both thinkers emphasized that the sexual drives conflict fundamentally with reality and society, as well as with one another. For Freud, of course, this was the fundamental message of his *Civilization and Its Discontents*. One ramification of this was the pervasive extent to which sexuality became covered up and regarded as a source of shame by society and individuals. Schopenhauer strongly emphasized this as well:

> The sexual impulse which is covered up everywhere and peeps up everywhere, in spite of all the veils thrown over it . . . the principal concern of all men is pursued secretly and ostensibly ignored as much as possible . . .

arrangements to subdue it, to imprison it, or at any rate to restrict it, and if possible to keep it concealed, or indeed so to master it that it appears only as an entirely subordinate and secondary concern of life.[104]

The act by which the will affirms itself and man comes into existence is one of which all in their heart of hearts are ashamed, and which therefore they carefully conceal . . .[105]

Compare Freud in just a couple of passages:

Young girls, who, after all, are systematically brought up to conceal their sexual life . . . [we must] spur such people on to abandon their secretiveness . . . In the matters of sexuality we are at present, every one of us, ill or well, nothing but hypocrites.[106]

Is it genuinely and seriously intended that later on they should consider everything connected with sex as something despicable and abhorrent from which their parents and teachers wish to keep them apart as long as possible?[107]

Freud, of course, from the outset recognized that "shame and morality are repressing forces." Freud wrote, "The sexual instinct has to struggle against certain mental forces which act as resistances, and of which shame and disgust are the most prominent."[108] Interestingly, for much of Freud's career he refused to comply with society's repressing forces and insisted on speaking in explicit "sexual" terms as opposed to the more socially acceptable "erotic."[109]

11. *Will/id operates according to principles of tension and pleasure.* The underlying energies for all we experience are in a constant state of tension. Schopenhauer wrote, "whereas everyone would really like to rest . . . everything is in permanent tension and forced movement."[110] This, of course, directly paralleled Freud's tension-reduction model: the id insists upon gratification of instinctual desires; such demands are tension-filled, and when satisfied, result in the reduction of tension. This is what Freud meant by the instincts operating according to the "pleasure principle"; pleasure consists purely of a reduction of tension. Furthermore, given that the will's/id's very nature while alive is to strive toward the satisfaction of instinctual demands, it could only achieve ultimate tension reduction by forfeiting its primary goal of existence. Once again, Schopenhauer and (eventually) Freud recognized death as fundamental to life. Another outcome of Schopenhauer's and Freud's model was to view human expe-

rience as necessarily consisting of conflict, suffering, periodic reductions of suffering, dissatisfaction and enmity with others. Since each individual will/id is continually striving to satisfy desires, fueled by an instinct to survive (at the expense of others), there is a universal conflict of interests among human individuals; humans are in essence in competition with one another. Furthermore, the ordinary life is inevitably unfulfilled.

12. *Will/id is manifested in the body.* Given that the will/id forms the core of our inner being the question naturally arises as to *how* we can gain access to it. The answer, for Schopenhauer and Freud (as well as Nietzsche), was that the body plays a pivotal role; all spoke of the primacy and primordiality of the body. It is the body that affords us direct insight as to the ultimate nature and basis of reality and how we are situated within it. Indeed, it is not even possible to conceive of will/id ("a seething cauldron of instinctual impulses") as being other than bodily in nature, and the reverse, bodily existence is, respectively for each thinker, willing/instinctual impulses seeking gratification. Indeed, as we have seen, this was a pivotal point for Freud in the development of his metapsychology: for him, the doctrine of psychoanalysis was understood as a superstructure which would eventually find as its foundation an "organic substructure" described in his metapsychological theory.[111] Compare this to Schopenhauer's observation that "[madness] depends more often [than not] on purely somatic causes."[112] For Freud, the id "contains everything . . . above all, the instincts which originate from the somatic organization."[113]

Schopenhauer emphasized that the body is primordial as the necessary condition for knowledge of the will. That is, the will is directly knowable only insofar as it appears through the body:

> The knowledge I have of my will, although an immediate knowledge, cannot be separated from that of my body. I know my will not as a whole, not as a unity, not completely according to its nature, but only in its individual acts, and hence in time, which is the form of my body's appearing . . .
> *Therefore, the body is the condition of knowledge of my will* [italics added].[114]

The reason for this is that the will and the body are identical, but we shall get to that in a moment. This knowledge of will is of a strange kind however, for

> it is the reference of a judgement to the relocation that a representation of perception, namely the body, has to that which is not a representation at all, but is *toto genre* different therefrom, namely will. I should therefore like to distinguish this truth from every other, and call it *philosophical*

> *truth par excellence.* We can turn the expression of this truth in different
> ways and say: My body and my will are one; or, what as representation
> perception I call my body, I call my will in so far as *I am conscious of it in
> an entirely different way comparable with no other;* or, My body is the *objectivity*
> of my will; or, Apart from the fact that my body is my representation, it is
> still my will [italics added].[115]

Hence, it is through the unique kind of consciousness that I have through
the body that I have direct inner awareness of the underlying will. "For us
immediately known changes precedes the application of the law of causality, and thus furnishes this with the first data."[116] I have a direct inner
awareness of impulses, energies, forces, desires, and so on. We might now
ask how it is that body gives us direct insight into the will. It is because the
will and the body are one identical being and as such form a unity; more
accurately, the body *is* the will (as well as its manifestation): "the body is a
function of the will . . . it is the metaphysical substratum of the body."[117]

> My teaching asserts that the whole body is the will itself . . . from this it
> follows that the will is everywhere equally and uniformly present in the
> whole body.[118]

> It alone among all objects is at the same time will and representation . . .
> body is the only real individual in the world, i.e., the only phenomenon
> of will, and the only immediate object of the subject.[119]

> The act of will and the action of the body, for they are directly identi-
> cal . . . the outer and the inner. Thus actual willing is inseparable from
> doing.[120]

As "nothing but the objectified will,"[121] "the objectified will-to-live itself,"[122]
the body was considered the *most real* of beings for Schopenhauer; hence,
"The body . . . is immediate object."[123] In addition, the body and will were
really just the same being experienced in two different ways. For example,
hunger is objectified in the body as digestive system and teeth.

One powerful philosophical ramification of this is that Schopenhauer's preceding analysis undercuts the subject–object dichotomy (introduced into understanding by the intellect) with which the existential
phenomenologists will later be concerned. It is in the will, and the will-as-
body, that the object coincides with the subject.[124] In doing so, Schopenhauer was transcending duality. Freud was arguably a fellow traveler when
he suggested, "The ego is first and foremost a body-ego."[125]

Not only was the body the condition for knowledge of the will, for
Schopenhauer, it was also the condition for knowledge of anything else:

> It happens that to everyone the thing-in-itself is known immediately in so far as it appears as his own body . . . Here, therefore, the body is for us immediate object, in other words, that representation which forms the starting-point of the subject's knowledge, since it itself with its immediately known changes precedes the application of the law of causality . . . precedes the application of the understanding . . .[126]

Freud clearly agreed:

> Another factor seems to have played a part in bringing about the formation of the ego and its differentiation from the id. A person's own body and above all its surface, is a place from which both external and internal perceptions may spring . . .[127]

It is this last insight that will have immense implications for and influence on the existential phenomenologists (for example, Merleau-Ponty).

Next, both agreed that there exists a reciprocal relationship between the body and the various mental functions.[128] Here, however, it is important to notice immediately a difference of emphasis between Schopenhauer and Freud with regard to the direction of this relationship. Schopenhauer was far more concerned with the way in which the body as will impacted the mind. For example, he argued that "madness . . . depends more often on purely somatic causes [as opposed to those of psychic origin]."[129] Freud strongly agreed that mental functions were rooted in somatic processes, ". . . neuroses have an organic basis";[130] spoke of "the somatic basis of the symptoms—a basis which is as a rule constitutional and organic";[131] and saw organic determinants as playing, at least at times, the decisive role in symptom formation.[132] He saw hysteria, for example, as having organic determinants: "I suspect that we are here concerned with unconscious processes of thought which are twined around a pre-existing structure of organic connections."[133] In addition, Freud wrote that he had often suspected "that something organic played a part in repression."[134] Freud was also clear that mental processes were *dependent upon* bodily functions.[135] Freud argued that "hysterical symptoms . . . cannot occur without the presence . . . of a pathological process in or connected with one of the bodily organs."[136] And again:

> There can be no question but that the libido has somatic sources, that it streams to the ego from various organs and parts of the body.[137]

> As psychoanalysis' . . . second fundamental hypothesis . . . it explains the supposedly somatic concomitant as being what is truly psychical.[138]

Finally, Freud asseverated that at times bodily functions dominated mental ones.[139]

Yet, contrary to Schopenhauer, Freud primarily focused his attention upon *the manner in which the mind affected the body*—a relation which, he insisted, had been all too often neglected.[140] For example, Freud noted that various states of mind are manifested as concomitant bodily changes;[141] or again, he explicitly defined the process of "conversion" as "the translation of a purely psychical excitation into physical terms."[142] Finally, Freud underscored this theme in his notion of "somatic compliance" in various contexts:

> We may ask ourselves whether the suppression of sexual component instincts which is brought about by environmental influences is sufficient in itself to call up functional disturbances in organs, or whether special constitutional conditions must be present in order that the organs may be led to an exaggeration of their erotogenic role and consequently provoke repression of the instincts. We should have to see in those conditions the constitutional part of the disposition to fall ill of psychogenic and neurotic disorders. This is the factor to which, applied to hysteria, I gave the provisional name of "somatic compliance."[143]

We should note that Schopenhauer too suggested that the psyche can and does impact bodily processes:

> The madness that has sprung from merely psychic causes can possibly bring about, through the violent inversion of the course of thought that produces it, even a kind of paralysis or other depravation of some parts of the brain . . .[144]

On the one hand, for Schopenhauer, the immediate appearance of the will was manifested through the body in mental life in several ways—pain/pleasure, emotions, perception, intellect, and so on. On the other hand, mental life can also affect the body. Instead of mistakenly thinking of pleasure/pain and emotions/passions as representations, Schopenhauer insisted that they were "immediate affections of the will in its phenomenon, the body,"[145] and, as such, something that we *undergo*.[146] Freud offered a similar description:

> Pain, too, seems to play a part in the process, and the way in which we gain new knowledge of our organs during painful illnesses is perhaps a model of the way by which in general we arrive at the idea of our body.[147]

Hence, the emotions have their seat in the organic body as well. Reciprocally, Schopenhauer noted, "the passions affect different parts of the body."[148]

> [Passions agitate] the body and its inner workings directly and immediately, and disturbs the course of its vital functions. This is specially discussed in *The Will in Nature*, second edition, p. 27.[149]

Not only do the passions affect the different parts of the body,[150] but "the individual or condition of the separate organs excites the passions and even the representations or mental pictures connected therewith."[151]

Similarly, Freud underscored the close connection between affects and somatic processes:

> The affects in the narrower sense are, it is true, characterized by a quite special connection with somatic processes; but, strictly speaking, all mental states, including those that we usually regard as "processes of thought," are to some degree "affective," and not one of them is without its physical manifestations or is incapable of modifying somatic processes. Even when a person is engaged in quiet thinking . . . the most powerful of all means by which the mind affects the body is the provocation of strong affects.[152]

As we have seen, since the will is that which is exclusively, immediately given, and known to us, only it can explain everything else.[153] Since we cannot ever get to the inner nature of things from without, it is the body (as will) that is a necessary starting point for the understanding of the *perception* of this world. Indeed, Schopenhauer asserted that ultimately perception is nothing more than the succession of changes in bodily states:

> Accordingly the brain, and hence the intellect, is certainly conditioned directly by the body, as the body again is by the brain, yet only indirectly, namely as something spatial and corporeal in the world of perception, but not in itself, in other words, as will.[154]

The reciprocal relation, however, is not symmetrical. Furthermore,

> this body is given in two entirely different ways. It is given in intelligent perception as representation, as an object among objects, liable to the laws of these objects. But it is also given in quite a different way, namely as what is known immediately to everyone, and is denoted by the word will.[155]

The body that conditions the intellect is a direct expression of the will and hence is independent and not subject to the representational function of the intellect, whereas the body conditioned by the intellect is a part of the world as constructed by the representational functions of the intellect. Thus, the functions of the intellect and perception are understood as that which can trigger the will, namely, the body into *action*.

The will manifests itself as *acts* of the body. Acts of will are identical with acts of body. To act I must do so through my body.

> Every true act of his will is also at once and inevitably a movement of his body; he cannot actually will the act without at the same time being aware that it appears as a movement of the body. The act of will and the action of the body . . . do not stand in the relation of cause and effect, but are one and the same thing, though given in two entirely different ways, first quite immediately and then in perception for the understanding . . .[156]

My bodily movements *as acts* are expressions of the will in the form of desire, impulse, force or energy.

> The action of the body is nothing but the act of will objectified, i.e., translated into perception . . . Every true, genuine, immediate act of will is also at once and directly a manifestation of the body; correspondingly, on the other hand, every impression on the body is also at once and directly an impression on the will.[157]

When I act, I am aware of my bodily movement in an entirely different way than I am of other events. I am aware of these movements as my own will uniquely and transparently expressing itself. Also, every bodily movement is an expression of desire, instinctual impulse: it is through our bodies that we strive, want, endeavor, and so on. It is in our body, furthermore, that we are aware of the minor role played by reason in our actions and hence just how little real control we exert over ourselves. One primary example Schopenhauer used repeatedly to illustrate this was sexual desire: sexuality underlies and explains the body's telos, in that it strives not merely to live but to perpetuate itself by procreating and protecting future generations.

It was at this juncture that Schopenhauer said something which shows in a striking way the nature of the alignment of his concerns with Freud's: "The fundamental theme of all the many different acts of will is the satisfaction of the needs inseparable from the body's existence in *health*."[158] The primary idea here is that the ultimate underlying reason for all acts of will is the maintenance of the individual and the propagation of the species. Schopenhauer subsequently elaborated on this point:

> The *physiatric* standpoint has at last asserted itself in pathology. Seen from this standpoint, diseases are themselves a healing process of nature, which she introduces in order to eliminate some disorder that has taken root in the organism by overcoming its causes . . . *naturae medicatrix* [healing power of nature]. In the healthy state, the will lies at the foundation of all organic functions, but with the appearance of disorders that threaten its whole work; it is vested with dictatorial power, in order to subdue the rebellious forces by quite extraordinary measures and wholly abnormal operations (the disease), and to lead everything back to the right track.[159]

One example of this is that "the body is self-repairing."[160]

A final important parallel between Schopenhauer and Freud on the body is that both conceived the body as the source of the unconscious. For Schopenhauer, this explicitly meant that willing through the body took place on the unconscious level: since willing was experienced through the body without consciousness, we must keep our eye on the body as the manifested source of the unconscious.[161] One example of this is the nerve. Schopenhauer pointed out that if the nerve is "*not* connected with the brain . . . the contraction is involuntary and unconscious, and thus an act serving organic life."[162] Other examples include the role of the instincts through the body, and especially the sexual instincts.

13. *Will/id is a force with which to be reconciled in order to function in society.* The instinctual desires and demands of the will/id create conflict and suffering. Fortunately, the development of consciousness and the intellect provide us with a means to satisfy these demands, hopefully in socially acceptable ways. Both Schopenhauer and Freud advocated the renunciation of individual desires as a way to best get along in our existence, while at the same time recognizing the tendency within society to attempt to unduly confine what was actually quite natural within each of us—namely, sexuality. A "healthy" person is one who successfully balances all the various demands from within and without and is brave enough to face the truth about his or her self by allowing unconscious material to become conscious, thereby loosening its grip. One way to reconcile the tensions between individual and society occurs through sublimation. Although Schopenhauer had little to say on this topic, his conception of the will discussed thus far certainly provided the opportunity for others like Nietzsche (and Freud) to come to an awareness of the importance sublimation

had in an individual's ability to cope with the tensions and conflicts between social and individual interests. And, in fact, Nietzsche certainly described sublimation in ways that clearly anticipated Freud's use of the term.

One goal of philosophy for Nietzsche was to distinguish among our "instincts" in terms of those that are "life-enhancing" and those that are "life-stultifying"; the idea being, of course, to encourage the former:

> since it is known that a single grain of historical cultivation is capable of breaking coarse and dull instincts and desires, or at least of *channeling them in the direction* of refined egoism [italics added].[163]

> . . . sublimations, in which the basic element seems almost to have dispersed and reveals itself only under the most painstaking observation . . . what if . . . the most glorious colours are derived from base, indeed from despised materials?[164]

This idea was quite clearly in line with Freud, when he described:

> shifting the instinctual aims in such a way that they cannot come up against frustration from the external world. In this, sublimation of the instincts lends its assistance. One gains the most if one can sufficiently heighten the yield of pleasure from the sources of psychical and intellectual work.[165]

> Instincts are induced to displace the conditions for their satisfaction, to lead them into other paths . . . Sublimation of instinct is an especially conspicuous feature of cultural development; it is what makes it possible for higher psychical activities . . . to play such an important part in civilized life.[166]

It was society, of course, which served as the primary restrictor of the instincts. Nietzsche, for example, wrote that "Society constrains instinctual impulses"; and insisted that instincts not permitted outward expression by society would turn inward and be used against the self, leading to *ressentiment*.[167] Compare this to Freud: "What happens in [the individual] to render his desire for aggression innocuous? . . . His aggressiveness is introjected and internalized . . . directed towards the ego."[168] Hence, both Nietzsche and Freud were heirs to Diderot's original observation that illness in modern man is based on society's demands that man give up the gratification of his instincts. They extended this by suggesting that frustrated aggressive drives became the root of guilt (Nietzsche's *ressentiment*) and hence of the conscience. Nietzsche wrote:

> This *instinct for freedom* forcibly made latent . . . this instinct for freedom pushed back and repressed, incarcerated within and finally able to discharge and vent itself only on itself: that, and that alone, is what the *bad conscience* is in its beginnings.[169]

To summarize, it was through the lines of inquiry opened up by Schopenhauer that Nietzsche was able to pursue and elaborate the relationship between our instinctual impulses, societal constraints, and the development of "guilt" within the individual's conscience. Schopenhauer and Freud shared a great deal in their respective conceptions of the will/id, and in the following chapter we will explore how these issues engaged both Schopenhauer's and Freud's concept of the unconscious—and how Nietzsche also believed that there must be unconscious mental processes—as well as the role freedom plays in human existence.

8

Of Philosophers and Madmen: Schopenhauer, Nietzsche, and Freud on the Unconscious, Freedom, and Determinism

> A human being often conceals the motives of his actions from everyone else, and sometimes even from himself, namely where he shrinks from acknowledging what it really is that moves him to do this or that.
> —Schopenhauer

For both Schopenhauer and Freud the will/id—as the true core of our being, thing-in-itself, and precondition for all that happens—is unconscious. Nietzsche rejected Schopenhauer's will, and the thing-in-itself; interestingly, he did not reject the concept of the unconscious. Indeed, Nietzsche credited Schopenhauer with calling to our attention "that mode of thought and knowledge of which we are unconscious."[1] These thinkers all, in fact, considered the notion of the unconscious as playing a ubiquitous, pivotal and prevalent role in mental life. Their thoughts on the unconscious (and consciousness) were remarkably similar: all gave similar evidence supporting the existence of unconscious phenomena, and all developed similar notions in regards to the repression of unconscious phenomena. Given their insistence upon a hidden, unconscious quality of the human mind, it comes as no surprise that their positions would have important and similar implications for the issue of freedom versus determinism, as well.[2]

Schopenhauer, Nietzsche, and Freud on the Unconscious

These thinkers all cited similar reasons and evidence for asserting the existence of unconscious mental processes; all referred to obvious gaps in consciousness which were not explainable purely on the conscious level, the nature of memories, and the peculiar phenomenon of dreams.

Schopenhauer referred to the "imperfection of the intellect," pointing out the "fragmentary nature of the course of our thoughts."

> The human consciousness and thinking are by their nature fragmentary, and therefore the theoretical or practical results obtained by putting such fragments together often turn out to be defective . . . Obviously a consciousness subject to such great limitations is little fitted to explore and fathom the riddle of the world.[3]

Nietzsche similarly emphasized the undeniable "intermittence" of consciousness throughout the beginning of *Human, All Too Human*.[4] And Freud justified the necessity of the concept of the unconscious,

> because the data of consciousness have a very large number of gaps in them; both in healthy and in sick people psychical acts often occur which can be explained only by presupposing other acts, of which, nevertheless, consciousness affords no evidence . . . All these conscious acts remain disconnected and unintelligible if we insist upon claiming that every mental act that occurs in us must also necessarily be experienced by us through consciousness.[5]

It was Freud's observation of these gaps in consciousness, in fact, that justified his extending beyond the limits of direct experience.[6] It was precisely this that made Freud's theory a *meta*-psychology, grounded Schopenhauer's belief that metaphysics was a necessary addition to science, and led Nietzsche to develop his psychological theory.

Memories lacking immediate consciousness also provided all three thinkers with evidence of unconscious thought processes. Schopenhauer pondered what we are to make of a memory of which we are not immediately conscious: all he said was, "it is latent." Freud extended the idea of "latent" thoughts and claimed that this further substantiated the existence of an unconscious.

> We can go further and argue, in support of there being an unconscious psychical state, that at any given moment consciousness includes only a

small content, so that the greater part of what we call conscious knowledge must in any case be for very considerable periods of time in a state
of *latency*, that is to say, of being psychically unconscious. When all our
latent memories are taken into consideration it becomes totally incomprehensible how the existence of the unconscious can be denied [italics
added].[7]

It was on this point that Nietzsche extended the notion of an unconscious
in a way that Schopenhauer did not, and that had a strong impact on
Freud. Nietzsche too spoke of memories that arise in us "from a common
root, from a fundamental will of knowledge."[8] He asserted "the human
being carries around with him the memory of all previous generations,"[9]
and "a memory analogous to our memory that reveals itself in heredity
and evolution and forms."[10] Here, of course, Nietzsche was an adherent of
the Lamarckian hypothesis which was so powerfully to influence Freud
later, culminating in his theory of a "phylogenetic history" which Freud
believed intrinsic to the human race (and foundational for his theory of
instincts).[11] Hence, both Nietzsche and Freud held that ancient and archaic memories (as well as individual childhood memories) were never
forgotten. For Freud, forgetting was considered nonexistent in the unconscious: "In the unconscious nothing can be brought to an end, nothing is past or forgotten."[12] Nietzsche underscored this point as well:

> Perhaps the human being is incapable of *forgetting* anything. The opera-
> tions of seeing and knowing are much too complicated for it to be pos-
> sible completely to efface them again; which means that from this point
> on, all forms that once have been produced by the brain and the nerv-
> ous system are repeated frequently in the same way [italics added].[13]

> The idea that is overcome is not annihilated, only driven back or subor-
> dinated. There is no annihilation in the sphere of spirit.[14]

Nothing is forgotten. Some memories—both on the level of the individual and of the human race—were simply not as accessible as others. The
very fact that we have memories which are sometimes accessible and sometimes not indicated that consciousness was not complete, that something
unconscious must be operative in mental functioning.

Finally, dreams provided further—and, for Freud, the strongest—
evidence of unconscious thought processes. Schopenhauer wrote:

> Nothing more clearly demonstrates the intellect's secondary, dependent,
> and conditioned nature than its periodical intermission. In deep sleep

all knowing and forming of representations entirely ceases; but the kernel of our true being . . . necessarily presupposed by the organic functions . . . *never* dares to pause, if life is not to cease . . . in sleep . . . the will alone operates according to its original and essential nature, undisturbed from outside . . . in sleep the whole force of the will is directed to the maintenance of the organism [italics added].[15]

Although Nietzsche did not accentuate dreams as much or exclusively in the same direction as did Schopenhauer and Freud, he did indicate once again the primordial aspect of dreams (of which Freud certainly made use):

In sleep and dreams we repeat once again the curriculum of earlier mankind . . . In the dream this piece of primeval humanity continues to exercise itself, for it is the basis upon which higher rationality evolved and continues to evolve in every human being: the dream takes us back again to remote stages of human culture and provides us with a means of understanding them better.[16]

Nietzsche also pointed out that our dreams express specific personal thoughts, feelings, and wishes that "we sometimes do not know or feel precisely while awake."[17] It was Freud, as we have seen, who greatly extended the significance of dreams as evidence of unconscious thought processes—claiming in his *Interpretation of Dreams* that dreams were "the royal road to the unconscious."[18] For Freud, dreams afforded us the opportunity to learn firsthand just how the inner workings of mental processes functioned.[19]

The evidence of an unconscious revealed several "truths" about ourselves for Schopenhauer, Nietzsche, and Freud: consciousness is merely the outer shell which conceals the inner depths of our (unconscious) being; we are not in control of our thoughts, but rather thoughts come when they will; the majority of our thoughts are unconscious; the unconscious predominates because it is the origin of all thought. As such, the unconscious is the organic, original source of all, including consciousness.

Schopenhauer insisted that the intellect was "a mere superficial force, essentially and everywhere touching only the outer shell, never the inner core of things."[20] Nietzsche strongly agreed:

One thinks that [consciousness] constitutes the *kernel* of man; what is abiding, eternal, ultimate, and most original in him. One takes consciousness for a determinate magnitude. One denies its growth and its intermittences. One takes it for the "unity of the organism" . . . This ridiculous overestimation and misunderstanding of consciousness

has the very useful consequence that it prevents an all too fast development of consciousness.[21]

Contrary to being the focal point of psychical existence, then, all three
agreed that consciousness actually *concealed* a great deal of mental life.
Schopenhauer:

> it must be that things exhibit themselves in a manner quite different
> from their own inner nature, and that therefore they appear as through
> a mask. This mask enables us always merely to assume, never to know,
> what is hidden beneath it; and this something then gleams through as
> an inscrutable mystery.[22]

Nietzsche:

> The decisive value of an action lies precisely in what is *unintentional* in
> it, while everything about it is intentional, everything about it that can
> be seen, known, *"conscious," still belongs to its surface and skin*—which, like
> every skin, betrays something but *conceals* even more [italics added].[23]

Freud:

> It is the much-abused privilege of conscious activity, wherever it plays a
> part, to conceal every other activity from our eyes.[24]

Nietzsche spoke often of that which is concealed by "consciousness"[25]
and which included various unconscious processes.[26] Perhaps most famously, he wrote "that all our so-called consciousness is a more or less fantastic commentary on an unknown, perhaps unknowable, but felt text."[27]

Hence, these thinkers all believed that consciousness played a comparatively minor role in our lives. Contrary to the strongly held beliefs
at the time—beliefs which contributed to the creation of science and philosophy—humans were not in control of even their own thoughts.
Schopenhauer wrote: "thoughts come not when *we* want them, but when
they want to."[28] This was the source of one of Freud's favorite quotations
from Nietzsche, to whom he mistakenly credited its original formulation.
Nietzsche wrote, "a thought comes when 'it' wishes, and not when 'I'
wish";[29] and Freud reiterated this point, "Thoughts emerge suddenly without one's knowing where they come from";[30] and "our most personal daily
experience acquaints us with ideas that come into our head we do not
know from where, and with intellectual conclusions arrived at we do not
know how."[31] Humans are not in control of their thoughts because the ma-

jority of thought processes take place on the unconscious level. Schopenhauer's characterization is justly famous here:

> Let us compare our consciousness to a sheet of water of some depth.
> Then the distinctly conscious ideas are merely the surface; on the other
> hand, the mass of the water is the indistinct, the feelings, the after-
> sensation of perceptions and intuitions and what is experienced in gen-
> eral, mingled with disposition of our own will that is the kernel of our
> inner nature . . . The whole process of our thinking and resolving sel-
> dom lies on the surface . . . Consciousness is the mere surface of the
> mind, and of this, as of the globe, we do not know the interior, but only
> the crust.[32]

Nietzsche constantly insisted:

> For the longest time, conscious thought was considered thought itself.
> Only now does the truth dawn on us that by far the greatest part of our
> spirit's activity remains unconscious and unfelt.[33]

> Man like every living being, thinks continually without knowing it; the
> thinking that rises to *consciousness* is only the smallest part of all this—
> the most superficial and worst part.[34]

Given that these thinkers insisted that most thoughts come from the
unconscious, it comes as no surprise that they asserted that it was unconsciousness which "predominates over consciousness."[35] For Schopenhauer, the will drives its servant, the intellect;[36] hence, "the intellect is the
secondary phenomenon, the organism the primary."[37]

> The will is the radical part of our real nature, and acts with original
> force, whereas the intellect, as something adventitious and in many ways
> conditioned, can act only in a secondary and conditional manner.[38]

Schopenhauer employed the metaphor "for the relation of the two is that
of the strong blind man carrying the sighted lame man on his shoul-
ders."[39] Nietzsche also, of course, held that unconsciousness predominates over consciousness. He emphasized, "consciousness is not the directing agent, but an organ of the directing agent."[40]

> "The impulses want to play the tyrant; one must invent a *counter-tyrant*
> who is stronger." . . . no one was any longer master over himself, the
> instincts turned *against* each other.[41]

Schopenhauer and Freud, interestingly, used reciprocal versions of the same metaphor. Schopenhauer wrote:

> In all these enhancements of the intellect, the will plays the part of the rider urging his horse with the spur beyond the natural measure of its strength.[42]

> For what bridle and bit are to an unmanageable horse, the intellect is to the will in man; it must be led by this bridle by means of instruction, exhortation, training, and so on; for in itself the will is as wild and impetuous an impulse . . .[43]

Freud wrote:

> Thus in its relation to the id [the ego] is like a man on horseback, who has to hold in check the superior strength of the horse; with this difference, that the rider tries to do so with his own strength while the ego uses borrowed forces . . . Often a rider, if he is not to be parted from his horse, is obliged to guide it where it wants to go; so in the same way the ego is in the habit of transforming the id's will into action as if it were its own.[44]

It was precisely for these reasons, among others, that Freud said "the ego is not master in its own house"—the unconscious id dominates mental processes.[45]

Furthermore, for Schopenhauer and Freud the ego (as having access to both unconscious and conscious material) rather than being "master," was in the position of guard. In Freud's words,

> the ego is obliged to guard against certain instinctual impulses in the id and to treat them as dangers. But it cannot protect itself from internal instinctual dangers as effectively as it can from some piece of reality that is not part of itself. Intimately bound up with the id as it is, it can only fend off an instinctual danger by restricting its own organization and by acquiescing in the formation of symptoms in exchange for having impaired the instinct. If the rejected instinct renews its attack, the ego is overtaken by all those difficulties which are known to us as neurotic ailments.[46]

Compare this formulation to Schopenhauer:

> The brain with the function of knowing is nothing more than a guard mounted by the will for its aims and ends that lie outside. Up in the

watch-tower of the head this guard looks round through the windows of the senses, and watches the point from which mischief threatens and advantage is to be observed, and the will decides in accordance with the report.[47]

Repression

With the unconscious as the foundation from which all thought processes emerge, Schopenhauer, Nietzsche, and Freud were able to account for phenomena that previously went unexplained. Recall that fundamental to Schopenhauer's will was the notion that humans are instinctual beings, striving to fulfill desires and needs, especially those which were self- and species-preserving (namely, sexual). One of the primary ways in which the unconscious served this purpose of self-preservation was through the process of repression.

For Freud, repression was a "turning something away, and keeping it at a distance, from the conscious";[48] it was considered an organic process, the body's way of defending itself from threatening ideas, trains of thought and/or instinctual impulses.[49] As we have seen, the seeds of this formulation of repression had its roots in both Schopenhauer[50] and Nietzsche.[51] For example, in *Ecce Homo* which Freud read in 1908, Nietzsche wrote, "an instinct of self-preservation . . . gains its most unambiguous expression as an instinct of *self-defense*. Not to see many things, not to hear many things, not to permit many things to come close . . ."[52]

All three thinkers agreed upon several key aspects of repression. Repression prevents certain ideas from arising in consciousness;[53] has as its source of resistance the will/id/unconscious itself as opposed to the intellect/ego/consciousness (which are strangers to what is repressed);[54] and occurs to prevent feelings of unpleasure or anxiety from arising.[55]

Unconscious ideas/emotions that are perceived as a potential threat are not allowed to reach consciousness as an act of protection;[56] yet their failure to receive admittance to consciousness causes a "shock" of pain and/or excitation within the system. Schopenhauer wrote:

> It knows, or in other words experiences from the self-same intellect, that [repressed ideas/impulses] would arouse in it any one of the emotions previously described . . . that [they] will cause it a shock of painful and unworthy emotion to no purpose . . . The will then decides in accordance with the last knowledge, and forces the intellect to obey. This is called "being master of oneself"; here obviously the master is the will, the servant the intellect, for in the last instance the will is always in command.[57]

One way in which pain may be aroused within us is that

> the good opinion we have of ourselves would inevitably suffer . . . we
> know that our real motive was not what we thought of it as being, but
> some other that we were unwilling to admit to ourselves, because it was
> by no means in keeping with our good opinion of ourselves.[58]

Nietzsche held similar ideas:

> People who comprehend a thing to its very depths rarely stay faithful to
> it for ever. For they have brought its depths into the light of day; and in
> the depths there is always much that is unpleasant to see.[59]

Interestingly, for all these thinkers that which is most often repressed is precisely that which is responsible for repression—human instinctual impulses. In other words, instincts of self-preservation are often
the impetus for repressing ideas, thoughts, and impulses because such
ideas, thoughts, and impulses are threatening to the delicate conscious:
consciousness does not want to know the inner workings of its own source.

What was considered the most fundamental to repression for Freud
and Nietzsche was the idea of "primal repression." Freud wrote:

> We have reason to assume that there is a primal repression, a first phase
> of repression, which consists in the psychical (ideational) representative
> of the instinct being denied entrance into the conscious.[60]

Here we have the most basic to our character, our human heritage, as that
which is most unacceptable to our conscious thoughts. Rather than admit
our instinctual life, we tend to be "frightened" by those demands which
impact us most. Hence, repression occurs to some extent out of a fear of
our own core.[61] Consequently, the source of our resistances in repression
lies in the most primordial aspect, the inner workings of the unconscious
will/id (and not in the intellect/ego which are strangers to the repressed
material). Schopenhauer wrote:

> [The will] curbs and restrains the intellect, and forces it to turn to other
> things . . . for the resistance then comes not from the intellect, which
> always remains indifferent, but from the will itself . . .[62]

Rather than reach consciousness, threatening material (ideas, emotions,
instinctual impulses which cause pain or unpleasure) deemed unacceptable gets pushed into the depths of the unconscious where it becomes dif-

ficult, even impossible to access. In essence, then, we "forget" that which we do not want to know. Nietzsche in particular recognized forgetting as an active form of repression:

> Forgetting is no mere *vis inertiae* [inertia] as the superficial imagine; it is rather an active and in the strictest sense positive faculty of repression . . .[63]

> That is the purpose of active forgetfulness, which is like a doorkeeper, a preserver of psychic order, repose, and etiquette . . .[64]

> Forgetting represents a force, a form of *robust* health . . .[65]

> We forget a great deal of our own past and deliberately banish it from our minds: that is to say, we want the image of ourselves that shines upon us out of the past, to deceive us and flatter our self-conceit—we are engaged continually in this self-deception . . . Those who conceal something of themselves *from themselves* and those who conceal themselves from themselves as a whole are, I think, alike in this, that they perpetrate a *robbery* in the treasure-house of knowledge: from which we can see against which transgression the injunction "know thyself" is a warning.[66]

Indeed, while speaking of the role the effort of fending-off pain or unpleasure has on forgetting, Freud specifically credited Nietzsche's insight:

> None of us has been able to portray the phenomenon and its psychological basis so exhaustively at the same time so impressively as Nietzsche, in one of his aphorisms . . . "I did this," says my memory, "I cannot have done this" says my pride and remains inexorable. In the end—memory yields.[67]

As we have seen earlier, Freud held not only that there are various types of forgetting motivated by repression[68] but that forgetting is often motivated by avoidance of unpleasure[69] and could be traced by unknown and unavowed motives—or, as one may say, to a *counter-will*.[70]

> There is a kind of forgetting which is distinguished by the difficulty with which the memory is awakened even by a powerful external summons, as though some internal resistance were struggling against its revival. A forgetting of this kind has been given the name of "repression" in psychopathology . . . we can assert quite definitely of "repression" that it does not coincide with the dissolution or extinction of the memory. What is

repressed cannot, it is true, as a rule make its way into memory without more ado; but it retains a capacity for effective action, under the influence of some external event, it may one day bring about psychical consequences which can be regarded as products of a modification of the forgotten memory and as derivatives of it and which remain unintelligible unless we take this view of them.[71]

Freud saw repression as necessarily involving ideas or trains of thoughts that would arouse unpleasant emotions or anxiety.[72] Early on, Freud specifically spoke of anxiety as a consequence of repression;[73] he later modified this to suggest that anxiety can be one of the primary motive forces leading to repression.[74]

Schopenhauer recognized the implications of the reverse process, whereby the development of what Freud called "neurotic anxiety" occurs:

> The will so mastered the intellect that it was quite incapable of glancing at the worst case of all . . . However, in decidedly melancholy dispositions, or those which have grown wiser through like experience, the process is indeed reversed, since apprehension and misgiving in them play the part formerly played by hope. The first appearance of a danger puts them into a state of groundless anxiety. If the intellect begins to investigate matters, it is rejected as incompetent, in fact as a deceptive sophist, because the heart is to be believed. The heart's timidity and nervousness are now actually allowed to pass as arguments for the reality and magnitude of the danger.[75]

Furthermore, both Schopenhauer and Freud recognized a connection between "madness" and repression via resistance. Not allowing unconscious thoughts or ideas to arise (resistance) creates a gap between the unconscious and consciousness; if or when this gap becomes too extreme, the will attempts to fill it with arbitrary material in order to make necessary connections. Schopenhauer wrote:

> In this resistance on the part of the will to allow what is contrary to it to come under the examination of the intellect is to be found the place where madness can break in on the mind . . . if, in a particular case, the resistance and opposition of the will to the assimilation of some knowledge reaches such a degree that that operation is not clearly carried through; accordingly, if certain events or circumstances are wholly suppressed for the intellect, because the will cannot bear the sight of them; and then, if the resultant gaps are arbitrarily filled up for the sake of necessary connexion; we then have madness.[76]

Compare Freud's thoughts on this issue:

> Human beings fall ill of a conflict between the claims of instinctual life
> and the resistance which arises within them against it . . .[77]

> No stronger impression arises from the resistances during the work of
> analysis than of there being a force which is defending itself by every
> possible means against recovery and which is absolutely resolved to hold
> on to illness and suffering.[78]

Given the complex interplays of conscious and unconscious thoughts
working at odds with one another, along with a strong resistance to overcoming what is repressed, the question of an appropriate way to uncover
the repressed is posed. How to bring about conscious awareness of that
which is repressed and highly resistant to exposure? Interestingly, Schopenhauer and Freud both recognized that unconscious repressed material
could only reach consciousness by "spying out and taking unawares . . . surprise the will in the act of expressing itself, in order merely to discover its
real intentions."[79] Here, in Schopenhauer, we witness the seeds of Freud's
fundamental rule of psychoanalysis—free association—as a means to deal
effectively with the resistances to uncovering repressed material.

Freedom and Determinism

The entire discussion on Schopenhauer's, Nietzsche's, and Freud's various
positions on the in-itself, will, unconscious, and repression engages another fundamental metaphysical issue—that of freedom and determinism. If the human being is intrinsically an interplay of unconscious and
conscious thoughts and instinctual impulses, both demanding satisfaction and forever running up against walls of unacceptability, how can
there possibly be any "free will"? Schopenhauer and Freud, in fact, denied
outright the notion of free will *in action*, because for them it would mean
something akin to an *unmotivated* will. As we have seen, there could be no
unmotivated will for Schopenhauer and Freud since the unconscious
will/id is the source of all human motivation.[80]

In light of the overwhelming overlapping qualities of Freud's and
Schopenhauer's positions on key issues, it is quite possible that Freud's entire psychoanalytic theory could be philosophically grounded by Schopenhauer's metaphysics; hence, Schopenhauer's thoughts on freedom and
determinism would be quite relevant to Freudian psychoanalysis. Indeed,

doing so will afford a highly plausible alternative interpretation of Freud's position from his own self-interpretation of "scientific determinism."

Schopenhauer was quite clear that freedom and necessity were compatible—that human beings are both free and determined. In his *Prize Essay on the Freedom of the Will*,[81] Schopenhauer wrote of "the compatibility of freedom with necessity, which is one of the finest and profoundest creations of that great mind, indeed of all humankind."[82]

> Every being without exception *acts* with strict necessity, but *exists* and is what it is by virtue of its *freedom*... In short, *determinism* stands firm ... [though] the *being and essence* of all things are the phenomenon of a really *free will*... To save freedom ... it had to be transferred from the action to the existence.[83]

Here, in a nutshell, is Schopenhauer's version of compatibilism: there is freedom of *being* and even *thought*, but no freedom of *action*.

In order to fully understand what Schopenhauer meant by the compatibility of freedom and necessity, it is important to consider how *the principle of sufficient reason* and law of causality functioned within his system. As heirs to Plato's and Kant's philosophies, Schopenhauer and Freud both subscribed to the same principle of sufficient reason.[84] Schopenhauer articulated it thus:

> Everything has a reason or ground which justifies us in everywhere asking why, this why may be called the mother of all sciences ... Nothing is without a ground or reason why it is.[85]

> Everything that happens, from the greatest to the smallest, happens necessarily ... by what we do we merely come to know what we are.[86]

This principle, as Schopenhauer employed it, had two significant, yet different implications that are also important to Freud's model of the mind. First, Schopenhauer claimed that there is a reason or explanation for *anything* that happens or exists—it is possible to make sense of anything from the highly significant to the smallest trifling. Second, everything that exists has a *ground* for its existence—for any *x*, there is some *y* in relation to which *x*'s existence can be either understood or explained.[87]

Freud's psychoanalysis conformed to Schopenhauer's principle of sufficient reason on both of these levels. On the first, he proclaimed in his *Psychopathology of Everyday Life:* "nothing in the mind is arbitrary or undetermined."[88] Everything—from the most insignificant memory slip, to amnesia concerning the most traumatic event of one's life—has a reason for its occurrence. On the second level, in his metapsychology, Freud made it clear that it is our organic, somatic infrastructure that *grounds* everything we experience.

For Schopenhauer and Freud, respectively, everything in the *phenomenal* world is "caused" in the deterministic sense—including human activity. Schopenhauer:

> Through [the law of causality] are mutually connected all the objects presenting themselves in the entire general representation, which constitutes the complex of the reality of experience.[89]

Freud:

> and in this way determination in the psychical sphere is still carried out without any gap.[90]

What did Schopenhauer mean by "causality" here? Schopenhauer wrote, "I call cause in the narrowest sense of the word that state or condition of matter which, while it brings about another state with necessity . . .";[91] and, "as regards the appearance and disappearance of these states . . . every *state* that appears must have ensured or resulted from a change that preceded it."[92]

> The only correct expression for the law of causality is this: *Every change has its cause in another change immediately preceding it.* If something happens, in other words, if a new state or condition appears, if something changes, then something else must have changed just previously.[93]

Schopenhauer's causation, then, is not a relationship among *things* as many philosophers have mistakenly claimed.[94] It is simply false to refer to the things themselves as causes or effects:

> On the other hand, it is quite wrong to call the objects, and not the state, the cause . . . there is absolutely no sense in saying that one object is the cause of another . . . the law of causality refers exclusively to changes, in other words, to the appearance or disappearance of states in time.[95]

In his deterministic account, Freud also spoke of the impact of events or states of affairs on subsequent ones: this is clearly demonstrated throughout his case histories and therapeutic papers, for example.[96]

Next, what is the "ground" of our experience? As we have seen, for Schopenhauer it was the underlying will; and for Freud, in psychic life, it was the id. Will and id were considered the necessary *underlying condition* for everything we experience, yet *they do not cause* our phenomenal world to be as it is. The will/id does not cause phenomena; rather, it is the necessary transcendental condition for the appearance of the phenomena that we experience. This is what Schopenhauer meant when he wrote:

> The a priori nature of the law of causality has at times not been seen at all . . . [seeing] the will as cause and the movement of the body as effect. But this fact is erroneous . . .[97]

> In general, therefore, the law of causality finds application to all things in the world, but not to the world itself, for this law is immanent to the world, not transcendent . . .[98]

It was through this distinction that Schopenhauer was able to claim that there is freedom of being but not freedom of action.

What form does this condition of the will take? For Schopenhauer,

> force is . . . what imparts to every cause its causality, in other words, the possibility of acting . . . Two things in nature, namely matter and the forces of nature, remain untouched by the chain of causality which is endless in both directions. These are the conditions of causality, whereas everything else is conditioned by it. For matter is that in which the states and their changes appear; the other (the forces of nature) that by which virtue of which alone they are able to appear at all . . . the forces of nature are shown to be identical with the will in ourselves, but that matter appears as the mere visibility of the will, so that ultimately it too can be regarded in a certain sense as identical with the will.[99]

Freud spoke of the id in the same way—as a "seething cauldron of forces/ desires."

Force and matter, then, form the underlying transcendental *conditions* necessary for the appearance of phenomena, which are subject to the principle of causality. All of this is a nice fit for Freud's tension-reduction model with instinctual impulses (forces) as the condition for the development of ideas—indeed, any experience whatsoever.

Freedom

We are now in a position to appreciate how freedom fits into Schopenhauer's and Freud's model of human experience. For Schopenhauer, the will was considered ultimately free in itself and functioned on at least three different, tightly interwoven levels: (1) the will is free to will as it does (unhindered); (2) the will "chooses" from among motives in terms of which has the strongest "stirring" power; and (3) freedom is the liberation of energies that comes with greater *awareness* of what the will desires and what the motives are which are acting upon it.

1. *The will/id is free to will as it does (unhindered).* On the most primordial level, it is will as thing-in-itself that is *absolutely free in its being.* As thing-in-itself, its being *is* to will freely. (That is, the underlying forces *are* what they are.) To say much more about it is, as Schopenhauer put it, to "run up against the limits of philosophy."

To say that the will is "absolutely free" means that it "determines itself," and as such, is "truly autonomous."[100] *In itself* will is absolutely free *from all hindrances.* Schopenhauer wrote: "This concept is *negative.* By it we understand simply the absence of everything that impedes and obstructs" the manifestation of some force (namely, will).[101] Here Schopenhauer distinguished among three forms of freedom: physical freedom is the exertion of physical force in the absence of material obstructions, intellectual freedom is the absence of cognitive disability, and moral freedom is the freedom of the will from constraints by motives. Schopenhauer spent a great deal of time explicating this last sense, in his essay *On the Freedom of the Will.* For him, it is a question of whether or not the will is able to will *as it wills* (free from externally imposed constraints). Since the will in itself is absolutely free, it is the source of our awareness of our moral responsibility:

> In the esse alone is freedom to be found . . . in what we do we recognize what we are. On this, and not on the alleged *liberum arbitrium indifferentiae,* rest the awareness of responsibility and the moral tendency of life.[102]

As we have seen, Schopenhauer pointed out that freedom belongs to the world as will. Part of what this means is that this freedom of the will is directly disclosed in emotional experience (affective states) through the body. One of the crucial feelings we have is our feeling of moral responsibility.

Furthermore, the will is independent from the law of causality (as a mere form of appearances).[103] This freedom of the will as man's own work is transcendentally prior to all knowledge—knowledge is merely added to illuminate it.[104]

2. *The will "chooses" from among motives, in terms of which has the strongest "stirring" power.* When motives enter into Schopenhauer's account of freedom, the play between will *as it is in itself* and the phenomenal manifesta-

tion of will as bodily existence become intertwined. Hence, an elaboration of what Schopenhauer meant by "motive" and how it functions within his paradigm is helpful. First, how did Schopenhauer define motive?

> The act of will . . . arises on the occasion of something that belongs to the consciousness of *other things* and thus is an object of the faculty of cognition. In this connection such an object is called a *motive*.[105]

Motives, then, are a form of causality, and hence lead to *necessary* outcomes in the phenomenal realm—motivation is merely causality passing through knowledge.[106] The exception to this, for Schopenhauer, was the motive of self-preservation (originating as an inner instinctual impulse), which is not caused, but is a condition for other motives to operate.

> But instinct is to a certain extent a real exception insofar as, by reason of it, the animal is set into motion in the whole of its mode of action not by motives proper, but by an inner urge and drive. But in the details of the particular actions and at every moment the latter receives again its closer determination through motives, and thus returns to the rule.[107]

Next, the intellect is the medium of the motive[108] and through it has knowledge of the external world.[109] Motive, then, as cognition simply "stirs" the will: as a *thought* (a representation), it exerts influence on the will.[110] At this point, the will is merely susceptible to motives; this does not mean that the will *necessarily acts* on these motives. It is only once the strongest motive is determined that it acts on the will which results in an *act of will*.[111] For example, it is possible for even the strongest instinctual impulses of the will (as an internal motive)—such as the preservation of life—to be overcome by stronger counter-motives (suicide, the sacrifice of life for others, and so on).[112] Nevertheless, it is the will that imparts to the motive the power to act on it:

> Here the inner moving force whose particular manifestation is called forth by the motive . . . [is] *will* . . . [It is] a determining ground of the will that is to be stirred here . . . I said just now "the will that is to be stirred here"; for . . . that which properly imparts to the motive the power to act, the secret spring of the motion that is produced by the motive, proclaims itself inwardly and immediately here to the being itself as that which is denoted by the word *will* . . .[113]

> Here we stand behind the scenes, so to speak, and learn the secret of the way in which the cause produces the effect according to its innermost

nature . . . The result of this is the important proposition: motivation is causality seen from within.[114]

The will as the determining ground for motives, then, is free to "choose" from among the various motives (which will potentially satisfy its desires) based on the extent to which these motives "stir" the will. Such choices are not caused even though the actions which arise from them are.

3. *Freedom is the liberation of energies that comes with greater awareness of what the will desires and what the motives are which are acting upon it.* For Schopenhauer, the broader the range of possible motives—the more expansive the knowledge and awareness in, and of, the phenomenal world—the freer the will. By enabling a person to explore the possibilities open to him/her—the range of possible motives—the intellect can *enable the will to develop capacities that would otherwise remain dormant.* Motives, then, could "stir" the will. The free will is, then, circumscribed by the range of motives to which it may respond; and in order to respond to a motive it must be *aware* (though not consciously, of course) of the motive. It is important to remember, however, that *such enhanced freedom of the will operates only on the level of awareness,* while our actions themselves are strictly caused. Schopenhauer clearly held that such an enhanced reflective awareness of the will is something quite worthy of pursuit. Rational understanding can enable the will to have a higher awareness of itself, and can thereby exert an influence on the will.

Schopenhauer put the point rather paradoxically: "The cerebrum is the place of motives, and through these the will here becomes free choice, in other words, more closely determined by motives."[115] However, motives as mere thoughts have another function: they can determine actions. Since we are the kind of beings who can reflect, we have the capacity to apprehend a much greater range of potential thoughts, since it "encompasses the absent, the past, and the future":

> Man has a far greater sphere of influence of motives and consequently also of choice than an animal has, restricted as it is to the narrowness of the present moment. As a rule, it is not the thing lying before his sensible intuition and present in time and space which determines his action, but rather mere thoughts, which he carries about in his head wherever he goes, and which make him independent of the impression of the present moment.[116]

> Fine, invisible threads (motives consisting of mere thoughts) guide his movements . . . A thought becomes motive, as does an intuition, as soon as it is able to act on the will that lies before it. But all motives are causes,

and all causality entails necessity. Now by means of his ability to think, a human being can represent to himself the motives whose influence he feels on his will in any order he likes, alternately and repeatedly, in order to hold them before the will; and this is called *reflecting*. He has a capacity for deliberation, and, by virtue of it, a far greater choice than is possible for the animal. In this way, he certainly is *relatively free*, namely from the immediate compulsion of objects that are present through intuition and act as motives on his will, a compulsion to which the animal is absolutely subject. A human being, on the other hand, determines himself independently of present objects, in accordance with thoughts, which are *his* motives. At bottom it is this relative freedom that educated but not deep thinking people understand by freedom of the will . . . But such freedom is merely relative, namely in reference to what is present through intuition . . . Only the *mode* of motivation is changed by it; on the other hand, the necessity of the effect of the motives is not in the least suspended or even only diminished. The *abstract* motive that consists in a mere *thought* is an external cause determining the will just as is the intuitive motive, which consists in a real object that is present. Consequently, it is a cause like every other and is even, like other causes, at all times something real and material insofar as it always rests ultimately on an impression received *from without* at some time and place. Its advantage lies merely in the length of the guiding wire. By this I mean that it is not, like the merely intuitive motives, bound to a certain *proximity* in space and time, but can operate through the greatest distance and longest time, by means of concepts and thoughts in a long concatenation.[117]

The point here is that even though humans have a greater latitude given the more complex nature of the motives that determine their actions, their actions are caused nonetheless.[118]

In summary, then, Schopenhauer's notion of freedom is intrinsic to our very being; it is the ground from which we *are* and act,

> when man abandons all knowledge of individual things . . . and sees through the *principium individuationis*. An actual appearance of the real freedom of the will as thing-in-itself then becomes possible.[119]

True freedom is to be found "in the whole being and essence *(existentia et essentia)* of the human being himself."[120]

> This freedom is transcendental, i.e., it does not emerge in the appearance but is present only insofar as we abstract outside all time, is to be thought of as the inner essence of the human being in himself . . .

Consequently, the will is indeed free, but only in itself and outside the appearance.[121]

Freedom, then, is not suspended by my treatment of the matter, but merely, moved up from the domain of individual actions, where it obviously is not to be found, into a higher region, which, however, is not so easily accessible to our cognition.[122]

Determinism and Necessity

For Schopenhauer, necessity arose out of freedom. In other words, from what a human *is* (as will), everything she or he *does* necessarily follows.[123] The will is the underlying transcendental condition for the manifestation of human actions in the phenomenal world, but, as such, it does not cause them. Instead, as actions appear in the phenomenal world, *they* are subject to the law of causality, hence all actions are necessarily determined to happen as they do.[124] In the phenomenal world, it is motives that determine human actions.

For Schopenhauer and Freud, human beings were seen in terms of an interplay between a will/id (which, as the underlying condition for any possible experience, when unhindered, is free) and competing motives (which, generally speaking, have their origin in the "external" world, are determined, and exert a stirring effect on the will). In Freudian terms, this was what he meant by the interplay between the id's primary process and the ego's secondary process.

In his account of the interplay through the intellect of the motives and the will, Schopenhauer's model paralleled Freud's account of the interactions between the ego and the id quite closely:

> The intellect or the faculty of cognition is the *medium of motives*. For through it motives act on the will, which is the real kernel of the human being. Only insofar as this medium of motives happens to be in a normal state or condition, fulfills its functions regularly, and thus presents to the will for choice the motives in an unfalsified manner as they exist in the real world can this will decide according to its nature, i.e., in accordance with the individual character of the human being, and thus manifest itself *unimpeded* in conformity with its very own essence. The human being is then *intellectually free*, i.e., his actions are the pure result of the reaction of his will to motives that lie in the outside world before him as also before everyone else . . . This intellectual freedom is *suspended* either through the permanent or temporary derangement of the medium of motives, the faculty of cognition, or by a faulty apprehension

of motives which is caused by external circumstances in the particular case. The former is the case in madness, delirium, paroxysm, and heavy drowsiness . . . motives are falsified and thus the will cannot decide as it would in existing circumstances if the intellect correctly transmitted them to it.[125]

It is important to note that conflict takes place on two levels: between the will and the motives (supplied by the "external" world); and among the motives themselves. For Freud, this conflict was manifested among the various parts of the personality—the id, ego, and superego.

How does one's inner essence as will engage outer motives (as that which is perceived or understood about the external world)? For Freud this question—namely, where the id aspires to gratification of its instinctual desires, and immediately runs into external motives supplied by society to block or delay its gratification—was of particular concern for humankind:

> The liberty of the individual is no gift of civilization. It was greatest before there was any civilization, though then, it is true, it had for the most part no value, since the individual was scarcely in a position to defend it. The development of civilization imposes restrictions upon it, and justice demands that no one shall escape these restrictions . . . What makes itself felt in a human community as a desire for freedom may be their revolt against some existing injustice, and so may prove favourable to a further development of civilization; it may remain compatible with civilization. But it may also spring from the remains of their original personality, which is still untamed by civilization and may thus become the basis in them of hostility to civilization. The urge for freedom, therefore, is directed against particular forms and demands of civilization or against civilization altogether. It does not seem as though any influence could induce a man to change his nature into a termite's. No doubt he will always defend his claim to individual liberty against the will of the group. A good part of the struggles of mankind centre round the single task of finding an expedient accommodation between this claim of the individual and the cultural claims of the group; and one of the problems that touches the fate of humanity is where such an accommodation can be reached by men of some particular form of civilization or whether this conflict is irreconcilable.[126]

Whether or not such impulses meet with resistance from society on their way toward satisfaction is another issue. Again, those impulses which are not allowed external expression become internalized in repression.

It is important to notice that Schopenhauer interpolated a step between willing and the act of will:

> For as long as the act of will is in the process of coming about, it is called
> wish, when complete it is called decision; but that it is complete is first
> shown to self-consciousness itself by deed, for until then the decision is
> changeable.[127]

Here "wish" simply operated on the level of the primary process for Freud.
Yet, it is important to draw a distinction between *freely thinking of oneself
willing* different occurrences and *freely willing* them: certainly we can do
the former, but we cannot do the latter (that is, will anything other than
what we will). One way in which this can happen is

> that in a given case, opposite acts of will are possible, and boast of their
> self-consciousness which, they imagine, asserts this. Thus [the philosoph-
> ically untutored] confuse wishing with willing; they can wish opposite
> things, but can will only one of them.[128]

What actions we actually carry out depends both upon what the will wills
(namely, desires) *and* which motive is the strongest in "stirring" it (which
motive the will discerns to be the strongest). However, as both Schopenhauer and Freud pointed out, we are not always consciously aware (and,
in fact, are most often *not* aware) of the effect of our motives on us, whether
because they originate in the will and are repressed before they attain
conscious awareness; because the will could get us to act based on its own
instinctual desires; or because of other factors, which we should now consider.

    We are now in a position to truly appreciate why these two thinkers
rejected an illusory kind of freedom on the same grounds.[129] Both rejected one notion of "free will" as an absurd illusion: "that two different
actions are possible to a given person in a given situation."[130] Yet both also
agreed that we have a perfectly viable notion of responsibility that is consistent with determinism.

    According to Schopenhauer it is easy to fall prey to such a "delusion
of an empirically given, absolute freedom of the will."[131] But how exactly
are we misled here?

> He may be led astray by the previously described immaterial nature of
> abstract motives, that consist of mere thoughts, since they are not tied to
> any present moment and environment and find again their *hindrances*
> only in mere thoughts as countermotives. Thus he may be so *led astray* as

to doubt their existence indeed the necessity of their efficacy, and to imagine that what is done can just as well be left undone; that the will decides by itself without cause . . . *All this taken together is therefore the source of that natural deception from which springs the error that in our self-consciousness lies the certainty of a freedom of our will* in the sense that the will determines itself without sufficient reasons [italics added].[132]

The point is that the illusion that our thoughts appear to lack obstructions in the form of counter-motives misleads us to believe that we freely could either do or not do act *x*. However, in the phenomenal world the will always acts in such a way as to comply with the principle of sufficient reason: there is always a reason why act *x* occurs. "A person [as] phenomenon of the will, is as such determined."[133] Even though competing motives try their "stirring power" on the will by cognition, and we have the illusion that we can choose from among various motives, in the end, "the stronger motive asserts its power over the will."[134]

According to Schopenhauer, what "the philosophically untutored" fail to do is to distinguish between *wishing* and *willing*.[135] When the act of will is in the process of coming into existence, at that stage opposite acts of will are *possible*—this is called *wishing*. When the actual act occurs, it can *will only one* of these wishes, namely, the strongest motive. The failure to draw this distinction is the chief source of that undeniable illusion that we are free to will what we choose.[136]

This position is precisely the same as Freud's:

There are also all the unfulfilled but possible futures to which we still like to cling in phantasy, all the strivings of the ego which adverse external circumstances have crushed, and all our suppressed acts of volition, which nourish in us the illusion of Free Will.[137]

Many people . . . contest the assumption of complete psychical determinism by appealing to a special feeling of conviction that there is free will. This feeling of conviction exists; and it does not give way before a belief in determinism. Like every normal feeling it must have something to warrant it . . . it is precisely with regard to the unimportant, indifferent decisions that we would like to claim that we could just as well have acted otherwise; that we have acted of our free—and unmotivated—will. According to our analyses it is not necessary to dispute the right to the feeling of conviction of having a free will. If the distinction between conscious and unconscious motivation is taken into account, our feeling of conviction informs us that conscious motivation does not extend to our motor decisions. But what is thus left free by the one side receives its motivation from the other side, from the unconscious; and in this way determination in the psychical sphere is still carried out without any gap.[138]

The similarity of Schopenhauer's and Freud's positions can hardly be a coincidence given all of the evidence adduced earlier, especially since we know that Freud read Schopenhauer's *Parerga und Paralipomena*, which refers to "the absurd fiction of a free will."[139] Freud also read there:

> A man can forget everything, absolutely everything, but not himself, his own true nature. For character is positively incorrigible because all man's actions flow from an inner principle by virtue whereof, under similar circumstances, he must always do the same thing and cannot do otherwise. The reader should peruse my prize-essay on the so-called freedom of the will and free himself from the erroneous idea.[140]

> After reading my prize-essay on *moral freedom*, no thinking man can be left in any doubt that such freedom is not to be sought anywhere within nature, but only without. It is something metaphysical, but in the physical world something that is impossible. Accordingly, our individual deeds are by no means free; on the other hand, the individual character of each one of us is to be regarded as his free act. He himself is such because he wills once for all to be such. For the will exists in itself, even in so far as it appears in an individual. Thus it constitutes the individual's primary and fundamental willing and is independent of all knowledge because it precedes this. From knowledge it obtains merely the motives wherein it successively develops its true nature and makes itself known or becomes visible. As that which lies outside time, however, it itself is unchangeable so long as it exists at all. Therefore everyone as such who exists now and under the circumstances of the moment, which, however, on their part occur with strict necessity, can never do anything other than what he is actually doing at that very moment.[141]

It is difficult to believe that Freud, on reading this, did not proceed immediately (if he had not already) to read Schopenhauer's essay on freedom, given the clarity, similarity, and cogency of the latter's remarks on the very issue which formed one of the foundational ideas of Freud's *Psychopathology of Everyday Life*.

Finally, even though both thinkers held that all human actions are not free, they agreed that this does not mean that we are not morally accountable for our true being. For example, Freud held that not only are we accountable for our actions, we are even accountable for our dreams: "Obviously one must hold oneself responsible for the evil impulses of one's dreams . . . it is a part of my own being."[142] Similarly, Schopenhauer wrote: "As a man is, so must he act; and hence guilt and merit attach not to his individual acts, but to his true nature and being."[143] In fact, it is here that Schopenhauer offered a highly significant propaedeutic for the development of an analysis of the psyche:

> But now where consciousness is rational and hence capable of nonintuitive cognition, i.e., concepts and thoughts, the motives become quite independent of the present moment and of the real environment, and thus remain hidden from the spectator. For now they are mere thoughts carried round by the human being in his head, yet their origination lies outside the head and often far away. Thus they may lie in his own experience of past years . . . Added to this is the fact that a human being often conceals the motives of his actions from everyone else, and sometimes even from himself, namely where he shrinks from acknowledging what it really is that moves him to do this or that. Meanwhile we see his actions ensue, and try by conjectures to ascertain the motives; for here we assume these just as firmly and confidently as we do the cause of every motion of inanimate bodies.[144]

Schopenhauer expanded upon this insight in a highly cogent manner:

1. Motives continue to exert an influence (or have an effect) on the person regardless of how long ago or far away they occurred. "In the higher and more intelligent animals the effect of the motives becomes more and more indirect."[145] Schopenhauer insisted that the effectiveness of motives has no specific duration or spatial-temporal proximity to current events.[146]
2. Motives, *while remaining as thoughts within a person's psychical life,* can become separate from the present moment and actual surroundings.[147]
3. With an ever-widening separation of those motives from the present moment and place, a person can come to lose a recognition of what their cause and effect relationship was, that is, their intelligibility in making sense out their experience:

> The cause and its effect become ever more widely separated, more clearly differentiated, and more heterogeneous from each other . . . The result of all this is that the connection between cause and effect loses its immediate comprehensibility and intelligibility.[148]

4. In conjunction with the above separation, the person may also find *hindrances* to any recognition of these motives by the existence of counter-motives, and hence be led so astray as to doubt the very existence of the original motive and/or its necessary efficacy.[149]

5. A person often *conceals* motives from others and self. First, as internal motives from whatever source can remain undisclosed to someone observing that person.[150] Second, and more important, a person might conceal motives from self and others while "shrinking from knowledge" of what their true motives are. Furthermore, "the necessity of [the] effect[s] [of motives] is concealed behind the conflict [among them] even from the person himself who acts."[151]

6. Lost or concealed motives are potentially discoverable by examining what a person does or how a person is:

> . . . the causes also appear less and less palpable and material, so that at last they are no longer visible to the eye, although still within reach of the understanding, which presupposes them with unshakable confidence, and also discovers them after a proper search.[152]

Motives can be recovered in terms of their interconnectedness with our experience. It is only with the clarity that hindsight affords that we are able to regain an understanding of the significance of the interconnectedness of our motives with our present experience:

> We frequently do not understand the true connection of important events in our own lives while they are going on or shortly after they have occurred, but only long afterwards. We do not easily recognize the significance of events and persons when they are actually present. It is only when they lie in the past that they stand out in all their significance after being given prominence by recollection, narrative, and description.[153]

We have seen Schopenhauer's claim that the principle of sufficient reason holds for everything, his deterministic account of the phenomenal world, and how motives can serve as causes within it. The most significant point in this for our purposes is that motives operate with the strict necessity of determinism *in the phenomenal realm*. Indeed, in a nutshell, Schopenhauer claimed that the strongest motive(s) + will (character) = necessary action in the phenomenal world. Where, then, is free will when it comes to action? Schopenhauer and Freud concurred that there is none. This does not, however, preclude other kinds of possibilities.

Through our ratiocinative faculty, for example, we can with conscious clarity, make "elective decisions"—weigh mutually exclusive motives against one another, and let them exert their "stirring" power on the will. The more powerful motive then "decides" the person with necessity.[154] (What "decides" which of the motives is the most powerful? The will, since it is stirred by each motive with differing degrees of strength.) Without the motive's "stirring" power on the will, there could be no decision.[155] From observation of our inner experience we know that this motive stirs this act of will. Hence, "explicit decisions" are consistent with will.[156]

> [The will] is determined by motives to which the character in each case regularly and necessarily always reacts in the same way. We see that, in virtue of the addition of abstract or rational knowledge, man has the advantage over the animal of an *elective decision*, which, however, simply makes him the scene of a conflict of motives, without withdrawing him from their control . . . Therefore this elective decision is certainly the condition of the possibility of the individual character's complete expression, but it is by no means to be regarded as freedom of the individual willing, in other words, as independence of the law of causality, whose necessity extends to man as to every other phenomenon.[157]

> The motives are almost always abstract representations; these are not shared by the spectator, and the necessity of their effect is concealed behind their conflict even from the person himself who acts. For only *in abstracto* can several representations lie beside one another in consciousness as judgments and chains of conclusions, and then, free from all determination of time, work against one another, until the strongest overpowers the rest, and determines the will. This is the complete *elective decision* or faculty of deliberation . . .[158]

This was precisely what Freudian psychotherapy was designed to do: to bring about awareness of (or make explicit) that which remained concealed (yet exerted its impact) in the human psyche, so that the patient was able to utilize his/her "elective decision." Ultimately, the idea is to be liberated from the oppressive effects—the huge amounts of anticathetic energy that go into keeping an awareness of them from our consciousness (repression)—that accrue from our lack of understanding their basis in the instincts.

In these last two chapters we have shown, in relatively detailed fashion, some of the ways in which Schopenhauer—and to a lesser extent, Nietzsche—anticipated a number of the most fundamental motifs of Freud's metapsychology. We contend that this alone enables us to better understand Freud's philosophical underpinnings and thereby strengthen it. Just as important, however, we believe that Schopenhauer's ideas provide Freud—with his self-ascribed "constitutional incapacity for philosophy"—access to substantial philosophical resources with which to respond more forcefully and cogently to criticisms lodged against him, posthumously, by the existential phenomenologists.

Part 2

Freud's Philosophical Engagement with Husserlian Phenomenology and Existential Phenomenology

9

A Propaedeutic to Freud and the Existential Phenomenologists

Every philosopher "takes something from the history" of past
philosophers, from past philosophical writings—just as he has at
his disposal, from the present philosophical environment, the
works that have most recently been added and put in circulation,
takes up those that have just appeared, and, what is possible
only in the case [of the present], makes more or less use of the
possibility of entering into a personal exchange of ideas with still
living fellow philosophers.
—Husserl

As we approach the historical engagement of Freud with the existential
phenomenologists it is crucial that we first consider the historical context
and role of one major philosophical contemporary of Freud, and *the* primary inspirational father of the existential phenomenologists, Edmund
Husserl. For it was Husserl, of course, who provided the existential phenomenologists with some of the initial methodological tools (however
modified to their own philosophical pursuits) or at least philosophical im-
petuses, which would furnish the grounding for their critical engagement
with Freud. An implicit set of questions immediately arises: what was
the historical—and is the philosophical—relationship between Husserlian phenomenology and Freudian psychoanalysis? Are the goals of the
two essentially identical or compatible (reciprocally supplementary to one
another), largely or marginally overlapping, or mutually exclusive?[1] Is
there a convergence which results in their merger? To what extent is a reconciliation of the two approaches possible? The answers to these questions will, of course, in the end identify what each has to offer the other, if
anything.

Before we consider directly Freud and Husserl's relationship to one
another in the following chapter, it is important to point out that a direct

historical convergence occurred between these two important thinkers, most notably through the works of Johann Herbart and Franz Brentano.[2]

Opposed to the route taken by the romanticists culminating in Schopenhauer's and Nietzsche's approaches, in keeping with the influence of British empiricism and in reaction to Kantian philosophy, Herbart and Brentano sought to place psychology in alignment with the natural sciences. Each undertook this project, though in highly discrepant ways,[3] and exerted a strong influence on the development of both Husserl's and Freud's philosophical approaches.

Herbart and Freud

It is well known that during Freud's youth Herbartian psychology was the predominant view in the field throughout Austria. It exerted its influence on Freud through several main avenues:

1. Gustaf Lindner's *Textbook of Empirical Psychology by Genetic Method,* described by its author as "a compendium of Herbartian psychology,"[4] had clearly been introduced to Freud during his final year at the Gymnasium.[5]
2. Freud's mentor in psychiatry, Theodor Meynert—who had also been influenced by Schopenhauer—was an admirer of Herbart's and had been powerfully influenced by him.[6]
3. Fechner had self-consciously constructed his psychology based on Herbart's (sheared of its metaphysical principles), which sought to extend the nomenclature of the natural sciences to psychology; and Fechner in turn exerted a strong influence on Freud's teachers, Brücke, Breuer, and Meynert, and—as we have seen—on Freud himself.
4. Freud certainly knew of Herbart's work via comments made to him by Brentano.[7]

Herbart conceived of psychology as a "mechanics of the mind" in which there are interactions among ideas (conceived as active agents) measurable in terms of quantity and force, hence a "mathematical psychology." Herbart believed that psychology was *supervenient* to physiology. This was an important advance for Freud beyond the medicine of his time that tended to reduce everything to the physiological level. Furthermore, Freud would clearly have appreciated Herbart's recognition of the empirical limits of science:

> Science knows more than what is actually experienced [in conscious-
> ness] only because what is experienced is unthinkable without examin-
> ing what is concealed. One must be able to recognize from what is expe-
> rienced the traces of what is stirring and acting "behind the curtains"![8]

According to Herbart, active ideas of varying degrees of strength
compete to be above the threshold of consciousness. The weaker ("inhib-
ited") ideas disappear from consciousness and form a mass of unconscious
ideas which continue to exert pressure against the ideas in consciousness in a continual conflict that results in the progressive adaptation of the
individual mind to personal and interpersonal situations. In this position,
Herbart obviously anticipated some of the primary ideas underpinning
Freud's position in, for example, *Civilization and Its Discontents,* particularly the conflict between acceptable and unacceptable ideas within society and their repression as part of individual adjustment.

Herbart also anticipated some of Freud's ideas concerning the existence of unconscious psychical processes playing a vital role in mental
life.[9] Herbart conceived of mental life dynamically, as the struggle among
active ideas to gain access to consciousness or remain unconscious and yet
produce indirect effects in consciousness: the notion that ideas are never
lost once they have become a part of an individual's mental life; that a
series of associations among ideas intersect in gnarls of "freely emerging
associations"; that ego awareness occurs when active ideas are occluded
in some way; and that striving for equilibrium governs mental processes
overall. All of these ideas are, *mutatis mutandi,* to be found in altered form
subsequently in psychoanalytic theory.

Herbart presaged Freud's formulation of "repression" *(verdrängt)*
and two aspects of his topographical conception of the unconscious. As
James Strachey noted in the *Standard Edition:*

> The term *"Verdrängung"* [repression] had been used by the early
> nineteenth-century psychologist Herbart and may possibly have come to
> Freud's knowledge through his teacher Meynert, who had been an
> admirer of Herbart.[10]

Here, Strachey was referring to Herbart's use of *verdrängt* in the latter's
Psychology as Science (1824). Herbart actually described an idea as *verdrängt*
when it was unable to reach consciousness due to competing ideas or
when it had been driven out of consciousness because of some conflicting
idea. However, Freud had been exposed to Herbart's use of the term in
Lindner's text even earlier at the Gymnasium:

A result of the fusion of ideas proves that ideas which were once in consciousness and for any reason have been repressed out of it are not lost, but in certain circumstances may return.[11]

It is interesting to note here that the exposure of Freud to the use of *verdrängt* in this sense had occurred in the form of a series of successive and mutually reinforcing waves. Freud was directly (or indirectly) affected by Schopenhauer's use of the term, as we saw earlier. Herbart was thoroughly familiar with Schopenhauer's philosophy as well.[12] Herbart employed the word in Schopenhauer's sense in his magnum opus *Psychology as Science*, which appeared six years after Schopenhauer's *World as Will and Representation*, volume one. Meynert, Freud's mentor, was clearly familiar with Schopenhauer's philosophy *and* an admirer of Herbart's; and again, Freud's experience at the Gymnasium certainly brought him into contact with the notion of repression through numerous sources. Given these successive waves of exposure, Freud's claim to originality is especially incredible: as stated earlier, the historical background makes his insistence that "the theory of repression quite certainly came to me independently of any source"[13] utterly fascinating from a psychoanalytic standpoint.

Herbart conceived of a topographical model of the mind in his analysis of two levels of thresholds in relation to consciousness. First, he described a "static threshold" where consciousness unblocks an idea from arising within it (which is somewhat akin to Freud's notions of "suppression" and the preconscious). Second, Herbart referred to a "mechanistic threshold" where fully repressed ideas continue to be antagonistic to various conscious ideas and exert indirect effects upon them. Given Herbart's clear anticipation of and influence on subsequent developments in Freudian psychoanalysis, it is useful for us to consider the relationship of Herbart's ideas to those of Husserl.

Herbart and Husserl

Herbart's psychology also exerted a great deal of influence on Husserl's analyses of mental processes. All one need do is compare large sections from Herbart's *A Text-book in Psychology*[14]—which contained the first articulation of the positions involved—with Husserl's *Analyses Concerning Passive and Active Synthesis*[15] to see highly congruent points from each concerning the psychical realm. Herbart contended that ideas become *forces* when they resist and struggle with one another for a place in consciousness. Once created, an idea is never lost from the psychical system; suppressed ideas remain as unconscious tendencies.[16] One idea has the capacity to prevent another from rising into consciousness. In order to become conscious, ideas must rise above a certain threshold.[17] A person can move ideas that are below the threshold into consciousness, and some ideas easily make the transition while others do not. The ones that move from the unconscious to consciousness are those which are most consonant with the system of ideas already in consciousness.[18] Other similarities include the notion that associative chains of ideas are in the unconscious that intersect at nodal points, free-floating ideas emerge from the unconscious, and so on.

One historical fact is quite noteworthy here: it is clear that Herbart's account of the psychic sphere had been substantially influenced by the philosophy of Leibniz. Indeed, it was Leibniz who was the originator of the idea of a threshold of consciousness. Ideas below it were unconscious, and above it were conscious. Herbart, and subsequently Husserl, took over this model. Also, in *Ideas II* and *Analyses Concerning Passive and Active Synthesis,* Husserl developed a notion of individual consciousnesses as *monadic* unities, as "minds":[19]

> The monad is a living unity that bears within itself an ego as the pole of being effective and being affected, and a unity of wakeful and concealed life, a unity of abilities, of "dispositions"; and what is concealed, "unconscious" . . .[20]

Similarly, Herbart had spoken of the universe as consisting of independent "reals" which sometimes lack consciousness.

Herbart, of course, had defined psychology as the "mechanics of the mind" involving attraction and repulsion. In spite of his aversion to the mechanistic model and the causality that accompanied it, Husserl shared Herbart's conception of ideas that actively struggle with one another to cross the threshold of consciousness. Like Husserl, as we shall see, Herbart referred to "concepts" being attracted to consciousness "by their own efforts"; "opposed concepts" as exerting a repulsive force upon one another, the suppressed concept as "unconscious"; and the suppressed concept as not dormant, but exerting an influence on conscious life. Hence, the unconscious was considered dynamic:[21]

> "The course of our thoughts is often so inconsequent, abrupt and apparently irregular"? Clearly, the course of conscious thought must be acted upon by events outside it.[22]

We should not fail to point out that Herbart also anticipated Husserl's distinctions between a study of the "statics" and "dynamics" of the mind and between the conscious separation of the act of conceiving from what is conceived—that is, the noesis–noema distinction that plays such a prevalent role in Husserl's transcendental phenomenology.

Brentano

Franz Brentano served as an especially prominent point of intersection in the history of philosophy in many ways. It is well known that he exerted an immense philosophical influence on the formation of Freud's and Husserl's ideas; he also had a considerable impact on others. For example, Heidegger credited Brentano's dissertation "On the different senses of being in Aristotle" for being the "lightening bolt" igniting his own ontological investigations. Brentano, of course, influenced analytic philosophy—Frege, Meinong, Russell, for example—as well.

Within the context of this book, Franz Brentano is an especially pivotal figure. As successive, avid students of his at the University of Vienna, Freud (1873–76) and Husserl (1883–86) had been so strongly impressed by Brentano that under his influence and encouragement each decided (in Freud's case, at least for a time) to pursue advanced work in philosophy. Freud openly acknowledged that "under Brentano's fruitful influence I have arrived at the decision to take my Ph.D. in philosophy and zoology."[23] Similarly, Husserl stated: "I was vacillating between studying in mathematics and devoting my life to philosophy, Brentano's lectures were the deciding factor."[24] Yet each rejected, in their respective ways, Brentano's conclusions about the possible existence of an "unconscious," and picked up his gauntlet concerning the challenge of developing a viable conception of the unconscious.[25]

Brentano and Freud

What was the philosophical appeal of Brentano—as Freud characterized him, this "splendid man, a scholar and philosopher,"[26] and "this damned clever fellow, a genius in fact"[27]—for Freud? Why did Freud voluntarily enroll in five of Brentano's courses—incidentally the only courses taken by Freud during his eight semesters at the University of Vienna that were not medical ones?[28]

Freud himself supplied part of the answer in his account of a visit to Brentano's home. First, Freud clearly identified with his heuristical approach: he said with admiration, "Brentano's great distinction is that he abhors all glib phrases, all emotionality, and all intolerance of other views."[29]

Second, and more important, Freud emphasized: "[Brentano] declared himself unreservedly a follower of the empiricist school which applies the method of science to philosophy and to psychology in particular (in fact, this is the main advantage of his philosophy, which alone renders it tolerable for me)."[30] Brentano sought to bridge the gap between science and philosophy by applying the method of the former to the latter. He strongly believed that contemporary psychologists (for example, Herbart) had failed to develop scientific procedures within their philosophical studies. While Brentano gave credit to Herbart for emphasizing the necessity for mathematizing psychology, he criticized his "complete failure of his attempt to discover actual determinations of quantity . . . by this method no progress is made toward the explanation of mental phenomena as revealed by experience."[31] Freud was clearly smitten with the idea of applying the "true methods" of the natural sciences to philosophy and psychology in order to establish the regularities of the laws of mental life. At this juncture, Brentano managed to inspire Freud to question his "materialist" proclivities.

Third, Brentano made it quite clear in his magnum opus, *Psychology from the Empirical Standpoint* (which was published during Freud's second year of study under him) that he sought "to eschew as much as possible all metaphysical theories."[32] As we have seen, Freud was more than sympathetic to such a view.[33]

Yet most important, Brentano's influence upon Freud was perhaps in the form of a challenge: Brentano's blatant rejection of the unconscious, coupled with his insistence upon basing philosophy on empirical grounds indirectly led Freud to attempt to retain the notion of an unconscious by approaching it scientifically and thereby providing it with the necessary scientific tools to render investigation into unconscious phenomena valid. Hence, Freud paid close attention to Brentano's rejection of the unconscious and attempted to avoid the problems into which those before him had fallen. Rather than following Brentano, then, Freud eventually composed what he believed was a way to save the unconscious from scientific obscurity.

Brentano's main position regarding the unconscious was that there was no scientific basis for asserting an unconscious. After reviewing the protracted historical arguments over the existence of the unconscious, Brentano rejected the conception as scientifically unsound.[34] He stated that his preference was to use the word "consciousness" "as synonymous with 'mental phenomenon,' or 'mental act': [hence] no mental phenomenon exists which is not consciousness of an object."[35] By "unconscious," then, Brentano meant "in a passive sense, speaking of a thing [that is, mental act] of which we are not conscious."[36]

What then was Brentano's primary argument for denying the existence of such an "unconscious"? He held that consciousness toward an object involved two primary aspects: consciousness toward an object as presented, and consciousness of itself as it is consciousness toward an object as presented (consciousness of the act of consciousness itself). From the second aspect, we know that we are automatically aware (conscious) of every occurring mental act. Since there are no mental acts of which we are unaware—that is, in which there is no presentation—there is no unconscious.[37]

Why, then, do we so easily fall prey to thinking that there is an unconscious? Brentano held that the degree of intensity with which the object is presented equals the degree of intensity of the corresponding mental act. Hence, in cases where there is an extremely low intensity involved we are inclined to overlook the conscious occurrence of such acts and are apt to think of them as unconscious.[38]

In the selections of *Psychology from the Empirical Standpoint* in which Brentano rejected the existence of the unconscious, he presented a rather detailed critique of the influential British psychologist Henry Maudsley. It is interesting to note that Maudsley was one of the most influential members of a British school of psychologists who directly influenced Freud's teachers in Vienna. This school developed a doctrine of unconscious mental processes within the context of a mind–body unity, a position that Freud might arguably be said to have ultimately assumed himself.

What is especially remarkable, however, is the fact that Maudsley's position, as characterized by Brentano, anticipated many of the fundamental underlying points of Freud's metapsychology. Was it, perhaps, the historical ambiance that spurred Freud to pick up the gauntlet—namely, Maudsley's "failure" and Brentano's challenge—and to develop his metapsychology, with the necessity of basing psychology upon physiology?[39]

In his *Physiology and Pathology of the Mind,* Maudsley lamented: "in the present state of physiological science, it is quite impossible to ascertain, by observation and experiment, the nature of those organic processes which are the bodily conditions of mental phenomena." Maudsley added that "there are really no grounds for expecting a positive science of mind at present."[40] As we have seen, Freud did much the same in his later writings as well.

Furthermore, Brentano quoted Maudsley as having written, "material conditions are the basis of consciousness."[41] This was clearly in anticipatory alignment with Freud's metapsychology. In fact, the following quote from Maudsley's *Physiology and Psychology of the Mind* could have been written by Freud:

The brain, of which all consciousness is a function, also has a *vegetative life*. It is subject to an organic metabolism which, of course, ordinarily goes on, in a healthy state, without our being conscious of it. Yet, pressing its way into consciousness, it is often the cause of abnormal phenomena. Involuntary emotions appear followed by a disorderly confusion of ideas.[42]

Brentano mentioned that Maudsley had also written that "mental life does not necessarily involve mental activity," and "mental activity does not necessarily involve consciousness." Here Brentano argued that Maudsley did not "give compelling evidence for the existence of unconscious ideas."[43]

Freud was later to pick up this gauntlet with a vengeance. Indeed, in a footnote added to the *Interpretation of Dreams*,[44] but composed in the year of the appearance of his metapsychological papers, Freud thought it important to quote Maudsley in regards to unconscious ideas: "It is a truth which cannot be too distinctly borne in mind that consciousness is not co-extensive with the mind."[45] Interestingly Maudsley, like Freud, accepted the Lamarckian hypothesis and was aware of a phylogenetic human history which was passed down from generation to generation. Freud was aware of this from Brentano's *Psychology from the Empirical Standpoint* where Brentano wrote, "Maudsley finally introduces the principle of heredity from generation to generation."[46]

> Just as the residues of previous mental life persist in the individual, they are also preserved in the species . . . the toilsome conscious activity of ordinary labor is the precondition for the unconscious creations of the richly endowed mind . . . It is clear once again that this influence of heredity is far removed from the realm of consciousness.[47]

Maudsley held views that were also in alignment with Herbart's and anticipated Husserl's notion of "apperceptive aftereffect," for example:

> Anything which has once been present, with a certain amount of completeness, in consciousness, leaves behind it a trace, a potential or latent idea, when it disappears from consciousness.[48]

Brentano and Husserl

It is important to note here one important influence by Brentano on Husserl as well. In his *Psychology from the Empirical Standpoint,* Brentano anticipated Husserl's distinction between "static" and "genetic" phenomenology by drawing a distinction between "descriptive psychology" (that is, "ascertaining the basic elements of mental phenomena") and "genetic

psychology" (determining "the laws governing their coming into existence, duration, and passing away").[49] The latter he regarded as predominantly physiological in nature. Ironically, as we shall see, it was precisely
this distinction which compelled Husserl to explore the very "unconscious" which Brentano had rejected earlier.

Both Husserl and Freud rejected Brentano's "proof" that "there
never exists within us a mental phenomenon of which we have no presentation."[50] Each in his own way accepted the challenge Brentano had articulated. As we shall see in the next chapter, it was partially Brentano's rejection of the unconscious (along with his undeniable influence on these
two remarkable students) which led Freud and Husserl to unwittingly
wander within similar domains; and possibly we shall find evidence of
something upon which the two might have agreed, had they had an inclination to find a meeting ground from within the recesses of their individual, archaeological discoveries.

An Intelligible yet Enigmatic Mutual Silence: Freud and Husserl

> In truth, this is a whole world—and if we could equate this subjectivity with the ψυχή [soul] of Heraclitus, his saying would doubtless be true of it: "You will never find the boundaries of the soul, even if you follow every road; so deep is its ground." Indeed, every "ground" that is reached points to further grounds, every horizon opened up awakens new horizons, and yet the endless whole, in its infinity of flowing movement, is oriented toward that *unity* of one meaning [italics added].
> —Husserl

> [The philosopher] knows that, in the process, historical tradition, as he understood it and used it, entered into him in a motivating way and as a spiritual sediment.
> —Husserl

Sigmund Freud lived from 1856 to 1939, and Edmund Husserl from 1859 to 1938. They spoke and worked in the same language, lived in relative proximity to one another,[1] shared common religious roots, and had mutual associates[2] and students (for example, Binswanger). Most important, they held in common certain specific philosophical-psychological concerns: the emergence of *meaning* in the psyche, its structure and operations, its relationship to the body, the functioning of memory in consciousness, unconscious operations in mental life, repression, and so on. Both men were, in their own ways, trying to apprehend those inaccessible dimensions of human existence which exert an impact upon the formation of meaning in consciousness, and thereby make the latter more comprehensible. And yet these two celebrated intellectuals not only failed to take substantial interest in one another's work but even neglected to acknowledge the importance of one another's work.

There were clearly significant differences between their paradigms, and, at times, their analyses operated at different levels; it is nevertheless remarkable that both shared many common features.[3] In general, both Husserl and Freud (1) undertook a regressive, archaeological inquiry into the affective histories of individuals and into the hidden recesses of the psyche; (2) acknowledged the existence and importance of "unconscious" intentionalities; (3) affirmed that entire associative chains of ideas can run their course without ever emerging into consciousness, and that they can help us to recover unconscious memories; (4) claimed that consciousness and the unconscious mutually modified one another; and (5) asserted that the ego is at the mercy (at least at times) of the underlying processes of the unconscious. In addition, both held that the unconscious (6) is rooted in instinctual life; (7) involves dynamic forces that continually conflict, and affect consciousness; (8) retains ideas interminably; (9) involves processes/ideas that are atemporal; and (10) is also a dimension of the ego. Furthermore, Freud and Husserl held that ideas require a certain force to reach the threshold of consciousness and when they do, they may only be fragmentary or confused in nature.

Given these commonalities it is—again, at the very least—prima facie enigmatic why neither held significant interest in nor even acknowledged the importance of the work of the other. Certainly they must have been aware on some level of one another's work.

On the surface, it would seem that since Husserl, as a phenomenologist, focused his attention primarily on the structures and acts of consciousness, while Freud, who took himself to be a natural scientist, devoted his primary attention to the nature and function of the unconscious, there could be no commonalities of philosophical-psychological concerns. We shall see that this explanation simply does not suffice, given the philosophical details of the historical context involved: hence, the puzzle of their silence remains.

Husserl and Freud: A Mutual Disregard

Paul Ricoeur once noted that no other philosophy has come so close to making room for the Freudian conception of the unconscious as the phenomenology of Husserl.[4] Given the historical influences by Herbart and Brentano this should come as no surprise. Yet if Ricoeur's remark is even remotely correct—and we shall show that it is—the natural question emerges as to why Husserl and Freud exhibited an ostensibly stubborn mutual disregard for one another.

There are no references to Husserl or his phenomenological project throughout Freud's writings.[5] In the reciprocal direction, in his earlier work, according to Husserl, any concern with an unconscious—presumably Freud's notion among others—leads to a "malaise"[6] and hence should be avoided; Husserl did, however, allude to the unconscious of depth psychology in his later work, while at the same time refusing any association with it.[7]

Why did Freud ignore Husserl's work? As we have seen, Freud had the greatest aversion for the esoteric quality of the "abstractness" of epistemology, one which was speculative and had no empirical grounding. Husserl's approach was well known as an abstract theory of perception and superficially had the appearance of simply equating consciousness with mental life. Hence, early on Freud likely viewed Husserl's work as yet another philosophy of consciousness (that is, transcendental idealism) that abstractly separated itself from concrete everyday life. Such characteristics epitomized precisely those aspects Freud most disliked about the majority of philosophers of his era.

The preceding might explain Freud's lack of interest in the "early" and "middle Husserl," but it does not explain the more mature Freud's lack of references to the "later" Husserl. Certainly Freud had indirect access to the later Husserl through his acquaintance with several key figures. Freud's colleague, Alfred Adler, was a student in Husserl's 1920s lectures on passive synthesis in which Husserl spoke of his own version of the unconscious and repression. Ludwig Binswanger, a psychiatrist and lifelong friend of Freud's,[8] had been very much influenced by Husserl and must have at least alluded to him at times during his conversations with Freud. Finally, both Husserl and Freud had common Germanic sources in nineteenth-century philosophy and psychology—Herbart, Lipps, Fechner—all of whom had developed some notion of the unconscious. Theodor Lipps was an especially interesting close historical connection between Freud and Husserl. We recall that it was Lipps whom Freud had credited with giving him the "courage and capacity" to undertake the unconscious as the problem of psychology; and Husserl, though initially critical of Lipps' "psychologism," was later on amiable terms with his work and proceeded to incorporate some of Lipps' ideas into his own brand of phenomenology.

Why did Husserl exhibit little interest in Freud's work? Husserl, throughout his career, would have viewed the early Freud's endeavors—for example, the *Project for a Scientific Psychology*—as well as his (later) metapsychology, as nothing more than the common "materialism" reflected within the "natural scientistic" psychology of the times. From this view-point, Freud was merely another victim of "the naturalistic prejudice" as a psychologist who had uncritically adopted Cartesian dualism with all of its concomitant shortcomings and problems.[9] By adopting such a "psycho-physical anthropology in the rationalistic spirit,"[10] Freud, like others, was led to "the incomprehensibility of functioning subjectivity."[11] For this rea-son, the early and middle Husserl would have perceived Freud as simply failing to conduct the necessary foundational analysis of the universal and necessary structures and acts of consciousness (transcendental subjectiv-ity). Thus, according to the Husserl of this time frame, Freud most likely would have been seen as plunged into the "malaise" of an investigation of the unconscious. Given (the early and middle) Husserl's insistence on "the suspension of the natural standpoint," he would not have been con-cerned with Freud's projects at all; instead Husserl focused exclusively upon the intuition of the essential content of conscious experience as a domain of "pure meanings." This topic would not have been accessible to one who started rigidly and uncritically from "the natural standpoint," but only to one who assumed the proper "phenomenological standpoint." As such, Husserl most likely viewed Freud as one more casualty of the prob-lematic natural standpoint and hence irrelevant to his own philosophical concerns.

Even for the later Husserl, any psychology which held such dualistic and physicalistic presuppositions was bound to fail, especially since it failed to engage the "life world" "through a radical, completely unpreju-diced reflection, which would then necessarily open up the transcendental-subjective dimension."[12]

> Why does the whole flowing life-world not figure at the very beginning
> of a psychology as something "psychic," indeed as the psychic realm
> which is primarily accessible, the first field in which immediately given
> psychic phenomena can be explicated according to types? . . . why is this
> experience not called psychological experience rather than "outer expe-
> rience" . . . ?[13]

Seeing Freud as an uncritical Cartesian and as operating from the natural standpoint, Husserl would have further criticized him for refer-ring to consciousness in terms more appropriately applied to material ob-jects: seeing the mind as a sort of container in which ideas are somehow contained; thinking of mental events as causing physical events and vice versa (and hence, holding that there is no human freedom); and seeing objects as simply physically given, and yet searching for the cause of an ob-ject's appearance in mental life (for example, Freud's primary process). Husserl's response was clear: "There is an immense difference between the essence of psychic subjectivity and the essence of a thing. From the start one must strictly avoid all the false analogizing which does violence [to this difference]."[14] We recall that Freud, at least at times, had analogized in just such a way (in the *Interpretation of Dreams*, where he compared the mind to a telescope, and so on).[15] Furthermore, we recall such late statements by Freud as, "the intellect and the mind are objects for scientific research in exactly the same way as any non-human things."[16]

For Husserl, it was simply a mistake to view psychology as Freud explicitly did at times, as a (naturalistic) science: "Psycho-analysis . . . is a part of science and can adhere to the scientific Weltanschauung."[17] Husserl objected to this view in the strongest possible terms:

> the task and method of natural science, is fundamentally and essentially different from the sense of objectivity, task, and method in the humanistic disciplines. This is as true of psychology as it is of the so-called concrete humanistic disciplines. One has expected the same objectivity from psychology as from physics, and because of this a psychology in the full and actual sense has been quite impossible; for an objectivity after the fashion of natural science is downright absurd when applied to the [mind],[18] to subjectivity . . . This is the ultimate sense of the objection that one must make to the philosophies of all times . . . that it was not able to overcome the naturalistic objectivism.[19]

Freud would have been perceived, by Husserl, as another natural scientist who "opposes philosophy to the sciences in another way, such that it stands on a plane with religion, into which we have grown historically."[20]

Furthermore, Husserl would have perceived Freud as a prototypical example of psychologists who failed to recognize "the incompatibility of the two directions of psychological inquiry," namely "the psychophysical" and "psychology based on inner experience":

> There were troublesome tensions between the [different] tasks which descended historically from Descartes: on the one hand, that of methodically treating [minds] in exactly the same way as bodies and as being connected with bodies as spatiotemporal realities, i.e., the task of investigating in a physicalistic way the whole life-world as "nature" in a broadened sense; and, on the other hand, the task of investigating [minds] in their being in-themselves and for-themselves by way of inner experience . . . The two tasks seemed obviously connected in respect to both method and subject matter, and yet they refused to harmonize.[21]

This had a number of ramifications from a Husserlian perspective. First, it led to the "questionable character of the concepts of 'outer' and 'inner' experience"[22] throughout Freud's theory and practice. Second, and more important, this was the philosophical reason why—according to Husserl—Freud's metapsychological and psychotherapeutic approaches would have been fundamentally incompatible.[23] Hence, he would have rejected Freud's claim to unity for his psychoanalytical approach as a whole.

Freud's natural-scientific approach to the unconscious simply presupposed the understanding that only transcendental phenomenology could offer;[24] the problematic of the unconscious could only be adequately dealt with after the phenomenological analysis of consciousness. Hence, from Husserl's standpoint, Freud had it reversed: consciousness is not constructed upon and hence a derivative of the unconscious (as with Schopenhauer); instead, a proper phenomenological analysis of consciousness provides the genuine grounding for an understanding of the various levels of "unconscious intentionalities."[25] In these terms, until a proper phenomenological investigation of consciousness had been conducted, Freud's approach was simply irrelevant.

To summarize, prima facie the answer as to why Husserl failed to take significant notice of Freudian psychoanalysis might be chalked up to Husserl's rejection of any and all thinkers (including Freud) who uncritically held Cartesian dualism, its resultant scientistic presuppositions, and naturalistic objectivism, as well as to Husserl's insistence on the a priori necessity of the investigation of the universal and necessary structures and acts of consciousness (along with the life-world in the later Husserl) prior to any supplemental investigations into the psyche (as Husserl might have perceived Freud's).

A Possible Convergence

However plausible and compelling this account may be, it does not remove the puzzle of mutual nonreference by both thinkers. Why? Nothing in the above account explains why Husserl and Freud *continued* to ignore one another in their later careers[26] when their theories arguably seem to have been converging—especially given that they shared mutual associates who must, surely, have informed them that this was the case.[27] This is especially interesting in the face of the historical fact that both were formally lecturing/writing on some of the same key concepts beginning at roughly the same time. For example, Husserl was formally developing his ideas on the lived-body, the importance of instincts, the unconscious, and repression in *Ideas II* as early as 1913 and extending to 1928, after which he only periodically mentioned such ideas; Freud had formalized his ideas on the unconscious, repression, and the instincts in his metapsychological papers of 1914.

Because of their similar interests and pursuits, some astonishing convergences took place between Husserl's and Freud's ways of understanding human experience. Specifically there were two primary points of convergence, which we will consider: that human beings are understood by Husserl and Freud as having both "body" and "mind" (psyche) in a unity; and that the psyche involves an unconscious which has an impact on consciousness.

Freud's "Body-Ego" and Husserl's "Bodily-Psychic" (Lived-Body)

First, both Freud and Husserl spoke of the psyche as indissolubly unified with the body. Arguably (and possibly unwittingly) transcending his earlier self-professed "dualism"[28] in his *The Ego and the Id*, Freud described the conscious ego as "first and foremost a body-ego."[29] Freud asserted this within the context of his claim that what is lowest and highest in the ego could be unconscious, the ego being ultimately grounded in the instincts. Or again:

> There can be no question but that the libido has somatic sources, that it streams to the ego from various organs and parts of the body . . . as psychoanalysis' . . . second fundamental hypothesis . . . it explains the supposedly somatic concomitant phenomena as being what is truly psychical . . .[30]

To better understand this we note that Freud was utterly convinced that his unifying metapsychology would show that all of our meanings and/or ideas are ultimately grounded in an "organic substructure."[31] Furthermore, he advocated the proposition that "what we call our ego behaves essentially passively in life, and that . . . we are 'lived' by unknown and uncontrollable forces,"[32] namely the instincts. It was the instincts which had *both* bodily and psychical attributes for Freud,[33] and hence, it was the intrinsic role that instincts played in his metapsychology which enabled Freud to view humans as a unity of mind and body.[34]

In parallel fashion, Husserl referred to the ego as "the Bodily-psychic," as involving the reciprocal relations between "man as nature" (bodily being) and "man as mind" (psychical being):[35]

> Humanistic science has to do with the [mind] . . . the [mind] is there in space-time where his living body is; and from there he lives into and acts upon the world . . . he constantly has a privileged experiential conscious-

ness of "his" living body . . . of always "living" and "being able to do" things through it as the affected ego and the ego holding sway.[36]

There is, in the obscure depths, a root soil . . . Every [mind] has a "natural side." This is precisely the underlying basis of subjectivity . . . To the natural side there belongs immediately the lower life of feelings, the instinctual life . . .[37]

Each free act has its comet's tail of nature . . . every act also has its natural side, namely its underlying basis in nature: what is pregiven as affecting is a formation of nature . . .[38]

In addition, it is important to note Husserl's emphasis that the "lived-body" has both primacy and primordiality (albeit a limited one):

On the plane of appearance the psychophysical natural unity, man or beast, is constituted as a unity that rests on bodily *foundations* and corresponds to the grounding function of apperception.[39]

The spirit (the soul, concrete personal being) is there in space-time where his living body is; and from there he lives into and acts upon the world.[40]

With each perception of an object, whatever it may be, the lived-body is, always there and always co-constituted . . . The lived-body remains the center . . .[41]

We have already seen how the body and psyche are indissolubly, interdependently related in Freud's metapsychology.[42] Similar to Freud's pursuits, then, Husserl investigated the "reciprocal relations" between the human mind (or "psyche") and nature ("body") in *Ideas II*[43] and saw them as a unity.[44]

Most important, Husserl and Freud shared the view that the intentional structures of consciousness are bound to the body. Husserl wrote:

For every human being, [groups of sensations] belong, in a way that is immediately intuitable, to the Body as to his particular Body, i.e., as a subjective objectivity distinguished from the Body as a mere material thing by means of this whole stratum of localized sensations. The intentional functions, however, are bound to this stratum . . . a human being's total consciousness is in a certain sense, by means of its hyletic substate, bound to the Body.[45]

Similarly, for Freud, it was through *the primary process* that images of what would satisfy one's bodily instinctual impulses were psychically formed, and would need to match the perception achieved through the secondary process of the external world for gratification.[46] The formation of meanings, then, ultimately originated in bodily processes for Freud as well.

Next both agreed that the ideas of consciousness engage and are affected by underlying instincts and drives. Husserl stated that the psyche's dependence on the body included "the sensuous sensations of feeling and instinct" which originated in the body,[47] and that "the whole life of consciousness is already affected by this dependency."[48] Remarkably, Husserl continued on to say that humans can be "driven irrationally" by allowing themselves to be "drawn by inclinations and drives which are blind."[49] Even more notably, Husserl quite clearly agreed with Freud on part of his description of "the original genesis" of "the personal ego." Husserl wrote, "a person [is] determined by drives, from the very outset and incessantly driven by original 'instincts' and passively submitting to them."[50] On this layer of the personal ego we are on "the lower level as 'pure' animality" which forms "the obscure depths, a root soil."[51] The higher psychical level of the personal ego

> finds itself dependent on an *obscure underlying basis* of traits of character, original and latent dispositions, and thereby dependent on nature . . . all life of the [mind] is permeated by the "blind" operation of associations, drives, feelings which are stimuli for drives and determining grounds for drives, tendencies which emerge in obscurity, etc. all of which determine the subsequent course of consciousness according to "blind" rules.[52]

This is a remarkable passage, indeed for it could have been written by Freud himself.

Finally, in his later work, *Analyses Concerning Passive and Active Synthesis,* Husserl offered the following astonishing remark:

> The wakeful ego with its lived-experiences . . . has a constant, broad horizon of background lived-experiences to which the ego is not present and "in" which it does not reside . . . affects may be intertwined with these background lived-experiences or with their objects, spilling over into a general atmosphere of well-being or malcontentment; even tendencies, lived-experiences of drive, may be rooted in them, which for instance incline away from malcontentment, but the ego is not present there. Belonging here are also flashes of insight, imaginings that arise, memories, theoretical insights that emerge or even *stirrings of the will,* decisions that are not however taken up by the ego . . . Only when the ego carries

> them out do they get the shape of *"ego cogito,"* of . . . "I carry out the stir-
> ring of the will," etc. Thus, the wakeful egoic life is distinguished from
> the egoic life that is not awake . . . and the two are distinguished by the
> fact that in the latter, no lived-experience in the specific sense of wake-
> fulness is there at all [italics added].[53]

This description marks one of the most compelling points of convergence
between Husserl's phenomenology and Freud's psychoanalysis. First, it
demonstrates Husserl's awareness that there are places where the "ego
is not present," "'in' which it does not reside," that is, is not consciously
aware; this, of course works nicely with Freud's own understanding of unconscious processes (which will be taken up in the next section). Second,
Husserl acknowledged that those same "constant, broad horizon of background lived-experiences" are involved in the individual's own feelings of
general well-being or dissatisfaction with the existing state of affairs
within his/her field of meaning; it is the latter, of course, which Freud
would view as a primary motivating factor for pursuing psychoanalytical
therapy. Third, and just as remarkably, Husserl employed the very same
concept as Schopenhauer—of the ego carrying out "the stirrings of the
will," that is, those strongest motivations which sway it; as we have seen,
Freudian metapsychology presupposed this very idea.

Thus, in the above analysis, we see Husserl's "bodily-psychic" as a
unity of mind–body, as having a "natural side" or "instinctual life" of which
the "wakeful ego" is not conscious. Here it is important to look more
closely at what exactly Husserl meant by "instincts." Husserl wrote of "the
instincts not as something supposedly transcendent to consciousness but
as primal lived experiences, always belonging to the content of the psychic
basis."[54] It is important to note just how closely this paralleled Freud's own
notion of instincts:

> An "instinct" appears to us as a concept on the frontier between the men-
> tal and the somatic, as the psychical representative of the stimuli origi-
> nating from within the organism and reaching the mind, as a measure of
> the demand made upon the mind for work in consequence of its con-
> nection with the body.[55]

We must also be careful to note some rudimentary divergences
of the two theories—ones upon which the existential phenomenologists
will subsequently seize. First, for Husserl, the will of the pure ego is able
to "freely" and "spontaneously" move the body.[56] For Schopenhauer and
Freud, the will/id, via the instincts, governs the ego through the body.
Furthermore, Husserl insisted that

the personal Ego is constituted not only as a person determined by drives, from the very outset and incessantly driven by original "instincts" and passively submitting to them, but also as a higher, autonomous, freely acting Ego, in particular one guided by rational motives, and not one that is merely dragged along and unfree.[57]

Hence, for Husserl we are an interplay between our determining instincts and the free and spontaneous metaphysical capacity of our personal ego (for undetermined acts based on reason).[58] Schopenhauer and Freud, of course, denied the existence of the latter, characterizing it as an "illusion." Finally, Husserl concluded *Ideas II* with the claim of "the ontological priority of the [mental] world over the naturalistic."[59] Husserl emphasized that the being of an ego not only includes but transcends the lived body:

> In my perceptual field I find myself holding sway as ego through my organs . . . though we are related through the living body to all objects which exist for us, are not related to them solely as a living body . . . But being an ego through the living body is of course not the only way of being an ego, and none of its ways can be severed from the others; throughout all their transformations they form a unity. Thus we are concretely in the field of perception, etc., and in the field of consciousness, how ever broadly we may conceive this, through our living body, but not only in this way, as full ego-subjects, each of us as the full-fledged "I-the-man."[60]

Hence, he viewed consciousness as having ontological primordiality over the body.[61] The conscious awareness of the free ego (the psychical level) is higher than the unfree ego driven by natural instinctual impulses. Certainly, if anything, precisely the opposite was true for Schopenhauer and Freud. Consciousness, for them, was more of an appendage through which the individual seeks to deal effectively with the demands of one's bodily instinctual impulses.

Husserl on the Unconscious

It is commonly acknowledged and even emphasized that Husserl's notion of the "unconscious" is *not* Freud's. Indeed, Husserl himself insisted on this point in his final work, which included his only (ostensible) reference to Freudian psychology:

> Let us not consider the fact that even the concept of "horizon"-consciousness [or of] horizon-intentionality contains very diverse modes

of an intentionality which is "unconscious" in the usual narrower sense
of the word but which can be shown to be vitally involved and cofunc-
tioning in different ways; these modes of intentionality have their own
modalities of validity and their own ways of changing them. Yet there are
still, over and above these, "unconscious" intentionalities, as can be
shown by a more detailed analysis. This would be the place for those
repressed emotions of love, of humiliation, of ressentiments, and the
kinds of behavior motivated by them which have been disclosed by
recent "depth psychology" (although this does not mean that we identify
ourselves with their theories). These too have their modes of validity
(certainties of being, certainties of value, volitional certainties and their
modal variations).[62]

In this passage Husserl quite clearly (1) distinguished his own notion of
unconscious intentionality from the unconscious intentionalities of "depth
psychology," (2) indicated that the former are more primordial than the
latter, and (3) acknowledged that the unconscious intentionalities disclosed by depth psychology "too have their modes of validity." It is important to note that Husserl not only did *not* reject the "unconscious" of
depth psychology, but conceded that it had something to contribute toward our understanding of the psyche. However, Husserl was quick to dis-
avow any identification with the views of depth psychology.

In spite of Husserl's obvious reservations, we contend that what has
not been sufficiently recognized (perhaps even by Husserl himself) are
the myriad ways Husserl's analysis, at times at least, closely resembled
Freud's approach to the unconscious both heuristically and contentually
speaking, and the extent to which the two converged. Indeed, it was Husserl himself who opened the door for a possible convergence between
phenomenology and psychoanalysis, in the above quotation.

We are able to trace historically the convergence of Husserl's and
Freud's theories of the unconscious back to Kant, who had spoken of the
attraction/repulsion of ideas. This influential idea was subsequently
picked up and developed by the German romanticists, who in turn exerted an influence on Husserl and Freud. Hence, it is not at all surprising
to find Husserl stress that the "positive affective force is the fundamental
condition of all life in dynamic connection and differentiation."[63]

Despite the fact that Husserl did not share the economic and dynamic model and operation of the censor in Freudian metapsychology,
there is still a striking similarity to Schopenhauer's and Freud's views here.
As we recall, for Freud, the will/id is the fundamental condition of all
mental life, and the intellect and consciousness are nothing without that
underlying affective force. This point is particularly interesting given

Husserl's own recognition that the ideas of consciousness engage and are affected by underlying instincts and drives. Husserl stated that the psyche's dependence on the body included "the sensuous sensations of feeling and instinct" and that "the whole life of consciousness is already affected by this dependency."[64]

It was in his *Ideas II* that we find one of Husserl's earliest references to and concern with the unconscious:

> [In the Ego] we find certain nexuses, the motivation-nexuses, which are determined by the sensuous lower level . . . the entirety of natural drives . . . the Ego thought of as purely passive which is mere nature and belongs within the nexus of nature . . . Here we have "unconscious" Ego-affections and reactions. What is affecting goes toward the Ego, though not toward the waking Ego . . . The Ego always lives in the medium of its "history," all its earlier lived experiences have sunk down but they have aftereffects in tendencies, sudden ideas, transformations or assimilations of earlier lived experiences, and from such assimilations new formations are merged together . . . All this has its natural course, thus even each free act has its comet's tail of nature . . . every act also has its natural side, namely its underlying basis in nature: what is pregiven as affecting is a formation of nature . . .[65]

Husserl delivered his earliest lectures and most extensive analysis on the unconscious from 1920 to 1926 in the *Analyses Concerning Passive and Active Synthesis: Lectures on Transcendental Logic.* Husserl subsequently sprinkled only brief and occasional references to the unconscious in his later works.

An important question to ponder is: what motivated Husserl to consider the possibility of unconscious intentionality in the first place? Why would a philosopher who had previously so pervasively preoccupied himself with the constituting processes of consciousness turn to the unconscious? In other words, why did Husserl find it necessary to conduct a "phenomenology of the unconscious" at all? First, we submit that such an endeavor was necessitated by Husserl's analysis of the "bodily-psychic," the pervasive affect of the instincts on consciousness, and so on, discussed above. Such concepts required the notion that some domain of the psychical apparatus be considered in a sense as "external" to consciousness. Next, the primary reason Husserl himself offered for investigating the unconscious was that his "static" phenomenological approach was unable to account for the gaps (or "breaks") of consciousness (for example, when we are sleeping) and what happens to ideas once they disappear from immediate conscious awareness.[66] Hence, the development of a "genetic" phenomenology was necessary.

> *Genetical intentional analysis* . . . is directed to the whole concrete nexus in which each particular consciousness stands, along with its intentional object as intentional. Immediately the problem becomes extended to include the other intentional references, those belonging to the *situation* in which, for example, the subject exercising the judicative activity is standing, and to include therefore, the *immanent unity of the temporality* of the life that has its *"history"* therein, in such a fashion that every single process of consciousness, as occurring temporally, has its own "history"— that is, its temporal genesis.[67]

It is interesting to note, as we have seen earlier, that Freud (as well as Schopenhauer and Nietzsche) offered precisely the same justification for the unconscious.[68] Recall that Freud wrote that the unconscious is "necessary because the data of consciousness have a very large number of gaps in them."[69] Also,

> at any given moment consciousness includes only a small content, so that the greater part of what we call conscious knowledge must in any case be for very considerable periods of time in a state of latency, that is to say, of being psychically unconscious. . . When all our latent memories are taken into consideration it becomes totally incomprehensible how the existence of the unconscious can be denied.[70]

> A conception—or any psychical element—which is now present to my consciousness may become absent the next moment, and may become present again, after an interval, unchanged, and as we say, from memory . . .[71]

Next, Husserl and Freud shared certain important similarities concerning *how they inquired* into the unconscious. Remarkably, Husserl conducted what might be described as a regressive, *archaeological inquiry*[72] into the most primordial processes underlying the various modes of thinking, of constituting consciousness—namely, the unconscious. Again, Freud held a similar stance. This was why Freud, for example, spoke of the need for "conclusions based on evidence derived from anthropological evidence . . . a neurotic's current conflict becomes comprehensible and admits of solution only when it is traced back to his pre-history."[73] However, we should be careful to emphasize that at first glance, unlike Freud, Husserl's attention was focused on identifying the lost origins and genuine foundations of logic or reason. Hence the subtitle of *Analyses Concerning Passive and Active Synthesis: Lectures on Transcendental Logic*. However, Husserl went on to take "conceptual thinking in general" to be the theme of logic which he investigated.[74] He then took "Thinking as a Sense Constituting Lived-Experience"[75] as a going back to "living, streaming life," and hence was not as far from Freud's pursuits as we might have first thought.

Drawing from the same historical-philosophical sources as Freud, Husserl too was influenced by the German romanticists who emphasized the importance of accessing the unconscious via an excavation of the dark, hidden recesses of the mind.[76] For instance, Husserl wrote that unconscious forces/connections "emerge out of the dark,"[77] and that "when there is no affection coming from the diverse objects, then these diverse objects have slipped into sheer nightfall, in a special sense, they have slipped into the unconscious."[78] In fact, Husserl described himself as conducting "a deep mining phenomenological investigation"[79] and "a phenomenology of the unconscious."[80] Hence: "The path of radical phenomenological investigation must trace the storied structure of constitution, and it must seek out and bring this structure to light."[81]

In order to truly understand the transcendental dimension of subjectivity, the "graduated" layers of the unconscious must be uncovered; this was why Husserl was to later say the "unconscious . . . naturally come[s] under the transcendental problem of constitution."[82] How did Husserl do this? Sharing an affinity with Freud's analysis of the human psyche which Freud undertook on both the collective and individual levels, Husserl proceeded by way of "regression,"[83] back from conscious thinking "to the broader nexus of the life of consciousness," and even more deeply "back . . . to the living, streaming life"; "back . . . to those acts and accomplishments that make up the most expansive part of our life," and "by beginning from below and ascending upward, to show how genuine thinking in all its levels emerges here, how it is motivated and is built-up in its founded accomplishment."[84] In other words, to trace the emergence of thinking from its genetic origins in passive syntheses; to trace "unconscious" motivations back up to conscious activities: this marked Husserl's move from "static" phenomenology to "genetic" phenomenology. Among other things, it included "originally instinctive, drive related preferences,"[85] leading back to "primordial elements,"[86] "the path is cleared from here toward a universal theory of genesis of a pure subjectivity, and in particular, initially in relation to its lower level of pure passivity."[87]

It was when Husserl moved to his "genetic" phenomenology (which includes the entire historically concrete individual)[88] that he realized the necessity of taking up the problem of an unconscious. Unlike in his *Logical Investigations,* he now saw the relevance of the unconscious for phenomenology.[89] It was only later, in his *Analyses Concerning Passive and Active Synthesis,* that Husserl explicitly developed "a phenomenology of the unconscious."

Husserl's problem was to explain how it was possible to phenomenologically grasp that which is directly involved in experience yet is ge-
netically prior to experience. Husserl now found himself in the position
of describing how it is that ideas of which we are no longer conscious (or
that have even been forgotten) continue to influence us in the present;
that is, he set off to explore our systems of "retentions" or "sedimentations"
to give us a fuller understanding of our conscious life. Husserl summarized
this point very nicely in *Cartesian Meditations*:[90] "beyond [the ego's living
present], only an indeterminately general presumptive horizon extends,
comprising what is strictly non-experienced but necessarily also meant."[91]

Husserl's Conception of the Unconscious

What did Husserl take the unconscious to be? He described it as "not a
dead nothingness but a limiting-mode of consciousness."[92] As such, the
unconscious is merely a nil of affective force: "a background or *subsoil* of
non-vivacity, of affective ineffectiveness (nil) belongs to every present."[93]
The unconscious, then, was conceived as a domain in which object-like
formations are not, or no longer, affective. Any present lived experience
or mental phenomena (an idea, a judgment, a perception, and so on) in
immediate consciousness undergoes "a gradual diminution of prominence" which, with the passage of time, reaches a limit at which it "sub-
sides into the universal substratum—the so called unconscious."[94] This is
important because

> the *whole intentional genesis* relates back to this substratum of sedimented
> prominences, which, as a horizon, accompanies every living present and
> shows its own continuously changing sense when it becomes "awakened."[95]

Hence, clearly this universal unconscious substratum played a crucial, pivotal role in the present and future formations of meanings in psychical
life for Husserl.

It is important to unpack these comments conceptually. First, this
substratum is only accessible according to Husserl through his "abstrac-
tive method." Through the use of his regressive, archaeological approach,
Husserl first descended from consciousness to the substratum of the unconscious and then, having reached bottom, ascended back up through
the complex sedimented layers of the unconscious to the level of consciousness. Doing this uncovered the relationship between the underneath of our lived experiences and the constituting levels of consciousness.
Accomplishing this demonstrated how consciousness and the unconscious mutually modify one another.

Second, Husserl showed how this substratum is composed of sedimented layers of previous meaning-experiences.[96] For Husserl, all earlier experiences "have sunk down" into this substratum;[97] and "Every present flows once more into this undifferentiated subsoil of the distant retention."[98] Interestingly, Freud employed the very same idea in his article entitled "The Mystic Writing Pad":

> I do not think it is too farfetched to compare the celluloid and waxed paper cover with the system *Pcpt.-Cs.* and its protective shield, the wax slab with the unconscious behind them, and the appearance and disappearance of the writing with the flickering-up and passing-away of consciousness in the process of perception.[99]

> [Our mental apparatus] has an unlimited receptive capacity for new perceptions and nevertheless lays down permanent—even though not unalterable—memory-traces of them . . . the permanent traces of the excitations which have been received are preserved in "mnemic systems" lying behind the perceptual system.[100]

Husserl characterized this "sinking down" during the retentional process as a "fading" or "clouding over" of mental phenomena which become progressively unclear and which lose their "distinguishing traits and prominences.[101] It is clear that the affective force accruing to them and to the whole is constantly diminished in the process."[102] Such mental phenomena or lived experiences lose their affective force completely (that is, become nil in their vivacity) and become "completely undifferentiated."[103] Freud, we should note, agreed that the unconscious had no organization.[104]

Next, in this substratum, the mental phenomena or lived experiences are "permanent possessions,"[105] "a habituality of the ego," "ready for a new associative awakening."[106] Compare Freud's comment that no ideas/ experiences are ever lost from psychic life: "In the unconscious nothing can be brought to an end, nothing is past or forgotten."[107] According to Husserl, when such ideas are reactivated in a new lived-context, they subsequently fade, to form yet another sedimented layer in the unconscious. This process goes on for the life of the individual.

One major implication of Husserl's theory here is that "the ego always lives in the medium of its 'history'";[108] and "The ego constitutes himself for himself in the unity of 'history.'"[109] Similarly for Freud, this point was crucial. Indeed, this was precisely the point of the "genetic" component of his metapsychology, and analysis of humankind's archaic heritage.

As we begin our ascent back up to consciousness, it is important to understand even more clearly how Husserl conceived of this substratum:

> Anything built by activity necessarily presupposes, as the lowest level, a
> passivity that gives something beforehand; and, when we trace anything
> built actively, we run into constitution by passive generation.[110]

Husserl's regressive archaeological inquiry, then, sought to unearth *passivity* as a dimension of human experience—that is, tracing motivations which ascend back up to consciousness.

As we now ascend from this substratum up to the wakeful ego (consciousness), Husserl noted other fundamental characteristics of the psyche. The ego is both *affected by* and *reacts to* this substratum. Husserl—like Freud, once again—acknowledged that consciousness and the unconscious mutually modify one another. Here, Husserl first referred to his distinction between the wakeful and nonwakeful ego: "what is affecting goes toward the Ego, though not toward the waking Ego . . ."[111] Hence, like Freud, Husserl conceived of part of the ego as including an unconscious.[112]

Next, according to Husserl, how do memories or past lived experiences which are nil exert an impact or "apperceptive aftereffect" on the active ego? How can they can influence current meaning formations?

> All [the ego's] earlier lived experiences have sunk down but they have
> aftereffects in tendencies, sudden ideas, transformations or assimilations
> of earlier lived experiences, and from such assimilations new formations
> are merged together.[113]

> When these habitual apperceptions become actually operative, the
> already given objects formed for the central Ego appear, affect him, and
> motivate activities.[114]

Compare this to Freud: "even when [an idea] is unconscious it can produce effects, even including some which finally reach consciousness."[115]

What did Husserl specifically mean by these "aftereffects"? The aftereffects involve "affection" which he defined as "the attraction *(Reiz)* given to consciousness, the peculiar pull that an object given to consciousness exercises on the ego; it is a pull that is relaxed when the ego turns toward it attentively."[116] As such, affection stimulates the ego into activity via "affective force":

> By affective force I mean a tendency directed toward the ego, a ten-
> dency whose reaction is a responsivity on the part of the ego. That is, in
> yielding to the affection—in other words, by being "motivated"—the
> ego takes up an endorsing position; it decides actively for what is entic-
> ing . . .[117]

It is through the affective force that the enticement of a memory or previous lived experiences exerts a pull on the active ego. Hence, affection is "a function of contrast"; we stand in "a relativism of affective tendencies."[118] Various affective forces (sensible data, feelings, and so on) "compete" for the attention of the ego, and the "strong ones" "win out," though the others continue to exert an attraction. This was why Husserl spoke of "a gradation of affective forces."[119] It is particularly noteworthy at this point that Husserl then suggested that among the victorious affections we can "even allow *originally instinctive, drive related* preferences" [italics added].

At this point, we might pause to wonder how this account is fundamentally different from Schopenhauer's and Freud's theories of motivation discussed earlier (see chapter 8). The difference between Husserl and Schopenhauer or Freud, on this score, is that for the latter *all* such affective forces are instinctual in nature, as intrinsic to the will/id. Compare Schopenhauer's and Husserl's analyses of "motivation." Schopenhauer wrote: "the object acting as motive needs only to be perceived or cognized . . . it is a determining ground of the will that is to be stirred here."[120] Compare this with Husserl:

> If we place ourselves on the terrain of the intentional relation between subject and object, the relation between person and surrounding world, then the concept of stimulus acquires a fundamentally new sense. Instead of the causal relation between things and men as natural realities, there is substituted the *relation of motivation* between persons and things, and these things are not the things of nature . . . but are experienced, thought, or in some other way intended . . . Phenomenologically, the unities of things . . . are points of departure for more or less "strong" tendencies. Already as conscious but not yet grasped (hovering in the background of consciousness), they draw the subject to themselves, and if the "stimulating power" is sufficient, the Ego "follows" the stimulus, "gives in" and turns in that direction.[121]

For Husserl, the strict and genuine *concept of will* designates only a special mode of activity which spreads over all other regions of consciousness insofar as all activity can occur in the form of voluntary activity.[122] When the ego reacts, it exerts a reciprocal "pull" which "neutralizes" the original affective force.

Husserl distinguished between "affective" and "pre-affective" synthesis. In alignment with his metaphorical archaeological inquiry, Husserl understood the battle among contrasting affective forces in terms of a three-dimensional *topography;* the psyche is viewed as involving various processes that are "in relief"[123]—have varying levels of prominence in a person's phenomenological field of meaning.[124] Affective syntheses manage to rise above the threshold of conscious awareness, preaffective syntheses do not. Compare this to Freud, where he wrote: "It is by no means impossible for the product of unconscious activity to pierce into consciousness, but a certain amount of exertion is needed for this task."[125] For Husserl, these are the sedimented layers comprising the "mine" or canyons of the unconscious. The unconscious has among its processes the formation of unities within it which Husserl calls "pre-affective" "intertwinings" of "affective hyletic unities":

> As the lowest level within passivity, the accomplishment of hyletic passivity, [the unconscious] fashions a constant field of pregiven objectlike formations of the ego, and subsequently, potentially a field of objectlike formations given to the ego . . . affective hyletic unities must become and intertwine with one another homogeneously in essential unity, initially in the hyletic sphere . . .[126]

For Husserl, this involved an "active passivity" on the unconscious level.[127] Furthermore, for Husserl, there is never a field of open pure possibilities, but our field of meaning and awareness have always already been *affected*.[128] Indeed, all of this is what makes it possible for a world of objects to be constituted in subjectivity at all. The main difference between Husserl and Freud on this score was that for Freud the instinctual impulses were considered the ultimate reservoir of our ideas (namely, the primary process) as they engage the processes of the ego (the secondary process); whereas for Husserl such impulses comprise but *one source* among others that affect consciousness.

Interestingly, there were times when Husserl's notion of "repression" sounded somewhat similar to Freud's. For example, Husserl wrote: "everything that is repressed sinks without support into the 'unconscious.'"[129] Furthermore, Husserl spoke (like Freud) of processes in the unconscious, which result in the incapacity of some ideas, memories, and so on to reach consciousness. At this juncture, however, such similarities take on a far different hue, due to Freud's introduction of the censor between the unconscious and the preconscious/consciousness (in his topographical model).

For Husserl, there was a *freer* (less restricted) two-way movement between consciousness and the unconscious; there were, in fact, only two restrictions on the movement involved. First, the only restriction on *recollection* was the fading of memory over time:

> The retentionally subsiding component formations remain . . . [a judger] can reach back and seize them again, each as having its identical

sense; also, in consequence of the new judgment-steps, they can undergo further accretions of sense in new formings.[130]

Every judging leads to a judgment–result that is, from then on . . . an *enduring 'result'* for the judger, an intellectual acquisition that is at his free disposal whenever he pleases.[131]

For Freud, Husserl's notion of the unconscious in the above was more akin to his own concept of the preconscious as that which can, at any time and given certain conditions, become conscious without any resistance (for example, the name of the capital of Oregon, or the high school one attended).[132] Here Freud admitted, "In what shape [memories] may have existed while present in the mind and latent in consciousness we have no means of guessing."[133] It is important to note that Husserl's genetic analysis offered some of the means for assisting Freud's theory on this score.[134]

However, it was the second restriction on movement that specifically brings us to Husserl's notion of repression. Husserl wrote: "We recognize as basic and essential that the superimposition of a new sense over a sense that is already constituted takes place through repression . . . Belief clashes with belief . . ."[135] Beliefs, memories, and so on "stand here in a mutual struggle."[136] When idea *x* has a stronger affective force in a specific context than competing ideas *y* and *z*, and thereby rises either to the unconscious ego (that psychical realm in which the affective forces in passivity are not nil, yet not conscious),[137] or to conscious awareness, *x* is said to have "repressed" the ideas *y* and *z*.[138] This was what Husserl meant when he wrote, "There is something like a possible competition and a kind of concealment of active tendencies by especially strong ones";[139] and

Are there not regulated inhibiting, weakening counter potencies which, by not letting affection arise any longer, also make the mergence of self-subsistent unities impossible, unities in other words that would not emerge at all without affection?[140]

And, though the others can continue to exert their own attraction or after-effect,

Is there not also a suppression of the affection in which the affection is repressed or covered over, but is still present, and is that not constantly in question here?

In particular: Affection of the *modus excitandi* of the ego, being irritated, conflict of affections. The one winning out does not annihilate the other ones, but suppresses them. (In the sphere of feelings or drives;

feelings, strivings, valuations, that come to naught due to certain motivations just like the absence of value becomes evident through clarifica-
tion, and the affection of value comes to naught through an appropriation coming from the inside. On the other hand, feelings, valuations
that are overcome, suppressed from the outside, suppressed in conflict,
while the conflict does not lead to any settlement, to any actual "peace.")
    Perseverance. Affections can be there, i.e., progressing from the
"unconscious," but suppressed.[141]

Another way this kind of process can occur, according to Husserl, is that
we can be affected anew "in the form of whims, free-floating ideas," and
so on.[142] "This is an affection, a mere expectation, directed toward the
ego, inviting it, so to speak, to a reaccomplishment."[143]
    Further parallels to Freud occur in Husserl's account of the various
ways in which sedimented memories or lived experiences can be "reactivated":

In its renewal, the original judgment can be newly accomplished *without
being completely articulated.* Word sequences presenting themselves associatively can produce the unity of a judgment but in a confused way, so
that nonsense is mingled with sense . . . Confused judgments of this kind
can be *"clarified,"* sense separated from nonsense . . .[144]

Freud, as we have noted above, would agree that repressed ideas, memories, and so on can and do exert an impact on conscious life even though
they themselves remain unconscious, or only *partially manifested* in consciousness.
    Husserl and Freud also shared several commonalities in the role "as-
sociation" plays in their respective approaches. First, Husserl and Freud
agreed that our memories of the past can always be "awakened" by a process of association and, once awakened, can always play a role in the formation of new meaning-experiences.[145] Second, on the level of the unconscious, Husserl observed that an "entire associative nexus" in the field
of consciousness can "run its course without being noticed."[146] In his discussion of the unconscious etiology of hysteria, Freud made the same
point: "we arrive by means of the analysis . . . at a series of experiences the
memories of which are linked together in association."[147] Later, Freud reiterated this point: "thanks to the pliability and ambiguity of associative
chains, the same event showed itself capable of stirring the second of the
complexes that lurked in [a person's] unconscious."[148]
    Furthermore, Husserl noted that it is possible for us to later recon-
struct the sequence of associations by recovering their past retentions,

to the extent that we are able to do so.[149] On this too, Freud clearly concurred. Indeed, it was this last process at which Freud had become quite skilled, as he untangled entire strings of associations by discovering the memories that unconsciously formed their basis in his *Psychopathology of Everyday Life*.[150] And finally, Husserl noted that it is "only once our memories are associatively awakened, [that] they can be temporally ordered."[151] Compare this with Freud:

> The processes of the system *Ucs.* are *timeless;* i.e., they are not ordered temporally, are not altered by the passage of time . . . Reference to time is bound up, once again, with the work of the system Cs.[152]

Hence, the unconscious for both thinkers was considered to be atemporal.

Husserl also offered an account of how it is possible to have illusory memories and how it is possible to disclose them as such, an account which paralleled Freud's discussion of "screen memories."[153]

> The illusion will be disclosed as illusion as soon as the affective force of the suppressed one becomes livelier and even now wins out . . . The illusory image will show itself in these transitions precisely as a conglomeration and fusion of different memorial images that are concordant in themselves, and the suppressed element within the fusion and its force of belief will come to life behind the fusion . . .
>
> Would it be conceivable that a reproductive intuition of ideally complete clarity could become negated by just any affective transformation, by just any synthesis with other rememberings? To pose such a question means to answer in the negative . . . All mixtures take place in the mode of unclarity. Only in unclarity can motivations, can expectations, potential coherent nexuses, their reciprocal fortifications and inhibitions, lose their efficacy, entire layers of the like can become, as it were, dimmed down; they lose their affective relief, fade away into the background. Every disclosure of an illusion is carried out in the transition to higher levels of clarity, just as every disclosure of a reproduced intuition through continual confirmation takes place in the progressive clarification of what is less clear.[154]

For Freud as well, the idea was to clarify (that is, uncover) the mixtures that had taken place in the unconscious processes.[155]

It is important to note that, according to Husserl, the ego is at the mercy of the underlying hyletic forces—namely, the processes of the unconscious—which, when initially awakened can at times overpower the ego. Ideas and memories can force their way into consciousness whether the ego likes it or not:

> All these occurrences of associative awakening and linkage take place in the domain of passivity without any participation by the ego. The awakening radiates from what is presently perceived; *the memories "rise up," whether we will or no* [italics added].[156]

Other examples from Husserl include: "A remote past suddenly dawns on me";[157] and, "A repressed memory or set of associations can 'emerge out of the dark,'" that is, can break through to conscious intuition.[158] In present experience, we can "involuntarily" reactivate retentions which are predicated on previous associations. Hence, at least at times, the ego is not master of its own field of meaning. This fact resembled not only Freud's claim that the ego "is not master in its own house," but that ideas often push their way into our consciousness without our solicitation (see chapter 8). Freud wrote, "Our most personal daily experience acquaints us with ideas that come into our head we do not know from where, and with intellectual conclusions arrived at we do not know how."[159]

Restrictions on a Merger between Freud and Husserl

Having delineated some crucial aspects of convergence between Husserl's and Freud's views, it now becomes apparent what prevents their merger. First and foremost, Husserl's unconscious does not operate according to the economics and dynamics of Freud's metapsychological model. We strongly concur with Ricoeur when he suggested,

> The gap between the passive genesis, in Husserl's sense, and the dynamics of instincts which Freud deciphers . . . [because of] the economic point of view: the notion of cathexis expresses a type of adhesion and cohesion that no phenomenology of intentionality can possibly reconstruct.[160]

Second, unconscious motivations are *exclusively* motivated by the underlying instinctual impulses (in accordance with the pleasure principle) for Freud, whereas for Husserl they are one set among others.[161] Of course, this fundamental difference has other ramifications as well. For example, the overpowering of the ego by the underlying forces of the unconscious is a far less prevalent phenomenon for Husserl than it was for Freud. In addition, for Husserl it was the ego that is awakened via the strongest affective attraction; for Schopenhauer or Freud it was the will/id that is awakened by the stirring power of whatever motive.[162]

Another point of divergence is that Husserl and Freud held fundamentally different positions on the role of rationality and freedom in human existence. Husserl held that we are "entirely free if [we are] not motivated passively, that is, if [we] do not carry out the consequence through affection but through 'rational motives.'"[163] For Freud, of course, the goal was to achieve rational insight into how the underlying forces are governing who we are and what we do, and thereby achieve a liberatory therapeutic effect; there is no such freedom from underlying motivations grounded in the will.

What is the outcome of all of this? Without forcing Husserl and Freud into one another's models, it is clear what each has to offer the other. Husserl, for example, offers Freud a way to understand what happens in the psyche to those ideas that fade from consciousness (without censorship operating) and yet have an aftereffect. Freud offers Husserl an explanation of why his account may fail to hold under the conditions when censorship is compelled to be operational. It would be important to establish when those conditions hold versus when they do not.

Finally, in light of all this, we conclude that the failure of the two to engage one another's work historically and to see the potential for a rapprochement was a missed opportunity. This missed opportunity had a direct and significant impact upon the existential phenomenologists we are about to consider.

11

Being versus Id: Heidegger's Critique of Freud's Worldview in the *Zollikon Seminars*

> The simple hardly speaks to us any longer in its simplicity
> because the traditional scientific way of thinking has ruined
> our capacity to be astonished about what is supposedly and
> specifically self-evident.
> —Heidegger

> But however much ado the philosophers may make, they cannot
> alter the situation . . . The benighted traveller may sing aloud in
> the dark to deny his own fears; but, for all that, he will not see an
> inch further beyond his nose.
> —Freud

We have just witnessed the failure of Freud and Husserl—contemporary intellectual giants in related fields of investigation—to notice or recognize each other's work. We now approach a similar situation in the case of Freud and Martin Heidegger.[1] Although Heidegger was thirty years younger than Freud, they shared the same language; lived relatively close to one another; had been directly influenced by the philosophy of Franz Brentano;[2] had close relationships with some of the same people (for example, the Swiss existential psychoanalysts Ludwig Binswanger and Medard Boss); and were both concerned about the emergence of meaning into the world and the development of psychology. Yet Freud did not once mention Heidegger—or anything even obliquely referring to him or his philosophy—in his major works composed after the publication of *Being and Time*.[3] Heidegger had little to say about Freud until relatively late in his philosophical career.

The History of Heidegger's Relationship to Freud

Historically speaking, Heidegger's familiarity with and general reaction to Freud's work is fairly clear. Medard Boss had been an analysand of Freud's over dozens of sessions in 1925,[4] and it was he—as a trained psychoanalyst—who initiated a relationship with Heidegger in 1947 and subsequently introduced him to Freud's metapsychological theory. In an essay on Daseinsanalysis, Boss poignantly described Heidegger's feelings toward Freud:

> Even before our first encounter, I had heard of Heidegger's abysmal aversion to all modern scientific psychology. To me, too, he made no secret of his opposition to it. His repugnance mounted considerably after I had induced him with much guile and cunning to delve directly for the first time into Freud's own writings. During his perusal of the theoretical, "metapsychological" works, Heidegger never ceased shaking his head. He simply did not want to have to accept that such a highly intelligent and gifted man as Freud could produce such artificial, inhuman, indeed absurd and purely fictitious constructions about Homo sapiens. This reading made him literally feel ill.[5]

What was the reason for Heidegger's strong distaste for Freud's metapsychological theory? According to Heidegger, Freud was the epitome of a great contemporary scientific mind uncritically adopting and subsequently becoming entrapped by the tacit ontological commitments of his philosophical heritage.[6] To understand what Heidegger had in mind, it is important to recall the following credo of Freud's: "[Psychoanalysis] must accept the scientific Weltanschauung . . . the intellect and the mind are objects for scientific research in exactly the same way as non-human things . . . Our best hope for the future is that intellect—the scientific spirit, reason—may in process of time establish a dictatorship in the mental life of man."[7] The reaction was twofold for Heidegger. First, Heidegger considered Freud to be a representative of "modern science" which, he pointed out, was "based on the fact that the human being posits himself as an authoritative subject to whom everything which can be investigated becomes an object."[8] Second, Freud was an unabashed advocate of "the dictatorship of scientific thinking" that Heidegger so vociferously opposed.[9]

In a speech in Meskirch in 1947, Heidegger made it clear that he saw psychoanalysis as a major threat: "the view that psychology—which long ago turned into psychoanalysis—is taken in Switzerland and elsewhere as a substitute for philosophy (if not for religion) . . ."[10] Heidegger concomitantly was worried about the spread of scientism generally in Europe: "The prevailing opinion nowadays is [that it is] as if science alone could provide objective truth. Science *is* the new religion. Compared to it, any attempt to think of *being* appears arbitrary and 'mystical.'"[11] Heidegger was concerned that not only was science becoming too powerful and hence its limitations no longer being seen, but that what was not within the realm of science was increasingly being excluded. In other words, science was taking over.

Although he was highly critical of science, Heidegger made it very clear that he did not advocate the "abandonment of science."[12] Rather he insisted on a reflective relationship to science, whereby one carefully thinks through its limitations. Unfortunately, according to Heidegger, science tended not to reflect on itself; and its increasing popularity removed it even further from self-reflection. He wrote: "The more the current effect and usefulness of science spread, the more the capacity and readiness for a reflection upon what occurs in science disappears. This is especially true insofar as science carries through its claim to offer, and to administer, *the* truth about genuine reality."[13]

For Heidegger, science had become blind to its methodological presuppositions. One of the unfortunate ontological outcomes of this was that science uncritically applied itself to domains inappropriate to it—for example, human existence. Psychology in general, and psychoanalysis in particular, made a mistake by trying to conform to the methodological approaches and tacit ontology of the natural sciences. Heidegger saw Freud's metapsychological theory as a primary example of the misapplication of the scientific method specifically to human beings. As such, Freud's metapsychology represented this process: "because truth is in essence freedom, historical man can, in letting beings be, also not let beings be the beings which they are and as they are. Then beings are covered up and distorted. Semblance comes to power."[14]

The power science enjoyed, according to Heidegger, was one that had come to dominate and control our modes of thinking, to distort certain phenomena, and thereby to cover up what it prevented us from seeing. How did Heidegger think scientism has dominated and distorted our thinking? For example, he said: "Until now, psychology, anthropology, and psychopathology have considered the human being as an object in a broad sense, as something present-at-hand, as a domain of beings . . ."[15] What did the inappropriate application of science prevent us from seeing? "The great decision is: Can we ever claim to determine human *being* according to natural scientific representation, that is, within the limitations of a science projected without regard to the specific being of human *being*?"[16] Heidegger insisted that to focus on human beings as objects of investigation is to miss their very being.

Since Heidegger was concerned that scientism and one of its primary manifestations, psychoanalysis, were quickly becoming the primary theoretical dominating influences in Europe, he clearly believed that he had to do something. To help stem this tide, Heidegger decided to take up Dr. Medard Boss's invitation to address large groups of psychiatrists (who had been primarily trained in the natural sciences) in what have come to be known as the *Zollikon Seminars*. He often said that he welcomed these opportunities where his philosophy could confront the natural sciences.

The German edition of the *Zollikon Seminars (Zollikoner Seminare)* was published in 1987. It includes detailed notes of the seminars themselves, conversations between Heidegger and Medard Boss, and correspondence from Heidegger to Boss. The actual seminars took place from 1947 to 1971, predominately in Dr. Boss's home. In these seminars, Heidegger—who was fifty-eight years old when they began, and hence relatively deep into his philosophical career—spoke directly and extensively about Freud and his psychoanalytic approach for the first time. Since the seminar participants were psychiatrists, psychotherapists, physicians, and so on, Heidegger was encouraged to be as clear as possible when discussing his own philosophical framework. Thus, the *Zollikon Seminars* affords an opportunity for people other than philosophers to have access to what might otherwise be inaccessible due to its abstract nature.

Aside from offering a critique of psychoanalysis, Heidegger's overall goal in these seminars was to present his own philosophical worldview in hopes of eliciting a new way of "seeing" among the participants—one which is able to let go of the need for empirical proof, logic, and so on, and to let the phenomena show themselves and be seen as they are.[17]

This chapter and the following (chapter 12) draw primarily from the *Zollikon Seminars,* since they contain the only written or verbal comments Heidegger made about Freud and psychoanalysis. The main goal of this chapter is to elaborate on Heidegger's overall concern with Freudian metapsychology, specifically Freud's scientific worldview. Although it is helpful for the reader to have a previous background in Heidegger's philosophy, some key aspects have been briefly summarized in order to help show the import of his specific critique.[18]

Heidegger's Critique of Freud's Worldview

Heidegger's general critique of Freudian metapsychology involved its fundamental methodological approach. As mentioned earlier, Heidegger was opposed to scientism in general and psychoanalysis in particular for the inappropriate application of the scientific method to human existence. Heidegger's overall critique of Freud, then, was (1) that Freud failed as a scientist because, although he adopted the scientific worldview, his theory did not remain "true" to scientific investigation; and (2) no study of human existence should utilize the scientific methodology. Such an approach, according to Heidegger, served to distort, conceal and confine human existence. Hence, much of Heidegger's critique of Freud contained references to his own philosophy, as well as alternative, more ontologically appropriate ideas. His intention was to show psychology and psychoanalysis a cogent alternative in hopes of breaking the hold of scientistic thinking.[19]

Freud as a Neo-Kantian

According to Heidegger, Freud's tacit ontology had its genesis in Cartesian philosophy with its quest for the development of a unified, comprehensive, scientific philosophy; and in Galilean-Newtonian physics, which contributed to Kantian and Neo-Kantian philosophy, and the Helmholtz school of physics. Heidegger was quite clear what he thought about Freudian theory: "Freud's metapsychology is the application of Neo-Kantian philosophy to the human being. On the one hand, he has the natural sciences, and on the other hand, the Kantian theory of objectivity."[20] To understand the essential thrust of Heidegger's overly laconic remark, it is necessary to briefly mention the historical context of Neo-Kantianism. Neo-Kantianism represented various philosophical trends owing their inspiration to Kant that were prominent in Germany between 1870 and 1920. However widely divergent, they shared the conviction that something can only be a "science" if it returned to the spirit of Kant; thus, their emphasis was on interpreting Kant's reflections as a more positivistic mixture of empiricism and rationalism.

Heidegger did not say which school of Neo-Kantianism he had in mind as influencing Freud.[21] A review of the various schools, based on Heidegger's understanding of Freudian psychoanalysis, shows that he must have had in mind the Neo-Kantianism of Helmholtz (and Friedrich Lange), who argued that physiology is "developed or corrected Kantianism." Helmholtz gave a genetic, physiological account of sense-perception with empirical analogies to Kant's transcendental psychology. He held that the sensible world is a product of the interaction between the human organism and an unknown reality: the world of experience is determined by this interaction. Sensory qualities are indications of unknown objects interacting with our sense organs. In his theory of the unconscious inferences, Helmholtz accepted the Kantian theory that perception involves judgment; the underlying principle in such unconscious inferences was considered to be the a priori principle of causation, which gives us the right to posit unknown causes of our sensations. Helmholtz sought to establish the physiological substratum for all mental events. Heidegger's interpretation of Freud—within what Heidegger took to be his somewhat limited historical flow—appears to be correct as far as it goes.

According to Heidegger, it was Kant who first explicitly articulated the essential characteristics of nature, as they are understood in the natural sciences. While doing so, Kant had been the first to make clear what "law" means in the natural sciences. "The representation of a universal condition, according to which a certain manifold can be posited in uniform fashion is called a rule, and when it must be so posited, [it is called] a law."[22] According to Heidegger, Freud simply assimilated Kant's pronouncements regarding the fundamental ways of understanding nature in the natural sciences.

Heidegger further claimed that Freud simply adopted Kant's theory of objectivity. He argued that Descartes was responsible for the emergence of the conception of the human being as a "subject," and our modern experience of "objectivity."[23] Building on this, Kant had taught us that there could be no scientific investigation of an object domain without our presupposing at least an implicit ontology. The problem according to Heidegger was, however, that Kant had merely equated the terms "transcendental" and "ontological."[24] Kant's ontology simply referred to another kind of object—albeit a transcendental one—to be investigated.

But how is causality understood in the natural sciences? Heidegger used a familiar example: "The rock gets warm because the sun is shining." This is grounded on empirical observation. But we are not only dealing with a sequence—our "because" means that there is a necessary condition of one after another. This was the causality of modern science as it dominated modern thought since Galileo and Newton; Kant, however, went further in his critique of pure reason. The necessary "one after another" led to the interpretation of an "effect determined by a cause." Kant wrote: "Everything that happens, that is, begins to be, presupposes something after which it follows according to a rule."[25] This "after which" referred not only to a temporal sequence, but to a rule that demonstrated its necessity.

Kant said, "Nature is the existence [*Da-sein*] of things as far as it [*Dasein*] is determined according to universal laws."[26] As a law of nature, causality is a law according to which phenomena constitute nature for the first time, and are able to become objects of experience. What did Kant mean by this? The objects we experience, we experience as a result both of what is presented to us from the noumenal world, and organized according to universal and necessary principles (categories) by the transcendental ego. What we perceive is an object as experienced in the phenomenal world.

How did this relate to Freudian psychoanalysis? Heidegger offered two hints. First, "What for Kant transcends [conscious] perception, for instance, the fact that the stone becomes warm *because* the sun is shining, is for Freud 'the unconscious.'"[27] In a section entitled "Concerning the 'Psychical Functions': Ego, Id, Super-Ego," Heidegger said: "This classification seems to be another nomenclature for sensibility [*Sinnlichkeit*], understanding [*Verstand*], and reason [*Vernunft*], that is, for the moral law or the categorical imperative [in the Kantian sense]."[28] Here Heidegger was, of course, referring to Kantian epistemological and moral theory.

As discussed in earlier chapters, Freud held that it was by means of investments of energy from the psychic reservoir (instinctual drives)—under which both internal and external stimuli are continuously modified[29]—that the psyche is enabled to produce perceptions of "the external world," as well as ideas in general. Recall that Freud wrote:

> Just as Kant warned us not to overlook the fact that our perception is subjectively conditioned and must not be regarded as identical with the phenomena perceived but never really discerned, so psychoanalysis bids us not to set conscious perception in the place of unconscious mental process which is its object. The mental, like the physical, is not necessarily in reality just what it appears to us to be.[30]

Thus analogous to the Kantian noumenal realm, Freud conceived both the unconscious id as the true psychical reality (with its basis in somatic processes), and the external world as ultimately unknowable. Indeed, Freud sometimes referred to the id or the unconscious as "mysterious substrata."

Why did Heidegger disapprove of these Kantian presuppositions in Freudian psychoanalysis? He expressed his general dissatisfaction in the first paragraph of the *Zollikon Seminars:* "Human existing in its essential ground is never just an object which is present-at-hand . . . all conventional, objectifying representations of a capsule-like psyche, subject, person, ego, or consciousness in psychology and psychopathology must be abandoned."[31] Heidegger believed that it was because of this way of conceiving human existence that what is most important gets covered—mainly, the ontological dimension of man.

The Ontological Dimension of Human Beings

Heidegger was very concerned that Freud's adherence to natural scientism simply made him oblivious to this "ontological dimension of man."

"According to natural science, the human being can be identified only as something present-at-hand in nature."[32] Hence, Heidegger believed that Freud's scientistic theory had to be abandoned in favor of an entirely different way of seeing: "This new view of the basic constitution of human existence may be called *Da-sein,* or being-in-the-world."[33] Freud's obliviousness, according to Heidegger, occurred on a variety of levels. Freud, among other things, failed to see the ontological, the clearing, the mystery, the very being of human being, as well as the ontological difference (beings versus being).

Ontical versus ontological inquiry

Heidegger drew a crucial distinction in his philosophy between "beings" and "being." On the one hand, the fundamental aspect of beings is that they are entities, which have defining characteristics. They include "things," processes, relations, events, and so on ("what there is"). Being, on the other hand, is the being of such entities ("that they are"). Heidegger called inquiries about entities (beings) "ontical inquiries." Since the sciences accumulate and are preoccupied with knowledge about particular entities, their relationships to one another, and so on, they conduct ontic inquiries, according to Heidegger. Focusing exclusively on entities— as he accused science of doing—leads to a preoccupation with beings to the exclusion (forgetting) of being.

On the other hand, inquiries into the meaning of being are what Heidegger called "ontological inquiry." Here one asks questions such as: What is the meaning of being? What does it mean that beings are? What does it mean to be as human? Being is not an entity, nor is it a property or category of entities.

Although it may have appeared that Freud was conducting an ontological inquiry, given that he was asking deep questions that were meant to get at the root of human existence, Heidegger pointed out that all of Freud's metapsychological theory remained solely on the ontical level— the level of things.[34] Heidegger maintained that Freud's metapsychological inquiry was only "ontical"—although it presupposed "thing-ontology"— and oblivious to the genuinely ontological dimension of human existence. That is, Freud inquired into what a human being is as an entity, not into what it means for a human to be as a process of concrete activity—as a self. He did not consider what must be presupposed for a human to "be" in the possible ways she/he is. As such, Freud's metapsychological theory failed to advance an understanding of what it means to be psychoanalytical, to be a self, and so on, by ignoring the crucial question of what it means to be human at all and the ontological question of how such experience is possible. Furthermore, not only did Freudian theory not address this question, it actually tended toward the preclusion of such an inquiry. It did this by simply preconceiving (faithful to his Cartesian-Kantian heritage) a human as an entity whose being is the same as all other entities: a human is an object or thing. In doing so, it tended to preclude the meaningfulness of the question of what it means to be human as a lived-experience.

There is a further point to be made, which is implicit in the above: not only did Freud's metapsychology give an ontologically inadequate answer to the question of what it means to be human, and how it is possible, but his scientifically based presuppositions about the nature of humans blatantly *distorted* what it means to be as a human being. As Heidegger would have said, Freud's theory presupposed that individuals are nothing more than things present-at-hand in the universe—objects that are ultimately reducible to quantifiable substances, relations, and events. If we as human beings are nothing more than this, how is it possible that we could ever come to reflect upon or wonder about our existence at all? How could a mere object become aware of and concerned about its own existence? It is an obvious fact that as human beings we do wonder about the meaning of existence: as a human being, I am aware of my ability to be or not to be. I am aware of not only being actual, but also of having possibilities. Clearly, an object cannot reflect upon its existence or be aware of its possibilities. Hence, according to Heidegger, human beings must be more than mere things, present-at-hand in the universe—as Freud had conceived them. Since Freud's metapsychology lacked any concept of the ontological function of reason, as the pursuit of the meaning of what it means to be, Heidegger concluded that Freud's theory was ontologically inadequate and anthropologically distortive. Heidegger wrote, "[it] fails to give an unequivocal and ontologically adequate answer to the question about the kind of Being which belongs to those entities which we ourselves are."[35]

The example of death: Freud's ontical approach versus Heidegger's ontological approach

To better illustrate what is at stake in the above distinction, it is useful to consider Freud's and Heidegger's individual approaches to a specific topic—death. Freud's primary analysis of the death instinct occurred within the context of his metapsychological theory. Indeed, he understood death as intrinsically embedded in this theory. For example, Freud explicitly defined an instinct as *"an urge inherent in organic life to restore to an earlier state of things."*[36] Recall that Freud conceived the "death instinct" (Thanatos) and the "life instinct" (Eros) as the two basic forms of instincts, which abide by the constancy principle as formulated by Fechner. This principle asserted that all living processes, including human beings, tend to return to the stability of the inorganic world. As such, Freud thought that this principle governed the existence of all life. In view of this, it was not surprising that Freud characterized the death instinct in the way he did:

> Everything living dies for *internal* reasons—becomes inorganic once again—then we shall be compelled to say that *the aim of all life is death.*[37]

> The function thus described would be concerned with the most universal endeavor of all living substance—namely to return to the quiescence of the inorganic world.[38]

As nothing more than a biological organism whose physiochemical processes tend to break down eventually (through the catabolic processes), humans, like all other life processes, wish to return to a quiescent level. Hence, Freud thought that every individual unconsciously desires his/her own death.

Freud's analysis of the unconscious wish for one's own annihilation involved no ontological inquiry (or even explicit ontological understanding) into the meaning of human existence and how it is possible. Instead, it was intended to show that humans, conceived metapsychologically as biological organisms, conform to what was understood by Freud as a physical law of the universe. Clearly, then, Freud's death instinct was not only consistent with the mechanistic-deterministic implications of his metapsychology, but was intrinsically embedded in it.

However, it was on the concrete level of everyday existence that Freud offered some acute observations on the pre-World War I adult's typical attitude toward death:

> We were of course prepared to maintain that death was the necessary outcome of life, that everyone owes nature a death and must expect to pay the debt—in short, that death was natural, undeniable, and unavoidable. In reality, however, we were accustomed to behave as if it were otherwise. We showed an unmistakable tendency to put death on one side, to eliminate it from life. We tried to hush it up . . . our habit is to lay stress on the fortuitous causation of death: in this way we betray an effort to reduce death from a necessity to a chance event . . . But this attitude of ours towards death has a powerful effect upon our lives. Life is impoverished, it loses interest . . . it becomes shallow and empty.[39]

According to Freud, it was the world war that necessitated a change in attitude toward death. It compelled us to acknowledge that death is an irrefragable fact—"people really die." It jolted us out of our deceitful complacency into an explicit recognition of the reality of death. As Freud tersely put it: "If you want to endure life, prepare yourself for death."

In Freud's writings on death as a human experience, some very interesting similarities can be found between his observations and Heidegger's analysis of death. First, both agreed on what they took to be an obvious fact: death is the inevitable outcome of human life. As Heidegger put it: "Dasein cannot outstrip the possibility of death . . . death is something impending."[40] Second, and more significantly, both underscored the proclivity of human beings in general to try to escape confrontation with the genuine meaning of death through various means of self-deceit. Like Freud, Heidegger suggested that "proximally and for the most part Dasein covers up its Being-towards-death, fleeing in the face of it."[41] Furthermore, he explicitly agreed with Freud that, in everyday life, "death is 'known' as a mishap which is constantly occurring."[42] Next, both men suggested that it was inappropriate, when one is searching for the truth, to evade an awareness of the reality of death. Freud wrote:

> Should we not confess that in our civilized attitude toward death we are once again living psychologically beyond our means, and should we not rather turn back and recognize the truth? Would it not be better to give death the place in reality and in our thoughts which is its due?[43]

Compare with Heidegger, "Our everyday falling evasion in the face of death is an inauthentic Being-towards-death."[44] They agreed, then, that in facing the reality of death one is also opening oneself up to the truth of one's everyday existence.

Finally, Freud and Heidegger both recognized that a genuine awareness of death invigorates an individual's sense of life. It contributes an urgency, which would otherwise be lacking. It is the awareness of death that discloses and enhances the true meaning and scope of the various ways of being. According to Freud, the experience of life without a true awareness of the possibility of death would be like "an American flirtation, in which it is understood from the first that nothing is to happen, as contrasted with a Continental love-affair in which both partners must constantly bear its serious consequences in mind."[45] Heidegger fully agreed: "With death, Dasein stands before itself in its own most potentiality-for-Being."[46]

Notwithstanding these obvious similarities, there were other highly significant divergences between these two thinkers' perspectives on death. First, Freud placed far less emphasis than did Heidegger on the necessity for the concrete individual to come to an explicit awareness of the inevitable termination of one's own personal existence. Instead, for the most part, it was enough for Freud that one comes to honestly acknowledge that persons in general do, in fact, die. Heidegger would have pointed out that by focusing on this point, Freud remained on the level of "everydayness" which possesses only a pre-authentic understanding of the meaning and import of death. Interestingly enough, Heidegger gave a concise description of what he took to be Freud's viewpoint:[47]

> In the publicness with which we are with one another in our everyday manner, death is "known" as something which is constantly occurring— as a "case of death." Someone or other "dies," be he neighbor or stranger. People who are no acquaintances of ours are "dying" daily and hourly. "Death" is encountered as a well-known event occurring within-the-world.[48]

By understanding death in this way, Freud succumbed to the temptation of what Heidegger referred to as "das Man" (the "they-self"), the tendency to cover up the true import of death as it would be authentically confronted by a reflective self. Heidegger pointed out that a true awareness of death affords a principle of individuation—that is, confers upon a concrete person a sense of his or her own personal individuality. Dying is something that no one else can do for me; by truly being aware of my own death as my most personal of possibilities, I am enabled to confront my true authentic self.

Second, for Freud, the death of persons was considered an ongoing occurrence in the world toward which one can adopt various psychological attitudes, whereas for Heidegger death was much more—it was a mode of existence for Dasein. "Let the term 'dying' stand for that way of Being in which Dasein is towards its death";[49] and, "death is a way to be which Dasein takes over as soon as it is."[50] A person has the capacity to relate their self to death in various ways. Death, as a mode of human existence, interpenetrates the various projects one undertakes in the world. It is in this way that the transitoriness of one's own existence is revealed. Death, then, is an immanent a priori structure of Being-in-the-world: Dasein exists as Being-towards-death (an end).

The third and foremost discrepancy between Freud's and Heidegger's viewpoints on death involved the nature and intent of their respective projects. According to Heidegger's interpretation, Freud was content to provide a description of the kinds of attitudes the average everyday adult exhibits toward the phenomenon of death[51] and to point out the advantage of truth over self-deceit when evaluating them. In Heideggerian terms, Freud was content to remain on the ontical level of analyzing everyday human existence as it manifested itself in concrete situations. For Heidegger the phenomenon of death was far more potent than this: it is precisely death which enables us to shift the focus of our inquiry into human existence from considerations about concrete ways of existing (the ontical level) to questions about what it means to be at all (the ontological level), and how these concrete ways of being are transcendentally possible. Indeed, it is ultimately the phenomenon of death that discloses temporality as the true ontological ground of existence. Furthermore, according to Heidegger, it is because death focuses upon our ownmost personal existence that death becomes the ground of authentic existence. This was why Heidegger suggested that "methodologically, the existential analysis is superordinate to the question of a biology, psychology . . . of death."[52]

In conclusion, Heidegger would have accused Freud of never achieving an ontological understanding of death. As a metapsychologist, Freud saw humans as mere biological organisms, which simply returned to inorganic substance. As such, Freud displayed no ontological understanding of the self as a process of lived concrete activity, which truly anticipated its own personal death. Heidegger would have contended that even as an observer of the world scene, Freud's psychological descriptions of death remained invariably on the level of everyday concerns and never explored the question more deeply. Freud was simply oblivious to the potential of the phenomenon of death as a catalyst for disclosing the true ontological understanding of human existence—for an inquiry into what the being of human is.

Ontological Inquiry as the Most Primordial Inquiry

Heidegger insisted that ontological inquiry—inquiry into what it means to be—was the most primordial form of inquiry of all. Any other form of inquiry presupposed some understanding of the meaning of being. For example, as a mode of inquiry, psychoanalysis made claims about what human beings are. Fundamental ontology examined how such claims were possible. Hence, fundamental ontology was presupposed by psychoanalysis (or any inquiry) because it considered how it was possible that we can be aware of any meaning whatsoever. Such an investigation aimed at ascertaining the a priori conditions necessary for the possible ways of being human, the necessary preconditions or structures by which any human experience whatsoever is possible and meaningful.

More specifically, Freudian psychoanalysis—conceived as a practical form of inquiry with two participants—tried to bring to light the truth concerning the unique manner in which a concrete existing individual human being relates to the world, others, and self. As a form of inquiry into the meaningful existence of an individual human being, it seems clear (given Heidegger's philosophy) that psychoanalysis must presuppose an understanding of what it means to be human in general. Understanding an individual's ways of being on the ontic level of everyday life presupposes an understanding of what it means to be human (that is, of the possible ways of being human). No complete psychoanalytical understanding of an individual is possible without a consideration of how it is possible for human existence in general to relate to its possibilities (what it means to be). Hence, Heidegger pointed out that ontological inquiry is prior to and grounds the very possibility of psychoanalytic inquiry.

The above argument applies to psychoanalytic activity specifically in three fundamental respects. First, as a *form of inquiry,* being psychoanalytical is a certain way or mode of being human; however, to be psychoanalytical one must have had the capacity to be—prior to any psychoanalytical activity. In other words, we must have had some a priori capacity within us which permitted us to relate in this way in the first place. Hence, we must ultimately be concerned with the question of the possible ways (the a priori conditions for such possibility) in which an individual can be said to be. The question of what it means to be, aims at ascertaining the a priori conditions for the possibility of the form of inquiry we call psychoanalysis.

Second, ontological analysis is not only prior to and foundational for psychoanalytical activity—it also affects our comprehension of psychoanalysis as an *activity.* When I view the patient and the world in the particular way a psychoanalyst does, I interpret that patient's utterances within my own conceptual framework in order to render them intelligible to me. Also, my own personality structure may color my understanding of how the patient relates to the world, others, and himself or herself. If I am to aid the patient in disclosing the truth of the way in which she or he exists in her or his relations, it will be necessary for me to be able to assess to what extent my own conceptual approach and personality structure is affecting my understanding while trying to assist the patient in apprehending that truth. For me to achieve this, I must explicate more fully my understanding of what it means to be a human, so that I may understand the structural possibilities of my existence and thereby eliminate idiosyncratic obstructions to my understanding of the patient's modes of relating (for example, as part of the process Freud referred to as "counter-transference").

Third, in its goal to understand the concrete ways in which a particular human being relates to the world, psychoanalysis must presuppose the prior inquiry into the possible ways in which a person can be said to be. No complete understanding of what a specific situation means to a particular individual (on the ontic level) is possible without a prior understanding of what the universal preconditions were for the possibility of experiencing that situation in the first place: that is, we must first delineate the horizons within which an individual's possibilities can be selected. For outside any ontological structural context, the interhuman assignment and interpretation of meaningful situations could not be explicitly and universally understood.

It is important to understand that, in the above it is not argued that there can be no understanding by a psychoanalyst of what a specific situation means to a particular individual without this understanding being ontologically grounded. Clearly analysts such as Freud must have had some understanding of the analysand prior to an explicit ontological grounding; else effective therapy would not have been possible in the past. Instead, it is argued that no complete understanding of the individual and psychoanalytical activity per se is possible until the everyday understanding (which the analyst already has) is sufficiently grounded in ontological understanding.[53] As discussed, one of the major functions of psychoanalysis is to clarify and make explicit the meaning of this everyday understanding (namely, the ontic level).

Genuine psychoanalytical inquiry, then, presupposes the understanding afforded by ontological inquiry. Such an inquiry is "ontological" in the sense that it investigates what it means to be human; it inquires into the very being of human reality. Furthermore, ontological inquiry discloses the "transcendental" dimension of its task by focusing upon the primordial question: what would have to be the nature of human existence, what would we have to presuppose about it, in order for any experience (way of being) to be possible? In other words, what would have to be the a priori conditions essential for the possible ways of being human? Heidegger would have claimed, then, that an ontological-transcendental analysis provides the conceptual elucidation necessary for humans to comprehend themselves in their concrete situations. Or again, since the transcendental analysis of the human being necessarily encompasses all of the possible ways in which a human self can exist, this inquiry forms the foundation for, and is prior to, the psychoanalytic form of inquiry.

In its practical endeavor to understand the truth concerning an individual's ways of relating, psychoanalysis not only presupposes some understanding of what it means to be, but also some comprehension of the essential nature of truth, meaning, understanding, and interpretation. Heidegger argued that an inquiry into the latter must be made on the level of ontological-transcendental analysis of human existence in general, before any grounded understanding of an individual's ways of being can be fully gained. Furthermore such an inquiry would provide the guidelines for understanding the meaning these concepts have for psychoanalytical activity per se.

Dasein as the proper point of departure for ontological inquiry

Heidegger suggested that since human beings (Dasein) are engaged in the clearing, wonder about their own being (their own being is an issue for them), and have at the outset at least an implicit understanding of that being (their own being), Dasein is the natural point of departure for such an inquiry. It is the necessary point of departure since, in order to elucidate the understanding of being intrinsic to Dasein's being it is crucial to have an antecedent understanding of Dasein's being per se. We must understand the way of being of the inquirer before we can truly understand the meaning of the results of any inquiry whatsoever.

What did Heidegger mean by *Dasein?* First, and foremost, Dasein is always already a situatedness in any situation (literally meaning, "to-be-there"). It is an openness in the sense of, "Here I am in my situation, open to possibilities, beings, and so on." Next, Dasein is always—in each case— a "mineness" in the sense of "I am my experience of meaning." Dasein exists as Being-in-the-world; that is, Dasein exists within a unified, concrete, experiential field of meaning. As such, its ways of Being-in-the-world include relating to objects, other Daseins, and itself. As clearedness, Dasein is always already engaged as existing in the clearing.

The clearing

Heidegger was convinced that the ontological dimension of humans could best be grasped by understanding the clearing. Yet he believed that not only had great minds like Freud failed to see the clearing, but even philosophy in general had continued to be oblivious to it.[54] To elucidate Heidegger's concept of the clearing it is useful to see it in terms of several of its intrinsically interrelated features.

1. *The clearing as presencing.* Heidegger conceived of the clearing as that which is necessary for the presencing of being, beings, thinking, meaning, and so on. He understood the clearing of being as the "open region" which prevails through being, through presence, as that which is necessary for anything at all to appear, to be present, or for anything to be absent; hence, the clearing of being makes possible the very appearance of beings.[55] To say that the clearing makes it possible for beings to appear does not imply that it is possible to separate the clearing from that which appears. Heidegger emphasized that in the clearing, being and beings are not separated from one another;[56] each is indissolubly rooted in the other.[57] The meaning of the clearing is to make possible the appearance

of what is given in everyday experience. Understanding the ontological meaning of the clearing as intrinsically related to the ontic everyday experience is what allows for humans to be unified experience (Being-in-the-world). Without separating the clearing from that which appears by virtue of the clearing, Heidegger brought to light the wholeness of experience. Furthermore, by not separating the ontic and ontological, the clearing can *not* be understood as a concrete being or place—for example, such as a clearing in the forest—for this would be to limit the clearing to the ontic level, and overlook the ontological all together.

Heidegger emphasized that the clearing of being is not something that could ever be actually seen or understood on the level of everyday objects. Instead, it can only be apprehended in reflective thinking.[58] In fact, being in the clearing is also presupposed and makes possible reflection itself. Hence, Heidegger believed that although Freud missed seeing the clearing (by remaining strictly on the ontic level), the clearing made possible Freud's metapsychological theory in the first place. As Heidegger poetically put it:

> The quiet heart of the opening is the place of stillness from which alone the possibility of the belonging together of Being and thinking, that is, presence and apprehending, can arise at all.[59]

2. *The clearing as most primordial.* Heidegger understood the clearing as what is most primordial. Heidegger described the clearing as "the free, the open."[60] This free openness is a "primal phenomenon."[61] According to Heidegger, there is nothing behind or underlying the clearing as, for example, in Kant's "noumenal world"—reality as it is in itself, prior to being organized in universal and necessary ways (the categories) by the transcendental ego—which in a sense exists behind what he called the "phenomenal world" (the everyday world as we experience it). For Heidegger, any speculative or dialectical thinking, originary intuition, and so on, is dependent upon openness in the first place. Da-sein is always already dependent on something showing itself to it (namely, being).[62]

> The imperceptible, ontological phenomena always already and necessarily show themselves *prior to* all perceptible phenomena. Before we can perceive a table as this or that table, we must receive-perceive that there is something presencing [Anwesen]. Ontological phenomena, therefore, are primary [in the order of being], but secondary in [the order of] being thought and seen.[63]

The ontological dimension, then, is the unreceived-unperceived, or as Heidegger later described it, the concealed (as well as the un-concealed).

3. *The clearing as granting being.* Heidegger wanted to underscore the point that the clearing grants being. The clearing, which affords the very presencing of being, grants, for example, the "spatiality" of Dasein. The clearing as openness grants giving and receiving; it grants not only the presencing of beings, but the presencing of presence itself. Heidegger said: "We must think aletheia, unconcealment, as the opening which first grants being and thinking and their presencing to and for each other."[64] The essential ground of human existing is the revealing-concealing mystery of being, which grants the human being his Da-sein.[65] Humans are, for Heidegger, recipients of the granted "gift" of being. Recognizing this aspect of the ontological level of human existence raises one's awareness of unified experience, and prompts humans to become aware of things/beings in terms of their *being* rather than seeking to exploit them and approaching them with the attitude of what use they can be.[66]

4. *The clearing and Dasein's clearedness.* Heidegger showed the indissoluble reciprocal interrelatedness of "the clearing" and "Dasein's clearedness." The importance of this point is underscored by the fact that it was the key sentence in Heidegger's very first lecture in the *Zollikon Seminars:* "To exist as Da-sein means to hold open a domain through its capacity to receive-perceive the significance of the things that are given to it [*Da-sein*] and that address it [*Da-sein*] by virtue of its own 'clearing' [*Gelichtetheit*]."[67] As discussed, the clearing makes possible the appearance of being, thinking, and so on. Heidegger also emphasized that the clearing is not separate from humans: being perceiving-receiving humans means the open engagement of the clearing while at the same time being the clearing. Here we are dealing with one of the most critical concepts in Heidegger's account: *vernehmen*. It is important to note that there is both an active and passive sense to Dasein's receiving-perceiving.[68] In its more active sense, *vernehmen* means to perceive—for example, what a judge comes to perceive after questioning some witnesses. In its existential-ontological meaning, *vernehmen* implies receiving or receptivity in the sense of "to listen in"—as in letting oneself in to the presencing of being. Hence, the human way of existing (as a standing open) consists of the capacities of perceiving what it encounters (beings) and receiving what addresses it (presence, being). On the one hand, the standing-open of human beings is a standing-out into the clearing.[69] Given this, the way in which humans exist is an openness for the thingness of things. If human beings' way of existing were not this openness, nothing would be able to appear. On the other hand, the openness for being, as which the human being exists, is claimed by the presence (being) of something.[70] Human beings are always already related to something unveiling itself to them.[71] Thereby, in this address, we are always already directed toward things disclosing themselves to us.[72]

As such, there is an indissoluble, reciprocal interrelatedness of human beings' way of existing as "standing-open" and the presencing of being.

This way of existing is an engaged openness: the extent to which and way in which Dasein is "open" forms the boundaries by which one may experience the presence of being and accept any being which one may encounter within the clearing for what it is. Hence, to let be is also to engage oneself with beings. When one engages the disclosedness of beings, one withdraws in the face of beings so that they might reveal themselves with respect to what and how they are.[73] Humans are summoned to the task of letting things show up in their full significance, their unified belongingness together, their simplicity and their greatness. In their Being-in-the-world, human beings always consist of a receptive-perceptive relatedness to what addresses them. In this address, humans are always already directed toward things disclosing themselves.[74]

Heidegger believed that humans could function on this deeper, more open level of existence—and not become preoccupied, one might even say obsessed, with the ontic. Given that humans are ontological beings as well as ontic, they could experience the more significant if they were able to remain open to the presencing of this deeper level. For example, Heidegger elucidated a more meaningful approach to existence in his discussion on the "sojourning" of human beings.

As sojourning beings, humans are dwelling in the clearing; humans take up a sojourn in the clearing, and concern themselves with things.[75] Human beings must always be understood as sojourning with what they encounter, namely, "as disclosure for what concerns it and what is encountered."[76] "Sojourning-with is the same . . . and at the same time as the letting come to presence of beings . . . in the sojourn lies that with which and with whom I sojourn, and how I comport myself toward [them]."[77] But what does this comportment mean? "This means that he must respond in such a way that he takes what he encounters into his care and that he aids it in unfolding its own essence as far as possible."[78]

5. The clearing of concealment and unconcealment. Heidegger emphasized that the clearing is always the clearing of concealment *and* unconcealment. Heidegger wrote, "clearing is never mere clearing, but always the clearing of *concealment.*"[79] For Heidegger, then, concealment had ontological priority over unconcealment, since in order for something to be un-concealed, it must first be concealed and awaiting the opportunity to show itself. However, Heidegger also emphasized that concealment and unconcealment are not opposites, but rather always presuppose one another as they engage the clearing. The clearing provides for the presencing of being, thinking, and so on, and the presencing is accepted to the extent that humans are open to receiving-perceiving. With the presencing, there is also what remains inaccessible. Heidegger wrote, "letting-be is intrinsically at the same time a concealing."[80] No matter how openly engaged humans are within the clearing, no matter how much unconcealing occurs, concealment is always also an aspect of presencing.

In general, Heidegger formulated concealment as the inaccessible manifesting itself as such.[81] This manifestation can occur in different ways and on various levels. The inaccessible, for example, may simply be temporarily beyond reach—that is, it may be concealed because it is not of concern or in focus; the inaccessible may also be something unavailable and incapable of being apprehended; the phenomenon itself may withdraw from the region of the clearing and be inaccessible, and in such a way that even this inaccessibility cannot be experienced. The self-manifestation of the inaccessible as such is what Heidegger referred to as the mystery. That the inaccessible becomes manifest itself at all is a mystery. Conversely, the concealing of the concealment is the mystery—namely, that the mystery is not even accessible to the extent that it is seen as inaccessible! Indeed, Heidegger described the mystery as the most primordial and unique obscurity. Furthermore, this mystery is pervasive and dominates the very being of human beings: the mystery has an impact upon us whether we know it or not.[82]

In more specific terms, concealment (as the inaccessible) can take place on many levels. For example, on the ontic level beings can become concealed by "hiding" and/or refusing to show themselves: keys and eyeglasses are notorious for concealing in this way; a patient in therapy may not authentically want to work out past trauma despite his/her choice to enter therapy. Beings can also remain concealed simply because they are not of concern, or what is of interest takes priority: he was wearing the eyeglasses, but was too busy searching for them to notice; she was so deeply engrossed in her book that she failed to notice the man sitting beside her on the bus. It is also possible for one being to hide another: he denied that his brother was an alcoholic, yet admitted that he did seem to have lapses in memory on occasion.

Concealment on the ontological level involves the concealment of the clearing. In this case, the "truth" of being might show itself in letting beings be what they are, yet also hide itself. Someone could have a mystical experience, for example, define it as a "religious experience," with all the attendant connotations from his/her previous experience, and hence conceal other possible understandings. In this case, truth is revealed while at the same time concealed. Or the truth of being might show itself in letting beings be what they are *not*, and manifest them in what Heidegger referred to as their "seeming-to-be." This kind of concealment includes errancy and mystery.[83] In this last case, Freud would serve as a classic example from Heidegger's perspective: here, there is a concealing of the concealment itself.

Heidegger believed that Freud was able to be unaware that he was concealing the ontological dimension of human beings. In failing to see the ontological dimension, Freud turned to that which was most readily available—beings. According to Heidegger, Freud took beings as his standard and in doing so strayed away from the mystery. Heidegger wrote: "The concealing of the concealed being as a whole holds sway in that disclosure of specific beings, which, as forgottenness of concealment, becomes errancy."[84] Hence, neglecting to see the deeper meaning, Freud's theory not only contributed to the concealment of humans, but also perpetuated what Heidegger believed was erroneous information.

Along similar lines, Heidegger also pointed out that when a particular way of interpreting the world comes to be taken as the ultimate truth, concealment happens in a most fundamental way. It was Freud—again serving as a classic example to illustrate Heidegger's point—who among others, with his uncritical and absolute adherence to the scientific Weltanschauung and its concomitant tacit ontology, fell prey to Heidegger's remark. Science presented itself as having the authoritative perspective on reality; as a result, science arrogated its most fundamental presuppositions as being beyond question and discussion. For Freud, this was the only reasonable way to go: only science could give genuine access to knowledge and reality.[85] However, Heidegger believed that if Freud had truly been able to come to a genuine understanding of this concealment, he might have been able to approach some kind of understanding of the truth of being.

Heidegger's discussion of the difference between ontological and ontical modes of inquiry, the "clearing," concealment and unconcealment, and so on, was intended to show that with regard to human existence science does not hold the ultimate, objective truth. Experience is a unified whole: if we do not think about it too long or analyze it too much, we recognize the unity of our existence. In trying to understand experience, then, we must begin with an inquiry which acknowledges this wholeness, and not with a scientific method which not only neglects the wholeness, but attempts to split it up, reduce, measure, and so on. In so doing, science can only reveal distortions; and yet, these distortions are somehow taken as *the* truth.

The Unspoken Dialogue: Heidegger's Specific Criticisms of Freudian Psychoanalysis

> Science is never able to critique philosophy because it is founded upon philosophy itself.
> —Heidegger

> Philosophy is not opposed to science, it behaves like a science and works in part by the same methods; it departs from it, however, by clinging to the illusion of being able to present a picture of the universe which is without gaps and is coherent, though one which is bound to collapse with every fresh advance in our knowledge.
> —Freud

As seen in the previous chapter, Heidegger was severely critical of Freudian psychoanalysis and its tacit ontology. Heidegger was convinced that Freud's uncritical adoption of the scientific Weltanschauung of his time prevented him from seeing what was ontologically significant. In the *Zollikon Seminars,* Heidegger also critiqued Freud's underlying philosophical presuppositions and specific elements within Freud's metapsychological theory. Although not systematic, and somewhat disorganized, Heidegger's critique of Freud was reasonably complete. It is also the case that Freud would not have been without any resources to respond; indeed, he would have had important rejoinders to many of Heidegger's objections. Certainly, during Freud's own lifetime and within his own circle of colleagues, he found himself frequently having to defend his position and justify his decision to go beyond the strict bounds of science. As discussed in earlier chapters, Freud ardently desired the respect of his fellow scientists, yet his experience in therapy showed him the limits of remaining within his scientific framework. Thus, he was compelled to go beyond scientific methodology to apply a regressive archaeological methodology, which synthesized a great deal of previous historical philosophical systems. Heidegger considered Freud's psychoanalysis strictly within the confines of scientific discovery, nonetheless, and hence Heidegger believed Freud to have ultimately failed both as a scientist and as one who purports to offer an accurate description of human existence.

This chapter is divided into two basic sections. The first section looks further at how Heidegger thought scientism affected Freud's most fundamental assumptions—as Heidegger understood them—and how scientistic thinking underlies and was intrinsic to various elements of Freud's theory. Heidegger's criticisms are organized so as to enhance their coherent flow. The second section of this chapter ponders the question: How would Freud have responded to Heidegger's criticisms? Obviously Freud would not have agreed with Heidegger's analysis of his metapsychological theory; and although Freud was not alive to hear what Heidegger had to say, Freud's writings give a fairly clear view of what his position was. This section provides "Freud" the opportunity to express that position in the face of Heidegger's critique.

Heidegger's Criticisms of Freud's Philosophical Presuppositions

Given Heidegger's critique of Freud's worldview, and Heidegger's alternative perspective, it is now important to consider *with greater specificity* what Heidegger thought about some of Freud's fundamental assumptions. Again, Heidegger's overall goal in discussing these during his *Zollikon Seminars* was to break the hold of the dictatorship of scientific thinking and its concomitant, tacit ontology, by conducting a critical reflection upon some of the most basic, interrelated philosophical presuppositions of Freud's metapsychological theory.

Heidegger argued that Freud made certain fundamental assumptions with regard to the nature and function of physical and psychical processes. Freud assumed that both the physical and psychical domains operated in the same mechanical way;[1] that they were ultimately grounded in somatic processes (forces);[2] and that psychical processes were transformable into somatic ones and vice versa. As a result, Freud considered both the physical and psychical as a continuous nexus of causal relations.[3] Such a view already presupposed that all human activity was necessarily subjectable to reductionistic, scientistic analysis,[4] in which everything that exists is measurable.[5] Hence, Freud postulated the complete explainability of psychical life[6] in causal terms.[7] However, since no "uninterrupted explainability" appeared in consciousness, Heidegger pointed out that Freud found it necessary to "invent the unconscious,"[8] and introduce the "fatal distinction" between the conscious and the unconscious;[9] to resort to the hypothesis of "unconscious purposes" as explanations;[10] and to mistakenly construct the idea of "unconscious motivation,"[11] thereby conflating "cause" and "motive."[12]

To see why Heidegger thought Freud's metapsychological theory ultimately failed, it is important to consider each of these fundamental assumptions from Heidegger's perspective.

Freud assumed that both the physical and psychical domains operated in the same mechanical way. Given his Cartesian heritage, Heidegger believed that Freud found himself uncritically accepting its metaphysical dualism between mind and body. Yet, Heidegger claimed that as a natural scientist, Freud was unable to successfully draw a distinction between the psychical and the physical in the first place. The physical is all that can be demonstrated via scientific means; hence, such a distinction was "ontologically false."[13]

Heidegger pointed out that by conceiving of humans as mechanical beings, one is compelled to construct an inaccessible reality beneath the perceived in order to explain how humans are also different from, for example, a microscope.[14] According to Heidegger, this was precisely what Freud did: he began with an inaccurate (mechanical) view of humans and was forced to construct his psychodynamic model in order to account for the "human quality" within the mechanism. Yet, the psychical mechanism presented a major problem for Freud. "What is the meaning of the psychical?" Heidegger asked. He pointed out that Freudian psychoanalysis inquired "about *processes* and about *changes in the psychical,* but *not* about what *psychical* is."[15] One of Freud's assumptions, in his own words, was that "the intellect and the mind are objects for scientific research in exactly the same way as non-human things."[16] Given this, Heidegger believed that it was therefore incumbent upon Freud to specify exactly what the psychical was as a measurable, mechanical thing. Obviously, Freud did not intend to present the psychical as the same thing as the physical, since he specifically conceived of both as different. Yet, Freud did believe that they operated in the same causally determined fashion. If this were "true," then it must be demonstrated and scientifically verifiable. Freud simply failed to accomplish this.

Furthermore, although it is possible to inaccurately view humans as strictly mechanical beings (Heidegger accused science of doing just that), Heidegger pondered the question: ought one to do so?[17] What are the implications of perpetuating such a view? Heidegger stressed that if we analyze human beings in the same way as mechanical beings we will lose track of our most significant questions and experiences. For example, we would lose our wonderment about our being: our being would no longer be an issue for us. Indeed, to conceive of ourselves as mechanical beings would lead to our no longer being able to account for significance—namely, that some thing or things would matter to us—at all. In other words, if we merely think of ourselves as objects to be investigated, how could it be at all a matter of concern to us that we are?

Freud believed that everything human is ultimately grounded in somatic processes (forces).[18] Once Freud split the human into two mechanisms—the psychical and the physical—Freud was forced to construct a psychodynamic model based on this inaccurate view of human nature in order to account for the connection between the two. Yet Heidegger pointed out that a scientific proof for this connection is impossible,

> since these foundations, according to the demands of science would have to be somatic due to the fact that in the natural sciences only what can be measured is "provable" therefore, the proof would be supported by only one of the two related domains, that is, by the somatic.[19]

In other words, what satisfied the claim of the natural scientist for valid knowledge must be provable and proven by the way of measurement, and measurement alone. It is only the somatic domain that can satisfy this requirement.

Hence, Heidegger believed that Freud's attempt to ground everything in somatic processes failed even by his own account: the psychical would have to disappear. A true scientist would not postulate an entire realm of human nature that cannot be scientifically validated.[20] This would leave Freud with the notion that the body is nothing more than a corporeal object. To do this, Heidegger thought, was to "eliminate the body as body."[21]

Instead of holding such a false position, Heidegger, of course, countered Freud's position with his own. According to Heidegger, bodily being presupposes Being-in-the-world—Dasein, as openness, as the ecstatic dwelling in the clearing of beings. Bodily being is the necessary yet insufficient condition for Dasein's Being-in-the-world. Being-in-the-world includes more than bodily being—the understanding of being, the limit of the horizon of Dasein's understanding of being, and so on. The most primordial ontological characteristics of Dasein include Being-in-the-world, openness, presence, ecstatic dwelling in the clearing, and so on: bodily being is "founded upon" Dasein's responsiveness to the clearing. Bodily being is possible because Being-in-the-world always already consists "of a receptive/perceptive relatedness to something which addresses us from out of the openness of our world."[22] As the ones who are addressed, we are always already directed toward the given facts of the world which are disclosed. It is due to this directedness that we are able to be bodily beings in the first place; Dasein's existence is the precondition for the possibility of bodily being.

Heidegger's response to Freud, then, was that while our bodily being is essential to our Being-in-the-world, it is our Being-in-the-world that is primordial from an ontological perspective. Hence, Heidegger accused Freud once again, of neglecting the unity of what it means to be human. Freud's conceptualization of the body remained solely on the corporeal level. Heidegger cautioned psychology as to this mode of approach: "the bodily being of man ought never to be considered as something merely present at hand," that is, merely as a physical object. "If I postulate human bodily being as something present-at-hand, I have already beforehand destroyed the body as body."[23]

Freud postulated that psychical processes are transformable into somatic ones, and vice versa. Heidegger pointed out that Freud neglected to explain how the transformation between the two could occur. According to Heidegger, since science holds the position that all subjects of study can be measured, it is incumbent upon the scientist to support any hypotheses (especially ones which include invisible things) with verifiable data. Yet Freud only asserted that the transformation occurred. Heidegger zeroed in on Freud on this point: "Is it not precisely the natural scientist who should no longer be unfamiliar with how a nonmaterial, optically invisible potentiality of comportment can be transformed into a 'bodily-material' reality?"[24]

Freud held that all human activity was necessarily subjectable to reductionistic, scientistic analysis.[25] Noting that nowhere in his writings did Freud indicate why he chose the word "analysis" for his theoretical endeavor,[26] Heidegger asked the psychologists, "What did Freud mean by 'analysis'?" They suggested that Freud meant by it the reduction of the symptoms to their origin, as in an analogy to chemical analysis, which also intends to go back to the elements.[27] Heidegger then observed that it was therefore a matter of a reduction to elements in the sense that the given—the symptoms—are dissolved into elements with the intention of explaining those symptoms by the elements thus gained. Heidegger concluded that analysis, therefore, in the Freudian sense, was considered a reduction in the sense of dissolution in order to develop a causal explanation.

However, Heidegger pointed out that analysis did not have to be limited to this reductionistic activity. He said, "But then not every reduction to 'from where' something exists and subsists is necessarily an analysis in the sense just stated."[28] For example, Heidegger noted that the ancient

Greeks had a different meaning of "analysis": "to loosen, for instance, to release a chained person from his chains, to liberate someone from captivity." This, according to Heidegger, seemed a more appropriate activity in which psychoanalysis could engage.[29]

Freud held that everything that exists is measurable.[30] Heidegger stated that, as a natural scientist, Freud simply presupposed that that which is real is founded on a precalculable nexus of causal relations *which are measurable.* "Science presupposes nature as a definite domain of beings which can be measured."[31] As such, measurability is one of the sciences' most basic presuppositions. Heidegger's critique, however, extended much farther than this; science insists on taking *exclusively* that which is measurable and quantifiable into account. By doing so, it disregards all other characteristics.[32] For Heidegger this led to some rather obvious questions: "Why can't there be something real which is not susceptible to exact measurement? Why not sorrow, for example?"[33] Are there "sorrow molecules" in teardrops? Heidegger insisted: "If the physiological dimension were the ground of the human then, for example, there would be 'farewell molecules.'"[34] Or again, "you can never actually measure tears. If you try to measure them, you measure a fluid and its drops at most, but not tears."[35] In addition, he pointed out that there are matters like presence of being, or freedom, which refuse any claim of measurability.[36] To insist on the exclusive use of measurement was to rule out of court other such highly significant dimensions of human existence at the outset.

Second, Heidegger pointed out that "what satisfies the natural scientist's claim for valid knowledge must be provable and proved by measurement."[37] Hence, Freud would then claim that the connection between psyche and soma must be measurable in some way. Heidegger stressed that this was an "unjustified claim" because it merely derived from the scientific *dogma* that only that which is measurable is real.

Freud postulated the complete explainability of psychical life in causal terms.[38] Heidegger interpreted Freud as holding the position that "only that which can be explained in terms of psychological, unbroken, causal connections between forces is actual and genuinely actual."[39] Here Heidegger understood Freud in the way that Freud, the scientist, typically understood himself (although Freud may not have completely understood the ramifications of this philosophical view)—as an unequivocal determinist. According to Heidegger's interpretation of Freud's theory, human phenomena were conceived as unbroken chains of explanations, that is, as involving the continuity of causal connections. For example, referring to *The Psychopathology of Everyday Life,* Heidegger noted that Freud presupposed that drives and forces cause phenomena and that the origins of so-called "parapraxes" can be explained by identifying those forces.[40]

Heidegger had several problems with the assumption that drives and forces cause phenomena. First, when Freud *postulated* this, he did not derive it from the psychical phenomena themselves but simply uncritically adopted the idea from natural science. Second, Freud conflated explanation with understanding.[41] Heidegger stressed that it is one thing to explain events in causal terms, it is quite another to make sense out of them in terms of the reasons behind their occurrence (see below, on Freud's conflation of "causation" and "motivation").

Furthermore, Heidegger observed that when a theorist—such as Freud—holds a deterministic view, that theorist is merely denying a preconceived notion of freedom that is represented in the natural sciences as a noncausal or acausal occurrence. This scientific notion of freedom involves a very narrow concept of freedom which contains both a positive and negative sense: we are free in the positive sense of having caprice in choice and inclination; we are free in the negative sense of being without constraints with respect to what we can and cannot do.[42] In each of these, freedom is preconceived as a *property* of man. As such, this preconception obstinately resists any other way of seeing freedom.

As a result, Heidegger believed that Freud's scientistic conception of freedom prevented him from recognizing a far more significant sense of freedom, whereby humans are "open for being claimed by the presence [being] of something."[43] This idea of freedom has nothing whatsoever to do with causal chains. Heidegger was quite explicit: "Being open for a claim lies outside the dimension of causality."[44] Hence, in Heidegger's conception of freedom, it is irrelevant whether one knows all or none of the causes of events Freud sought to analyze, for example, in *The Psychopathology of Everyday Life*. For Heidegger, what remained unapprehended in the scientific concept of freedom was the ontological dimension. On an ontological level, "freedom" is not dependent upon humans: freedom is more of a metaphorical "realm" within which one lives one's life, that is, in the Open (see in chapter 11, on "the clearing"). As such, one can be more or less open to this mode of existence. The more one is open, the more freedom is disclosed; the less one is open, the more freedom becomes concealed from that life. Yet regardless of how an individual lives, freedom is intrinsic to existence. It is more an issue of the extent to which one allows oneself to be open, to participate within the openness: the openness itself is "there" regardless of any human choice. In other words, freedom is a condition of being human. It cannot be "escaped," it can only be concealed.

Heidegger's notion of freedom involved what he called a "letting beings be." Humans participate insofar as they are openly engaged in this letting beings be. As Heidegger explained, "To let be, that is—to let beings be as the beings which they are—means to engage oneself with the open region and its openness into which every being comes to stand, bring that openness, as it were, along with itself."[45] It is as though one "steps back" into the open region and becomes a presence which allows all presences to show themselves. Hence, one must shed, for example, one's prejudgments in order to really "apprehend" what is being presented: "To engage oneself with the disclosedness of beings is . . . to withdraw in the face of beings in order that they might reveal themselves with respect to what and how they are."[46]

Also in relation to Heidegger's notion of freedom, is the sense of "exposure." Freedom ex-poses itself to humans as a possibility for existence. Humans are likewise exposing themselves when freedom becomes unconcealed. In remaining open to the experience of freedom, the concealed suddenly opens up to disclose what is truly real—what was before inaccessible is brought into awareness. Heidegger wrote, "As this letting-be, it ex-poses itself to the beings as such and transposes all comportment into the open region. Thus freedom, as this letting-be is ex-posing."[47]

In order for Dasein to let itself in on beings, it must be by its very constitution open and let itself in on the openness so that all beings comport themselves in the open.[48] This process by which Dasein lets itself in on the open is ek-static by its very essence. Hence it is by this process that Dasein stands outside itself in the direction of the open. Dasein's ek-sistence is transcendence and thereby goes beyond the beings that open to the open itself, to the world, to being. Dasein transcends beings into the open itself.[49]

Heidegger's notion of freedom is difficult to articulate. He would have acknowledged that this is, in part, do to the concealment which has taken place through the overvaluing and domination of scientistic thinking. However, Heidegger's description of freedom can be seen in its more open presencing by observing the play of a toddler prior to mastering language: a child often appears simply to engage in interest and joy, fascination and delight, without needing or attempting to categorize, analyze, judge and evaluate. Because a toddler has not yet learned to conform to social rules, she/he does not have to shed all the labels and judgments in order to simply be. As many people have witnessed, sometimes in embarrassment, there is an innocent curiosity which does not know the socially appropriate response to differences in humans. Hence, the child often appears to enjoy a more open, unconcealed freedom without the constraints of adulthood. It is this kind of freedom, one that springs from openness and joy, of which Heidegger reminds us. Recognizing that even as adults we participate more or less in this freedom brings to light that we can allow freedom to become even more unconcealed by engaging actively in the open, and by withdrawing in the face of beings revealing themselves.

It is the ability to "withdraw" in order that beings can present themselves freely, which allows for the unconcealment of truth. Yet, according to Heidegger, it was precisely scientism's unwillingness to withdraw (especially in its methodological application to humans) that served to confine not only scientific truth, but also human freedom. This was the ontological freedom from which science turned away, and hence was unable to recognize.

Returning to Heidegger's criticisms of Freud's philosophical presuppositions, Heidegger also expressed concerns with Freud's notion of "motivation." In fact, Heidegger professed not to know what the psychologists meant by motivation in the first place. In a letter to Boss in 1960, Heidegger asked a series of questions:

> Does it mean the human being as Ego, the *motivating* one, or the Ego within the human being otherwise still *motivated?* Are "human motivations" a medley of influences? Are causation and motivation distinguished from each other? Or is the fatal distinction between the conscious and the unconscious hidden behind this whole (excuse me) hodgepodge?[50]

Heidegger concluded that as one of the primary representatives of the development of naturalistic scientism, Freud was guilty of egregiously conflating "cause" and "motive." In his analysis, since Freud the determinist conceived everything as grounded in the somatic forces, "motive" too was understood as "a cause producing some event." Heidegger's rejoinder was to point out that what is causal and what is purposive—namely, a motive—are not the same.[51]

How are they different? Heidegger was explicit on this.

> *Motive* is the ground for acting this way or that, that is, for moving oneself for this or for that. Ground does not mean an efficient cause here, but it means the "for what," the "reason for." Something unconscious cannot be a "reason for" because such a "reason for" presupposes conscious awareness. Therefore, the unconscious is unintelligible.[52]

Or again, "Motive is a reason [ground of action], and this involves the fact that it is known and represented as such in contrast to a cause which merely acts on its own."[53] In other words, a motive (a reason) is not something that determines one from behind—as with Freud's "instincts," for example—but rather something standing in front, that is, a task in which Dasein is involved. The primary point here, for Heidegger, was that reasons do not necessarily make something happen, whereas causes do.

Heidegger took this distinction and applied it to that of which Freud was oblivious—the ontological dimension. Being "open for being claimed by something," means that this claim is "the ground of action, the motive." "What claims [the human being] is the motive for human response."[54] Hence, according to Heidegger, as human beings we are free and open for being claimed by the presence (being) of something. Our response to the presence of something is our motive. "Cause," on the other hand, has no place in human existence. According to Heidegger, Freud's deterministic stance was simply mistaken, and primarily an outcome of his misapplication of science to human existence. As such, these mistaken assumptions became manifest in specific elements throughout Freud's theoretical framework.

Heidegger's Criticism of Specific Freudian Concepts

Heidegger argued that since Freud could find no "uninterrupted explainability" in consciousness, he found it necessary to "invent the unconscious,"[55] thereby introducing the "fatal distinction" between the "conscious" and the "unconscious";[56] to resort to the hypothesis of "unconscious purposes" as explanations;[57] and to mistakenly construct the idea of "unconscious motivation."[58]

Here Heidegger referred to Freud's "Justification for the Conception of the Unconscious" in his metapsychology papers. It is important to be reminded of Freud's explicit formulation on this point:

> [The unconscious] is necessary because the data of consciousness are exceedingly defective; both in healthy and in sick persons mental acts are often in process which can be explained only by presupposing other acts, of which consciousness yields no evidence. These include not only the parapraxes and dreams of healthy persons, and everything designated a mental symptom or an obsession in the sick; our most intimate daily experience introduces us to sudden ideas of the source of which we are ignorant, and to results of mentation arrived at we know not how. All these conscious acts remain disconnected and unintelligible if we are determined to hold fast to the claim that every single mental act per-

formed within us must be consciously experienced; on the other hand, they fall into a demonstrable connection if we interpolate the unconscious acts we infer.[59]

Heidegger believed that it was because of Freud's presupposition that everything is caused, that his theory necessitated the creation of certain concepts like the unconscious to explain human phenomena that could not be explained within a causal (scientific) framework. It was not, then, that such aspects of human nature actually exist and can be studied, but rather that these constructs were conceived as a "necessary and legitimate" idea to conceal the fact that the scientific framework is inappropriately applied to human existence.

Furthermore, Heidegger argued, since a "motive" is a "reason for," "something unconscious cannot be a 'reason for' because such a 'reason for' presupposes conscious awareness."[60] Hence the notion of "unconscious motives" makes no sense. Heidegger concluded that Freud's notion of the unconscious was unintelligible.

To better illustrate the reasons behind Heidegger's rejection of Freud's notion of the unconscious, and his formulation of a better alternative, Boss raised the example of the act of leaving something behind.[61] Psychoanalysts have suggested that when one, for example, leaves an umbrella behind in a friend's room, this is an expression of an unconscious wish to return there later. In the psychoanalytic hypothesis, the "leaving behind" is isolated as a fact, which must then be explained in terms of some kind of unconscious intention.

Heidegger denied that there were any unconscious intentions involved in such instances. Instead, such acts of forgetting merely indicated that something was no longer considered thematically by a person in its presence. If, on the one hand, I departed from the home of a person I care deeply about, my attention may have been focused upon that person and my desire not to leave—my umbrella was still present, but it was something of which I was not thematically aware. If, on the other hand, I departed from the home of a person to whom I was indifferent, I would not, Heidegger insisted, forget my umbrella—had I left it behind, it was that I neglected to attend to it. Only departing in the rain would matter in this case. My visit with a person to whom I was indifferent was simply finished. Hence, Freud's attribution of an unconscious intention was, Heidegger claimed, a pure hypothesis which failed to help us understand the above phenomena any better.[62]

What about memories that are so painful that they become (according to Freudian theory) repressed into the unconscious? Heidegger believed that he could phenomenologically account for everything involved here without having to resort to a notion of the unconscious. Heidegger claimed that when someone forgets some painful event, she/he simply did not want to think about it. Take, for example, a situation in which I let a painful memory slip away from me. When I let this memory slip away, I increasingly preoccupied myself with something else so that this uncomfortable thought could slip away. In order to be a painful event to me, however, I must know about it. Now, I might try to avoid myself while I continue to be afflicted by this painful event, but in this avoidance of myself I am still present to myself, albeit in an unthematic way. The more I engage in this avoidance, the less I know about this avoidance—I am completely absorbed in this avoidance in a nonreflective manner. In Heidegger's opinion, this was all we needed in order to understand the process from an existential phenomenological point of view. Hence, Heidegger concluded that Freud was simply mistaken in claiming that "repression" necessitated the hypothesis of an unconscious.[63]

It might be argued that Heidegger's concept of "concealment" (see chapter 11) contains similar elements to Freud's notion of repression. However, in the *Zollikon Seminars* Heidegger clearly asserted that "concealment is not the antithesis of consciousness."[64] "Concealment is not a hiding as is Freud's 'repression'" since, even if repression existed, it would have a special way and manner of being in the clearing.[65] The kind of hiding involved in Freud's repression (if it existed) would be a representation; by way of contrast, "withdrawal in the clearing" is a matter of dealing with the phenomenon in itself. The phenomenon withdraws itself from the domain of the clearing and is inaccessible—so inaccessible that we can no longer experience it in its inaccessibility.[66] As we have seen earlier, Heidegger emphasized that the clearing is always the clearing of concealment, which means that the inaccessible manifests itself as the inaccessible (that is, as simply or momentarily inaccessible). Hence, Heidegger insisted that this concept of concealment was more primordial and conceptually unrelated to Freud's notions of "repression" and the "unconscious."

Heidegger did not limit his criticism of Freudian concepts to the unconscious. He also explicitly objected to Freud's libido theory.[67] Heidegger argued, for example, that when Freud reduced wishing, willing, and urge to "instincts" (or "drives"), he thereby eliminated human being. How so? By always searching for an explanation, Freud neglected to realize how phenomena are given in the first place. He objectified human beings with his "mythical drives"[68] and was unable to ascertain anything about the very being of human beings.

Heidegger insisted that one cannot understand Being-in-the-world—specifically, the structure of care[69]—from such psychical acts as wishing, willing, and so on. Conversely, thoughts such as "I wish I had x" are grounded in the structure of Being-in-the-world. "Willing, wishing, propensity, and urge are ways of enacting being-in-the-world."[70] Hence, it is not possible to construct Being-in-the-world from such psychical acts: Being-in-the-world is always already presupposed. Furthermore, Heidegger emphasized that the threefold, basic structure of Being-in-the-world must always be taken into consideration. He alluded to a passage from *Being and Time*: "The being of Dasein means ahead-of-itself-being-already-in (the world) as being alongside (entities encountered-within-the world)."[71] Such threefoldness is equi-primordial, whereas psychical acts such as wishing always refer to modifications of all three structural aspects of care. All three structural aspects (Being-ahead-of-oneself, Always-already-being, and Being-alongside) are always involved in our field of meaning—none are ever lost. For Heidegger, the crucial point is that Freud's theory becomes intractable when one realizes that one cannot construct the significance or meaningfulness of Being-in-the-world from such psychical acts as wishing, urging, propensities, and so on.[72] Rather, to be meaningful, to have significance, such psychical acts must always already presuppose Being-in-the-world.

Similarly, Freud's conceptions of "introjection," "projection," "empathy," and "transference" turn out to be contrived constructions predicated upon a subject–object model which is oblivious to the primordiality of Being-in-the-world.[73] In addition, such Freudian conceptions presuppose, yet abstract from, the Being-with dimension of Dasein which is intrinsic to the unity of Being-in-the-world.[74] As an *existentiale,* Being-with is that structure which is always presupposed and makes it possible for us to experience any of our possible ways of relating to others.

Freud's Response to Heidegger

One cannot help but wonder how Freud would have responded to Heidegger's extensive barrage of criticisms. Obviously, since Heidegger did not appear to discuss any of Freud's theory during his lifetime, Freud was never afforded the opportunity to address those criticisms. Hence, in what follows, "Freud" is provided with an opportunity to respond posthumously to Heidegger's criticisms. While doing so, only some of the most important points taken from Freud's perspective are provided; but Freud's "response" is as close to his own articulated position on the issues concerned as possible.[75]

First and probably foremost, against Heidegger, the aspect of Freud as an enlightenment thinker would have insisted that any investigatory enterprise worth being called such (for example, psychoanalysis) must accept the scientific Weltanschauung. Freud defined a Weltanschauung as

> an intellectual construction which solves all the problems of our existence uniformly on the basis of one overriding hypothesis, which, accordingly, leaves no question unanswered and in which everything that interests us finds its fixed place.[76]

But why did Freud insist on accepting the scientific Weltanschauung? Freud asserted that it is natural science that gives us access to knowledge. Given this, the contribution of psychoanalysis to science was its extension of research to the mental field.[77]

Furthermore, according to Freud, it was psychoanalysis that served as the ground of philosophy[78]—and not the reverse, as Heidegger asseverated.[79] Freud's point was twofold here. First, Freud conceived his "metapsychology" as the ground for everything, including psychoanalysis itself as well as philosophy. The structures his metapsychology elucidated were intended (among other things) to demonstrate how it was possible for there to be any formation of meaning in human experience at all. Second, one's philosophical perspective was seen as always antecedently founded upon the psychodynamic processes that occur within the philosopher.[80] From Freud's point of view, one could only wonder about the nature of Heidegger's childhood and the traumatic events that would have led him to contrive such opaque, bizarre reflections and speculations.

To Freud's mind, then, how did Heidegger go astray? Freud certainly could not argue that Heidegger "over-estimated the epistemological value of our logical operations," as he had argued against other philosophers.[81] Instead, Freud would have been critical of Heidegger for "accepting other sources of knowledge such as intuition."[82] Such intuition leads to a kind of mysticism which science must do everything within its power to overcome, or at least to avoid.[83] As previously discussed, Heidegger would have conceded this point by acknowledging that he had proposed the viability of alternative modes of thinking, and being open to the presencing of being.[84] Finally, Freud might have claimed that as a philosopher Heidegger "clung to the illusion that [he] can present a picture of the universe that is without gaps and is coherent."[85] Heidegger, of course, would have denied that this accurately characterized his project at all, for to do so would have been to engage in philosophical anthropology, which was not his philosophical concern. Instead, Heidegger's was an inquiry into the meaning of being, and hence an ontological inquiry.[86]

Next, Freud would have rejected in the strongest possible terms Heidegger's criticisms that he had simply invented the unconscious, and merely divided the psychical into consciousness and the unconscious. For Freud, the concept of the unconscious formed the very locus of his entire metapsychological theory, and the division between consciousness and the unconscious was "the fundamental premise of psycho-analysis."[87] As we recall, Freud insisted: "Our assumption of the unconscious is necessary and legitimate, and . . . we possess numerous proofs for its existence."[88] Freud argued that without the hypothesis of the unconscious, it would not have been possible to understand the common, everyday pathological processes in mental life. Indeed, it would not have been possible to understand in any depth the normal everyday experiences of human beings in general.[89]

Why specifically was the concept of the unconscious necessary, according to Freud?[90] It was needed to explain the gaps in consciousness, atypical acts that are out of character for a person, the reasons and/or causes behind parapraxes, psychical symptoms, and dreams in healthy people. Without it we would be unable to account for various aspects of our most personal ordinary everyday experience: when ideas pop into our heads from some unknown origin, when we arrive at intellectual conclusions without knowing how, and so on. Such acts remain disconnected and unintelligible unless "we interpolate between them unconscious acts which we have inferred."[91] The crucial point for Freud was that the concept of the unconscious leads to a significant gain in meaning—that alone made it "perfectly justifiable" for Freud's theory to transcend the limits of empirical observation. Indeed, that was why he developed his metapsychology in the first place.

Why was the concept of the unconscious considered "legitimate," according to Freud?[92] It was in alignment with the conventionally accepted modes of thinking. For example, when we assume that others have consciousness, we do not have immediate certainty, yet we continue to make this assumption. Hence, if we can assume that there is within us that which we cannot directly observe—and hence parallels the idea "as if it is in someone else"—it is just as reasonable to hold the idea of an unconscious as well. Furthermore, allowing nonempirically verifiable concepts into scientific study is especially legitimate when their adoption contributes to a more comprehensive explanation of human experience (dreams, "slips of the tongue," unintended actions, and so on).

Freud might have pointed out that despite Heidegger's obvious rejection of the unconscious and unconscious reasons, he himself had to admit that there is at the very least something else at work. Heidegger's own theory included concepts that Freud would have concluded were not entirely conscious—"call to conscience," "they-self," "concealment," and so on all indicate a sort of "unconscious" phenomena.[93]

Freud would have responded to Heidegger's denial of unconscious *reasons,* by asserting that the major thrust of psychoanalysis is to bring unconscious reasons into awareness. Without unconscious reasons, psychoanalysis would have no point. For if it were simply a matter of uncovering the unconscious *desires,* then along deterministic lines what was going to be, would be anyway, regardless of psychoanalytic intervention.

Freud also argued that philosophers (like Heidegger) simply could not make sense of the unconscious for a variety of reasons.

> To most people who have been educated in philosophy the idea of anything psychical which is not also conscious is so inconceivable that it seems to them absurd and refutable by logic. I believe this is only because they have never studied the relevant phenomena of hypnosis and dreams, which—quite apart from pathological manifestations—necessitate this view.[94]

Freud was attempting to convince philosophers (and others) to suspend their empiricistic thinking in order that something quite extraordinary might be discovered about the human mind. Freud truly believed that his experience as a psychoanalyst, along with his studies on human nature, necessitated the concept of the unconscious. Philosophers were not in the position, perhaps, to understand this.

> Experience (gained from pathological material, of which the philosophers were ignorant) of the frequency and power of impulses of which one knew nothing directly and whose existence had to be inferred like some fact in the external world, left no alternative open.[95]

Heidegger, then, simply had not sufficiently studied dreams, hypnosis, and various pathological materials; neither did he have any relevant concrete experience with psychoanalysands undergoing therapy. Heidegger's judgment, then, was based on ignorance.

For Freud, despite his expostulations, Heidegger would simply have been seen as yet another victim of "the dogma of philosophers, i.e., that psychical life = consciousness."[96] Had he had the opportunity, perdurance, and patience to read Heidegger, Freud would have pointed out that in his argument that the unconscious is unintelligible, Heidegger had put his cards on the table: "Something unconscious cannot be a 'reason for' because such a 'reason for' presupposes conscious awareness."[97] Heidegger simply assumed that for person y to have a motive x, y must be conscious of x. Hence, for Freud, Heidegger simply presupposed that there are no unconscious motives, which was to simply engage in *petitio principii*.

Finally, Freud could have responded to Heidegger's analysis of "leaving behind the umbrella" in the following way. Freud would claim that Heidegger's depiction of this situation was far too simple in terms of how his concepts of repression and the unconscious operate. Heidegger, once again, was merely begging the question by assuming that a person would not forget his/her umbrella if one particular reason did not hold. His inadequate analysis of the umbrella neglected the complex processes of the unconscious. For example, it might be the case that the color of the umbrella was associated with a repressed traumatic event of childhood that occurred in a shopping center, hence one might very well forget his or her umbrella based on an unconscious purpose or motive.

Freud would assert that Heidegger's account was inadequate for a variety of reasons. First, in Heidegger's description there was the non sequitur that the person "also knows about this painful event, otherwise it could not be a painful event."[98] Freud, however, was prepared for this.

> To begin with it may happen that an affect or an emotion is perceived, but misconstrued. By the repression of its proper presentation it is forced to become connected with another idea, and is now interpreted by consciousness as the expression of this other idea. If we restore the true connection, we call the original affect "unconscious," although the affect was never unconscious but its ideational presentation had undergone repression.[99]

In other words one might not know the content of the painful event as an idea, and yet still feel its pain. Next, against Heidegger, Freud pointed out that forgetting can occur for a number of singular or combined reasons—as in Freud's concept of "overdetermination"—although it must always have at least one reason. It could be a hysterical symptom, an expression of hostility, an expression of guilt, motivated by avoidance of pain, and so on.

How would Freud have responded to Heidegger's charge that it was incumbent upon him as a natural scientist to account for the connection between the physical and the mental, and that Freud had simply failed to do so? On one level, Freud would have responded by saying that throughout his theory he argued that it is the instincts that provided the link between the mind and the body. Originating in organic processes, instincts are responsible for the development of psychical representatives (wishes, as ideas and images) with an affective charge in the mental apparatus whose goal is the diminution of unpleasurable bodily excitation. For

Freud, this accounted for how meaning emerges into the world. Second, Freud did concede that the problem raised by Heidegger is difficult. Freud wrote, "the leap from the mental to the physical is . . . puzzling."[100]

> Every attempt to go on from [brain anatomy] to discover a localization of mental processes, every endeavor to think of ideas as stored up in nerve-cells and of excitations as traveling along nerve-fibres, has miscarried completely.[101]

> In view of the intimate connection between the things that we distinguish as physical and mental, we may look forward to a day when paths of knowledge, and let us hope, of influence will be opened up, leading from organic biology and chemistry to the field of neurotic phenomena. That day still seems a distant one . . .[102]

Freud also wrote, "Meanwhile, we shall have to reserve discussion of what lies between the terminal points of the brain and consciousness for 'philosophical thought.' "[103] Heidegger, no doubt, would have found these to be unsatisfying responses, especially in light of the stark lack of progress on this score.

Next, how would Freud have responded to Heidegger's charge that he merely conflated "motive" with "cause" in his metapsychological theory? This is a difficult question given our claim that even though Freud seemed, at least at times, to take himself to be a typical determinist in the standard scientific sense of the term, his position is more philosophically grounded in Schopenhauerean metaphysical theory. Seen within the context of Schopenhauer's philosophy, Heidegger's analysis would simply fail to apply, since the impetus of Heidegger's criticism failed to consider Freud's "determinism" in an alternative way from the standard scientific context (see chapter 17). However, within the scientific framework within which Freud consciously participated, he would have likely conceded that he equated "motive" and "cause." Freud's metapsychological theory held that all psychical as well as physical events are strictly determined. All human psychical activities are seen as ultimately traceable to somatic processes which, given their material, physicochemical nature, are governed by the laws of nature. These somatic processes are determined by the organism's physical environment and hereditary structure. Since the instincts are either somatic processes or grounded in them, they are determined; since they also are responsible for meaning-formations such as wishes, these psychical meaning-formations also must be determined. According to Freud's metapsychology, then, any occurrence outside this causal chain would literally be "meaningless." Indeed, it was the above linkage of meaning and causality that permitted Freud to equate "motive" with "cause" in his metapsychological theory.[104]

This was most clearly visible in his concept of "overdetermination." By it Freud meant that any given object-choice—that is, an object which would satisfy and thus eliminate the instinctual tension—might satisfy a multiplicity of instincts. Thus the selection of a particular object-choice could have several "motives" or "causes." In his metapsychological theory, Freud tended not to distinguish between the two.[105] Hence, he would likely have responded to Heidegger's allegation that his metapsychological theory conflated "motive" and "cause" by pointing out that the two are necessarily interchangeable, and, hence, to equate the two is not the same as to conflate them. Thus, Freud would have likely agreed that this position was true for his metapsychological theory.[106]

In summary, Freud would simply have dismissed Heidegger's criticism that he was oblivious to the ontological dimension (of human *being*, the clearing, concealment, and so on). Freud consciously found such "mystical" viewpoints simply distasteful: Heidegger's approach was exactly the kind of view that the scientific Weltanschauung was specifically designed to combat and overcome. Freud's concern was clear: "Once science has been disposed of, the space vacated may be filled by some kind of mysticism."[107] Furthermore, even if Freud had conceded that he was egregiously oblivious to the ontological dimension, he probably would have pointed out that his theory still made significant contributions to the understanding of everyday human existence (on the ontical level). To fall short in ontological understanding does not entail that what one says on the everyday level of human experience is insignificant. Indeed, the posthumous success, power, and influence of Freudian psychoanalysis are a testament to this fact.

("Lack" of) Fathers and Sons: Sartre and Freud

> Every existing thing is born without reason, prolongs itself out of weakness and dies by chance.
> —Sartre

> The moment a man questions the meaning and value of life, he is sick, since objectively neither has any existence; by asking this question one is merely admitting to a store of unsatisfied libido to which something else must have happened, a kind of fermentation leading to sadness and depression.
> —Freud

Sartre is a spectacular example of a philosopher who employed the notions of "apprehending" and the "inaccessible" in a dialectical tension throughout his philosophical career. He both spoke of nothing as hidden in human experience—as our having access to everything—and yet asserted that a great deal of that which *is*, is "inapprehensible."

Early in his philosophical career, in the early sections of *Being and Nothingness,* Sartre made clear his position that with regard to human experience "nothing is hidden." He concurred with Nietzsche's repudiation of "the illusion of worlds-behind-the-scene."[1] In line with Hegel's rejection of the Kantian noumenal realm, Sartre held "what [the phenomenon] is, it is absolutely, for it reveals itself as it is . . . it is absolutely indicative of itself."[2] Being is not concealed in some way behind the phenomena, but rather "is simply the condition of all revelation."[3] And yet, as such, "Being will be disclosed to us by some kind of immediate access."[4] Immediate access, for Sartre, included experiences such as boredom, nausea, and so on. These are the phenomena of being as it is manifested.

For Sartre, there are also those features of human experience which are accessible to us but have been hitherto unapprehended. The for-itself is a hidden reality insofar as it remains unreflected upon; my original choice is typically unrevealed as a manifestation of my pursuit of the fundamental project of being the in-itself-for-itself.[5] However, Sartre went much further and spoke of the unknowable or inapprehensible throughout *Being and Nothingness*. Even though the being of the phenomenon is coextensive with the phenomenon, it is not subject to the condition that it exists only insofar as it reveals itself. Hence being surpasses the knowledge which we have of it and provides the basis for such knowledge.[6] There are many other features of human experience that are inapprehensible as well: (1) when another person looks at me, I experience the inapprehensibility of the subjectivity of the Other as this subjectivity experiences itself—such apprehension of the Other is an ontological impossibility;[7] (2) "I am inaccessible to myself"[8] because I cannot make myself an object for myself;[9] (3) my senses are inapprehensible; (4) my body, or my flesh,[10] is inapprehensible; (5) it is impossible for me to apprehend the evanescent contingency which the for-itself has derived from the in-itself (facticity)—it is impossible to grasp facticity in its brute nudity[11] or as it happens;[12] (6) it is impossible to apprehend the in-itself-for-itself as a metaphysical being;[13] and (7) freedom assumes death as the inapprehensible limit of its subjectivity.[14]

This dialectical tension in Sartre's position is clearly demonstrated by considering two examples. First, Sartre developed his account of existential psychoanalysis in order to reveal how original choices manifested an individual's fundamental pursuit of being: such original choices were not immediately accessible and required some assistance in accessing them. Second, Sartre's analysis of the for-itself included "an apprehension of being as a lack of being."[15] Sartre wrote, "the fissure within consciousness is a nothing except . . . that it can have being only as we do not see it."[16] Nothingness is apprehended as a "rupture" in being, as such it "does not refer us elsewhere to another being; it is only a perpetual reference of self to self."[17] As illustrated by this example, Sartre's approach was quite self-consciously, transcendentally circular in nature—he was simultaneously speaking of what it is we apprehend, while noting that he was identifying (in this case, nothingness) that which makes possible our capacity for apprehending in the first place. To do so, he believed, was to establish the connection of consciousness with the world.

In Sartre's view, if there were no such thing as consciousness, there would be no distinctions or differentiations within the realm of being. Borrowing from Spinoza's and Hegel's basic principle that "all determination is negation," Sartre claimed that determinate reality with its differentiations is possible only because one thing is distinguished from another, and this means that there must be negations in being.[18] It is consciousness which introduces determinations into reality by introducing negations. What is it about consciousness that makes it possible to introduce nothingness into the world? Consciousness at its very core is itself a nothingness. As we shall see, this dialectical tension in Sartre's position resulted in a particularly tumultuous engagement with Freudian psychoanalysis.

Sartre's Engagement with Freudian Psychoanalysis

Among the major existential phenomenologists, Sartre exhibited the most profound and protracted interest in Freud's work. Freud was one of the select few intellectual figures who pervaded the entire span of Sartre's adult intellectual life. His reading of Freud and final comments spanned a period of over fifty-five years (1920–75). Yet throughout his philosophical development Sartre exhibited a *tempestuous ambivalence* toward Freudian psychoanalysis. Generally speaking, the nature of Sartre's ambivalence diachronically moved from an initial reaction of outright repugnance, to seeing Freud's psychoanalysis as an innocuous interpretive mythology, and ended in a willingness to incorporate it into the most viable synthesis of a worldview possible.[19] Synchronically, Sartre's reaction to Freud was at various times one of repugnance versus curiosity; intense critique of its principles and underlying thing-ontology (a causalism that reduced consciousness to a "thing") versus acknowledgement of the truth of some of its insights; less intense critique versus respectful portrayal and utilization of some of Freud's ideas; to critique versus incorporation of Freud's method into a synthesized worldview.

Obviously Sartre's relationship to Freudian psychoanalysis was extremely complex. In fact, one might even say that, in good Hegelian style, Sartre assimilated and incorporated Freudian psychoanalysis while at the same time rejecting it. Sartre embraced this point by describing himself as a "critical fellow-traveller" of psychoanalysis.[20] He unquestionably knew and acknowledged that Freud was on to something very important in pursuit of that which had hitherto been inaccessible, yet he largely rejected the language, theoretical worldview, and techniques which Freud employed in his approach to apprehending it. In the end, Sartre's idea was to correct Freud's ontological inadequacy while salvaging its merits and useful results.

Sartre's Familiarity with and Ambivalence toward Freud's Work

In his student years (1924–29), Sartre first encountered Freud by reading *The Psychopathology of Everyday Life* for a philosophy course during his first year at the École Normale Supérieure (1924–25). While at the École, he also read *The Interpretation of Dreams*.[21] Sartre's attitude toward Freud's work, during this period at least, was ostensibly quite unambiguous: he experienced "a deep repugnance for psychoanalysis in [his] youth."[22] Sartre emphasized that he was especially "deeply shocked" by the idea of the unconscious and the "inevitable" biologistic-mechanistic language used to explain its functions. Sartre's philosophical training, steeped as it was in the Cartesian tradition, made it nearly impossible for him to understand Freud's position. Sartre felt he was unable to even begin to assimilate the complex mental processes and cultural descriptions Freud had adumbrated in, for example, *The Psychopathology of Everyday Life:* "when you read all that, your breath is taken away."[23] They were simply "too far removed from rational, Cartesian thinking,"[24] and as such, foreign to Sartre's primary philosophical concerns.

In *The Prime of Life,* Simone de Beauvoir elaborated on Sartre's and her attitudes toward Freudian psychoanalysis during 1929 and the following several years.[25] She acknowledged that during that time psychoanalysis "was beginning to spread in France" and "many young people were rallying" to it.[26] Yet she and Sartre maintained "only a rudimentary knowledge" which was ever "so sketchy" of it. Here, de Beauvoir confirmed Sartre's recollection: "We had hardly read any Freud apart from his books *The Interpretation of Dreams* and *The Psychopathology of Everyday Life.*"[27] This being the case, the natural question arises as to why they were not inclined to investigate it more extensively.

It is at this juncture that we witness what were possibly the first seeds of Sartre's (and de Beauvoir's) ambivalence toward Freudian psychoanalysis. On the one hand "certain aspects of it interested us": "We looked favorably on the notion that psychoses, neuroses, and their various symptoms had a meaning, and that this meaning must be sought in the patient's childhood."[28] On the other hand, this consideration was outweighed by a plethora of concerns:

> We rejected psychoanalysis as a tool for exploring a normal human being. We were put off by their dogmatic symbolism and the technique of association which vitiated them for us. Freud's pansexualism had an element of madness about it . . . Above all, the importance it attached to the uncon-

scious, and the rigidity of its mechanistic theories, meant that Freudian-
ism, as we conceived it, was bound to eradicate human free will.[29]

The tenor of de Beauvoir's account clearly showed that especially during
this period she and Sartre were experiencing a call to arms. "We were concerned with safeguarding [freedom's] existence—for it was in danger."
This was why, then, when they read *The Psychopathology of Everyday Life* and
The Interpretation of Dreams they had "absorbed the letter rather than the
spirit of these works."[30] In doing so, they thought that they could escape
the pernicious effects the shadow Freudian thought had cast over their
own Zeitgeist.

Sartre apparently maintained this attitude in the earlier part of his
teaching years (1931–37) as he delved "deeper into the doctrine of Freud."[31]
Simone de Beauvoir pointed out that Sartre was so engrossed by psychoanalysis, that by 1932 he had already generated a theory designed to make
Freud's notion of the unconscious superfluous.[32] Interestingly enough, in
one of his earliest pieces of fiction, "Childhood of a Leader" (1938),[33] Sartre
metaphorically expressed Freud's strong influence on him by focusing on
such Freudian notions as sexuality, dreams, childhood experiences, pa-
rental relationships with children, and so on. However, Sartre clearly maintained a skeptical attitude toward psychoanalysis as he parodied these ideas.
A couple of examples clearly illustrate this. In one case, Sartre had one of
its characters articulate his thoughts on psychoanalysis as an ephemeral
intellectual fad, whose most vital insights were already articulated by Plato,
with nothing to add. In another case, two of the primary protagonists were
self-congratulatory as to the size of their complexes.

It was during the years between *The Emotions: Outline of a Theory*
(1937)[34] and *Being and Nothingness* (1943) that Sartre offered his most extensive and sustained philosophical reflection on Freud, and it was during
this time that Sartre was most intensely ambivalent toward Freudian
psychoanalysis. Indeed, Sartre's preoccupation with psychoanalysis was so
strong in *The Emotions* that while he devoted its first chapter to the other
rival theories he wished to refute (William James, Pierre Janet, Wolfgang
Köhler), psychoanalysis received a separate chapter (one of three).

In *The Emotions*, Sartre credited psychoanalysis with being the first
to recognize the significance of the hiddenness of meaning in psychic life
and appreciated the symbolic connection it established among emotions
as "gratifications of sexual tendencies." Furthermore, he wrote:

> As for us, we do not reject the results of psychoanalysis when they are
> obtained by comprehension. We limit ourselves to denying any value
> and any intelligibility to its subjacent theory of psychic causality.[35]

Sartre, then, rejected in no uncertain terms the principle of explanation that psychoanalysis purported to give. Yet, like Merleau-Ponty, he sought to salvage the merits of psychoanalysis while providing it with a more appropriate philosophical grounding.

In *Being and Nothingness,* Sartre dealt specifically with Freudian psychoanalysis in two extensive sections.[36] Early in this text, Sartre claimed that Freud's theory of human nature served as a perfect example of bad faith. Later he pointed out what was useful from Freudian psychoanalysis, and what served as an impetus and a point of departure for—that is, contrasted it with—the development of his own form of existential psychoanalysis.

On the negative side, Sartre criticized Freud for (1) holding an incoherent theory of an unconscious and all of the ramifications that ensued from it; (2) the mechanistic-causal underpinnings of his theory of the unconscious, which Sartre claimed were inconsistent with its teleological features (the purposiveness of human behavior); (3) holding a vague, arbitrary, and exiguous theory of motivation; (4) advocating the irreducibility of an a priori biological theory which failed to convincingly show its connection to human action;[37] and (5) failing to account for the emergence of meaning (namely, intentionality) in the world (the phenomenological reality of interpersonal relationships, love, sexual desire, and so on).

On the positive side, Sartre credited Freudian psychoanalysis with being the first to recognize the crucial importance of the existence of hidden structures underlying psychical acts. Moreover, Sartre refused to reject several of the most important theoretical concepts of Freudian psychoanalysis. For example, not only did Sartre *not* reject the notion of the Oedipus complex in *Being and Nothingness,* he employed analogical complexes (for example, the Acteon and Jonah complexes).[38] Furthermore, Sartre never repudiated the existence of the ego in this context— he merely made it an object of pre-reflective consciousness. These comments will be further explored when we consider Sartre's analysis of Freudian psychoanalysis in the following chapters.

In his psychobiography *Baudelaire* (1947), Sartre engaged in what might be regarded as an ongoing debate with Freud in such a way that his ambivalence for Freudian psychoanalysis was equally apparent.[39] Traditional themes, such as overdetermination, defense mechanisms, the Oedipus complex, and so on, appeared throughout the text. However, Sartre understood himself to be showing that meaning structures such as the Oedipus complex were still merely secondary—they had an underlying pursuit (as choice) of being which operated on a more fundamental level. Soon thereafter, in a discussion of his paper "Consciousness and Knowledge," delivered at the French philosophical society in 1948, Sartre argued that instrumentally speaking, the concept of the unconscious was useless and superfluous.[40]

However, manifesting his deep ambivalence for Freud once again, in 1951 Sartre alluded to the significant contributions made by psychoanalysis:

> . . . the existentialist's stress on the basest function: The reason why we speak of even the most humble functions of the body is that we must not pretend to have forgotten that the spirit descends into the body, or . . . the psychological into the physiological . . . in my view the writer ought to grasp man whole . . . There is an interaction between sex and thought, as we have been taught by psychoanalysis, to which we owe a considerable enhancement of psychology, and which is not yet sufficiently known.[41]

In 1957, John Huston asked Sartre to write a screenplay for a film on Freud he was contemplating. He regarded Sartre as the "ideal man to write the Freud screenplay . . . He knew Freud's works intimately and would have an objective and logical approach."[42] Sartre himself noted the irony of this request and his acceptance of it, given his well-known and unwavering philosophical opposition to the notion of Freud's unconscious.[43] Meanwhile, lacking money, Sartre tackled this project seriously and with a great deal of enthusiasm.[44] He spent hundreds of hours working on what was to become an ill-fated manuscript. Sartre reputedly gave a 400-page manuscript (in French) to Huston, who said it was much too long for a Hollywood screenplay and returned it for revision. Supposedly Sartre reworked the lengthy manuscript and later returned to Huston with his revised manuscript of more than 800 pages![45] Due to its inordinate length it was unacceptable as a screenplay for a roughly ninety-minute film—by Sartre's own admission, it would have lasted eight or nine hours. The manuscript (and its revisions) have been subsequently published in *The Freud Scenario*.[46]

In recounting his intention regarding the screenplay, and subsequently *The Freud Scenario*, Sartre's sympathy toward Freud and his work (which, of course, constituted part of his ambivalence) was evident:

> What we tried to do was to show Freud not when his theories had made him famous, but at the time, around the age of thirty, when he was utterly wrong; when his ideas had led him into hopeless error. You know that at one point he seriously believed that what caused hysteria was fathers raping their daughters. We begin in that period, and follow his career up to the discovery of the Oedipus Complex.

That, for me, is the most enthralling time in the life of a great discoverer—when he seems muddled and lost, but has the genius to collect himself and put everything in order. Of course, it is difficult to explain this development to an audience ignorant of Freud. In order to arrive at the right ideas, one must start by explaining the wrong ones . . .[47]

Sartre's experience with *The Freud Scenario* contributed to his ambivalence toward Freud. For though Sartre was not in agreement with most of Freud's ideas (the unconscious, repression, and so on), he developed an immense respect for the person, and treated Freud's work in a very respectful manner throughout the manuscript. For example, he portrayed Freud as having the courage to examine in an open-minded way the evidence he encountered in the therapeutic context.

Though Sartre admitted that his work with the Freud manuscript led him to "rethink" his ideas regarding the unconscious,[48] Sartre also found himself becoming *more* critical of the inadequacies he perceived in psychoanalysis, specifically its lack of dialectics. Sartre believed that Freudian psychoanalysis was unable to show how phenomena not only derived from one another, but how each conditioned future occurrences while simultaneously retaining and superseding past occurrences. Freudian psychoanalysis was merely "syncretic" in Sartre's eyes.[49]

It is important to note here that although John Huston's decision to recruit Sartre for his screenplay was based on his opinion that Sartre was an expert on Freudian psychoanalysis, Sartre's actual exposure to Freud's writings was quite limited. At the time, Freud had published extensively in the field of psychoanalysis, and these works were easily accessible to Sartre in his research for the project. Yet Sartre indicated that he merely reread the *Interpretation of Dreams,* read Freud's autobiographical study, and (since he wanted to focus on the early Freud) read the *Studies on Hysteria.* Sartre also consulted some critical commentaries on Freud's work, along with the biography of Freud that had been recently published by E. Jones. After having conducted this research, Sartre claimed in an interview (May 1975) that he "had acquired an average, satisfactory knowledge of Freud."[50] It is obvious that Sartre's engagement with Freud's actual works did not exactly constitute a thorough and comprehensive reservoir of information from which to draw.

At this juncture, we shall adduce one prototypical example to illustrate the *profound* extent of the limitation of Sartre's understanding of Freudian psychoanalysis. In *Being and Nothingness,* while comparing his own existential psychoanalysis to Freud's, Sartre declared that for both forms "there are no primary givens such as hereditary dispositions, character."[51] This is a remarkable statement given that Freud emphasized the following crucial threads of psychoanalysis throughout almost his entire intellectual career: "the role of heredity in the aetiology of neurosis," "hereditary disposition to neurosis," "heredity factors and acquired characters," "phylogenetic inheritance," and "archaic heritage."[52] Indeed, Freud was forthright on this point:

> What was acquired by our forefathers certainly forms an important part of what we inherit . . . it does not imply any mystical overvaluation of heredity if we think it credible that, even before the ego has come into existence, the lines of development, trends and reactions which it will exhibit are already laid down for it. The psychological peculiarities of families, races, and nations . . . allow of no other explanation. Indeed, more than this: analytic experience has forced on us a conviction that even particular psychical contents, such as symbolism, have no other sources than hereditary transmission, and researches in various fields of social anthropology, make it plausible to suppose that other, equally specialized precipitates left by early human development are also present in the archaic heritage.[53]

One can see from the references involved here that all of Freud's remarks on this subject occurred in those numerous works of Freud's with which Sartre was not familiar.

It is also the case that Sartre had no direct personal experience with psychoanalytic therapy. However, there is a great deal of evidence to show that he was especially interested in the process during the interval he was writing his autobiography, *The Words*.[54] For example, Jean-Bertrand Pontalis—a psychoanalyst and friend of Sartre's—observed:

> I recall that in order to carry through this autobiography which was turning into a "self-analysis," Sartre decided to note down his dreams . . . To undergo projective tests. That he even envisaged embarking on analysis. What did psychoanalysis represent to him? A useful, no doubt indispensable, instrument of knowledge; but an *instrument* that once he had set to work he would succeed in appropriating.[55]

What occurred here was, of course, no more than an expression of intellectual curiosity on Sartre's part—he was curious about the process of the psychoanalytic method. In light of this, Sartre went so far as to request that Pontalis analyze him.[56] Pontalis, a consummate professional, appropriately declined.

Sartre's ambivalence toward Freudian psychoanalysis continued into his later years. For instance, in 1964 he made it clear that Freud had, indeed, been one of the primary thinkers who had exerted an immense impact on his intellectual life.[57] And in retrospect, on the topic of his *Freud Scenario,* Sartre offered a summary of the film as he envisioned it:

> The subject of the scenario is really: a man sets about knowing others because he sees this as the only way of getting to know himself; he realizes he must carry out his research upon others and upon himself simultaneously. We know ourselves through others, we know others through ourselves.[58]

For the philosopher of *Being and Nothingness* and the *Critique of Dialectical Reason,* this theme held a special attraction. Sartre rejected the scientistic ideal of attaining objectivity through detachment. Instead, he held that the dialectic discloses itself only to an investigator whose inquiries are immersed within his or her personal experience, as well as being those that seek to modify the universe itself.[59] When Freud analyzed his own dreams and himself along with conducting an analysis on others, he changed the history of human thought while discovering the truth about himself.[60]

It was in his *Search for a Method*[61] and *Critique of Dialectical Reason,*[62] that Sartre's ambivalence not only continued, but manifested itself in a different form. In the *Search for a Method,* Sartre held that it was fine that psychoanalysis had no theoretical foundation as long as it was accompanied by "in certain works of Freud—a completely innocuous mythology."[63] Sartre continued this point of view in his *Critique of Dialectical Reason:*

> What psychoanalysts lack is opposition, at least in certain respects (for there is dialectical conflict between the id, the superego and the ego). They have nonetheless constructed a rationality . . . the analysed subject appears a true whole . . . The truth is, however, that his being is passivity, at least in "classical" psychoanalysis.[64]

It was the Marxist interpretation of history and methodological approach which the later Sartre saw as providing the theoretical foundation for everything, including psychoanalysis. Sartre came to strongly believe, nonetheless, that psychoanalytic ideas could make valuable contributions to the most complete understanding of an individual.

In 1969, during a torrent of controversy, Sartre expressed his deep-seated ambivalence by expressing both sympathy for and strong reservations about Freudian psychoanalysis: "I am not a 'false friend' of psychoanalysis, but a critical fellow-traveller, and I have neither the desire, nor the wherewithal, to ridicule it."[65] In the incident of "The Man with the

Tape-recorder," on the one hand, Sartre objected specifically to certain aspects of psychoanalytic practice. Indeed, he was unsparingly direct: "the psychoanalytical relationship is, by its very nature, a violent one."[66] More specifically, it "represents a tragedy of impossible reciprocity" between the participants, and one whereby interpretations are imposed upon the analysand. The result is that she/he is made to be a "passive object (i.e., a thing)." On the other hand, Sartre softened his critique by going on to acknowledge the "immense gains of psychoanalytic knowledge," noting that some techniques of traditional psychoanalysis (for example, the couch method) may be necessary at times, but that "no progress will be made unless both approaches [namely, face-to-face encounter of mutually engaged subjects and the couch method] are grasped together."[67]

In an interview entitled "The Itinerary of a Thought" a dramatic change occurred with regard to Sartre's ambivalence. He wrote,

> . . . the manner in which [Freud] the psychoanalytic object suffers from a kind of mechanistic cramp. This is not always true, for there are moments when he transcends this. But in general this language produces a *mythology* of the unconscious which I cannot accept. I am completely in agreement with the *facts* of disguise and repression, as facts. But the *words* "repression," "censorship," or "drive"—words which express one moment a sort of finalism and the next moment a sort of mechanism, these I reject.
>
> Psychoanalytic theory is . . . a "soft" thought. It has no dialectical logic to it . . . what is missing in conventional psychoanalytic accounts is the idea of dialectical irreducibility . . . I do not believe in the unconscious in the form in which psychoanalysis presents it to us.[68]

Here we see a softening of Sartre's position on Freudian concepts. His early rejection of such notions as "repression," "censorship," and "drive" evolved into a more informed and deeper understanding which, though not exactly accepting, was certainly more open to the spirit of Freudian concepts.

With this deeper appreciation of the meaning underlying Freudian psychoanalysis, Sartre was able to come to some kind of resolution in his own philosophical struggle. In his final major project, on Flaubert,[69] Sartre worked toward a synthesis of Freudian and existential psychoanalysis, along with Marxist methodology. It is also apparent that in his later works Sartre made freer use of Freudian language as he attempted a dialectical reconciliation of existential psychoanalysis and Marxism. Apparently, the core reason for this was the fundamental shift in Sartre's position on the nature and extent of human freedom. Early on, Sartre had objected as vociferously as possible to Freud's theory of psychic causality;[70] no conditioning factors on human action at all were admissible. Later, Sartre expressed amazement that he could have ever believed such a thing.[71] Hence, it is not surprising to see Sartre temper his later remarks on Freudian psychoanalysis in this regard.

At the end of this conflicted itinerary of thought, one major point remains clear: Sartre, by his own admission, never possessed a very extensive knowledge of Freudian psychoanalysis. And it was this, in particular, which led him to commit some very serious errors while critically reflecting on Freud's system and which also places some of the cogency of his criticism in abeyance. This will become apparent in the following chapters, as well as in many of the "Freudian" responses to Sartre's criticisms.

14

"The Science That Never Was": Sartre's Critique of Freudian Metapsychology

Strictly speaking, there are only two sciences; psychology . . . and natural science.
—Freud

Quite frankly, I do not believe in the existence of psychology. I have not done it, and I do not believe it exists.
—Sartre

Sartre's criticisms of Freudian metapsychology were extensive and complex, reflecting at times his deep-seated ambivalence. Even very early on, Sartre seemed genuinely to appreciate psychoanalysis's serious acknowledgment that there was more to being human than surface appearances. Psychoanalysis's recognition that there are deeper meanings and interpretations to human activity, that everything in human activity is meaningful, that we are mysterious even to ourselves, and so on, were tremendous insights and could contribute toward a fuller human understanding. Yet the instrument used in an attempt to uncover these mysteries—namely, the instrument of science—as Sartre perceived it, was seriously flawed. Insofar as Freud was a scientist and made use of scientific explanations, psychoanalysis suffered.

Due to the complexity of Sartre's criticisms, the following critique is organized into four major sections within which more specific criticisms are developed. This has the added benefit of allowing "Freud" to respond to each major criticism without losing contact with the specific arguments.[1] In general, Sartre accused Freud (1) of uncritically adopting science as providing an explanation for human nature, while (a) holding two incompatible scientific explanations (mechanistic and finalistic) which conflated causality and purpose, (b) misunderstanding the distinction between "explanation" and "comprehension" (understanding) and purporting to offer the former by reifying and dissecting consciousness, and (c) losing sight of the individual within the universal; (2) of misapplying the scientific method to the self, thereby (a) misrepresenting the self as a thing, (b) splitting the "thing" that was self into a subject and object, (c) consequently failing to account for the emergence of meaning, and (d) falsely presenting humans as causally determined; (3) of sacrificing human freedom and thus robbing humans of what is intrinsic to their being—freedom, creativity, anguish, temporality, and moral responsibility; and (4) of splitting up consciousness and developing the notion of an unconscious, exemplifying all of Freud's fundamental mistakes. This final point will be taken up in the next chapter.

The Misapplication of Scientific Explanation

Sartre accused Freud of having assumed that scientific reflection and observation were the only true sources of knowledge. Hence the mind was considered an object for scientific research just like anything else.[2] This was the attitude and approach toward human beings which most offended Sartre. Even with his "softening" toward Freudian psychoanalysis later in life, Sartre never came to the point of embracing the practice of applying scientific methodology to human beings. "Quite frankly," he said in a 1972 interview, "I do not believe in the existence of psychology."[3] Typical of Sartre's humor, he boldly conveyed his total rejection of psychology as a science (that is, as anything other than mere psychobiography). This was not only because psychology treated humans as objects to be investigated and was therefore fundamentally misguided from the start, but because of the nature of the theory of explanation it presupposed.

Freud's Presupposed Theories of Explanation as Incompatible

According to Sartre, Freud's adoption of the scientific perspective presupposed a mechanistic account of human nature whereby humans were understood to be rigidly subject to the principle of cause and effect (Freud's determinism). Within this framework, however, Sartre contended that Freud could not account for his notions of, for example, "repression" and "resistance." For to say that a person is caused to do *x* is not the same as to say that a person purposively does *x*. One must have a *purpose* in order for repression and resistance to be possible at all. In other words, Sartre believed that one must have an "intent" or "meaning" in order to engage in Freud's repression or resistance. Hence, Sartre believed that Freud was forced to go beyond this purely mechanistic account to incorporate a "finalistic" or teleological account of human nature.[4] Sartre must have had in mind Freud's statement:

> The individual does actually carry on a twofold existence: one to serve his own purposes and the other as a link in a chain, which he serves against his will, or at least involuntarily. The individual himself regards sexuality as one of his own ends; whereas from another point of view he is an appendage to his germ-plasm, at whose disposal he puts his energies in return for a bonus of pleasure . . . This makes it probable that it is special substances and chemical processes which perform the operations of sexuality and provide for the extension of individual life into that of the species.[5]

This allowed Freud to introduce purpose into his explanation; yet Sartre pointed out that these two kinds of scientific explanations—"mechanistic" and "finalistic"—were incompatible.

Sartre also saw an incompatibility between the scientific explanation presupposed in Freud's theoretical account of human nature and Freud's attempt to "comprehend" via his therapeutic approach. According to Sartre, it was the psychoanalytic theoretician who got caught in the transcendent bonds of a rigid causal web, while the practitioner flexibly approached an understanding of the analysand through the bonds of comprehension.[6] In these two distinct frameworks, Freud wound up conflating *explanation* with *description* (understanding). Sartre expressed it this way several years later: Freudian psychoanalysis is "a study based on comprehension that is hidden beneath an analytic and explanatory myth."[7] It was only the "explanatory myth" to which Sartre denied any value and intelligibility. Such "explanations" were about as far as one could get from genuinely understanding human reality.

Comprehension/Understanding versus Explanation

Early in his philosophical career Sartre was impressed by the fact that psychoanalysis (beginning with Freud) had put us in a better position to understand people by initiating the emphasis on "the signification of psychic facts; that is, it was the first to insist upon the fact that every state of consciousness is the equivalent of something other than itself."[8] Sartre did not deny that psychoanalytical interpretations of states of consciousness enabled us to make, at least at times, "internal" sense (what Sartre called "comprehension") of the phenomena of consciousness. However, to retain the truth of the Cartesian cogito, Sartre insisted that it was crucial to see that in order for "comprehension" to occur there could be no separation between "the signification, and the thing signified."[9] Hence we must understand from *within* the structure of consciousness the meaning of its acts: on this level, nothing was to be understood as being in some way *behind* consciousness. Sartre thought that psychoanalysis recognized this in one fundamental way: "for [it] there is always an internal analogy between the conscious fact and the desire which it expresses, since *the conscious fact symbolizes with the complex which is expressed.*"[10] Hence, signification was to be considered "constitutive" of consciousness itself—it was seen as intrinsic to the very nature of consciousness, as "an interstructural bond of consciousness." This was what Sartre called an "immanent bond of *comprehension.*" As such, everything was to be understood (even by psychoanalysts) as occurring within consciousness itself. So far, so good. But what then was Sartre's problem with psychoanalysis at this early point of his philosophical career?

Sartre's problem was with what he called "the very principle of psychoanalytic explanation." With it, psychoanalysis mistakenly made the phenomenon of consciousness "the symbolic realization of a desire repressed by censorship." Under the causal pressure of a transcendent fact—namely, the repressed desires/libidinal impulses of the id—we fall into the theory "which makes the relation of thing signifying a causal relation." By doing so, "the thing signified is entirely cut off from the thing signifying."[11] Thus Freud was interpreted by Sartre as appealing to epiphenomenal psychical forces governed by the law of cause and effect. The conscious fact was considered the effect (that is, a thing) of the thing signified. The connection between the two was then understood as external and passive. What bothered Sartre about this? The answer is apparently twofold. First, this was to conceive "of consciousness as *a thing* in relation to the thing signified." Yet how could consciousness as *thing* be related to another thing?[12] Second, it was to admit that consciousness is "established as a signification without being conscious of the signification which it establishes."[13] The fundamental problem was that Freudian metapsychology claimed to look for explanatory factors which lie underneath human experience and yet were considered outside of it. Sartre believed this to be a "flagrant contradiction." How can that which signifies—consciousness—not be conscious of what it signifies?[14] Furthermore, to make this kind of separation showed a blatant disregard for the Cartesian cogito, and made consciousness into "a secondary and passive phenomenon."

Hence, Sartre approved more or less of psychoanalysis insofar as it operated on the level of meaning with the intention of furthering our *understanding*. However, by offering a scientific *explanation*, which moved to an account of materialistic process (divided and separated), he created an unbridgeable cleft between the two.

> It is the profound contradiction of all psychoanalysis to introduce *both* a bond of causality and a bond of comprehension between the phenomena which it studies. These two types of connection are incompatible.[15]

The Failure of Freud's Explanations to Account for the Individual

In addition to the incompatibility of Freud's explanations, Sartre asserted that in actuality the mechanistic and finalistic theories of explanation each failed. Such theories proceeded "from the postulate that an individual fact is produced by the intersection of abstract, universal laws."[16] In other words, the fact to be explained is conceived simply as a combination of typical, abstract desires encountered in *any* person. Prior to any concrete individual, there exists a hypothesized abstract, universal schemata into which the individual must fit. Sartre's reaction to this was to assert that not only are postulations of such universal schemata logically absurd (he did not deem it necessary to say why), they simply failed to explain how it was that any *particular individual project* comes about. In other words, Freud's universal theory failed to fill crucial gaps in grasping the uniqueness of the person, though it attempted to do so by either resorting to unknowns (i.e., inexplicable original givens) or mechanistic interpretations.[17] By resorting to mechanistic interpretations in order to explain individual uniquenesses, Freud simply begged the question concerning the truth of the mechanistic model from the beginning.

Freud's Response on the Issue of Scientific Explanation

Of course Freud the "scientist" would most likely not have felt the force of Sartre's criticisms on the topic of scientific explanation.[18] Freud would have even agreed with Sartre's observation that he (Freud) felt it necessary to go beyond strictly a mechanistic account of human nature, to incorporate purpose. Yet Freud would have argued that the mechanistic and finalistic explanations do not *conflate* "cause" and "purpose." Rather such explanations underscore the fact that both cause and purpose are to be regarded as indissolubly related. This was an aspect intrinsic to Darwinian evolutionary theory.

Darwinian evolutionary theory ubiquitously provided the interpretive framework of German reflection during Freud's own formative years by offering a unified worldview grounded in biology. Hence, this was the prevalent conception of humankind held by most nineteenth-century German-speaking physicians. Freud was no exception: his scientific framework was constructed with its primary purpose consisting of the explanation of human beings as biological organisms. The basic unfulfilled internal sources of energy, which motivate the organisms to act, are the biological needs of procreation and hunger. Hence, instinctual desires are by nature teleologically oriented. They are crucial for the preservation and survival of the species. In doing so they serve the purposes of Nature rather than the idiopathic purposes of the individual—that is, the id is prepersonal. Hence, as part of his metapsychology, Freud sought to integrate the biological, physiological, and psychological dimensions of human reality. Instead of being mutually exclusive forms of explanation, mechanism and teleology are interwoven in Freudian metapsychological theory.

Sartre's further criticism that, by offering a "universal" account of human nature, Freud's theory failed to explain individual uniqueness would have also been lost on Freud. Freud would have pointed out that all disciplines necessarily form universal schemata, which are what further human understanding, and that some are more comprehensive than others. In fact, Freud would have definitely pointed a finger at philosophy—particularly metaphysics—as being quite guilty of creating "comprehensive" systems which actually explained and reflected very little of reality. Indeed, Freud would have insisted that this is equally true of Sartre's own existential psychoanalysis. As previously discussed, this was a major criticism Freud launched against philosophy, in fact, and was a reason for his decision to renounce the discipline in pursuit of the "true knowledge" science could offer. Furthermore, Freud would have added that a *truly* scientific approach to human nature would only develop theoretical explanations based on actual observations of individuals. This was one very valuable contribution his therapeutic practice afforded him. It was from his extensive experience working with individuals that he was enabled to develop his universal theory—one he believed to be in a constant state of revision and evolution precisely because of his scientific observations. Hence, Freud would have asserted that Sartre's claim that the individual gets lost in the universal had no merit.

The Misapplication of the Scientific Method to the Self

From Sartre's point of view, Freud's uncritical adherence to Cartesian ontology led him to hold some disastrous presuppositions. It led to conceiving of self as a thing, falsely split the self into subject and object, failed to account for the emergence of meaning in the world, and mistakenly conceived of humans as determined.

The Self as a Thing: All Reality Is Objective Reality

According to Sartre, one primary philosophical presupposition of Freud's was the claim that all reality is composed of "things," that is, the psyche and the material world are substantial beings. Sartre clearly recognized Freud to be taking the psyche to be merely a thing—a substantialized self, conceived as a physical mechanism.[19] Sartre was, of course, utterly opposed to any such materialistic reductionism.[20] Indeed, his goal was to provide a philosophical foundation for realism and thereby avoid idealism without lapsing back into a mechanistic materialism.[21] Furthermore, advocacy of mechanistic materialism was just another form of the claim that there is a universal human nature, which of course Sartre rejected in the strongest possible terms, because he believed it precluded the possibility of meaning and human dignity.[22]

Sartre was convinced that Freud fell prey to precisely that which Descartes had been criticized for having done: "for having conceived that thought as cogito, grasping itself, is at the same time substance, which is to say, a being-in-itself endowed with opacity and total adequacy to itself."[23] As far as Sartre was concerned, then, Freud's notion of the psyche simply presupposed Cartesian substance whose attribute was thought.

On this point Sartre could not have been clearer in his "refusal to consider man as capable of being analyzed and reduced to original givens, to determined desires (or 'drives'), supported by the subject as properties by an object."[24] Such reductionistic materialism simply reduced human beings to bundles of physical instinctual desires in the same way "the complex personality of an adolescent" is reduced to "a few basic desires, as the chemist reduces compound bodies to merely a combination of simple bodies."[25] According to Sartre, Freud's metapsychology theory failed to adequately deal with this problem since it was simply another form of materialism, which sought "to produce a substance in terms of another substance."[26] In this framework, "the *man* disappears." We cannot find the person who has had experiences. Instead, "we encounter a useless, contradictory metaphysical substance."[27] For Sartre, Freud's theory presupposed a substantial self which was, prior to its being acted upon by the desires of experience: "a sort of indeterminate clay which would have to receive [desires] passively."[28] He asserted that "[we] should never have to resort to this idea of substance which is inhuman because it is well this side of the human."[29] As such, this idea of substance was "only a caricature" of human existence. Human beings are nonsubstantial beings, humans are not things: as such, Sartre believed that the individual person was the initial project ("original choice") that constituted him/her as the original relation to self, world, and others, in the unity of his/her internal relations and of a fundamental project.[30]

Self as Split into Subject and Object

A related philosophical presupposition of Freud's metapsychological theory, according to Sartre, was the idea that the subject–object dichotomy is intrinsic to our intellectual operations and research. Sartre's response to this was, of course, equally clear. Coming out of the phenomenological tradition of (the later) Husserl and Heidegger, Sartre recommended that we eschew presupposing the duality of the subject–object and instead recognize the indissoluble engagement of consciousness as being-in-the-world as a unified totality.

Given what seems prima facie to be a metaphysical dualism—the for-itself as subjectivity and the in-itself as objectivity—it might seem that Sartre would have been in sympathy with Freud concerning the subject–object dichotomy. Such an interpretation from Sartre's point of view could not have been further from his intentions.

For Sartre, the for-itself *is* only when it is engaged and in a situation.[31] A situation is comprised of the interplay between two aspects of reality: the facticity (the given beings of the world) and the transcendence (freedom) of the for-itself. Sartre described the relation between the for-itself and situation as "being-there." It is by "being-there" that the object takes on meaning for the for-itself: the situation is identified and defined by that meaning, being-in-the-situation defines the human reality. Sartre wrote, "the For-itself feels a profound solidarity of being with [the In-itself] ";[32] hence "the inextricable connection of freedom and facticity in the situation,"[33] "world" and "person" are mutually necessary conditions of the existence of the other.[34] Subject and object are never understood as *separate* in any sense of the term; for Sartre there is no subject–object dichotomy.

From this it is clear how Sartre reacted to Freud's assumption that his metapsychology presupposed that human existence is a mind–body dualism, connected via the instincts. Sartre attacked any form of Cartesian mind–body dualism:

> The problem of the body and its relations with consciousness is often obscured by the fact that while the body is from the start posited as a certain *thing*. . . if after grasping "my" consciousness in its absolute interiority and by a series of reflective acts, I then seek to unite it with a certain living object composed of a nervous system, a brain, [etc.] whose very matter is capable of being analyzed chemically into atoms . . . then I am going to encounter insurmountable difficulties.[35]

Sartre thought that this characterization, of course, would include Freud's metapsychology in his interpretation.

Sartre's own solution to the irresolvable difficulties of a Cartesian mind–body dualism was to conceive human existence as intrinsically an embodied consciousness. In doing so, he sought to reestablish the indissoluble unity of mind and body: "Being-for-itself must be wholly body and it must be wholly consciousness; it can not be *united* with a body."[36] In a sense, "the body is nothing other than the for-itself."[37] What does this mean? Not that the in-itself (the given as object) is somehow "in" the for-itself, for that would make the latter into an object as well. Why is the body not a thing? As it is "a transcended transcendence, then the perception of it cannot *by nature* be of the same type as that of inanimate objects."[38] Instead, Sartre was making a transcendental point: "the body is a necessary characteristic of the for-itself . . . the very nature of the for-itself demands that it be [a] body; that is, that its nihilating escape from being should be made in the form of an engagement in the world."[39] As a permanent structure of my being, the body is "the necessary condition of the world."[40] Sartre went even further, claiming that "my body is coextensive with the world"; that is, the body is always in a situation as the fact of my being-in-the-world.[41] The body is the totality of meaningful relations to the world. As such, it is "the total center of reference which things indicate,"[42] "which I am without being able to know it."[43] Hence, the body is included as one of the structures of non-thetic consciousness; "The body is *lived* and not *known*."[44] Or, "I exist my body, this is its first dimension of being";[45] "consciousness exists its body,"[46] meaning, "my consciousness exists a corporeal form which arises on the body-as-totality which it exists."[47]

Sartre also spoke of a "psychic body": "This consciousness is affectivity in its original upsurge."[48] For example, it is illness as it is felt (yet not known) in one's suffering. "It is the projection on the plane of the in-itself of the intra-contexture of consciousness, [it] provides the implicit matter of all the phenomena of the psyche."[49] Here Sartre meant that insofar as psychic body was existed by consciousness it is captured by and projected into the in-itself. It represents the tendency of each psychic object to be externalized outside the person. "In so far as the body is the contingent and indifferent matter of all our psychic events, the body determines a *psychic space.*"[50]

> [The psychic body as suffering] is nonetheless a real characteristic of the psyche—not that the psyche is united to a body but that under its melodic organization the body is its substance and its perpetual condition of possibility . . . It is this which is the basis of the mechanistic and chemical metaphors which we use to classify and to explain the events of the psyche . . . It is this, finally, which motivates and to some degree justifies psychological theories like that of the unconscious . . .[51]

Sartre was offering an account, here, of how someone like Freud could have generated the theory he did. In Freudian terms, the physicalistic id generates an image, which was then compared by the ego to its perceptions of "external objects." But this merely has the appearance of showing how meaning emerges into the world.

The Failure of Meaning to Emerge into the World

If Freud was correct in conceiving of human beings (or the human psyche) as things, how is meaning ("intentionality") possible at all? In other words, if all of reality is truly composed of discrete things, which are strictly physical objects, how can something that is not an object—such as meaning—emerge from them? For Sartre, Freud's metapsychology was unable to account for how meaning emerges into the world.

First, given his conception of the ego as a passive thing, Freud was unable to coherently account for how it is that meaning emerges into the world in the first place. Sartre argued that an ego (like Husserl's or Freud's) cannot belong to the domain of consciousness (the for-itself) since if it did it would be "a nucleus of opacity."[52] This was so, because Freud claimed that the "ego" belonged to "the system of things that are outside of consciousness."[53] To view the ego in this way would be to shatter the unity of consciousness, obliterate its transparency, and place into consciousness something of which it would not be conscious and something which did not exist as consciousness.[54]

Second, Freud's metapsychology was simply another form of materialism which sought "to produce substance in terms of another substance,"[55] that is, to produce psychical substance from material substance.

But given such a substance's isolation "in its being by its total positivity,"[56] it could not produce anything (such as meaning) beyond its own material being. Here, Sartre illustrated his point by considering Freud's own position. Freud wrote: "The psychical processes [are] qualitatively determined states of specifiable material particles."[57] Sartre's counter was direct and to the point:

> The nerve is not meaningful; it is a colloidal substance which can be
> described in itself and which does not have the quality of transcendence;
> that is, it does not transcend itself in order to make known to itself by
> means of other realities what it is. Under no circumstances could the
> nerve furnish the basis for meaning.[58]

Sartre's position was clear—meaning simply could not have its origin in a thing, or an in-itself.

Freud's theory, then, was another example of the violent insertion of those "idols" or "phantoms" which Freud referred to as "instincts"[59] ("drives," "energies," "forces," and so on) into the psyche. As such, they were incomprehensible since they were merely given "as in-itself existents."[60] From them, representations were said to be formed as psychical events. This would be an impossibility.

Sartre made a similar point later, when he asserted that all empirical psychologists—of whom Freud would be a prime example—held that desire existed in humans as if it were somehow "contained" by consciousness. Sartre insisted that we "beware of considering these desires as little psychic entities dwelling in consciousness,"[61] and that "by holding that the meaning of the desire is inherent in the desire itself [Freud for example] avoids everything which could evoke the idea of transcendence."[62] The specific problem with this from Sartre's perspective was that to hold such a position was simply to preclude the very possibility of transcendence as intentionality—that consciousness *is* consciousness of something. The empirical psychologists introduced a mysterious account of nothing more than magical transformations—material substance into psychical meaning.

Sartre believed that his alternative theory of meaning truly accounted for the emergence of meaning. In *Being and Nothingness,* he took himself to be rendering a transcendental account of human experience. His basic questions were: what ontological relations make all experience possible? And more specifically: how in general could an object exist for consciousness?[63] This introduced the problem of intentionality: how did meaning emerge into the universe? His general solution to the problem of intentionality was to establish that "it is through the for-itself that the meaning of being appears."[64] He wrote, "We can apprehend [instincts] only as the result of projecting into the in-itself a relation of immanent being of the for-itself and this ontological relation is precisely lack."[65] The in-itself and for-itself are always already in a unity—in their ontological relation to one another.[66] And it is because the for-itself nihilates the in-itself that this is always a unity in terms of the emergence of meaning.

Borrowing from Hegel's *Phenomenology of Spirit*[67] and *Science of Logic*,[68] Sartre held that a profound tension exists between opposing elements in human existence. Hegel distinguished between two major aspects of the human being: (1) as an in-itself, each human is a given, natural being with desires and needs; and (2) as opposed to all other animals, the human being is reflective about self and the environment; as a for-itself, each person goes beyond the "givens" of the universe. A human being is able to go beyond everyday concerns, think about the universe, and reflect on her or his place in it. In this way, human existence introduced a rupture into the fullness (Sartre called this the "plenum") of being—introduced nothingness, the for-itself as consciousness. Here we have an apprehension of being as a lack of being. When one questions one's existence and takes a stand on an answer, one raises various interminable possibilities of changing the universe, of making it "not" as it was. Such consciousness understands that it is "not" whatever else is; consciousness realizes that it will "not" remain what it is, and so on.

Without consciousness, Sartre believed, there would be no distinctions made in the world. In order for distinctions to be drawn by someone, there must be a being that introduces negations into the world. Here Sartre borrowed from Spinoza's and Hegel's principle that "determination is negation."[69] What makes determinate reality possible is the fact that some being makes distinctions; for this to be possible there must be a being that introduces negations into being; that being itself must be "nothingness" else none of the above would be possible. This being is consciousness itself. Since consciousness is intrinsically nothingness, it is consciousness which makes it possible for nothingness to be in the world. Furthermore, the nothingness that is consciousness experiences the lack of its nothingness and constantly desires to fill itself up. Life consists of striving and the desire to restore being to fullness—to rid itself of "nothingness." But this desire perpetuates itself and, in Hegel's words, "can find no peace." For Sartre, this was the tragic finale of human existence: it desires to be what it cannot be—the in-itself-for-itself, or in other words, God.[70]

Thus, in order to account for the emergence of meaning, Sartre believed that it was necessary to introduce his own ontological account of the human desire to be the in-itself-for-itself. This was fundamental to human existence and was considered more ontologically appropriate than any of Freud's mechanistic explanations.

Humans as Causally Determined

For Sartre, one of the most important criticisms of Freud's mechanistic and finalistic explanation in its misapplication to human beings was that it adopted and imposed a deterministic account of human existence. Since the human psyche was conceived to be grounded as a mechanism and a teleologically oriented biological organism it was, according to Freud, governed by the principle of cause and effect—human beings are "thoroughly determined."[71]

Sartre's criticism of Freud's determinism was closely related to his criticism of Freud's thing-ontology. He wrote, "By identifying consciousness with a causal sequence, one transmutes it into a plenitude of being."[72]

> It is not necessary to understand by this that on the one hand, some external cause (an organic trouble, an unconscious impulse, [etc.]) could determine that a psychic event—a pleasure, for example—produce itself . . . This would be moreover to make the psychic event a thing . . .[73]

In spite of Freud's deterministic proclivities, Sartre, interestingly enough, believed that he shared with him the same fundamental question concerning the origin of any individual action. Both asked: under what conditions is it possible that this particular person has performed this particular act? Sartre, then, believed that both he and Freud were conducting transcendental inquiries on the same question but arriving at entirely different answers.

In a dense and somewhat tangled paragraph in *Being and Nothingness*,[74] Sartre offered his understanding of Freud's answer to this question. While doing so, Sartre made several crucial distinctions. First, he asserted that Freud was not exclusively a proponent of a "horizontal psychic determinism." In other words, Freud, according to Sartre, refused to interpret an action merely by its temporal psychical antecedent(s). Freud's position, then, was *not* to be understood simply as a linear sequence of causes and effects on the psychical level. Instead, Sartre claimed that Freud also held a position of "vertical determinism" which included a form of libidinal causation from "underneath," pushing up from below, in whatever form it appeared. The ego was considered as unwittingly driven by the forces of prethematic libidinal instincts. Or, as Sartre put it: "Affectivity for Freud is at the basis of the act in the form of psychophysiological instincts."[75]

Furthermore, Sartre added, it was "through the intermediacy of history Freud's vertical determinism remains axised on an horizontal determinism." What Sartre apparently meant by this was that one's vertical determinism—the libidinal forces operating *within* oneself—was employed as a fixed reference for determining the position of a series of points. The actions caused by these libidinal forces, then, were based on an individual's "horizontal determinism" as well—their concrete history and *external* situation. That is, one explains an act by showing how its simultaneously existing underlying desire(s) (which is based on a yet deeper, more profound complex) engages one's unfolding historical and external set of circumstances. The instinctual impulses of the id and "external reality" engage in such a way that we are able to explain (post facto) why a person acted specifically in the way that she/he did. For Freud, for example, the basic patterns of a person's life were established early on in childhood, and because of this the individual has a proclivity to repeat them—what he called "repetition compulsion."

With this more developed form of determinism, then, Freud was able to explain human activity as occurring in a more complex web of causal connections. Sartre, of course, completely rejected both forms of Freud's determinism.

Freud's Response on the (mis)Application of Science to the Self

It is unclear whether Freud would have accepted Sartre's characterization of his theory as "mechanistic" had he understood the full ramifications that it entailed from a philosophical orientation.[76] However, as we have witnessed, those figures who were likewise accused of being mechanistic—Descartes, Fechner (the constancy principle), Meynert, Brücke, Helmholtz, and so on—obviously influenced Freud's intellectual development. Out of this tradition, Freud clearly viewed human beings as complex organisms whose physical instinctual impulses formed the foundation of self. These instinctual impulses (as well as the desires they manifested) were understood explicitly as entities which provided the ground for and were manifested in the psyche. It is clear that, taking natural science and the explanatory model it afforded, Freud presupposed that all beings operated, at least at first, in terms of matter and motion. In his *Project for a Scientific Psychology* he insisted:

> The intention of the project is to furnish us with a psychology which shall be a natural science; its aim, that is, is to represent psychical processes as quantitatively determined states of specifiable material particles and so make them plain and void of contradictions.[77]

Hence, for example, Freud conceived of the nervous system as a self-regulating mechanism maintaining a certain equilibrium of energy.[78]

Freud, however, most likely would not have conceded that his theory was purely "mechanistic," nor that it failed to account for the emergence of meaning. According to Freud the metapsychologist, meaning was considered to be that which resulted from the primary and secondary processes. It was ultimately reducible to the interplay of biologically based instinctual impulses, which were evolving with the activities of the various functions of the personality (id, ego, superego). Hence, Freud conceived desire to be biological instinct. In other words, meaning emerges from the instinctual desires.[79]

Perhaps the fundamental disagreement between Freud and Sartre, then, was whether or not desire was considered biological or merely an expression of consciousness in nature. Again, for Freud, desires have their roots in obscure physiological processes believed to be unconscious and hence quite inaccessible. Certainly the aim of desire included the cessation of an unpleasant state of tension (the pleasure principle), but the specificity of desire (why a person desires a particular object) resided in the plasticity of the instincts. Given this plasticity, objects of desire were believed connected to previous object-choices, which conditioned (or possibly even determined) them.

For Freud, when Sartre rejected the idea that consciousness may be acted upon by anything outside itself—for example, as emanating from an id or even unconscious affectivity—he then had the problem of accounting for what motivated a specific desire in its choice of an object. Freud most likely would have seen Sartre's solution to this problem as merely verbal, tautological, and perhaps even "magical."

Furthermore, when Sartre claimed that there could be no unconscious intentionality, Freud would have vociferously disagreed. He would have pointed out that there is a regular connection between the meaning of a psychical event and what it stands for (symbolizes). Freud may have even argued that on this point especially, his theory had an advantage over Sartre's because such a claim was capable of and had been validated repeatedly in the therapeutic context. In addition, Freud was able to find out from others what truly happened in the past. Perhaps he would have made the point too that when Sartre said that humans desire to appropriate others and the world, his theory was no less "deterministic" than

Freud's. That is, if this was considered an aspect of our nature, in what sense do we genuinely have the choice to do otherwise?

This introduces another issue between Sartre and Freud, that of determinism. Sartre's characterization of Freud's determinism in several instances was overly simplistic. Sartre wrote,

> Freud . . . aims at constituting a vertical determinism. In addition because of this bias his conception necessarily is going to refer to the subject's past . . . Consequently, the dimension of the future does not exist for psychoanalysis. Human reality loses one of its ekstases and must be interpreted solely by a regression toward the past from the standpoint of the present.[80]

Freud's "symptom formation," for example, was far more complicated, or to put it more philosophically, "dialectical" in nature than Sartre interpreted it to be. It involved not only a compromise of sorts between desire and repression, but also served as a reaction to both the present set of circumstances as well as future anticipations.

In addition, it should be noted that Freud was not always consistent in his position on determinism (see chapter 17). At least at times, Freud seemed to consider himself a psychical determinist;[81] and, he was relatively clear on one major point—when it came to psychical life, "nothing in the mind is arbitrary or undetermined."[82] Recall that Freud wrote, "determination in the psychical sphere is carried out without any gap."[83] He also stated quite boldly, "free will is an illusion."[84] Freud believed that one of the primary aspects attaching us to free will was "all the strivings of the ego which adverse external circumstances have crushed."[85] Such strivings were considered (vertically) determined insofar as they have their ultimate basis in the libidinal processes of the id, which engage and are crushed (horizontally determined) by external reality.

> The apportioning of the determining factors of our life between the "necessities" of our constitution and the "chances" of our childhood may still be uncertain in detail; but in general it is no longer possible to doubt the importance precisely of the first years of our childhood.[86]

Sartre's characterization of Freud's determinism failed to account for Freud's therapeutic approach: in therapy, a major goal was to provide the ego with resources for uncovering and genuinely understanding the past and overcoming its unilaterally determining features so that it could pursue its own chosen direction for development in the future. Successful psychotherapy, then, could afford a person genuine liberation, to enable him/her to live life within the scope of his/her own conscious control, and to be open to the world with greater flexibility. We will take up the issue of Freud's determinism again later.

The Ultimate Sacrifice: Freedom and Responsibility

Sartre believed that Freud was very quick to surrender human freedom to a deterministic explanation of human nature. This renouncement (along with its implications) was probably what Sartre ultimately found most appalling in Freud's metapsychology. In order to understand precisely what Sartre believed Freud to be sacrificing, it is useful to consider Sartre's concept of freedom. To facilitate the discussion it is worthwhile to distinguish between three levels of freedom:

> F1 = the freedom of decision or choice (in the sense that I may choose among various alternatives)
>
> F2 = the freedom of trying to implement or execute a choice (once having chosen, the freedom of trying to put that choice into effect)
>
> F3 = the freedom of actually implementing or executing a choice (the freedom of successfully achieving, attaining, acquiring, and so on, that choice once it has been made)

It is important to note at the outset that in *Being and Nothingness,* Sartre did not use the word "freedom" as it is commonly understood, meaning, "to obtain what one has wished" (F3). For Sartre, to be "free" (as an ontological concept) meant "to project an end," that is, to "by oneself determine oneself to wish" (an act is a projection of the for-itself toward what it is not, to be free = to act, to be is to do).[87] Sartre, then, did not consider the notion of success to be necessarily important to freedom, but rather conceived freedom to be autonomous choice. At this point it is clear Sartre was speaking of F1.

According to Sartre, freedom is at the heart of human existence. It is the very being of the being-for-itself: freedom is the human being putting his/her past out of play by secreting his/her own nothingness.[88] What this means is that the for-itself has a permanent possibility to break off with its own past, to tear itself away from what it is, and project itself into that which it can be. Human freedom, then, is not simply a characteristic of human existence, but rather it precedes human existence and makes it possible.

For Sartre, since freedom creates itself incessantly, it can only be described—never defined. That is, "Freedom has no essence. It is not subject to any logical necessity."[89] If freedom were defined, it would lose its meaning; for freedom is the being of the for-itself which Sartre described as "being what it is not and not being what it is." That which has yet to complete itself cannot be defined as an aggregate of "entities."

It is important to note here that although freedom lacks "essence" for Sartre, it is still the foundation of all essentiality. By virtue of the fact that the for-itself "is," it incessantly transcends the world in the direction of its own possibilities and hence constantly reveals the essentiality (namely, meaning) of the world it has transcended.

Sartre maintained that not only is freedom the state of being of the for-itself, but that the for-itself is "condemned to freedom."[90] By this, Sartre meant that individuals are free but lack the freedom not to be free. Since freedom is precisely the nothingness at the heart of the for-itself, human reality is forced to make itself rather than to simply be. The for-itself, in order to be, must choose itself—but it cannot choose itself as freedom (for it is freedom)—hence, we are condemned to be free. And since humans are condemned to be free, they are responsible for the world's essentiality and for themselves as "fundamental projects."

However, Sartre did not understand freedom (as for-itself) to be "free-floating": freedom is always engaged with and limited by the givens (beings which humans have not created in the world).[91] Freedom is necessarily connected to these givens (its facticity).[92] The mutually necessary interplay between an individual's freedom and these givens comprise any situation.[93] "There is freedom only in a situation and there is situation only through freedom."[94]

As engaged in the world, freedom is both limited and unlimited. Freedom is limited by obstacles—resistances it encounters as part of the givens (past, others, space, death, environment, and so on). Such givens (facticity) are a necessary condition for the very possibility of freedom itself.[95] Yet such givens have meaning only through human reality (as the for-itself nihilates the in-itself = intentionality = the bestowal of meaning).[96] Freedom is also unlimited—it is total, unconditioned, and infinite.[97] It is unlimited in terms of the attitudinal disposition I assume in my situation at any given time. Finally, human freedom cannot, according to Sartre, be relative to a particular situation: since freedom is human nothingness, and nothingness is absolute in that it is the condition of the for-itself, human freedom is absolute.

> For human reality, to be is to choose oneself, nothing comes to it either
> from the outside or from within which it can receive or accept . . . Thus

freedom is not a being; it is the being of man, i.e., his nothingness of being . . . If we start by conceiving of man as a plenum, it is absurd to try to find in him afterwards moments or psychic regions in which he would be free . . . Man cannot be sometimes slave and sometimes free; he is wholly and forever free or he is not free at all.[98]

For Sartre, then, freedom (F1, F2) and determinism are necessarily mutually exclusive states of affairs.[99]

Engagement also means that my freedom does more than conceive a choice—it acts to try to realize it (F2). Sartre wrote: "choice, being identical with acting, supposes a commencement of realization in order that the choice may be distinguished from the dream and the wish."[100] And human beings cannot be conceived as determined. When Freud adopted a deterministic view of human nature, he perpetuated a distorted and dangerous myth. In Sartre's view, Freud's metapsychology failed to offer a realistic account of human existence and rendered some of the most fundamental aspects of human experience illusory. For example, human creativity and anguish were made impossible; human temporality was severely truncated; and consequently, there could be no human responsibility.

Creativity and Anguish

By making freedom impossible, Freud's determinism precluded any account of human creativity and human anguish. For, according to Sartre, human creativity presupposes freedom. Yet "every ideology (e.g., determinism) undertakes to destroy the very idea of creation. Current forms of psychology (behaviorism, psychoanalysis) have no way of explaining or describing inventiveness. They have even gotten rid of the idea."[101]

Human anguish also remained unaccounted for in Freud's determinism. Sartre pointed out that anguish[102] in its essential structure is consciousness of freedom. If psychic determinism were true "we should suddenly appear to ourselves as things in the world."[103] We would not have the capacity to continually choose from among possibilities, nor to confront the fact that nothing guarantees the validity of self-chosen values.[104] Furthermore, Freud's determinism provided an excuse to "flee from our anguish by attempting to apprehend ourselves as an Other or as a thing."[105] Sartre argued that we must face anguish as an intrinsic part of the human condition and not attempt to cover it up (thereby fleeing from who we are and avoiding our moral responsibility to be sincere about who we are) by "constituting it in an unconscious psychic phenomenon."[106]

Truncated Temporality

Freud's determinism truncated the temporality intrinsic to human existence—it cut off the future in human experience. According to Sartre, Freud contended that it was the past that entirely constituted all of our actions (for example, the complex preexists its symbolic manifestation). It was exclusively the "intermediacy of history" (and external circumstances), which determined why instinctual drives fixated on any particular object at any specific moment. Sartre concluded that psychoanalysis only acknowledged human history and neglected any future.

> Consequently the dimension of the future does not exist for psychoanalysis. Human reality loses one of its ekstases and must be interpreted solely by a regression toward the past from the standpoint of the present.[107]

Rejecting what he understood by Freud's deterministic account, Sartre emphasized that the "past does not determine our acts"; it "is without force to constitute the present and to sketch out the future."[108] Yet it is interesting to note that Sartre's description of how the for-itself engages its past sounds very much like Freud's own account:

> [The for-itself] has to be its own past, and this past is irremediable . . . If the past does not determine our actions, at least it is such that we can not take a new decision except in terms of it . . . this is to recognize the past's immense importance as a backdrop and a point of view . . . all which I am I have to be in the mode of having-been. Thus, the importance of the past can not be exaggerated . . .[109]

Once we bestow meaning on our past in light of a certain end (for Freud, this would be when the id forms an image of that which will satisfy its desires), "from then on it imposes itself upon us and devours us . . . We are compelled to adopt these conducts."[110]

Yet what Freud failed to understand, according to Sartre, was that "I am the being through whom the past comes to myself and to the world."[111] Even more generally, Freud failed to see that nothingness is the transcendental condition for temporality itself. Sartre wrote, "this nothingness which separates human reality from itself is at the origin of time."[112] Hence, there can be no past for an in-itself like Freud's id, nor can there be previous events which determine present events: "We refuse a priori to grant a past to the in-itself."[113]

Analogous to Freud, Sartre wrote:

> What originally constitutes the being of the For-itself is this relation to a
> being which *is not* consciousness, which exists in the total night of iden-
> tity and which the For-itself is nevertheless obliged to be, outside and
> behind itself . . . the For-itself feels a profound solidarity of being with it
> and indicates this by the word *before*. The In-itself is what the For-itself
> was before. In this sense . . . our past . . . is lost in a progressive obscura-
> tion back to that darkness which is nevertheless still *ourselves*.[114]

> [My past] is the origin and springboard of all my actions; it is that con-
> stantly given density of the world which allows me to orient myself and to
> get my bearings. It is myself insofar as I aim at myself as a person (there
> is also a structure to-come of the Ego).[115]

However, Sartre's objection to the empirical psychologists (among whom
he included Freud) was that they "psychologize" the past and thereby "remove any way for accounting for it."[116] According to Sartre they do this

> by the naive way in which psychologists take recourse in the unconscious
> in order to distinguish the three "nows" of the psychic: they call *present*
> the "now" which is present to the consciousness. Those which have
> passed into the future have exactly the same characteristics, but they wait
> in the limbo of the unconscious; and if we take them in that undifferen-
> tiated environment, it is impossible to distinguish past from future
> among them. A memory which survives in the unconscious is a past
> "now" and at the same time, inasmuch as it awaits being evoked, it is a
> future "now."[117]

The problem for Sartre was that this resulted in psychic form containing
"two co-existing contradictory modalities of being," since it is already
made and appears in the cohesive unity of an organism and simultaneously can exist only through a succession of "nows," each of which is isolated in an in-itself. Applying this to Freudian theory, in the first case, the
id is a unified being in which the temporal modes of past, present, and future are not distinguished; and yet, in the second case, the id exists in a
succession of instances which involve a material state of affairs at each
point. The id cannot simultaneously both be temporal (in the Aristotelian
sense of a series of discrete now points) and be atemporal.

Furthermore, since the psyche is the objectification of the ontological unity of the for-itself (in Freud's case, the id) and hence cannot be its
own synthesis thereby merely having the unitary characteristic of a given

(the atemporal id), Sartre held that it then followed that the total cohesion of the psychic form was rendered unintelligible. "There is a sort of magic cohesion between the successive 'now' state[s]" of the id.[118] "The result is a total action at a distance by means of a magic influence of one on the other."[119]

> The fact that this action at a distance is totally magic and irrational proves better than any analysis the futility of attempts on the part of intellectualistic psychologists to remain on the level of the psychic and yet deduce this action to an intelligible causality by means of an intellectual analysis . . . this somewhat arbitrary reduction of the great psychic forms to more simple elements accentuates the magic irrationality of the inter-relations which psychic objects support . . . It is necessary to give up trying to reduce the irrational element in psychic causality. This causality is a degradation of the ekstatic for-itself, which is its own being at a distance from itself, into an in-itself which is what it is at its own place.[120]

Given its causal model, Freud's theory (as well as others) failed to explain in any cogent manner how it was that the discrete series of "nows" flowed into one another, given their discrete quality.

One further consequence of the above was that Freud's metapsychological theory was not able to account for the existence and functioning of memory. Sartre pointed out, "If we want remembering to remain possible, we must on this hypothesis admit a recollecting synthesis."[121] Sartre argued that Freud could not account for the meaning of a past being, since memory presupposes an ontological relation which unites the past to the present (through transcendence).[122] There could be no such recollecting synthesis (transcendence) in Freud's account, hence he was unable to account for memory.

Just as important, Sartre was extremely critical of what he perceived to be Freud's failure to recognize the crucial significance of the temporal mode of the future in his theory.

> What-is [the past] . . . takes on its meaning only when it is surpassed toward the future . . . the very nature of the past comes to the past from the original choice of a future . . . In order for us to "have" a past, it is necessary that we maintain it in existence by our very project towards the future . . .[123]

Here, of course, we see a direct influence on Sartre by Heidegger. Both held that it is primarily (though certainly not exclusively) because we as human beings are futurally directed, with a kind of cumulative goal-directedness, that it is possible for us to reflect and experience meaning at all. It is the distinctive "futural" character in the temporal unfolding of human existence that so fundamentally distinguishes it from physical beings.

The result was that for Sartre, Freud offered a severely temporally truncated description of human existence since human reality identifies and defines itself by the ends which it pursues. Any viable theory concerning human reality must take into account the crucial role the future plays within it.

No Responsibility

According to Sartre, Freud's determinism perpetuated a very dangerous myth—that humans are not responsible for their actions. Sartre was clear:

> The ultimate meaning of determinism is to establish within us an unbroken continuity of existence in-itself . . . the motive provokes the act as the physical cause its effect . . . the refusal of freedom can be conceived only as an attempt to apprehend oneself as being-in-itself . . . trying to take causes and motives as things . . . We attempt to hide from ourselves that their nature and weight depend each moment on the meaning which I give to them . . .[124]

According to Sartre, by conceiving of human beings as determined things, theories like Freud's generated deceptive pictures which enabled people to hide from the fact that they were responsible for the bestowal of meaning in the world. Failure to acknowledge this further concealed the fact that humans are morally responsible for who they are and what they do (or don't do). Freud's explanation was a sophisticated excuse for avoiding moral responsibility via a refusal of authenticity, and nothing more. According to Sartre, Freud's metapsychology and theory of human nature were nothing more than vehicles providing humans with excuses for what they do and thereby absolving them of any moral responsibility whatsoever. In short, the very generation of Freud's metapsychological theory was itself a form of bad faith. It focused exclusively upon elements of human facticity while denying the existence of human freedom. Bad faith was defined by Sartre as the vacillation in any situation between an exclusive focus on our transcendence (our freedom) and our facticity (the givens that are intrinsic to existence). By focusing exclusively on the one side of our facticity, freedom is neglected. Sartre could not be more explicit on this point:

Psychological determinism . . . is first an attitude of excuse . . . or if you prefer, the basis of all attitudes of excuse . . . it is given as a faith to take refuge in, as the ideal end toward which we can flee to escape anguish. That is made evident on the philosophical plane by the fact that deterministic psychologists do not claim to found their thesis on the pure givens of introspection. They present it as a satisfying hypothesis, the value of which comes from the fact that it accounts for the facts—or as a necessary postulate for establishing all psychology . . . it is an illusion due to the mistaken belief that we are the real causes of our acts.[125]

Freud's Response to Freedom and Responsibility

As mentioned, Freud would have most likely considered Sartre's description of horizontal and vertical determinism overly simplistic. He probably would have also disagreed with the conclusions Sartre reached in his interpretation of psychoanalysis. Contrary to Sartre's position, Freud believed that his theory accounted for creativity; he would deny having "truncated temporality"; and, most important, he would have opposed the idea that his form of determinism absolved humans of any moral responsibility whatsoever.

First, contrary to what Sartre argued, creative activity is perfectly intelligible within the Freudian model. Far from dispensing with the idea, Freud wrote full articles on the subject of "creativity." To take but one example, in his work "Creative Writers and Day-Dreaming" (1908),[126] Freud argued that the unreality of a writer's world of fantasy could be (and often is) a source of pleasure, one which would be absent without that unreality. Freud wrote: "The motive forces of phantasies are unsatisfied wishes, and every single fantasy is the fulfilment of a wish, a correction of unsatisfying reality."[127] According to Freud, something in the present arouses a creative subject's wishes in such a way as to bring back a memory (usually from childhood) of an earlier experience in which this wish was fulfilled. It presently creates a situation relating to the future in which that wish is fulfilled—a day-dream. In this way, "past, present and future are strung together on the thread of the wish that runs through them."[128] The wish is thus fulfilled through a creative work. Hence, "a piece of creative writing, like a day-dream, is a continuation of, and a substitute for, what was once the play of childhood."[129]

Metapsychologically speaking, such "creativity" was considered to be a form of what Freud called "sublimation." Freud was quite explicit in what he meant by his concept of sublimation:

> Sublimation is a process that concerns the object-libido and consists in the instincts directing itself towards an aim other than, and remote from, that of sexual gratification . . .[130]

> This enables excessively strong excitations arising from particular sources of sexuality to find an outlet and use in other fields, so that a not inconsiderable increase in psychical efficiency results from a disposition which in itself is perilous.[131]

Sublimation for Freud was a sophisticated way of warding off the development of neurosis while permitting the satisfaction of instinctual impulses through socially and culturally accepted means. Furthermore, its connection with Freud's metapsychology is clear: "the ability to sublimate, must be traced back to the organic bases."[132] For Freud, it was the id's inability to make fine discriminations between objects which necessitated the displaceable quality of instinctual energy. The instinctual impulses were seen to be extremely "malleable," in that one of them could replace another or take over another's intensity. They also exhibited a strong capacity for changing their object—for taking a more easily attainable one in its place.[133] It was this malleability and/or interchangeability of the instinctual impulses and their object-choices which Freud argued accounted for the illusion of what a philosopher like Sartre would think of as "free creativity."

But if the above substitutions and choices were not free for human creativity, how did Freud account for the occurrence of a specific displacement? The direction a particular displacement took was determined in two ways. First, it could be determined by how closely the substitute impulse resembled the original. Here "success" was determined by the amount of tension reduction accomplished. However, Freud emphasized that tension was seldom completely reduced. Consequently the individual was compelled to explore more adequate ways of reducing tension. According to Freud, this accounted for the diversity and variability of human behavior in general. Without the displaceable nature of psychic energy, humans would be relegated to simple rigid patterns of behavior, driven by instincts. Second, Freud pointed out that the environmental influence of societal and cultural sanctions and proscriptions helped dictate acceptable displacements. Hence, even the highest cultural achievements—philosophy (including Sartre's!), art, music, and so on—were considered respectable forms of sublimation, which were seen as ultimately rooted in the organic energetics of his metapsychoanalytic theory.[134] For Freud, then, creativity and determinism were far from incompatible ideas.

Next, Sartre's position that psychoanalysis "cut off the future" would have struck Freud as simply mistaken. The very point of psychotherapy, as conceived by Freud, was to enable the patient to truly grasp his or her past and to become free to move in different directions in the future. Freud would have declared that it was common sense that since we have future plans, goals, aspirations, and so on, what we do now in relationship to our past is related to the future. He would also have denied that he ignored the unity of temporality. To cite but one example, Freud spoke of the "wish" as a primary component of his theory: wishing was considered a phenomenon in which the past, present, and future were seen as bound together, as if there were a thread running through them. In other words, for the content of a wish to be understood one must understand that, by its very nature, it necessarily involves all three modes of temporalization.[135]

For Freud, issues involving temporality would not emerge with regard to instinctual desires (for example, the id is not temporal). On this most basic level, cognition does not enter in its organizing function. In line with Kant and more specifically the noumenal world, the primal forces of the id have no organizing processes which would contribute any understanding or knowledge of temporal sequences. It is only when desires make their way into consciousness that they even become subject to the organizing principles of temporality, causality, and so on. In this sense, then, Freud obviously departed from the typical psychological determinism of his time. With the introduction of the id—the "true reality" and a nontemporal, noncausal condition for human activity—humans are only "determined" insofar as their actions and thoughts are subject to the categories of causality, temporality, and so on.

Does all of this imply, as Sartre proposed, that humans are somehow exempt from responsibility? For Freud, the answer was a resounding *No!* He was, in fact, quite adamant about humans taking responsibility for their decisions and actions, even for what would seem the most "blameless" of all—our dreams.[136]

> Obviously one must hold oneself responsible for the evil impulses of one's dreams. What else is one to do with them? Unless the content of the dream (rightly understood) is inspired by alien spirits, it is part of my own being . . . If I seek to classify the impulses that are present in me according to social standards into good and bad, I must assume responsibility for both sorts; and if, in defense, I say that what is unknown,

unconscious and repressed in me is not my "ego," then I shall not be basing my position on psychoanalysis, I shall not have accepted its conclusions . . .

It is true that in the metapsychological sense this bad repressed content does not belong to my "ego"—that is, assuming that I am a morally blameless individual—but to an "id" upon which my ego is seated. But this ego developed out of the id, it forms with it a single biological unit . . .[137]

Obviously Freud was very much opposed to the idea that determinism precluded responsibility. Despite the logical argument that "if we cannot do otherwise, we are not responsible for our actions," Freud would not have accepted the conclusion. He refused to believe that logic excuses us from what is fundamentally a human issue: to take responsibility for who we are and what we do, regardless of how we got there. The idea that we are, for the most part, unconscious and hence not aware of our most basic selves serves not as an excuse, but rather as a warning. Recognizing this fact about ourselves should entice us all the more to delve deeply into our hidden selves, so that we could have an awareness of what it is exactly, for which we are responsible!

In fact, it could be argued that Freud's primary therapeutic goal of bringing about awareness of unconscious, repressed material was simultaneously an attempt to show patients precisely that they *were* responsible for their decisions and actions, and that they could do otherwise. As long as one is held captive by unconscious desires and forbidden memories, there is a compulsion to repeat; only by awareness of the condition by which one has been compelled is one freed from the compulsion and able to not engage in past behaviors or symptoms. And hence, only through awareness is one able to fully exercise that fundamental responsibility we have for who we are and what we do.

The Master of Self-Deception: Sartre on Freud

> I have to say that I was incapable of understanding [Freud] because I was a Frenchman with a good Cartesian tradition behind me, imbued with a certain rationalism, and I was therefore deeply shocked by the idea of the unconscious.
> —Sartre

> [We should] avoid the perilous reef of the unconscious which psychoanalysis meets at the start.
> —Sartre

> The more we seek to win our way to a metapsychological view of mental life, the more we must learn to emancipate ourselves from the importance of the symptom of "being conscious."
> —Freud

Despite Sartre's ambivalence toward Freudian psychoanalysis, his position regarding the *unconscious* remained relatively consistent throughout his career.[1] Simone de Beauvoir recalled that it was as early as 1932 that Sartre held a theory which was specifically designed to render the notion of the unconscious superfluous.[2] Sartre later wrote: "I was . . . deeply shocked by the idea of the unconscious . . . I must say that I remain shocked by what was inevitable in Freud . . . I do not believe in the unconscious in the form in which psychoanalysis presents it to us today."[3] What compelled Sartre to oppose continuously Freud's notion of the unconscious? The answer is protracted and extensive. Obviously, this chapter will not provide us enough space to fully develop Sartre's argument against the unconscious, but some key elements will hopefully shed light on this discussion.

Considerations of a Philosophical Nature

Sartre's own "Cartesian" heritage formed the background for his disapproval. Descartes had, of course, insisted that the mind is a unity, that is, indivisible: "it is one and the same mind that wills, understands and has sensory perceptions."[4] The mind remains an indissoluble unity because whatever happens—there remains a single center of consciousness, a single center of awareness and control.

Yet, Freud did not share Sartre's loyalty to Descartes, nor was he "philosophically constituted." (Freud, with the exception of courses from Brentano, lacked formal philosophical training.) Hence, he borrowed a variety of philosophical ideas from, at times, discrepant philosophical systems without attending to the inherent inconsistencies among them. Perhaps one of Sartre's main frustrations with the "unconscious," then, was the extent to which it reflected Freud's haphazard philosophical approach.[5] Sartre felt that while Freud purported to adopt a Cartesian mechanistic view of humans, he mixed it with a finalistic, teleological account as well. Philosophically speaking, the two did not go together, or, at the very least, not without numerous mistakes.

The Unconscious as a Misinterpretation of Self-Deception

Ever true to his transcendental proclivities, Sartre's critique of the Freudian unconscious in *Being and Nothingness* occurred in the context of his discussion of how "bad faith" was possible at all.[6] Sartre defined "bad faith" as a lie to ourselves within the unity of a single consciousness—the motive being, to escape the responsible freedom which comprises our very being (that is, to hide the truth of its import for our existence).[7] How does bad faith do this? Consciousness bestows meaning insofar as it vacillates at its own convenience between the two primary aspects of any situation—our transcendence (freedom) and our facticity (our necessary connection to given features of the world, namely, those beings which we engage with our freedom). The two are perfectly capable of a harmonious coordination, in what Sartre called "sincerity."[8] However, often when we try to account for why we did a particular act, we vacillate between an appeal to our transcendence and to our facticity, and form an explanation to suit our purposes rather than to reflect any truth in the situation. In other words, we often fail to take the unitary nature of a situation into account and instead seek to absolve ourselves from any responsibility for our actions.

We consequently make excuses for ourselves (that is, deceive ourselves) by either focusing on the external forces which (we claim) made us do a particular act (for Sartre, a perfect example was found in the Freudian instincts); or, we focus on our freedom to do otherwise now and in the future, rather than address what we actually did at the time. At this critical juncture, Sartre posed the question: how is such self-deception possible? Given that humans are unified consciousness, how can they lie to themselves and yet believe the lie? This strikes us as incomprehensible and yet it seems to be, in fact, what people do.[9]

The attempt to resolve this ostensible paradox, Sartre said, prompted some to posit the existence of an unconscious region of the mind. Rather than acknowledge the unity of the psyche, psychoanalysis resorted to the hypothesis of a censor to reestablish the duality of the deceiver and the deceived. How? They held the position that reality consists of the engagement of our instincts along with the linear causal background of our individual histories. Hence, human beings are essentially composed of instincts and the facts of consciousness that arise from them. The individual was considered to have the same relation to the facts of consciousness (forgetting, dreams, and so on) as the deceived is to the behavior of the deceiver. The facts of consciousness and the behavior of the deceiver both reveal a truth to the person or the deceived respectively. "Thus the subject deceives himself about the *meaning* of his conduct, he apprehends it in its concrete existence but not in its *truth*."[10] Why? She or he is unable to derive it from its original historical context and from a psychophysical realm that is foreign to her or him.

Thus what Freudian psychoanalysis did, according to Sartre, was to break up the unity of the psyche. Sartre characterized it bluntly: "I *am* the ego but I *am not* the *id*."[11] As ego, I am immediately conscious of phenomena; but I am not my id, insofar as I receive my psychical facts passively and must speculate about their origin and meaning. My speculations will be confirmed as true depending upon the number of conscious facts it explains. Finally, and most important for the purposes of Sartre's analogy, "I hold no privileged position in relation to my unconscious psyche." "I stand in relation to my 'id,' in the same position as the Other (i.e., an 'external' observer of the deepest level of the psyche)."[12] This was what Sartre referred to a few years later as "the final type of alienation."[13] This brings us to Sartre's famous conclusion:

> Thus psychoanalysis substitutes for the notion of bad faith, the idea of a lie without a liar; it allows me to understand how it is possible for me to be lied to without lying to myself since it places me in the same relation to myself that the Other is in respect to me; it replaces the duality of the

deceiver and the deceived, the essential condition of the lie, by that of the "id" and the "ego."[14]

Since Freud held that the ego was deceived by the id, there could be a lie without a liar. According to Sartre, the processes of the id were, as such, epistemologically inaccessible to the processes of the ego for Freud.

In response to this position, Sartre suggested that a fair question to ask here would be: when I experience "resistance" to the truth of an idea in therapy, what is it in me that resists? It cannot be the ego, Sartre said, because the ego is

> *envisaged as a psychic totality of the facts of consciousness;* this could not suspect that the psychiatrist is approaching the end since the ego's relation to the meaning of its own reactions is exactly like that of the psychiatrist himself [italics added].[15]

In addition, it was the ego that made the decision to pursue therapy in the first place! Furthermore, Sartre claimed that in light of Freud's theory the source of the resistance could not be the "complex" either, since it seeks to express itself in consciousness. Sartre held that there was only one other possible source:

> The only level on which we can locate the refusal of the subject is that of the censor. It alone can comprehend the questions or the revelations of the psychoanalyst as approaching more or less near to the real drives which it strives to repress—it alone because it alone knows what it is repressing.[16]

Sartre maintained that this appeal to a censor raised two fundamental kinds of questions. First, how can we conceive of a knowledge which is ignorant of itself? In order to judge what is to be repressed or not to be repressed, the censor must know the content of what is before it. As Sartre stated it: "How could the censor discern the impulses needing to be repressed without being conscious of discerning them?"[17] Sartre's conclusion was that since all knowing must be conscious of knowing, the notion and operation of Freud's censor was self-contradictory: "It must be the consciousness (of) being conscious of the drive to be repressed, but precisely in order not [to] be conscious of it."[18] It is not possible for me to know and not know the same thing at the same time.

Sartre raised a related example in a much later section of *Being and Nothingness*.[19] Sartre discussed resistance—the situation in therapy when a patient lies or terminates therapy in order to avoid the truth about himself or herself. Freud explained this phenomenon by claiming that the patient somehow senses that the therapist is near to the truth, and this causes an unconscious anxiety. But, according to Sartre, to suppose some hidden operation of an unconscious anxiety and to use such a notion to explain resistance does nothing to further our understanding. For, in order to resist the truth, the unconscious would have to be apprised of the impending discovery of the truth without being conscious of it. Once again, Sartre pointed out that this was contradictory.

The second major question Sartre posed was: how is it possible for the repressed drive to "disguise itself"? Psychoanalysis denied (rightly, according to Sartre) that the repressed drive possessed any consciousness of being repressed—of being repelled because it constituted some kind of threat, or even of pursuing a project of disguise. Given its complete lack of consciousness, Sartre claimed that it simply did not make sense to speak of repressed drives disguising themselves (which presupposes a consciousness of doing so) so that they could emerge into consciousness.

A related question for Sartre was: how is it possible to consciously experience pleasure or anguish when a drive succeeds in its purpose, unless consciousness had—at least on some level—some understanding of the goal to be attained which it both desires yet is repulsed by? Such descriptions simply could not be explained by a mechanistic theory (one which imposed divisions upon the psyche), but must involve a veiled appeal to a purpose (a "finality"). The result for Sartre was undeniable: "By rejecting the conscious unity of the psyche, Freud is obliged to imply everywhere a magic unity linking distant phenomena across obstacles."[20] Freud's unconscious instinct was magically constituted by the capacity for being repressed. In other words, by dividing up the psyche, Freud could not account for any connectedness among the various components. Hence, any explanation of a connection took on a magical, unknowable quality. Repression, by ubiquitously affecting the instincts, modifies them, "and magically provokes its symbolism."[21] Reciprocally, consciousness is magically modified by repression's symbolic meaning while at the same time being unable to apprehend it in any clear manner.

What was wrong with this "explanation by magic" according to Sartre? First, it was inferior in principle. Not only did it not truly enable us to gain a better understanding of the psyche in any way whatsoever, but obscured it: "One thinks that magic is to allow the mind to move among things. But it is also and in the first place the obscuring of the mind by thingness."[22] Second, it involved mutually contradictory, yet complementary structures which simultaneously implied and destroyed one another.

During the act of hiding something from oneself, one simultaneously strives to uncover the meaning of that which is hidden while repressing and disguising it. According to Sartre, this meant nothing more than to say that the censor was itself in bad faith. The result was that psychoanalysis failed in dealing effectively with the problem of bad faith. Instead, it offered "a mere verbal terminology" which simply inserted a censor that was in bad faith between consciousness and the unconscious. The ultimate outcome, then, was that Freud's indissolubly connected notions of the unconscious, repression, and the instincts ended up making bad faith into a concrete reality, and yet failed to explain how it was possible. In Sartre's view, unable to make sense of the phenomena of self-deception, Freud resorted to the conception of the unconscious.

Sartre's Refutation of Unconscious Processes

Sartre attempted to further refute the notion of unconscious processes on two interconnected levels, through his analysis of the intrinsic nature of intentionality—the idea that all consciousness is necessarily consciousness of something. This of course presupposed his rudimentary claim that "there is nothing in consciousness which is not consciousness" (that is, there is no subject or something which is "behind" consciousness in some way).[23] First, "consciousness of something necessarily implies a consciousness of self, under penalty of falling into the unconscious."[24] Since we always have a consciousness of self upon which we can direct our consciousness, Sartre argued that there can be no such process as *unconscious repression,* for it would entail a form of consciousness which would not be a consciousness of what was repressed. Similarly, "the idea of an unconscious pleasure is totally absurd."[25] Second, Sartre's rejection of consciousness as a repressing agent was indissolubly linked to his general rejection of any mechanistic explanation of these processes. He asked that we reject this "materialistic mythology of psychoanalysis" (that is, the conceiving of the unconscious as a physical object),[26] and "all the metaphors representing the repression as the impact of blind forces."[27] The psychoanalyst persisted in claiming that the unconscious was physical (comprised of physical forces). Sartre claimed that to do so was to make "of it something passive and inert."[28] But this, then, gave rise to another fundamental contradiction of psychoanalysis: the idea that the unconscious was considered physical while consciousness was not; the unconscious was conceived as acting upon consciousness which was "not a kind of passivity." There could be no "intermediate" notion to which we can appeal.

The fundamental reason why such psychical processes could not be accounted for in causal terms was that they were inherently teleological in nature. The sheer impossibility of causally explaining intentional, goal-directed behavior was so obvious, Sartre thought, that it required no justification at all: "there is no presence of a thing-being to itself."[29] Faithful to his Cartesian tradition, Sartre defended the metaphysical irreducibility of the mental to the physical domain.

Sartre's Quest for an Alternative

Without an unconscious to explain various phenomena, Sartre was faced with the burden of an alternative account. He seemed to believe, at least for a period, that his notion of bad faith could account for some of these phenomena.

> I can interpret each particular psychological fact in one meaning or in another, and the meaning sticks or it doesn't. If I act very much in good faith the meaning sticks; if not, it doesn't.[30]

In other words, if we are in bad faith and attempting to shirk our responsibility, we engage in self-deception; if we act sincerely, we recognize the truth about ourselves. According to Sartre there need not be anything hidden behind such phenomena (as in Freud's "unconscious processes"). To posit such a hidden phenomena, again, was unnecessary and distortive;[31] it ignored the fact that consciousness is consciousness through and through, that it is lucid, transparent: "If a belief is belief, that is because it believes itself as a belief or because it is contested as a belief."[32] But if *all* belief is consciousness of belief, does this necessarily mean that we have knowledge of any particular belief? How did Sartre prevent himself from falling back into an appeal to an unconscious? Sartre's answer was his famous distinction between *knowledge* (reflective or positional consciousness) and *awareness* (pre-reflective, non-thetic or prepositional consciousness). Sartre described them as "two radically different phenomena."[33] We are aware of the world through non-thetic consciousness yet we do not know it on a reflective level.[34] However, "it is not to that extent an unconscious if it is not a faculty of knowledge."[35] For example, as I type this sentence I am conscious of this typing activity without knowing through direct reflection this very activity (unless I turn to reflect upon it).

In the discussion period following a typically ignored lecture before the French philosophical society, Sartre was confronted directly by a psychoanalyst—M. Salzi—on his position on the unconscious. Salzi challenged him to explain how psychoanalytic cures were possible if there were no unconscious. Sartre replied by arguing that on ontological grounds the unconscious did not exist, but that perhaps he was being too quick since it would do nothing to convince the psychoanalysts whose experience was to the contrary. From an instrumentalist point of view, Sartre argued that not only was the unconscious a useless tool, it was "an illusion." To substantiate this, Sartre unconvincingly argued, "one could also appeal to different notions." However, instead of revealing what those were, he simply said that he knew of a psychoanalyst—Wilhelm Steckel—who was perfectly able to conduct his work without having to have recourse to the unconscious.[36]

It should be noted that in a section in *Being and Nothingness* Sartre also alluded to Steckel's comment: "Every time that I have been able to carry my investigations far enough, I have established that the crux of the psychosis was conscious."[37] In addition, Sartre claimed that Steckel offered cases of bad faith for which Freudian psychoanalysis was unable to account.

However, about fifteen years later, some of those closest to Sartre strongly believed that he eventually recognized and admitted his earlier account to have been false. For example, his close friend Pontalis, a well-respected psychoanalyst, observed:

> It seems to me undeniable that Sartre succeeded in making percept-ible—hence first and foremost in making perceptible to himself—a certain number of phenomena which could no longer be adequately accounted for by the notion of "bad faith" that he had long promoted to "counter" Freud . . . But can one regard hysterical complaints as lies, especially when they affect vital functions . . . as was the case with patients treated by Breuer and Freud . . . but we cannot help feeling that Sartre sympathized with those women telling their "stories."[38]

Freud's Response

Freud's introduction of the "unconscious" was met with much suspicion and protest from the scientific and philosophical communities. It is no surprise, then, that many of Sartre's criticisms were directly addressed by Freud, despite the fact that Freud never came in personal contact (as far as we know) with Sartre. Basically, "Freud's" response to Sartre would have centered on certain key configurations of ideas. Freud would have argued that (1) Sartre's characterization of consciousness as exclusively involving intentionality, along with a spectrum of gradations, simply (and crassly) begged the question concerning the existence of the unconscious; (2) Sartre's alternative proposal to the unconscious failed to account for a variety of phenomena (such as previously acquired ideas, memory, the occurrence of dreams, parapraxes, the processes of hypnosis, and so on), all of which required the explanatory notion of the unconscious in the first place; and (3) Sartre's portrayal of the Freudian psyche was completely mistaken and based on an oversimplification and misunderstanding of Freud's writings. Due to the extensive nature of this response, each of these points will be considered individually.

Sartre begged the question of the existence of the unconscious

From a Freudian point of view, Sartre would have been a spectacular example of philosophers who fall prey to the (philosophical) prejudice that mental life is equatable with consciousness, and by doing so begged the question of the (non)existence of the unconscious. There are a number of key ways in which Sartre did this. We shall focus on two of them.

First, while developing his philosophy of mind as a theory of consciousness, Sartre prima facie equated consciousness with psychical reality.

> Insofar as consciousness *makes itself,* it is never anything but what it appears to be. Therefore, if it possesses a signification it should contain it in itself as a structure of consciousness . . . If the cogito is to be possible, consciousness is itself the *fact,* the *signification,* and the *thing signified.*[39]

In *Being and Nothingness,* Sartre simply presupposed a Cartesian position concerning the unity and transparency of the psyche. This precluded any possible existence of a divided mind which was, at least, partially opaque. Sartre proclaimed: "For the law of being in the knowing subject is to-be-conscious";[40] and, "The law of being of the for-itself, as the ontological foundation of consciousness is to be itself in the form of presence to itself."[41]

> Ontology alone in fact can take its place on the plane of transcendence and from a single viewpoint apprehend being-in-the-world with its two terms, because ontology alone has its place originally in the perspective of the cogito.[42]

All of this was already to restrict consciousness within the boundaries Sartre selected (namely, as that which makes itself), and hence to identify consciousness with psychical life. In doing so, Sartre obviously begged the question of whether unconscious psychical processes exist.[43] How did Sartre do this, specifically? Following the phenomenological tradition in which he was immersed, consciousness was understood as fundamentally intentional in nature. Consciousness was always consciousness *of* some kind of object.[44] This, Sartre believed, was true for all psychical processes (perceptions, emotions, intentions, desires, and so on). Furthermore, Sartre argued that all such intentionality necessarily involves some kind of self-consciousness (that is, a "pre-reflective," "non-positional," or "non-thetic" consciousness—which was an implicit consciousness of being conscious of an object). Sartre offered a reductio ad absurdum argument against the existence of the unconscious:

> If my consciousness were not consciousness of being conscious of that table, it would then be consciousness of that table without consciousness of being so. In other words, it would be a consciousness ignorant of itself, an unconscious consciousness—which is absurd.[45]

This reasoning ruled out *ob ovo* the very possibility of an unconscious psychical process. More simply put, Sartre's argument was that since consciousness was equatable with intentionality, there could be no such thing as unconscious intentionality.

Yet in relation to this argument, Freud needed only to point out that with regard to consciousness, there was no necessary contradiction of a consciousness that was not conscious of itself as consciousness. Hence there was no need to posit a level of implicit consciousness which was a self-consciousness of the consciousness of an object. More important, there was no reason to make the assumption that all intentional psychical processes must be, on some level, self-conscious. For example, if someone desires something, it is not necessarily the case that one is aware that one is conscious that one desires that something. For Freud, all of this can, and often does, occur on the unconscious level (without contradiction!).

A second argument, which Sartre adduced in favor of the existence of a pre-reflective cogito, was to offer a phenomenological analysis of the experience of counting cigarettes.[46] For example, I may not explicitly realize what I am doing, while I am counting cigarettes. As Sartre put it: "The consciousness of man in action is non-reflective consciousness."[47] Yet if asked, Sartre argued, I could always give an immediate report of what I am doing. However, Sartre's example of counting cigarettes was only *one* illustration. He failed to show that the same can be done in *all* instances, and in order to make his case he would have had to do so. Yet, there are clearly times when we cannot give an immediate report of what we are doing. For example, when one of the authors was new to lecturing he (evidently) had the habit of twirling his curly hair (probably to help assuage any anxiety he was feeling), but had someone asked what he was doing with his body while lecturing he would not have known to report that he was twirling his hair with his fingers—indeed, he had no aware-ness of this on any level, whatsoever.[48] These examples would all be, more or less, understood within Freud's framework as a matter of bringing *pre-conscious* material to the level of consciousness.[49]

Sartre also claimed that the unconscious was based merely on the recognition that there are different gradations in the clarity of that which is in consciousness: "not all signification has to be perfectly explicit. Many degrees of condensation and clarity are possible."[50] In a quotation that could have been addressed directly to Sartre, Freud wrote:

> A new turn taken by criticisms of the unconscious deserves consideration at this point. Some investigators, who do not refuse to recognize the facts of psycho-analysis but who are unwilling to accept the unconscious, find a way out of the difficulty in the fact, which no one contests, that in con-sciousness (regarded as a phenomenon) it is possible to distinguish a great variety of gradations in intensity or clarity. Just as there are pro-cesses which are very vividly, glaringly, and tangibly conscious, so we also experience others which are only faintly, hardly even noticeably con-scious; those that are most faintly conscious are, it is argued, the ones to which psycho-analysis wishes to apply the unsuitable name "uncon-scious." These too, however (the argument proceeds), are conscious . . . if sufficient attention is paid to them.[51]

Freud rebutted this argument *toute à fait*. (1) Such references to "gradations of clarity in consciousness" are inconclusive and, since they have no evidential value, "for practical purposes they are worthless." For Freud it would be as silly as trying to infer from the dubious claim "there are varying degrees of vitality" the conclusion "therefore there is no death." (2) To include "what is unnoticeable" under the concept of "what is conscious" would be to wreak havoc with "the one and only piece of di-rect and certain knowledge that we have about the mind."[52] (3) A con-sciousness about which one knows nothing is far more absurd than some-thing mental that is unconscious. Freud was explicit on this point: "Now let us call 'conscious' the conception which is present to our conscious-ness and of which we are aware, and let this be the only meaning of the term 'conscious.'"[53] And, (4) such talk ignored the dynamic conditions in-volved in mental life: (a) it ignored the immense difficulty and tremen-dous effort required to remain focused on this "unnoticed" something; and (b) when this was achieved, consciousness—instead of immediately recognizing it for what it was—opposed and disavowed it as something en-tirely foreign.

On this last point, from a Freudian viewpoint Sartre failed to understand what was directly experienced concerning the unconscious in the psychotherapeutic context. Freud wrote:

> To most people who have been educated in philosophy the idea of anything psychical which is not also conscious is so inconceivable that it seems to them absurd and refutable simply by logic. I believe this is only because they have never studied the relevant phenomena of hypnosis and dreams, which—quite apart from pathological manifestations— necessitate this view. Their psychology of consciousness is incapable of solving the problems of dreams and hypnosis.[54]

Hence:

> Seeking refuge from the unconscious in what is scarcely noticed or unnoticed is after all only a derivative of the preconceived belief which regards the identity of the psychical and the conscious as settled once and for all.[55]

There is no doubt that Freud would have held Sartre to be a victim—and not alone—of *petitio principii.*

Sartre failed to account for unconscious phenomena

Freud would have argued that Sartre failed to offer an account of mental phenomena that would seem to involve "preconscious" and "unconscious" processes. First, Sartre neglected to account for the status of ideas which have been previously acquired and are not immediately conscious yet can be brought to consciousness with little effort. Suppose one thinks of the name of the hospital in which one was born. Before one thinks of it—just now—what was the nature of the existence of the idea of that hospital? Such ideas are left, by Sartre, in a sort of psychological limbo. He failed to show us how we are to account for such latent memories. Sartre's position had the misfortune of holding that we are conscious of everything that we can remember, even before we remember it. Freud demonstrated that this was simply not how we are in our psychological being.

Furthermore, Freud observed that people typically acquire various kinds of material without necessarily being conscious of it on the preconscious level, and that much of such material never becomes conscious at all. If Freud is correct here, it follows that people are able to become conscious of something in memory without first having consciousness of the original event as it occurred. Freud would refer to experiments in hypnosis where witnesses to some event could be brought to be consciously aware of something they had not previously noticed. Such evidence strongly undermines Sartre's claim that such cases were impossible, given his account of the nature of consciousness. Similarly, by rejecting the unconscious, Sartre failed to account for why dreams, parapraxes, hypnotic processes, and so on occur in the way in which they do.

In addition, Sartre was one more philosopher who had no explicit experience of the unconscious in the therapeutic context and hence could not have any knowledge of it. Since Sartre had no such direct experience, he spoke of things he knew nothing about:

> Yet we have been obliged to recognize and express as our conviction that no one has a right to join in a discussion of psycho-analysis who has not had particular experiences which can only be obtained by being analysed oneself.[56]

Sartre mischaracterized Freud's position on the nature of the psyche
Had Freud addressed Sartre's critique of the unconscious, he would have most likely included him among those critics who were in need of a thorough rereading (or even reading) of his work.[57] Sartre's blatant misunderstanding of Freud's model of the psyche was so extensive, it requires a section of its own.

1. Sartre (mis)equated Freud's notions of consciousness and the unconscious with the ego and the id (and the repressed), respectively. Sartre accused psychoanalysis of separating consciousness from the unconscious by means of the censor. It established "a veritable duality and even a trinity (Id, Ego, Superego expressing themselves through the censor) . . ."[58] Here, Sartre simplistically failed to distinguish between Freud's "topographical" and subsequent "structural" models. The first involved the distinction between consciousness, the preconscious, and the unconscious; the second, the distinction between the id, ego, and superego. Sartre simply conflated the two systems. An accurate account of Freud's latter model reveals that the interrelationship among the components of the structural model is not nearly so simple as Sartre made them out to be.[59]

As Strachey noted, Freud's use of the notion of the "ego" was not unambiguous: "it denotes a particular part of the mind characterized by special attributes and functions."[60] For example, Freud thought of the (progenitor of the) ego as including an unconscious—that is, in the descriptive sense, a preconscious—as early as *The Interpretation of Dreams*.[61]

Freud came to believe that it was simply not practicable to regard the repressed as coinciding with the unconscious, and the ego with the preconscious and conscious;[62] the distinguishing mark of consciousness versus unconscious is ambiguous. "A part of the ego, too—and Heaven knows how important a part—may be Unconscious, undoubtedly is Unconscious."[63] And again, "It is certain that much of the ego is itself unconscious, and notably what we may describe as its nucleus."[64] Freud was also explicit that the superego had an unconscious as well:

> . . . in quite important situations the super-ego and the ego can operate unconsciously, or—and this would be still more important—that portions of both of them, the ego and the super-ego themselves, are unconscious. In both cases we have to reckon with the disagreeable discovery that on the one hand (super-) ego and conscious and on the other hand repressed and unconscious are far from coinciding.[65]

Finally, one need only peruse the diagram Freud offered in his later writings,[66] eleven years prior to the publication of *Being and Nothingness*, to see how mistaken Sartre was in his identification of the two systems.

2. Sartre understood Freud's view of the psyche as literally having discrete ("a veritable duality") and opposing divisions within it. Again, Sartre claimed that psychoanalysis "separate[d] consciousness from the unconscious by means of the censor";[67] and, "By the distinction between the 'id' and the 'ego,' Freud has cut the psychic whole into two. I am the ego but I am not the id."[68]

In terms of the topographical model, Sartre clearly had in mind Freud's diagrams (with which we know he was familiar from the beginning of his studies at the École), represented in both *The Interpretation of Dreams*[69] and (its predecessor) in a letter to Fliess of December 6, 1896.[70] It is true that both diagrams were concerned with the function and ostensibly discrete functional structures of the psyche.[71] It is also true that in his *Lectures on Psychoanalysis* Freud alluded to a spatial description of the topographical systems—though he described it as "crude" and "incorrect."[72] Such descriptions were not, Freud believed, to be taken literally.

Far more serious however is the point that Freud was quite explicitly opposed to a Sartrean description of the ego and id as discrete and opposing forces. Freud wrote, "We should be quite wrong if we pictured the ego and the id as two opposing camps."[73] "The ego is not sharply separated from the id; its lower portion merges into it."[74] Freud emphasized why he held this view in no uncertain terms:

> We were justified, I think, in dividing the ego from the id, for there are certain considerations which necessitate that step. On the other hand

the ego is identical with the id, and is merely a specially differentiated part of it. If we think of this part by itself in contradistinction to the whole, or if a real split has occurred between the two, the weakness of the ego becomes apparent. But if the ego remains bound up with the id and indistinguishable from it, then it displays its strength . . . The ego is, indeed, the organized portion of the id.[75]

Furthermore, Freud saw the superego as forming part of the ego.[76] Again, even in *The Interpretation of Dreams,* Freud was already careful on this point: "Strictly speaking, there is no need for the hypothesis that the psychical systems are actually arranged in *spatial* order."[77]

I hope you do not take the term too anthropomorphically, and do not picture the "censor of dreams" as a severe little manikin or a spirit living in a closet in the brain and there discharging his office; but I hope too that you do not take the term in too "localizing" a sense, and do not think of a "brain-centre," from which a censoring influence of this kind issues, an influence which would be brought to an end if the "centre" were damaged or removed. For the time being it is nothing more than a serviceable term for describing a dynamic relation.[78]

3. Sartre oversimplified Freud's notion of the nature and functioning of the censor within Freud's various models. In *Being and Nothingness,* Sartre described his understanding of Freud's censor as "conceived as a line of demarcation with customs, passport division, currency control, etc."[79] Where was this line? Sartre said only that the censor "separate[s] the unconscious from the conscious."[80] Superficially speaking, this was true—Freud said,

You have long been aware that this censorship is not an institution peculiar to dream-life. You know that the conflict between the two psychical agencies, which we—inaccurately[81]—describe as the "unconscious repressed" and the "conscious," dominates our whole mental life . . .[82]

However, Sartre's account of Freud was clearly a gross oversimplification. In his argument, Sartre did not even take note of the major divisions Freud drew within his topographical model—consciousness, the preconscious, and the unconscious. As a result, he also failed to note that Freud discussed more than one level of censorship at work within this model; it is clear that Freud spoke of the process of censorship both between the preconscious and the conscious,[83] and between the unconscious and the preconscious.[84] What is odd about Sartre's neglect regarding these distinctions is that they prominently occurred as early as *The Interpretation of*

Dreams as well as later in *Introductory Lectures on Psycho-analysis,* texts with which Sartre was clearly familiar. The reason that this point is so important is that Sartre's criticism of Freud's censor was monolithic and failed to take into account the subtleties and nuances of the different ways in which they operated.

Next, Sartre seemed unacquainted with the fact that in his later writings Freud seemed to equate, in explicit fashion, the censor with his notion of the superego: "repression is the work of this super-ego and that it is carried out either by itself or by the ego in obedience to its orders."[85]

From this last remark, it might be tempting to take this as Freud's general position on the extent of egological repression[86] vis-à-vis the superego, but this would be to exacerbate Sartre's oversimplification of Freud's position even more extensively. Freud's writings themselves do not conform to this general pronouncement throughout his career.[87] The evidence to the contrary—that is, that superegological repression was but one form of repression—was clearly Freud's predominant position.[88] With his obvious sensitivity to the complexity of the processes of repression, Freud discussed: examples where egological repression was not only *not* in compliance with the superego, but actually opposed it;[89] cases where the superego's behest may have been involved;[90] cases where the superego may have been involved among others;[91] cases where the superego (or earlier forms of it) may be involved, but not to the exclusion of the other parts of the personality;[92] and cases where the superego may be responsible for various pathological states.[93]

The greatest preponderance of cases, however, were those (1909–38) whereby Freud discussed egological repression with no mention of the superego (or related concepts) being involved at all.[94] Indeed, Freud said as one of his final statements on the subject: "There is a danger of overestimating the part played in repression by the super-ego."[95] In his autobiographical account of the development of ego repression, there was no mention of the superego in its early development.

> The ego drew back, as it were, on its first collision with the objectionable instinctual impulse; it debarred the impulse from access to consciousness and to direct motor discharge, but at the same time the impulse retained its full cathexis of energy. I named this process *repression* . . .[96]

Finally, it should be noted in light of Sartre's first mistake (above), especially with regard to the point of the ego also having an unconscious, Sartre put himself into a position of completely missing Freud's description of the operation of the censor on the level of the ego (namely, egological repression).[97] Sartre wrote,

It is a fair question to ask what part of himself can thus resist. It can not be the "Ego," envisaged as a psychic totality of the facts of consciousness, this could not suspect that the psychiatrist is approaching the end since the ego's relation to the meaning of its own reactions is exactly like that of the psychiatrist himself.[98]

Sartre obviously missed a fundamental aspect of Freud's last theoretical model. Freud wrote, for example, "we have to reckon with the disagreeable discovery that on the one hand (super-) ego and conscious and on the other hand repressed and unconscious are far from coinciding."[99] In egological repression, Freud thought the ego selected those kinds of repression which would best comply with the requirements of the reality principle—if the id made dangerous demands threatening the person's well-being, they would need to be repressed by the ego. "The ego fends off the danger by the process of repression."[100] Here, in particular, Freud explicitly maintained that the functions of censorship were to be understood as the responsibility of the ego.[101]

4. *Sartre misconceived the Freudian ego (that is, consciousness) as passive.* Sartre wrote:

> The first result of such a [psychoanalytic] interpretation is to establish consciousness as a thing in relation to the thing signified . . . in this case it is necessary to renounce entirely the Cartesian cogito and make of consciousness a secondary and passive phenomenon.[102]

> By separating consciousness from the unconscious by means of the censor, psychoanalysis has not succeeded in dissociating the two phases of the act, since the libido is a blind conatus toward conscious expression and since the conscious phenomenon is a passive, faked result.[103]

Obviously, Sartre characterized Freud's "ego" as a "psychic totality of the facts of consciousness"[104] which was passively tossed about by the demands of the id.

Having obviously run into this interpretation of the ego as passive antecedently,[105] Freud's rejoinder was sharp and to the point:

> Just as the ego controls the path to action in regard to the external world, so it controls access to consciousness. In repression it exercises its power in both directions . . . In [*The Ego and the Id*] I drew a picture of its dependent relationship to the id and to the superego and revealed how powerless and apprehensive it was in regard to both and with what an

effort it maintained its show of superiority over them. This view has been widely echoed in psycho-analytic literature. Many writers have laid much stress on the weakness of the ego in relation to the id and of our rational elements in the face of the daemonic forces within us; and they display a strong tendency to make what I have said into a corner-stone of a psycho-analytic *Weltanschauung*. Yet surely the psycho-analyst, with his knowledge of the way in which repression works, should, of all people, be restrained from adopting such an extreme and one-sided view.[106]

Freud immediately followed this statement with: "I must confess that I am not at all partial to the fabrication of *Weltanschauungen*. Such activities may be left to philosophers . . ."[107]

Anyone (or almost anyone, it seems) generally familiar with Freud's writings knows that Freud conceived of the ego as an active agent on a variety of levels. Consider the following quotes from Freud, for example: "it is the mental agency which supervises all its own constituent processes . . .";[108] "the ego seeks to bring the influence of the external world to bear upon the id and its tendencies, and endeavours to substitute the reality principle for the pleasure principle . . .";[109] "the ego can gain control over the id . . .";[110] "By virtue of its relation to the perceptual system it gives mental processes an order in time and submits them to 'reality-testing'";[111] "By interposing the processes of thinking, it secures a postponement of motor discharges and controls the access to motility . . . the ego's position is like that of a constitutional monarch . . .";[112] "The ego develops from perceiving instincts to controlling them, from obeying instincts to inhibiting them . . . Psychoanalysis is an instrument to enable the ego to achieve a progressive conquest of the id";[113] "As a frontier creature, the ego tries to mediate between the world, and the id . . ."[114] Also,

All our analyses go to show that the transference neuroses originate from the ego's refusing to accept a powerful instinctual impulse in the id or to help it find a motor outlet, or from the ego's forbidding that impulse the object at which it is aiming. In such a case the ego defends itself against the instinctual impulse by the mechanism of repression. The repressed material struggles against this fate. It creates for itself, along paths over which the ego has no power, a substitutive representation (which forces itself upon the ego by way of a compromise)—the symptom. The ego finds its unity threatened and impaired by this intruder, and it continues to struggle against the symptom, just as it fended off the original instinctual impulse. All this produces the picture of a neurosis. It is no contradiction to this that, in undertaking the repression, the ego is at bottom following the commands of its super-ego—commands which, in their turn, originate from influences in the external world that have found representation in the super-ego. The fact remains that the ego *has* taken sides with those powers . . .[115]

We must not be surprised if the ego on its part can bring its influence to bear on the processes in the id. I believe the ego exercises this influence by putting into action the almost omnipotent pleasure-unpleasure principle by means of the signal of anxiety.[116]

Indeed, there is a virtually endless stream of examples from Freud on this point. Obviously, the ego was primarily conceived by Freud as active and not simply pushed around by the instinctual forces of the id, the moral demands of the superego, and the requirements of external reality. Indeed, it was the ego that was actively trying to coordinate all of the demands made on it as the executor of the personality.

From a Freudian point of view, Sartre would be a philosopher who attributed a straw man Weltanschauung to psychoanalysis, only to then show why it was deficient. Any psychoanalyst worth his/her salt would have known, given their intimate knowledge of repression, to avoid being "restrained from adopting such an extreme and one-sided view."[117]

Had Freud had the patience and forbearance to read Sartre's writings about him—had he been alive (*Being and Nothingness* was published four years after his death)—he probably would have wondered about Sartre's inconsistencies in his account of psychoanalysis. For at times Sartre was very careful in his approach:

Considered more closely the psychoanalytic theory is not as simple as it first appears. It is not accurate to hold that the "id" is presented as a thing in relation to the hypothesis of the psychoanalyst, for a thing is indifferent to the conjectures which we make concerning it, while the "id" on the contrary is sensitive to them when we approach the truth.[118]

A natural question for Freud to have asked was why Sartre did not accord the Freudian ego the same point concerning its status—not as a passive thing, but as an active agent? As the executor of the personality, clearly the Freudian ego was not merely at the mercy of the id's demands!

Indeed, Freud may have himself identified one of the primary reasons for Sartre's misunderstanding, while specifically addressing the question of his ostensibly contradictory discussions regarding the activity/passivity of the ego (placing emphasis on the one at the expense of the other, at times).

> To return to the problem of the ego. The apparent contradiction is due
> to our having taken abstractions too rigidly and attended exclusively now
> to the one side and now to the other of what is in fact a complicated state
> of affairs.[119]

This is a remarkable statement by Freud, for it alluded not only to a deficient tendency in himself, but also unintentionally demonstrated one of
Sartre's own ideas, that of "bad faith." Sartre, by focusing on the ego as passive and not considering its active side—despite the immense evidence to
the contrary—was in his own terms in "bad faith" (and hence, the "master" of self-deception). Furthermore, while it was true that Freud spoke at
times as if the ego were passive, it is crucial to observe that these were most
frequently occasions when a person was ill and out of balance. One of the
goals of Freudian psychoanalysis was precisely to restore the unifying and
harmonious functioning of the psyche, so that the person could assume
more active control of his or her life.

In conclusion, there is a sense in which, historically speaking, Freud
and Sartre evolved in opposite directions on the issue of the extent to
which we are conditioned by environment, and to what extent we are free
to change it and ourselves. The mature Sartre came to realize increasingly
the strong impact of the conditioning factors of our environment upon
us—while always insisting upon a measure of freedom. Freud, always emphasizing the determining features of human existence, nevertheless recognized that we have the capacity to choose to do something about what
we have felt compelled to repeat in the past, so that we can increasingly
become master in our own house!

The Poetic Weight of the Body: Merleau-Ponty's Reposturing of Freudian Psychoanalysis

> The best . . . would perhaps be . . . to learn to read Freud the way
> we read a classic, that is, by understanding his words and
> theoretical concepts, not in their lexical and common meaning,
> but in the meaning they acquire from within the experience
> which they announce and of which we have behind our backs
> more than a suspicion . . . perhaps we should continue calling it
> the unconscious—so long as we do not forget that the word is
> the index of an enigma—because the term retains, like the algae
> or the stone that one drags up, something of the sea from which
> it was taken.
> —Merleau-Ponty

Maurice Merleau-Ponty's reaction to Freudian psychoanalysis was quite different than the existential phenomenologists discussed in previous chapters. In general, he was far more receptive to Freudian theoretical insights, even though he sought to reposture them in what he believed was the philosophically more viable context of an existential phenomenological framework.[1] This raises some very interesting questions: what, in the end, is the relationship of the goals of existential phenomenology to Freudian psychoanalysis? To some, there never seemed to be a natural meeting ground between the world of consciousness and the world of the unconscious, while to others, existential phenomenology and Freudian psychoanalysis appear to be entirely consistent. Are the goals of the two essentially identical, compatible, or possibly mutually exclusive? Do they converge, and if so, to what extent? Is there a convergence, which results in their merger? To what extent is a reconciliation between the two possible?

This chapter will address these questions from Merleau-Ponty's point of view. We shall do this while examining Merleau-Ponty's attitude toward Freudian psychoanalysis as it evolved throughout the course of his philosophical development; and considering what Freud's reaction to Merleau-Ponty's interpretation/reposturing of his thought would have been. Merleau-Ponty's major and original contributions toward an understanding of the relationship existing between existential phenomenology and Freudian psychoanalysis will be "fleshed" out while some of the deficiencies and unresolved problems involved in his suggestions will be noted.

Merleau-Ponty's Attitude toward Freudian Psychoanalysis

In his first book, *The Structure of Behavior,* Merleau-Ponty engaged in a strong critique of objectivist psychology. Here, Merleau-Ponty believed that one of his essential tasks was to disclose "the abuse of causal thinking in explanatory theories," while showing how one might properly conceive that which is of value in them.[2] Merleau-Ponty felt that by focusing upon the Freudian psychoanalytic system as his example, he could effectively accomplish both. It was his belief that it is beneficial to glean what is of value in Freudian psychoanalysis and resituate it within an existential phenomenological framework.

Merleau-Ponty first alluded to the characteristic objectivist phraseology of the Freudian system. Freud, in his discussions and descriptions of the psychological mechanisms (the formation of complexes, repression, and so on), had written in such a way as to suggest a psychical content of unconscious forces and entities. Freud, in fact, has been traditionally interpreted in just this way. Without questioning Freud's account of the libidinal infrastructure, Merleau-Ponty wanted to inquire as to whether or not those actual conflicts and psychological mechanisms of which Freud had spoken, necessarily required the system of causal notions by which he had interpreted them. Merleau-Ponty's answer was that such causal thinking was dispensable. He contended that what was important in Freud's theory could just as easily be shown through the use of nonobjectivist language. In a highly significant passage, Merleau-Ponty wrote:

> Development should be considered, not as the fixation of a given force on outside objects which are also given, but as a progressive and discontinuous structuration of behavior. Normal structuration is one which reorganizes conduct in depth in such a way that infantile attitudes no longer have a place or meaning in the new attitude; it would result in perfectly

integrated behavior, each moment of which would be internally linked with the whole. One will say that there is repression when integration has been achieved only in appearance and leaves certain relatively isolated systems subsisting in behavior which the subject refuses both to transform and to assume. A complex is a segment of behavior of this kind, a stereotyped attitude, an acquired and durable structure of consciousness with regard to a category of stimuli.[3]

It is clear that Merleau-Ponty did not wish to deny the facts which Freud described, but rather Freud's interpretations of them.

Contrary to Freud, Merleau-Ponty asserted that the complex should not be viewed as some entity subsisting deep within us, sporadically producing its effects on the surface. Instead, the problem is to understand how certain separated dialectics (involving the interchange between person and the world) and mental automations (that is, nonobjective ones) possessing an internal logic, can be constituted in the flux of consciousness. Paul Ricoeur made the same observation: "Freud's discovery operates on the level of effects of meaning, but he continues to express it in the language and through the concepts of energetics of his masters."[4] In other words, one must understand how such rigid and stable structures arise. This problem, once again, is not solved by attributing entitative status, possessing their own causal efficacy, to complexes. Instead, what is required by the facts that Freud described is "only the possibility of a fragmented life of consciousness which does not possess a unique significance at all times."[5]

According to Merleau-Ponty, the possibility of fragmentation is attributable both to the ambivalence of consciousness and the levels of meaning within human life. During the moments of fragmentation, the subject is guided by the immediate feeling of the forbidden or the permitted, without investigating the meaning of the prohibitions. In this case, "the pretended unconsciousness of the complex is reduced to the ambivalence of immediate consciousness."[6] Freud's complexes and psychological mechanisms, instead of having causal efficacy, only manifested the return to a more primitive manner of organizing behavior, that is, a withdrawal from complex structures toward more facile ones. But, then, according to Merleau-Ponty, Freud's description of mental functioning would represent only fragmentary behavior—behavior which is pathological. At this point, Merleau-Ponty saw Freud's work as constituting a tableau of anomalies, not one of human existence. Merleau-Ponty translated Freud's causal explanation of behavior into a more "appropriate" language, one depicting the inadequacy of the structurations achieved by the subject.

However, Merleau-Ponty observed that along with the mechanisms Freud depicted, "a true development, a transformation of human existence would be possible." He contended that Freudian mechanisms (namely, primitive and inadequate structurations) would function in some cases, while in others they would be transcended. The behavior of some persons would be explicable solely in terms of the history of the libido. Others would believe that they had succeeded in transcending the biological and social dialectic while actually failing to do so. Still others would actually be capable of integrating their existence by unifying it with all of the successively higher orders, the physical, the vital, and the mental. Such people, according to Merleau-Ponty, would have achieved the fullest humanity. For these people, Freud's causal explanations would be merely "anecdotal," since they would have integrated their behavior so as to transcend those primitive ways of organizing the world represented by the Freudian complexes and psychological mechanisms.

Unfortunately, Freud's limited view of development, according to Merleau-Ponty, revealed his failure to escape from the classical debate between "mentalists" and "materialists." For Merleau-Ponty, the artificial distinction of the mental and the somatic prevented Freud's theory from disclosing knowledge of the "normal" person (an integrated human). Merleau-Ponty pointed out that the processes of both the mental and the somatic do not unfold in isolation, but are integrated into a cycle of more extensive action. Higher levels of behavior both assume and reorganize the lower levels. He wrote, "It is not a question of two de facto orders external to each other, but of the two types of relations, the second which integrates the first."[7] The body of the normal subject is not distinct from the psychological. Similarly, mind is not a new kind of being added to vital or psychological being in order to constitute a person. Instead, "mind" is a new form of unity which is unable to stand by itself, and is inseparable from the very orders it integrates. Once behavior is considered "in its unity" and in its human meaning, it is clear that one is not dealing with a material reality or mental reality, but with a significative totality or structuration which belongs neither to the external world nor to internal life.

Merleau-Ponty pointed out that Freud failed because he conceived of complexes as rigid slices of behavior that were not integrated in a coherent and flexible field of meaning. He failed to understand that human "instincts" could not exist apart from the mental dialectic, and that this dialectic was inconceivable outside of the concrete situations in which it was embodied. Freud, then, was a casualty of one of the major quagmires of thought, the subject–object dichotomy.

Apparently, Merleau-Ponty did not transcend this position in *Phenomenology of Perception*. It was in this book, however, that Merleau-Ponty elaborated upon his attitude toward Freudian psychoanalysis within the context of his perspective on sexuality and the body. In the chapter entitled, "The Body in its Sexual Being," Merleau-Ponty's goal was to clarify the primary way in which human beings illuminate their experience. He described the body as the place where this appropriation of the world occurs. He claimed that it is necessary to describe that realm of experience which has significance and reality only to the individual (namely, affection), so that it is possible to discover the rudimentary relationship between the embodied subject and its world. In seeing how an object begins to exist through desire, one is able to better understand how objects can exist in general.

First, Merleau-Ponty showed the inadequacy of empirical psychology's conception of sexuality as a mixture of stimuli, representations, and reflexes. He pointed out that an analysis of several abnormal cases revealed that this is not the case: sexual incapacity did *not* result in the loss of certain representations or a weakening in the capacity for satisfaction. Instead, the sexually incapacitated person lacks the "power of projecting before himself a sexual world . . . [He] no longer asks of his environment, this mute and permanent question which constitutes normal sexuality."[8] In this case, there is an erotic perception (or rather, its lack), which is quite distinct from objective perception. Instead of being an intentionality, which is pure "awareness of something," it aims at another body through one body; it occurs in the world and not in a consciousness. In other words, something has a sexual significance, when it exists for the body. This "erotic comprehension" is, once again, not of the order of intellectual understanding, rather it is desire which comprehends "blindly" by linking body to body. Hence, sexuality involves an intentionality which both follows and yields to the general flow of existence. Normal sexuality gives perception an erotic structure. It is one of the fundamental modes in which an individual, on the level of the bodily-subject, discloses sense in the world as existence and as an expression of self.

> We discover both that sexual life is one more form of original intentionality and also brings to view the vital origins of perception, motility and representation by basing all these "processes" on an "intentional arc" which gives way in the patient, and which, in the normal subject, endows experience with its degree of vitality and fruitfulness.[9]

For Merleau-Ponty, sexuality was *one* of the fundamental modes of existence, but as such it was not seen as an autonomous cycle. In *this mode of existence* both the individual and the world are active and passive, so that the sense expressed in the world is the expression of self in a concrete situation. Hence, whatever the form of the sexual situation, Merleau-Ponty stressed that affectivity, activity, and cognition (as the three "sectors" of existential orientation toward the world), constituted one structure; each was viewed as having the relationship of reciprocal expression toward the others. It was from this perspective that Merleau-Ponty concurred with what he called "the more lasting discoveries of psychoanalysis."

He suggested that the fundamental significance of psychoanalysis was *not* to have made psychology biological, nor was it to have given an explanatory theory of humans in terms of their sexual infrastructure. Instead, the true achievement of psychoanalysis, in Merleau-Ponty's opinion, was "to discover a dialectical process in functions thought of as 'purely bodily' and to *reintegrate* sexuality into the human being."[10] Psychoanalysis led to a discovery of relations and attitudes in sexuality that formerly had been claimed to exist in consciousness. According to Merleau-Ponty, Freud knew that the libido was not an instinct but rather a sort of teleological activity, a general power engaging structures of behavior. Through reintegrating sexuality into the human being, Freud showed how it projected a person's manner of being toward the world—toward time and other people. A correct exegesis of sexual symptoms would reveal that they represented the *whole* attitude of the subject.

Merleau-Ponty's reinterpretation of Freud involved knowing what was to be understood by sexuality. Psychoanalysis was seen as representing a *double trend of thought*. First, it emphasized the sexual substructure of life; Merleau-Ponty reinterpreted this in terms of the bodily-subject as the fundamental level of existence. Second, psychoanalysis "'expands' the notion of sexuality to the extent of absorbing into it the whole of existence."[11] This occurred insofar as the sense, born on the level of biological existence, can be taken up by human existence on the conscious and free level. Sexuality, then, becomes a *real mode of our being-in-the-world*, a manner of being in the physical and interhuman world.

Generalizing the notion of sexuality in the preceding way caused conclusions of psychoanalysis to remain ambiguous. This ambiguity raised questions concerning the relationship between sexuality and existence. For Merleau-Ponty, it was nonsense to say—as Freud did—that all existence has sexual significance. If that were the case, existence would be simply another name for the sexual life. Again, this would be to misconceive sexuality as a separate function definable in causal terms. Conversely, it is not the case that every sexual phenomenon has an existential significance, for the *sexual life is not a mere reflection of existence*. The sexual life is a sector of life bearing a special relation to the epiphenomenal. However, it was clear to Merleau-Ponty that the mode of sexuality was a highly important one in existential orientations toward the world—as

Freud correctly saw. Hence, Merleau-Ponty believed that it was important to avoid the dissolution of sexuality into the more general intentionality of existence and to refuse to artificially restrict existence to the narrow confines of sexual intentionality.

What, then, is the true relationship between sexuality and existence? According to Merleau-Ponty, sight, hearing, sexuality—and the body— are not merely manifestations of tools of personal existence; rather, the body takes up and absorbs into itself the existence of sight, hearing, and sexuality as it is anonymously given. The life of the body and the life of the psyche were seen by Merleau-Ponty as involved in a relationship of recip- rocal expression; the bodily event invariably has a psychic meaning. The relationship between sexuality and existence, then, is one of sign and sig- nification, and one of expression and the expressed. The body as expres- sion does not merely convey the significance (express its modalities of ex- istence), it is "filled with it."

Merleau-Ponty elucidated the meaning of this relationship in the example of the girl whose mother had forbidden her to see the boy she loved, and consequentially experienced aphonia. Her loss of speech sig- nified her refusal of coexistence with other persons. Her refusal had be- come generalized at the level of that most intersubjective dimension of her existence, speech. In this case, it becomes clear how it is possible to judge through the sexual significance of symptoms their more general significance in relation to the fundamental dimensions of existence— past and future, self and others, and so on. Furthermore, the girl's expe- rience of aphonia was not voluntary. She experienced a "disease of the Cogito . . . [her] consciousness has become ambivalent and not a deliber- ate refusal to declare what one knows."[12] The girl "lost" her voice in the same way one loses one's memory.

Merleau-Ponty agreed with psychoanalysis when it asserted that lost memories belong to an area of rejected life, insofar as it retains a specific meaning; forgetfulness was seen as an act. Psychoanalysis also correctly demonstrated that resistance does not set the memory resisted before us as an object; no specific memory is rejected. Instead, resistance was directed against particular categories or areas of experience. Freud's example was of a man who had left a book, which was a gift from his estranged wife, in a drawer and had forgotten about it until he and his wife had been reconciled once again.[13] Though the man had not lost the book, he did not know where it was. He had blocked out everything even remotely related to his es- tranged wife. Merleau-Ponty pointed out that our memories and our body are enveloped in "generality," and "hence sensory messages or memories are expressly grasped and recognized by us only insofar as they adhere gen- erally to that area of our body and our life to which they are relevant."[14]

The fact that our bodies and memories are enveloped in "general-ity" is what allows for the possibility of self-deception in the form of "bad faith" or "metaphysical hypocrisy." Generality allows anyone facing an intolerable situation to escape into it via the impersonality of the body. Such self-deception is not voluntary (as opposed to Sartre's conception). However, it is always possible for freedom to "derail the dialectics of bad faith, the fact remains that a night's sleep has the same power."[15] Merleau-Ponty's point was, that which can be overcome by this "anonymous force" (as, for example, with sleep) must be of the same nature as that which overcomes. Loss of speech, for example, assumes a structure in the same way one goes to sleep. It is not by willing it, but by "soliciting" it (through mimicry). Similarly, any decision to interrupt it must come from a level lower than the "will."

To ensure such metamorphosis, the role of the body is crucial. The body can symbolize existence essentially because it brings it into being and actualizes it:

> Bodily existence which runs through me, yet does so independently of me, is only the barest raw material of a genuine presence in the world. Yet at least it provides the possibility of such presence, and establishes our first consonance with the world. I may very well take myself away from the human world, and set aside personal existence, but only redis-cover in my body the same power, this time unnamed, by which I am condemned to being.[16]

According to Merleau-Ponty, the body expresses existence, but the process of signification is one in which the thing expressed does not (unlike conventional theory) exist apart from the expression. Clearly, Merleau-Ponty wanted to emphasize the point that body and existence form an intimate union: each presupposes the other. He wrote, "body is solidi-fied or generalized existence, and existence a perpetual incarnation . . . This incarnate significance is the central phenomenon of which body and mind, sign and significance are abstract moments."[17] Finally, existence was conceived by Merleau-Ponty, not as a set of facts, but instead as the ambiguous setting of their intercommunication, the point when an interpenetration of their boundaries occurs. In short, existence is their "woven fabric."

From all of this, Merleau-Ponty's ultimate conclusion was that "ambiguity is the essence of human existence, and everything we live or think has always several meanings."[18] The ambiguity of the body consists in the fact that its multitudinous parts permeate and interpenetrate one another, rather than existing in isolation. Hence sexuality, being one of the major modes of our existential orientations in the world, exists as interfused with existence; existence and sexuality mutually permeate.

Given the above discussion, Merleau-Ponty's attitude toward Freudian psychoanalysis in the *Phenomenology of Perception* becomes clear. He suggested that Freudian psychoanalysis never excluded the description of psychological motives and that it certainly was not in opposition to the phenomenological method. Indeed, he contended that Freudian psychoanalysis had actually been ancillary to existential phenomenology's development (though unwittingly) by declaring that "every human action 'has a meaning'" and by attempting to understand events without recourse to mechanical circumstances.[19] Furthermore, psychoanalysis allowed for the expansion of the notion of sexuality so as to absorb into it the whole of existence. By doing so, the true relationship existing between sexuality and existence can be explored. The two exist as *interwoven (and inseparable) intentionalities*. Multiple meanings result from the ambiguity of the bodily-subject because its numerous parts permeate and interpenetrate one another.

Elsewhere, in the last portion of his concurrent essay entitled, "Cézanne's Doubt,"[20] Merleau-Ponty defended psychoanalysis against the demand for inductive rigor. He suggested that psychoanalytical intuition should not be discredited simply because Freud's explanations appear arbitrary and lacking in evidence. Merleau-Ponty agreed that, according to the rules of inductive logic, a doctrine that interjects sexuality everywhere cannot demonstrate its effectiveness anywhere. This would be to exclude all different cases antecedently, thereby precluding the possibility for counterevidence. However, according to Merleau-Ponty, appealing to such logic allows for only a verbal triumph over psychoanalysis.

It is important to note that Merleau-Ponty was offering a strong defense of Freud against, for example, Ludwig Wittgenstein: the latter contended in his "Conversations on Freud" that Freud's interpretations, methods, and techniques never showed where the right solution was, resulted in pure speculation and mythology, appealed to insufficient evidence, and so on.[21] Merleau-Ponty suggested that it was not reasonable to discount the complex correspondences which psychoanalysis discovered between the child and adult. Also, psychoanalysis had shown the correct linkage between echoes, illusions, repetitions, and so on, from one moment in life to another. Furthermore, Merleau-Ponty pointed out that psychoanalysis was not intended as an explanatory theory with cause and effect relations (as he had held from the very beginning); instead, it indicated motivational relationships, which were in principle merely possible. Our past, for example, should not be understood as a force determining our future, but as an ambiguous symbol, which is antecedently applicable to several possible sequences of events. Merleau-Ponty's basic point was that in all of our lives, our birth and past define fundamental dimensions which can be found in all acts, yet which do not impose any particular act. The decisions that transform us are always involved in a factual situation, one to be accepted or refused. It is the incarnation for us of the value we give it. Psychoanalysis sought to describe the mutual interpenetration of meaning between past and future; it attempted to show how life questions itself concerning its final meaning. Clearly, then, we would err if we required inductive rigor from it. Life is involved in a circular movement—past and future are mutually predicative—where everything symbolizes everything else. "Psychoanalysis does not make freedom impossible; it teaches us to think of this freedom concretely, as a creative repetition of ourselves, always in retrospect, faithful to ourselves."[22]

Reversing a judgment made in *The Structure of Behavior,* Merleau-Ponty, in a later essay entitled "Man and Adversity," attempted to show that psychoanalysis had transcended the superficial mind–body dichotomy while deepening the notion of flesh, that is, animate body. He contended, once again, that psychoanalysis can be and traditionally has been interpreted in narrowly defined mechanistic terms, and that this was consistent with the earlier writings of Freud. Merleau-Ponty believed, however, that Freud transcended this view toward the modern notion of the experienced body. Freud overturned the concept of instinct so that humans, in the mechanistic sense, had no sexual instincts. For Freud, a child's attachment to his mother, instead of being instinctual, was understood as *mental.*

> For Freud, the ultimate psychological reality is the system of attractions and tensions which attaches the child to parental images, and then through these to all the other persons, a system within which he tries out different positions in turn, the last of which will be his adult attitude.[23]

Merleau-Ponty saw Freud as revealing that instinct was enveloped in a central demand for absolute possession, which, instead of being a mechanistic act, existed on the order of consciousness. Insofar as Freud explained the psychological by the body, he disclosed the psychological *meaning* of the body, its "latent logic." Body was seen as the vehicle, the fulcrum, and the steadying factor of human life. To remain on the level of mechanistic explanations would preclude one from thinking about the body's relationship to life as a whole—about the way in which body and personal existence are interwoven. "With psychoanalysis mind passes into body, as inversely body passes into mind."[24]

However, according to Merleau-Ponty, psychoanalysis had done little to reformulate more adequately our idea of the mind. In this case, Freud had satisfied himself with a structure of inadequate ideas. To account for his greatest discovery, the osmosis between the anonymous life of the body and the person's official life, Freud found it necessary to introduce the unconscious. It was conceived as being between the organism and the self, and was considered as a sequence of deliberate acts. According to Merleau-Ponty (as even Freud knew) the unconscious was an insufficiently developed idea. Hence, he suggested that it was important to search for the right formulation of Freud's provisional idea. Merleau-Ponty believed that, according to Freud, it was the unconscious that decided which aspects would be permitted into "official existence," which aspects would be repressed, and so on. The unconscious, then, was not an unknowing, but rather an unformulated and unrecognized form of knowing. Freud's characterization of the unconscious in this way placed him "on the point of discovering what other thinkers have more appropriately named *ambiguous perception.*"[25] In ambiguous perception we encounter a consciousness which eludes its objects at the moment it attempts to specify them; a consciousness which does not know its objects, yet is aware of them (as Sartre saw); and finally, a consciousness which subtends our express acts and understandings. Merleau-Ponty's conclusion, then, was that Freud had an increasingly clear view of the body's mental function and the mind's incarnation. In this sense, it would appear that what Freud really had meant by the "unconscious" was the incarnate consciousness of Merleau-Ponty's philosophy.

In his later years, Merleau-Ponty continued to affirm the permanent importance of psychoanalysis for existential phenomenological descriptions of experience. He saw psychoanalysis as facilitating the development of a greater conspectus from which to understand the immense diversity of the human life-worlds.

First, concerned that his earlier analysis of perception and the perceived world might have failed to go deep enough in understanding the origin of meaning in experience, Merleau-Ponty turned his attention to the lowest levels of awareness and the problem of passivity.[26] In his *Themes from the Lectures at the Collège de France, 1952–1960,* Merleau-Ponty agreed with Sartre's criticism of Freud for having introduced a second thinking subject (namely, the "unconscious") whose creations were simply received by the first. However, Merleau-Ponty contended that Sartre erroneously granted a monopoly to consciousness, viewing the unconscious as a particular instance of bad faith. Such a position was not only mistaken, but overlooked Freud's most "interesting" insight: "the idea of a symbolism which is primordial, originary, the idea of a 'non-conventional thought' enclosed in a 'world for us,' which is the source of dreams and more generally of the elaboration of life."[27]

Merleau-Ponty recognized that the unconscious was not reducible to a phenomenological description predicated on intentionality or some form of consciousness. But how then could he relate the unconscious to conscious thought? His answer was that the *unconscious possesses an intentionality uniquely its own,* which exists in a dynamic relationship to the intentionalities of the subject.[28] Improving upon Freud's position: instead of belonging to different phenomena, the conscious and unconscious were recognized as two structures belonging (albeit in different ways) to the same phenomenon. Merleau-Ponty now recognized the validity of a wholly anonymous level, which underlies explicit consciousness, including the body's operative intentionality. Freud's contribution, then, was to have revealed that the analysis of a given behavior invariably discloses several layers of signification, each possessing its own truth. The multitude of conceivable exegeses was the articulation of a life-blend in which every choice has many meanings, none of which is the one true one.[29]

In the cryptic working notes of *The Visible and the Invisible,* a further shift was conspicuous. Here Merleau-Ponty viewed Freudian philosophy as one of the *flesh,* rather than the body. He wrote: "The Id, Ego, unconscious are to be understood on the basis of *flesh.*"[30] Merleau-Ponty wanted to interpret Freud on the basis of his new and radical understanding of incarnation (a complete articulation of which transcends the scope of this chapter). Quasi-perception discloses that there is, in the body, a character of being perceived by others and of its participation in the perceived world. Merleau-Ponty contented that, like subjectivity, this facet of the body was crucial to perception. As a complementarity of the body, it was considered to be the nexus between human existence and the world of things because they were composed of the same material. Hence, the body must be cognitive of the world while being *of* it. This guaranteed the body's insertion into the world. Instead of being material, the "flesh" of the world in which humans participate was believed to be its very *being.* In the relationship of the visible and invisible, self-consciousness, ideas, and so on, are invisible, yet they are found in the visible when the body-world objects and human consciousness encounter one another: each "derives itself from the 'brute' or 'raw *being*' which announces itself to perception."[31]

To take an example from Freudian psychoanalysis, Merleau-Ponty claimed that instead of being the *cause,* "feces give rise to a character only if the subject lives them in a way as to find in them a dimension of *being.*"[32] Merleau-Ponty stressed that it was necessary to understand that for the child, the relationship with feces was "a concrete ontology." To be "anal" explained nothing. Instead, Merleau-Ponty pointed out that it was essential to have the ontological capacity to take a being as representative of Being. That was why, he suggested, we need an ontological psychoanalysis, not an existential one.

It was in one of Merleau-Ponty's later pieces—his preface to a book by the French psychoanalyst, Angelo Hesnard[33]—that he presented the clearest account and summation of his views regarding the relationship of phenomenology and psychoanalysis, as well as his attitude toward the latter. Merleau-Ponty first reiterated his primary reasons for reformulating particular Freudian concepts within the framework of what he conceived to be a better philosophy. As discussed, Merleau-Ponty had, throughout the course of his philosophical development, been quite careful to distinguish between psychoanalysis (as "properly" interpreted) and a scientistic or objectivist ideology.[34] The "pitiless hermeneutic" of the latter had led to a plethora of misunderstandings between Freud and his interpreters, and even, Merleau-Ponty suggested, between Freud and himself. For example, *sexuality conceived as the nerve of human interaction* had been confused with sexuality thought of as a function of the organism, that is, as an objective process. Similarly, the Oedipus complex as a system of references and dimensions had been assiduously misconstrued and referred to as a cause. To conceive Freudian psychoanalysis in mechanistic terms, then, was to fail to comprehend its true significance. Hence, Merleau-Ponty contended, it was important to reformulate a more fruitful *hermeneutic* for it.

This reformulation consisted of conceiving of the Freudian unconscious as a more *primordial consciousness,* the repressed as a realm of experience which had yet to be integrated, the body as a natural complex, and communication as a relation between incarnate beings who are either well or poorly integrated. With this interpretation, Merleau-Ponty believed that he had eliminated one of the greatest obstacles to understanding Freud. Freudian psychoanalysis was now understood as it should be. Merleau-Ponty wrote, "it is the human body which discovers its symbolic or poetic weight."[35] In this way, it became possible to properly understand those symbolic matrices, systems of equivalencies constructed by the past abbreviations, and distortions of simple acts of which Freud had so acutely described.

Given the above, the role of existential phenomenology becomes clear. Merleau-Ponty contended that existential phenomenology would supplement psychoanalysis with certain categories and means of expression which were essential for it to become complete.

> Phenomenology permits psychoanalysis to recognize "psychic reality" without equivocation, the "intra-subjective" essence of morbid formations, the fantastic operation that reconstructs a world on the margin of, and counter to, the true world, a lived history beneath the effective history—a world called illness.[36]

Reciprocally, psychoanalysis would be of aid to phenomenology:

Freudian thought, in turn, confirms phenomenology in its description of a consciousness that is not so much knowledge or representation as investment; it brings to phenomenology a wealth of concrete examples that add weight to what it has been able to say in general of the relations of man with the world and of the interhuman bond.[37]

Merleau-Ponty claimed that *this reciprocal encounter of existential phenomenology and psychoanalysis* would lead to a better philosophy, a "humanism of truth" without metaphysics.

In the second half of his preface to Hesnard's book, Merleau-Ponty said that although he still agreed with his earlier views (depicted above), he had philosophically matured in such a way that he felt the need to modify his thoughts on the relations of existential phenomenology and psychoanalysis, and the tacit philosophy of the latter. He suggested that it would be quite easy, on a superficial reading of Husserl, to fail to distinguish existential phenomenology (as properly conceived) from a philosophy of consciousness. However, it was clear that Husserl, during the later execution of his program, encountered fragments of being which were not able to be subsumed under the correlation of the noesis–noema. Examples included the body as "subject–object," as lived, and the passage of interior time, which is not a system of acts of consciousness. For Husserl, philosophy was no longer a pure regard on pure objects (that is, an exact knowledge), but rather "what was sought" by the successive generations of philosophers. Intentionality's object (namely, this world) was no longer conceived as the object of a "phenomenological positivism" (an object that is what it is, exactly adjusted to the acts of consciousness). Merleau-Ponty wrote: "Consciousness is now the 'soul of Heraclitus,' and Being, which is around it rather than in front of it, is a Being of dreams, by definition hidden."[38]

Merleau-Ponty was referring to Husserl's recognition in *The Crisis of European Sciences and Transcendental Phenomenology* that the intentionality of "subjectivity" has many levels of "stratum" which lie deeper and deeper and which lead back to an obscure horizon.[39] He thought that by descending into its own substratum in this way, phenomenology was "converging" more than ever with Freudian research.

Merleau-Ponty warned against two possible dangers, however. The first, and perhaps greatest, was that phenomenological idealism (continuing to view intentionality as a relation of ideal objects) would encourage the acceptance of Freudian psychoanalysis in an "idealist" form. In this sense, phenomenology would have succeeded *too well*. Just as a phenomenological idealism was inadequate, so would a Freudian one. The second, was the possibility of adopting the "pitiless hermeneutic" of mechanistic and energetic metaphors in Freudian psychoanalysis. To accept psychoanalysis as an objectivistic ideology would be neither satisfying nor philosophically comprehensible.

To avoid the above dangers, Merleau-Ponty recommended that instead of understanding Freud's expressions and theoretical concepts in their lexical and common/ordinary meanings, we see the meanings they acquire from within the experience which they announce, and of which we have behind our backs much more than a suspicion.[40] With all its difficulties, one might ask, why retain the term "unconscious" (that atemporal and indestructible element in us)? Merleau-Ponty's answer was a poetic one: "the term retains, like the algae or the stone that one drags up, something of the sea from which it was taken."[41] The "unconscious" retains its immersion within the intentional field of our historicity.

At the end of his essay, Merleau-Ponty laconically admonished us not to assume that phenomenology was saying clearly what psychoanalysis had said only obscurely. Instead, it was by what phenomenology disclosed as its limits—that is, its latent content or unconscious—that it was in harmony with psychoanalysis:

> Their agreement is, rather, precisely in describing man as a timber yard in order to discover, beyond the truth of immanence, that of the Ego and its acts, that of consciousness and its objects, of relations which a consciousness cannot sustain: man's relations to his origins and his relations to his models.[42]

Freud spoke of the id, superego, and so on, while Husserl wrote of an ever-deepening subjectivity leading back, by regressive, archaeological analysis, to an obscure horizon.

Merleau-Ponty's final opinion, then, was that phenomenology and psychoanalysis, once properly understood, "converge" without resulting in their merger. They are not parallel but rather are both directed toward the same latency. It was for the above reasons, that Merleau-Ponty advocated a rapprochement between phenomenology and Freudian psychoanalysis.

Freud's Reaction to Merleau-Ponty's Reinterpretation of Psychoanalysis

Having delineated Merleau-Ponty's attitude toward Freudian psychoanalysis and its relation to existential phenomenology, as it evolved throughout the course of his philosophical development, it is important to consider how Freud would have reacted to Merleau-Ponty's reposturing of his thought within an existential phenomenological philosophy. Freud's generally anti-phenomenological attitude has been well documented by Ricoeur.[43] Ricoeur pointed out that there was, in Freud's thought, a movement from a descriptive concept of the unconscious which was adjectival (the quality of being unconscious) to a systematic concept which was substantive (unconscious forces, energies).[44] The latter involved the recognition of the causal efficacy of ideas as representatives of instincts. Thus, instead of taking "consciousness" as the fundamental concept to be investigated, as some phenomenologists have, Freud focused upon *instinctual* desire and the unconscious as primary.[45]

Now, it is crucial to note that Freud would not have rejected phenomenology per se. Rather, he would have rejected a phenomenology (and psychology) of consciousness—that is, of the early Husserlian or Sartrean variety.[46] Freud ubiquitously entreated us to "abandon the overvaluation of the property of being conscious" and not equate mind with consciousness. He emphasized that it is "totally incomprehensible how the existence of the unconscious can be denied . . . that there exist psychical acts which lack consciousness";[47] and he encouraged opposition in the face of "the majority of philosophers [in declaring] . . . that the idea of something psychical being unconscious is self-contradictory."[48]

It would seem, then, that Freud would have applauded Merleau-Ponty's antipathy toward any Cartesian-like adherence to the term "consciousness" and supported his assertion that consciousness must be reinserted back into the world—that the idealist's notion of a detached cogito must be rejected. Thus, Freud would undoubtedly have liked Ricoeur's and Merleau-Ponty's suggestions that there are no longer "immediate givens of consciousness," that there is only a "wounded cogito."[49] Freud would most likely have welcomed Ricoeur's interpretation that "the aim of psychoanalysis' concrete critique of the cogito is to deconstruct the false cogito—the fakery of immediate consciousness."[50] He probably would have also agreed with Merleau-Ponty's (and Ricoeur's) description of the incarnation of instinctual desires as the "archaeology of the subject."[51] Furthermore, Freud would have appreciated the fact that Merleau-Ponty, unlike most of the philosophers of his day, never (even in his earliest writings) considered the idea that something psychical could be unconscious to be a contradiction in terms.

Freud would have had high regard for Merleau-Ponty's recognition of the true meaning of his various concepts, which have been grossly misunderstood in what have come to be the traditionally accepted interpretations. Freud has, for example, been interpreted by such diverse philosophers as Sartre[52] and Wittgenstein[53] as assigning fixed meanings in his interpretation of symbols and as advocating a strict determinism.

In the first case, Merleau-Ponty pointed out that to interpret Freud's theory as assigning fixed meanings to symbols is to misunderstand his concept of the overdetermination of meaning/symbols, in which symbols may represent a multiplicity of instinctual desires, a multilayer of structure, affective signification, and so on.[54] Indeed, Freud himself said that symbols are ambiguous.[55] He wrote, "No one has a right to complain because the actual phenomenon expresses the dynamic factor ambiguously."[56] Clearly, he would have agreed with Merleau-Ponty's recognition of a wholly ambiguous level, which underlies explicit consciousness. Freud wrote:

> I must confess that I have tried to translate into the language of our normal thinking what must in fact be a process that is neither conscious nor preconscious, taking place between quotas of energy in some unimaginable substratum.[57]

In the second case, Merleau-Ponty knew that to interpret Freud as advocating a strict determinism was to overlook the fact that he often denied "an inevitable sequence of events which could not be otherwise determined."[58] As discussed, Merleau-Ponty agreed with Freud that our past should not be necessarily understood as a force determining our future, but as an ambiguous symbol which is applicable to several possible sequences of events. Indeed, Freud acknowledged, long before Merleau-Ponty, the dangers involved in pandeterminism. For example, occasionally Freud explicitly rejected the complete "objectification" of the psyche which his metapsychology seemed to entail.[59] Freud would sometimes appear to agree with Merleau-Ponty's depiction of freedom as inextricably interwoven with determinates beyond our control—as an intrinsic feature of the "woven fabric of human existence." Freud wrote: "we are 'lived' by unknown and uncontrollable forces. We have all had impressions of the same kind, even though they may not have overwhelmed us to the exclusion of all others."[60]

Furthermore, Freud and Merleau-Ponty may have been in prima facie agreement on other points as well. First, both recognized that the importance of the phenomenon was the meaning it has for the subject.[61] Second, both agreed that in order for ideas to become conscious, it is necessary for them to be associated with language.[62] Finally, both viewed the "repressed" event surviving only as a "manner of *being*,"[63] though Merleau-Ponty explored these points to a far greater extent than did Freud.

Despite what might have been his approval of the preceding aspects of Merleau-Ponty's philosophy and reinterpretation of psychoanalysis, however, it is evident that there is much in it Freud would have found objectionable.

Freud's Objections to Merleau-Ponty's Resituation of Psychoanalysis

First, how would Freud have reacted to the early Merleau-Ponty's suggestion that we consider the unconscious (Ucs.) as a *lower* form of integrated
consciousness (Cs.)? In his last major theoretical work, *The Ego and the Id,*
Freud's response was directly applicable:

> But why do we not rather remain in agreement with the philosophers
> and instead in a consistent way distinguish the Pcs. and the Ucs. from the
> conscious psychical? The philosophers would then propose that the Pcs.
> and the Ucs. should be described as two *species* or *stages* of the "psychoid,"
> and the harmony would be established. But endless difficulties in exposi-
> tion would follow, and the one important fact, that these two kinds of
> "psychoid" coincide in almost every respect with what is admittedly psy-
> chical would be forced into the background in the interests of a preju-
> dice dating from a period in which these psychoids, or the most impor-
> tant part of them, were still unknown.[64]

Freud, then, clearly agreed with the more mature Merleau-Ponty's
position that the term "unconscious" be kept since it connotatively retains
something of the historical context from which it is taken. As we have repeatedly seen, Freud was ubiquitously vigilant that there always be a sufficient watershed against the prejudice of equating "consciousness" with
"psychical."

Second, Freud would have strongly rejected—on a number of levels—Merleau-Ponty's criticism that his work constituted a "tableau of
anomalies" and was thus inadequate for a full understanding of human
existence. It was always Freud's conviction that through the study of "abnormal" processes and disturbances we could learn about the workings of
the normal mind (something the psychology of consciousness could not
do).[65] This was one of the reasons Freud considered his clinical research
to be so important. In *The Interpretation of Dreams,* for example, one of his
most important discoveries was precisely that through his study of dreams
we were afforded access to the unconscious life of all humans—pathological or otherwise. Similarly, in *The Psychopathology of Everyday Life,*[66]
Freud attempted to explain how some "abnormal" processes or disturbances occur in even "normal" people throughout their everyday existence. Indeed, for Freud, "it is not scientifically feasible to draw a line of
demarcation between what is psychically normal and abnormal"; the distinction necessarily becomes blurred.[67]

Clearly, Freud could have aptly pointed out that Merleau-Ponty also relied heavily upon the existential phenomenological perspectives of "abnormal" subjects—for example, Schneider—throughout his *Phenomenology of Perception* to gain a better understanding of the functions of the "normal" human mind. Merleau-Ponty's rebuttal would have been that Freud was correct about his reliance upon anomalies to better understand human existence, but that he did not do this to the point of *excluding* the use of other valuable heuristical approaches—for example, Gestalt psychology—whereas Freud had. The question remains as to whether Freudian psychoanalytic theory, method, and technique offered us a sufficient basis for fully understanding human existence. It is clear that Merleau-Ponty thought not.

Third, the mature Freud would have strenuously objected to Merleau-Ponty's interpretation of his term "libido" in only the sexual sense, and for attributing to him the failure of seeing sexuality as but one of the fundamental modes of human existence (that is, of equating sexuality and existence).

It must be acknowledged that Freud himself, to some extent, was responsible for Merleau-Ponty's misinterpretation of his theory. As we have seen, in his early writings Freud had indeed used the term "libido" to denote only sexual energy.[68] It was only when he later revised his theory of motivation that "libido" was defined as the energy of all life instincts.[69] More important is the fact that in his *Three Essays on Sexuality*[70]—where he studied only the sexual instincts most intimately—Freud came strongly across as a pansexualist; but later, Freud shifted his focus from consciousness to the aims of the instincts. He suggested, "the primacy of the aim over the object (of instincts) is most clearly seen in the sexual instincts."[71] This accounts for Freud's concentration on the sexual instincts. Even here, Freud understood that the sexual instincts were *only one* group among the life instincts with which they interact; they just happened to exhibit certain phenomena more clearly than did some of the other instincts.[72]

Thus, Merleau-Ponty and the later Freud agreed that sexuality was only one mode of human existence, which interacts with others. However, Freud continued on to suggest that it was "the sexual instincts which alone can be observed *in isolation*."[73] This would have been unacceptable to Merleau-Ponty's position, which stressed that sexuality was but one mode, inextricably intertwined within the "woven fabric" of human existence: "All human 'functions' from sexuality to mobility and intelligence are rigorously unified in one synthesis, it is impossible to distinguish in the total being of man a bodily organization to be treated as a contingent fact."[74]

Fourth, Freud would have believed that Merleau-Ponty (and Sartre) misinterpreted him in their criticisms of the Freudian unconscious as the introduction of a second subject or consciousness. From his early writings on, Freud had been opposed to the idea of thinking of the unconscious as a second consciousness.[75] He argued instead, that there are only unconscious mental states (that is, unconscious psychical acts), and though they may form a system, they remain states of a person whose other mental states are conscious or preconscious.

Indeed, Freud offered several arguments against the idea of a second consciousness: he argued (1) that it was a gratuitous assumption founded upon the abuse of the word "conscious" and that philosophers "have no right to extend the meaning of this word so far as to make it include a consciousness of which its owner himself is not aware";[76] he stated (2) that it was an unintelligible idea, and that the idea of a second consciousness lacking its most important characteristic (namely, self-consciousness or awareness) deserved no discussion; he pointed out (3) that since analysis demonstrated that the various latent mental processes seem to enjoy a high degree of mutual independence (as though they know nothing of one another), we would have to assume the existence of an unlimited number of states of consciousness all unknown to us and one another; he argued (4) that the idea of a second consciousness conceives the division between the conscious as a kind of brute fact resembling an unbridgeable geological fissure, and in consequence, it is utterly unable to do justice to the dynamic factors involved in "inadmissibility to consciousness"; and he proposed (5) what he considered to be "the most weighty agreement of all":

> We have to take into account the fact that analytic investigation reveals some of these latent processes as having characteristics and peculiarities which seem alien to us, or even incredible, and which run directly counter to the attributes with which we are familiar. Thus we have grounds for modifying our inference about ourselves and saying that what is proved is not the existence of a second consciousness in us, but the existence of psychical acts which lack consciousness.[77]

Hence, Freud most likely would have asserted that Merleau-Ponty and Sartre failed to grasp his crucial distinction between unconscious psychical acts and an unconscious consciousness. Freud, too, would have rejected the latter as a most objectionable concept.

One could argue, perhaps, that the above "debate" between Freud and Merleau-Ponty and Sartre was merely a dispute over verbal terminology. On one level, Merleau-Ponty and Sartre recognized the existence of a pre-reflective consciousness and operative intentionality that intrinsically involved a consciousness that lacks self-awareness: they simply chose to call this "consciousness." Freud, on the other hand, chose to place the latter concepts and functions under the rubric "unconscious" and "preconscious," reserving the term "consciousness" for a concept intrinsically involving "self-awareness." On another level, this debate was more fundamental. Freud's terms were predominately predicated upon a physicalistic energetics, while Merleau-Ponty's and Sartre's terms involved descriptive fields of intentionality.

Fifth, it is possible that Freud would have agreed with the early Merleau-Ponty when he suggested that Freud remained within a subject–object framework. Indeed, at times Freud believed that such a framework was intrinsic to human nature. (It is unclear that Freud himself was clear as to the ramifications of this dualism. We shall take this up again in chapter 17.) Freud distinguished between external and internal perception.[78] It was the id, which conceived the true psychic reality—that is, the *inner* world which existed before the individual had experience of the external world. To deal with the demands and/or restrictions of the external world, a secondary process develops (belonging to the ego), forcing the desires of the id to be subservient to the reality principle. This secondary process consists of discovering or producing reality by means of a plan of action that develops through thought and reason. Obviously Freud, at least at times, would have been distrustful of Merleau-Ponty's claim to (and need for) having overcome the subject–object dichotomy. He would have rejected Merleau-Ponty's assertion that truth or meaning does not inhabit an "inner" man, that "thought is no internal thing."[79]

Sixth, as previously discussed, the later Merleau-Ponty thought Freud had transcended a mind–body dualism by conceiving the "instincts" as interpenetrating and fusing the orders of consciousness and body. Here, Merleau-Ponty no longer interpreted Freud as conceiving of the instincts as existing apart from the mental dialectic (as he had earlier).

Paul Ricoeur strongly supported Merleau-Ponty's position in his book *Freud and Philosophy: An Essay on Interpretation*. He contended that for Freud:

1. The introduction of narcissism deepens our notion of instinct; it forces us to conceive of instincts as more radical than any subject–object relation. Instincts are the reservoir of energy underlying all the distributions of energy between the ego and objects.[80]
2. The notion of the "ego-instinct" symmetric with that of the "object-instinct" makes instinct a structure prior to the phenomenal relation of subject–object.[81]
3. Psychoanalysis never confronts one with bare forces but always with forces in search of meaning; this link between force and meaning makes instinct a psychical reality or more exactly, the limit concept at the frontier between the organic and the psychical.[82]

Did Freud, via his concept of "instinct," transcend a mind–body dualism and a subject–object inquiry standpoint in spite of himself, as Merleau-
Ponty and Ricoeur contended? To answer this question sufficiently, it is
important to recall how Freud defined this crucial concept.

> An "instinct" appears to us as a concept on the frontier between the men-
> tal and the somatic, as the psychical representative of the stimuli origi-
> nating from within the organism and reaching the mind, as a measure of
> the demand made upon the mind for work in consequence of its con-
> nection with the body.[83]

Though it is clear that Freud considered himself, at least at times, to be
advocating a kind of "interactive dualism" here, he was also arguably in
the process of transcending it via his analysis of the body-ego later (as we
saw earlier, in the Husserl chapter). One, then, can discern a metaphysically ambivalent and evolving Freud on this issue.

Finally, it should by now be fairly evident that Freud would have
been conflicted regarding Merleau-Ponty's comments concerning the
possibility of a rapprochement between phenomenology and psychoanalysis. It is undeniable that Freud accorded importance to consciousness.
He explicitly said that consciousness must be the point of departure for
all of his investigations, that all knowledge is invariably bound up with
consciousness.[84] However, it is crucial to bear in mind that what Freud
meant by "consciousness" was the fleeting consciousness of moments
(which is certainly not the consciousness of most existential phenomenologists). To the extent that existential phenomenology could describe
the latter in all their immediacy, it could aid psychoanalysis in giving it a
secure starting point in investing the real processes underlying such phenomena. Freud agreed that it would allow us to observe the normal–
abnormal manifestations of the "phenomenological perspective of the
subject" (Freud's own words).[85] However, this for Freud was only to remain
on an inadequate, "surface" level. He wrote, "Acts of consciousness are immediate data and cannot be further explained by any sort of description."
It was only from the perspective of dynamics or economics that they could
be explained.[86] Again, it was the metaphysics of his metapsychology (the
real processes involved in energetics) that grounded everything—even
meaning. Thus, while Freud might have agreed that existential phenomenology and psychoanalysis could be mutually beneficial insofar as each
clarifies its own realm and thus makes it easier to see their proper relationship, he would have rejected Merleau-Ponty's claim that their mutual
encounter would lead to a "humanism of truth without metaphysics."

Freud, then, would probably have agreed with Merleau-Ponty that it would be on the level of meaning or hermeneutics, that phenomenology would tend to converge with psychoanalysis without being parallel. At the same time, it would most likely be the metapsychological level of economics–energetics, which would have prevented their merger. The reason for the latter being that phenomenology did not and could not operate on this level, since it offered only descriptions and not explanations. Finally, it is pretty clear Freud would have discerned the relation of phenomenology and psychoanalysis to be one of complementarity: the descriptions provided by phenomenology permitted a better understanding of the structures of a person's conscious life, while the explanations of psychoanalysis enabled us to ferret out the real metaphysical processes underlying them.

Part 3

A Rapprochement between Freudian Psychoanalysis and Existential Phenomenology

17

Freud's Philosophically Split Personality: The Existential Phenomenological Perspective

As we have seen from the previous chapters on the existential phenomenologists, each individual thinker had much to say in response to Freud's metapsychology. We are now in a position to crystallize those critiques of Freudian psychoanalysis and to identify the general, fundamental, philosophical presuppositions that underlie Freudian psychoanalysis *from an existential phenomenological perspective*. Given this perspective's philosophical presuppositions, certain inconsistencies become apparent within Freud's metapsychology—inconsistencies upon which the existential phenomenologists all tended to agree. In response to the apparent inconsistencies in Freudian psychoanalysis, in fact, Medard Boss asserted that there were two distinct Freuds: Freud the scientist, and Freud the humanist. As a psychoanalyst who highly valued Freudian therapy, Boss proposed that we reject Freud's metapsychology while retaining Freud's valuable therapeutic advice. He believed that Freudian therapy could be salvaged from the remains of Freud's metapsychology precisely because the two were inconsistent.

We shall consider Boss's proposal and demonstrate that—contrary to any "philosophical split"—Freudian psychoanalysis was intrinsically unified, as Freud had insisted. Borrowing from Freud's historical-philosophical background discussed in the first part of this book, we shall show that it was Freud's philosophical heritage—via Schopenhauer's influence above all—that provides Freud with additional philosophical resources to reassert his unified psychoanalysis.

Presuppositions of Freud's Metapsychological Theory

In general, the existential phenomenologists saw Freud as holding a Cartesian thing-ontology and mechanistic framework, which offered a scientific explanation of human behavior and precluded the genuine possibility of human freedom. What were the specific philosophical presuppositions that underlie this critique and is there textual evidence within the corpus of Freud's works to substantiate it?

1. *Only objective "beings" or "things" exist.* Throughout Freud's account of the universe, everything that is, is a thing—including human beings. Examples from Freud include: "Analysts are at bottom incorrigible mechanists and materialists";[1] and, "the intellect and the mind are objects for scientific research in exactly the same way as any non-human objects."[2]

2. *Two forms of objective reality exist—the psychical and the material.* Freud himself asserted that he was indeed a "dualist": "If [I] had to choose among the views of the philosophers, [I] could characterize [myself] as a dualist. No monism succeeds in doing away with the distinction between ideas and the objects they represent."[3]

3. *The subject–object dichotomy is intrinsic to our mental operations.* Freud ostensibly uncritically adopted the Cartesian subject–object dichotomy. He asserted, for instance: "This anti-thesis ego—non-ego (external), i.e., subject–object . . . remains, above all, sovereign in our intellectual activity and creates for research the basic situation which no efforts can alter."[4]

4. *"Material reality" is the independently existing external world of things.*[5]

5. *"Psychical reality"—that is, the mind—as an object, consists of internal mechanistic processes.* For example, Freud wrote: "The psychical processes [are] qualitatively determined states of specifiable material particles."[6]

Freud, then, transcended his Cartesian roots by hypothesizing:

6. *Psychical reality includes unconsciousness.*[7]

7. *Psychical reality is powered by an energy analogous to, and reciprocally transformable with, material–physical energy; psychical (instinctual) energy exists.*[8] In order for the psychical instrument to operate, Freud thought it must be powered. Here he was seen as borrowing from his nineteenth-century sci-

entific heritage: "We assume as other sciences have led us to expect, that in mental life some kind of energy is at work."[9] Freud assumed that, though energy occurs in various forms (electrical, mechanical, chemical, and so on), the energy that powers the organism essentially is the same as the energy that powers the universe. Following the lead of the physics of his time, Freud simply defined psychical (instinctual) energy in terms of the work it performed.[10] Since thinking, perceiving, remembering, and so on, as psychological activities are forms of work, Freud simply inferred that they must involve a psychic form of energy. Freud also subscribed to the principle of the conservation of energy: though energy may be transformed from one form to another, it can never be lost from the total system.[11] Thus, Freud assumed that physiological energy could be transformed into psychical energy, and vice versa, and has a constant and quantifiable amount.

8. *Psychical energy is ultimately derivable from bodily–organic (mechanistic) processes.*[12] Freud wrote:

> . . . the aims of our psychology. We seek not merely to describe and to classify phenomena, but to understand them as signs of an interplay of forces in the mind . . . We are concerned with a dynamic view of mental phenomena. On our view the phenomena that are perceived must yield an importance to trends which are only hypothetical.[13]

> The normal and abnormal phenomenal manifestations observed by us (that is, the phenomenology of the subject) need to be described from the point of view of their dynamics and economics (i.e., from the point of view of the quantitative distribution of the libido).[14]

9. *Mind and body are connected via the instincts.* The instincts are responsible for the development of mental processes and images. Freud defined instincts:

> The forces which we assume to exist behind the tensions caused by the needs of the id are called the instincts. They represent the somatic demands upon the mind . . . they are the ultimate cause of all activity.[15]

> We can distinguish an instinct's source, object and aim. Its source is a state of excitation in the body, its aim is the removal of that excitation; on its path from its source to its aim the instinct becomes operative psychically.[16]

> An "instinct" appears to us as a concept on the frontier between the mental and the somatic, as the psychical representative of this stimuli originating from within the organism and reaching the mind, as a measure of the demand made upon the mind for work in consequence of its connection with the body.[17]

Freud thought, then, that an instinct was an inborn psychical representative (a wish) of an inner somatic source of excitation (a need). As such, he believed that the instincts constituted the total amount of psychic energy in each person's id. By describing the instincts as inborn psychical representatives (wishes) of an inner somatic source of excitation (needs), Freud indirectly sought to account for the genesis of meaning in his system. Instincts can be seen as having a "meaning bestowal" function (and "intentionality") of their own. In a sense, they "intend" pleasure or the reduction of bodily excitation in the form of "wishes." Wishing, then, was Freud's basic vector of meaning; phenomena and things are "meaningful" insofar as they serve to gratify instinctual impulses.

It was particularly Heidegger who alluded to the Kantian-like characteristics of Freud's metapsychology, without specifying them.[18] We shall do this for him. The epistemological relationship between the psychical apparatus and the "objective" external world has the following Kantian-like characteristics.

10. *Cathexes via the psychical reservoir, continuously modify internal and external reality; the ego knows a "phenomenal" world.*[19] By postulating an intentional psychical apparatus powered by psychical energy, Freud thought he could account for the epistemological relationship between the subjective psychical apparatus and the objective "external" world. For Freud, it was by means of investments of energy (cathexes) from the psychic reservoir (instinctual drives), under which both internal and external stimuli are continuously modified, that the psyche is enabled to produce perceptions of the external world (as well as ideas in general).[20]

11. *The real natures of the independently existing world and the underlying psychical processes are ultimately unknowable.*[21] Thus, analogous to the Kantian noumenal realm, Freud conceived both the unconscious id as the true psychical reality and the external world as ultimately unknowable. Freud strongly concurred with Kant's admonition regarding our perception of the external world by means of the sense-organs (that is, the system perception-unconsciousness). He insisted that we must "not overlook the fact that our perceptions are subjectively conditioned and must not be regarded as identical with what is perceived though unknowable."[22] In this

sense, "external reality is always unknowable"; we can only asymptotically approach a perceptive undistorted reality.[23]

12. *Space and time are "forms of thought."*[24] Although it is not generally recognized, Freud agreed with the Kantian theorem that space and time are "necessary forms of mental acts." According to Freud, one of the functions of the preconscious systems—those ideas and processes which are capable of entering consciousness at any time and are not repressed—is to give mental events an order in time.[25] Freud explained this by saying that it is the "discontinuous method of functioning of the system *Pcpt-Cs* [which] lies at the bottom of the origin of the concept of time."[26] Freud meant that so long as the perceptive-consciousness is invested with energy, it receives perceptions and passes them on to the unconscious memory systems; when the investment of energy is withdrawn from the perceptive-consciousness system, it stops. The origin of time, then, is rooted in this sporadic functioning of the perceptive-consciousness system. It is the id which provides the exception to the Kantian theory of space and time as forms of thought: in the unconscious psychical processes of the id, ideas (and so on) are not ordered temporally and no changes are produced by the passage of time; wishful impulses immured there are immortal.[27] Here, with the id, Freud introduced a kind of noumenal world into the inner life of humans. He also agreed with Descartes and Kant that scientific reflection and observation are the only true sources of knowledge.[28]

13. *Humans are causally determined.* Transcending both his Cartesian and Kantian heritages, Freud went on to infer that since humans are mechanistic beings they are causally determined—psychically and materially. Free will is an illusion.[29] Given this presupposition, Freud's metapsychological theory ubiquitously held that all psychical as well as physical events are strictly determined.[30] All human psychical activities are seen as ultimately traceable to somatic processes, which, given their material physicochemical nature, are governed by the causal laws of nature. These somatic processes, which ground the instincts, are determined by the organism's physical environment and hereditary structure.[31] Since the instincts are either themselves somatic processes or grounded in them, they are causally determined. Since they are also responsible for meaning-formations as wishes, these psychical meaning-formations also must be causally determined. According to Freud's metapsychology then, it could be said that any occurrence outside this causal chain would literally be "meaningless."

In conclusion, there is substantial evidence throughout the corpus of Freud's writings that he, on at least some level, held those fundamental philosophical presuppositions within his metapsychological theory which form the basis of the critique lodged by the existential phenomenologists.

Philosophical Difficulties with Freudian Metapsychology

The above leaves Freud with some rather transparent philosophical difficulties, particularly for an existential phenomenologist. Freud's self-ascribed "lack of constitutional capacity" for philosophy may have made him oblivious to such concerns.

First, it is important to note the blatant inconsistencies among Freud's ontological and epistemological presuppositions. Freud's system simultaneously held two different forms of epistemological dualism: the Cartesian internal, psychical world versus the external, material world, and the Kantian phenomenal world versus the noumenal world. Obviously, Freud could not have it both ways, and yet, due to his lack of epistemological sophistication, the inconsistency never occurred to him.

Furthermore, Freud unwittingly inherited some of the philosophical problems of traditional Cartesianism. For example, Freud conceived of the ego as subject and non-ego as object—yet both were also conceived as objectifiable forms of being. At the onset, then, a fundamental contradiction in his position is apparent. On the one hand, Freud conceived of the id as representing the inner world of subjective experience, which has no contact with objective reality. Yet later, Freud presupposed that all forms of reality (including the id as part of the psyche) exist as objective beings. In Cartesian terms, Freud, in the first case, considered the *res cogitans* to exist independently of the *res extensa;* in the second, he presupposed that the *res cogitans* was in some peculiar way part of the realm of the *res extensa.*[32] In other words, the id was to be purely subjective, yet somehow existing within objective reality. This contradiction is embedded in Cartesian dualism, from an existential phenomenological point of view.

Next, by conceiving of two distinct realities—an internal, subjective reality of the unconscious id, and an objective reality of a body and a "world" outside of and apart from the subjective reality—Freud had the added problem of finding a way to bridge all the gaps. He sought to account for the connection between ego and non-ego via his theory of instincts. By introducing instincts, he thought he could explain both the connection between the ego (as a knowing subject) and the external world, and the connection between the mind and the body. Hence, his theory of instincts formed the crucial core of his metapsychology. Unfortunately Freud's instinct theory was riddled with many irresolvable problems at crucial points.

First, as mentioned earlier, Freud was never clear in his own mind what the actual nature of the instincts is. He at various times conceived them as the psychical representative of somatic forces, as an amalgamation of idea and quota of affect (psychical impulses), as a nonpsychical impulse, and finally as organic and physical forces themselves. Ultimately, Freud had to admit that we "know nothing of them"—that they are "quotas of energy in some unimaginable substratum."[33]

Second, Freud never really specified how physical forces are transformed into psychical energies, and vice versa. In his final theoretical work he noted:

> We assume, as other natural sciences have led us to expect, that in mental life some kind of energy is at work; but we have nothing to go upon which will enable us to come nearer to a knowledge of it by analogies with other forms of energy.[34]

Instead of developing explanations, Freud offered only descriptions:

> Discharge from the system Ucs. passes into somatic innovation that leads to the development of affect.[35]

> The most abundant sources of this internal excitation are what are described as the organism's instincts—the representatives of all the forces originating in the interior of the body and transmitted to the mental apparatus.[36]

> In conversion hysteria the instinctual cathexis of the repressed idea is changed into the innervation of the symptom. How far and in what circumstances the unconscious idea is drained empty by this discharge into innervation . . . had better be reserved for a special investigation of hysteria.[37]

No such "special investigation" appeared throughout the rest of Freud's writings. All he said was that when the somatic excitation reached a certain level, it somehow converted into psychical excitation.

Again, when discussing anxiety, Freud expressed his awareness that he could not account for the transformation of psychical energies:

> I believed I had put my finger on a metapsychological process of direct transformation of the libido into anxiety. I can now no longer maintain this view. And, indeed, I found it impossible at the time to explain how a transformation of that kind was carried out.[38]

He went on to simply admit, *non liquet* ("it is not clear").

Probably the gravest unresolved difficulty of Freud's theory from an existential phenomenological perspective was its failure to account for how "forces," "energies," "impulses," and so on, are transformed into meaningful ideas and vice versa. Freud asseverated:

> It is a general truth that our mental activity moves in two opposite directions: either it starts from the instincts and passes through the system *Ucs.* to Conscious thought-activity; or, beginning with an instigation from outside, it passes through the system *Cs.* and *Pcs.* till it reaches the *Ucs.* cathexes of the ego and objects.[39]

However, Freud failed to give a comprehensible explanation of this transformational movement in either direction.

Freud had, of course, tried to solve this problem of transformation of energy via his notion of instincts. To try to account for the first direction, Freud said that an instinct, during the course of its path from its organic source to the attainment of its aim, becomes mentally operative; it develops physical representatives by which one understands an idea, which is cathected with a definite quota of psychical energy. That is, the id is somehow able to form an image or idea of something that would satisfy its instinctual impulse. In the other direction, the ego, as having as its "outermost peripheral layer," "perception-consciousness" (Pcpt.-Cs), receives external stimuli which is somehow meaningfully organized (with the help of internal impulses), and then compared with the image or idea formed by the internal stimuli alone. All of this, however, remains quite mysterious!

When considered closely, Freud's account of the transformation of meanings into forces and vice versa had, for the existential phenomenologists, in effect really accounted for nothing at all. Instead of reconciling "ideas" with "quotas of affects," all he did was to tie mind and body, ego and non-ego together by simply treating forces (wishful impulses) as meanings (wishes, images, ideas), and vice versa. He did not show how it is possible that wishful impulses form meaningful ideas, or the reverse. Nor did Freud explain how it is possible for a biological organism to develop a "perception-consciousness" in the first place—how it is possible that an organic configuration of mass and energy can have the capacity of organizing, into meaningful ensembles, stimuli received from an external world. Freud, in fact, conceded the inadequacy of his explanation here: "every attempt to go on from (brain anatomy) to discover a localization of mental process, every endeavor to think of ideas as stored up in nerve-cells and of excitations as traveling along nerve-fibres, has miscarried completely."[40]

At the crucial points in his accounts of the above transformations, then, Freud failed to provide us with the causal explanation his scientific Weltanschauung required. If Freud was correct in saying that psychoanalysts are "incorrigible mechanists and materialists,"[41] he himself had an obligation to give a satisfactory account of the above transformations: this would seem a necessary requirement if he were going to remain loyal to his scientific credo.

For much of his career the lacunae in his account did not seem to have greatly disturbed Freud the scientist. He occasionally admitted in passing that "the leap from the mental to the physical" is "puzzling."[42] However, he believed that it was just a matter of time:

> In view of the intimate connection between the things that we distinguish as physical and mental, we may look forward to a day when paths of knowledge, and let us hope, of influence will be opened up, leading from organic biology and chemistry to the field of neurotic phenomena. That day still seems a distant one.[43]

> Our provisional ideas in psychology will some day be based on an organic substructure.[44]

Conceiving it to be like any other natural science, Freud thought that psychoanalysis would sooner or later be able to account for the gap and transformational processes between the mental and physical realms. However, he abandoned this hope in his last major theoretical work:

> Psychoanalysis makes a basic assumption . . . i.e., we know two kinds of things about what we call our psyche (or mental life): first, its bodily organ and scene of action, the brain (or nervous system) and, on the other hand, our acts of consciousness, which are immediate data and cannot be further explained by any sort of description. Everything that lies between is unknown to us, and the data do not include any direct relation between these two terminal points of our knowledge. If it existed, it would at the most afford an exact localization of the processes of consciousness and would give us no help toward understanding them.[45]

The discussion of this "basic assumption" Freud reserved for "philosophical thought." Here Freud must be understood as having essentially conceded that psychoanalysis cannot be, through natural scientific means, based upon an organic substructure. In his framework, Freud moved from his understanding of the reciprocal movement between instinctual impulses and thought-activity in organic processes as a basic truth which will sooner or later be scientifically validated to a recognition that his dualism was so fundamental that to account for the relation between the two he had to rely on scientifically unverifiable assumptions.

Furthermore, Freud neglected to explain the nature of certain critical concepts of which he made a great deal of use—for example, consciousness and unconsciousness. For Freud, they were systems of psychical life engaged in intermingling processes. But what were they really? What were their substantial natures? Since one of Freud's major assumptions was that the psyche can be scientifically studied like any other object, it would be reasonable to ask these questions and expect a relevant response. Freud, however, was ubiquitously evasive:

> The question as to the ultimate nature of this Unconscious is no wiser or more profitable than the older one as to the nature of consciousness.[46]

> There is no need to characterize what we call "conscious": it is the same as the consciousness of philosophers and of everyday opinion.[47]

> "What do you mean by the 'mental apparatus'? And what may I ask is it constructed of?" It will soon be clear what the mental apparatus is; but I must beg you not to ask what material it is constructed of. That is not a subject of psychological interest. Psychology can be as indifferent to it as, for instance, optics can be to the question of whether the walls of a telescope are made of metal or cardboard . . . we recognize in human beings a mental organization which is interpolated between their sensory stimuli and the perception of their somatic needs on the one hand and their motor acts on the other, and which mediates between them for a particular purpose . . . Now there is nothing new in this. Each one of us makes this assumption without being a philosopher, and some people even in spite of being philosophers.[48]

This was a peculiar sort of response. For if it is true that "the psychical processes [are] qualitatively determined states of specifiable material particles," and that "the somatic concomitant is what is truly psychical," it would seem important from a scientific viewpoint to elaborate on the nature of the material out of which the psychical apparatus is composed. Was this not the entire purpose of Freud's metapsychology in the first place?

The result of all of this is that Freud's metapsychological theory, according to the existential phenomenologists, could not adequately reconcile its conception of humans as both a mechanistic being, driven by instinctual impulses, and a consciousness, aware of internal and external meanings, ideas, and so on. He could account for neither their substantive natures nor their transformational processes. Here he could offer only descriptions, not explanations—and it was the latter that his metapsychology required.

The reason for Freud's discomfort was clear. He was caught between his loyalty to the scientific "credo"—which dictates that humans are just one more researchable object in the universe—and the necessity for employing scientifically unverifiable assumptions because of the intrinsically different nature of the psychical realm. Freud found himself in the odd position of being a scientist who made and relied upon scientifically unverifiable assumptions.

Freud's Philosophically Split Personality?

In the face of the above kind of ostensibly intractable philosophical difficulties, Medard Boss attempted to salvage Freud's significant contributions by arguing that the above presuppositions applied only to his metapsychological theory, whereas his therapeutic techniques were far more conciliatory to an existential perspective. How did he do this? Boss wrote:

> The two ways of understanding man inherent in psychoanalytic therapy and psychoanalytic theory differ so much from each other that they amount, at times, to clear-cut *contradictions*, especially in regard to their most important features [italics added].[49]

Boss argued that this was especially true of the issue of determinism versus free will:

> The intrinsic harmony of psychoanalytic therapy and analysis of *Dasein* becomes *particularly evident* in their common underlying conception of human freedom . . . as being able to choose. They mean choice between two decisions. Freud's writings, insofar as they deal with practical psychoanalytic technique, abound with references to freedom.[50]

If Boss was correct, then there is a clear-cut contradiction between Freud's theory, which held a hard determinism (at least according to the existential phenomenologists), and Freud's therapy, which "presupposed" human freedom. This would go far in mitigating the philosophical destruction of Freud undertaken by the existential phenomenologists. Let us examine the cogency of Boss's claim.

The critical question here, of course, is whether and to what extent these two orientations share a "common underlying conception of human freedom"? What was Boss's evidence for this claim? He alluded to only three passages in Freud's therapeutic papers:[51]

> One best protects the patient from injuries brought about through carrying out one of his impulses by making him promise not to take any important decisions affecting his life during the time of his treatment— for instance, not to choose any profession or definite love-object . . .
>
> At the same time one willingly leaves untouched as much of the patient's personal freedom as is compatible with these restrictions . . .[52]

> Transference-love has perhaps a degree less of freedom than the love which appears in ordinary life and is called normal . . .[53]

> To achieve this overcoming, she has to be led through the primal period of her mental development and on that path she has to acquire the extra piece of mental freedom which distinguishes conscious mental activity— in the systematic sense—from unconscious.[54]

In the above, what else could Freud have meant but a freedom which involved deliberations among various options (that is, the existentialist notion of "choice")? Indeed, prima facie, there is additional cogent evidence supporting Boss's claim that Freud referred to the human capacity for freedom throughout what are primarily (though not exclusively) Freud's therapeutic writings.[55]

It is highly significant to note what Freud said when he addressed the very task of therapy:

> We try to restore the ego, *to free it from its restrictions,* and to give it back the command over the id which it has lost owing to its early repressions [italics added].[56]

> Only then will [psychoanalysis], thanks to having strengthened the patient's ego, succeed in replacing by a correct solution the inadequate decision made in his early life.[57]

The goal of Freud's therapy, then, was clear: by making conscious the repressed material formed during early childhood and uncovering and eliminating the resistances, Freud enabled the analysand to achieve greater self-knowledge, and consequently an increase in self-control over his/her impulses.[58] Hence, in line with Boss's thinking, Freud's psychoanalytic treatment was designed to expand the horizons of the individual's freedom through the "widening of his intellectual horizon . . . and liberating enlightenment that the treatment brings with it."[59] Or again: "the freeing of someone from his neurotic symptoms, inhibitions and abnormalities of character . . ."[60] Psychoanalytic treatment attempted to expand the analysand's possibilities to their outermost limits.[61] It accomplished this by helping the patient to ascertain and grasp the truth about himself or herself (overcome resistances to repressed ideas, and so on).

Second, it would seem that Freud *must* have recognized the existence of freedom as the necessary condition for the very implementation of the "fundamental rule" (namely, free association) in therapy, which "has the greatest importance for cure": "[the analysand] is to tell us not only what he can say intentionally and willingly . . . but . . . everything else as well that his self-observation yields him, everything that comes into his head . . ."[62] By asking the analysand to "let him-/her-self go" and say everything that crosses his/her mind, Freud presupposed that the analysand had the freedom to comply or not comply with this request.[63] He openly acknowledged the possibility that the patient might feel "at liberty . . . to disregard the fundamental rule of psycho-analysis."[64] In a similar vein, the patient had other options, for example: "each person makes a selection from the possible mechanisms of defence, that he always uses a few only of them and always the same ones."[65] Freud recognized a complementary function of the fundamental rule for the analyst as well:

> The doctor must put himself in a position to make use of everything he is told for the purposes of interpretation and of recognizing the concealed unconscious material without substituting a censorship of his own for the selection that the patient has forgone.[66]

It is apparent here that Freud acknowledged the analyst's capacity to choose to adopt this stance during the course of therapy.

Freud recognized that various options were open to the analyst during the therapeutic process, for example: "In interpreting a dream during an analysis a choice lies open to one between several technical procedures."[67] Freud, which is highly significant, was very careful to insist that during the course of therapy the analyst must be, in the maximally appropriate way, respectful of the analysand's autonomy: "there is nothing we would rather bring about than that *the patient should make his decisions for himself* " [italics added].[68] The eventual *independence of the patient* is the analyst's ultimate object.[69]

> The patient should be educated to liberate and fulfill his own nature, and not to resemble ourselves . . . psychoanalysis should [not] place itself in the service of a particular philosophical outlook on the world and should urge this upon the patient in order to ennoble him. I would say that after all this is only tyranny . . ."[70]

In summary, there is strong prima facie evidence within Freud's own writings to substantiate Boss's claim of a fundamental contradiction between the determinism of Freud's metapsychological theory and the capacity of human freedom presupposed in his papers on therapeutic technique.

Freud as Unified

Although there is evidence in support of a philosophically split Freud, as Boss proposed, Freud himself staunchly insisted that he always remained unified in his psychoanalytic approach. In fact, he believed that his therapeutic practice sprang from a scientific grounding in his metapsychological theory. Indeed, Freud described his metapsychology as "designed to clarify and carry deeper the theoretical assumptions on which a psychoanalytic system could be founded."[71] It would "provide a stable theoretical foundation for psycho-analysis."[72] Hence, all psychoanalytic ideas, techniques, and approaches would be grounded in it.[73] It could, in fact, be argued that the "humanistic" side of Freud was actually motivated by scientific impulses; from his clinical experience, Freud the scientist formulated hypotheses (his metapsychological theory) and then sought to confirm or deny them (his therapeutic practice). When practice (empirical investigations) did not support his theory, Freud modified that theory. And when certain therapeutic approaches seemed to fail in producing the desired results, Freud modified his techniques (for example, Freud gave up hypnosis in favor of analysis, and later modified analysis to include a more open, less interpretative approach). Even the very notion of health—what every therapist desires for her or his patients—had to be considered within Freud's theoretical framework: "It is impossible to define health except in metapsychological terms, i.e., by reference to the dynamic relations between the agencies of the mental apparatus which have been recognized—or (if that is preferred) inferred or conjectured by us."[74]

Throughout his writings on therapy and technique, Freud continually reemphasized the importance of his metapsychology. He admitted that the actual practice of psychoanalysis was different from his theoretical account of human nature: his theory was to make sense of the process as a whole, while therapy was to engage the patient in order to heal. Obviously the two were not the same, and hence involved different considerations. When discussing therapeutic technique, Freud never abandoned his theoretical foundation; it always served, at least implicitly, as the backdrop for clinical interpretation. It was just that each was to be dealt with from its own respective approach.

> In speaking to you I need not rebut the objection that the evidential value in support of the correctness of our hypotheses is obscured in our treatment as we practise it to-day; you will not forget that this evidence is to be found elsewhere, and that a therapeutic procedure cannot be carried out in the same way as a theoretical investigation.[75]

At times, however, even in therapy the practice and theory of psychoanalysis interacted. When it was time for the analyst to disclose his/her interpretation of the unconscious material, for example, the analyst relied heavily upon the metapsychology.

> The treatment is made up of two parts—what the physician infers and tells the patient, and the patient's working-over of what he has heard. The mechanism of our assistance is easy to understand: we give the patient the conscious anticipatory idea [the idea of what he may expect to find] and he then finds the repressed unconscious idea in himself on the basis of its similarity to the anticipatory idea.[76]

And again, when analysts ran up against problems that seemed difficult to understand, Freud suggested a return to the theoretical in order to deepen and explain their understanding of the process. Recall that Freud wrote:

> If we are asked by what methods and means this result is achieved [namely, the "taming of the instinct"], it is not easy to find an answer. We can only say: "We must call the Witch to our help after all!" [Goethe, *Faust*, I.6]—the Witch Metapsychology. Without metapsychological speculation and theorizing—I had almost said "phantasying"—we shall not get another step forward. Unfortunately, here as elsewhere, what our

> Witch reveals is neither very clear nor very detailed. We have only a
> single clue to start from—though it is a clue of the highest value—
> namely, the antithesis between the primary and the secondary
> processes . . .[77]

Hence, although theory and therapy were recognized as distinct from one another, and thus requiring different approaches, Freud held strong to his conviction that the two were necessarily interrelated, and hence unified.

It would not have seemed contradictory to Freud, then, that a therapist should on the one hand hold biologically based theoretical positions, while on the other hand treating patients *as if* they were free, autonomous beings, capable of making decisions and assuming responsibility for those decisions.[78] For Freud, humans were conceived as both biologically determined and "free." Freud's "free will," however, was itself a biological fact of human existence (as opposed to being contra-causal); as we have seen, it was by virtue of human mental processes, which were grounded in physical instinctual impulses, that the conviction of "free will" truly existed.

> Many people, as is well known, contest the assumption of complete psy-
> chical determinism by appealing to a special feeling of conviction that
> there is a free will. This feeling of conviction exists; and it does not give
> way before a belief in determinism . . . the feeling that we have is rather
> one of psychical compulsion . . .[79]

As with any psychical compulsion, the therapist's role was not to deny the existence of free will, but rather to understand the motivating force behind the compulsion. And like all compulsions, the feeling of free will originated, according to Freud, in an instinctual need.

> According to our analyses it is not necessary to dispute the right to the
> feeling of conviction of having a free will. If the distinction between con-
> scious and unconscious motivation is taken into account, our feeling of
> conviction informs us that conscious motivation does not extend to all
> our motor decisions . . . But what is thus left free by the one side receives
> its motivation from the other side, from the unconscious; and in this way
> determination in the psychical sphere is still carried out without any
> gap.[80]

If Freud was guilty of treating his patients "as if" they had free will, then, it was not evidence of an inconsistency between theory and practice, but rather the utilization of a therapeutic technique that was grounded in a psychically determined metapsychology.

For Freud, humans were first and foremost biological organisms: the fact that humans possess mental processes of a "very elaborately organized nature" does nothing to change their fundamentally biological nature. Freud wrote that all mental processes are "at bottom motives, instinctual impulses."[81] Thus, note once again Freud's grounding of everything in an organic substructure (that is, his metapsychology), even within his papers on technique. Freud held that these complex mental processes function in various ways to assist us in our survival. When something happens to threaten our survival, the mental processes work to protect us. According to Freud, material that is unacceptable in some way becomes blocked from consciousness. Such material then becomes inaccessible, whereby it is relegated to the unconscious areas of mental functioning.

Freud believed that the amount of energy invested in keeping unacceptable material in the unconscious unduly confined the person, for as long as the energy was geared toward repression, it could not be used in other, more productive ways. Hence, the "freedom" therapy afforded individuals was purely on the mental, biological level. Its purpose was to bring about an understanding of the instinctual impulses, which motivated the patient to exhibit abnormal symptoms. Freud wrote:

> But the patient knows nothing of these elementary motives or not nearly enough. We teach him to understand the way in which these highly complicated mental formations are compounded; we trace the symptoms back to the instinctual impulses which motivate them; we point out to the patient these instinctual motives, which are present in his symptoms and of which he has hitherto been unaware—just as a chemist isolates the fundamental substance, the chemical "element," out of the salt in which it had been combined with other elements and in which it was unrecognizable. In the same way, as regards those of the patient's mental manifestations that were not considered pathological, we show him that he was only to a certain extent conscious of their motivation—that other instinctual impulses of which he had remained in ignorance had cooperated in producing them.[82]

Hence, for Freud, therapy primarily consisted in working with the mental processes to make conscious the repressed, unconscious material so that the individual need not invest his or her energies in repression. The "motive force" could be freed, thereby allowing the person liberation from, for example, compulsively repetitive activities. "Freedom," then, consisted of the manipulation of biological energies, its concomitant raising to conscious awareness, and the redirecting of those energies. Any other notions of "freedom," such as the freedom about which Boss spoke, were based upon misunderstandings, psychical compulsions, and/or a lack of awareness of the biological nature of humans within Freud's metapsychological theory.

Schopenhauer's Obviation of Freud's "Philosophically Split Personality"

Given the previous discussions, it is irrefragable that Freudian psycho-analysis was vulnerable to the critique lodged by the existential phenom-enologists. Yet he himself lacked the resources to refute the existential phenomenologists on a philosophical level. If we consider the previous chapters on the historical-philosophical influences that engaged Freud's development of psychoanalysis, it is equally clear that Freudian psycho-analysis encompassed far more than the critique of Freud's supposed Cartesianism–Kantianism lodged by the existential phenomenologists. In-deed, such an overly simplified "historical" account tended more to "de-contextualize" Freud historically than the reverse.[83]

Indeed, it was Schelling who may have been the pivotal point in the history of ideas for Freudian psychoanalysis. On the one hand, Schelling had anticipated the existentialist critique: "So far as I am *free*, I am not a *thing* at all, not an *object* . . . But what is caught up in mere mechanism can-not step out of the mechanism and ask: How has all of this become pos-sible?"[84] On the other, Schelling offers the solution that enables Schopen-hauer and Freud to transcend the critique lodged by the existential phenomenologists: "But now mechanism alone is far from being what constitutes Nature. For as soon as we enter the realm of organic nature, all mechanical linkage of cause and effect ceases for us."[85]

If we understand Schopenhauer's thought as the philosophical cul-mination of the successive waves of philosophical strains exerting an im-pact upon Freud, it would seem that, at least prima facie, it should be con-sidered as potentially providing the philosophical grounding for Freudian psychoanalysis. Indeed, we contend it is Schopenhauer's metaphysical po-sition that affords Freud the philosophical resources with which to defend his position against the existentialist thinkers in a unified manner, as co-gently as possible. It does so by treating the key configuration of topics for Freud—the body, the unconscious, the instincts/will/id—in a truly uni-fied manner. As we have seen in the chapters on the philosophical rela-tionship between Freud's and Schopenhauer's systems, Freud himself was, to some extent, on the way to this realization.

From a "Freudian" philosophical viewpoint, much is to be gained by explicitly resituating Freud entirely within the Schopenhauerean model.[86] As we shall see, many—though certainly not all—of the existential phenomenological critiques simply dissolve.

Recall that the goal of Freud's metapsychology was to show how everything is grounded in an organic substructure. With his analysis of the will as the underlying transcendental condition for the emergence of all that is, Schopenhauer showed how it was *the body* which enabled us to apprehend directly the hitherto inaccessible noumenal realm as will. This model has a number of advantages in relation to the existential phenomenological critique. First, it affords Freud's system a metaphysical *unity* that undercuts their charges of a Cartesian, mechanistic conception of human beings and its unbridgeable dualistic account, as well as all the problems that stem from its uncritically held subject–object dichotomy. This occurs on a variety of interrelated levels.

For Schopenhauer, human beings are unified manifestations of the will, which involve indissoluble biological processes and meaning-formations. As such, this is not reducible to a mechanistic conception of humankind. Humans are not ontologically conceived as objects or things, according to this model. Hence, all the above Cartesian presuppositions and the unresolved problems that emerge from them are obviated. Minds (as active, thinking, unextended substances) and bodies (as passive, unthinking, extended substances) are no longer understood as mechanistic objects—and Freud, then, is not in the position of having to say exactly what they "are" as objects.

Schopenhauer's metaphysics undercuts the subject–object dichotomy intrinsic to Cartesian dualism: "an actual identity . . . of the subject with the object is *immediately given*."[87] There is no inner and outer world, and there is no ontological distinction between mind and body in the Cartesian sense. As a result, Freud need not get caught up in the problem of explaining the metaphysical relationships between the internal/external world—how, for example, mental ideas represent external material objects—and the interactive dualism involved in the mind–body problem. The need for Freud's tergiversatory descriptions of what the instincts "are" is thereby removed.

Next, resituating Freud within Schopenhauerean metaphysics enables Freud to retain (on his own terms) certain descriptive advantages of the dualism of Kantian epistemological model while recognizing the necessity to modify it. Noumena (by itself inaccessible as the id for Freud) is always already *unified* in human beings with phenomena (the psychical representatives of instinctual processes of the id) through *the body*. As we have seen, Freud himself was arguably a fellow traveler with Schopenhauer's transcendence of duality here: "The ego is first and foremost a bodily ego."[88] In this way, Freud can avoid the problem of having to account for the transformation of bodily forces into psychical energies (and vice versa), and bodily forces into psychical meaning (and vice versa).

We should also note the irony that the existential phenomenologists ignored Schopenhauer, given that the body plays such an important role, as we have seen, in their analysis.

Finally, resituating Freudian psychoanalysis within Schopenhauerean metaphysics has the additional advantage of mitigating (though by no means eliminating) the existential phenomenological critique of Freud's lack of freedom in his deterministic model. Among the essential differences between the existential phenomenologists and Schopenhauer/ Freud is that the former assert that intrinsic to the human condition: (1) there is spontaneous and creative *free choice;* (2) there is freedom of *action* in the phenomenal world; and (3) there is *no grounding* for freedom. Schopenhauer and Freud denied all three assertions: there is no free-floating, spontaneous, ungrounded (that is, unmotivated action) freedom.

As we have seen, for Schopenhauer freedom really means the removal of hindrances to the will and the will "choosing" which motive "stirs it" in the strongest way. Freedom is the liberation of energies that comes with greater awareness of what the will desires and what the motives are which are acting on it. The broader the range of possible motives, the freer the will. As the transcendental condition for the phenomena that occur, the will, then, does not *cause* the phenomena to happen, it merely makes their occurrence possible in the transcendental sense. In the phenomenal world, everything, to be sure, is "caused"—but not in the sense of one object (the cause) forcing another object to move (the effect). Rather, the state of affairs x necessarily—that is, in accordance with the principle of sufficient reason—precedes the state of affairs y, and so forth. For example, a person's sexually abusive childhood (x) is followed by an unconscious unwillingness to face x due to the immense pain that would occur in doing so (y), and hence she or he represses it and does not face it (z . . .). Or again, according to Schopenhauer this is what gives Freud's technique of "free association" merely the appearance of being "free":

> Here too the will is determined by the law of motivation according to
> which [the will] *is also the secret director of the so-called association of ideas* . . .
> Here it seems as though something quite unconnected with anything
> else has entered our consciousness. That this, however, cannot occur, is,
> as I have said, precisely the root of the principle of sufficient reason . . .
> Every picture or image that is suddenly presented to our imagination,
> also every judgement that does not follow its previously existing ground

or reason, must be produced by an act of will which has a motive . . . as soon as a link in a series of representations has come to us, we at once recall all the others, often apparently against our will [italics added].[89]

There is a "determinism" here of sorts, but it is not of the causal mechanistic variety ascribed to Freud by the existential phenomenologists.[90]

The way in which we are "free," from the Schopenhauerean and "Freudian" perspectives, is in our capacity to be able to come to a conscious awareness of our underlying motives. For example, Schopenhauer explained:

> Only [a human being's] *cognition* can be corrected; thus he may come to see that the particular means formerly employed by him do not lead to the end he has in view, or that they entail more disadvantage than gain; he then changes the means but not the ends . . . the motives operate with necessity, but they have to pass through *cognition*, the medium of the motives. Cognition, however, is capable of the most manifold extension, of constant correction in innumerable degrees; all education works to this end. Cultivation of reason by cognitions and insight of every kind is morally important, because it opens the way to motives which would be closed off to the human being without it. As long as he was unable to understand them, they were nonexistent for his will.[91]

This is precisely Freud's position on the educational, psychotherapeutic function of psychoanalysis[92]—it liberates analysands by enabling them to understand their true motives, by consciously showing them the way to the outside of Plato's cave.[93]

Resituating Freud entirely within the paradigm of Schopenhauerean metaphysical theory thus enables us to truly see to what extent Freudian psychoanalysis and phenomenology/existential phenomenology *converge* in the crucial role *the body* plays in their analyses of human existence. At the same time, it shows more accurately what specifically *prevents their merger:* the analysis of freedom as unhindered will which is "stirred" by the strongest motive versus a spontaneously creative, ungrounded free choice through which one can act and engage the world of facticity. It is the latter which will always preclude the possibility of a complete merger between the two orientations.[94]

Finally, Schopenhauer made it clear that it is this will which enables human beings to turn against themselves as a phenomenon insofar as they have truly grasped the nature of their will. This led to his anticipation of one motivation for becoming something akin to a psychoanalyst:

The breaking free from the bondage to the will occurs even more fully
and radically when a knowing subject recognizes himself and others as
manifestations of the same will. Seeing that suffering is a necessary concomitant of the will's activity, such a subject will express his liberation
through sympathy, compassion.[95]

On this score, Schopenhauer favorably quoted Ovid: "He helps the mind
best who once for all breaks the tormenting bonds that ensnare and en-
tangle the heart."[96]

Unfortunately, helping others could only go so far toward liberating
humanity in general. Hence, unlike the optimism of the existential phenomenologists, Schopenhauer, Nietzsche (in the final analysis), and Freud
all shared a pessimism about the human capacity to overcome their primordial state of being governed by instinctual impulses. Schopenhauer
was convinced that the best we could do, generally, was to seek ephemeral
respite from the demands of the will in aesthetic and philosophically con-
templative experiences. Nietzsche, while rejecting (yet, ultimately, never
quite escaping) Schopenhauer's brand of pessimism,[97] urged us to have a
yea-saying attitude while embracing such intrinsic features of the human
condition. Freud, on the other hand, suggested that all we could really do
was to endure with resignation such a predicament: "Attempts at flight
from the demands of instinct are, however, in general useless."[98]

Ultimately, they were pessimistic about the capacity of human beings in general to transcend what could only be considered a relatively insignificant existence. However, all three acknowledged the importance of
maximizing the possibilities of those fortunate few who could genuinely
contribute to the human condition. In this way, they shared a guarded optimism about the world: we each have the potential to alleviate some of the
suffering by developing a greater awareness and understanding of ourselves and humanity in general, but we certainly cannot escape it. To put
this in the context of our topic: we have access to the inaccessible through
ever-evolving awareness of and courage to glimpse what is hidden, yet we
can never hope to change what is intrinsic to our very being—our innermost instinctual nature.

18

Unification of Freudian Psychoanalysis through an Archaeological Methodology

Under such flattering colors and make-up as well, the basic text of homo natura must again be recognized.

To translate man back into nature; to become master over the many vain and overly enthusiastic interpretations and connotations that have so far been scrawled and painted over that eternal basic text of homo natura; to see to it that man henceforth stands before man as even today, hardened in the discipline of science, he stands before the rest of nature, with intrepid Oedipus eyes and sealed Odysseus ears, deaf to the siren songs of old metaphysical bird catchers who have been piping at him all too long, "you are more, you are higher, you are of a different origin!"
—Nietzsche

The overman is the meaning of the earth. Let your will say: the overman shall be the meaning of the earth! I beseech you, my brothers, remain faithful to the earth, and do not believe those who speak to you of otherworldly hopes!
—Nietzsche

Freud assumed the role of Zarathustra upon the summit of the glacier of human consciousness, shining his lantern into the dark and hidden recesses of the unconscious mind, and was not always welcomed as bearing the light of truth. Neither the scientists of his day nor the philosophers who desired the revelation of something optimistic in human nature appreciated his account of the human unconscious. For Freud, humans were essentially one species of animal that had evolved, for better or worse, into conscious beings who could not escape the instinctual ancestry of their past. And although consciousness could provide the tools for awareness, liberation was limited to understanding and not action.

The existential phenomenologists wanted something more than an instinctually deterministic account of human nature, which stripped humanity of its freedom and responsibility. For the most part, they rejected Freud on the basis of his adherence to and misapplication of the scientific methodology and accused him of overstepping the boundaries of science with the introduction of a nonscientifically verifiable unconscious. Yet, as we have seen, in relegating Freud within a scientific and contradictory Cartesian–Kantian framework, the existential phenomenologists neglected to honor their own demands that any theoretical framework be critiqued within the full historical context from which it arose.

It is relatively clear to what extent the existential phenomenologists were familiar with the works of Freud. From Boss, we know that Heidegger "generally perused" Freud's metapsychological papers[1] and his articles on therapeutic technique.[2] Heidegger only directly referred to Freud's *Psychopathology of Everyday Life*.[3] Sartre was at most familiar with Freud's *Studies in Hysteria, The Interpretation of Dreams, The Psychopathology of Everyday Life, An Autobiographical Study,* and possibly his *Introductory Lectures on Psycho-analysis*. Merleau-Ponty referred only to Freud's *Introductory Lectures on Psycho-analysis* and *Five Lectures on Psycho-analysis* in his magnum opus *The Phenomenology of Perception*. Based on this limited exposure to Freud's writings, it can hardly be argued that any of the existential phenomenologists were thoroughly familiar with Freud's work. As a result, this led to some specific misunderstandings and subsequent mischaracterizations of Freud's position (especially on the part of Sartre). We submit that had they been more extensively familiar with Freud's psychological works (which extend to twenty-three volumes) and sought to situate Freud within the full context of his philosophical heritage, they might have been able to see the greater depth and unity of his metapsychology, as grounded in Schopenhauer's philosophy.

When the existential phenomenologists (and scientists) criticized Freud, they did so from the standpoint of their own a priori interpretive frameworks and hence wound up understanding Freud from an unduly narrow perspective. It is by looking into a fuller account of the philosophical-historical confluences which fed into the ultimate development of his theory that we are enabled to truly understand it.

Freud as Synthesizer

As we have witnessed, through the application of a regressive archaeological investigation (a "philosophography") of the philosophical background of Freudian psychoanalysis, Freud's work represents a culmination and synthesis of many great ideas throughout the history of Western philosophy. Briefly, in Bacon and the Philosophes, Freud found the philosophical grounding of science and an appreciation and optimism that science could indeed yield insights into the hidden recesses of the human mind. In addition, Bacon contributed to Freud's tentative optimism that reason could potentially provide the tools not only for humans to establish scientific reflection as "sound philosophy," but to successfully deal with the internal strife between human beings' natural instincts and the restrictive demands of civilization.

From Kant, Freud understood that our perceptions are subjectively conditioned (for example, space and time are necessary forms of thought), that there is a distinction between reality as it actually *is* versus reality as it appears to us. Freud concurred with Kant that the psyche is largely inaccessible (the mind included an inner "noumenal" realm, an unconscious) and not necessarily what it appears to be and that dreams—properly understood—had the capacity to disclose our hidden natures. Freud also found further confirmation, in Kant, of the antagonism between human desires and societal constraints that only few could deal with rationally.

The Greeks—Empedocles and Plato—provided Freud with precious remnants from our human past prior to social evolution/repression and served as one of the primary inspirations in Freud to be, at times, highly speculative as to the underlying, most fundamental forces operative in the universe. Their insights revealed some of the most basic themes in human existence, themes with which the human mind continues to grapple: how, for example, to reconcile polarities, to understand the tensions of unity versus separation in their various forms (love versus strife, attraction versus repulsion, Eros versus Thanatos). Plato exerted an especially prominent influence on Freud. As we have seen, Freud was consciously influenced by Plato's theory of reminiscence; insight of Eros as underlying, preserving, and uniting everything; and awareness of the importance of dreams in disclosing the underlying meaning of our desires. Unconsciously, Freud was impacted by Plato in his recognition that humans have desires/ideas that are inaccessible to them, and are capable of becoming their own masters when their appetites are properly tempered; and in the development of his tripartite theory of the self, which involves the self-mastery of desires, conflicts among parts of the self, and appetites as the chief and strongest element within us. Furthermore, Plato and Freud shared methodological similarities for approaching the inaccessible. Since some memories are inaccessible and there are powerful resistances to knowing the truth, a person is liberated when she or he knows the truth.

Generally speaking, Freud was affected by the romanticists' recognition that humans are neither separate nor separable from Nature; that a deeper look into human nature reveals our human past and hence that which is most fundamental; that society as a human creation has served, among other things, to distort and remove humans from their ancient roots; and that what is necessary is to rediscover those roots in the search for the inaccessible.

Goethe, as we have seen, served as *a primary impetus* for the direction of Freud's intellectual development. In addition, Goethe provided a new "view" of science as involving archetypal phenomena and polarities, while expressing an antipathy for epistemology and reservations about metaphysics. His reverence for historically rooted ideas was concretely manifested in his reclamation and reinforcement of Plato's identification of the unity of Eros and the maze of passions, which underlie our dreams.

Schiller and Schelling, rejecting the sharp bifurcation between reason and desires, emphasized the limited resources of reason while elevating the instincts and passions in our understanding of the universe, and sought to explore the unconscious processes in dreams, mental maladies, and nature in general. Schelling, in particular, conceived of all reality as consisting of an indeterminate, unconscious, striving will which created reason. Furthermore, Schelling and Goethe shared the same notion of freedom with Schopenhauer and Freud.

Finally, Schopenhauer conceived of the noumenal world (namely, as will) in much the same way as Freud (as id). Schopenhauer, of course— and, at times, Nietzsche—held the same notions of the unconscious, repression, sexuality, the body, the relationship between dreams and madness, and the death instincts.

A regressive archaeological investigation reveals the extent to which Freud was able to synthesize, consciously and unconsciously, those major figures in his past and present intellectual environment. It also puts us in a better position to understand to what extent Freud transcended those theories which had influenced him.

Benefits of an Archaeological Investigation into Freudian Psychoanalysis

In chapter 1, we noted the dialectical tendencies intrinsic to Freud's intellectual development. This schema now enables us to understand the extent to which philosophical influences contributed to—that is, provided the roots for the development of—these dialectical tendencies. It also affords us the opportunity to consider the degree to which Freud reconciled these dialectical tendencies within himself.

First, Freud exhibited a marked ambivalence toward philosophy. Freud shared Bacon's and the Enlightenment's critique of philosophy as speculative. Indeed, Freud often chastised Empedocles, Schopenhauer, and Nietzsche on this score. Yet he appealed to their theories for confirmatory reasons when it suited his purposes. At times, even Freud could not restrain himself from engaging in speculative philosophical inquiry, particularly in *Beyond the Pleasure Principle*.

Similar to Bacon, Freud was anti-systematic and critical of the completeness sought by philosophers. Nevertheless, like Schopenhauer, he systematically sought an all-encompassing account of human experience in his metapsychology.

Freud claimed he was opposed to the construction of worldviews. He subscribed, however, to various (occasionally conflicting) worldviews such as the "scientific" worldview, "Goethe's" view of nature, Schopenhauer's worldview, and so on.

Freud agreed with Bacon and the Philosophes that observation was the basis of science, yet he extended his concept of science to cover unobservable domains of human experience (in accordance with Romanticism, Schopenhauer, and Nietzsche).

In line with the Philosophes, Freud employed rationality to explore humankind's irrational impulses. Yet, analogous with Schopenhauer, Freud saw that that which forms the irrational basis of human existence is the very source of rationality itself.

Finally, Freud saw human action as determined, and yet viewed humans as responsible, and capable of a certain liberation. As we have seen, it is Schopenhauer who provides Freud a way of reconciling the latter. Indeed, Schopenhauer provides Freud with the means to either resolve or come to terms with all the above dialectical tendencies.

Given these dialectical tendencies, it is tempting to conclude that Freud had a philosophically split personality, as Boss and others have claimed. Prima facie, this claim has some basis in Freud's writings. This is, however, as we have shown, to mistake the dialectical tendencies as constituting a split in Freud's synthesizing mind between his theory and his therapeutic practice. Freud was consistent in seeing his metapsychology as providing, among other things, the basis for his therapeutic practice. There is, in fact, a clear dialectical *unity* in Freud's synthesis. Undoubtedly the philosophical influences upon Freud contributed in different ways to this unity. Bacon and the Philosophes—along with all of those who were subsequently affected by them and who had an impact on Freud, such as Herbart, Fechner, Helmholtz, and so on—generated the basis of Freud's scientific concerns; while the Greeks, romanticists, Schopenhauer, and Nietzsche contributed to Freud's humanistic concerns. Freud sought to push the boundaries of what was taken during his own time to be "science"—via the influence of philosophers who inspired and thereby enabled him to transcend the scientistic orientation he himself had so doggedly pursued—so as to more adequately encompass that which formed the primal elements underlying such humanistic concerns. It is for this reason that Freud could properly claim to be seeking unity in his metapsychological account of human experience.

To what extent did the historical influences upon Freud necessitate these dialectical tendencies? What we see within Freud as an individual, as we saw in Kant the individual, is a reflection of the Hegelian dialectical movement throughout history.[4] It is precisely that dialectical basis which propels great individuals/historical epochs forward to greater and greater syntheses. Given our archaeological exploration of Freud's historical psyche, it is clear how the emergence of Freudian metapsychology is an ideal illustration of this process.

There were not, then, two "Freuds." Rather, what we witness is the historical emergence of a great synthesizing mind in the process of dialectically working itself out. The culmination of this process in Freud's mind was the unified account of human experience offered by his metapsychological theory. There is a great irony in this dialectical result, however. Freudian metapsychological theory is not metaphysically grounded in Hegelian philosophy. Instead, as we have seen, it gains its genuine metaphysical foundation in Schopenhauer's philosophy—the great antithesis to Hegel's philosophy in the sense that "Kantian" noumena are not only *not* meaningless, but are accessible. The dialectical process itself (as manifested in Freud's intellectual heritage) is a manifestation of the underlying cosmic will.[5]

Indeed this comprises the very essence of this book: in our archaeological inquiry, we have witnessed the uncovering *in* Freud (and *by* Freud) of that which has been "lost" historically for whatever reason (namely, repressed) and then rediscovered later in a very powerful manner. Here it is useful to recall that for Freud, the "uncanny" *(unheimlich)* is something which is secretly familiar, which has undergone repression and then returned from it. A primary example of this is Freud's concrete application of the Lamarckian thesis concerning the phylogenetic transmission of ideas in a collective unconscious. That which continually reemerges as "inaccessible" and which Freud is able to access is precisely our phylogenetic history—the Oedipus complex, for example—as it relates to the unconscious and various dimensions of the self and, globally, for humankind.

Our archaeological inquiry has also placed us in a better position to appreciate the extent to which Freud understood himself philosophically and psychoanalytically. It is clear that Freud did not truly grasp the sophisticated philosophical nuances involved in such epistemological positions as Cartesian interactive dualism, Kantian theory, Schopenhauerean metaphysics, and so on. Yet he tried to incorporate various facets of these into his metapsychology theory—at times inconsistently and at others with a great deal of success. We have also come to see the extent to which he was on the way to transcending his own self-understanding with regard to the philosophical positions on dualism and determinism. In terms of the *unity* of his own system, it is far more coherent to understand Freud as a Schopenhauerean, as opposed to his self-professed Cartesianism–Kantianism. Freud himself insisted that psychoanalysis could help us better understand why great thinkers develop the ideas they do. Psychoanalytically, we have witnessed that, despite Freud's expostulations to the contrary, his own theory accounts for the falsity of his historical version of his self-proclaimed "greatest discoveries" (for example, the theory of repression).

The Engagement of Freudian Psychoanalysis and Existential Phenomenology

In considering Freud's work within a fuller account of the historical-philosophical context, the nature of the engagement of his insights with those of the existential phenomenologists has also become clearer. Reciprocally, we are now in a better position to appreciate the extent to which Husserl's phenomenology and existential phenomenology have engaged Freudian psychoanalysis. We have shown that there are good reasons for thinking that Ricoeur and Merleau-Ponty are correct—that ultimately phenomenology and psychoanalysis converge without merging. At the same time they are complementary to one another: each has something to offer the other. What prevents a merger between Freudian psychoanalysis and phenomenology/existential phenomenology are their differing conceptions of freedom. There is an irreconcilable difference between the phenomenologists and the existential phenomenologists, who advocate the idea that human existence at the very least includes a spontaneous, productive, and creative capacity to make choices and act in the world based on those choices, and Schopenhauer and Freud, for whom no such capacity really exists (in any significant sense).

In spite of this fundamental difference, Husserl and Merleau-Ponty come closest to providing a bridge between existential phenomenology and Freudian psychoanalysis. This is due to the weight they accord (1) the interplay between conscious and unconscious psychical/bodily processes in their analysis, (2) the idea that thoughts arise when *they* will and not when *we* will them, (3) the view that psychical life is a continuous thread of activity, and (4) the lived-body, that is, the instinctual processes as the subsoil of psychical life.

The body is the most real of beings for Schopenhauer and Freud. Hence, Schopenhauer and Freud would have been more closely aligned with Husserl and the French existential phenomenologists in the debate among the existential phenomenologists on the primordiality of bodily being. All would concur that (1) the body undercuts the subject–object dichotomy (subject and object coincide, thus transcending duality for all involved); (2) it is the body that is the necessary starting point for the understanding of perception; and (3) the fundamental theme of all acts of will is inseparable from the body's existence in health.

Convergence in Bodily Being: The Question of the Ontological Primordiality of the Body within Existence

One essential theme that played a pivotal role in both apprehending the inaccessible and unifying the converging traditions of Freudian psychoanalysis and phenomenology/existential phenomenology is *bodily being*. Each of the thinkers within these traditions, in varying degrees, saw the body as playing a central and unifying role in affording direct insight as to the ultimate basis of reality/existence. Hence, bodily being can serve as a final conceptual fulcrum by which we can enhance our understanding of the varying reactions to Freudian psychoanalysis by these German and French philosophers. On this issue, it was the French existential phenomenologists who—with some irony—were far closer to Schopenhauer and Freud than were the Germans.

As we have seen, the primacy of the body is of paramount importance within Schopenhauerean metaphysical theory and Freudian metapsychology in this regard. Indeed, the universe as they understood it was *inconceivable* without the body. Not coincidentally, it was the French existential phenomenologists—as those who were most affected by and responsive to Freudian psychoanalysis—who came the closest to Schopenhauer's and Freud's positions concerning the *primacy* and *primordiality* of the body.[6] For example, Merleau-Ponty wrote: "Neither body nor existence can be regarded as the original of the human being, since they presuppose each other, and because the body is solidified or generalized existence, and existence a perpetual incarnation."[7] Similarly, Sartre: "To say . . . that there is a world or that I have a body is one and the same thing";[8] "My body is co-extensive with the world, spread across all things";[9] "the body is identified with the whole world inasmuch as the world is the total situation of the for-itself and the measure of its existence."[10]

While there are significant differences between Sartre and Merleau-Ponty on the nature of the body,[11] it is still important to note that they shared certain crucial commonalities. Both held that it is our bodies that make our experience transcendentally possible in the first place.[12] Since we are our body as being-in-the-world, we perceive the world through it.[13] My consciousness transcendentally requires the presence of my body, for the latter permits me to be situated in the world. The body, then, is ultimately understood by both thinkers to be "equi-primordial" with existence. Body and existence presuppose each other in order to *be* at all—modally speaking, they are reciprocally implicative.

At this juncture it is interesting to note that while these thinkers both credited Husserl with having powerfully influenced the development of their thought, each chose to move beyond his position to stances which are arguably closer to Schopenhauer's and Freud's. Indeed, Husserl had developed a powerful account of the lived-body in his *Ideas II*,[14] and in the lectures he had delivered from 1920 to 1926, which have appeared in the form of the *Analyses Concerning Passive and Active Synthesis*.[15]

Husserl agreed with the French concerning the intrinsic nature of the human condition, including bodily being: "with each perception of an object, whatever it may be, the lived-body is, always there and always co-constituted";[16] "The lived-body remains the center of everything that surrounds it";[17] concrete personal being "is there in space-time where his living body is; and from there he lives into and acts upon the world";[18] and, lived-bodies are the center of orientation in the world.[19] However, Husserl then remarked that the ego encompasses more than the lived-body itself:

> Though we are related through the living body to all objects which exist for us [we] are not related to them solely as a living body . . . being an ego through the living body is of course not the only way of being an

ego . . . We as living in wakeful world-consciousness, are constantly active on the basis of our passive having of the world; it is from there, by objects pregiven in consciousness, that we are affected; it is to this or that object that we pay attention, according to our interests; with them we deal actively in different ways; through our acts they are "thematic" objects.[20]

The being of an ego (with its interests) is not confined to being an ego through the living body.

Indeed, Husserl even pushed this point to the extent that he asserted the primordiality of consciousness over the body:

It is *thinkable* that there would be no Bodies at all and no dependence of consciousness on material events in constituted nature, thus no empirical souls, whereas absolute consciousness would remain over as something that cannot simply be cancelled out.[21]

This is the "transcendental residue" Husserl described in his *Ideas I*.[22] Schopenhauer and Freud, of course, could not relate to such an idealism in their theories. Neither could Heidegger, but from a different vantage point. It was Heidegger who, among the existential phenomenologists, held a position furthest from Schopenhauer's and Freud's. It is important to understand the historical context for this being the case, to fully understand the philosophical implications involved.

Among his ontological competitors, it was specifically Sartre who criticized Heidegger for having almost entirely neglected the significance of the body in *Being and Time*.[23] Indeed, Heidegger had parenthetically mentioned the (lived) body only once in that work: "(This 'bodily nature' hides a whole problematic of its own, though we shall not treat it here.)"[24] Twenty years later in his "Letter on Humanism," Heidegger held the same perspective: "A chemical and physical approach to the body, probably hides rather than reveals the specifically human aspect of the body."[25] Heidegger discussed Sartre's reproach with Boss, during a vacation in 1963[26] and again in 1972.[27] In the latter, and in an earlier seminar on Heraclitus, Heidegger acknowledged that bodily being is the most difficult to understand, and that he simply had not known what else to say in 1927.[28] However, Heidegger said just a bit more in the very next year: "Dasein is thrown, factical, thoroughly amidst nature through its bodiliness . . ."[29]

At first blush, it appears that when Heidegger did address the question of the body late in his career, he agreed with the claim of the French phenomenologists. He wrote, for instance, "the bodying forth of the human being's body co-determines the human-being's being-in-the-world";[30]

"Bodying forth *[Leiben]* always belongs to being-in-the-world";[31] and that everything which we call our bodily being belongs essentially to existence.[32] However, Heidegger was utterly convinced that the French (and by implication, Schopenhauer and Freud) had failed to see the problem of the body in an ontologically primordial way.[33] In his lectures, *Zollikon Seminars,* Heidegger directly confronted the French philosophers' criticism of his lack of consideration on the topic of the human body, stating that since the French lacked an adequate word for "bodily being" *(das Leiben),* "it is very difficult to see the real problem of the phenomenology of the body."[34] According to Heidegger: "The French psychologists also misinterpret everything as an expression of something interior instead of seeing the phenomenon of the body in the context of which men are in relationship to each other."[35] Later in his lectures, Heidegger further commented, "as for the French authors, I am always disturbed by [their] misinterpretation of being-in-the-world; it is conceived either as being present-at-hand or as the intentionality of subjective consciousness . . ."[36] Obviously, Heidegger believed that the French had failed to understand the underlying thrust of his phenomenological description of Dasein, and hence considered their criticisms to be unfounded.[37]

Ultimately, then, why did Heidegger reject—directly Sartre, and indirectly Merleau-Ponty, Schopenhauer, Freud—the claim of the ontological equi-primordiality of the body with existence? Heidegger's response[38] is most easily understood when viewed as a series of interconnected claims:

Bodily being belongs essentially to existence. Heidegger wrote, for example, "as factical, Dasein is among other things in each case dispersed in a body."[39] "Yet, the human being would not be able [to do this] if he consisted only of a 'spiritual' receiving-perceiving and if he did not also have a bodily nature."[40] Bodily being is always already involved in the experience of that which is present.[41] Bodily being codetermines Dasein's existence as Being-in-the-world.[42]

Bodily being presupposes Being-in-the-world (that is, Dasein, as openness, as the ecstatic dwelling in the clearing of beings).[43] Bodily being is the necessary yet insufficient condition for Dasein's Being-in-the-world.[44]

Bodily being does not encompass Being-in-the-world. Being-in-the-world includes more than bodily being—the understanding of being, the limit of the horizon of Dasein's understanding of being, and so on.[45] Yet it is not merely added on to bodily being.[46]

The most primordial ontological characteristics of Dasein include Being-in-the-world, openness, presence, ecstatic dwelling in the clearing, and so on. Bodily being is "founded upon" Dasein's responsiveness to the clearing.[47] One must begin with the basic constitution of human existence as existence—

as a domain of the openness toward a world, in light of which the significant features of what is encountered addresses man.[48]

*Bodily being is possible because our Being-in-the-world always already con-
sists "of a receptive/perceptive relatedness to something which addresses us from out
of the openness of our world, from out of that openness as which we exist."*[49] As the
ones who are addressed, we are always already directed toward the given
facts of the world which are disclosed. It is due to this very directedness
that we are able to be bodily beings in the first place. Dasein's existence is
the precondition for the possibility of bodily being.[50]

Heidegger's response to the French, and to Schopenhauer and Freud,
then, was that while our bodily being is essential to our Being-in-the-
world, it is our Being-in-the-world—our openness to that which addresses
us in the clearing, Dasein's receptive-perceptive relatedness, our dwelling
as ecstatic being, our understanding of being, and so on—which is most
fundamentally *primordial* from an ontological perspective.[51] Heidegger,
then, would no doubt have accepted Merleau-Ponty's, Sartre's, Schopenhauer's, and Freud's premises that the lived-body and existence "presuppose each other"—and yet deny their conclusions, in that neither "can be
regarded as the original of the human being." He would point out that
each presupposes the other in different ways. Bodily being is necessary for
us to be related to the world in any situation. Being-in-the-world is necessary for there to be any relations at all, since it is primarily an understanding of being in which anything else is possible: existence is ontologically more primordial than bodily being.

This was the reason Heidegger was reticent to mention bodily being
more than six times in *Being and Time*. To become too concerned with one
aspect of being could have reduced his inquiry to philosophical anthropology, which is precisely what he wanted to avoid. Further, to concentrate
on bodily being without always recognizing its groundedness in Being-in-
the-world, tempts one to slip into a Cartesian dualism—something to
which, in fact, Heidegger accused the French and Freud of having fallen
prey. Bodily being may be a worthy focus of inquiry, but it was not something Heidegger felt necessary to pursue. Dasein's Being-in-the-world as
receptive-perceptive openness was more primordial than bodily being,
from an ontological perspective.

Heidegger's insistence on an ontological grounding for any inquiry
into the being of Dasein, of course, is what sets him apart from Freudian
psychoanalysis most fundamentally. It was precisely this which motivated
the *Zollikon Seminars* in the first place, and which provides the most resistance to a convergence with Freudian psychoanalysis. For Heidegger, Freud
operated purely on the ontical level and was oblivious to the ontological
dimension of human existence.

Freudian Psychoanalysis's Contribution to Philosophy and the Existential Phenomenologists

Freud was convinced that insofar as philosophy is constructed on psychology it could not avoid taking the contributions of psychoanalysis properly into account.[52] For example, by enabling philosophers to become familiar with unconscious processes they could better understand the relationship between the mind and body. More generally, Freud's archaeology of the mind assumed as one of its primary tasks to translate "metaphysics into metapsychology."[53] In other words, to glean from the philosophical creations of the human mind facts about its universal and necessary (that is, transcendental) structure and what made such creations possible. Freud was confident that ultimately this would enable us to better understand the meaning and origins of philosophical creations: it is this, Freud contended, that would permit us to overcome "the doubt as to which of the countless philosophical systems should be accepted, since they all seemed to rest on an equally insecure basis."[54] Freud's metapsychology sought to provide that secure basis.

Freud observed that a first attempt to do this would be to turn to concepts in the minds of ancient philosophers, but even this he discerned to be too "elusive." Instead, he insisted that it is important to study subjects "closer to hand"—for example, "the mental life of the child is important for the psychological understanding of philosophical concepts."[55]

> By examining the primitive psychological situations which were able to provide the motive for [philosophical] creations, it has been in a position to reject certain attempts at an explanation that were based on too superficial a psychology and to replace them by a more penetrating insight.[56]

It is crucial to bear in mind here that Freud was operating on two different, yet interrelated levels simultaneously. He was speaking both of the mental life of the childhood of individual thinkers and the childhood of all humankind. In both, phylogenetic memories and other unconscious processes rooted in our instincts are operative during the construction of philosophical creations (worldviews). It is important to note that the instincts comprise an essential part of our facticity for the existential phenomenologists as well. Freud's analysis helps us to gain clarity as to the nature of our instinctual life and how it grounds human experience.

It was Nietzsche who first saw this most clearly, and insisted "psychology is now the path to the most fundamental problems":[57]

> By far the greater part of conscious thinking must still be included
> among instinctive activities, and that goes even for philosophical think-
> ing . . . most of the conscious thinking of a philosopher is secretly guided
> and forced into certain channels by his instincts.[58]

> . . . *psychology of philosophers:* their most alienated calculations and their
> "spirituality" are still only the last pallid impression of a physiological
> fact . . . everything is instinct, everything has been directed along cer-
> tain lines from the beginning.[59]

No matter how much fuss philosophers make during the course of their
philosophical reflection, Nietzsche and Freud insisted that we, as philosophers (or anyone else), must face up to this instinctual rootedness of humanity.

Second, psychoanalysis can enable us to understand the underlying
forces that led a particular philosopher to generate a particular worldview.

> Psychoanalysis can supply some information which cannot be arrived at
> by other means, and can thus demonstrate new connecting threads in the
> "weaver's masterpiece" spread between the instinctual endowments, the
> experiences, and the works of the artist [or philosopher] . . . it seems to
> me that thanks are due to psychoanalysis if, when it is applied to a great
> man, it contributes to the understanding of his great achievement.[60]

> There is yet another way in which philosophy can derive a stimulus from
> psychoanalysis, and that is by itself becoming a subject of psychoanalytic
> research. Philosophical theories and systems have been the work of a
> small number of men of striking individuality. In no other science does
> the personality of the scientific worker play anything like so large a part
> as in philosophy. And now for the first time psychoanalysis enables us to
> construct a "psychography" of the personality. It teaches us to recognize
> the affective units—the complexes dependent upon the instincts—
> whose presence is to be presumed in each individual, and it introduces
> us to the study of the transformations and end-products arising from
> these instinctual forces. It reveals the relations of a person's constitu-
> tional disposition and the events of his life to the achievements open to
> him owing to his peculiar gifts . . . psychoanalysis can indicate subjective
> and individual motives behind philosophical theories which have osten-
> sibly sprung from impartial logical work . . .[61]

Freud noted that there were psychoanalysts who had already conducted
some initial investigations along these lines: "A beginning has been made

by Hitschmann and von Winterstein in throwing psycho-analytic light on philosophical systems and personalities, and here there is much need both of extended and of deeper investigation."[62] During some early meetings of the Viennese Psychoanalytic Society (in which Freud was an active participant), Eduard Hitschmann had raised the general question: "What is it that causes a man to remain a philosopher?"[63] Attempting to address this question, he conducted preliminary psychoanalytic inquiries into, interestingly enough, the philosophies of Schopenhauer and Nietzsche. For example, Hitschmann explicitly argued: "a philosopher's subjective views may be determined by his personal characteristics; this is beautifully illustrated in [Nietzsche's] *Genealogy of Morals* . . ."[64]

Freud himself, of course, never conducted such an explicit psychoanalysis of a philosopher in an extensive manner. The closest he came, possibly not so coincidentally, was a cursory analysis of the one philosopher with whom he shared *the value of this very approach*—Nietzsche. During a discussion on Nietzsche's *Ecce Homo* at a meeting of the Viennese Psychoanalytic Society in 1908, Freud remarked on Nietzsche's personality development:

> Nietzsche was a paretic . . . To all of us, he is an enigmatic personality . . . We just have not succeeded in understanding Nietzsche's personality. One could look at the matter this way: this is an individual about whom we lack some prerequisite information. Some sexual abnormality is surely present . . . From his childhood, one thing stands out; he lost his father at an early age and grew up in a family of women . . . he begins with great perspicacity—endopsychic perception, as it were—to recognize the strata of his self. He makes a number of brilliant discoveries in himself. But now illness takes hold. Nietzsche is not satisfied with correctly fathoming these connections, but projects the insight gained about himself outward as a general imperative . . . mankind has created for itself through projection a moral view of the world that mirrors endopsychically perceived elements.[65]

> The degree of introspection achieved by Nietzsche had never been achieved by anyone, nor is it likely ever to be reached again. What disturbs us is that Nietzsche transformed "is" into "ought," which is alien to science. In this he has remained, after all, the moralist . . . The most essential factor must still be added: the role that paresis played in Nietzsche's life. It is the loosening process resulting from paresis that gave him the capacity for the quite extraordinary achievement of seeing through all layers and recognizing the instincts at the very base [of everything].[66]

Interestingly enough, Freud was considerably more reticent about analyzing Nietzsche much later, in 1934. In fact, Freud seemed to do everything he could to dissuade Arnold Zweig from writing a book that subjected Nietzsche to psychoanalysis:

> But with Friedrich Nietzsche there is something that goes beyond what is usual. There is also an illness, and that is harder to explicate and reconstruct; that is to say, there are no doubt psychical processes in a certain sequence, but not always psychical motives generating them, and one can go very much astray in trying to unravel these.[67]

> For me two things bar the approach to the Nietzsche problem. In the first place one cannot see through anyone unless one knows something about his sexual constitution, and with Nietzsche this is a complete enigma . . . In the second place he had a serious illness and after a long period of waning symptoms a general paralysis became manifest. Everyone has conflicts. With general paralysis the conflicts fade into the background of the etiology.[68]

Freud also participated in a discussion of Alfred Winterstein's "Psychoanalytic Observations on the History of Philosophy" in which the following topics were discussed:

> Which elements of a philosophical system are of heterogeneous origin; what role the unconscious plays in philosophical production; to what extent the validity of a philosophical position is affected by psychoanalysis; and, finally, which philosophy of life is the only one that, from the standpoint of psychoanalysis, can come under discussion.[69]

> Winterstein took as his point of departure the sexual investigation of the young child, from which, according to Freud's presentation the neurotic brooder and the researcher are found among the philosophers; they show traits that bear a particularly striking resemblance to the obsessional neurotic and to the system-formations of some mental patients.[70]

Freud, of course, is famous for his claim that philosophers are quite akin to "neurotics."

> . . . the forms assumed by the different neuroses echoed the most highly admired productions of our culture . . . e.g., philosophy . . . the delusions of paranoics have a unpalatable external similarity and internal kinship to the systems of our philosophers.[71]

Hence, philosophers would be ideal candidates for psychoanalysis![72]

Psychoanalyzing Sartre

Here a perfect philosophical candidate for psychoanalysis, from Freud's point of view, would have been Sartre. First, Sartre himself had arrived at the conclusion in his *Critique of Dialectical Reason* that his life's work had been dominated by a *neurosis* stemming from his childhood.[73] Second, Sartre is an especially good candidate for psychography given the complex *ambivalence* he felt toward Freudian psychoanalysis itself. Such ambivalence is understood from Freud's viewpoint as the simultaneous existence of contradictory tendencies, attitudes, or feelings in the relationship to a single object. Borrowing the term from Eugen Bleuler, Freud wrote: "Ambivalence in the emotional trends of neurotics is the best explanation of their ability to enlist their transferences in the service of *resistance*" [italics added].[74] Furthermore, in his later years, Freud tended to give an increased significance to ambivalence in the theory and treatment of the Oedipus conflict.[75] Placed in conjunction with Freud's idea that a person's worldview is nothing more than a reflection of the metapsychological processes within them, it is apparent what Freud would have had to say about the origin and generation of Sartre's philosophy.[76]

Sartre would be a spectacular example of philosophers who "identified the mental with the conscious." Such an opinion is attributable to the fact that

> philosophers have formed their judgment on the unconscious without being acquainted with the phenomena of unconscious mental activity, and therefore without any suspicion of how far unconscious phenomena resemble conscious ones or of the respects in which they differ from them.[77]

Unconscious forces lurk beneath the surface to form—in this case, Sartre's—worldview. Knowing this, on some level, led to Sartre's ambivalence toward Freudian psychoanalysis.

How did this play out in Sartre's specific situation? A compelling interpretation is that Sartre felt a classic Oedipus conflict in relation to the loss of his father at the age of one and what were ostensibly traumatic separations from his mother when she remarried and Sartre was sent to live with his grandparents.[78] Indeed, Sartre characterized these years (1916–20) as among the worst years of his life: "I detest my childhood and everything of it that survives."[79]

Sartre's struggle with his Oedipus complex is most apparent in his book *The Words:*

> There is no good father, that's the rule. Don't lay the blame on men but on the bond of paternity, which is rotten. To beget children, nothing

better; to have them, what iniquity! Had my father lived, he would have lain on me at full length and would have crushed me. As luck had it, he died young . . . I move from shore to shore, alone and hating those invisible begetters who bestraddle their sons all their life long. I left behind me a young man who did not have time to be my father and who could now be my son. Was it a good thing or a bad? I don't know. But I readily subscribe to the verdict of an eminent psychoanalyst: I have no Superego![80]

Sartre then added somewhat *sardonically* (an attitude which discloses the accuracy of the interpretation from a psychoanalytic point of view):

Actually my father's early retirement [that is, death] had left me with a most incomplete "Oedipus complex." No superego, granted. But no aggressiveness either. My mother was mine; no one challenged my peaceful possession of her. I knew nothing of violence and hatred; I was spared the hard apprenticeship of jealousy.[81]

Confirming this interpretation, Sartre continued on to say that the family bond which attracted him "was not so much the amorous temptation as the taboo against making love: fire and ice, mingled delight and frustration; I liked incest if it remained platonic."[82]

But what does all of this have to do with Sartre's *ambivalence* toward Freudian psychoanalysis? Sartre, of course, was justly famous for his rather bleak view of the gratuitous contingency of existence: "Every existing thing is born without reason, prolongs itself out of weakness and dies by chance."[83] For Freud such a view merely represented some unresolved libidinal processes:

The moment a man questions the meaning and value of life, he is sick, since objectively neither has any existence; by asking this question one is merely admitting to a store of unsatisfied libido to which something else must have happened, a kind of fermentation leading to sadness and depression.[84]

Sartre's description of metaphysical nausea was nothing more than a manifestation of an underlying, unresolved neurotic complex.[85] Clearly, a repressed Oedipus conflict may have been part of its basis, but another clue ironically (that is, unconsciously) is afforded by Sartre himself.

In *Being and Nothingness*, Sartre described the Freudian censor as in a situation of ambivalence: "Psychoanalysis has merely localized this double activity of repulsion and attraction on the level of the censor."[86] Sartre, as his own (unconscious) censor, is arguably sympathetic to the hidden impulses while being antipathetic to them! Hence his rejection of the Freudian unconscious may have its basis in that which was repressed during the course of the development of his Oedipus complex. Sartre's rejection of the Freudian idea of the unconscious may be related to his resistance to giving any kind of ontological status to his own submerged proclivities, for these would radically place in jeopardy his notion of the absolute freedom of humans as their very being.

Furthermore, while discussing the psychography of a personality, which helps to construct one's philosophical worldview, Freud was careful to allude to the "social conditions in the causation of neurosis . . . the forces which, operating from the ego, bring about the restriction and repression of instinct owe their origin essentially to compliance with the demands of civilization."[87] Sartre himself conceded the point when he alluded to his reaction of repugnance to and noncomprehension of the Freudian unconscious as grounded in the dominance of Cartesianism in his philosophical milieu. For all the above reasons, psychoanalysis (Freud would have argued) can assist our understanding of the factors underlying the very formative processes of Sartre's philosophy.

What do we gain by conducting such "psychographies"? Freud pointed out that we achieve a greater understanding of the evolution and development of the ideas and systems generated by great thinkers and hence a greater understanding of those ideas and systems themselves. Taking Freud seriously on this point, the methodology of this book included a "psychography" (or rather a "philosophography") of sorts conducted on Freud, in relation to his claim to originality regarding the psychical process of repression. The point of showing that Freud repressed the origins of his theory of repression was not, of course, one-upmanship on the part of philosophy, but rather serves to illustrate precisely the value of Freud's theory of psychoanalysis as it applied to Freud himself (namely, as one of the great thinkers). It is a concrete illustration and confirmation of Freud's own theory in its application to Freud's intellectual life—an investigation into the underlying forces/meanings for a thinker believing as she/he does.

We might now ask whether the development of such psychographies via psychoanalysis is not merely a matter of "psychologizing" from a philosophical point of view and hence of committing a version of "the genetic fallacy." In other words, was Freud not advocating that we reject the justification/validity of a philosophical position based on the noncognitive origins embedded within the life history of the thinker? Is this ultimately not to *reduce* ideas to nothing more than their instinctual origins?

Freud was clear that, by tracing the underlying forces which led to the generation of a particular philosophical claim or worldview, we would not be thereby entitled to dismiss its validity/truth. He wrote, "the fact that a theory is psychologically determined does not in the least invalidate its scientific truth."[88] Freud's thinking here, not surprisingly once again, had Nietzsche as his philosophical predecessor:

> If there is anything in which I am ahead of all psychologists, it is that my eye is sharper for that most difficult and captious kind of backward inference in which the most mistakes are made: the backward inference from the work to the maker, from the deed to the doer, from the ideal to him who needs it, from every way of thinking and valuing to the want behind it that prompts it.[89]

Nietzsche asked, what motivates a thinker to construct philosophical positions in the first place? What needs or wants is one seeking to satisfy or are indeed satisfied by doing so?[90] Nietzsche's crucial point, in terms of its implications for Freud, was that even though there is a significant difference between the validity of philosophical position *x* and the psychological origins that lead a person to hold philosophical position *x*, it does not follow that we should ignore the underlying factors for how it was that *x* developed. Certainly the latter is not necessarily relevant as to whether *x* is sound or unsound, but the latter does contribute to our understanding as to why *x* arose in the first place, in a particular person. The latter can certainly enhance our understanding and appreciation of that person and of the meaning of *x* for that person's intellectual development as well as its implications for humankind's collective psyche. Nietzsche's and Freud's point was this: it is useful to uncover the psychic motives that draw humankind to certain philosophical ideas, because we can better understand those ideas via their origin in humankind's collective psyche as well as individual psyches.

Furthermore, Freud offered a methodological certainty about the role of unconscious ideas and impulses during the psychotherapeutic process:

> But of this I am certain—that any one who sets out to investigate the same region of phenomena [namely, unconscious ideas and impulses] and employs the same method will find himself compelled to take up the same position, however much philosophers may expostulate.[91]

That is, Freudian psychoanalysis provides an understanding of unconscious processes on a level (for example, working-through), which cannot possibly be truly understood unless one has actually gone through the therapeutic process involved in psychoanalysis (or at least some kind of commensurate psychotherapeutic process). One must ponder the question as to whether or not the phenomenologists/existential phenomenologists could have genuinely comprehended what Freud meant by liberation (freeing the analysand) in the psychotherapeutic context, since they themselves never took the opportunity to grasp it as a lived-experience. It is somewhat ironic—given their emphasis on the importance of reflection engaging lived-experience—that they failed to realize this.

Existential Phenomenologists' Contribution to Psychoanalysis

One of the claims by Freud was that psychoanalysis had a great deal to offer philosophers by looking at the psychoanalytical underpinnings and/or origins of their ideas. It is equally true, however, that philosophers have a great deal to offer psychoanalysis by examining the philosophical underpinnings and/or origins of its ideas. Both traditions have theories concerning the grounding of meaning that can reciprocally reinforce one another!

First and foremost, the phenomenologists and existential phenomenologists offer a clearer understanding of the operations of the various levels of meaning involved in consciousness. Husserl and the existential phenomenologists propose "a new way of seeing" that transcends the confines of both scientific methodology and Freud's own understanding of the scientific approach, insofar as they uncritically adhere to a thing-ontological framework. Husserl, in particular, assists us in understanding what happens to ideas when they fade into the unconscious (when the censor is not operating), and their aftereffects in consciousness.

From a Heideggerian standpoint, philosophy can offer Freudian psychoanalysis (1) an ontological analysis that discloses how such positions as Freudian psychoanalysis are possible in the first place; (2) an ontological grounding of the spatialization, temporality, sexuality, and so on, of the body; (3) an alternative, yet complementary account to Freud's regarding how concealment is the inaccessible manifesting itself per se; and (4) an account of how there are other levels of the inaccessible beyond those to which Freud alluded.

By reclaiming the Greek sense of the word "analysis," Heidegger also enables psychoanalysis to engage in a "freeing activity" on a multiplicity of levels. First, analysts and analysands are "freed from" their unreflectively held ontological commitments. As a theoretical mode of inquiry, psycho-analysis would be in a position to "let beings be," free from any precon-ceived "dogmatic constructions"—free, for example, from the propensity to cling so tightly and uncritically to the "scientistic" Weltanschauung. On the level of psychoanalytic therapy, the therapeutic process would be freed of the danger of the uncritical imposition of theoretical frameworks by therapists on the analysands. Second, everyone involved in the thera-peutic process could then be "freed to" be open to whatever presences it-self. Applying to both the analyst and the analysand, this would result in the "transformation in the listener's way of seeing and in awakening the sense in which the questions must be asked."[92] This would enable indi-viduals to have a greater horizon of possibilities in which they could gain genuine self-knowledge.

Sartre also provides some important insights for psychoanalysis. His ambivalence toward Freudian psychoanalysis acted as a catalyst to "in-spire"[93] the creation of his own version of psychoanalysis—"existential psychoanalysis"—with its own proposals for a suitable ontological ground-ing.[94] Sartre could never bring himself to accept the existence of an un-conscious dimension of human existence, nor could he accept that there is a grounding to how human existence comports itself in the world, since any such grounding would completely prevent freedom. Yet he refused to abandon "the immense gains of psychoanalytic knowledge" and came to accept some of the methodological devices of psychoanalysis.[95]

Indeed, one of the contributions to psychoanalysis by the later Sartre was his work on an appropriate method that could be employed in order to reconcile and synthesize what are, prima facie, incompatible forms of historical explanations and/or descriptions—namely, Freudian psycho-analysis, in combination with his own version of existential psychoanalysis and Marxian philosophy—in order to gain as complete a picture of the individual as possible.[96]

In his book, *Search for a Method,* Sartre pointed out that

> [Marxists] have forgotten their own childhoods . . . They have not yet
> understood that sexuality is only one way of living the totality of our
> condition—at a certain level and within the perspective of a certain indi-
> vidual venture. Existentialism, on the contrary, believes that it can inte-
> grate the psychoanalytic method which discovers the point of insertion
> for man and his class—that is, the particular family—as a mediation
> between the universal class and the individual. The family in fact is con-
> stituted by and in the general movement of History, but is experienced,
> on the other hand, as an absolute in the depth and opaqueness of child-
> hood.[97]

Hence, coupled and rationalized with Marxism, Freudian and existential psychoanalysis could be useful.[98] Sartre believed that this type of method was necessary in order to achieve the most encompassing and deepest understanding of the individual as she or he is embedded in her or his historical context. This was why Sartre insisted,

> we must be able, in our regressive investigation, to make use of the whole of contemporary knowledge to elucidate a given undertaking or social ensemble . . . we use the whole of knowledge in order to decipher the human ensembles which constitute the individual and which the individual totalises by the very style in which he lives them.[99]

In such a synthesis, Sartre emphasized the importance of some ideas which had their origins in Freudian theory: in order to comprehensively understand a person in his/her project it is necessary to go back to significant events in that individual's childhood. This was precisely why Sartre discussed the childhoods of Flaubert and Baudelaire in his later books *The Family Idiot* and *Baudelaire*.[100] Indeed, Sartre commented that "*The Family Idiot* is the sequel to *Search for a Method*."[101]

Sartre's original attempt to establish his "totalizing" method, however, gave way to a new insight—namely, that a complete, "totalizing" self-comprehension by the individual is never possible. The later Sartre admitted to a level of human experience he called *le vécu*, which formed an integral part of our dialectical field of meaning. Hence, in *The Family Idiot* Sartre replaced his earlier notion of consciousness with *le vécu*, "lived experience." He defined it as "the terrain in which the individual is perpetually overflowed by himself and his riches and consciousness plays the trick of determining itself by forgetfulness."[102]

While being careful to deny that it is preconscious, unconscious, or consciousness, Sartre described *le vécu* somewhat enigmatically as "the equivalent of conscious-unconscious."[103] The notion of *le vécu* demonstrates forcibly and paradoxically the impossibility of the subject being fully self-conscious, or fully self-knowing, for *le vécu* is a "constant totalization" of the "dialectical process of psychic life,"[104] but one which—by the law of the hermeneutic circle—cannot include its own totalizing process in the totalization it effects.

> What I call *le vécu* is precisely the whole of the dialectical process of psychic life, a process that remains necessarily opaque to itself for it is a constant totalization, and a totalization that cannot be conscious of what it is. One may be conscious, in fact, of an external totalization, but not of a totalization that also totalizes consciousness.[105]

In this sense, according to Sartre, *le vécu* reveals the ultimately impossible regression of reflexive self-knowledge.

Interestingly, then, although Sartre to the very end rejected Freud's unconscious, his own notion of *le vécu* certainly acknowledged a hidden quality and limitation upon human understanding of self. Thus, an amplification of Sartre's notion of lived-experience would be useful as supplementary to the Freudian notion of the unconscious.

Merleau-Ponty also contributed a great deal to our understanding of the relationship between existential phenomenology and Freudian psychoanalysis. He showed, among other things, that it was on the descriptive level of meaning that existential phenomenology and Freudian psychoanalysis converge without the methodologies involved in their investigations being parallel. Both understood that the intentionality of subjectivity had many "strata," and that this was one of the senses in which both aimed at the same latency. Furthermore, Merleau-Ponty knew that it was the meta-physical level of energetics which prevented their merger; for psychoanalysis dealt on the level of an explanatory energetics, which founded Freud's metapsychology. Existential phenomenology, on the other hand, dealt primarily on the level of meaning by giving a descriptive analysis of concrete lived experience. Thus, while rapprochement between existential phenomenology and Freudian psychoanalysis was considered possible, their merger was not.

It was Merleau-Ponty's untiring refusal (throughout his writings) to adopt the "energetic" language of psychoanalysis (and its concomitant metapsychology), which permitted him to resituate Freud's sovereign insights of human experience within a existential phenomenological framework. In doing this, Merleau-Ponty was able to offer a means for dialogue between existential phenomenology and Freudian psychoanalysis on the level of meaning. As a result, he managed to make a great deal of progress toward establishing the rapprochement he so fervently advocated.

We have seen how Merleau-Ponty resituated Freud's insights within the structure of concrete lived-experience. Similarly, the transcendental nature of Merleau-Ponty's inquiry was ubiquitous in his reposturing of Freud. From the very beginning, Merleau-Ponty had: in (1) *The Structure of Behavior* inquired as to the necessary conditions for the possibility of various structures of consciousness (including Freud's); in (2) *Phenomenology of Perception* shown that it was the body that provided the possibility of existence, and elaborated on how sexuality and existence must permeate one another even for Freud; and later, in (3) *The Visible and the Invisible,* indicated how those objects upon which Freud focused had the ontological capacity to take being as representative of being (a way to find a dimension of being in those objects upon which Freud focused). In this last, Merleau-Ponty showed how descriptions of concrete existence have an ontological dimension with reference to the fundamental structures of embodied-consciousness. Merleau-Ponty recognized the immense importance of both transcendental and ontological inquiry for the formation of any comprehensive psychoanalysis.[106] Thus, Merleau-Ponty offered a cogent way of properly integrating existential phenomenology with Freudian psychoanalysis by providing a description of unified concrete lived-experience and the significant results of his transcendental and ontological inquiry into the general structures of Being-in-the-world. Furthermore, even if Merleau-Ponty could somehow be shown to be in error, one accomplishment cannot be taken from him: he has shown not only how meaningful dialogue between Freudian psychoanalysis and existential phenomenology, philosophy, and/or psychology is possible, but *why it is necessary.*

Finally, it was the engagement of Freudian psychoanalysis by the existential phenomenologists which spawned the development of various forms of existential psychoanalysis and psychology. Heidegger's *Being and Time* served as the philosophical foundation for the development of Ludwig Binswanger's "existential psychoanalysis"[107] and Medard Boss's "Daseinsanalysis."[108] Sartre's *Being and Nothingness* served, of course, as the philosophical grounding for his own "existential psychoanalysis" within which it appeared. In addition, Sartre's approach has exerted a strong impact on the existential psychologies of R. D. Laing and Rollo May.[109] Merleau-Ponty's existential phenomenology played a significant role in stimulating and contributing to the investigations of various significant French "psychoanalysts." For example, both Angelo Hesnard[110] and Henri Ey[111] were significantly influenced by Merleau-Ponty's notion of the body-subject immersed within concrete lived-experience, of an unconscious intentionality, and so on, and have tried to demonstrate the possibility and necessity for a rapprochement from a psychoanalytic point of view.

Final Thoughts on Apprehending the Inaccessible

Perhaps there is one issue upon which all of the philosophers discussed in this book (except Nietzsche) can agree, and that is that there is some mystery to our existence, something familiar yet hidden, that apparently permeates our very being and all of Nature. The tradition of Western philosophy has included an attempt to make sense of this elusive aspect of our existence by utilizing the tools we have been given, most frequently reason. Yet for all our efforts to gain some rational hold over this mystery, we find that either we fail to bring about a clear understanding, or we find temporary satisfaction in our metaphysical theories only to encounter others who tear them asunder once again, revealing the inadequacies of our constructs. It is as though these endeavors are repetitions of Sisyphus's fate to push his boulder up a great mountain only to come crashing down, leaving us in the wake of its descent. Still, we dust ourselves off, seek some "alternative" method of access, and begin to rebuild and rework our theories with the renewed hope of success.

Freud began this same architectural endeavor with confidence in science and rationality. In his effort to build something upon the foundations of science, however, he found that an archeological excavation was also required. And at times he stood in awe of those who had come before him, with their unique contributions to this human struggle. He looked upon Plato's Aristophanes, for example, and found what he believed to be the origin of human instincts: Eros (and Thanatos) developed from "*a need to restore an earlier state of things.*"[112] Freud contemplated that the sexual instincts may have been biologically based in an early evolutionary process whereby "living substance at the time of its coming to life was torn apart into small particles, which have ever since endeavored to reunite through the sexual instincts."[113] This is a remarkable speculation. What Freud was hypothesizing is that human instinct, the very life energy of humanity and the underlying motivation for all human activity, operated according to this principle of unity to separation to unity. In other words, there was, at one time, a primordial *unity* to Being; for whatever reason that unity was disrupted and a separation occurred. From that moment forward, a process (that is, series of stages) of "working through" the ostensible separation emerged. The culmination of this process is the re-establishment and/or re-cognition of *unity* within the individual *and* the universe as a whole.[114]

The above process (unity→separation→unity) occurs in the history of Western philosophical thought on two interrelated levels. First, from a bird's eye view, it manifests as an expression of humankind's consciousness coming to know itself in the unfolding of history. Second, it transpires *within individuals* as the expressions of that long dialectical process—as we have seen, for example, in Freud's intellectual evolution. As Hegel observed: "The advanced Spirit is thus the inner soul of all individuals; but this is an unconscious inwardness which the *great men* bring to consciousness for them."[115] This also occurs during psychotherapeutic practice: when the person establishes a harmonious cooperation among the various parts of the self (psyche), she or he recovers health. For example, the separation of reason and the emotions especially works itself through ("liberation") in the therapeutic process. Schelling articulated this point particularly well: "Originally in man there is an absolute equilibrium of forces and of consciousness. But he can upset this equilibrium through freedom, in order to reestablish it through freedom. But only in equilibrium of forces is there health."[116] One of the fascinating outcomes of all this is that both sets of worldviews refer to *the gaining of unity as "liberation"* (namely, health). This in itself is yet another expression and confirmation of the multilevel unity (vertically and horizontally) involved.

From a Freudian standpoint, it is here that we see the *unity* afforded between practice (psychotherapy) and theory (metapsychology). Freud sought to bring about unified individuals in the psychotherapeutic context and simultaneously developed a unified theory of human experience. Recall that the idea underlying the development of metapsychology for Freud was to provide a foundation for the *unity* of all of psychoanalysis— its theory, practice, techniques, and so on. This quest for unity is *the* primary thread linking Freud with all of those figures we have considered in relation to his philosophographical formation. It should come as no surprise, then, that all of the philosophers within this book are on a quest for unity, as they seek to apprehend the inaccessible. Empedocles spoke of the unified processes of love and strife. Plato considered this everyday world as a manifestation of the underlying Being (namely, the Good) which makes it possible. Bacon (in his *Great Instauration*) and the Philosophes saw in reason the possibility of providing a unified worldview. Kant, in particular, recognized the necessity for unifying the noumenal world (as the underlying condition for the possibility of all that is) with the phenomenal world. The romanticists assimilated this theme in their attempts to reconcile the polarities of existence within a unity. Hegel, of course, emphasized the quest for unity throughout his philosophical development. He was famous for arguing that

> [the fluid nature and] the diversity of philosophical systems as the progressive unfolding of truth . . . makes them moments of an organic unity in which they not only do not conflict, but in which each is as necessary as the other; and this mutual necessity alone constitutes the life of the whole.[117]

Schopenhauer (not Nietzsche) proceeded to identify this underlying being which provides the unifying perspective for all that is—cosmic will.[118] Freudian metapsychology represents the culmination of this process, gathering all of these related ways of dealing with this theme together.[119]

Interestingly, although the existential phenomenologists were often highly critical of Freud's metapsychology, they shared in this quest for *unity* as well. Heidegger sought to recover the unity of Being from Heraclitus, in this "destruction of ontology." Here we have, once again, a manifestation of Nietzsche's notion of atavism. In his analysis of Being-in-the-world as a unified being in *Being and Time,* Heidegger wrote, "unity makes up what we call the world."[120] Sartre sought the unity of the in-itself and for-itself; the tragic finale being that the two are impossible as the fundamental reality of human reality. Yet on a different level, meaning is possible *only because* the for-itself engages (that is, nihilates) the in-itself. Merleau-Ponty, on the other hand, found the lived-body to be equiprimordial with lived experience. It is not surprising, then, that Merleau-Ponty was the most receptive of the existential phenomenologists to Freudian psychoanalysis.

How specifically is Freudian metapsychology an expression of this pursuit for unity? Seeing separation (that is, gaps) in consciousness, Freud attempted to account for the unity of psychical life. To do so he sought the deepest level of self in the unconscious. He discovered that the deepest level of the unconscious is grounded in the instincts, and the instincts are grounded in the body. At the same time, it was the universal instincts of Eros and Thanatos that unified Freud's whole system. Both Eros (by its very nature, libido unifies) and Thanatos (a desire for a return to the unity of a tensionless state) seek a return to unity. Another way to put this: for Freud, the "uncanny" *(unheimlich)* is something which is secretly familiar, which has undergone repression and then returned from it.

Freud's intellectual development reflected the schemata of separation and unity as well. For example, in his adoption of the scientistic worldview, he utilized a tool that is by necessity an "analysis"—a breaking up, separation—of the world into its component parts. Yet, in his speculative work *Beyond the Pleasure Principle,* Freud also sought to reestablish unity via the principles of Eros and Thanatos. By utilizing rationality, which comprehends via distinctions, in order to explore the irrational, which lacks the capacity and organizing function to make distinctions, Freud clearly demonstrated the dialectical tension between unity and separation.

Furthermore, Freud was aware that it was precisely the *denial* of unity which results in suffering/illusion. For example, when a person becomes confined in reason, it is this separation of his or her emotions that results in suffering/illusion without the person being able to even recognize the basis of his or her suffering. Freud argued that this occurred on the profoundest level when philosophers, who had never been through genuine therapy and hence had no true understanding of what was involved, simply equated mental life with consciousness or relegated the unconscious to some mystical domain.

As we have seen, the existential phenomenologists interpreted Freud as a "dualist"—as advocating that which is somehow "behind the scene" as separate from that which "appears."[121] But the source of the dualism stems not from the "evolving" Freud—even though, in his attempt to be "scientific" he sometimes spoke in this way—but from the existential phenomenologists themselves through their insistence that Freud was "mechanistic," "thing-oriented," and so on. Rather, we contend that Freud was in the process of himself (unconsciously) overcoming this dualistic quality—in, for example, his notion of the body-ego. Hence, what are taken as dualisms in Freud are "unities" which get mistaken for the former—mind–body, intellect–instincts, consciousness–unconsciousness. That which is the underlying condition for the possibility of all that is, should never be understood as somehow "separate" from that which is— but rather as forming an indissoluble interconnectedness with all that is.

Perhaps what Freud heralds to us most vociferously in his Zarathustrian role is that through our endeavor to apprehend the inaccessible we must look deeper into ourselves, with the courage to embrace what we find. As Schopenhauer emphasized: "Man carries the ultimate fundamental secrets within himself, and this fact is accessible to him in the most immediate way. Here only, therefore, can he hope to find the key to the riddle of the world, and obtain a clue to the inner nature of all things."[122] Our most basic instinctual being is not to be concealed from consciousness, locked away in the darkness of unconsciousness; such self-imposed bondage merely serves to strengthen those organic energies which rage forth, demanding expression. Rather, our most inner nature provides us with our primary and sole access to "truth." As Nietzsche's Zarathustra proclaimed, "Behind your thoughts and feelings, my brother, there stands a mighty ruler, an unknown sage—whose name is self. In your body he dwells; he is your body."[123] Hence, "Become who you are!"[124]

Notes

Preface

1. We might point out that there are other compelling reasons for writing a book on Freud and the existential phenomenologists than those previously listed. For example, the preponderance of philosophical books on Freud have been written within the Anglo-American analytic tradition dominant in this country. As a result alternative, and what are arguably more unified approaches to Freud, have been marginalized. As we shall demonstrate, such approaches have a great deal to contribute toward a deeper understanding and appreciation of Freud's worldview.

2. In particular, it will also enable us to be in a stronger position to evaluate the cogency of the criticisms of Freud that are raised specifically by the existential phenomenologists.

3. It is also the case that Freud himself often failed to acknowledge and appreciate the synthesizing nature of his work. On several occasions, he denied that his project involved a pursuit of a synthesis at all. For example, in reaction to James Jackson Putnam's metaphysics Freud wrote, "I feel no need for a higher synthesis in the same way that I have no ear for music" (Nathan G. Hale, ed., *James Jackson Putnam and Psychoanalysis; Letters Between Putnam and Sigmund Freud, Ernest Jones, William James, Sandor Ferenczi, Morton Prince, 1877–1917,* trans. Judith Bernays Heller [Cambridge, Mass.: Harvard University Press, 1971], 105). And again, in a letter to Putnam, Freud wrote: "For my part I have never been concerned with any comprehensive synthesis, but invariably with certainty alone." In a letter to Lou Andreas-Salomé, Freud wrote: "Naturally I do not always agree with you. I so rarely feel the need for synthesis. The unity of this world seems to me so self-evident as to not need emphasis" (Ernst Pfeiffer, ed., *Sigmund Freud and Lou Andreas-Salomé: Letters,* trans. William and Elaine Robson-Scott [New York: W. W. Norton & Company, 1972], 32).

4. With Jean-Martin Charcot as the obvious exception to this general point.

5. Freud was also greatly influenced by ideas neither specifically scientific nor philosophical. However, we shall not treat the literary influences on Freud—Shakespeare, for example—since our interest is in rediscovering/uncovering the much neglected philosophical influences which provided much of the intellectual resources leading to the development of psychoanalysis.

6. Sigmund Freud, *The Standard Edition of the Complete Psychological Works of Sigmund Freud,* trans. and ed. James Strachey, vol. I (London: Hogarth Press, 1960),

xvi. Citations from the Standard Edition (hereafter abbreviated as *SE*) are by volume and page number.

7. When forced to leave his home in Vienna due to the German invasion during World War II and antisemitism, Freud was required to be highly selective in what he would retain for his library. Among those books chosen were an impressive array of philosophy books! See Harry Trosman and Roger Dennis Simmons, "The Freud Library," in *Journal of the American Psychoanalytic Association*, vol. 21 (1973), 646–87.

8. Ernest Jones, *The Life and Works of Sigmund Freud*, vol. 2 (New York: Basic Books, 1955), 415.

9. Richard Rorty, "The Challenge of Relativism," in *Debating the State of Philosophy: Habermas, Rorty, and Kolakowski*, ed. Jozef Niznik and John Sanders (Westport, Conn.: Praeger, 1996), 52.

10. Sigmund Freud, *The Freud Reader*, ed. Peter Gay (New York: W. W. Norton & Company, 1989), xiii.

11. Sigmund Freud, *The Origins of Psychoanalysis: Letters to Wilhelm Fliess*, trans. Eric Mosbacher and James Strachey (New York: Basic Books, 1954).

12. To borrow Ricoeur's usage of the term. Paul Ricoeur, *Freud and Philosophy: An Essay on Interpretation*, trans. Denis Savage (New Haven: Yale University Press, 1970), 439–58.

Introduction

Epigraphs: Johann Wolfgang von Goethe, *Maxims and Reflections*, trans. Peter Hutchinson (New York: Penguin Books, 1998), No. 537; Friedrich Nietzsche, *Human, All Too Human*, trans. R. J. Hollingdale (Cambridge: Cambridge University Press, 1996), 179–80; Arthur Schopenhauer, *The World as Will and Representation*, vol. 2, trans. E. F. J. Payne (New York: Dover, 1966), 179; *SE* XXII, 73; Martin Heidegger, *Zollikon Seminars*, trans. Franz Mayr and Richard Askay (Evanston: Northwestern University Press, 2001), 183.

1. Various strains of "Eastern philosophy" have, of course, pursued such domains as well—for example, "Brahman" in Hinduism, the "Tao" in Taoism—though these transcend the scope of this book.

2. Heraclitus believed that one cannot know the psyche regardless of how endless the search: "The soul is undiscovered, though explored forever to a depth beyond report" (*Fragments: The Collected Wisdom of Heraclitus*, trans. Brooks Haxton [New York: Viking Penguin, 2001], 45). It is interesting to note that Freud himself was a participant in a discussion in which *these specific philosophers* were approached via one way of apprehending the inaccessible, in a presentation by Hautler entitled "Mysticism and the Comprehension of Nature," before the Vienna Psychoanalytic Society in 1907 (Herman Nunberg and Ernst Federn, eds., *Minutes of the Vienna Psychoanalytic Society*, vol. 1, trans. M. Nunberg [New York: International Universities Press, 1975] 146ff.; see vol. 2, 329).

3. Immanuel Kant, *Political Writings,* trans. H. B. Nisbet (Cambridge: Cambridge University Press, 1970), 42.

4. Schopenhauer, *World as Will and Representation,* vol. 2, 194.

5. Yet of the major figures with whom we will be dealing in this book, it is Friedrich Nietzsche who, arguably, most radically called into question the very project of "apprehending the inaccessible" itself, as we will see.

6. Friedrich Nietzsche, *Unfashionable Observations,* trans. Richard T. Gray (Stanford: Stanford University Press, 1995), 174.

7. Friedrich Nietzsche, *Twilight of the Idols,* in *The Portable Nietzsche,* trans. Walter Kaufmann (New York: Viking, 1968), 475.

8. *SE* VI, 253.

9. *SE* XX, 96.

10. *SE* VII, 265–67; *SE* XI, 219–30; *SE* XII, 109–57; *SE* XVII, 157–68; *SE* XX, 204–5; *SE* XXIII, 209–54.

11. *SE* XXII, 90; *SE* XXIII, 145.

Chapter 1

Epigraphs: Friedrich Nietzsche, *Beyond Good and Evil: Prelude to a Philosophy of the Future,* trans. Walter Kaufmann (New York: Vintage Books, 1989), 27; Friedrich Nietzsche, *The Gay Science: With a Prelude in Rhymes and an Appendix of Songs,* trans. Walter Kaufmann (New York: Vintage Books, 1974), 157; *SE* IV, 100.

1. Our language and metaphor here, of course, have roots in G. W. F. Hegel, *Phenomenology of Spirit,* trans. A. V. Miller (New York: Oxford University Press, 1977), 6–7.

2. Friedrich Nietzsche, *The Will to Power,* ed. Walter Kaufmann, trans. Walter Kaufmann and R. J. Hollingdale (New York: Vintage Books, 1967), 518.

3. Friedrich Nietzsche, *Human, All Too Human,* trans. R. J. Hollingdale (Cambridge: Cambridge University Press, 1996), 119. James Strachey's earlier comment about Freud's having a mind of "two cultures" is clearly an illustration of what Nietzsche had in mind here.

4. We shall focus upon only the philosophical influences and will not discuss areas such as literature, music, and so on, which also had their impact on Freud's intellectual development.

5. *SE* XIX, 261.

6. *SE* XVIII, 235.

7. Freud himself acknowledged this: "psychoanalysis can indicate the subjective and individual motives behind [great thinkers'] theories" (*SE* XIII, 179).

8. *SE* XIV, 143; *SE* XIX, 261.

9. Letter from Freud to Marie Bonaparte, January 11, 1927. Quoted in Ernest Jones, *The Life and Works of Sigmund Freud,* vol. 3 (New York: Basic Books, 1965), 131.

10. *SE* XXIII, 245. See also: Herman Nunberg and Ernst Federn, eds., *Min-*

utes of the Vienna Psychoanalytic Society, vol. 1, trans. M. Nunberg (New York: International Universities Press, 1975), 360.

11. *SE* XIX, 261.

12. *SE* XIV, 13.

13. Compare this to Nietzsche: "everywhere, originality out of forgetfulness" (*Unpublished Writings from the Period of "Unfashionable Observations,"* trans. Richard T. Gray [Stanford: Stanford University Press, 1995], 153). Also: *"Originality.*—Not that a man sees something new as the first one to do so, but that he sees something old, familiar, seen but overlooked by everyone, *as though it were new,* is what distinguishes true originality" (*Human, All Too Human,* 261).

14. Sigmund Freud, *The Origins of Psychoanalysis: Letters to Wilhelm Fliess,* trans. Eric Mosbacher and James Strachey (New York: Basic Books, 1954), 141; Jones, *Life and Works of Sigmund Freud,* vol. 1, 172; vol. 2, 432; vol. 3, 41. See also: Sigmund Freud, *The Letters of Sigmund Freud,* ed. Ernst Freud, trans. Tania Stern and James Stern (New York: Basic Books, 1975), 232; *The Complete Letters of Sigmund Freud to Wilhelm Fliess, 1887–1904,* ed. J. M. Masson (Cambridge, Mass.: Harvard University Press, 1985), 159.

15. Walter Boehlich, ed., *The Letters of Sigmund Freud to Eduard Silberstein,* trans. Arnold Pomerans (Cambridge, Mass.: Belknap Press, 1990), 95.

16. Jones, *Life and Works of Sigmund Freud,* vol. 3, 41–42.

17. Freud, *Origins of Psychoanalysis: Letters to Wilhelm Fliess,* 141.

18. *SE* XX, 253.

19. One suggestive way to explain the reasons for Freud's attitude might include Nietzsche's insight: "the noble riches in the psychic economy of the philosopher which had made him feel defensive and small" (*Beyond Good and Evil,* 122); it is important to take this in conjunction with Freud's later reason (i.e., "embarrassment") for avoiding Nietzsche because of Nietzsche's wealth of ideas.

20. *SE* XV, 97–98.

21. *SE* XX, 96.

22. Ibid.

23. Freud, *Letters of Sigmund Freud,* 375.

24. Freud, *Freud to Eduard Silberstein,* 52.

25. *Minutes of the Vienna Psychoanalytic Society,* vol. 1, 359.

26. Ibid., vol. 2, 335. It is noteworthy that Nietzsche himself could not have agreed more with Freud's point: "the level to which all modern philosophy has gradually sunk, this rest of philosophy today, invites mistrust and displeasure, if not mockery and pity. Philosophy reduced to 'theory of knowledge,' in fact no more than a timid epochism and doctrine of abstinence—a philosophy that never gets beyond the threshold and takes pains to *deny* itself the right to enter—that is philosophy in its last throes, an end, an agony, something inspiring pity. How could such a philosophy—*dominate!*" (*Beyond Good and Evil,* 123).

27. *Minutes of the Vienna Psychoanalytic Society,* vol. 2, 335.

28. Jones, *Life and Works of Sigmund Freud,* vol. 1, 29.

29. *SE* XIV, 15.

30. Ibid., 15–16.

31. Freud, *Origins of Psychoanalysis: Letters to Wilhelm Fliess,* 126.

32. Jones, *Life and Works of Sigmund Freud*, vol. 1, 41–42.

33. *SE* XIV, 15–16.

34. Jones, *Life and Works of Sigmund Freud*, vol. 1, 172.

35. Freud, *Freud to Eduard Silberstein*, 70.

36. Freud, *Origins of Psychoanalysis: Letters to Wilhelm Fliess*, 260–61.

37. *SE* XIV, 15–16.

38. *SE* XX, 59.

39. Seen by Walter Kaufmann in the autograph department of Goodspeed's Book Shop in Boston, November 1978; Walter Kaufmann, *The Discovery of the Mind: Freud versus Adler and Jung* (New York: McGraw-Hill, 1980), 16. See also: *SE* XXII, 178.

40. *SE* XXII, 175.

41. Nathan G. Hale, ed., *James Jackson Putnam and Psychoanalysis; Letters Between Putnam and Sigmund Freud, Ernest Jones, William James, Sandor Ferenczi, Morton Prince, 1877–1917*, trans. Judith Bernays Heller (Cambridge, Mass.: Harvard University Press, 1971), 170.

42. *SE* XIX, 253.

43. *SE* XXII, 181. See also: *SE* XXII, 158.

44. *SE* XIII, 73. See also: *SE* XIV, 96–7; *SE* XVII, 261.

45. *SE* XXII, 158.

46. Compare: *SE* XVIII, 253–54.

47. *SE* XIX, 217, 214ff.

48. *SE* XXII, 160.

49. *SE* XIX, 214.

50. *SE* XII, 260. See also: *SE* XXIII, 286.

51. As we have seen and will see, Freud was clearly aware and affected by major counter-examples to this general attitude—Herbart, Lipps, Fechner, Schopenhauer, Nietzsche, and so on.

52. Here Freud clearly fell prey to Nietzsche's insight: "sometimes lack of respect for individual philosophers that had involuntarily generalized itself into lack of respect for philosophy" (*Beyond Good and Evil*, 122).

53. *SE* XIII, 178.

54. *SE* XVIII, 253–54. See also: *SE* XIX, 253, 20, 191.

55. *SE* XIX, 217. Also: 214ff. One example of this oddity is that when pressed to define what he meant by "consciousness," *a notion of crucial importance to his metapsychology*, Freud simply deferred to the definitions given by the philosophers (*SE* XXIII, 159).

56. *SE* XIX, 217. Also: 214ff.

57. Hegel, *Phenomenology of Spirit*, 2.

58. Ibid.

59. *SE* XXII, 177.

60. *Minutes of the Vienna Psychoanalytic Society*, vol. 2, 174.

61. Nietzsche: "how can something originate in its opposite, for example, rationality in irrationality, the sentient in the dead, logic in unlogic . . . truth in error" (*Human, All Too Human*, 12).

62. Freud: "the view which held that the psychical is unconscious in itself,

enabled psychology to take its place as a natural science like any other . . . to arrive at what is described as an 'understanding' of the field of natural phenomena in question. This cannot be effected without framing fresh hypotheses and creating fresh concepts; but these are not to be despised as evidence of embarrassment on our part but deserve on the contrary to be appreciated as an enrichment of science" (*SE* XXIII, 158).

63. Freud: "As a result of a little speculation, we have come to suppose that this instinct is at work in every living creature, and is striving to bring it to ruin and to reduce life to its original condition of inanimate matter" (*SE* XXII, 211).

64. *SE* IX, 49.

Chapter 2

Epigraphs: *SE* XX, 253; Goethe's Mephistopheles (*Faust*, I.4) quoted by Freud (*SE* XIX, 149).

1. *SE* XXII, 138, 153, 156; *SE* XVIII, 235.
2. *SE* XIV, 222n, 78; *SE* XX, 58–59; *SE* XVIII, 453ff.
3. *SE* XXIII, 225.
4. *SE* VI, 259.
5. *SE* XIV, 222n.
6. Ibid., 78.
7. *SE* XVII, 253.
8. *SE* XIV, 167.
9. *SE* XX, 58–59.
10. It should be noted that the situation is a bit more complicated than this. Freud had earlier developed a conscious/preconscious/unconscious topographical model (*SE* XIV, 180–85). Freud only later superseded it with the above, structural viewpoint (*SE* XXIII, 156).
11. *SE* VII, 180ff.; *SE* XXIII, 156.
12. *SE* VII, 242; *SE* X, 143, 147; *SE* XIII, 180ff.; *SE* XX, 242; *SE* XXIII, 153–56.
13. *SE* XXIII, 185. It is also important to point out that Freud discussed in depth humanity's phylogenetic history or prehistory within each individual unconscious. This will be discussed further in the following sections and chapters.
14. *SE* XIX, 152.
15. *SE* VII, 43n.
16. *SE* XVII, 159.
17. *SE* VII, 266.
18. *SE* XX, 205.
19. *SE* XXIII, 220.
20. *SE* VII, 258–59.
21. Ibid., 261.
22. Ibid., 260.
23. Ibid., 260–61.
24. *SE* XII, 91–93. See also: *SE* XXIII, 174.

25. *SE* XII, 91–93.
26. *SE* IV, 93.
27. Ibid., 100.
28. *SE* IV–V.
29. *SE* XV, 150.
30. *SE* XXII, 12–13.
31. *SE* XV, 165.
32. Ibid., 199. One of the phylogenetic themes Freud came to recognize as prevalent throughout history was the "Oedipus complex." Freud (along with Otto Rank) applied his analytic technique to historical expressions of the Oedipus complex and strove to substantiate his theory by tracing the Oedipus complex throughout literature and even scientific investigation—for example, Darwin and the primal horde. Freud also showed how earlier renditions of the Oedipus complex, beginning with Sophocles, underwent their own distortions—for example, Shakespeare's *Hamlet* represented a distorted rendition of the Oedipus complex—leading Freud to conclude that our historical "awareness" underwent a social repression. See, for example: *SE* IV, 264; *SE* XIII; *SE* XV, 207–8; *SE* XVII, 261–62; *SE* XX, 68; *SE* XXI, 252; *SE* XXIII, esp. 192.
33. *SE* XV, 101.
34. *SE* V, 359–60.
35. *SE* XV, 151.
36. *SE* V, 608.
37. *SE* XI, 142.
38. *SE* XVI, 436–37; *SE* XII, 155–56.
39. *SE* XII, 155–56.
40. Ibid., 139–40.
41. Ibid., 374.
42. *SE* XI, 145.
43. Ibid.

Chapter 3

Epigraphs: Marquis de Condorcet, "The Future Progress of the Human Mind," in *The Portable Enlightenment Reader,* ed. Isaac Kramnick (New York: Penguin Books, 1995), 30; *SE* XXII, 171.

1. *SE* XXII, 181.
2. While it is accurate to suggest that Freud's intellectual heritage was deeply embedded in the traditions of the Enlightenment, it is far too simple—as we shall see—to characterize him as a "loyal philosophe," as some major intellectual historians have claimed.
3. *SE* XI, 65.
4. Before we proceed to note these commonalities, it might be useful to stop and note a parallel in their historical situations. Each stood before a secure and powerful tradition as rebels introducing radically new insights and methodologies

into the acquisition of human knowledge. Bacon revolted against the dominating edifice of scholasticism as providing the foundation of knowledge; Freud took on the powerful materialism of medicine, the reductionist tendencies of psychology, and the intimidating worldviews of philosophy. The dissident comportment of these two men is reflected in many of the similarities listed in this section.

5. There are some other important similarities as well, which are not relevant to our project—both, for example, were critical of religion for derailing knowledge and tempting us into an all too comfortable illusion.

6. Francis Bacon, *Meditationes Sacrae* [1597] (Kila, Mont.: Kessinger Publishing Company, 1912).

7. Francis Bacon, *Novum Organum*, trans. Peter Urbach and John Gibson (Chicago and La Salle: Open Court, 1994), 43.

8. *SE* XXII, 171. See also: *SE* XXI, 15–19, 21, 90–94; *SE* XXII, 171, 177–78, 181.

9. *SE* XIX, 219.

10. Bacon wrote, for example, that *false philosophy* is *"Sophistical, Empirical,* and *Superstitious" (Novum Organum,* 68).

11. Bacon, *Novum Organum,* 55.

12. Both Bacon and Freud strenuously objected to the contrivances of fantasy to which philosophers are prone. Bacon referred to these as *Idols of the Cave.* See: *Novum Organum,* 54, 61–62, 63–64.

13. Bacon, *Novum Organum,* 55–56, 66–75.

14. Ibid., 55, 64.

15. Ibid., 64.

16. Ibid., 55.

17. Ibid., 64.

18. Ibid., 58.

19. Aristotle was his favorite whipping boy here. See: Bacon, *Novum Organum,* 66–68.

20. Bacon, *Novum Organum,* 60.

21. Ibid., 64–66.

22. Ibid., 126.

23. Similarly, Descartes in his *Discourse on the Method for Rightly Conducting the Reason* spoke of a practical philosophy that masters nature. See: *The Philosophical Works of Descartes,* trans. Elizabeth S. Haldane and G. R. T. Ross (London: Cambridge University Press, 1968), 79–130.

24. Bacon, *Novum Organum,* 61–62.

25. Ibid., 56.

26. *SE* XVIII, 59.

27. Bacon, *Novum Organum,* 64.

28. *SE* XVIII, 59.

29. *SE* XX, 266.

30. Compare: Bacon, in Richard Popkin, ed., *The Philosophy of the 16th and 17th Centuries: Readings in the History of Philosophy* (New York: The Free Press, 1966), 83–88; *SE* XXII, 159, 171.

31. *SE* XIV, 117.

32. Bacon, *Novum Organum*, 47–48.

33. Ibid., 48–49.

34. Ibid., 66–68.

35. Popkin, *Philosophy of the 16th and 17th Centuries*, 84.

36. *SE* XXII, 160–61, 171; *SE* XIV, 117.

37. Bacon: "It is rather the case that all our perceptions, both of our sense and of our minds, are reflections of man, not of the universe, and the human understanding is like an uneven mirror that cannot reflect truly the rays from objects, but distorts and corrupts the nature of things by mingling its own nature with it" (*Novum Organum*, 54).

38. Popkin, *Philosophy of the 16th and 17th Centuries*, 84.

39. Bacon, *Novum Organum*, 60.

40. Ibid.

41. Ibid.

42. It should be noted that Rousseau is a significant figure here as well; Freud showed some familiarity with Rousseau's *Confessions*. See: *SE* VII, 193.

43. Ernest Jones, *The Life and Works of Sigmund Freud*, vol. 2 (New York: Basic Books, 1955), 415. There are additional reasons why Freud might have been particularly impressed by Voltaire: Freud was familiar with the life and ideas of Voltaire from a book he had read—and retained, in his selective library in London—by Carl Linneas. He could not have helped being impressed by Voltaire's characterization of all supernaturalistic religion as predicated on nothing more than superstition and ignorance, and he would have applauded Voltaire's contention that human existence by itself is significant and livable, without having to resort to some sort of transcendental domain.

44. Like Freud, neither Voltaire nor Diderot was a systematic philosopher seeking to generate his own original worldviews.

45. Kramnick, *Enlightenment Reader*, 52–53.

46. Ibid., 17–21.

47. Ibid., 371.

48. Ibid., 266. Rousseau also focused on love/sexuality as the strongest natural forces, which serve to bind our most basic elements into a coherent unity. Rousseau, in anticipation of Freud, extended this idea to note that the plasticity of the sexual instincts of human beings can be channeled in such ways as to be more spiritually directed (Freud's notion of sublimation).

49. On this point, Diderot offered a critique of sexual repression in Western civilization.

50. *SE* XVI, 337; *SE* XXI, 251; *SE* XXIII, 192.

51. *SE* XXI, 251. Of course Freud (and Otto Rank) gathered numerous other examples of historical evidence of a recognition of the Oedipus complex—for example, in Greek mythology (namely, Sophocles) and Shakespeare's *Hamlet*.

52. Herman Nunberg and Ernst Federn, eds., *Minutes of the Vienna Psychoanalytic Society*, vol. 1, trans. M. Nunberg (New York: International Universities Press, 1975), 133, 320, 322.

53. Immanuel Kant, *Critique of Pure Reason*, trans. Norman Kemp Smith (New

York: St Martin's Press, 1965); Immanuel Kant, *Critique of Judgement*, trans. J. H. Bernard (New York: Hafner, 1968); *SE* VIII, 12.

54. *SE* XIV, 171.

55. *SE* V, 613.

56. Immanuel Kant, *Anthropology from a Pragmatic Point of View*, ed. Hans H. Rudnick, trans. Victor Lyle Dowdell (Carbondale, Ill.: Southern Illinois University Press, 1978), 18–19. This was the origin of the metaphor—various versions of which Schopenhauer and Fechner were to pick up on much later—which so greatly impacted Freud.

57. *SE* XVIII, 28.

58. Kant, *Critique of Pure Reason*, 77.

59. *SE* XXII, 74. The reference here is to Kant (*SE* XVIII, 28).

60. Letter from Freud to Marie Bonaparte, August 21, 1938. Quoted in Jones, *Life and Works of Sigmund Freud*, vol. 3, 466.

61. It is difficult to know what to make out of the following very late pronouncement by Freud concerning this point: "Space may be the projection of the extension of the psychical apparatus. No other derivation is probable. Instead of Kant's *a priori* determinants of our psychical apparatus. Psyche is extended; knows nothing about it" (*SE* XXIII, 300).

62. *Minutes of the Vienna Psychoanalytic Society*, vol. 2, 336.

63. *SE* I, 149.

64. *SE* IV, 90.

65. Ibid., 70–71.

66. *SE* XIII, xiv.

67. Ibid., 22.

68. *SE* XXII, 164.

69. *SE* XIX, 167.

70. *SE* XXII, 61.

71. Immanuel Kant, *Kant: Political Writings*, ed. Hans Reiss, trans. H. B. Nisbet (New York: Cambridge University Press, 1991), 41. This idea goes hand in hand with Kant's conception of the underlying basis of everything as a developing organism (see *Critique of Judgement*).

72. Reiss, *Kant: Political Writings*, 44.

73. Ibid., 54–55.

74. Immanuel Kant, *The Classification of Mental Disorders*, trans. and ed. Charles T. Sullivan (Doylestown, Penn.: The Doylestown Foundation, 1964), 14.

75. *SE* XXII, 159.

76. Ibid.

77. *SE* XXII, 159. It must be noted that Freud, of course, could not accept the general trend of Enlightenment thinkers to downplay the nonrational aspects of nature.

78. Although Freud was, arguably, quite ambivalent about this.

79. *SE* XXI, 54.

Chapter 4

Epigraphs: John Burnet, *Early Greek Philosophy* (New York: Meridian Book, 1969), 220; *SE* XXIII, 247.

1. *SE* IX, 246. The book is Theodor Gomperz, *Griechische Denker* (Leipzig: Veit & Company, 1896–1909).

2. And even further, Freud speculated in *Totem and Taboo*.

3. It was in light of this point that Otto Rank, a colleague and friend of Freud's, endeavored to research numerous historical writings looking for examples of the Oedipus complex.

4. *SE* XXIII, 245.

5. G. S. Kirk and J. E. Raven, *The Presocratic Philosophers: A Critical History with a Selection of Texts* (New York: Cambridge University Press, 1969), 360.

6. Empedocles' concerns as a doctor included: *"some seeking prophecies, while others, for many a day stabbed by grievous pains, beg to hear the word that heals all manner of illness"* (Kirk and Raven, *Presocratic Philosophers*, 321, see 412).

7. Although in a way that transcended Freud's own understanding/awareness.

8. *SE* XXIII, 245.

9. Freud: "We need not feel greatly disturbed in judging our speculation upon the life and death instincts by the fact that so many bewildering and obscure processes occur in it" (*SE* XVIII, 60).

10. *SE* XXIII, 245.

11. *SE* XVIII, 7, 24, 30, 41, 55n, 60, 61n.

12. *SE* XXIII, 245.

13. Ibid., 245–46.

14. Ibid., 149.

15. *SE* XVIII, 7, 60.

16. Ibid., 59.

17. Goethe's Faust (*Faust*, I.6) in search of the secret of youth unwillingly seeks for the Witch's help (*SE* XXIII, 225n2).

18. *SE* XXIII, 225.

19. *SE* III, 160.

20. Kirk and Raven, *Presocratic Philosophers*, 324, 345.

21. Ibid., 323.

22. Ibid., 330.

23. Burnet, *Early Greek Philosophy*, 205–7; Kirk and Raven, *Presocratic Philosophers*, 326–27.

24. Burnet, *Early Greek Philosophy*, 207; Kirk and Raven, *Presocratic Philosophers*, 324.

25. *SE* XXIII, 246.

26. *SE* X, 140n.

27. See also: *SE* XVIII, 47, 49, 54; *SE* XXIII, 148; *SE* XIX, 40, 45, 48; *SE* XXI, 120.

28. Kirk and Raven, *Presocratic Philosophers*, 327.

29. Burnet, *Early Greek Philosophy*, 209. Freud does, however, fail to note that though Empedocles' concepts were fundamentally cosmological, he also viewed them from a biological point of view. He, for example, conceived Aphrodite as the

personification of Love having the same sexu al impulses toward union that characterize human bodies (Kirk and Raven, *Presocratic Philosophers*, 328).

30. Freud quotes Capelle's formulation here (*SE* XXIII, 246). See: W. Capelle, *Die Vorsokratiker* (Leipzig, 1935), 186.

31. Kirk and Raven, *Presocratic Philosophers*, 339.

32. *SE* XVIII, 40–41.

33. For Freud, "This concurrent and mutually opposing action of the two basic instincts gives rise to the whole variegation of the phenomena of life" (*SE* XXIII, 149). See also: *SE* XXII, 209.

34. We should be careful to note here that Freud did not think that this formula could be applied to Eros alone: "To do so would presuppose that living substance was once a unity which had later been torn apart and was now striving towards re-union" (*SE* XXIII, 149).

35. Freud notes this point: *SE* XVII, 58n.

36. Kirk and Raven, *Presocratic Philosophers*, 351–55.

37. Ibid., 354–55. It is important to notice the "waves" of successive historical influence here. This doctrine (1) is similar to that of Buddhism and Hinduism; and (2) had a considerable influence on Plato. Subsequently, (1) and (2) exerted a great deal of influence on the philosophy of Schopenhauer.

38. *SE* XXIII, 245. See also: Kirk and Raven, *Presocratic Philosophers*, 337; Burnet, *Early Greek Philosophy*, 242–44.

39. It is important to note, however, that Empedocles does not offer an account of how well adapted organisms are prone to reproduce their own type.

40. It is important to bear in mind here Freud's comment that he could "never be certain, in view of the wide extent of my reading in early years" (*SE* XXIII, 245), the nature and extent of the influence of others on his thinking.

41. Franz Brentano, *Psychology from an Empirical Standpoint*, eds. Oskar Kraus and Linda L. McAlister, trans. Antos C. Rancurello, D. B. Terrell, and Linda L. McAlister (New York: Humanities Press, 1973), 177–79.

42. Ernest Jones, *The Life and Works of Sigmund Freud*, vol. 1 (New York: Basic Books, 1955), 56.

43. *SE* IV, 67; *SE* V, 620.

44. Herman Nunberg and Ernst Federn, eds., *Minutes of the Vienna Psychoanalytic Society*, vol. 1, trans. M. Nunberg (New York: International Universities Press, 1975), 114.

45. *SE* XX, 24.

46. For example, he synthesized the positions of Heraclitus, Parmenides, and Empedocles—see, for example, the speech of Eryximachus in Plato's *Symposium*, where the meaning of "love" is extended to include "attraction" and "harmony," on the issue of permanence versus change.

47. In saying this, we want to emphasize that we do not wish to ignore highly significant differences; but we do not believe that such differences mitigate the importance of the parallels to which we shall allude.

48. Jones, *Life and Works of Sigmund Freud*, vol. 1, 56.

49. *SE* XVIII, 57; *SE* VII, 136.

50. The Greek word "Eros," which can be translated as "desire" or "love,"

refs to intense attachment and desire, frequently to sexual desire and to the god (Eros) who personified that state of desire and attachment.

51. *SE* XVIII, 58.

52. *SE* XI, 170.

53. Although Freud took this up again in *Totem and Taboo* and *Moses and Monotheism.*

54. Plato, *Meno,* 821aI–2; *Theaetetus,* 150c3–d2. All citations of Plato's dialogues are from Edith Hamilton and Huntington Cairns, eds., *The Collected Dialogues of Plato Including the Letters* (Princeton: Princeton University Press, 1961). References will include only the dialogue title and paragraph location, for easy reference.

55. Plato, *Meno,* 82e4.

56. *SE* XIX, 38.

57. *SE* XVIII, 256; *SE* XIV, 182.

58. *SE* XVIII, 91. See also: *SE* XIX, 218; *SE* XX, 209.

59. O. Pfister, "Plato als Vorläufer der Psychoanalyse," in *International Zeitung Psychoanalyse,* vol. 7 (1921), 264.

60. *SE* XIX, 218.

61. *SE* XVIII, 60n.

62. *SE* VII, 134.

63. Plato, *Symposium,* 211b.

64. *SE* XXII, 209. See also: *SE* XIX, 45.

65. *SE* XIX, 218.

66. One example of this for Plato was to create with another person a life of shared actualization and appreciation of beauty (Plato, *Symposium,* 211b). It is arguable, of course, that there are several significant points of divergence between Plato and Freud here, some of which the latter may have failed to sufficiently appreciate: (1) for Plato, Eros involved a contemplation of the Forms and eternal apprehension of the Good (the underlying principle which governs the unity of all that is), while a more narrowly specified sexual Eros was secondary—in contrast, sexuality was always a primary component of Eros for Freud; (2) for Freud, the origin of Eros was a manifestation of physical, bodily instincts, whereas for Plato, it was eternal and spiritual in nature.

67. *SE* XVIII, 91; *SE* VII, 134. There is, of course, debate as to whether or not this view of Eros was in fact Plato's view at all, since it is arguably difficult to reconcile with the idea of reason as the rational desire of the good, the latter of which is truly Eros.

68. *SE* XIX, 35, 218; Plato, *Symposium.*

69. See chapter 2 for a brief elaboration of Freud's dream theory.

70. Plato, *Timaeus,* 87d.

71. *SE* XV, 122. See also: *SE* IV, esp. 67; *SE* V; *SE* XV, 156; A. A. Brill, ed., *The Basic Writings of Sigmund Freud* (New York: Modern Library, 1966), 548.

72. Plato, *Republic,* 576b.

73. Ibid., 571a–b.

74. This is not surprising given the influence Sophocles had on both.

75. Plato, *Republic,* 571d; 574c–e. In addition, he spoke of such desires explicitly in the myth of "Gyges" in *Republic.*

76. *SE* XI, 46–7. See also: *SE* XIII, 17, 129.

77. Plato, *Timaeus*, 71b4–5, c4, 72a1.

78. There is a difference in emphasis that should be noted, however, between the two. Plato much more typically spoke of dreams as directly manifesting our desires, while according to Freud, this was far more an atypical occurrence. See also: Plato, *Theaetetus*, 158a; *Timaeus*, 46a, d.

79. *SE* XX, 266.

80. Plato, *Phaedrus*, 246–55; *Republic*, 434–44; *Timaeus*, 69d.

81. Although on a speculative level, perhaps this was really not all that surprising after all. Freud may have merely avoided Plato's theory despite its similarities, to avoid any confusions that could potentially result from a comparison of the two and to base, or so he claimed, his theory solely on his observations of his patients.

82. Plato, *Phaedrus*, 246b.

83. *SE* XIX, 25.

84. *SE* XXII, 77.

85. Plato, *Phaedrus*, 256d; *Republic*, 440b. Freud, of course, sought to make the ego master in its own house (*SE* XVII, 143).

86. *SE* XVIII, 91; *SE* VII, 134; *SE* XXIII, 149.

87. Neither Plato nor Freud really clearly or precisely specified the ontological nature of these parts, but at the very least they were seen as *capacities* of sorts with which we deal in our world.

88. Plato, *Republic*, 434d–441c.

89. *SE* XIX, 25.

90. It is arguable that there is a significant difference between Plato and Freud on this score. For Plato, the rational part of the self has desires of its own (*Republic*, 485d), namely, the desire for learning becomes specifically the desire for philosophy (and other disciplines); whereas for Freud, it would not seem that the rational part—the ego—has desires of its own. However, this prima facie difference may not be so great after all, given that Freud claimed that once the needs of the id have been satisfied, the ego is then free to use its excess energies to generate the highest works of civilization.

91. *SE* XIX, 30–39; Plato, *Republic*, 436b–438a, 440b; *Phaedrus*, 237e, 245b, 248a–b.

92. Plato, *Symposium*, 187a.

93. Plato, *Republic*, 438a–439d; *SE* XIX, 30–34; *SE* XXII, 158–82.

94. Plato, *Phaedrus*, 254b–e, 256a–b.

95. Plato, *Republic*, 431a. See also: *Republic*, 439c, 440a.

96. Ibid., 441e.

97. Ibid., 440b, 441e.

98. Ibid., 440d, 441e; *Phaedrus*, 254b–e, 256a–c.

99. *SE* XIX.

100. *SE* XX, 201; *SE* XIX, 149; Plato, *Republic*, 580c–581b.

101. Plato, *Republic*, 581c, 441e, 573d–574a, 589b.

102. Ibid., 485d.

103. *SE* XIX, 44.

104. *SE* XVI, 345. See also: *SE* XIX, 218.

105. *Phaedrus,* 249c; *SE* XIX, 45.
106. *SE* XX, 201; *SE* XIX, 149; Plato, *Republic,* 580c–581b, 587a.
107. Plato, *Republic,* 442d.
108. Ibid., 564a.
109. Ibid., 439c.
110. Ibid., 439c.
111. Ibid., 444e, 441d–e, 442a–d, 443e; *SE* XX, 201; *SE* XIX, 149.
112. This is especially true in light of the following passage from Plato:

> Of our unnecessary pleasures and appetites there are some lawless ones,
> I think, which probably are to be found in us all, but which, when controlled
> by the laws and the better desires in alliance with reason, can in some men be
> altogether got rid of, or so nearly so that only a few weak ones remain, while in
> others the remnant is stronger and more numerous.
>
> What desires do you mean? he said.
>
> Those, said I, that are awakened in sleep when the rest of the soul, the
> rational, gentle and dominant part, slumbers, but the beastly and savage part,
> replete with food and wine, gambols and repelling sleep, endeavors to sally
> forth and satisfy its own instincts. You are aware that in such case there is noth-
> ing it will not venture to undertake as being released from all sense of shame
> and all reason. It does not shrink from attempting to lie with a mother in fancy
> or with anyone else, man, god, or brute. It is ready for any foul deed of blood;
> it abstains from no food, and, in a word, falls short of no extreme of folly and
> shamelessness.
>
> Most true, he said.
>
> But when, I suppose, a man's condition is healthy and sober, and he goes to
> sleep after arousing his rational part and entertaining it with fair words and
> thoughts, and attaining to clear self-consciousness, while he has neither
> starved nor indulged to repletion his appetitive part, so that it may be lulled to
> sleep and not disturb the better part by its pleasure or pain, but may suffer
> that in isolated purity to examine and reach out toward and apprehend some
> of the things unknown to it, past, present, or future, and when he has in like
> manner tamed his passionate part, and does not after a quarrel fall asleep with
> anger still awake with him, but if he has thus quieted the two elements in his
> soul and quickened the third, in which reason resides, and so goes to his rest,
> you are aware that in such case he is most likely to apprehend truth, and the
> visions of his dreams are least likely lawless.
>
> I certainly think so, he said.
>
> This description has carried us too far, but the point that we have to notice
> is this, that in fact there exists in every one of us, even in some reputed most
> respectable, a terrible, fierce, and lawless brood of desires, which it seems are
> revealed in our sleep (*Republic,* 571b–572b).

113. Plato, *Republic,* 442a.
114. Ibid., 580e.
115. Ibid., 442c, 580e, 588d.
116. *SE* XX, 194.

117. Plato, *Republic,* 573e–574a.
118. Ibid., 571a–572b.
119. Ibid., 439a–d.
120. Ibid., 439–40b, 561.
121. *SE* XVIII, 244.
122. Plato, *Republic,* 439d.
123. Ibid., 561.
124. Ibid., 437, 580e; *SE* XX, 200; *SE* XXII, 78.
125. Plato, *Republic,* 607a; *SE* XXII, 74.
126. Plato, *Phaedrus,* 246–56.
127. Plato, *Republic,* 439a.
128. Ibid., 588c; *SE* XXII, 73.
129. *SE* XIX, 23.
130. Plato, *Republic,* 571c–d.
131. Plato, *Timaeus,* 72a–b.
132. Plato, *Republic,* 440b–441e, 561c, 589b; *Phaedrus,* 237e, 245b, 254b–e, 256 a–b.
133. Plato, *Republic,* 536c–d.
134. Ibid., 440d.
135. Ibid., 441c; *SE* XIX, 25.
136. Plato, *Republic,* 441c, e, 442c; *SE* XIX, 17, 55.
137. Ibid.
138. Plato, *Republic,* 572; *SE* XVIII, 109.
139. Plato, *Republic,* 485d.
140. Ibid., 431a.
141. *SE* XXII, 80, 201; *SE* XIX, 56.
142. *SE* XVII, 143.
143. *SE* XX, 194.
144. Plato, *Phaedrus,* 252b.
145. Plato, *Meno,* 821aI–2; *Theaetetus,* 150c3–d2.
146. *SE* XII, 108.
147. Plato, *Meno,* 82e. Although both seemed to hold that there was a truth that the philosopher/therapist recognized and which was ultimately to be understood by the other person.
148. Plato's allegory of the cave is clearly a powerful illustration of this idea, not only for philosophy but for psychotherapy as well.
149. Freud directly credited Plato on this point: "Nor was I then aware that in deriving hysteria from sexuality I was going back to the very beginnings of medicine and following up a thought of Plato's. It was not until later that I learnt this from an essay by Havelock Ellis" (*SE* XX, 24).
150. Plato, *Republic,* 515c. It was Heidegger who pointed out that one of the major senses of *analyein* in Greek is "releasing from chains" (*Zollikon Seminars,* trans. Franz Mayr and Richard Askay [Evanston: Northwestern University Press, 2001], 148).
151. *SE* XIX, 50n.

Chapter 5

Epigraphs: Johann Wolfgang von Goethe, *Maxims and Reflections*, trans. Peter Hutchinson (New York: Penguin Books, 1998), No. 1080; Friedrich Schiller, *Essays: Aesthetical and Philosophical, Including the Dissertation on the "Connexion Between the Animal and Spiritual in Man"* (London: Bell and Sons, 1875), 406; Schelling quoted by Freud, *SE* XVII, 224; *SE* XVII, 245.

1. *SE* XX, 8.

2. Douglas Miller, ed., *Johann Wolfgang von Goethe: Scientific Studies*, vol. 12 of *Collected Works in 12 volumes*, trans. Douglas Miller (Princeton: Princeton University Press, 1988), 3–4.

3. *SE* XX, 8n4.

4. This scenario is rather amusing in light of Goethe's own comment: "After all it's pure idiocy to brag about priority; for it's simply unconscious conceit, not to admit frankly that one is a plagiarist" (quoted in Lancelot Whyte, *The Unconscious Before Freud* [New York: Basic Books, 1960], v). Compare this to Nietzsche, "everywhere, originality out of forgetfulness" (*Unpublished Writings from the Period of "Unfashionable Observations,"* trans. Richard T. Gray [Stanford: Stanford University Press, 1995], 153).

5. Even though Goethe himself, at times, referred to Romanticism as "sickly."

6. There is a very real sense in which Rousseau—as the commonly regarded father of European Romanticism (yet also a member of the French Enlightenment)—lurks in the background of the development of German Romanticism. First with Kant, then Schiller and Goethe: he influenced all these figures with his emphasis on the lost unity of nature and humanity, and the elevation of nature and the passions as the key to the self, with the reciprocal demotion of reason and the intellect, and civilization (the self as personal versus social); with the problems of the human condition deriving from society; along with his dynamic and teleological conception of history. Freud did not refer to Rousseau much at all; however, it is clear that he was familiar with his *Confessions* (see *SE* VII, 193).

7. *SE* XXI, 208. See also: *SE* V, 613; *SE* XXIII, 125; Ernest Jones, *The Life and Works of Sigmund Freud*, vol. 2 (New York: Basic Books, 1955), 415.

8. Jones, *Life and Works of Sigmund Freud*, vol. 2, 183.

9. The philosophers Goethe, Schiller, and Schelling were all discussed during meetings of the Vienna Psychoanalytic Society (Herman Nunberg and Ernst Federn, eds., *Minutes of the Vienna Psychoanalytic Society*, vol. 1, trans. M. Nunberg [New York: International Universities Press, 1975], 27, 66, 193, 339).

10. Freud retained a volume entitled *Foundations of Naturephilosophy*, by Rudolf Hermann Lotze, in his London library as well as Kant's *Brief writings of Naturephilosophy*.

11. *SE* XIX, 215. This is fascinating, since Freud must have been somewhat aware of the dialectic working in himself—the idea that he at times identified with *Naturphilosophie* and at other times with science.

12. Indeed, in 1907, Freud was a participant in a discussion of a presentation in which "Schelling, in particular" was characterized as a representative of the ro-

manticists—of the interrelating of the mystic drive with the drive to understand nature (*Minutes of the Vienna Psychoanalytic Society,* vol. 1, 147).

13. *SE* V, 20; *SE* VII, 283.

14. However, according to Freud's colleague and friend, Ludwig Binswanger, Freud acknowledged the importance of human spirit. In a discussion between these two men, Freud said: "Yes, spirit is everything . . . *Mankind has always known that it possesses spirit; I had to show it that there are also instincts.* But men are always unsatisfied, they cannot wait, they always want something whole and ready-made; *but one has to begin somewhere and only very slowly move forward*" (Ludwig Binswanger, *Being-in-the-World: Selected Papers of Ludwig Binswanger,* trans. Jacob Needleman [New York: Harper & Row, 1967], 182–83).

15. *SE* XXI, 206.

16. Ibid., 207.

17. Ibid., 208. It is interesting to compare Freud's description of Goethe with Strachey's description of Freud in the preface of this text.

18. *SE* XXI, 208–12.

19. Ibid., 210.

20. Goethe, *Maxims and Reflections,* No. 664.

21. Quoted in *Characteristics of Goethe; from the German of Falk, von Müller, &c.,* ed. and trans. Sarah Austin (London: Effingham Wilson, 1833), 76.

22. *SE* XVIII, 38–40, 44–45, 55.

23. *SE* XXI, 212.

24. Ibid.

25. Miller, *Goethe: Scientific Studies,* vol. 12, 28–29.

26. *SE* XXII, 160–61.

27. Nathan G. Hale, ed., *James Jackson Putnam and Psychoanalysis; Letters Between Putnam and Sigmund Freud, Ernest Jones, William James, Sandor Ferenczi, Morton Prince, 1877–1917,* trans. Judith Bernays Heller (Cambridge, Mass.: Harvard University Press, 1971), 170.

28. Goethe, *Maxims and Reflections,* No. 546.

29. This is one of the reasons why Freud's instinct theory is more akin to Empedocles', Plato's, and the romanticists' theories than to what was, then or now, science.

30. Goethe, *Maxims and Reflections,* No. 64.

31. Miller, *Goethe: Scientific Studies,* vol.12, 25, 31, 194–95, 206, 271, 275, 296, 303.

32. Ibid., 6, 19, 155–56, 267, 275, 302.

33. *SE* VII, 16. This was in reference to Goethe's *Faust* (I.6).

34. *SE* II, 206n; *SE* V, 386n, 419n, 424, 456, 466, 519; *SE* VI, 24, 96–97, 100n, 182n, 217, 219, 225, 226, 239n, 246; *SE* XVIII, 268; *SE* XXII, 73.

35. *SE* V, 428n; *SE* VI, 245; *SE* VII, 59n; *SE* VIII, 30, 45, 221n; *SE* XI, 63; *SE* XII, 129; *SE* XIV, 40, 319n; *SE* XV, 31, 36; *SE* XVIII, 45, 77n, 134; *SE* XX, 221; *SE* XXII, 142; *SE* XXIII, 101n.

36. Goethe, *Maxims and Reflections,* No. 412. Here one sees an example of Plato's influence on Goethe, given the former's description of the conflict between the appetites and morality.

37. Schiller, *Essays*, 408. See also: 417.

38. Goethe aptly pointed out that it was Kant who was the primary counterexample here: "Kant deliberately confines himself within a certain sphere and is always ironically pointing beyond it" (Goethe, *Maxims and Reflections*, No. 1198).

39. Rousseau is the visible source of the movement which led to the discovery of the role of will and emotion in the processes that lie below the threshold of consciousness.

40. Freud also realized that at times, reason could be used to *prevent* psychological progress!

41. Kant credited Rousseau with being "the very first *to discover beneath the varying forms which human nature assumes the deeply concealed nature of man*" (*Deutsche Akademie der Wissenschaften*, XX [Berlin, 1900], 58).

42. Goethe, *Maxims and Reflections*, No. 1080.

43. Indeed, even Kant spoke of "Sense perceptions and sensations of which we are not aware but whose existence we can undoubtedly infer, that is, obscure ideas in both man and animals, constitute an immeasurable field. The clear ideas, on the other hand, contain infinitely few instances of sense perceptions and sensations which reveal themselves to consciousness. It is as if just a few places on the vast map of our mind were illuminated" (*Anthropology from a Pragmatic Point of View*, ed. Hans H. Rudnick, trans. Victor Lyle Dowdell [Carbondale, Ill.: Southern Illinois University Press, 1978], 19). This is a metaphor which Schopenhauer and Freud seized upon later, as we shall see. Kant continued on to say that such considerations belong to "physiological anthropology with which we are not properly concerned."

44. Goethe, *Maxims and Reflections*, No. 536.

45. Johann Wolfgang von Goethe, *Conversations and Encounters*, vol. 2, trans. and ed. David Luke and Robert Pick (Chicago: H. Regnery Co., 1966), 254.

46. Goethe, *Maxims and Reflections*, No. 957.

47. Ibid., No. 1005.

48. Stephen Spender, ed., *Great Writings of Goethe* (New York: Mentor Books, 1958), 40.

49. *SE* V, 613.

50. Friedrich Schiller, *Briefwechsel mit körner*, vol. 1 (Berlin, 1847), 381.

51. Schiller, *Essays*, 61–62, 101.

52. *SE* XVII, 226.

53. Though as we shall see, Freud did not share important facets of Schelling's philosophy—where, for example, nature and spirit were linked in a series of developments by unfolding powers together forming one great organism, in which nature was seen as dynamic visible spirit and spirit invisible nature.

54. Eduard von Hartmann, *Philosophy of the Unconscious in Three Volumes*, vol. 3, trans. William Coupland (New York: Macmillan, 1884), 155–59. See also: *SE* IV, 134; *SE* V, 528.

55. F. W. J. Schelling, *Ideas for a Philosophy of Nature: As Introduction to the Study of This Science*, trans. Errol E. Harris and Peter Heath (New York: Cambridge University Press, 1995), 10.

56. F. W. J. Schelling, *System of Transcendental Idealism*, trans. Peter Heath (Charlottesville: University Press of Virginia, 1978), 204.

57. Ibid., 219. See also: F. W. J. Schelling, *Philosophical Inquiries into the Nature of Human Freedom,* trans. James Gutmann (La Salle, Ill.: Open Court, 1936), 36.

58. Schelling, *System of Transcendental Idealism,* 206–7.

59. Schelling, *Ideas for a Philosophy of Nature,* 177.

60. Ibid., 11. See also: Schelling, *Philosophical Inquiries,* 41.

61. Schelling, *Ideas for a Philosophy of Nature,* 78–79.

62. Schelling, *Philosophical Inquiries,* 24, 34–35.

63. Ibid., 24, 34–36.

64. Schelling, *Ideas for a Philosophy of Nature,* 10–11.

65. *SE* XXI, 117.

66. *SE* XX, 200.

67. *SE* XXI, 117.

68. *SE* XVII, 217–56. It is interesting to note Heidegger's use of *unheimlich* as in the sense of "uncanny," of "not-being-at-home" (unhomelike): "In anxiety one feels 'uncanny' . . ." (*Being and Time,* trans. John Macquarrie and Edward Robinson [New York: Harper & Row, 1962], 233). What is interesting here is that both Heidegger and Freud spoke of "anxiety" as intrinsic to the experience of the "uncanny"—although for Freud it involved fear that something threatening would emerge into consciousness, while for Heidegger it was anxiety about one's Being-in-the-world which one does not want to face. Heidegger even went so far as to say that "Anxiety is often conditioned by 'physiological' factors" (*Being and Time,* 234). However there is a fundamental difference between the two: for Heidegger, only because Dasein is anxious in the very depths of its being does it become possible for anxiety to be elicited "physiologically." For Freud, it was because humans experience threats to the gratification of their instincts that ideas which are threatening get repressed, which can then manifest in "physiological" form. We also note the etymological connection with Heidegger's use of the word *Geheimnis* for "mystery." See: Martin Heidegger, *Zollikon Seminars,* trans. Franz Mayr and Richard Askay (Evanston: Northwestern University Press, 2001), 171n.

69. *SE* XVII, 224–26.

70. Ibid., 241.

71. Goethe wrote, "The main ideas in the [*Critique of Judgement*] were completely analogous to my earlier work and thought" (Miller, *Goethe: Scientific Studies,* vol. 12, 29).

72. Goethe, *Maxims and Reflections,* No. 1070.

73. Miller, *Goethe: Scientific Studies,* vol. 12, 8. See also: vol. 12, 28, 49.

74. Schiller, *Essays,* 428.

75. Ibid., 420.

76. Ibid., 63. See also: 418, 424.

77. Schelling, *Ideas for a Philosophy of Nature,* 10.

78. Once again, Freud felt the need to shy away from any mention of "spirit" which might get misconstrued in some form that resembled—or approached—a "higher" being in humans. It was precisely because Freud saw the id as forever retaining all memories—individual and phylogenetic—that he was suspicious of those who attributed mystical/spiritual significance to humans. All this, in Freud's view, was rooted in primitive humans. He wrote: "Of all the erroneous and super-

stitious beliefs of mankind that have supposedly been surmounted there is not one whose residues do not live on among us to-day in the lower strata of civilized peoples or even in the highest strata of cultural society. What has once come to life clings tenaciously to its existence. One feels inclined to doubt sometimes whether the dragons of primaeval days are really extinct" (*SE* XXIII, 229).

79. Goethe, *Maxims and Reflections*, No. 1213.

80. Schelling, *Ideas for a Philosophy of Nature*, 30.

81. Goethe, *Maxims and Reflections*, No. 575.

82. *SE* XIV, 117.

83. Miller, *Goethe: Scientific Studies*, vol. 12, 24.

84. *SE* XIV, 117.

85. Goethe, *Maxims and Reflections*, No. 575.

86. Ibid., No. 1230.

87. As discussed previously, Freud recognized Goethe's discovery/application of free association and gave Goethe credit—in his acceptance speech for the Goethe Prize—for having utilized free association. See Goethe's *Faust:* "To bear all—naked truths, And to envisage circumstances all calm. That is the top of sovereignty." Also: "Everything that liberates our mind without at the same time imparting self-control is pernicious" (*Maxims and Reflections*, No. 504).

Freud was not as generous in giving credit to Schiller, who also anticipated Freud's important technique. At an international conference (1908) on psychoanalysis which Freud attended, Otto Rank read a passage he had discovered in Schiller's correspondence in which he advised a friend to release his imagination from the restraint of critical reason by employing a flow of free association (Jones, *Life and Works of Sigmund Freud*, vol. 2, 42; Schiller, *Briefwechsel mit Körner*, vol. 1 [1847], 381–85). Freud directly acknowledged the import of Schiller's suggestion (*SE* IV, 102–3). However, in "A Note on the Prehistory of the Technique of Analysis" (*SE* XVIII, 264), Freud denied that Schiller had in fact any influence on the choice of psychoanalytic technique, and credited a letter by Ludwig Borne for "having brought to light the fragment of cryptomnesia which in so many cases may be suspected to be behind apparent originality."

88. Friedrich Schiller, *On the Aesthetic Education of Man, in a Series of Letters*, trans. Reginald Snell (New York: F. Ungar Publishing Company, 1965).

89. Given Plato's account earlier, one cannot help but feel his overwhelming influence on this conception.

90. Johann Wolfgang von Goethe, *Faust I & II*, ed. and trans. Stuart Atkins (Cambridge, Mass.: Suhrkamp/Insel Publishers, 1984), 23.

91. Goethe, *Geheimnisse* [1776] (Stuttgart: Verlag der Christengemeinschaft, 1935).

92. Schelling, *Ideas for a Philosophy of Nature*, 10.

93. Ibid.

94. *SE* XVII, 161.

95. Immanuel Kant, *Metaphysical Foundations of Natural Science*, trans. James Ellington (Indianapolis: Bobbs-Merrill, 1970), 57, 59. Schelling, of course, took this idea directly over from Kant (*Ideas for a Philosophy of Nature*, 154).

96. As we have seen, Empedocles was a clear predecessor on this score. As an

example of Plato's influence on Goethe, compare earlier remarks on Plato and Freud's personality theory with *Faust:* "Two souls, alas! reside within my breast, and each is eager for a separation: / in throes of coarse desire, one grips / the earth with all its senses; / the other struggles from the dust / to rise to high ancestral spheres" (*Faust I & II*, 1112–17).

97. Miller, *Goethe: Scientific Studies,* vol. 12, 155–56.

98. Ibid., 6.

99. Schelling, *Ideas for a Philosophy of Nature,* x.

100. Miller, *Goethe: Scientific Studies,* vol. 12, 6.

101. F. W. J. Schelling, *The Ages of the World,* trans. Jason M. Wirth (Albany: State University of New York, 2000), 83–89.

102. *SE* XIV, 133–40.

103. *SE* XI, 170.

104. *SE* XVIII, 117–21.

105. Goethe, *Maxims and Reflections,* No. 716.

106. *SE* XV, 199.

107. *SE* XIII, 142–43.

108. Goethe, *Maxims and Reflections,* No. 412.

109. *SE* XV, 207–8.

Chapter 6

Epigraph: *SE* XX, 59–60.

1. *SE* XVII, 143–44; *SE* XVIII, 178.

2. *SE* XVII, 143–44.

3. Herman Nunberg and Ernst Federn, eds., *Minutes of the Vienna Psychoanalytic Society,* vol. 2, trans. M. Nunberg (New York: International Universities Press, 1975), 31–32.

4. Ernest Jones, *The Life and Works of Sigmund Freud,* vol. 2 (New York: Basic Books, 1955), 415; *SE* XVII, 143–44.

5. Arthur Schopenhauer, *The World as Will and Representation,* vol. 2, trans. E. F. J. Payne (New York: Dover, 1966), 201. Nietzsche wrote, "It is the stillest words that bring on the storm. Thoughts that come on doves' feet guide the world" (*Ecce Homo,* trans. Walter Kaufmann [New York: Vintage Books, 1969], 219). Nietzsche referenced this quote in *Thus Spoke Zarathustra* (*The Portable Nietzsche,* trans. Walter Kaufmann [New York: Viking, 1954], 258). And again, "anything truly productive is offensive" (*Untimely Meditations,* trans. R. J. Hollingdale [New York: Cambridge University Press, 1983], 35). This is an interesting comment in light of Freud's own characterization of himself as the bearer of painful truths that people did not want to face.

6. Schopenhauer, *World as Will and Representation,* vol. 1, xv.

7. Like Freud, Schopenhauer saluted Empedocles' recognition that it is only through strife/conflict that nature exists—that "if strife did not rule in things,

then all would be a unity" (*World as Will and Representation,* vol. 1, 147; see also vol. 1, 222–23, 410; vol. 2, 274).

8. It is significant that there were fewer than a half-dozen more philosophers Schopenhauer referenced throughout his magnum opus—for example, Aristotle, Spinoza, and Leibniz.

9. Nietzsche's outright rejection of the "thing-in-itself" sets him apart from both Schopenhauer and Freud.

10. Friedrich Nietzsche, *The Birth of Tragedy,* trans. Walter Kaufmann (New York: Vintage Books, 1967).

11. Franz Brentano, *Psychology from an Empirical Standpoint,* eds. Oskar Kraus and Linda L. McAlister, trans. Antos C. Rancurello, D. B. Terrell, and Linda L. McAlister (New York: Humanities Press, 1973), 103–9, 115–16.

12. Eduard von Hartmann, *Philosophy of the Unconscious in Three Volumes,* vol. 3, trans. William Coupland (New York: Macmillan, 1884), 149–50.

13. *SE* VI, 119.

14. *SE* XXIII, 297.

15. Jones commented, "Freud described [Lou Andreas-Salomé] as the only real bond between Nietzsche and himself"(*Life and Works of Sigmund Freud,* vol. 3, 213).

16. Ernst Freud, ed., *The Letters of Sigmund Freud and Arnold Zweig,* trans. William Douglas Robson-Scott (New York: New York University Press, 1970), 78.

17. *Minutes of the Vienna Psychoanalytic Society,* vol. 1, 98, 239, 322, 355–61, 357–59, 365–66; vol. 2, 25–33, 56, 329–30, 334–36, 372–73, 411, 491, 501, 535; vol. 3, 54, 63, 211, 265, 266, 292, 313, 334, 350; vol. 4, 55, 84, 101–2.

18. *Minutes of the Vienna Psychoanalytic Society,* vol. 4, 101–2.

19. Two facts are particularly noteworthy about this: first, Freud did not acknowledge Schopenhauer's forerunner status until five years later; and second, the above presentation was the *only one,* as far as we can discern, in the entire history of the meetings of the Vienna Psychoanalytic Society *not* to have included a discussion after a presentation.

20. Schopenhauer, *World as Will and Representation,* vol. 2, ch. 32 ("On Madness"), 399–402.

21. *Minutes of the Vienna Psychoanalytic Society,* vol. 2, 372–73.

22. Friedrich Nietzsche, *On the Genealogy of Morals,* trans. Walter Kaufmann and R. J. Hollingdale (New York: Vintage Books, 1969); discussed in *Minutes of the Vienna Psychoanalytic Society,* vol. 1, 355–61.

23. *Minutes of the Vienna Psychoanalytic Society,* vol. 1, 358.

24. Ibid., vol. 2, 25–33.

25. Friedrich Nietzsche, *Daybreak: Thoughts on the Prejudices of Morality,* trans. R. J. Hollingdale, ed. Maudemarie Clark and Brian Leiter (New York: Cambridge University Press, 1997).

26. *Minutes of the Vienna Psychoanalytic Society,* vol. 3, 113.

27. Freud said, for example, that Nietzsche was "a person of our time with such a living influence" (Jones, *Life and Works of Sigmund Freud,* vol. 3, 459).

28. *SE* XX, 59–60.

29. Peter Gay, *Freud: A Life for Our Time* (New York: Anchor Books, 1988), 46n.

This was found in a letter from Freud to Lothar Bickel, June 28, 1931. See also: *SE* XX, 60.

30. *Minutes of the Vienna Psychoanalytic Society*, vol. 1, 359–60.

31. *SE* XIV, 15–16.

32. *Minutes of the Vienna Psychoanalytic Society*, vol. 1, 359; vol. 2, 32.

33. Freud referred to Schopenhauer's *Parerga and Paralipomena* in his *Interpretation of Dreams* and quoted directly from it in *Beyond the Pleasure Principle*, in 1920 (*SE* XVI, 50, 101). *The Interpretation of Dreams* was actually published in 1899, but its title page was postdated into the new century. See Strachey's introduction: *SE* IV, xii.

34. Freud himself explicitly referenced some key points of Schopenhauer's philosophy, which are strewn throughout Schopenhauer's collection of essays, *Parerga und Paralipomena*. It is clear that Freud read sections from both volumes of this voluminous work as early as 1899 and subsequently. See: *SE* XXIV, 138–39.

35. *SE* IV, 36.

36. Ibid., 66.

37. Ibid., 90.

38. *SE* XIII, 87.

39. *SE* XIV, 15.

40. *SE* XVII, 143–44.

41. *SE* VII, 134. See also: *SE* XIX, 218, 223–24; *SE* XX, 59–60; *SE* XXII, 107.

42. *SE* XX, 59.

43. *SE* XVIII, 49–50. Freud's comments are based on an essay Schopenhauer wrote entitled "Essay on Spirit Seeing and Everything Connected Therewith," in which he employed his famous and powerful metaphor: "Therefore, as I have shown in the *World as Will and Representation*, vol. 2, chaps. 17 and 22, the intellect is a mere superficial force, essentially and everywhere touching only the outer shell, never the inner core of things" (*Parerga and Paralipomena*, vol. 1, trans. E. F. J. Payne, [Oxford: Clarendon Press, 1974], 301; see *World as Will and Representation*, vol. 2, 176). Given this—and especially in light of the myriad close similarities we are about to consider—it is implausible that Freud did not *immediately* proceed to read Schopenhauer's magnum opus as well. (As we have seen, Freud's intellectual interests and pursuits certainly inspired him to read the ancient Greeks, the Enlightenment figures, the romanticists, and so on.) Indeed, Freud's translator, James Strachey was utterly convinced that when Freud (in 1917) referred to Schopenhauer's "words of unforgettable impressiveness admonish[ing] mankind of the importance, still so greatly under-estimated by it, of its sexual craving" (*SE* XVII, 144) and "The incomparable significance of sexual life had been proclaimed by the philosopher Schopenhauer in an intensely impressive passage" (*SE* XIX, 218), Freud was referring to a specific passage in Schopenhauer's *The World as Will and Representation* (vol. 2, ch. 42). We also note that the same idea appeared in a different part of Schopenhauer's work, than the aforementioned passage (in *World as Will and Representation*, vol. 2, 400); Otto Rank had brought this passage to Freud's attention in 1909 (*SE* XII, 28; *SE* XIV, 15).

44. *SE* XVII, 144.

45. *SE* XXII, 107. See also: *SE* XIII, 87.

46. *SE* XVII, 144; *SE* XXII, 107.

47. *SE* XVII, 144.

48. *SE* XX, 59. It is important to note that Freud, as we shall see, was simply mistaken on this point. Schopenhauer emphasized the importance of empirical observations and of ensuring the compatibility of his metaphysics with the empirical claims of science.

49. *SE* XX, 59–60.

50. As we have seen earlier, there is evidence to suggest that Freud was intellectually intimidated by the discipline of philosophy.

51. Schopenhauer, *Parerga and Paralipomena*, vol. 1, 129.

52. Freud was directly intellectually influenced by Lipps and had marked a passage about the unconscious as the basis for consciousness (in Lipps' *Komik und Humor* [1898]). In fact, Freud gave Lipps lavish credit for inspiring him to write his book, *Jokes and Their Relation to the Unconscious:* "It is this book [*Komik und Humor*] that has given me the courage to undertake this attempt as well as the possibility of doing so" (*SE* VIII, 147–48). Freud referred to Lipps twice in his discussion of the concept of the unconscious—early in 1900, and twice in 1940 at the end of his career. This suggests a strong and sustained interest in his work. This is confirmed by the fact that Freud's personal library in London contains a dozen books by Lipps, works dated from 1883–1902. (We might note for future reference that this was well after Schopenhauer's works!)

In addition, Fechner's influence on psychoanalysis is evidenced by the fact that Freud quoted him in the *Interpretation of Dreams, Jokes and Their Relation to the Unconscious,* and *Beyond the Pleasure Principle.* It was from Fechner's philosophy of nature that Freud borrowed several basic concepts that he incorporated into his metapsychology. Freud took from Fechner the concept of mental energy (*SE* I, 296, 312; *SE* XIX, 159), the "topographical" concept of the mind (*SE* IV, 48; *SE* V, 536), and employed the constancy principle (*SE* I, 296, 315; *SE* XIX, 47; *SE* XX, 78). Freud's London library contains several works by Fechner as well.

53. *SE* XX, 59.

54. Sigmund Freud, *The Origins of Psychoanalysis: Letters to Wilhelm Fliess,* trans. Eric Mosbacher and James Strachey (New York: Basic Books, 1954), 261–62.

55. Once again it is important to note that Schopenhauer tried as well to render his metaphysical speculations consistent with science, although his criticism of science must have been well known.

56. *SE* I, 312; *SE* XVIII, 8–9.

57. *SE* V, 611.

58. *SE* XXIII, 286.

59. Given Freud's critique of metaphysics cited earlier, it is interesting to see him resort here to a metaphysician *as metaphysician* to support the plausibility of his view.

60. *SE* VII, 134.

61. *SE* X, 196n.

62. *SE* XIX, 261.

63. *SE* IX, 22, 105.

64. *SE* VI, 169–70.

65. Ibid., 40. See also: *SE* VI, 19-20.

66. *SE* VI, 136.

67. Unless, of course, we are willing to believe that Freud was simply lying.

68. *SE* XXI, 212.

69. *SE* XIII, 178–79.

70. *SE* XXII, 107.

71. *SE* XVIII, 49–50. Here Freud quoted directly from Schopenhauer's *Parerga and Paralipomena* (vol. 1, 213).

72. *SE* XXII, 107.

73. *SE* X, 140.

74. *SE* XXII, 108.

75. Ibid., 107.

76. Schopenhauer, *World as Will and Representation*, vol. 2, 350.

77. Ibid., 351.

78. Ibid., 360.

79. It is interesting to note that, in the very same paragraph in which Freud made this point, he *accurately* described various fundamental ideas of Schopenhauer's philosophy.

80. With respect to Schopenhauer, it was due to these striking similarities that James Strachey included an "Extract From Schopenhauer's *The World as Will and Idea*" in the *Standard Edition*! See: *SE* XIX, 223–24.

81. This is especially noteworthy given that book-length studies have been conducted on the relationship of Nietzsche's philosophy to the development of Freudian psychoanalysis, while *comparatively* few have been done, *by way of a truly extensive, detailed analysis,* on the relationship of Schopenhauer's philosophy to Freud.

Chapter 7

Epigraphs: Arthur Schopenhauer, *The World as Will and Representation*, vol. 2, trans. E. F. J. Payne (New York: Dover, 1966), 560; *SE* XXII, 73.

1. Schopenhauer, *World as Will and Representation*, vol. 2, 194–95. See also: vol. 2, 318, 515.

2. Schopenhauer, *World as Will and Representation*, vol. 2, 191–200.

3. Ibid., vol. 1, 99.

4. Ibid., vol. 2, 195.

5. Arthur Schopenhauer, *Parerga and Paralipomena*, vol. 2, trans. E. F. J. Payne, (Oxford: Clarendon Press, 1974), 18–19.

6. Schopenhauer, *World as Will and Representation*, vol. 2, 164.

7. Schopenhauer, *Parerga and Paralipomena*, vol. 2, 3.

8. Schopenhauer, *World as Will and Representation*, vol. 2, 219. See also: vol. 2, 376–98.

9. Schopenhauer, *Parerga and Paralipomena*, vol. 2, 8, 17. Freud clearly missed this point, in his understanding of Schopenhauer's philosophy.

10. Schopenhauer, *World as Will and Representation*, vol. 2, 180, 184. Schopen-

hauer would occasionally visit asylums to observe inmates, to confirm or disconfirm his theories (*World as Will and Representation*, vol. 1, 22).

11. Arthur Schopenhauer, *Schopenhauer's On the Will in Nature: A Discussion of the Corroborations from the Empirical Sciences that the Author's Philosophy has Received Since its First Appearance*, trans. E. F. J. Payne, ed. David E. Cartwright (New York: St Martin's Press, 1992), 3. See also: "Preface."

12. Schopenhauer, *On the Will in Nature*, 21.

13. Schopenhauer, *World as Will and Representation*, vol. 2, 178.

14. Ibid., 181.

15. Ibid., 184.

16. Ibid., 183.

17. Ibid.

18. Ibid., 185.

19. Ibid., 642.

20. Ibid., vol. 1, 100.

21. Ibid., vol. 2, 195.

22. Ibid., vol. 1, 292.

23. Ibid., vol. 2, 197, 643.

24. *SE* XVII, 143–44.

25. *SE* I, 317.

26. Schopenhauer, *World as Will and Representation*, vol. 2, 182, 189, 199, 239; *SE* XXII, 73; *SE* XXIII, 197.

27. Schopenhauer, *World as Will and Representation*, vol. 2, 206, 642.

28. Ibid., 179, 195, 197–98, 643; *SE* XXII, 73–74.

29. Schopenhauer, *World as Will and Representation*, vol. 2, 179, 197–98; *SE* XXII, 73–74; *SE* IV, *SE* V, as well as his therapeutic writings.

30. Schopenhauer, *World as Will and Representation*, vol. 2, 197–98, 274.

31. Ibid., 182, 195.

32. Ibid., 197–98.

33. Ibid., 197–98, 560, 640.

34. Ibid., 641–42; *SE* XXII, 73–74.

35. Schopenhauer, *World as Will and Representation*, vol. 2, 197–98, 560, 640–42.

36. Ibid., 560. See also: vol. 2, 640–42.

37. Schopenhauer, *World as Will and Representation*, vol. 2, 196; *SE* XXII, 73–4; *SE* XXIII, 96.

38. Schopenhauer, *World as Will and Representation*, vol. 2, 201, 277; *SE* XXIII, 96.

39. Schopenhauer, *World as Will and Representation*, vol. 2, 342.

40. Ibid., 559.

41. Schopenhauer, *Parerga and Paralipomena*, vol. 1, 214.

42. *SE* I, 315. Early in his career, Freud used a different terminology: "endogenous quantities of excitation ascend . . . the mainspring of the psychical mechanism . . . only periodically become psychical stimuli . . . in the interior of the system there arises the impulsion which sustains all psychical activity. We know this power as the *will*—the derivative of the *instincts*" (*SE* I, 315–17). As Strachey noted: "These 'endogenous stimuli' are thus the precursors of the 'instincts'" (*SE* I, 297).

43. Schopenhauer, *World as Will and Representation*, vol. 2, 342; *SE* XVIII, 7; *SE* XXIII, 145.

44. Ibid., 342, 559; *SE* XVIII, 34–5; *SE* XXII, 106, 96 221.

45. Schopenhauer, *World as Will and Representation*, vol. 2, 342; *SE* XIV, 122–25.

46. Schopenhauer, *World as Will and Representation*, vol. 2, 342, 540.

47. Ibid., 538.

48. *SE* XVIII, 24–25.

49. *SE* XIV, 122.

50. Schopenhauer, *World as Will and Representation*, vol. 2, 560; *SE* XXI, 46–53.

51. Schopenhauer, *World as Will and Representation*, vol. 2, 350, 360; *SE* XVIII, 50; *SE* XVIII, 258.

52. Schopenhauer, *World as Will and Representation*, vol. 1, 311, 313; *Parerga and Paralipomena*, vol. 1, 223; *SE* XVIII, 36, 38.

53. *SE* XVIII, 50. Freud quoted from Schopenhauer's *Parerga and Paralipomena* (vol. 1, 223). See also: *World as Will and Representation*, vol. 2, 512.

54. *SE* XVIII, 44, 52.

55. Ibid., 52–53. Freud was not consistent on this distinction however. Earlier he equated the ego instincts with being "self-preservative" (*SE* XIV, 115–16, 124–26, 135–39).

56. Schopenhauer, *World as Will and Representation*, vol. 2, 512; *Parerga and Paralipomena*, vol. 1, 223; *SE* XVIII, 49–53, 259; *SE* XXI, 101–3, 118–24, 137–41.

57. It is in this sense that Freud agreed with the all-encompassing notion of Eros in Plato. See chapter 4.

58. *SE* XIII, 157–58.

59. *SE* XXIII, 188.

60. Ibid., 187.

61. Ibid., 145. See also: *SE* XXIII, 206. In a footnote to this, Freud added: "This oldest portion of the psychical apparatus remains the most important throughout life."

62. Schopenhauer, *World as Will and Representation*, vol. 2, 207–8.

63. Ibid., 235.

64. *SE* XXII, 73–74.

65. Ibid.

66. Schopenhauer, *World as Will and Representation*, vol. 2, 206–7, 239.

67. *SE* VII, 134.

68. Schopenhauer, *World as Will and Representation*, vol. 2, 570.

69. Ibid., 535.

70. Ibid., 237.

71. Ibid., 511.

72. Ibid., vol. 1, 329.

73. Ibid., vol. 2, 514.

74. Ibid., vol. 1, 330.

75. Ibid., vol. 2, 513.

76. *SE* XVIII, 91. See also: *SE* XIX, 218; *SE* XX, 209.

77. Schopenhauer, *World as Will and Representation*, vol. 2, 513.

78. Ibid., vol. 1, 329; vol. 2, 511.

79. Ibid., vol. 2, 513.

80. Ibid., 514.

81. Ibid., 512.

82. Ibid., vol. 1, 329. See also: *SE* XIV, 78.

83. Letter from Freud to Dr. Ernest Jones, 1913, in reference to Jung. Quoted in *The Great Thoughts*, comp. George Seldes (New York: Ballantine Books, 1985), 151.

84. Quoted in *The Great Thoughts*, 152. See also: *SE* XXI, 79–80, 84, 97, 103, 179.

85. Schopenhauer, *World as Will and Representation*, vol. 2, 513; *SE* XXII, 209.

86. Schopenhauer, *World as Will and Representation*, vol. 2, 513.

87. *SE* VI, 276.

88. *SE* VIII, 101. See also: *SE* VIII, 110–11.

89. Schopenhauer, *World as Will and Representation*, vol. 2, 513.

90. Ibid., 513; *SE* XII, 222.

91. *SE* VII, 47, 51.

92. *SE* XVI, 370.

93. *SE* IX, 186–87.

94. Schopenhauer, *World as Will and Representation*, vol. 2, 514; *SE* XIV, 125.

95. Schopenhauer, *World as Will and Representation*, vol. 2, 511. See also: vol. 2, 514.

96. Ibid., 542.

97. Ibid., 511.

98. *SE* XIV, 125. See also: *SE* XIV, 78.

99. Schopenhauer, *World as Will and Representation*, vol. 1, 108.

100. Ibid., 330.

101. Ibid., 330.

102. *SE* XXIII, 152.

103. *SE* XX, 113–16; *SE* XXIII, 154–56.

104. Schopenhauer, *World as Will and Representation*, vol. 2, 513.

105. Ibid., 56.

106. *SE* III, 266.

107. In "The Sexual Enlightenment of Children" (1907), *SE* IX.

108. *SE* VII, 162. See also: *SE* VII, 164, 219, 231; *SE* XI, 96.

109. *SE* I, 221, 269.

110. Schopenhauer, *World as Will and Representation*, vol. 2, 359.

111. *SE* XIV, 78.

112. Schopenhauer, *World as Will and Representation*, vol. 2, 401.

113. *SE* XXIII, 145.

114. Schopenhauer, *World as Will and Representation*, vol. 1, 101–2.

115. Ibid., 102–3. See also: vol. 2, ch. 18.

116. Ibid., vol. 1, 19.

117. Ibid., vol. 2, 214.

118. Ibid., 230.

119. Ibid., vol. 1, 104.

120. Ibid., vol. 2, 248.

121. Ibid., 100–102.

122. Ibid., 312.

123. Ibid., vol. 1, 5.

124. Arthur Schopenhauer, *On the Fourfold Root of the Principle of Sufficient Reason,* trans. E. F. J. Payne (La Salle, Ill.: Open Court, 1974), 207–11.

125. *SE* XIX, 26. We shall take up this topic again in the final chapter, when discussing Freud's professed "dualism."

126. Schopenhauer, *World as Will and Representation,* vol. 1, 19–20.

127. *SE* XIX, 25.

128. Schopenhauer, *World as Will and Representation,* vol. 2, 176; *SE* VII, 284.

129. Schopenhauer, *World as Will and Representation,* vol. 2, 401.

130. *SE* VII, 113.

131. Ibid., 41.

132. Ibid., 84, 102, 114.

133. Ibid., 15.

134. Sigmund Freud, *The Origins of Psychoanalysis: Letters to Wilhelm Fliess,* trans. Eric Mosbacher and James Strachey (New York: Basic Books, 1954), 231, letter 75.

135. *SE* VIII, 202, 222.

136. *SE* VII, 40–41.

137. *SE* XXIII, 151.

138. Ibid., 158.

139. *SE* VIII, 223.

140. *SE* VII, 284–86.

141. Ibid., 286, 288.

142. Ibid., 53.

143. *SE* XI, 218. See also: *SE* VII, 40–41, 52–53, 113; *SE* XII, 248.

144. Schopenhauer, *World as Will and Representation,* vol. 2, 402.

145. Ibid., vol. 1, 100.

146. Ibid., 643.

147. *SE* XIX, 26.

148. Schopenhauer, *Parerga and Paralipomena,* vol. 2, 176. See also: *World as Will and Representation,* vol. 2, ch. 20.

149. Schopenhauer, *World as Will and Representation,* vol. 1, 101.

150. Ibid., vol. 2, ch. 20.

151. Schopenhauer, *Parerga and Paralipomena,* vol. 2, 176.

152. *SE* VII, 293.

153. Schopenhauer, *World as Will and Representation,* vol. 1, 643.

154. Ibid., vol. 2, 259.

155. Ibid., vol. 1, 100.

156. Ibid., 100–101.

157. Ibid.

158. Ibid., 327.

159. Ibid., vol. 2, 260.

160. Schopenhauer, *Parerga and Paralipomena,* vol. 2, 173. Such thoughts directly paralleled Freud's emphasis on the necessity of various processes throughout therapy.

161. Schopenhauer, *World as Will and Representation,* vol. 2, 135–36.

162. Ibid., 252.

163. Friedrich Nietzsche, *Unfashionable Observations,* trans. Richard T. Gray (Stanford: Stanford University Press, 1995), 156. See also: Friedrich Nietzsche, *The Will to Power,* ed. Walter Kaufmann, trans. Walter Kaufmann and R. J. Hollingdale (New York: Vintage Books, 1967), 359.

164. Friedrich Nietzsche, *Human, All Too Human,* trans. R. J. Hollingdale (Cambridge: Cambridge University Press, 1996), 12.

165. *SE* XXI, 79.

166. Ibid., 97.

167. Friedrich Nietzsche, *On the Genealogy of Morals,* trans. Walter Kaufmann and R. J. Hollingdale (New York: Vintage Books, 1969), 84.

168. *SE* XXI, 123.

169. Nietzsche, *Genealogy of Morals,* 87.

Chapter 8

Epigraph: Arthur Schopenhauer, *The World as Will and Representation,* vol. 1, trans. E. F. J. Payne (New York: Dover, 1966), 301.

1. Friedrich Nietzsche, *Unpublished Writings from the Period of "Unfashionable Observations,"* trans. Richard T. Gray (Stanford: Stanford University Press, 1995), 12.

2. Given the importance of these similarities, and the importance they will have for our later argument that the existential phenomenologists have misconstrued Freud's position, we will have significantly greater recourse to quotations from the philosophers themselves in this chapter. We will do so to illustrate as cogently as possible just how closely their positions resembled one another and why this leads to a radically different, yet more cogent, account of Freud's position concerning the issue of freedom and determinism.

3. Schopenhauer, *World as Will and Representation,* vol. 2, 137–39.

4. See also: Friedrich Nietzsche, *The Gay Science: With a Prelude in Rhymes and an Appendix of Songs,* trans. Walter Kaufmann (New York: Vintage Books, 1974), 85.

5. *SE* XIV, 166.

6. Ibid., 167.

7. Ibid.

8. Nietzsche, *Gay Science,* 16.

9. Nietzsche, *Unpublished Writings,* 52.

10. Friedrich Nietzsche, *The Will to Power,* ed. Walter Kaufmann, trans. Walter Kaufmann and R. J. Hollingdale (New York: Vintage Books, 1967), 343.

11. Jean Baptiste Lamarck (1744–1829) was the first biologist to formulate a comprehensive theory of evolution. He was renowned for his theory on the inheritance of acquired characteristics, which held that under certain conditions, characteristics that were acquired during an animal's lifetime (for example, bodily alterations resulting from dramatic environmental changes) could be preserved by heredity and transmitted to future offspring. Lamarck's theories were repudiated during his lifetime, and he died in poverty. Despite the fact that Lamarck's ideas had met with vehement opposition from the scientific community, Freud "re-

mained from the beginning to the end of his life . . . an obstinate adherent of this discredited Lamarckism" (Ernest Jones, *The Life and Work of Sigmund Freud*, vol. 3 [New York: Basic Books, 1965], 311). Freud's intention was to publish articles illustrating the psychoanalytic significance of Lamarckism—in its relationship, for example, to the transmission of unconscious memories, the omnipotence of thoughts, and so on. However, Freud eventually abandoned his plans, perhaps out of practical concerns for the future of Freudian psychoanalysis (Jones, *Life and Work of Sigmund Freud*, vol. 3, 309–14). It is interesting to note that there are contemporary biologists who are reconsidering Lamarck's theories—neo-Lamarckism—in relation to the functioning of the immune system, embryonic development, and so forth.

12. *SE* V, 577.

13. Nietzsche, *Unpublished Writings*, 31. See also: *Unpublished Writings*, 48, 52; Friedrich Nietzsche, *Daybreak: Thoughts on the Prejudices of Morality*, trans. R. J. Hollingdale, ed. Maudemarie Clark and Brian Leiter (New York: Cambridge University Press, 1997), 78; Friedrich Nietzsche, *On the Genealogy of Morals*, trans. Walter Kaufmann and R. J. Hollingdale (New York: Vintage Books, 1969), 57, 58.

14. Nietzsche, *Will to Power*, 323.

15. Schopenhauer, *World as Will and Representation*, vol. 2, 240–41.

16. Friedrich Nietzsche, *Human, All Too Human*, trans. R. J. Hollingdale (Cambridge: Cambridge University Press, 1996), 17–18. See also: *Daybreak*, 314.

17. Nietzsche, *Human, All Too Human*, 230.

18. *SE* V, 608.

19. We should also be careful to note that Schopenhauer, Nietzsche, and Freud shared a number of further thoughts concerning dreams:

> Dreams are just as important and meaningful as waking life. Schopenhauer: *Parerga and Paralipomena*, vol. 2, trans. E. F. J. Payne, (Oxford: Clarendon Press, 1974), 4. Nietzsche: *Beyond Good and Evil: Prelude to a Philosophy of the Future*, trans. Walter Kaufmann (New York: Vintage Books, 1989), 106; *Daybreak*, 75. Freud: *SE* XV, 89–91; *SE* XXIII, 166–71.
>
> Dreams have a hidden meaning for our lives. Schopenhauer: *Parerga and Paralipomena*, vol. 1, 237. Nietzsche: *The Birth of Tragedy*, trans. Walter Kaufmann (New York: Vintage Books, 1967), 45; *Human, All Too Human*, 230. Freud: *SE* IV, 36; *SE* V, 608.
>
> In dreams, everything is interconnected in accordance with reason. Everything has a meaning or sense; nothing is insignificant. Schopenhauer: *World as Will and Representation*, vol. 1, 16. Nietzsche: *Birth of Tragedy*, 34. Freud: *SE* V, 513.
>
> As a form of thinking, dreams have the same underlying organic basis, which is mysterious. Schopenhauer: *Parerga and Paralipomena*, vol. 1, 237–8; vol. 2, 4. Nietzsche: *Daybreak*, 76. Freud: *SE* IV, 33–42.
>
> Dreams are wish-fulfillments. Schopenhauer: *Parerga and Paralipomena*, vol. 2, 217. Nietzsche: *Daybreak*, 75. Freud: *SE* I, 340; *SE* IV, 144.
>
> In dreams, primeval memories continue to exercise themselves on humans. Nietzsche: *Human, All Too Human*, 17–18; *Daybreak*, 157. Freud: *SE* V, 549.

20. Schopenhauer, *Parerga and Paralipomena*, vol. 1, 301.

21. Nietzsche, *Gay Science*, 85. See also: *Human, All Too Human*, 193; *Will to Power*, 376.

22. Schopenhauer, *World as Will and Representation,* vol. 2, 195. See also: vol. 2, 318, 535.

23. Nietzsche, *Beyond Good and Evil,* 44.

24. *SE* V, 63–64.

25. Nietzsche, *Beyond Good and Evil,* 44; *Gay Science,* 82–83.

26. Nietzsche, *Beyond Good and Evil,* 146; *Thus Spoke Zarathustra,* in *The Portable Nietzsche,* trans. Walter Kaufmann (New York: Viking, 1954), 146; *Daybreak,* 133; *Human, All Too Human,* 40, 193, 209–43, 245–47, 263, 285–86, 290, 296, 302–5, and so on.

27. Nietzsche, *Daybreak,* 76.

28. Schopenhauer, *Parerga and Paralipomena,* vol. 2, 51.

29. Nietzsche, *Beyond Good and Evil,* 24. See also: *Human, All Too Human,* 183; *Will to Power,* 274.

30. *SE* XVII, 141.

31. *SE* XIV, 166–67.

32. Schopenhauer, *World as Will and Representation,* vol. 2, 135.

33. Nietzsche, *Gay Science,* 262.

34. Ibid., 298–99. See also: *Gay Science,* 301; *Will to Power,* 337–38, 376.

35. Schopenhauer, *World as Will and Representation,* vol. 2, 142.

36. Ibid., 135, 208.

37. Ibid., 201. See also: 240.

38. Ibid., 219. See also: 220.

39. Ibid., 209.

40. Nietzsche, *Will to Power,* 284.

41. Nietzsche, *Twilight of the Idols,* in *The Portable Nietzsche,* trans. Walter Kaufmann (New York: Viking, 1954), 477.

42. Schopenhauer, *World as Will and Representation,* vol. 2, 221.

43. Ibid., 213.

44. *SE* XIX, 25.

45. *SE* XVII, 143

46. *SE* XX, 156.

47. Schopenhauer, *World as Will and Representation,* vol. 2, 241. Schopenhauer's account of the mind directly paralleled many (though, by no means, all) of those aspects shared by Plato and Freud, as we have seen earlier. He agreed with both that:

> The self has parts. Schopenhauer, of course, spoke of the Will and the intellect as distinct functions throughout his analysis. "Will and intellect . . . separate out very distinctly" (*World as Will and Representation,* vol. 2, 224). See also: *World as Will and Representation,* vol. 2, 206, 209–13, 215, 224, 400; *SE* XIX, 19–27. It is the intellect/ego that has contact with the external world which is discerned as a threat to or a source of satisfaction of the Will's/Id's needs. See: *World as Will and Representation,* vol. 2, 241; *SE* XIV, 133–40; *SE* XIX, 21–25; *SE* XXIII, 199–206.
>
> Conflicts occur among the parts of the self. The functions of the will and the intellect are frequently counter to one another. See: *World as Will and Representation,* vol. 2, 206, 213, 215, 220, 221–24, 400; *SE* XVII, 138, 208, 260.

Parts of the self try to temper and train other parts. The intellect and the will try to mutually temper one another. See: *World as Will and Representation,* vol. 2, 206, 213, 215, 220, 400; *SE* XVII, 25–28.

Parts of the self can and do form alliances with other parts. At times the intellect and the will work cooperatively to achieve their goals. See: *World as Will and Representation,* vol. 2, 220–24.

Any part of the self has the potential/capacity to become the dominant part. See: *World as Will and Representation,* vol. 2, 206, 215, 220, 224. For the most part, it is the will that forms the dominant wing of the personality, yet there are rare times when this can occur with the intellect—for example, in cases of genius. See: *World as Will and Representation,* vol. 2, 215, 220.

Different parts can and do dominate/rule the self at different times. See: *World as Will and Representation,* vol. 2, 206, 209, 213, 215, 220, 224, 240. In the case of genius it is possible that with "an abnormally predominant development of the intellect" that "the intellect [can] directly impede the will" (*World as Will and Representation,* vol. 2, 220).

The healthy person is one whose parts each fulfills its own respective proper functions/tasks. A harmonious coordination of the parts is possible, yet rare. See: *World as Will and Representation,* vol. 2, 220. At times, Schopenhauer spoke of the mentally healthy person as one who has a coherent and continuous memory and rational reflection. See: *World as Will and Representation,* vol. 2, 401. For Schopenhauer, a harmonious coordination of the intellect and the will are rare, as well.

48. *SE* XIV, 147.

49. Ibid., 144–57, 177–85; *SE* XVI, 295–96; *SE* XX, 91–110.

50. Schopenhauer, *World as Will and Representation,* vol. 2, 208–10.

51. Nietzsche, *Human, All Too Human,* 107–80; *Gay Science,* 37, 41; *Genealogy of Morals,* 84; *Will to Power,* 202–3.

52. Friedrich Nietzsche, *Ecce Homo,* trans. Walter Kaufmann (New York: Vintage Books, 1969), 252.

53. Schopenhauer: *World as Will and Representation,* vol. 2, 208. Nietzsche: *Human, All Too Human,* 179–80; *Gay Science,* 37, 41; *Will to Power,* 202–3; *Genealogy of Morals,* 58, 84; *Ecce Homo,* 252. Freud: *SE* V, 567; *SE* XIV, 144–57, 177–85; *SE* XVI, 295–96; *SE* XX, 91–110.

54. Schopenhauer: *World as Will and Representation,* vol. 2, 208–10. Nietzsche: *Human, All Too Human,* 179–80. Freud: *SE* XII, 103; *SE* XIV, 149, 181.

55. Schopenhauer: *World as Will and Representation,* vol. 2, 208–10. Nietzsche: *Human, All Too Human,* 179. Freud: *SE* VI, 147n2; *SE* IX, 60–61; *SE* XX, 93.

56. Schopenhauer: *World as Will and Representation,* vol. 2, 208. Nietzsche: *Human, All Too Human,* 179–80; *Gay Science,* 37, 41; *Will to Power,* 202–3; *Genealogy of Morals,* 58, 84; *Ecce Homo,* 252–53. Freud: *SE* V, 567; *SE* XIV, 144–57, 177–85; *SE* XVI, 295–96; *SE* XX, 91–110.

57. Schopenhauer, *World as Will and Representation,* vol. 2, 208.

58. Ibid., 209–10.

59. Nietzsche, *Human, All Too Human,* 179.

60. *SE* XIV, 148. See also: *SE* XX, 94.

61. *SE* IV, 149, 181.

62. Schopenhauer: *World as Will and Representation,* vol. 2, 208, 209–10. Nietzsche: *Human, All Too Human,* 179–80. Freud: *SE* XIV, 149, 181; *SE* XII, 103.

63. Nietzsche, *Genealogy of Morals,* 57.

64. Ibid., 58.

65. Ibid.

66. Nietzsche, *Human, All Too Human,* 224.

67. *SE* VI, 147n.2. Nietzsche's quote came from *Beyond Good and Evil,* 80. Strachey noted that "Freud had had his attention drawn to this saying by the 'Rat Man,' whose case history was published very shortly before the date of this footnote (1909d), *Standard Ed.,* 10, 184" (*SE* VI, 147n2).

68. *SE* VI, 4–7, 19–24, 39–45, 154–61.

69. Ibid., 19–20, 22, 40, 136–39, 142–48, 275.

70. Ibid., 154–61.

71. *SE* IX, 34.

72. *SE* III, 171–72; *SE* V, 461, 467–68, 556–57; *SE* XX, 111, 117; *SE* XXI, 153–54.

73. *SE* XIV, 153, 155.

74. *SE* XX, 221, 93. For all three, in fact, repression occurs to prevent feelings of unpleasure or anxiety from arising. Schopenhauer: *World as Will and Representation,* vol. 2, 208–10. Nietzsche: *Human, All Too Human,* 179. Freud: *SE* VI, 147n2; *SE* IX, 60–61; *SE* XX, 93.

75. Schopenhauer, *World as Will and Representation,* vol. 2, 217. See also: vol. 2, 207.

76. Schopenhauer, *World as Will and Representation,* vol. 2, 400.

77. *SE* XXII, 57. See also: *SE* XX, 29, 267.

78. *SE* XXIII, 242.

79. Schopenhauer, *World as Will and Representation,* vol. 2, 209.

80. This, we believe, is what inspired Freud to advocate in no uncertain terms the position of "scientific determinism." Here, however, it is important to consider again Freud's "antipathy" toward philosophical analysis; Freud never gave a clear and carefully worked out description of the issue of freedom and determinism within Freudian psychoanalysis. Yet his metapsychological theory and therapeutic practice presupposed and operated in relation to this issue in a highly significant fashion.

81. Arthur Schopenhauer, *Prize Essay on the Freedom of the Will,* ed. Günter Zöller, trans. Eric F. J. Payne (New York: Cambridge University Press, 1999).

82. Schopenhauer, *Prize Essay on the Freedom of the Will,* 86. Schopenhauer credited Kant with having this insight originally. See: Immanuel Kant, *Critique of Pure Reason,* trans. Norman Kemp Smith (New York: St Martin's Press, 1965), 474.

83. Schopenhauer, *World as Will and Representation,* vol. 2, 320–21.

84. Schopenhauer quoted Plato's *Meno:* "For even true opinions are not of much value until someone ties them together by reasoning from a cause" (*On the Fourfold Root of the Principle of Sufficient Reason,* trans. E. F. J. Payne [La Salle, Ill.: Open Court, 1974], 5).

85. Schopenhauer, *Fourfold Root of the Principle of Sufficient Reason,* 5–6.

86. Schopenhauer, *Prize Essay on the Freedom of the Will,* 53–54.

87. The existentialists reject the second implication and might accept various versions of the first. However, as we shall see, this in itself enabled Schopenhauer to offer Freud resources for a philosophical defense of his metapsychology.

88. *SE* VI, 242.

89. Schopenhauer, *Fourfold Root of the Principle of Sufficient Reason,* 53.

90. *SE* VI, 254. See also: *SE* VI, 46; *SE* IX, 105, 109; *SE* XI, 29, 38, 52, 137; *SE* XV, 28, 106–9; *SE* XVIII, 238, 240. Among those individual predecessors for this determinist conception of the human will, Schopenhauer cited Voltaire, Kant, Goethe, and Schelling (*Prize Essay on the Freedom of the Will,* ch. 4, 71–80), all of whom, as we have seen, exerted an immense influence on Freud.

91. Schopenhauer, *World as Will and Representation,* vol. 2, 115.

92. Schopenhauer, *Fourfold Root of the Principle of Sufficient Reason,* 53.

93. Schopenhauer, *World as Will and Representation,* vol. 2, 42.

94. Schopenhauer believed that the notion of "cause" had become too generalized in abstract thinking and was subsequently misused by "extending causality to the thing absolutely, and thus to its entire essence and existence and consequently to matter as well" (*World as Will and Representation,* vol. 2, 43; see vol. 2, 39, 41). Rather, causality was a relationship among changes or *states* of things (*World as Will and Representation,* vol. 2, 39).

95. Schopenhauer, *Fourfold Root of the Principle of Sufficient Reason,* 55. Nietzsche, too, held at times that causality is merely a matter of a succession of temporal states (*Unpublished Writings,* 149, 192; *Will to Power,* 270, 284; *Daybreak,* 77). Nietzsche wrote, "Suppose someone were thus to see through the boorish simplicity of this celebrated concept of 'free will' and put it out of his head altogether, I beg of him to carry his 'enlightenment' a step further, and also put out of his head the contrary of this monstrous conception of 'free will': I mean 'unfree will,' which amounts to a misuse of cause and effect. One should not wrongly reify 'cause' and 'effect,' as the natural scientists do . . . according to the prevailing mechanical doltishness" (*Beyond Good and Evil,* 29).

96. As we shall see later, the existential phenomenologists will strongly criticize (arguably, erroneously) Freud for holding a causally mechanistic theory of human nature, whereby one configuration of objects (or at least material processes) causally act upon another configuration of objects and hence have certain effects. It is not clear that this criticism has anything to do with Freud's position in the first place.

97. Schopenhauer, *World as Will and Representation,* vol. 2, 36.

98. Ibid., 43.

99. Ibid., 44–45.

100. Ibid. vol. 1, 272, 285.

101. Schopenhauer, *Prize Essay on the Freedom of the Will,* 3.

102. Ibid., 87.

103. Ibid., 86.

104. Schopenhauer, *World as Will and Representation,* vol. 1, 293.

105. Schopenhauer, *Prize Essay on the Freedom of the Will,* 12.

106. Schopenhauer, *Fourfold Root of the Principle of Sufficient Reason,* 72; *Prize Essay on the Freedom of the Will,* 27.

107. Schopenhauer, *Prize Essay on the Freedom of the Will*, 30. The instinctual drive for self-preservation obviously held enormous significance for Freud's theory as well. For Freud, it is the instinctual energies of the id that fuel all possible developments of experience—the action of motives, aspirations, fears, and so on.

108. Schopenhauer, *Fourfold Root of the Principle of Sufficient Reason*, 72.

109. Ibid., 70–71.

110. Schopenhauer, *World as Will and Representation*, vol. 1, 298.

111. Ibid.

112. Schopenhauer, *Prize Essay on the Freedom of the Will*, 5.

113. Ibid., 28–29.

114. Schopenhauer, *Fourfold Root of the Principle of Sufficient Reason*, 213–14.

115. Schopenhauer, *World as Will and Representation*, vol. 2, 248.

116. Schopenhauer, *Prize Essay on the Freedom of the Will*, 30.

117. Ibid., 31.

118. Schopenhauer noted that there remains here an ambiguity concerning the sources of human nature/action: "the borderline has not yet been clearly and incontestably drawn between what in those impulses is original and peculiar to human nature, and what is added by moral and religious education" (*Prize Essay on the Freedom of the Will*, 9). This involves the "ambiguity" (though on a different level) which the existential phenomenologists made so much of later.

119. Schopenhauer, *World as Will and Representation*, vol. 1, 301. Nietzsche commented on this aspect of Schopenhauer's "freedom": "Schopenhauer makes that striking distinction which is very much more justified than he really dared to admit to himself: 'the insight into the strict necessity of human actions is the boundary line which divides *philosophical* heads from *the others*.' This mighty insight . . ." (*Human, All Too Human*, 222).

120. Schopenhauer, *Prize Essay on the Freedom of the Will*, 87.

121. Ibid., 86.

122. Ibid., 88.

123. Ibid.

124. Schopenhauer, *World as Will and Representation*, vol. 1, 288; *Prize Essay on the Freedom of the Will*, 86.

125. Schopenhauer, *Prize Essay on the Freedom of the Will*, 89.

126. *SE* XXI, 95–96. See also: *SE* IV, 621. Freud spoke of "impulses which force their way through to consciousness . . . such impulses often meet with no psychical obstacles to their progress."

127. Schopenhauer, *Prize Essay on the Freedom of the Will*, 15.

128. Ibid.

129. Nietzsche also insisted that the notion of "freedom of the will" is a "primary," "fundamental" error (*Human, All Too Human*, 22, 306), and "free will . . . the dominant feeling from which we cannot get loose" (*Will to Power*, 352). See also: *Daybreak*, 77; *Twilight of the Idols*, 499; *Beyond Good and Evil*, 28–29; *Gay Science*, 285. Although Nietzsche shared many of Schopenhauer's concerns, and anticipated Freud's, the reasons behind his position transcend the scope of this book.

130. Schopenhauer, *Fourfold Root of the Principle of Sufficient Reason*, 72.

131. Schopenhauer, *World as Will and Representation*, vol. 1, 290. See also: vol. 1, 115.

132. Schopenhauer, *Prize Essay on the Freedom of the Will*, 36.

133. Schopenhauer, *World as Will and Representation*, vol. 1, 115.

134. Schopenhauer, *Prize Essay on the Freedom of the Will*, 43.

135. Ibid., 15.

136. Nietzsche agreed: "*On the 'realm of freedom.'*—We can think many, many more things than we can do or experience" (*Daybreak*, 77).

137. *SE* XVII, 236.

138. *SE* VI, 253–54.

139. Schopenhauer, *Parerga and Paralipomena*, vol. 1, 124. See also: vol. 2, 234.

140. Schopenhauer, *Parerga and Paralipomena*, vol. 1, 454.

141. Ibid., vol. 2, 226–27. Note that this is what Freudian psychoanalysis does. It merely makes known the motives behind what we have done, do, and will do.

142. *SE* XIX, 133.

143. Schopenhauer, *Parerga and Paralipomena*, vol. 2, 236.

144. Schopenhauer, *Prize Essay on the Freedom of the Will*, 35.

145. Ibid., 34.

146. Schopenhauer, *Fourfold Root of the Principle of Sufficient Reason*, 70. The important aspect of the above for Freud would be Schopenhauer's recognition that the motive's effectiveness bears no relation to how long it lasts, nor how close the subject is to it (space or time).

147. Schopenhauer, *Prize Essay on the Freedom of the Will*, 36.

148. Ibid., 32.

149. Ibid., 36.

150. Schopenhauer, *World as Will and Representation*, vol. 1, 298.

151. Ibid.

152. Schopenhauer, *Prize Essay on the Freedom of the Will*, 39.

153. Schopenhauer, *Parerga and Paralipomena*, vol. 2, 593.

154. Schopenhauer, *Fourfold Root of the Principle of Sufficient Reason*, 72.

155. Ibid., 212–13.

156. Schopenhauer, *Prize Essay on the Freedom of the Will*, 10.

157. Schopenhauer, *World as Will and Representation*, vol. 1, 301.

158. Ibid., 298.

Chapter 9

Epigraph: Edmund Husserl, *The Crisis of European Sciences and Transcendental Phenomenology: An Introduction to Phenomenological Philosophy*, trans. David Carr (Evanston: Northwestern University Press, 1970), 392.

1. Ricoeur famously argued, of course, that not only are the two *not* identical, but *they fail to intersect at all*: "[. . .] phenomenology is not psychoanalysis. However slight the separation, it is not nil, and phenomenology does not bridge the gap . . . [Freud's] type of archeological excavation has no parallel in phenomenology" (*Freud and Philosophy: An Essay on Interpretation*, trans. Denis Savage [New Haven: Yale University Press, 1970], 390). We shall argue that Ricoeur is mistaken in his claim that they do not intersect at all.

2. The Helmholtz school was an important factor in Freud's theoretical development, especially through Brücke, but it is beyond the scope of our discussion to include it here.

3. It is natural to wonder what Brentano, who was a toddler when Herbart died, thought of Herbart's philosophy. Freud offered a brief account from his student days: "He utterly condemned [Herbart's] a priori constructions in psychology, thought it unforgivable that Herbart had never deigned to consult experience or experiment to check whether these agreed with his arbitrary assumptions . . ." (Walter Boehlich, ed., *The Letters of Sigmund Freud to Eduard Silberstein,* trans. Arnold Pomerans [Cambridge, Mass.: Belknap Press, 1990], 102).

4. G. Lindner, *Lehrbuch der empirischen Psychologie nach genetischer Methode* (Wien: Carl Gerold's Sohn, 1858), Preface.

5. *SE* XIV, 162.

6. Ernest Jones, *The Life and Works of Sigmund Freud,* vol. 1 (New York: Basic Books, 1955), 372–76.

7. Boehlich, *Sigmund Freud to Eduard Silberstein,* 102.

8. G. Hartenstein, ed., *Johann Friedrich Herbart's Sämmtliche Werke,* vol. 2 (Leipzig: L. Voss, 1850–52), 19.

9. We should be careful to note that Herbart derived his ideas about the dynamics of an unconscious and the threshold of consciousness from Leibniz.

10. *SE* XIV, 143.

11. Lindner, *Lehrbuch der empirischen Psychologie,* 63.

12. Upon reading Schopenhauer's *The World as Will and Idea* in 1920 (this preceded Herbart's own major work by four years), Herbart wrote: "Mr. Schopenhauer belongs to the class of people who, taking the Kantian philosophy as their starting-point, occupy themselves with trying to improve it according to their own mind . . . Schopenhauer the clearest, the cleverest and the most approachable" (J. F. Herbart, review [1820] reprinted in Volker Spierling, ed., *Materialien zu Schopenhauer's 'Die Welt als Wille und Vorstellung'* [Suhrkamp, Ffm., 1984], 109). Herbart was irrefragably referring to Schopenhauer's assertion that "the subject knows itself only as a willer, not as a knower" (Arthur Schopenhauer, *On the Fourfold Root of the Principle of Sufficient Reason,* trans. E. F. J. Payne [La Salle, Ill.: Open Court, 1974], 208). As a student of Fichte's, Herbart emphasized that in his *Sittenlehre,* Fichte had argued directly for the conclusion that it is only as willing that I "find myself" (Hartenstein, *Herbart's Sämmtliche Werke,* vol. 4, 18–22). In his review of 1820, Herbart used this passage in Fichte to support his assessment of Schopenhauer as a highly unoriginal thinker. In the second volume of the *The World as Will and Representation,* Schopenhauer counter-blasted with: "There is more to be learnt from each page of David Hume than from the collected philosophical works of Hegel, Herbart, and Schleiermacher taken together" (trans. E. F. J. Payne [New York: Dover, 1966], 582). In *Parerga and Paralipomena,* vol. 1, Schopenhauer denied that Herbart was even a "genuine philosopher" as included within "the generic characteristic of the philosophical works of the nineteenth century is that of writing without really having something to say" (trans. E. F. J. Payne [Oxford: Clarendon Press, 1974], 163; see vol. 1, 171, 176, 180, 182). What were the reasons for Schopenhauer's antipathy? Other than the fact that it was Herbart, and not Schopenhauer, who was appointed to fill Kant's vacated chair at Königsberg, there

is also the following doctrinal difference: for Herbart, the feelings, the desires, and the will have their origin in the presentation; for Schopenhauer, it was precisely the reverse. *All of this is particularly interesting, given that we will argue that had not these polemics occurred at this time, and had a rapprochement—if not dialectical synthesis—occurred, it may have preempted the subsequent mutual disregard by Husserl and Freud of one another's work. A missed opportunity, indeed!*

13. *SE* XIV, 15.

14. Johann Herbart, *A Text-book in Psychology*, trans. M. K. Smith (New York: Appleton, 1891), sec. 4, 8–11.

15. Edmund Husserl, *Analyses Concerning Passive and Active Synthesis: Lectures on Transcendental Logic*, trans. Anthony J. Steinbock (Dordrecht: Kluwer Academic Publishers, 2001).

16. Herbart, *Text-book in Psychology*, sec. 10. This was quoted by Gustaf Lindner, in his *Lehrbuch der empirischen Psychologie.*

17. Herbart, *Text-book in Psychology*, sec. 11.

18. Herbart, *Text-book in Psychology*, sec. 127. Leibniz originated this idea as well.

19. Edmund Husserl, *Ideas Pertaining to a Pure Phenomenology and to a Phenomenological Philosophy, Second Book: Studies in the Phenomenology of Constitution*, trans. Richard Rojcewicz and André Schuwer (Dordrecht: Kluwer Academic Publishers, 1989), 115. (This book will be cited in short-title as *Ideas II.*)

20. Husserl, *Analyses Concerning Passive and Active Synthesis*, 635.

21. The latter idea came directly from Leibniz.

22. Hartenstein, *Herbart's Sämmtliche Werke*, vol. 5, 20.

23. Boehlich, *Sigmund Freud to Eduard Silberstein*, 95.

24. Linda L. McAlister, *The Philosophy of Brentano* (London: Duckworth, 1976), 47.

25. Although Brentano's influence on Husserl is widely known—intentionality, descriptive versus genetic psychology, and so on—his impact on Freud is not at all apparent because Freud clearly developed his psychoanalysis in inconsistent directions from Brentano. Hence, we will concentrate our discussion of Brentano's influence primarily on Freud.

26. Boehlich, *Sigmund Freud to Eduard Silberstein*, 71.

27. Ibid., 95.

28. Brentano's courses were the only formal training in philosophy Freud ever received.

29. Boehlich, *Sigmund Freud to Eduard Silberstein*, 104.

30. Ibid., 102.

31. Franz Brentano, *Psychology from an Empirical Standpoint*, ed. Oskar Kraus, trans. Antos C. Rancurello, D. B. Terrell, and Linda L. McAlister (New York: Humanities Press, 1973), 66.

32. Brentano, *Psychology from an Empirical Standpoint*, 64. This helps account for the fact that Brentano did not even deign to consider Schopenhauer's approach to the unconscious, given its intrinsically metaphysical characteristics.

33. Freud also took over Brentano's notion of "intentionality," and modified it for his own purposes—namely, the id forms an image of an object that will

gratify its wish (the primary process). Perception was understood as an active process fueled by psychic energy ("cathexis").

34. Interestingly, Brentano listed four different ways in which some philosophers/psychologists had tried to prove the existence of the unconscious (*Psychology from an Empirical Standpoint*, 105), yet none of them included Schopenhauer's approach!

35. Brentano, *Psychology from an Empirical Standpoint*, 102. It is important to note that Brentano was not taking himself to be merely defining mental life as consciousness, but rather as describing "the natural boundaries of a homogeneous class [of phenomena]" (*Psychology from an Empirical Standpoint*, 101). However, for Freud, Brentano was undoubtedly another philosopher who fell prey to the convention of simply equating consciousness with mental life.

36. Brentano, *Psychology from an Empirical Standpoint*, 102–3n.

37. Ibid., 137.

38. Here is the historical origin of Husserl's later description of the unconscious as the zero-point of affective force.

39. Brentano, *Psychology from an Empirical Standpoint*, 54, 63.

40. Henry Maudsley, *Physiology and Pathology of the Mind* (New York: Appleton, 1871), 7.

41. Brentano, *Psychology from an Empirical Standpoint*, 56.

42. Maudsley, *Physiology and Pathology of the Mind*, 22ff.; in Brentano, *Psychology from an Empirical Standpoint*, 56.

43. Brentano, *Psychology from an Empirical Standpoint*, 57.

44. *SE* V, 612n.

45. Freud quoted from Maudsley, *Physiology and Pathology of the Mind*, 15.

46. Brentano, *Psychology from an Empirical Standpoint*, 58.

47. Ibid.

48. Ibid., 57.

49. Ibid., 7, 44.

50. Ibid., 137.

Chapter 10

Epigraphs: Edmund Husserl, *The Crisis of European Sciences and Transcendental Phenomenology: An Introduction to Phenomenological Philosophy*, trans. David Carr (Evanston: Northwestern University Press, 1970), 170; Husserl, *Crisis of European Sciences and Transcendental Phenomenology*, 394–95.

1. Indeed, they even lived within the same city, Vienna, early in their careers (1874–76).

2. Alfred Adler attended Husserl's lectures of 1920 to 1926.

3. We will consider these more specifically when we consider the extent to which Husserlian phenomenology and Freudian psychoanalysis converge.

4. Paul Ricoeur, *Freud and Philosophy: An Essay on Interpretation*, trans. Denis Savage (New Haven: Yale University Press, 1970), 376. However, Ricoeur contin-

ued on to say: "It is well to mention at the very start that this attempt is also bound to fail . . . it is a true approximation, one that comes very close to the Freudian unconscious, but misses it in the end." We shall argue that the two sets of analyses rather than resembling one another, in the end, converge to a point of overlapping intersection, through which each can be useful, as supplementary, to the other.

5. The term "phenomenology" is employed in Freud's final theoretical work, *An Outline of Psychoanalysis*, in a way irrelevant to Husserl's project (*SE* XXIII, 156). Freud's usage bears no discernible relation to Husserl's and merely states that "phenomenology" is the recording of normal and abnormal phenomena which we observe.

6. Edmund Husserl, *Logical Investigations*, vol. 1, trans. J. N. Findlay (New York: The Humanities Press, 1976), 413. As early as 1900 in his *Logical Investigations*, Husserl said that if we relegate intuitions "to the unnoticed or the unconscious, one merely adds to one's malaise, since one is sacrificing the self-evidently given intention in favour of what is unobservable" (vol. 1, 412).

7. Husserl, *Crisis of European Sciences and Transcendental Phenomenology*, 170.

8. Binswanger had conducted his internship under Eugen Bleuler, one of the first psychiatrists to respond to Freud's work, and worked under Bleuler's assistant, Carl Jung. It was Carl Jung who first introduced Binswanger to Freud, initiating a friendship that lasted a lifetime.

9. Husserl, *Crisis of European Sciences and Transcendental Phenomenology*, 315.

10. Ibid., 60–62.

11. Ibid., 67.

12. Ibid., 211–12.

13. Ibid., 220.

14. Ibid., 327.

15. Here, of course, we see Husserl sharing one of the most common themes held among the more existentially inclined phenomenologists—namely, that the human psyche is not a thing.

16. *SE* XXII, 159.

17. Ibid., 181.

18. In order to avoid any misunderstandings, given the misleading connotative features of the word "spirit," in this context we prefer to translate the German *Geist* as "mind," as opposed to "spirit," as the translators of *Ideas II* have done. Please note: wherever Rojcewicz and Schuwer have translated *Geist* as "spirit," our citations will read "mind."

19. Husserl, *Crisis of European Sciences and Transcendental Phenomenology*, 337.

20. Ibid., 389. Compare: *SE* XXII, 158–82.

21. Husserl, *Crisis of European Sciences and Transcendental Phenomenology*, 214.

22. Ibid., 219

23. The fundamental incompatibility of Freud's metapsychology and his therapeutic approach, was taken up by Medard Boss—a colleague and analysand of Freud's—as well. Boss claimed there were actually two "Freuds"—Freud the scientist, and Freud the humanist. Boss rejected Freud's scientism, while incorporating his therapeutic humanistic concerns by resituating Freudian therapy within a Heideggerian framework. See chapter 17 for further elaboration on this point.

24. Husserl, *Crisis of European Sciences and Transcendental Phenomenology*, 188–89.

25. Ibid., 237.

26. Of course, it could simply have been that each had formed a habitual way of seeing the other's work as irrelevant to his own project, for the reasons given above, and hence continued to disregard that work.

27. It is understandable, the reservations Freud might have had toward Husserl's static analysis as focusing on consciousness—but why ignore his genetical analysis?

28. It is unclear that Freud clearly understood what the term "dualism" meant philosophically, or the philosophical implications/ramifications it entailed for the development of metaphysical problems. He may simply have been—and probably was—oblivious to such philosophical concerns.

29. *SE* XIX, 27.

30. *SE* XXIII, 151, 158.

31. *SE* XIV, 78.

32. *SE* XIX, 23.

33. Freud, at times, tergiversated as to which attribute to emphasize; sometimes describing instincts as "psychical representatives" (*SE* XIV, 121–22), at times as organic forces (*SE* XIV, 177; *SE* XX, 73, 96, 106, 221), and at other times as both (*SE* VII, 168; *SE* XIV, 111–12).

34. See chapters 17 and 18.

35. Edmund Husserl, *Ideas Pertaining to a Pure Phenomenology and to a Phenomenological Philosophy, Second Book: Studies in the Phenomenology of Constitution*, trans. Richard Rojcewicz and André Schuwer (Dordrecht: Kluwer Academic Publishers, 1989), 151. (This book will be cited in short-title as *Ideas II*.)

36. Husserl, *Crisis of European Sciences and Transcendental Phenomenology*, 324.

37. Husserl, *Ideas II*, 292.

38. Ibid., 350.

39. Edmund Husserl, *Ideas: General Introduction to Pure Phenomenology*, trans. W. R. Boyce Gibson (New York: Collier Books, 1972), 150. (This book will be cited in short-title as *Ideas I*.)

40. Husserl, *Crisis of European Sciences and Transcendental Phenomenology*, 324.

41. Edmund Husserl, *Analyses Concerning Passive and Active Synthesis: Lectures on Transcendental Logic*, trans. Anthony J. Steinbock (Dordrecht: Kluwer Academic Publishers, 2001), 584–85. See also: *Crisis of European Sciences and Transcendental Phenomenology*, 331.

42. Recall as well that one of the main reasons Freud began his research into madness was his recognition that bodily symptoms could have mental "causes."

43. Husserl, *Ideas II*, 151, 142. See also: *Crisis of European Sciences and Transcendental Phenomenology*, 106–7.

44. Husserl, *Ideas I*, 149, 150. See also: *Analysis Concerning Passive and Active Synthesis*, 544.

45. Husserl, *Ideas II*, 160.

46. *SE* XXIII, 198; *SE* I, 332–5; *SE* V, 588.

47. Husserl, *Analyses Concerning Passive and Active Synthesis*, 198.

48. Husserl, *Ideas II*, 142.

49. Ibid., 233.

50. Ibid., 267.

51. Ibid., 292.

52. Ibid., 289.

53. Husserl, *Analyses Concerning Passive and Active Synthesis*, 19.

54. Husserl, *Crisis of European Sciences and Transcendental Phenomenology*, 346.

55. *SE* XIV, 121–22.

56. Husserl, *Ideas II*, 159.

57. Ibid., 267–68.

58. Ibid., 289.

59. Ibid., 294–316.

60. Husserl, *Crisis of European Sciences and Transcendental Phenomenology*, 108.

61. Husserl, *Ideas II*, 308.

62. Husserl, *Crisis of European Sciences and Transcendental Phenomenology*, 237.

63. Husserl, *Analyses Concerning Passive and Active Synthesis*, 219.

64. Husserl, *Ideas II*, 142.

65. Ibid., 350.

66. Husserl, *Analyses Concerning Passive and Active Synthesis*, 151–53.

67. Edmund Husserl, *Formal and Transcendental Logic*, trans. Dorion Cairns (The Hague: Martinus Nijhoff, 1969), 316.

68. Although Freud, of course, offered different kinds of examples—parapraxes, dreams, and so on.

69. *SE* XIV, 166.

70. *SE* XIV, 167.

71. *SE* XIII, 260.

72. See: Ricoeur, *Freud and Philosophy*, 419–58, where he applied the term to Freud's investigations.

73. *SE* XIV, 63.

74. Husserl, *Analyses Concerning Passive and Active Synthesis*, 9.

75. Ibid., 13.

76. See Goethe, Schelling, and so on, in chapter 5. It is also interesting to recall on this point that Schopenhauer had spoken of it as "a subterranean passage."

77. Husserl, *Analyses Concerning Passive and Active Synthesis*, 249. Also: 201.

78. Ibid., 221.

79. Ibid., 170.

80. Ibid., 201.

81. Ibid., 270.

82. Husserl, *Crisis of European Sciences and Transcendental Phenomenology*, 188.

83. Husserl, *Analyses Concerning Passive and Active Synthesis*, 27.

84. Ibid., 32.

85. Ibid., 198.

86. Ibid., 515–16.

87. Ibid., 163.

88. Husserl, *Formal and Transcendental Logic*, 316.

89. Husserl, *Logical Investigations:* "the supposed unconscious events are in any case wholly irrelevant for pure phenomenology" (vol. 1, 413).

90. Edmund Husserl, *Cartesian Meditations: An Introduction to Phenomenology*, trans. Dorion Cairns (The Hague: Martinus Nijhoff, 1969).

91. Husserl, *Cartesian Meditations*, 23.

92. Edmund Husserl, *Edmund Husserl's Experience and Judgment: Investigations in a Genealogy of Logic*, ed. Ludwig Landgrebe, trans. James S. Churchill and Karl Ameriks (Evanston: Northwestern University Press, 1973), 279. See also: Husserl, *Formal and Transcendental Logic*, 319.

93. Husserl, *Analyses Concerning Passive and Active Synthesis*, 217.

94. Husserl, *Formal and Transcendental Logic*, 319.

95. Ibid.

96. Husserl, *Analyses Concerning Passive and Active Synthesis*, 244–45.

97. Husserl, *Ideas II*, 350.

98. Husserl, *Analyses Concerning Passive and Active Synthesis*, 476.

99. *SE* XIX, 230–31.

100. Ibid., 228.

101. Husserl, *Formal and Transcendental Logic*, 319.

102. Husserl, *Analyses Concerning Passive and Active Synthesis*, 217–18. Also: 200.

103. Ibid., 219.

104. *SE* XXII, 73–74.

105. Husserl, *Experience and Judgment*, 197.

106. Ibid., 279.

107. *SE* V, 577.

108. Husserl, *Ideas II*, 350.

109. Husserl, *Cartesian Meditations*, 75.

110. Ibid., 78.

111. Husserl, *Ideas II*, 350.

112. *SE* XIX, 24; *SE* XVIII, 19–20; *SE* XXII, 69–71, 75, 78–9.

113. Husserl, *Ideas II*, 350.

114. Husserl, *Cartesian Meditations*, 79.

115. *SE* XIV, 166.

116. Husserl, *Analyses Concerning Passive and Active Synthesis*, 195.

117. Ibid., 90–91.

118. Ibid., 197.

119. Ibid. Schopenhauer spoke of a "conflict of motives" in much the same way earlier. See, for example: Arthur Schopenhauer, *Prize Essay on the Freedom of the Will*, ed. Günter Zöller, trans. Eric F. J. Payne (New York: Cambridge University Press, 1999), 32.

120. Schopenhauer, *Prize Essay on the Freedom of the Will*, 28–29.

121. Husserl, *Ideas II*, 199.

122. Husserl, *Analyses Concerning Passive and Active Synthesis*, 282.

123. Ibid., 280.

124. We cannot help but note that both Schopenhauer and Freud used precisely the same idea. See chapter 8.

125. *SE* XIII, 262.

126. Husserl, *Analyses Concerning Passive and Active Synthesis*, 210.

127. Husserl, *Ideas II*, 349.

128. Husserl, *Analyses Concerning Passive and Active Synthesis*, 277.

129. Ibid., 517.

130. Husserl, *Formal and Transcendental Logic*, 320.

131. Ibid., 321.

132. *SE* XIV, 173; *SE* XXIII, 162.

133. *SE* XIII, 260.

134. Ricoeur claimed, we believe mistakenly: "The unconscious of phenomenology is the preconscious of psychoanalysis" (*Freud and Philosophy*, 392). While it is true that Husserl developed a phenomenological elaboration of those areas of mental life in his own concepts of the prethematic—namely, what is able to become conscious in a further act of thematizing or recollection—which Freud called the preconscious, Husserl's conception of the unconscious was much more than this.

135. Husserl, *Analyses Concerning Passive and Active Synthesis*, 70.

136. Ibid., 73.

137. Ibid., 515.

138. Ibid., 94–95.

139. Ibid., 197.

140. Ibid., 201.

141. Ibid., 518–19.

142. Husserl, *Experience and Judgment*, 279.

143. Ibid., 280.

144. Ibid., 281.

145. Husserl, *Formal and Transcendental Logic*, 322; *SE* VI, 2–7.

146. Husserl, *Analyses Concerning Passive and Active Synthesis*, 167.

147. *SE* III, 198.

148. *SE* X, 137.

149. Husserl, *Analyses Concerning Passive and Active Synthesis*, 168.

150. *SE* VI, 2–5.

151. Husserl, *Experience and Judgment*, 178.

152. *SE* XIV, 187.

153. *SE* V, 43–52.

154. Husserl, *Analyses Concerning Passive and Active Synthesis*, 250–51.

155. *SE* VI.

156. Husserl, *Experience and Judgment*, 179.

157. Husserl, *Analyses Concerning Passive and Active Synthesis*, 476.

158. Ibid., 249.

159. *SE* XIV, 166–67.

160. Ricoeur, *Freud and Philosophy*, 393.

161. *SE* XIV, 187.

162. This is what would make the two approaches complementary rather than antithetical—their concerns overlap and merge without being identical.

163. Husserl, *Ideas II*, 350.

Chapter 11

Epigraphs: Martin Heidegger, *Zollikon Seminars*, trans. Franz Mayr and Richard Askay (Evanston: Northwestern University Press, 2001), 102; *SE* XX, 96.

1. To be sure, there were rudimentary differences (which will become progressively apparent as we proceed) between Freud and Heidegger, given their fundamentally discrepant worldviews and methodological approaches. Even so, these similarities should give reason for pause. The irresistible question arises as to why such influential giants in the history of ideas virtually ignored the writings and thoughts of the other throughout their careers. Freud completely ignored Heidegger, and Heidegger had not read Freud nor written/spoken about him until relatively late in his philosophical career—he was fifty-eight years of age. (See Medard Boss's account of Heidegger's initial reading of and reaction to Freud in the following section.)

2. Freud had been a student of Brentano's: *SE* VIII, 31n6, 237–38; Herbert Spiegelberg, *Phenomenology in Psychology and Psychiatry: A Historical Introduction* (Evanston: Northwestern University Press, 1972), 128. Heidegger referred to Brentano's work as the "lightning bolt" in his own dissertation of being: Spiegelberg, *Phenomenology in Psychology and Psychiatry*, 202. See also: Martin Heidegger, *Being and Time*, trans. John Macquarrie and Edward Robinson (New York: Harper & Row, 1962), 258.

3. These include: *Civilization and Its Discontents* (1930), *SE* XXI; *New Introductory Lectures on Psychoanalysis* (1933), *SE* XXII; *Moses and Monotheism* (1939), *SE* XXIII; *An Outline of Psycho-analysis* (1940), *SE* XXIII. Freud composed dozens of other essays after 1927.

4. Spiegelberg mistakenly stated that Freud and Boss never met (*Phenomenology in Psychology and Psychiatry*, 334). Boss recounted many of his experiences as an analysand of Freud's, during a visit with the authors of this book in 1989. He further stated that Freud was very generous and gave him money for food, since he was at that time a penurious student.

5. Medard Boss, "Martin Heidegger's Zollikon Seminars," in *Heidegger and Psychology: A Special Issue from the Review of Existential Psychology and Psychiatry*, ed. Keith Hoeller (Seattle: 1988), 9.

6. Heidegger wrote, "any science is grounded in a tacit ontology of its object domain" (*Zollikon Seminars*, 122).

7. *SE* XXII, 171.

8. Heidegger, *Zollikon Seminars*, 94.

9. Ibid., 274.

10. Heinrich Wiegand Petzet, *Encounters and Dialogues with Martin Heidegger, 1929–1976*, trans. Parvis Emad and Kenneth Maly (Chicago: The University of Chicago Press, 1993), 49.

11. Heidegger, *Zollikon Seminars*, 18.

12. Ibid.

13. Ibid., 94.

14. Martin Heidegger, "On the Essence of Truth," in *Martin Heidegger: Basic Writings*, ed. David Farrell Krell (New York: Harper & Row, 1977), 130.

15. Heidegger, *Zollikon Seminars*, 153.

16. Ibid., 27.

17. It is interesting to note that, historically speaking, Freud in essence asked the same of his fellow scientists with the introduction of the unconscious. Given this, it is somewhat odd that Heidegger was not more sympathetic to Freud's plight.

18. Heidegger's philosophy can most succinctly be summarized in the phrase "hermeneutical phenomenological ontology." First, and foremost it is "ontological" because it asks the question: What does it mean to be as *Dasein?*, rather than What is man?, which is an inquiry about objects. It is "phenomenological" because it offers a descriptive analysis of the universal and necessary structures for the possibility of any meaningful human experience (for example, what must be presupposed in order to engage in any inquiry in the first place). By means of it, we move from an implicit everyday understanding of what it means to be as a human being to an explicit, ontological understanding of what it means to be. While doing so, distortions and concealments are stripped away. It is "hermeneutical" because it understands itself, methodologically, as an interpretive process of human experience as it occurs within an overall historical flow and context. It is concerned with the interpretation of the being who interprets the world. As such, concrete everyday human experience is the text to be interpreted.

19. In a highly significant passage in "The Ways of Psycho-analytic Therapy," Freud wrote, "we cannot accept . . . that psycho-analysis should place itself in the service of a particular philosophical outlook on the world and should urge this upon the patient to ennoble him. I would say that this is only tyranny" (*SE* XVII, 165–66). In addition, Freud observed that an individual often permits him-/herself to be absorbed in an anonymous group mentality. When this occurs one willingly forfeits his/her distinctness, freedom and its concomitant responsibility (*SE* XVIII, 74, 86–90). Heidegger would also point out that because Freud so rigidly adhered to the scientific Weltanschauung, he in effect, was urging a particular philosophical outlook on his colleagues and patients. According to Heidegger, this was just another form of tyranny.

20. Heidegger, *Zollikon Seminars*, 207.

21. Indeed, most of the Neo-Kantian theories espoused ideas that would seem to be quite contrary to Freudian metapsychology. For example, the Neo-Kantians had the general tendency to separate the human sciences from the natural sciences—there was a growing dissatisfaction with the epistemic authority of the natural sciences—and to conceive of the noumenal world as a limiting concept rather than an existent, albeit unknowable realm. Hence, the phenomenal world was conceived as reality, which was constructed by the mind.

22. Immanuel Kant, *Critique of Pure Reason*, trans. Norman Kemp Smith (New York: St Martin's Press, 1965), A 113.

23. Heidegger, *Zollikon Seminars*, 99.

24. Ibid., 128.

25. Kant, *Critique of Pure Reason*, A 113.

26. Immanuel Kant, *Prolegomena to Any Future Metaphysics*, trans. Lewis White Beck (New York: The Bobbs-Merrill Company, 1950), para. 14.

27. Heidegger, *Zollikon Seminars*, 208.

28. Ibid., 174.

29. *SE* V, 615–16.

30. *SE* XIV, 171. See also: *SE* V, 615–16.

31. Heidegger, *Zollikon Seminars*, 3–4.

32. Ibid., 26.

33. Ibid., 4. See also: Martin Heidegger, *Being and Time*, trans. John Macquarrie and Edward Robinson (New York: Harper and Row, 1962), 27n. It should be noted that Heidegger almost always used the term *Dasein*, instead of "human being," in order to emphasize the kind of *being* that belongs to human being as the situated awareness of what it means to be as a human being. Dasein is discussed further in this chapter, in the section titled, "Dasein as the proper point of departure for ontological inquiry."

34. Freudian psychoanalysis is a classic example of such a mode of inquiry, and as such, Heidegger would regard it as a form of *philosophical anthropology*, asking the question: what is man? See: Heidegger, *Zollikon Seminars*, 122, 125–26.

35. Heidegger, *Being and Time*, 75.

36. *SE* XVIII, 36.

37. Ibid., 38.

38. Ibid., 62. See also: *SE* XIX, 40–47; *SE* XXII, 107; *SE* XXIII, ch. 2.

39. *SE* XIV, 289–90.

40. Heidegger, *Being and Time*, 294.

41. Ibid., 295.

42. Ibid., 296.

43. *SE* XIV, 299.

44. Heidegger, *Being and Time*, 303.

45. *SE* XIV, 290.

46. Heidegger, *Being and Time*, 294.

47. Heidegger neglected the fact that Freud saw death (Thanatos) as one of the primary instincts of will—death is more than what Heidegger claimed for Freud. Thus, Freud would say that death is one of the primary motivating forces, though unconscious, and hence repressed.

48. Heidegger, *Being and Time*, 296–97.

49. Ibid., 291.

50. Ibid., 289.

51. Once again, for Freud this would be to say that on a conscious level, this is how people tend to conceive death; but on the unconscious level, death is much more.

52. Heidegger, *Being and Time*, 292.

53. For Freud, this would be a grounding in his metapsychology.

54. Heidegger, *Basic Writings*, 386. Indeed, Heidegger wrote that the clearing, "the opening as such as it prevails through Being, through presence, remains unthought in philosophy."

55. Heidegger, *Basic Writings*, 384, 386.

56. Heidegger, *Zollikon Seminars*, 204–5.

57. Heidegger explicitly emphasized in *Being and Time* that the ontological and ontical levels are never understood as separate but as indissolubly rooted in one another (28–35).

58. Heidegger, *Zollikon Seminars*, 204.

59. Heidegger, *Basic Writings*, 387.
60. Heidegger, *Zollikon Seminars*, 13.
61. Heidegger, *Basic Writings*, 385.
62. Ibid.
63. Heidegger, *Zollikon Seminars*, 6.
64. Heidegger, *Basic Writings*, 387.
65. Heidegger, *Zollikon Seminars*, 4. Professor Franz Mayr is to be credited with this formulation.
66. This resembles the traditional Native American belief that humans do not own the land, but rather are the caretakers of it.
67. Heidegger, *Zollikon Seminars*, 4.
68. Ibid. The clear articulation of this distinction is attributable to Professor Franz Mayr.
69. Heidegger, *Zollikon Seminars*, 206.
70. Ibid., 217.
71. Ibid., 231.
72. Ibid., 232.
73. Ibid., 216–17.
74. Ibid., 232.
75. Ibid., 144.
76. Ibid., 159.
77. Ibid., 160.
78. Ibid., 231. It is important to note that even though the above seems to be Heidegger's most consistent position, there were times when Heidegger emphasized Dasein's clearedness over the clearing. In *Being and Time*, Dasein's clearedness is emphasized. "To say that Dasein is 'illuminated' means that as Being-in-the-world, Dasein is cleared in itself in such a way that it is itself the clearing. Dasein is its disclosedness" (133). "Only by this clearedness is any illuminating or illumining, any awareness, 'seeing,' or having of something, made possible" (350–51; see 321).
79. Heidegger, *Zollikon Seminars*, 183.
80. Heidegger, *Basic Writings*, 132.
81. Heidegger, *Zollikon Seminars*, 182–83.
82. Furthermore, one might ask: why are some able to see this mystery while others are not? That is part of the mystery itself (on one level).
83. Heidegger, *Basic Writings*, 135.
84. Ibid., 136.
85. *SE* XXII, 159.

Chapter 12

Epigraphs: Martin Heidegger, *Zollikon Seminars*, trans. Franz Mayr and Richard Askay (Evanston: Northwestern University Press, 2001), 200; *SE* XXII, 160.
1. Heidegger, *Zollikon Seminars*, 20.

2. Heidegger, *Zollikon Seminars,* 186.

3. Ibid., 6–7.

4. Ibid., 80, 113.

5. Ibid., 7–8.

6. Ibid., 208.

7. Ibid., 113.

8. Ibid., 207–8.

9. Ibid., 254.

10. Ibid., 169.

11. Ibid., 186–87.

12. Ibid., 20–24.

13. Ibid., 199–202.

14. Actually, as we shall see, Freud conceived humans as organic biological processes, not mechanical ones at all.

15. Heidegger, *Zollikon Seminars,* 20.

16. *SE* XXII, 159.

17. Heidegger, *Zollikon Seminars,* 20.

18. Ibid., 186–87.

19. Ibid., 80.

20. It is this line of thinking, in fact, which led to Skinnerian Behaviorism, for example.

21. Heidegger, *Zollikon Seminars,* 170.

22. Ibid., 232.

23. Ibid., 170.

24. Ibid., 233.

25. Ibid., 79–80, 113–14.

26. Ibid., 113–14.

27. Heidegger was inaccurate on this point. Freud discussed why he gave up hypnosis and the power of suggestion in favor of analysis, using the analogy of painting versus sculpture (see chapter 2, on psychotherapeutic practice). More akin to sculpture, Freud wrote, "Analytic therapy, on the other hand, does not seek to add or to introduce anything new, but to take away something, to bring out something, and to this end concerns itself with the genesis of the morbid symptoms and the psychical context of the pathogenic idea which it seeks to remove" (*SE* VII, 261).

28. Heidegger, *Zollikon Seminars,* 113–14.

29. Freud could be said, in fact, to have done precisely this.

30. Heidegger, *Zollikon Seminars,* 6–7.

31. Ibid., 213.

32. Ibid., 25–26.

33. Ibid., 7.

34. Ibid., 155.

35. Ibid., 81.

36. Ibid., 207–8.

37. Ibid., 80.

38. Ibid., 207–8.

39. Ibid., 7.

40. Ibid., 5.

41. Ibid., 207–8.

42. Martin Heidegger, *Martin Heidegger: Basic Writings,* ed. David Farrell Krell (New York: Harper & Row, 1977), 128.

43. Heidegger, *Zollikon Seminars,* 217. See also: *Basic Writings,* 126–30.

44. Heidegger, *Zollikon Seminars,* 217.

45. Heidegger, *Basic Writings,* 386.

46. Ibid., 128.

47. Ibid., 128.

48. Ibid., 127.

49. Ibid., 127–30. See also: *Zollikon Seminars,* 216–20, 232–33.

50. Heidegger, *Zollikon Seminars,* 254.

51. Ibid., 21.

52. Ibid., 186.

53. Ibid., 200.

54. Ibid., 217.

55. Ibid., 207–8.

56. Ibid., 254.

57. Ibid., 169.

58. Ibid., 186–87.

59. *SE* XIV, 161.

60. Heidegger, *Zollikon Seminars,* 186.

61. Ibid., 168–69.

62. Ibid.

63. Ibid., 169–70.

64. Ibid., 182.

65. Ibid., 183.

66. Ibid., 182–83.

67. Ibid., 173.

68. Ibid.

69. "Care" is the structure which unifies the interrelated structures of Being-with, Being-in, and the-world. It enables us to be concerned about various aspects of our existence. See: Martin Heidegger, *Being and Time,* trans. John Macquarrie and Edward Robinson (New York: Harper and Row, 1962), sect. 39.

70. Heidegger, *Zollikon Seminars,* 172.

71. Ibid., 237.

72. Ibid., 172.

73. Ibid., 163, 182.

74. Ibid., 162–65.

75. In the final two chapters of this book, we take up other significant Freudian rejoinders to the existential phenomenologists in general, based on our historical understanding of Freud.

76. *SE* XXII, 158.

77. Ibid., 159.

78. *SE* XVIII, 251–52.

79. Heidegger, on the other hand, said "the task of reflecting on what natural science is constantly focused upon belongs not to natural science but to philosophy" (*Zollikon Seminars,* 25–26).

80. *SE* XIII, 178–79. See also: *SE* VI, 259; *SE* IX, 115–27; *SE* XI, 212; *SE* XIII, 161–62, 178–99; and chapter 18, endnotes 54, 55, 69.

81. *SE* XXII, 160–61. Indeed, Heidegger agreed that such "calculative" modes of thinking have been egregiously predominant and exclusionary of other ways of thinking in Western cultures. See: Martin Heidegger, *Discourse on Thinking,* trans. John M. Anderson and E. Hans Freund (New York: Harper & Row, 1966).

82. *SE* XXII, 160–61.

83. Ibid., 175.

84. Heidegger, *Zollikon Seminars,* 162.

85. *SE* XXII, 160–61.

86. Heidegger, *Zollikon Seminars,* 122, 125–26.

87. *SE* XIX, 13.

88. *SE* XIV, 161.

89. *SE* XIX, 13.

90. *SE* XIV, 161.

91. Ibid., 167.

92. Ibid., 576–77.

93. See: Heidegger, *Being and Time,* for further elaboration of these types of phenomena.

94. *SE* XIX, 13.

95. *SE* XX, 31–32.

96. Ibid.

97. Heidegger, *Zollikon Seminars,* 186.

98. Ibid., 169.

99. *SE* XIV, 177–78.

100. *SE* XVI, 258.

101. *SE* XIV, 175.

102. *SE* XX, 231.

103. *SE* XXIII, 144–45.

104. *SE* XII, 260.

105. *SE* VII, 31, 60; *SE* V, 480; *SE* XI, 38.

106. There is substantial evidence that Freud, despite his own general account, did not equate "motive" and "cause" in his therapeutic papers. There is, for example, no question that in his case studies on the etiology of neurosis, Freud presupposed free, intentional, and purposive motives in seeking to understand the meaningful and historical contexts in which they were embedded. Thus, "motives" were understood by Freud as "purposes" and "intentions" for the sake of gaining some advantage. Here, there was often no reference to any underlying causal network. See, for example: *SE* I, 117; *SE* X, 199–200; *SE* XIV, 53–56; *SE* XVI, 263–69, 449.

107. *SE* XXII, 175.

Chapter 13

Epigraphs: Jean-Paul Sartre, *Nausea*, trans. Lloyd Alexander (New York: New Directions, 1964), 133; letter from Freud to Marie Bonaparte, April 13, 1937, quoted in Ernest Jones, *The Life and Works of Sigmund Freud*, vol. 3 (New York: Basic Books, 1955), 465.

1. Jean-Paul Sartre, *Being and Nothingness: An Essay on Phenomenological Ontology*, trans. Hazel. E. Barnes (New York: Philosophical Library, 1956), xlvi.

2. Sartre, *Being and Nothingness*, xlvi.

3. Ibid., xlix.

4. Ibid., xlviii.

5. Ibid., 162.

6. Ibid., lix.

7. Ibid., 270, 408.

8. Ibid., 271.

9. Ibid., 275.

10. Ibid., 401.

11. Ibid., 82–84.

12. Ibid., 556.

13. Ibid., 566.

14. Ibid., 547. Much later in his career, in his concept of *le vécu*, Sartre asserted that any total self-knowledge by a person is impossible. See: Jean-Paul Sartre, *Between Existentialism and Marxism*, trans. John Mathews (New York: William Morrow & Company, 1974), 41–42.

15. Sartre, *Being and Nothingness*, 83.

16. Ibid., 78.

17. Ibid.

18. Ibid., 14–15.

19. There is, however, one point upon which Sartre never wavered throughout his entire philosophical career—his rejection of Freud's notion of the unconscious, in whatever way it was conceived (as interpretive myth, as a thing instantiating deterministic causes, as a separate realm which preempts our freedom, and so on). See: Sartre, *Between Existentialism and Marxism*, 39.

20. Sartre, *Between Existentialism and Marxism*, 199.

21. Interview with Sartre in May 1975; in Paul Arthur Schilpp, ed., *The Philosophy of Jean-Paul Sartre* (La Salle, Ill.: Open Court, 1981). Simone de Beauvoir's *Force of Circumstance*, trans. Richard Howard (New York: G. P. Putnam's Sons, 1965), added the possibility that Sartre had read Freud's *Introduction to Psychoanalysis* as well.

22. Sartre, *Between Existentialism and Marxism*, 36.

23. Ibid.

24. Schilpp, *Philosophy of Jean-Paul Sartre*, 12.

25. Simone de Beauvoir, *The Prime of Life*, trans. Peter Green (New York: Harper & Row, 1976), 22–23.

26. French culture was being permeated by psychoanalysis. For example, beyond the works of Merleau-Ponty which we discuss in chapter 16, a series of

works appeared which explicitly took Freudian ideas seriously, for example: Georges Politzer's *Critique des fondements de la psychologie: la psychologie et la psychanalyse* (1928), Roland Dalbiez's *La méthode psychanalytique et la doctrine freudienne* (1936), and Gaston Bachelard's *La psychanalyse du feu* (1938).

27. De Beauvoir, *Prime of Life*, 23.

28. Ibid.

29. Ibid.

30. Ibid.

31. Schilpp, *Philosophy of Jean-Paul Sartre*, 12.

32. De Beauvoir, *Force of Circumstance*, 134.

33. Jean-Paul Sartre, "Childhood of a Leader," in *The Wall (Intimacy) and Other Stories*, trans. Lloyd Alexander (New York: New Directions, 1969).

34. Jean-Paul Sartre, *The Emotions: Outline of a Theory*, trans. Bernard Frechtman (New York: Philosophical Library, 1948).

35. Sartre, *The Emotions*, 48.

36. See: *Being and Nothingness*, pt. 1, ch. 2; pt. 4, ch. 2. No other psychological theorists appear nearly so prominently throughout the text.

37. Sartre wrote, "empirical psychoanalysis has decided upon its own irreducible . . . investigation" (*Being and Nothingness*, 571).

38. However, it is important to note that for Sartre such complexes were not irreducible in the way they were for Freud, that is, they can be traced back to an individual's "original choice" as it pertains to the pursuit of being. Hence, they were merely secondary structures for Sartre.

39. Jean-Paul Sartre, *Baudelaire*, trans. Martin Turnell (New York: New Directions, 1950).

40. Jean-Paul Sartre, "Consciousness and Knowledge," in *Readings in Existential Phenomenology*, ed. Nathaniel Lawrence and Daniel O'Connor (Englewood Cliffs, New Jersey: Prentice Hall, 1967).

41. Michel Contat and Michel Rybalka, eds., *The Writings of Jean-Paul Sartre*, trans. Richard C. McCleary (Evanston: Northwestern University Press, 1974), 258.

42. John Huston, *An Open Book* (New York: A. A. Knopf, 1980), 294.

43. Jean-Paul Sartre, *Life/Situations*, trans. Paul Auster and Lydia Davis (London: André Deutsch, 1978), 72.

44. For a fee of $25,000 to $550,000, depending on which secondary source one believes.

45. These numbers also vary between 300 and more than 1,600 pages, depending on the secondary source.

46. Jean-Paul Sartre, *The Freud Scenario*, ed. J. B. Pontalis, trans. Quinton Hoare (Chicago: The Chicago University Press, 1985).

47. Contat and Rybalka, *Writings of Jean-Paul Sartre*, 608.

48. Sartre, *Life/Situations*, 72.

49. We shall discuss this criticism in the subsequent chapters on the later Sartre's critique of Freudian psychoanalysis.

50. Schilpp, *Philosophy of Jean-Paul Sartre*, 12. This last comment is another concession by Sartre himself that before 1957 he had a limited knowledge of

Freud. This, along with Simone de Beauvoir's comment in *The Prime of Life*, clearly shows the limited extent to which he was familiar with Freud's writings.

51. Sartre, *Being and Nothingness*, 569.

52. *SE* I, 139–40, 195–200; II, 12, 104; III, 137–39, 143–56; VII, 138–41, 154–55; VIII, 101–3; X, 141–44; XI, 21; XII, 209, 281–82; XIII, 158; XIV, 131; XV, 199; XVI, 354–55, 361–62, 371, 378, 408, 411; XVII, 21–22, 86, 97, 119–21, 193, 203–4, 261–62; XIX, 38, 36–38; XX, 151; XXII, 81; XXIII, 98–101, 145, 183–84.

53. *SE* XXIII, 240–41.

54. Jean-Paul Sartre, *The Words*, trans. Bernard Frechtman (New York: G. Braziller, 1964).

55. Sartre, *Freud Scenario*, xv.

56. Indeed, John Huston actually did try to hypnotize Sartre. The result was "total failure." "Occasionally you encounter someone like that . . . hypnotically impregnable" (Robert LaGuardia, *Monty: A Biography of Montgomery Clift* [New York: Arbor House, 1977]). See also: Sartre, *Freud Scenario*, ix.

57. Contat and Rybalka, *Writings of Jean-Paul Sartre*, 438.

58. Sartre, *Freud Scenario*, 505.

59. There is arguably a dialectic, as well, between one's transcendence and facticity in Sartre's descriptions in *Being and Nothingness*.

60. And here, once again, we have the Hegelian motif of the individual mirroring within his/her own psyche the evolutionary point of development/progression of the Absolute spirit.

61. Jean-Paul Sartre, *Search for a Method*, trans. Hazel E. Barnes (New York: Vintage Books, 1968).

62. Jean-Paul Sartre, *Critique of Dialectical Reason, Vol. I: Theory of Practical Ensembles*, ed. Jonathan Rée, trans. Alan Sheridan-Smith (London: New Left Books, 1976).

63. Sartre, *Search for a Method*, 61. Here Sartre seems to be approaching the position of the later Merleau-Ponty (see chapter 16, below).

64. Sartre, *Critique of Dialectical Reason*, 17–18n6.

65. Sartre, *Between Existentialism and Marxism*, 199.

66. Ibid., 202.

67. Ibid., 204–5. Sartre apparently was unaware of the fact that Freud already recognized this on a profound level.

68. Sartre, *Between Existentialism and Marxism*, 37–39.

69. Jean-Paul Sartre, *The Family Idiot: Gustave Flaubert, 1827–1857*, trans. Carol Cosman (Chicago: The University of Chicago Press, 1993).

70. See, for example: Sartre, *The Emotions*, 48; *Being and Nothingness*, 457–60.

71. De Beauvoir, *Prime of Life*, 22.

Chapter 14

Epigraphs: *SE* XXII, 179; Sartre in Paul Arthur Schilpp, ed., *The Philosophy of Jean-Paul Sartre* (La Salle, Ill.: Open Court, 1981), 38.

1. Of course, such an extensive critique cannot be fully developed in such a limited space.

2. Also see chapter 17.

3. Schilpp, *Philosophy of Jean-Paul Sartre*, 38.

4. Jean-Paul Sartre, *Being and Nothingness: An Essay on Phenomenological Ontology*, trans. Hazel. E. Barnes (New York: Philosophical Library, 1956), 51–52.

5. *SE* XIV, 78.

6. Here Sartre himself implicitly recognized the merit to Boss's claim that there were two Freuds.

7. Jean-Paul Sartre, *Notebooks for an Ethics*, trans. David Pellauer (Chicago: The University of Chicago Press, 1992), 276.

8. Jean-Paul Sartre, *The Emotions: Outline of a Theory*, trans. Bernard Frechtman (New York: Philosophical Library, 1948), 43.

9. Sartre, *The Emotions*, 46. Sartre is not claiming here that the meaning of all our psychic acts is therefore clear and immediately explicit but that many "degrees" are possible.

10. Sartre, *The Emotions*, 47.

11. Ibid., 44–45.

12. This is, of course, the problem of intentionality.

13. Sartre, *The Emotions*, 46.

14. This is an early version of Sartre's basic critique of the Freudian notion of the unconscious in *Being and Nothingness*.

15. Sartre, *The Emotions*, 48.

16. Sartre, *Being and Nothingness*, 558.

17. Ibid.

18. Throughout this series of "Freud's" responses, we shall consider Sartre's objections from the viewpoint of Freud's self-professed "scientism."

19. See, for example: Jean-Paul Sartre, *Between Existentialism and Marxism*, trans. John Mathews (New York: William Morrow & Company, 1974), 37–38; *The Emotions*, 46; *Notebooks for an Ethics*, 198, 428; *Being and Nothingness*, liv, 25, 34, 43. Freud is not always mentioned by name in these references, but it is clear that Freud is a prime example of Sartre's critique in each context.

20. Despite the fact that Sartre discerned some conclusions of Marx's dialectical materialism to be true (*Between Existentialism and Marxism*, 39), Sartre for the same reason rejected what he took to be a claim by the mature Marx that within "dialectical materialism" there was a "dialectic of nature, in the sense of a natural process which produces and resolves man into an ensemble of physical laws" (*Between Existentialism and Marxism*, 37).

21. Sartre, *Between Existentialism and Marxism*, 36–37.

22. See: Jean-Paul Sartre, "Existentialism," in *Existentialism and Human Emotions*, trans. Bernard Frechtman (New York: Castle, 1947).

23. Jean-Paul Sartre, "Consciousness and Knowledge," in *Readings in Existential Phenomenology*, ed. Nathaniel Lawrence and Daniel O'Connor (Englewood Cliffs, New Jersey: Prentice Hall, 1967), 128.

24. Sartre, *Being and Nothingness*, 561.

25. Ibid., 558.

26. Ibid., 176.
27. Ibid., 561.
28. Ibid.
29. Ibid.
30. Ibid., 563.
31. Ibid., 483–84, 489, 494–95, 549.
32. Ibid., 139.
33. Ibid., 495.
34. Ibid., 104.
35. Ibid., 303.
36. Ibid., 305.
37. Ibid., 309.
38. Ibid., 347.
39. Ibid., 309.
40. Ibid., 328.
41. Ibid., 318. See also: 347, 365.
42. Ibid., 320.
43. Ibid., 318.
44. Ibid., 324, 330.
45. Ibid., 351.
46. Ibid., 329.
47. Ibid., 334.
48. Ibid., 337.
49. Ibid.
50. Ibid., 338.
51. Ibid.
52. Ibid., li, liv, lix, 28, 102–3, 557; *Readings in Existential Phenomenology,* 123; *Notebooks for an Ethics,* 438; *Between Existentialism and Marxism,* 37–38; Jean-Paul Sartre, *The Transcendence of the Ego: An Existentialist Theory of Consciousness,* trans. Forrest Williams and Robert Kirkpatrick (New York: The Noonday Press, 1957).
53. Schilpp, *Philosophy of Jean-Paul Sartre,* 36.
54. Sartre, *Being and Nothingness,* 77–78.
55. Ibid., 176.
56. Ibid., 79.
57. *SE* I, 295.
58. Sartre, *Being and Nothingness,* 560.
59. We translate *Trieb* as "instincts" rather than "drives."
60. Sartre, *Being and Nothingness,* 199.
61. Ibid., 557.
62. Ibid.
63. Ibid., 176.
64. Ibid., 181.
65. Ibid., 199.
66. Ibid., 217.
67. G. W. F. Hegel, *Phenomenology of Spirit,* trans. A. V. Miller (New York: Oxford University Press, 1977).

68. G. W. F. Hegel, *Science of Logic*, trans. A. V. Miller (Atlantic Highlands, New Jersey: Humanities Press International, 1993).

69. Sartre, *Being and Nothingness*, 14–15.

70. Hegel and Sartre, of course, completely disagreed over the possibility of resolving this tension between the in-itself and the for-itself. Sartre denied its possibility since it would necessitate the fusion of contradictory beings. Hegel believed that through a process of rational "dialectic" this rupture between the for-itself (as subject) and in-itself (as object) would eventually be resolved.

71. Sartre, *Being and Nothingness*, 458–60; *Notebooks for an Ethics*, 197.

72. Sartre, *Being and Nothingness*, 25–26.

73. Ibid., liv.

74. Ibid., 458.

75. Ibid.

76. This issue is taken up again in the final chapter of this book.

77. Sigmund Freud, *The Origins of Psychoanalysis: Letters to Wilhelm Fliess*, trans. Eric Mosbacher and James Strachey (New York: Basic Books, 1954), 355.

78. *SE* I, 137; *SE* II, 10, 153–4; *SE* III, 46.

79. Sartre would, of course, have repeated that this could not occur, given Freud's mechanistic view. Most likely this argument would have been lost on Freud.

80. Sartre, *Being and Nothingness*, 458.

81. *SE* VI, 242.

82. Ibid.; *SE* IX, 104–5, 109; *SE* XI, 29, 38, 52; *SE* XVIII, 238, 240, 264.

83. *SE* VI, 253–54. See also: *SE* V, 514–15.

84. *SE* XVII, 236.

85. Ibid.

86. *SE* XI, 137.

87. Sartre, *Being and Nothingness*, 483.

88. Ibid., 28.

89. Ibid., 438.

90. Ibid., 439, 485.

91. Sartre, *Being and Nothingness*, 484.

92. Freedom presupposes a relation to the given—the plenum of being (Sartre, *Being and Nothingness*, 486)—in order to emerge in the heart of being as nothingness (*Being and Nothingness*, 484). Hence, Sartre's account is not dualistic.

93. Sartre, *Being and Nothingness*, 549, 495.

94. Ibid., 489.

95. Ibid., 494.

96. Ibid., 489.

97. Ibid., 479, 537, 547, 555.

98. Ibid., 441.

99. It is important to add that Sartre emphasized throughout *Being and Nothingness* that the for-itself is only when it is engaged and in a situation. This is crucial for Sartre's position, and he has often been misunderstood on this score. (See: *Being and Nothingness*, 104, 291, 327, 450, 478, 481, 483–84, 489, 494–95, 549). A situation is comprised of the interplay between two aspects of reality: the facticity

(the givens of the world with which freedom concretely engages and is necessarily connected) and the transcendence (freedom) of the for-itself. Sartre described the relation between the for-itself and situation as "being-there." It is by "being-there" that the object takes on meaning for the for-itself—the situation is identified and defined by that meaning—"being-in-the-situation defines the human reality" (*Being and Nothingness*, 569). According to Sartre, human reality encounters resistances and obstacles which it did not create, but these obstacles have meaning only in and through the free choice which is human reality.

100. Sartre, *Being and Nothingness*, 483. See also: 327, 484.

101. Sartre, *Notebooks for an Ethics*, 511.

102. In a Kierkegaardian sense.

103. Sartre, *Being and Nothingness*, 34.

104. Ibid., 31.

105. Ibid., 43.

106. Ibid., 44.

107. Ibid., 458.

108. Ibid., 496.

109. Ibid.

110. Ibid., 503.

111. Ibid., 496.

112. Ibid., 102.

113. Ibid., 114.

114. Ibid., 138–39.

115. Ibid., 141.

116. Ibid.

117. Ibid., 165. Here Sartre is alluding to Freud's characterization of the id as atemporal.

118. Sartre, *Being and Nothingness*, 166.

119. Ibid., 168.

120. Ibid., 168–69.

121. Ibid., 111.

122. Ibid., 110–11.

123. Ibid., 497.

124. Ibid., 440.

125. Ibid., 40. Also: 561. We shall consider Sartre's point more specifically when we consider his argument that the Freudian notion of the unconscious is the perfect example of bad faith, in the following chapter.

126. *SE* IX, 141–53.

127. Ibid., 146.

128. Ibid., 147–48.

129. Ibid., 152.

130. *SE* XIV, 94. See also: *SE* XXII, 97–98.

131. *SE* VII, 238. See also: *SE* VII, 178.

132. *SE* XI, 122–23. See also: *SE* XI, 132–36.

133. *SE* XVI, 345; *SE* XIV, 126.

134. *SE* VII, 156–57.

135. *SE* IX, 147–48.
136. *SE* IV, 68–70. See also: *SE* XIX.
137. *SE* XIX, 133.

Chapter 15

Epigraphs: Jean-Paul Sartre, *Between Existentialism and Marxism*, trans. John Mathews (New York: William Morrow & Company, 1974), 37; Jean-Paul Sartre, *Being and Nothingness: An Essay on Phenomenological Ontology*, trans. Hazel. E. Barnes (New York: Philosophical Library, 1956), 461; *SE* XIV, 193.

1. Sartre, *Between Existentialism and Marxism*, 37–9.

2. Simone de Beauvoir, *The Prime of Life*, trans. Peter Green (New York: Harper & Row, 1976), 134; Jean-Paul Sartre, *Notebooks for an Ethics*, trans. David Pellauer (Chicago: The University of Chicago Press, 1992), 194–98.

3. Sartre, *Between Existentialism and Marxism*, 37–39.

4. Descartes insisted that the mind is indivisible. Of course, the mind contains distinct thoughts, and one might even distinguish distinct faculties within it; but these nonspatial divisions did not, for Descartes, constitute "parts": "since it is one and the same mind that wills, and understands and has sensory perceptions" (René Descartes, *The Philosophical Writings of Descartes*, vol. 2, trans. J. Cottingham [Cambridge: Cambridge University Press, 1984], 59).

5. Yet, as we have seen, Freud's theory is easily and naturally grounded in Schopenhauer's philosophy.

6. Sartre, *Being and Nothingness*, 51–54. Given this, it is not at all surprising that Kant had, as early as 1797, recognized the ostensibly paradoxical nature of self-deception (taken as a lie to myself): "The reality of many an *internal* lie, of which men may be guilty, is easy to set forth; yet to explain its possibility seems more difficult. Since a second person is required whom one intends to deceive, deceiving oneself deliberately seems in itself to contain a contradiction" (Immanuel Kant, *The Metaphysical Principles of Virtue*, trans. James Ellington [Indianapolis: Bobbs-Merrill, 1964], 91). One might also note that even Hegel spoke in a similar way in his *Phenomenology of Spirit*: "its fear of the truth may lead consciousness to hide, from itself and others, behind the pretension that its burning zeal for truth makes it difficult or even impossible to find any other truth . . . it flees" (trans. A. V. Miller [New York: Oxford University Press, 1977], 52). Consciousness occasionally retreats in terror from its endless self-transcendence; Nietzsche as well: "By lie I mean: wishing *not* to see something that one does see; wishing not to see something *as* one sees it. Whether the lie takes place before witnesses or without witnesses does not matter. The most common lie is that with which one lies to oneself; lying to others is, relatively, an exception" (*The Antichrist*, in *The Portable Nietzsche*, trans. Walter Kaufmann [New York: Viking, 1954], 639–40).

7. Sartre wrote: "This original project of bad faith is a decision in bad faith on the nature of faith" (*Being and Nothingness*, 68). However in the very next sentences he stated: "Let us understand clearly that there is no question of a reflec-

tive, voluntary decision, but of a spontaneous determination of our being. One puts oneself in bad faith as one goes to sleep and one is in bad faith as one dreams." One might now inquire, in what sense is this a decision? Also, why could Freud not argue that the impulses of the id are "spontaneous determinations of our being" in the same way?

8. Sartre, *Being and Nothingness*, 56.

9. Sartre's account for how "bad faith is possible requires . . . that there be an imponderable difference separating being from non-being in the mode of being human reality" (*Being and Nothingness*, 66).

10. Sartre, *Being and Nothingness*, 50.

11. Ibid.

12. Sartre, *Notebooks for an Ethics*, 428.

13. Ibid., 411.

14. Sartre, *Being and Nothingness*, 51.

15. Ibid., 52.

16. Ibid.

17. Ibid., 53.

18. Ibid.

19. Ibid., 474.

20. Ibid., 54.

21. Ibid.

22. Sartre, *Notebooks for an Ethics*, 428.

23. Jean-Paul Sartre, "Consciousness and Knowledge," in *Readings in Existential Phenomenology*, ed. Nathaniel Lawrence and Daniel O'Connor (Englewood Cliffs, New Jersey: Prentice Hall, 1967), 124.

24. Sartre, *Readings in Existential Phenomenology*, 122.

25. Ibid., 124.

26. Ibid., 138.

27. Sartre, *Being and Nothingness*, 52.

28. Sartre, *Readings in Existential Phenomenology*, 138.

29. Ibid., 128.

30. Ibid., 139.

31. Here we might ask, is this not what Sartre himself ended up doing?

32. Sartre, *Readings in Existential Phenomenology*, 140.

33. Ibid., 122.

34. Ibid., 141, 125.

35. Ibid., 141.

36. Ibid.

37. Sartre, *Being and Nothingness*, 54.

38. Jean-Paul Sartre, *The Freud Scenario*, ed. J. B. Pontalis, trans. Quinton Hoare (Chicago: The Chicago University Press, 1985), xii–xiii.

39. Jean-Paul Sartre, *The Emotions: Outline of a Theory*, trans. Bernard Frechtman (New York: Philosophical Library, 1948), 46.

40. Sartre, *Being and Nothingness*, li.

41. Ibid., 77.

42. Ibid., 603.

43. Sartre developed his doctrine on the existence of a pre-reflective consciousness in part to avoid this.

44. Here Sartre's brand of realism obviously transcends what is arguably Husserl's transcendental idealism.

45. Sartre, *Being and Nothingness,* 14.

46. Ibid., liii.

47. Ibid., 36.

48. He may still have this mode of bodily comportment, and still not know he is doing it, despite having become very comfortable with the process of lecturing.

49. Unless there are reasons for thinking that other past motivating factors were entering in.

50. Sartre, *The Emotions,* 46. As we saw earlier, this objection was raised by Brentano (see chapter 9).

51. *SE* XIX, 16n.

52. Sartre might point out that it is Freud who now is question begging.

53. *SE* XII, 260.

54. *SE* XIX, 13.

55. *SE* XIX, 16n.

56. *SE* XXII, 69.

57. *SE* IV, 93.

58. Sartre, *Being and Nothingness,* 53.

59. Compare: *SE* XIX; *SE* XXII, 68–70.

60. *SE* XIX, 3–11.

61. *SE* V, 540n, 558.

62. *SE* XIX, 27.

63. Ibid., 18. See also: *SE* XIV, 192–93; *SE* XIX, 17, 23, 27.

64. *SE* XVIII, 19–20, 75n.

65. *SE* XXII, 69. See also: *SE* XIX, 39, 52; *SE* XXII, 69–71, 75, 78–79; *SE* XXIII, 162.

66. *SE* XXII, 78.

67. Sartre, *Being and Nothingness,* 53.

68. Ibid., 50.

69. *SE* V, 541.

70. *SE* I, 234, letter 52.

71. From the diagrams alluded to, it is clear that for the later Freud the systems were not discrete. He was quite explicit on this point: "The ego is after all only a portion of the id" (*SE* XXII, 76). And again: "After making the separation [of these dynamic relations] we must allow what we have separated to merge together once more" (*SE* XXII, 79).

72. *SE* XVI, 296.

73. *SE* XX, 97.

74. *SE* XIX, 24.

75. *SE* XX, 97.

76. *SE* XIX, 28. See also: *On Narcissism: An Introduction* (*SE* XIV), and *Group Psychology and the Analysis of the Ego* (*SE* XVIII).

77. *SE* V, 537.

78. *SE* XV, 140.

79. Sartre, *Being and Nothingness,* 50. The origins of Sartre's interpretation obviously derived from his reading of the *Introductory Lectures on Psycho-analysis,* where Freud employed his analogy of the large entrance hall (the unconscious), a drawing room (consciousness), and a watchman between the two who decides which ideas, mental impulses, and so on, will be permitted entry from the unconscious to consciousness (*SE* XVI, 295–96). Yet even here, Freud was careful to distinguish between the conscious, preconscious, and the unconscious (*SE* XVI, 296).

80. Sartre, *Being and Nothingness,* 53.

81. The reason it is inaccurate for Freud is that the conflict occurs not only between the components of the personality but within them as well (for example: *SE* XXII, 58; *SE* XIX, 17, with intra-ego conflicts), which is precisely one of the major points Sartre failed to recognize.

82. *SE* XXII, 15.

83. *SE* V, 615, 617–18; *SE* XIV, 173, 186, 191, 193–94, 224–26.

84. *SE* IV, 235–36; *SE* V, 553, 567–68, 607, 611, 615, 617–18; *SE* XIV, 173, 186, 191, 193–94, 224–26.

85. *SE* XXII, 69. This is prima facie important since it could be argued that since Sartre did not think the censor could be in either the id or ego, it must by modus tollens be thought to be in the superego, for Freud, though this is an inference that Sartre himself did not explicitly draw.

86. The reason this is important here is that during the course of his argument against the censor, Sartre explicitly denied the possibility that the ego could ever be responsible for repression at all (*Being and Nothingness,* 52).

87. Freud only made this general pronouncement in four other citings during roughly the same years (*SE* XIX, 34, 52, 150, 197).

88. Freud held a notion of the ego and egological repression prior to the development of the superego—his position seems to have been relatively consistent throughout its development. Freud's view of the ego as a coherent structure performing certain functions extends back as far as Freud's *Project for a Scientific Psychology,* of 1895 (*SE* I, 322–24).

89. *SE* XIX, 52.

90. *SE* XX, 91.

91. *SE* XI, 24; *SE* XVI, 429; *SE* XX, 90, 224.

92. *SE* IX, 123; *SE* XIV, 95.

93. *SE* XIV, 247.

94. *SE* III, 170; *SE* V, 558; *SE* XI, 24, 34, 37, 146, 215–16; *SE* XIV, 53, 184, 188; *SE* XV, 147; *SE* XVI, 298, 359, 373, 380, 382, 410; *SE* XVII, 110, 138, 260; *SE* XVIII, 19–20, 23, 246, 249, 256, 410; *SE* XIX, 17, 150; *SE* XX, 44, 56, 90, 91–92, 95, 97, 100, 153, 163–64, 209, 220–21, 241–42, 256; *SE* XXII, 96; *SE* XXIII, 127, 185, 236–37.

95. *SE* XX, 94.

96. *SE* XX, 29–30.

97. *SE* XXIII, 127, 185, 227, 236–37, 303.

98. Sartre, *Being and Nothingness,* 52.

99. *SE* XXII, 69.

100. *SE* XXIII, 127.

101. Ibid., 162. See also: *SE* XIX, 17.

102. Sartre, *The Emotions*, 46.

103. Sartre, *Being and Nothingness*, 53.

104. Ibid., 52.

105. "[Georg Groddeck] is never tired of insisting that what we call our ego behaves essentially passively in life, and that, as he expresses it, we are 'lived' by unknown and uncontrollable forces" (*SE* XIX, 23). It is interesting to note how closely this part of Sartre's critique resembles this formulation.

106. *SE* XX, 95.

107. Ibid., 96.

108. *SE* XIX, 17.

109. Ibid., 25.

110. Ibid., 20.

111. *SE* XIV, 188.

112. *SE* XIX, 55.

113. Ibid., 55–56.

114. Ibid., 56.

115. Ibid., 149–50.

116. *SE* XXII, 93.

117. *SE* XX, 95.

118. Sartre, *Being and Nothingness*, 51.

119. *SE* XX, 97.

Chapter 16

Epigraph: Maurice Merleau-Ponty, "Phenomenology and Psychoanalysis: Preface to Hesnard's *L'Oeuvre de Freud*," in *The Essential Writings of Merleau-Ponty*, ed. Alden Fisher (New York: Harcourt, Brace & World, 1969), 86.

1. It is important to note that throughout this chapter and the next, the term "phenomenology" refers to Merleau-Ponty's "reinterpretation" of Husserlian phenomenology as it pertains to the development of Merleau-Ponty's own brand of existential phenomenology.

2. Maurice Merleau-Ponty, *The Structure of Behavior*, trans. Alden Fisher (Boston: Beacon Press, 1963), 176.

3. Merleau-Ponty, *The Structure of Behavior*, 177.

4. Paul Ricoeur, *The Conflict of Interpretations: Essays in Hermeneutics* (Evanston: Northwestern University Press, 1974), 166–67.

5. Merleau-Ponty, *The Structure of Behavior*, 178.

6. Ibid., 179.

7. Ibid., 180–81.

8. Maurice Merleau-Ponty, *Phenomenology of Perception*, trans. Colin Smith (New York: Humanities Press, 1962), 156.

9. Merleau-Ponty, *Phenomenology of Perception*, 157.

10. Ibid., 158.

11. Ibid., 159.

12. Ibid., 161.

13. *SE* XV, 55.

14. Merleau-Ponty, *Phenomenology of Perception*, 162.

15. Ibid., 163. It is obvious from this that Merleau-Ponty rejected Sartre's view of the relationship of his ontological concept of freedom to "bad faith." See also: 434–56.

16. Merleau-Ponty, *Phenomenology of Perception*, 165–66.

17. Ibid., 166.

18. Ibid., 169.

19. Ibid., 158.

20. Maurice Merleau-Ponty, *Sense and Non-Sense*, trans. Hubert L. Dreyfus and Patricia A. Dreyfus (Evanston: Northwestern University Press, 1964), 24–25.

21. Ludwig Wittgenstein, *Lectures and Conversations on Aesthetics, Psychology and Religious Belief,* ed. Cyril Barrett (Berkeley: University of California Press, 1973), 41–52. There are many points in this essay where Wittgenstein was, at best, unfair to Freud, or simply misunderstood him.

22. Merleau-Ponty, *Sense and Non-Sense*, 25.

23. Maurice Merleau-Ponty, *Signs*, trans. Richard C. McCleary (Evanston: Northwestern University Press, 1964), 228.

24. Merleau-Ponty, *Signs*, 229. See also: Maurice Merleau-Ponty, *Themes from the Lectures at the Collège de France, 1952–1960,* trans. John O'Neill (Evanston: Northwestern University Press, 1970), 130.

25. Merleau-Ponty, *Signs*, 229–30. It seems clear that Merleau-Ponty was referring to Sartre's notion of consciousness in *Being and Nothingness*, that is, pre-reflective/reflective consciousness.

26. Merleau-Ponty, *Themes from the Lectures at the Collège de France*, 46–52.

27. Ibid., 49.

28. Ibid., 50.

29. Once again, critics such as Wittgenstein seem to have misunderstood Freud, in thinking that he was attempting to give the one true solution to the analysis of any given behavior/dream. Freud argued the contrary. See: *SE* XIX, 16.

30. Maurice Merleau-Ponty, *The Visible and the Invisible,* ed. Claude Lefort, trans. Alphonso Lingis (Evanston: Northwestern University Press, 1968), 270.

31. Merleau-Ponty, *The Visible and the Invisible,* 270.

32. Ibid., 269.

33. A. Hesnard, *L'Oeuvre de Freud et son importance pour le Monde Moderne* [trans. Alden L. Fisher] (Paris: Payot, 1960), 5–10.

34. See: Merleau-Ponty, *The Visible and the Invisible,* 232, 269–70; *Themes from the Lectures at the Collège de France,* 130; as well as Merleau-Ponty's other writings.

35. Merleau-Ponty, *Essential Writings of Merleau-Ponty,* 83.

36. Ibid., 81.

37. Ibid., 82.

38. Ibid., 85.

39. Husserl wrote: "In truth, this is a whole world—and if we could equate this subjectivity with the ψυχή [soul] of Heraclitus, his saying would doubtless be

true of it: 'You will never find the boundaries of the soul, even if you follow every road; so deep is its ground.' Indeed, every 'ground' that is reached points to further grounds, every horizon opened up awakens new horizons, and yet the endless whole, in its infinity of flowing movement, is oriented toward that unity of one meaning" (*The Crisis of European Sciences and Transcendental Phenomenology: An Introduction to Phenomenological Philosophy*, trans. David Carr [Evanston: Northwestern University Press, 1970], 170).

40. Merleau-Ponty, *Essential Writings of Merleau-Ponty*, 86.

41. Ibid.

42. Ibid., 86–87.

43. Paul Ricoeur, *Freud and Philosophy: An Essay on Interpretation*, trans. Denis Savage (New Haven: Yale University Press, 1970), 117–22, 424–28; *Conflict of Interpretations*, 100, 242–43.

44. *SE* XII, 261–63, 266; *SE* XIV, 172; *SE* XIX, 3–4.

45. *SE* XIV, 103–236.

46. It is interesting to note that the early Husserl responded reciprocally by suggesting in his *Logical Investigations:* "the supposed unconscious events are in any case wholly irrelevant for pure phenomenology" (vol. 1, trans. J. N. Findlay [New York: The Humanities Press, 1976], 413).

47. *SE* XIV, 167–70.

48. *SE* XXIII, 158.

49. Ricoeur, *Conflict of Interpretations*, 172.

50. Ibid., 242–43.

51. Merleau-Ponty, *Essential Writings of Merleau-Ponty*, 86.

52. Jean-Paul Sartre, *Being and Nothingness: An Essay on Phenomenological Ontology*, trans. Hazel. E. Barnes (New York: Philosophical Library, 1956), 47–54, 557–75.

53. Wittgenstein, *Lectures and Conversations*, 41–52.

54. Merleau-Ponty, *Themes from the Lectures at the Collège de France*, 50; *Phenomenology of Perception*, 158n. See also: Ricoeur, *Freud and Philosophy*, 341–42, 499–506, 523–24, 542–43.

55. *SE* V, 353.

56. *SE* XIX, 16.

57. *SE* XXII, 90.

58. *SE* XIV, 226–27.

59. Ibid., 156–57.

60. *SE* XIX, 23.

61. *SE* XXIII, 285; *SE* IX, 322–24; Merleau-Ponty, *Phenomenology of Perception*, viii–xi, 158; *Essential Writings of Merleau-Ponty*, 81–87.

62. *SE* XIV, 201–2; Merleau-Ponty, *Phenomenology of Perception*, 183; *Signs*, 90; Maurice Merleau-Ponty, *Consciousness and the Acquisition of Language*, trans. Hugh J. Silverman (Evanston: Northwestern University Press, 1976), 4.

63. *SE* XIX, 156–7; Merleau-Ponty, *Phenomenology of Perception*, 84.

64. *SE* XIX, 15.

65. *SE* XXIII, 195–96; *SE* XII, 263.

66. *SE* VI.

67. *SE* XXIII, 195.
68. *SE* VII, 123–47; *SE* XI, 214n; *SE* XIV, 114–15.
69. *SE* XVIII, 255–59.
70. *SE* VII, 123–47.
71. *SE* XIV, 127.
72. Ibid., 121n; *SE* XVIII, 49–54, 252–59.
73. *SE* XIV, 125.
74. Merleau-Ponty, *Phenomenology of Perception*, 170. Also: 166.
75. *SE* III, 45–51; *SE* XII, 263; *SE* XIV, 170–71.
76. *SE* XII, 263.
77. *SE* XIV, 170.
78. *SE* XIX, 23, 25; *SE* XXIII, 196–208.
79. Merleau-Ponty, *Phenomenology of Perception*, xi, 57, 183.
80. Ricoeur, *Freud and Philosophy*, 127.
81. Ibid., 132.
82. Ibid., 151.
83. *SE* XIV, 121–22. See also: *SE* VII, 168.
84. *SE* XIX, 18–19.
85. *SE* XIX, 23.
86. *SE* XXIII, 151.

Chapter 17

1. *SE* XVIII, 179.
2. *SE* XXII, 159.
3. Herman Nunberg and Ernst Federn, eds., *Minutes of the Vienna Psychoanalytic Society*, vol. 4, trans. M. Nunberg (New York: International Universities Press, 1975), 136. See also: *SE* I, 103–13; *SE* XX, 247; *SE* XXIII, 144–45, 151, 158.
4. *SE* XIV, 134.
5. Ibid., 368; *SE* XVII, 248.
6. See: *SE* I, 295, 305, 322, 334, 360–62, 368–70, 375; *SE* V, 536–37; *SE* XXIII, 163.
7. *SE* XIV, 166–204; *SE* XII, 260–66.
8. *SE* I, 295.
9. *SE* XXIII, 163.
10. *SE* VII, 168.
11. *SE* XIV, 85–86, 119–22.
12. *SE* XXIII, 151, 158.
13. *SE* XXII, 67.
14. *SE* XXIII, 156.
15. Ibid., 148.
16. *SE* XXII, 96.
17. *SE* XIV, 121–22.
18. Martin Heidegger, *Zollikon Seminars*, trans. Franz Mayr and Richard Askay (Evanston: Northwestern University Press, 2001), 207–8.

19. *SE* XIV, 171.

20. *SE* V, 615–16.

21. *SE* XXIII, 196; *SE* VI, 229.

22. *SE* XIV, 171.

23. *SE* XXIII, 196; *SE* VI, 229.

24. *SE* XXII, 74, 76; *SE* XVIII, 28.

25. *SE* XIV, 188.

26. *SE* XIX, 231.

27. *SE* XXII, 74; *SE* I, 252; *SE* V, 577–78; *SE* VI, 275; *SE* XIV, 187; *SE* XVII, 10–11; *SE* XVIII, 28.

28. *SE* XXII, 158–82. Also see our section on Bacon, in chapter 3.

29. *SE* XVII, 236; *SE* VI, ch. XII.

30. *SE* V, 514; *SE* VI, 89–90, 239–41; *SE* IX, 105; *SE* XI, 29, 38, 52; *SE* XV, 106–9, 144; *SE* XVIII, 238.

31. See, for example: *SE* XII, 66; *SE* XIV, 131; *SE* XV, 254; *SE* XVIII, 36–37, 74, 143; *SE* XIX, 35–36, 48; *SE* XX, 93, 129–30, 151; *SE* XXIII, 145–46, 167.

32. Freud found himself in this self-contradictory position precisely because he sought to extend the philosophical presuppositions underlying his scientific Weltanschauung to the mental apparatus of human beings. He sought to investigate the psychical realm by eliminating from consciousness/unconsciousness their most essential aspect—nonobjectivity.

33. *SE* XXII, 90.

34. *SE* XXIII, 163–64.

35. *SE* XIV, 187–88.

36. *SE* XVIII, 34.

37. *SE* XIV, 184.

38. *SE* XX, 109.

39. *SE* XIV, 204.

40. Ibid., 78.

41. *SE* XVIII, 179.

42. *SE* XV, 258.

43. *SE* XX, 231.

44. *SE* XIV, 78. See also: *SE* IV, 41–42; *SE* VII, 13; *SE* XI, 21; *SE* XVIII, 60.

45. *SE* XXIII, 144–45.

46. *SE* XX, 32.

47. *SE* XXIII, 159.

48. *SE* XX, 194–95.

49. Medard Boss, *Psychoanalysis and Daseinsanalysis,* trans. Ludwig B. Lefebre (New York: Dacapo Press, 1982), 58.

50. Boss, *Psychoanalysis and Daseinsanalysis,* 67.

51. *SE* XII, 153, 168, 170.

52. Ibid., 153.

53. Ibid., 168.

54. Ibid., 170.

55. *SE* VII, 254, 266; *SE* XII, 106, 107, 115–17, 134–35, 153–54, 168, 170; *SE* XVI, 433–34, 440; *SE* XVII, 165; *SE* XVIII, 151, 250–51; *SE* XIX, 109; *SE* XX, 205; *SE* XXIII, 216, 220, 239–40.

56. *SE* XX, 205. See also: *SE* VII, 266; *SE* XII, 106.
57. *SE* XXIII, 220.
58. *SE* VII, 266; *SE* IX, 226; *SE* XII, 117, 118, 140–42, 147–48; *SE* XVII, 159, 162.
59. *SE* XVI, 440.
60. *SE* XXIII, 216.
61. *SE* XVII, 164–65; *SE* XVIII, 250–51.
62. *SE* XXIII, 174. See also: *SE* XII, 91–93, 134.
63. *SE* XII, 154.
64. *SE* XII, 107. See also: *SE* XII, 134–35; *SE* XXIII, 220.
65. *SE* XXIII, 240.
66. *SE* XII, 115.
67. *SE* XIX, 109.
68. *SE* XVI, 433.
69. *SE* XII, 106.
70. *SE* XVII, 165.
71. *SE* XIV, 222n.
72. Ibid., 105.
73. Ibid., 78.
74. *SE* XXIII, 226n.
75. *SE* XI, 142.
76. *SE* XI, 141–42.
77. *SE* XXIII, 225.
78. Of course one explanation for why Freud used the terms "freedom," "choice," "decisions," and so on, is that he was presenting his therapeutic approach to colleagues and the public in general. Such words have an everyday use, and since Freud was not necessarily intending to defend his position to the philosophical community, he may not have found it necessary to be careful in his word choice.
79. *SE* VI, 253.
80. Ibid., 253–54.
81. *SE* XVII, 160.
82. Ibid.
83. The irony here, of course, is that all of the existential phenomenologists insisted that to truly understand any great thinker, one must consider *all* of the primary strains of thought that exerted an impact upon them.
84. F. W. J. Schelling, *Ideas for a Philosophy of Nature: As Introduction to the Study of This Science,* trans. Errol E. Harris and Peter Heath (New York: Cambridge University Press, 1995), 13–14.
85. Schelling, *Ideas for a Philosophy of Nature,* 30.
86. It is interesting to note that Schopenhauer's philosophy was either ignored (Brentano, Husserl) or vilified (Herbart) by the predecessors of the existential phenomenologists, and subsequently almost completely ignored by the existential phenomenologists themselves. It is natural to wonder why Schopenhauer was not taken, with Freud, as a primary target of attack by the existential phenomenologists.
87. Arthur Schopenhauer, *On the Fourfold Root of the Principle of Sufficient Rea-*

son, trans. E. F. J. Payne (La Salle, Ill.: Open Court, 1974), 211. There is an interesting irony here, in that the existential phenomenologists have almost entirely ignored Schopenhauer's metaphysical position, throughout their writings. Yet it was Schopenhauer who pointed out that it is *the intellect* that introduced the distinction between the subject and object in the first place. It is precisely this point that provides one of the fulcrums for the existential phenomenological critique of Cartesianism and scientism across the board.

88. *SE* XIX, 26.

89. Schopenhauer, *Fourfold Root of the Principle of Sufficient Reason*, 215–16.

90. A viable alternative interpretation is that Schopenhauer and Freud do not remain within the parameters of the standard free will/determinism debate, but see the issue in different terms than those in which it is usually couched—in a way which is more akin, for example, to the notion of "karma" that certain "Eastern" philosophical approaches such as Hinduism and Buddhism hold. As the self goes through life, one acquires energies that seem to attach to the self—which are never lost—with one's actions being an expression of those various energies. Schopenhauer acknowledged the *Upanishads* as one of three primary influences on the development of his philosophy (*The World as Will and Representation*, vol. 1, trans. E. F. J. Payne [New York: Dover, 1966], xv, 3–4). The historical influences on Freud may now be understood in a different way: such historical influences on a person may be seen as groupings of states, which change during the course of temporal transitions.

91. Arthur Schopenhauer, *Prize Essay on the Freedom of the Will*, ed. Günter Zöller, trans. Eric F. J. Payne (New York: Cambridge University Press, 1999), 45–46.

92. *SE* XVI, 440; *SE* XVII, 164–65.

93. It is important to note that Nietzsche had the same insight: "This would also prevent personalities from becoming 'free'—that is to say, truthful to themselves and truthful to others in both word and deed" (*Unfashionable Observations*, trans. Richard T. Gray [Stanford: Stanford University Press, 1995], 118). And again: "[. . .] the free, ever freer spirit begins to unveil the riddle of that great liberation which had until then waited dark, questionable, almost untouchable in his memory" (*Human, All Too Human*, trans. R. J. Hollingdale [Cambridge: Cambridge University Press, 1996], 9).

94. One way to see the ineradicable antithesis involved here is in the stark contrast between Schopenhauer's and Sartre's positions on metaphysical grounding of freedom. *For Schopenhauer such a grounding is absolutely necessary:*

> Every being, of whatever kind, will always react in accordance with its peculiar nature to the occasion of the influencing causes . . . Here we must remember that every *existentia* presupposes an *essentia;* that is to say, everything that is must also be *something*, must have a definite essence. It cannot *exist* and yet at the same time be *nothing*, thus something like the *ens metaphysicum* [metaphysical being], i.e., something that *is* and only *is*, without any determinations and qualities, and consequently without the definite mode of action that flows from these . . . an *existentia* without *essentia* is unable to furnish a reality. For everything that is must have a nature essential and peculiar to it, by virtue of

which it is what it is, which it always maintains and the manifestations of which are called forth by causes with necessity; whereas this nature itself is by no means the work of those causes, nor can it be modified through them. But all this is just as true of the human being and his will as of all the other beings in nature. He too has an *essentia* in addition to an *existentia*, i.e., he has fundamental essential qualities that constitute his very character and require only occasioning from without in order to come forth . . . Closely considered, the freedom of the will means an *existentia* without *essentia;* this is equivalent to saying that something *is* and yet at the same time *is nothing*, which again means that it *is not* and thus is a contradiction (*Prize Essay on the Freedom of the Will*, 51).

For Sartre, such a grounding of freedom would make it impossible, since freedom as the being of the for-itself is precisely what it is and is not.

95. Schopenhauer, *World as Will and Representation*, vol. 1, 295. See also: vol. 1, 478; *Complete Essays of Schopenhauer, Seven Books in One Volume*, trans. T. Bailey Saunders (New York: Willey Book Company, 1942), bk. 6, 96.

96. Schopenhauer quoted Ovid's *Remedia Amoris*, in *World as Will and Representation*, vol. 1, 307.

97. Nietzsche sought to reject Schopenhauer's pessimism (*The Birth of Tragedy*, trans. Walter Kaufmann [New York: Vintage Books, 1967], 24); he claimed: "Schopenhauer was not strong enough for a new Yes" (*The Will to Power*, ed. Walter Kaufmann, trans. Walter Kaufmann and R. J. Hollingdale [New York: Vintage Books, 1967], 525).

98. *SE* XIV, 184.

Chapter 18

Epigraphs: Friedrich Nietzsche, *Beyond Good and Evil: Prelude to a Philosophy of the Future*, trans. Walter Kaufmann (New York: Vintage Books, 1989), 161; Friedrich Nietzsche, *Thus Spoke Zarathustra*, in *The Portable Nietzsche*, trans. Walter Kaufmann (New York: Viking, 1954), 125.

1. *SE* XIV.

2. Boss is quoted in Martin Heidegger, *Zollikon Seminars*, trans. Franz Mayr and Richard Askay (Evanston: Northwestern University Press, 2001), 309.

3. Heidegger, *Zollikon Seminars*, 5.

4. Recall Hegel's idea that dialectical conflicts are reflected not only in historical epochs but within great individuals themselves! See: G. W. F. Hegel, *Phenomenology of Spirit*, trans. A. V. Miller (New York: Oxford University Press, 1977), 33.

5. In the same way that Freud (and Schopenhauer) and Marx are dialectically synthesized subsequently by the critical theorists.

6. This is part of the reason the general lack of reference to Schopenhauer's metaphysics in the writings of Sartre and especially in those of Merleau-Ponty is somewhat puzzling from an historical point of view.

7. Maurice Merleau-Ponty, *Phenomenology of Perception,* trans. Colin Smith (New York: Humanities Press, 1962), 166.

8. Jean-Paul Sartre, *Being and Nothingness: An Essay on Phenomenological Ontology,* trans. Hazel. E. Barnes (New York: Philosophical Library, 1956), 318.

9. Ibid.

10. Ibid., 309.

11. We note, of course, that while their conclusion concerning the ontological primacy of the body is the same, the ontological analyses surrounding Merleau-Ponty's and Sartre's developments of it are quite different. The place where Sartre and Merleau-Ponty part ontological company occurs most clearly when the former insists:

> We have laid down as the foundation of the revelation of the body as our original relation to the world, i.e., our very upsurge into the midst of being. It is only in a world that there can be a body, and a primary relation is indispensable in order that this world may exist: the ontological primordiality of the nihilating activity of the For-itself (*Being and Nothingness,* 325).

12. Merleau-Ponty, *Phenomenology of Perception,* 164–65; Sartre, *Being and Nothingness,* 328.

13. Merleau-Ponty, *Phenomenology of Perception,* 203–6; Sartre, *Being and Nothingness,* 345, 365.

14. Edmund Husserl, *Ideas Pertaining to a Pure Phenomenology and to a Phenomenological Philosophy, Second Book: Studies in the Phenomenology of Constitution,* trans. Richard Rojcewicz and André Schuwer (Dordrecht: Kluwer Academic Publishers, 1989), 160–69. Hereafter: *Ideas II.*

15. Edmund Husserl, *Analyses Concerning Passive and Active Synthesis: Lectures on Transcendental Logic,* trans. Anthony J. Steinbock (Dordrecht: Kluwer Academic Publishers, 2001), 50–52, 271, 373–74, 543–44, 584–86, 631–33.

16. Husserl, *Analyses Concerning Passive and Active Synthesis,* 584.

17. Ibid., 585. See also: Edmund Husserl, *The Crisis of European Sciences and Transcendental Phenomenology: An Introduction to Phenomenological Philosophy,* trans. David Carr (Evanston: Northwestern University Press, 1970), 331.

18. Husserl, *Crisis of European Sciences and Transcendental Phenomenology,* 324.

19. Ibid., 331.

20. Ibid., 108.

21. Husserl, *Ideas II,* 308n.

22. Edmund Husserl, *Ideas: General Introduction to Pure Phenomenology,* trans. W. R. Boyce Gibson (New York: Collier Books, 1972), sect. 49.

23. Boss referred to this in Heidegger's *Zollikon Seminars,* 157, 231.

24. Martin Heidegger, *Being and Time,* trans. John Macquarrie and Edward Robinson (New York: Harper & Row, 1962), 123.

25. Martin Heidegger, *Martin Heidegger: Basic Writings,* ed. David Farrell Krell (New York: Harper & Row, 1977), 210.

26. Heidegger, *Zollikon Seminars,* 157.

27. Ibid., 231.

28. Martin Heidegger, *Heraklit, Seminar Wintersemester 1966/67 mit Eugen Fink,* in *Heidegger Gesamtausgabe,* vol.15 (Frankfurt am Main: V. Klostermann, 1970), 243.

29. Martin Heidegger, *The Metaphysical Foundations of Logic,* trans. Michael Heim (Bloomington: Indiana University Press, 1984), 166. See also: 137.

30. Heidegger, *Zollikon Seminars,* 93.

31. Ibid., 97.

32. Ibid., 231–32.

33. Despite the fact that Merleau-Ponty addressed the lived body extensively, Heidegger's response to the French on these points was directed only to Sartre in his lectures (*Zollikon Seminars,* 157, 231). It is, in fact, remarkable that Heidegger, in his extensive analysis of over fifty pages on the problem of the body, did not refer to Merleau-Ponty at all, though it is clear he was aware of Merleau-Ponty's work. This is especially curious given the fact that it was Merleau-Ponty who had been most positively influenced by Heidegger in his magnum opus, the *Phenomenology of Perception.*

Those closely involved with Heidegger and his writings addressed Merleau-Ponty's work. Indeed, Boss credited Merleau-Ponty with having improved on Sartre's translation of Heidegger's notion of Dasein. As opposed to Sartre's *être-dans-le-monde,* which tended to reify human beings, Boss preferred Merleau-Ponty's choice of *être-au-monde,* which underscored the sense of the directional nature of existential intentionality.

Heidegger's lack of reference is all the more interesting given that Merleau-Ponty's account of the body came the closest (among the French existential phenomenologists) to his own descriptions in the *Zollikon Seminars.* Some of these similarities in the analysis of bodily being included:

> Gesture and expression: Merleau-Ponty, *Phenomenology of Perception,* 139, 184–89. Heidegger, *Zollikon Seminars,* 84, 88. Medard Boss, *Existential Foundations of Medicine and Psychology,* trans. Stephen Conway and Anne Cleaves (New York: Jason Aronson, 1979), 102.
>
> Bodily being and spatiality: Merleau-Ponty, *Phenomenology of Perception,* 100, 139. Heidegger, *Being and Time,* 419. Medard Boss, *Existential Foundations of Medicine and Psychology,* 86–93, 104; *Psychoanalysis and Daseinsanalysis,* trans. Ludwig B. Lefebre (New York: Dacapo Press, 1982), 43.
>
> Refusal to see the body as merely a corporeal, self-contained object: Merleau-Ponty, *Phenomenology of Perception,* part 1. Heidegger, *Being and Time,* 419; *Zollikon Seminars,* 231–32. Boss, *Existential Foundations of Medicine and Psychology,* 102, 127–31; *Psychoanalysis and Daseinsanalysis,* 140.
>
> Phantom limb analysis: Merleau-Ponty, *Phenomenology of Perception,* 81–89. Heidegger, *Zollikon Seminars,* 221.
>
> Boss made similar observations to Merleau-Ponty's, such as how injury to the brain impairs human ways of relating to the world: Boss, *Existential Foundations of Medicine and Psychology,* 202. Merleau-Ponty, *Phenomenology of Perception,* 103–9.

34. Heidegger, *Zollikon Seminars,* 89.

35. Ibid., 91.

36. Ibid., 272.

37. Merleau-Ponty himself eventually conceded Heidegger's point: "The problems that remain after this first description [of the *Phenomenology of Perception*]: they are due to the fact that in part I retained the philosophy of 'consciousness'" (Maurice Merleau-Ponty, *The Visible and the Invisible*, ed. Claude Lefort, trans. Alphonso Lingis [Evanston: Northwestern University Press, 1968], 183; see 165–67, 179).

38. This was echoed and developed by Boss: *Existential Foundations of Medicine and Psychology*, 100–105, 200; *Psychoanalysis and Daseinsanalysis*, 140.

39. Heidegger, *Metaphysical Foundations of Logic*, 176. Also, Boss: "Existence is that which bodies forth" (*Existential Foundations of Medicine and Psychology*, 105; see 130).

40. Heidegger, *Zollikon Seminars*, 231.

41. Ibid., 200.

42. Ibid., 88–89, 93–94, 96–97. As we have seen above, Heidegger, Sartre, and Merleau-Ponty agree on this point.

43. Heidegger, *Zollikon Seminars*, 86–87, 93–94, 196–97.

44. Ibid., 186.

45. Ibid., 196–97.

46. Ibid., 200.

47. Ibid., 186.

48. Ibid., 231.

49. Ibid., 232.

50. Ibid. Also, Boss: "We see because we are world luminating and disclosing" (*Psychoanalysis and Daseinsanalysis*, 140).

51. It is worth noting that Binswanger and Boss, far from being oblivious to Merleau-Ponty's analysis, raised similar criticisms to it. Ludwig Binswanger: "Even [the] phenomenological descriptions properly outlined and developed by Merleau-Ponty fail to go far enough. [He] stops with describing phenomena and their relationships without being interested in the fundamental ontological structure of existence" (*Journal of Existential Psychiatry*, vol. 3 [January 1959], 163). In his *Existential Foundations for Medicine and Psychology*, Medard Boss credited the French philosophers—J.-P. Sartre, M. Merleau-Ponty, A. de Waelhens, G. Marcel, and P. Ricoeur—for "pointing insistently to the necessity for reconsidering the human body." According to Boss, however, the French philosophers only advanced a "half-step" beyond the natural scientific concept of the body, due to their inability to escape their Cartesian heritage. See: *Existential Foundations for Medicine and Psychology*, 127–28, 129–31.

52. *SE* XIII, 178. It is important to note that an actual debate occurred between a philosopher, James Jackson Putnam, and Freud on the nature of the relationship between psychoanalysis and philosophy. Putnam argued that the two ought to be understood as "equiprimordial" in relation to understanding human existence—that is, "supplemental" to the other. See: James Jackson Putnam, "A Plea for the Study of Philosophic Methods in Preparation for Psychoanalytic Work," *Journal of Abnormal Psychology*, vol. 6 (October–November 1911), 249, 249–63. In addition, Putnam, an enthusiastic supporter of psychoanalysis (*SE* XX, 51),

made an impassioned plea on behalf of doing philosophy prior to psychoanalytic work: "the psychoanalyst should not neglect that portion of the knowledge of the mind, which he can get only by philosophic methods . . ." ("Plea for the Study of Philosophic Methods," 253).

53. *SE* VI, 259.

54. Nathan G. Hale, ed., *James Jackson Putnam and Psychoanalysis; Letters Between Putnam and Sigmund Freud, Ernest Jones, William James, Sandor Ferenczi, Morton Prince, 1877–1917,* trans. Judith Bernays Heller (Cambridge, Mass.: Harvard University Press, 1971), 55.

55. Herman Nunberg and Ernst Federn, eds., *Minutes of the Vienna Psychoanalytic Society,* vol. 1, trans. M. Nunberg (New York: International Universities Press, 1975), 149–50. See also: *SE* IX, 115–27; *SE* XIII, 161–62.

56. *SE* XIII, 185.

57. Nietzsche, *Beyond Good and Evil,* 32.

58. Ibid., 11.

59. Friedrich Nietzsche, *The Will to Power,* ed. Walter Kaufmann, trans. Walter Kaufmann and R. J. Hollingdale (New York: Vintage Books, 1967), 251.

60. *SE* XI, 212.

61. *SE* XIII, 179.

62. *SE* XIV, 38.

63. *Minutes of the Vienna Psychoanalytic Society,* vol. 1, 357.

64. Ibid.

65. *SE* VI, 258–59. Here Freud not so coincidentally referenced precisely that passage in which he argued for the need for a transformation of metaphysics into metapsychology!

66. *Minutes of the Vienna Psychoanalytic Society,* vol. 2, 31–32.

67. Letter to Arnold Zweig, May 11, 1934. Ernest Jones, *The Life and Works of Sigmund Freud,* vol. 3 (New York: Basic Books, 1965), 459–60.

68. Letter to Arnold Zweig, July 15, 1934. Jones, *Life and Works of Sigmund Freud,* vol. 3, 190.

69. *Minutes of the Vienna Psychoanalytic Society,* vol. 4, 133.

70. Ibid., 134.

71. *SE* XVII, 261.

72. Heidegger might himself be seen as an excellent candidate for psychoanalysis, especially in light of his historic decision to join the Nazi party. For example, Erich Fromm made the point that Freud's analysis of group psychology and the attraction of authoritarian personalities would make such acts more comprehensible within an individual's life-flow.

73. Michel Contat and Michel Rybalka, eds., *The Writings of Jean-Paul Sartre,* trans. Richard C. McCleary (Evanston: Northwestern University Press, 1974), 34.

74. *SE* XII, 107.

75. *SE* XX, 102.

76. *SE* XIV, 38.

77. *SE* XIII, 178–79.

78. Freud's classic formulation can be found in *SE* XIX, 32: ". . . from this the Oedipus complex originates. His identification with his father then takes on a hos-

tile colouring and changes into a wish to get rid of his father in order to take his place with his mother."

79. Jean-Paul Sartre, *The Words*, trans. Bernard Frechtman (New York: G. Braziller, 1964), 102.

80. Sartre, *The Words*, 11.

81. Ibid.

82. Ibid., 34n.

83. Jean-Paul Sartre, *Nausea*, trans. Lloyd Alexander (New York: New Directions, 1964), 133.

84. Freud to Marie Bonaparte, August 13, 1937. Jones, *Life and Works of Sigmund Freud*, vol. 3, 465.

85. Here Freud's diagnosis is inconsistent with his recognition that identifying the underlying metapsychological underpinnings of a worldview does not negate its validity/truth.

86. Sartre, *Being and Nothingness*, 53.

87. *SE* XIII, 188.

88. Ibid., 178–79.

89. *The Portable Nietzsche*, trans. Walter Kaufmann (New York: Viking, 1954), 670.

90. Nietzsche's answer is that belief in the transcendent is sustained at the expense of focusing on this world and our creative possibilities within it. The idea is to eliminate the impetus for the development of (at least certain) metaphysical ideas, which are suspect by their very nature, by identifying the factors that led to their emergence in the first place.

91. *SE* VII, 113.

92. Heidegger, *Zollikon Seminars*, 259.

93. Sartre, *Being and Nothingness*, 569.

94. Ibid., 557–615.

95. Jean-Paul Sartre, *Between Existentialism and Marxism*, trans. John Mathews (New York: William Morrow & Company, 1974), 204.

96. Sartre, *Between Existentialism and Marxism*, 44.

97. Jean-Paul Sartre, *Search for a Method*, trans. Hazel E. Barnes (New York: Vintage Books, 1968), 62.

98. Sartre, *Between Existentialism and Marxism*, 43.

99. Jean-Paul Sartre, *Critique of Dialectical Reason, Vol. I: Theory of Practical Ensembles*, trans. Alan Sheridan-Smith (London: New Left Books, 1976), 55.

100. In *The Family Idiot*, Sartre spent the first couple hundred pages exploring the determining/conditioning factors governing Flaubert's childhood (along with his social environment) so that we could better understand the adult Flaubert.

101. Jean-Paul Sartre, *The Family Idiot: Gustave Flaubert, 1827–1857*, trans. Carol Cosman (Chicago: The University of Chicago Press, 1993), ix.

102. Sartre, *Between Existentialism and Marxism*, 39.

103. Jean-Paul Sartre, *Life/Situations*, vol. 9, trans. Paul Auster and Lydia Davis (London: André Deutsch, 1978), 108, 110–11.

104. Sartre, *Life/Situations*, vol. 9, 111.

105. Ibid. See also: *Between Existentialism and Marxism*, 41.

106. It is important to note that Heidegger implicitly, and Sartre explicitly—"the last discoveries of phenomenological ontology are the first principles of psychoanalysis" (*Being and Nothingness*, 735)—have in different ways come to the same realization.

107. See: Ludwig Binswanger, *Being-in-the-world: Selected Papers of Ludwig Binswanger*, trans. Jacob Needleman (New York: Harper & Row, 1967). Also, we should be careful to note that Binswanger credited Husserl's phenomenology with being a primary impetus for the development of his approach.

108. See: Boss, *Psychoanalysis and Daseinsanalysis; Existential Foundations of Medicine and Psychology.*

109. See: R. D. Laing, *The Politics of Experience* (New York: Pantheon, 1983); Rollo May, *Existential Psychology* (New York: Random House, 1969); *Existence: A New Dimension in Psychiatry and Psychology*, ed. Rollo May, Ernest Angel, Henri F. Ellenberger (New York: Basic Books, 1958).

110. A. Hesnard, *L'Oeuvre de Freud et son importance pour le Monde Moderne* (Paris: Payot, 1960).

111. Henri Ey, *Consciousness: A Phenomenological Study of Being Conscious and Becoming Conscious*, trans. John H. Flodstrom (Bloomington: Indiana University Press, 1978).

112. SE XVIII, 57; *SE* VII, 136.

113. *SE* XVIII, 58.

114. This is a schema that is common to a variety of Eastern traditions: Hinduism, Buddhism, Zen, and so on. In the West this is, of course, the Schellingian–Hegelian dialectical process of Being having become alienated from itself and running through a necessary process which regains the sought after reunification.

115. Hegel, *Phenomenology of Spirit*, 33.

116. F. W. J. Schelling, *Ideas for a Philosophy of Nature: As Introduction to the Study of This Science*, trans. Errol E. Harris and Peter Heath (New York: Cambridge University Press, 1995), 11.

117. Hegel, *Phenomenology of Spirit*, 2.

118. Nietzsche rejected the metaphysical pursuit for unity throughout his writings.

119. Although it transcends the scope of this text, we must be careful to note that such a quest for unity is clearly characteristic of, among other traditions/ orientations: Jungian psychology, Hinduism, Buddhism (the movement from no-self to self to no-self), Taoism, Confucianism, and Zen.

120. Heidegger, *Being and Time*, 415.

121. See the first two pages of Sartre's *Being and Nothingness*.

122. Arthur Schopenhauer, *The World as Will and Representation*, vol. 2, trans. E. F. J. Payne (New York: Dover, 1966), 179.

123. Nietzsche, *Thus Spoke Zarathustra*, 146.

124. Ibid., 351.

Index

About the Authors

Richard Askay is a professor of philosophy at the University of Portland. He has published articles on continental philosophy and critical thinking and is researching the relationship of scientific cosmological theory to metaphysics. With Franz Mayr, he translated and annotated Heidegger's *Zollikon Seminars,* also published by Northwestern University Press.

Jensen Farquhar is a psychotherapist and an editor in the fields of psychology and philosophy. Her research interests include philosophy and education, feminism, and Eastern thought.

Consulting Editors